I0071537

Strategic, Sustainable, and Innovative Entrepreneurship

Compiled and Edited by:

Jonathan H. Westover, Ph.D.
Utah Valley University

First printed/published in 2015 in the USA
by HCI Press
as part of Leading Innovative Organizations series

Library of Congress Cataloging-in-Publication Data

Strategic, Sustainable, and Innovative Entrepreneurship/ Jonathan H. Westover, editor.
        p. cm. -- (Leading Innovative Organizations series)
ISBN-13: 978-0692532171; ISBN-10: 069253217X (HCI Press)
1. Sustainability. 2. Innovation. 3. Entrepreneurship I. Westover, Jonathan H.

Table of Contents

Chapter 1: History 1

Chapter 2: Sustainability Innovation in Business 19

Chapter 3: Framing Sustainability Innovation and Entrepreneurship 31

Chapter 4: Entrepreneurship and Sustainability Innovation Analysis 57

Chapter 5: Energy and Climate 103

Chapter 6: Clean Products and Health 137

Chapter 7: Buildings 177

Chapter 8: Biomaterials 223

About the Editor

Dr. Jonathan H. Westover is an Associate Professor of Management and Associate Director of the Center for the Study of Ethics at Utah Valley University, specializing in international human resource management, organizational development, and community-engaged experiential learning. He is also a human resource development and performance management consultant. Already a recipient of numerous research, teaching, and service awards and fellowships early in his academic career, Jonathan also recently was named a Fulbright Scholar and was visiting faculty in the MBA program at Belarusian State University (Minsk, Belarus), and he is also a regular visiting faculty member in other graduate business programs in the U.S., UK, France, Poland, and China. Prior to his doctoral studies in the Sociology of Work and Organizations, Comparative International Sociology, and International Political Economy (University of Utah), he received his B.S. in Sociology (Research and Analysis emphasis, Business Management minor, Korean minor) and MPA (emphasis in Human Resource Management) from the Marriott School of Management at Brigham Young University. He also received graduate certificates in demography and higher education teaching during his time at the University of Utah. His ongoing research examines issues of globalization, labor transformation, work quality characteristics, and the determinants of job satisfaction cross-nationally.

Acknowledgements

This text was compiled, edited, and adapted from open source texts at http://www.saylor.org/books and created under a Creative Commons Attribution-NonCommercial ShareAlike 3.0 License without attribution as requested by the work's original creator or licensee. Please contact me for a free copy of the e-text. I would like to thank the many anonymous individuals who contributed their own wisdom and writing to this edited work, particularly those who contributed to the text *Sustainability, Innovation, and Entrepreneurship*. Of course, this text would not be possible without each of their important contributions. Most of all, I would like to publically thank my wife (Jacque) and my six wonderful children (Sara, Amber, Lia, Kaylie, David, and Brayden) for all of their love and support!

Preface

This book offers students and instructors the opportunity to analyze businesses whose products and strategies are designed to offer innovative solutions to some of the twenty-first century's most difficult societal challenges. A new generation of profitable businesses is actively engaged in clean tech, renewable energy, and financially successful product system design and supply chain strategies that attempt to meet our economic development aspirations while addressing our social and ecological challenges. This textbook offers background educational materials for instructors and students, business cases illustrating sustainability innovation, and teaching notes that enable instructors to work effectively and accelerate student learning.

The industrial revolution marked an era of tremendous growth, innovation, and prosperity in many parts of the world—but those achievements also have had unintended consequences that are increasingly obvious. Climate change, pollution, water scarcity, toxins in products and food, and loss of ecosystem services and biological diversity, among other problems, pose serious threats that may undermine the remarkable human progress achieved. Major forces behind these challenges are the unprecedented global population explosion and advances in technology that have caused dramatic increases in industrial production, energy use, and material throughput. As a consequence, technology races to keep pace with the demand for land, water, materials, energy, and food. At the same time, technology is being applied to address the growing volume of waste that disrupts and impairs natural systems worldwide, including our bodies and physical health. These burdens fall most heavily on those least able to avoid the adverse impacts, fight for resources, or protest: children and the poor.

We know that those same natural systems being undermined by industrialization provide the critical ecological services on which we depend for life, health, and the pursuit of prosperity. Furthermore, it is implicitly assumed our health must be sacrificed in the name of economic growth, as evident in growing environmental health problems and chronic health threats such as asthma, diabetes, and cancer that accompany expanded economic activity worldwide.

While some people observe the entrenched business paradigm and the deteriorating state of natural systems with a resigned, "what can *I* do?" mentality, innovative entrepreneurial individuals and firms naturally see opportunity. The resulting entrepreneurial activity, what we discuss as *sustainability innovation*, represents a wave of change that is moving rapidly into mainstream business. Pioneers, whether building enterprises within large organizations or starting new ventures, aim for the profitable provision of needed goods and services to meet demand *while at the same time* contributing to ecological and human health and larger community prosperity. This book is about these innovators. Studying them, through example and analyses, helps us to understand alternative business models, a new-century mind-set, and a future in which prosperity can be extended to greater numbers of global citizens.

The book was written in response to the paucity of teaching materials that enable instructors to integrate sustainability concepts in their business courses. Business students are poorly served by an education that omits the useful scholarly literature and advances made over the past few decades. Nor is their education complete if they are not aware of global ecological and environmental health trends and their implications for business. Available business cases that touch on larger societal and ecological challenges often view the problems as ethical concerns or as unavoidable Environmental, Health, and Safety (EH&S) expenses, or even exclusively the concern of regulators, policy folks, and corporate lawyers. A gap exists in management curricula between conventional business practices that assume infinite resources and safe waste disposal on the one hand, and the sustainability innovation that today's new market conditions demand. There are now well-developed and vetted frameworks, analyses, and tools, such as cradle-to-cradle design, green chemistry, industrial ecology, The Natural Step, and markets for ecological services, as well as newly forged and creative ways of collaborating and organizing to maximize innovative outcomes. These ideas are explored. Emphasis in the collection is on private sector examples, but social enterprise and entrepreneurship cases are also included.

Case Examples

- As the first company to deliver aesthetically appealing, ecologically friendly home-cleaning products to mainstream retailers (as opposed to just natural products stores), Method, created in the early 2000s, has changed the rules of that game to such an extent that major consumer packaged goods global companies followed the lead of these upstart entrepreneurs.
- Project Frog was formed to fill the market gap between the expensive conventional school buildings that school

districts could no longer afford and the less-than-adequate and sometimes toxic trailers often seen next to public schools to accommodate growth in student populations. FROG's buildings are less expensive, naturally lit, monitored with custom-adjusted, state-of-the-art climate control technology, and far superior and healthier learning environments for children.

- Frito-Lay's (owned by PepsiCo) Casa Grande manufacturing facility in Arizona provides a systems innovation example of a large firm experimenting with one site to demonstrate strategic and operating benefits from going off-grid. A carbon footprint analysis, extensive eco-efficiency measures, and renewable energy for process heating and electricity needs combine to create cutting-edge innovation in production facility management.

The sustainability pioneers that we spotlight throughout this book represent a small subset of a much larger pool of entrepreneurial activity and innovation whose ranks are rapidly expanding. They are forging viable commercial paths that optimize across financial goals, strategic thinking, operating protocols, and high-quality goods and services with ecological stability, human health, and community prosperity considerations built in. These efforts *are* the company's strategy to succeed. Collectively, though not necessarily visible from their dispersed locations around the world, these creative individuals and firms are fueling a massive wave of innovation. This innovation is even more essential today than it was a decade ago to meet the rapidly growing needs of global markets, as billions more people aspire to higher prosperity and quality of life within the limits of finite resources.

Chapter 1:
History

1.1 Environmental Issues Become Visible and Regulated

LEARNING OBJECTIVES

1. Gain an understanding of environmental issues' historical antecedents.
2. Identify key events leading to regulatory action.
3. Understand how those events shaped eventual business actions.

Sustainability innovations, currently driven by a subset of today's entrepreneurial actors, represent the new generation of business responses to health, ecological, and social concerns. The entrepreneurial innovations we will discuss in this book reflect emerging scientific knowledge, widening public concern, and government regulation directed toward a cleaner economy. The US roots of today's sustainability innovations go back to the 1960s, when health and environmental problems became considerably more visible. By 1970, the issues had intensified such that both government and business had to address the growing public worries. The US environmental regulatory framework that emerged in the 1970s was a response to growing empirical evidence that the post–World War II design of industrial activity was an increasing threat to human health and environmental system functioning.

We must keep in mind, however, that industrialization and in particular the commercial system that emerged post–World War II delivered considerable advantages to a global population. To state the obvious: there have been profoundly important advances in the human condition as a consequence of industrialization. In most countries, life spans have been extended, infant mortality dramatically reduced, and diseases conquered. Remarkable technological advances have made our lives healthier, extended education, and made us materially more comfortable. Communication advances have tied people together into a single global community, able to connect to each other and advance the common good in ways that were unimaginable a short time ago. Furthermore, wealth creation activity by business and the resulting rise in living standards have brought millions of people out of poverty. It is this creative capacity, our positive track record, and a well-founded faith in our ability to learn, adapt, and evolve toward more beneficial methods of value creation that form the platform for the innovative changes discussed in this text. Human beings are adept at solving problems, and problems represent system feedback that can

inform future action. Therefore, we begin this discussion with a literal and symbolic feedback loop presented to the American public in the 1960s.

Widespread public awareness about environmental issues originated with the publication of the book **Silent Spring** by Rachel Carson in 1962. Carson, a biologist, argued that the spraying of the synthetic pesticide dichlorodiphenyltrichloroethane (DDT) was causing a dramatic decline in bird populations, poisoning the food chain, and thus ultimately harming humans. Similar to Upton Sinclair's 1906 book The Jungle and its exposé of the shocking conditions in the American meatpacking industry, Silent Spring was a dramatic challenge to the chemical industry and to the prevalent societal optimism toward technology and post–World War II chemical use. Its publication ignited a firestorm of publicity and controversy. Predictably, the chemical industry reacted quickly and strongly to the book's threat and was critical of Carson and her ideas. In an article titled "Nature Is for the Birds," industry journal Chemical Week described organic farmers and those opposed to chemical pesticides as "a motley lot" ranging from "superstition-ridden illiterates to educated scientists, from cultists to relatively reasonable men and women" and strongly suggesting Carson's claims were unwarranted. [1] Chemical giant Monsanto responded directly to Carson by publishing a mocking parody of Silent Spring titled The Desolate Year. The book, with a "prose and format similar to Carson's…described a small town beset by cholera and malaria and unable to produce adequate crops because it lacked the chemical pesticides necessary to ward off harmful pests." [2] Despite industry's counteroffensive, President Kennedy, in part responding to Carson's book, appointed a special panel to study pesticides. The panel's findings supported her thesis. [3] However, it wasn't until 1972 that the government ended the use of DDT. [4]

Figure 1.1 "DDT Accumulation in the Food Chain" shows how toxins concentrate in the food chain. Humans, as consumers of fish and other animals that accumulate DDT, are at the top of the food chain and therefore can receive particularly high levels of the chemical. Even after developed countries had banned DDT for decades, in the early part of the twenty-first century the World Health Organization reapproved DDT use to prevent malaria in less developed countries. Lives were saved, yet trade-offs were necessary. Epidemiologists continue to associate high concentration levels with breast cancer and negative effects on the neurobehavioral development of children. [5]

Figure 1.1 DDT Accumulation in the Food Chain

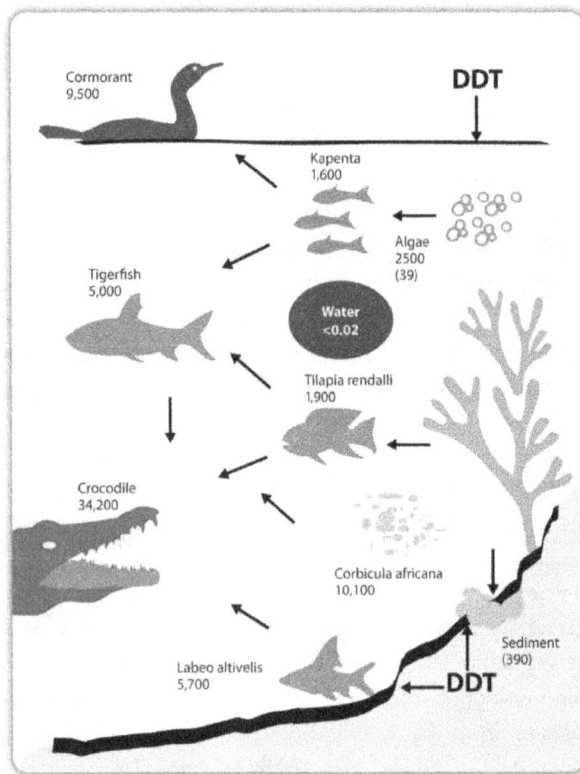

DDT levels, shown in nanograms per gram of body fat for animals in Lake Kariba in Zimbabwe, accumulate in the food chain.
Source: Håkan Berg, Martina Kiibus, and Nils Kautsky, "DDT and Other Insecticides in the Lake Kariba Ecosystem, Zimbabwe," Ambio 21 (November 1992): 444–50.

Throughout the 1960s, well-publicized news stories were adding momentum to the call for comprehensive federal environmental legislation. The nation's air quality had deteriorated rapidly, and in 1963 high concentrations of air pollutants in New York City caused approximately three hundred deaths and thousands of injuries. [6] At the same time, cities like Los Angeles, Chattanooga, and Pittsburgh had become infamous for their dense smog. Polluted urban areas, once considered unpleasant and unattractive

inconveniences that accompanied growth and job creation, were by the 1960s definitively connected by empirical studies to a host of respiratory problems.

Urban air quality was not the only concern. Questions were also being raised about the safety of drinking water and food supplies that were dependent on freshwater resources. In 1964, over a million dead fish washed up on the banks of the Mississippi River, threatening the water supplies of nearby towns. The source of the fish kill was traced to pesticide leaks, specifically endrin, which was manufactured by Velsicol. [7] Several other instances of polluted waterways added to the public's awareness of the deterioration of the nation's rivers, streams, and lakes and put pressure on legislators to take action. In the mid-1960s, foam from nonbiodegradable cleansers and laundry detergents began to appear in rivers and creeks. By the late 1960s, Lake Erie was so heavily polluted that millions of fish died and many of the beaches along the lake had to be closed. [8] On June 22, 1969, the seemingly impossible occurred in Ohio when the Cuyahoga River, which empties into Lake Erie, caught fire, capturing the nation's attention. However, it was not the first time; the river had burst into flame multiple times since 1968.

Influenced by these events and the proliferation of environmental news stories and public discourse, citizens of industrialized countries had begun to shift their perceptions about the larger physical world. Several influential books and articles introduced to the general public the concept of a finite world. Economist Kenneth Boulding, in his 1966 essay "The Economics of the Coming Spaceship Earth," coined the metaphors of "**spaceship Earth**" and "spaceman economy" to emphasize that the earth was a closed system and that the economy must therefore focus not on "production and consumption at all, but the nature, extent, quality, and complexity of the total capital stock." [12] Paul Ehrlich, in the follow-up to his 1968 best seller The Population Bomb, borrowed Boulding's metaphor in his 1971 book How to Be a Survivor to argue that in a closed system, exponential population growth and resource consumption would breach the carrying capacity of nature, assuring misery for all passengers aboard the "spaceship." [13] Garrett Hardin's now famous essay, "The Tragedy of the Commons," was published in the prestigious journal Science in December 1968. [14] It emphasized the need for new solutions to problems not easily addressed by technology, referring to pollution that involved public commons such as the air, water, soil, and oceans. These commonly used resources are shared in terms of access, but no single person or institution has formal responsibility for their protection.

Another symbolic turning point came in 1969 during the Apollo 11 mission, when the first photograph of the earth was taken from outer space. The image became an icon for the environmental movement. During that time period and subsequently, quotations proliferated about the new relationship between humans and their planetary home. In a speech at San Fernando Valley State College on September 26, 1966, the vice president of the United States Hubert H. Humphrey said, "As we begin to comprehend that the earth itself is a kind of manned spaceship hurtling through the infinity of space—it will seem increasingly absurd that we have not better organized the life of the human family." In the December 23, 1968, edition of Newsweek, Frank Borman, commander of

Apollo 8, said, "When you're finally up at the moon looking back on earth, all those differences and nationalistic traits are pretty well going to blend, and you're going to get a concept that maybe this really is one world and why the hell can't we learn to live together like decent people."

KEY TAKEAWAYS

- By the 1970s, the public began to recognize the finite resources of the earth and to debate its ability to sustain environmental degradation as environmental catastrophes grew in size and number.
- Chemical contaminants were discovered to accumulate in the food chain resulting in much higher concentrations of toxins at the top.
- Key events and publications educated citizens about the impact of human activities on nature and the need for new approaches. These included the Santa Barbara oil spill, *Silent Spring*, and "The Tragedy of the Commons."

EXERCISES

1. How do you think Americans' experience of abundance, economic growth, and faith in technology influenced perceptions about the environment?
2. How did these perceptions change over time and why?
3. Compare your awareness of environmental and health concerns with that of your parents or other adults of your parents' generation. Name any differences you notice between the generations.
4. What parallels, if any, do you see between today's discussions about environmental issues and the history provided here?

[1] "Nature Is for the Birds," *Chemical Week*, July 28, 1962, 5, quoted in Andrew J. Hoffman, *From Heresy to Dogma: An Institutional History of Corporate Environmentalism* (San Francisco: New Lexington Press, 1997), 51.
[2] Andrew J. Hoffman, *From Heresy to Dogma: An Institutional History of Corporate Environmentalism* (San Francisco: New Lexington Press, 1997), 51.
[3] Andrew J. Hoffman, *From Heresy to Dogma: An Institutional History of Corporate Environmentalism* (San Francisco: New Lexington Press, 1997), 57.
[4] A ban on DDT use went into effect in December 1972 in the United States. See US Environmental Protection Agency, "DDT Ban Takes Effect," news release, December 31, 1972, accessed April 19, 2011, http://www.epa.gov/history/topics/ddt/01.htm.
[5] Brenda Eskenazi, interviewed by Steve Curwood, "Goodbye DDT," *Living on Earth*, May 8, 2009, accessed November 29, 2010, http://www.loe.org/shows/segments.htm?programID=09-P13-00019&segmentID=3; Theo Colburn, Frederick S. vom Saal, and Ana M. Soto, "Developmental Effects of Endocrine-Disrupting Chemicals in Wildlife and Humans," *Environmental Health Perspectives* 101, no. 5 (October 1993): 378–84, accessed November 24, 2010, http://www.pubmedcentral.nih.gov/articlerender.fcgi?artid=1519860. DDT, along with several other chemicals used as pesticides, is suspected endocrine disruptors; the concern is not just with levels of a given toxin but also with the interactive effects of multiple synthetic chemicals accumulating in animals, including humans.
[6] G. Tyler Miller and Scott Spoolman, *Living in the Environment: Principles, Connections, and Solutions*, 16th ed. (Belmont, CA: Brooks/Cole, 2009), 535.
[7] Andrew J. Hoffman, *From Heresy to Dogma: An Institutional History of Corporate Environmentalism* (San Francisco: New Lexington Press, 1997), 52.
[8] G. Tyler Miller and Scott Spoolman, *Living in the Environment: Principles, Connections, and Solutions*, 16th ed. (Belmont, CA: Brooks/Cole, 2009), 535.
[9] "America's Sewage System and the Price of Optimism," *Time*, August 1, 1969, accessed March 7, 2011, http://www.time.com/time/magazine/article/0,9171,901182,00.html#ixzz19KSrUirj.
[10] "Apollo 8 hand-held Hasselblad photograph of a half illuminated Earth taken on 24 December 1968 as the spacecraft returned from the first manned orbit of the Moon. The evening terminator crosses Australia, towards the bottom. India can be seen at upper left. The sun is reflecting off the Indian ocean. The Earth is 12,740 km in diameter, north is at about 1:00. (Apollo 8, AS08-15-2561)"; NASA, "Earth—Apollo 8," *Catalog of Spaceborne Imaging*, accessed March 7, 2011, http://nssdc.gsfc.nasa.gov/imgcat/html/object_page/a08_h_15_2561.html.
[11] Andrew J. Hoffman, *From Heresy to Dogma: An Institutional History of Corporate Environmentalism* (San Francisco: New Lexington Press, 1997), 57–58.
[12] See Kenneth E. Boulding, "The Economics of the Coming Spaceship Earth," in *Environmental Quality in a Growing Economy*, ed. Henry Jarrett (Baltimore: Johns Hopkins University Press, 1966), 3–14.
[13] Philip Shabecoff, *A Fierce Green Fire: The American Environmental Movement* (New York: Hill & Wang, 1993), 95–96.
[14] Kenneth E. Boulding, "The Economics of the Coming Spaceship Earth," in *Valuing the Earth, Economics, Ecology, Ethics*, ed. Herman Daly and Kenneth Townsend (Cambridge, MA: MIT Press, 1993), 297–309; Paul Ehrlich, *The Population Bomb* (New York: Ballantine Books, 1968); Paul Ehrlich, *How to Be a Survivor* (New York: Ballantine Books, 1975).

1.2 Business Shifts Its Focus

LEARNING OBJECTIVES

1. Understand the initial framework for US environmental regulation.
2. Explain why and how companies changed their policies and practices.

In response to strong public support for environmental protection, newly elected president Nixon, in his 1970 State of the Union address, declared that the dawning decade of the 1970s "absolutely must be the years when America pays its debt to the past by reclaiming the purity of its air, its waters and our living environment. It is literally now or never." [1] Nixon signed into law several pieces of legislation that serve as the regulatory foundation for environmental protection today. On January 1, 1970, he approved the **National Environmental Policy Act (NEPA)**, the cornerstone of environmental policy and law in the United States. NEPA states that it is the responsibility of the federal government to "use all practicable means…to improve and coordinate federal plans, functions, programs and resources to the end that the Nation may…fulfill the responsibilities of each generation as trustee of the environment for succeeding generations." [2] In doing so, NEPA requires federal agencies to evaluate the environmental impact of an activity before it is undertaken. Furthermore, NEPA established the Environmental Protection Agency (EPA), which consolidated the responsibility for environmental policy and regulatory enforcement at the federal level.

Also in 1970, the modern version of the Clean Air Act (CAA) was passed into law. The CAA set national air quality standards for particulates, sulfur oxides, carbon monoxide, nitrogen oxide, ozone, hydrocarbons, and lead, averaged over different time periods. Two levels of air quality standards were established: primary standards to protect human health, and secondary standards to protect plant and animal life, maintain visibility, and protect buildings. The primary and secondary standards often have been identical in practice. The act also regulated that new stationary sources, such as power plants, set emissions standards, that standards for cars and trucks be established, and required states to develop implementation plans indicating how they would achieve the guidelines set by the act within the allotted time. Congress directed the EPA to establish these standards without consideration of the cost of compliance. [3]

To raise environmental awareness, Senator Gaylord Nelson of Wisconsin arranged a national teach-in on the environment. Nelson characterized the leading issues of the time as pesticides, herbicides, air pollution, and water pollution, stating, "Everybody around the country saw something going to pot in their local areas, some lovely spot, some lovely stream, some lovely lake you couldn't swim in anymore." [4] This educational project, held on April 22, 1970, and organized by Denis Hayes (at the time a twenty-five-year-old Harvard Law student), became the first Earth Day. [5] On that day, twenty million people in more than two thousand communities participated in educational activities and demonstrations to demand better environmental quality. [6] The unprecedented turnout reflected growing public anxiety. Health and safety issues had become increasingly urgent. In New York City, demonstrators on Fifth Avenue held up dead fish to protest the contamination of the Hudson River, and Mayor John Lindsay gave a speech in which he stated "Beyond words like ecology, environment and pollution there is a simple question: do we want to live or die?"[7] Even children's books discussed the inability of nature to protect itself against the demands, needs, and perceived excesses associated with economic growth and consumption patterns. The 1971 children's book The Lorax by Dr. Seuss was a sign of the times with its plea that someone "speak for the trees" that were being cut down at increasing rates worldwide, leaving desolate landscapes and impoverishing people's lives.

Global Science, Political Events, Citizen Concern

Pollution control typified the corporate response to environmental regulations from the genesis of the modern regulatory framework in the 1970s through the 1980s. **Pollution control** is an end-of-the-pipe strategy that focuses on waste treatment or the filtering of emissions or both. Pollution control strategies assume no change to product design or production methods, only attention to air, solid, and water waste streams at the end of the manufacturing process. This approach can be costly and typically imposes a burden on the company, though it may save expenses in the form of fines levied by regulatory agencies for regulatory noncompliance. Usually pollution control is implemented by companies to comply with regulations and reflects an adversarial relationship between business and government. The causes of this adversarial attitude were revealed in a 1974 survey by the Conference Board—an independent, nonprofit business research organization—that found that few companies viewed pollution control as profitable and none found it to be an opportunity to improve production procedures. [12] Hence, from a strictly profit-oriented viewpoint, one that considers neither public reaction to pollution nor potential future liability as affecting the bottom line, pollution control put the company in a "losing" position with respect to environmental protection.

The environmental regulatory structure of the United States at times has forced companies into a pollution control position by mandating specific technologies, setting strict compliance deadlines, and concentrating on cleanup instead of prevention. [13] This was evident in a 1986 report by the Office of Technology Assessment (OTA) that found that "over 99 percent of federal and state environmental spending is devoted to controlling pollution after waste is generated. Less than 1 percent is spent to reduce the generation of waste." [14] The OTA at that time noted the misplaced emphasis on pollution control in regulation and concluded that existing technologies alone could prevent half of all industrial wastes. [15]

Economists generally agree that it is better for regulation to require a result rather require a means to accomplishing that result. Requiring pollution control is preferred because it provides an incentive for firms to reduce pollution rather than simply move hazardous materials from one place to another, which does not solve the original problem of waste generation. For example, business researchers Michael Porter and Claas van der Linde draw a distinction between good regulations and bad regulations by whether they encourage innovation and thus enhance competitiveness while simultaneously addressing environmental concerns. Pollution control regulations, they argue, should promote resource productivity but often are written in ways that discourage the risk taking and experimentation that would benefit society and the regulated corporation: "For example, a company that innovates and achieves 95 percent of target emissions reduction while also registering substantial offsetting cost reductions is still 5 percent out of compliance and subject to liability. On the other hand, regulators would reward it for adopting safe but expensive secondary treatment." [16] Regulations that discouraged innovation and mandated the end-of-the-pipe mind-set that was common among regulators and industry in the 1970s and 1980s contributed to the adversarial approach to environmental protection. As these conflicts between business and government heated up, new science, an energy crisis, and growing public protests fueled the fire.

Global Science, Political Events, Citizen Concern

In 1972, a group of influential businessmen and scientists known as the Club of Rome published a book titled The Limits to Growth. Using mathematical models developed at the Massachusetts Institute of Technology to project trends in population growth, resource depletion, food supplies, capital investment, and pollution, the group reached a three-part conclusion. First, if the then-present trends held, the limits of growth on Earth would be reached within one hundred years. Second, these trends could be altered to establish economic and ecological stability that would be sustainable far into the future. Third, if the world chose to select the second outcome, chances of success would increase the sooner work began to attain it. [17] Again, the notion of natural limits was presented, an idea at odds with most people's assumptions at the time. For the people of a country whose history and cultural mythology held the promise of boundless frontiers and limitless resources, these full-Earth concepts challenged deeply held assumptions and values.

Perhaps the most dramatic wake-up call came in the form of political revenge. Americans were tangibly and painfully introduced to the concept of limited resources when, in 1973, Arab members of the Organization of Petroleum Exporting Countries (OPEC) banned oil shipments to the United States in retaliation for America's support of Israel in its eighteen-day Yom Kippur War with Syria and Egypt. Prices for oil-based products, including gasoline, skyrocketed. The so-called oil shock of 1973 triggered double-digit inflation and a major economic recession. [18] As a result, energy issues became inextricably interwoven with political and environmental issues, and new activist groups formed to promote a shift from nonrenewable, fossil fuel–based and heavily polluting energy sources such as oil and coal to renewable, cleaner sources generated closer to home from solar and wind power. However, with the end of gasoline shortages and high prices, these voices faded into the background. Of course, a strong resurgence of such ideas followed the price spikes of 2008, when crude oil prices exceeded $140 per barrel. [19]

In the years following the 1973 energy crisis, public and government attention turned once again toward the dangers posed by chemicals. On July 10, 1976, an explosion at a chemical plant in Seveso, Italy, released a cloud of the highly toxic chemical called dioxin. Some nine hundred local residents were evacuated, many of whom suffered disfiguring skin diseases and lasting illnesses as a result of the disaster. Birth defects increased locally following the blast, and the soil was so severely contaminated that the top eight inches from an area of seven square miles had to be removed and buried. [20] Andrew Hoffman, in his study of the American environmental movement in business, noted that "for many in the United States, the incident at Seveso cast a sinister light on their local chemical plant. Communities became fearful of the unknown, not knowing what was occurring behind chemical plant walls....Community and activist antagonism toward chemical companies grew, and confrontational lawsuits seemed the most visible manifestation." [21]

Over time, these developments built pressure for additional regulation of business. Politicians continued to listen to the concerns of US citizens. In 1976, the Toxic Substance Control Act (TSCA) was passed over intense industry objections. The TSCA gave the federal government control over chemicals not already regulated under existing laws. [22] In addition, the Resource Conservation and Recovery Act (RCRA) of 1976 expanded control over toxic substances from the time of production until disposal, or "from cradle to the grave." [23] The following year, both the CAA and Clean Water Act were strengthened and expanded. [24]

In the late 1970s, America's attention turned once again to energy issues. In 1978, Iran triggered a second oil shock by suddenly cutting back its petroleum exports to the United States. A year later, confidence in nuclear power, a technology many looked to as a viable alternative form of energy, was severely undermined by a near catastrophe. On March 29, 1979, the number two reactor at Three Mile Island near Harrisburg, Pennsylvania, lost its coolant water due to a series of mechanical failures and operator errors. Approximately half of the reactor's core melted, and investigators later found that if a particular valve had remained stuck open for another thirty to sixty minutes, a complete meltdown would have occurred. The accident resulted in the evacuation of fifty thousand people, with another fifty thousand fleeing voluntarily. The amount of radioactive material released into the atmosphere as a result of the accident is unknown, though no deaths were immediately attributable to the incident. Cleanup of the damaged reactor has cost $1.2 billion to date, almost twice its $700 million construction cost. [25] In large part due to the Three Mile Island incident, all 119 nuclear power plants ordered in the United States since 1973 were cancelled. [26] No new commercial nuclear power plants have been built since 1977, although some of the existing 104 plants have increased their capacity. However, in 2007, the Nuclear Regulatory Commission received the first of nearly twenty applications for permits to build new nuclear power plants. [27]

One of the most significant episodes in American environmental history is **Love Canal**. In 1942, Hooker Electro-Chemical Company purchased the abandoned Love Canal property in Niagara Falls, New York. Over the next eleven years, 21,800 tons of toxic chemicals were dumped into the canal. Hooker, later purchased by Occidental Chemical Corporation, sold the land to the city of Niagara Falls in 1953 with a warning in the property deed that the site contained hazardous chemicals. The city later constructed an elementary school on the site, with roads and sewer lines running through it and homes surrounding it. By the mid-1970s, the chemicals had begun to rise to the surface and seep into basements. [28] Local housewife Lois Gibbs, who later founded the Citizens' Clearinghouse for Hazardous Wastes, noticed an unusual frequency of cancers, miscarriages, deformed babies, illnesses, and deaths among residents of her neighborhood. After reading an article in the local newspaper about the history of the canal, she canvassed the neighborhood with a petition, alerting her neighbors to the chemical contamination beneath their feet. [29] On August 9, 1978, President Carter declared Love Canal a federal emergency, beginning a massive relocation effort in which the government purchased 803 residences in the area, 239 of which were destroyed. [30]

In the face of vehement industry opposition, the states and the federal government managed to put in place a wide-ranging series of regulations that defined standards of practice and forced the adoption of pollution control technologies. To oversee and enforce these regulations, taxpayers' dollars now funded a large new public bureaucracy. In the coming years, the size and scope of those agencies would come under fire from proindustry administrations elected on a platform of smaller government and less oversight and intervention.

In the meantime, the creation of the EPA compelled many states to create their own equivalent departments for environmental protection, often to administer or enforce EPA programs if nothing else. According to Denise Scheberle, an expert on federalism and environmental policy, "few policy areas placed greater and more diverse demands on states than environmental programs." [32] Some states, such as California, continued to press for stricter environmental standards than those set by the federal government. Almost all states have seen their relationships with the EPA vary from antagonistic to cooperative over the decades, depending on what states felt was being asked of them, why it was being asked, and how much financial assistance was being provided.

Despite growing public awareness and the previous decade of federal legislation to protect the environment, scientific studies were still predicting ecological disaster. President Carter's Council on Environmental Quality, in conjunction with the State Department, produced a study in 1980 of world ecological problems called The Global 2000 Report. The report warned that "if present trends continue, the world in 2000 will be more crowded, more polluted, less stable ecologically, and more vulnerable to disruption than the world we live in now. Serious stresses involving population, resources, and the environment are clearly visible ahead. Despite greater material output, the world's people will be poorer in many ways than they are today." [33]

Despite forecasts like this, the election of Ronald Reagan in November of 1980 marked a dramatic decline in federal support for existing and planned environmental legislation. With Reagan's 1981 appointments of two aggressive champions of industry, James Watt as secretary of the interior and Anne Buford as administrator of the EPA, it was apparent that the nation's environmental policies were a prime target of his "small government" revolution. In its early years, the Reagan administration moved rapidly to cut budgets, reduce environmental enforcement, and open public lands for mining, drilling, grazing, and other private uses. In 1983, however, Buford was forced to resign amid congressional investigations into mismanagement of a toxic waste cleanup, and Watt resigned after several statements he made were widely viewed as insensitive to actions damaging to the environment. Under Buford's successors, William Ruckelshaus and Lee Thomas, the environmental agency returned to a moderate course as both men made an effort to restore morale and public trust.

However, environmental crises continued to shape public opinion and environmental laws in the 1980s. In December 1984, approximately forty-five tons of methyl isocyanine gas leaked from an underground storage tank at a Union Carbide pesticide plant in Bhopal, India. The accident, which was far worse than the Seveso incident eight years earlier, caused 2,000 immediate deaths, another 1,500 deaths in the ensuing months, and over 300,000 injuries. The pesticide plant was closed, and the Indian government took Union Carbide to court. Mediation resulted in a settlement payment by Union Carbide of $470 million. [34] Over twenty-five years later, in 2010, courts in India were still determining the culpability of the senior managers involved.

This disaster produced the community "right to know" provision in the Superfund Amendments and Reauthorization Act (SARA) of 1986, requiring industries that use dangerous chemicals to disclose the type and amount of chemicals used to the citizens in the surrounding area that might be affected by an accident. [35] The right to know provision was manifested in the Toxics Release Inventory (TRI), in which companies made public the extent of their polluting emissions. This information proved useful for communities and industry by making both groups more aware of the volume of pollutants emitted and the responsibility of industry to lower these levels. The EPA currently releases this information at http://www.epa.gov/tri; other pollutant information is available at http://www.epa.gov/oar/data.

In 1990, Thomas Lefferre, an operations vice president for Monsanto, highlighted the sensitizing effect of this new requirement on business. He wrote, "If…you file a Title III report that says your plant emits 80,000 pounds of suspected carcinogens to the air each year, you might be comforted by the fact that you're in compliance with your permit. But what if your plant is two blocks from an elementary school? How comfortable would you be then?" [36

Until the mid-1980s, environmental disasters were perceived to be confined to geographically limited locations and people rarely feared contamination from beyond their local chemical or power plant. This notion changed in 1986 when an explosion inside a reactor at a nuclear plant in Chernobyl in the Ukraine released a gigantic cloud of radioactive debris that standard weather patterns spread from the Soviet Union to Scandinavia and Western Europe. The effects were severe and persistent. As a result of the explosion, some 21,000 people in Western Europe were expected to die of cancer and even more to contract the disease as a result. Reindeer in Lapland were found to have levels of radioactivity seven times above the norm. By 1990 sheep in northwest England and Wales were still too radioactive to be consumed. Within the former Soviet Union, over 10,000 square kilometers of land were determined to be unsafe for human habitation, yet much of the land remained occupied and farming continued. Approximately 115,000 people were evacuated from the area surrounding the plant site, 220 villages were abandoned, and another 600 villages required "decontamination." It is estimated that the lives of over 100,000 people in the former Soviet Union have been or will likely be severely affected by the accident. [37]

Other environmental problems of an international scale made headlines during the 1980s. Sulfur dioxide and nitrogen oxides from smokestacks and tailpipes can be carried over six hundred miles by prevailing winds and often return to ground as acid rain. As a result, Wheeling, West Virginia, once received rain with a pH value almost equivalent to battery acid. [38] As a result of such deposition, downwind lakes and streams become increasingly acidic and toxic to aquatic plants, invertebrates, and fish. The proportion of lakes in the Adirondack Mountains of New York with a pH below the level of 5.0 jumped from 4 percent in 1930 to over 50 percent by 1970, resulting in the loss of fish stocks. Acid rain has also been implicated in damaging forests at elevations above two thousand feet. The northeastern United States and eastern Canada, located downwind from large industrialized areas, were particularly hard hit. [39] Rain in the eastern United States is now about ten times more acidic than natural precipitation. Similar problems occurred in Scandinavia, the destination of Europe's microscopic pollutants.

A 1983 report by a congressional task force concluded that the primary cause of acid rain destroying freshwater in the northeastern United States was probably pollution from industrial stacks to the south and west. The National Academy of Sciences followed with a report asserting that by reducing sulfur oxide emissions from coal-burning power plants in the eastern United States, acid rain in the northeastern part of the country and southern Canada could be curbed. However, the Reagan administration declined to act, straining relations with Canada, especially during the 1988 visit of Canadian Prime Minister Brian Mulroney. [40] Acid rain was finally addressed in part by the Clean Air Act Amendments of 1990.

The CAA, a centerpiece of the environmental legislation enacted during what might be called the first environmental wave, was significantly amended in 1990 to address acid rain, ozone depletion, and the contribution of one state's pollution to states downwind. The act included a groundbreaking clause allowing the trading of pollution permits for sulfur dioxide and nitrogen oxide emissions from power plants in the East and Midwest. Plants now had market incentives to reduce their pollution emissions. They could sell credits, transformed into permits, on the Chicago Board of Trade. A company's effort to go beyond compliance enabled it to earn an asset that could be sold to firms that did not meet the standards. Companies were thus enticed to protect the environment as a way to increase profits, a mechanism considered by many to be a major advance in the design of environmental protection.

This policy innovation marked the beginning of market-oriented mechanisms to solve pollution problems. The Clean Air Interstate Rule (CAIR) expanded the scope of the original trading program and was reinstated after various judicial challenges to its method. The question of whether direct taxes or market solutions are best continues to be debated, however. With President Obama's election in 2008, the question of federal carbon taxes in the United States versus allowing regional and national carbon markets to evolve became a hot topic for national debate.

Another problem that reached global proportions was ozone depletion. In 1974, chemists Sherwood Rowland and Mario Molina announced that chlorofluorocarbons (CFCs) were lowering the average concentration of ozone in the stratosphere, a layer that blocks much of the sun's harmful ultraviolet rays before they reach the earth. Over time, less protection from ultraviolet rays will lead to higher rates of skin cancer and cataracts in humans as well as crop damage and harm to certain species of marine life. By 1985, scientists had observed a 50 percent reduction of the ozone in the upper stratosphere over Antarctica in the spring and early summer, creating a seasonal ozone hole. In 1988, a similar but less severe phenomenon was observed over the North Pole. Sensing disaster, Rowland and Molina called for an immediate ban of CFCs in spray cans.

Such a global-scale problem required a global solution. In 1987, representatives from thirty-six nations met in Montreal and developed a treaty known as the Montreal Protocol. Participating nations agreed to cut emissions of CFCs by about 35 percent between 1989 and 2000. This treaty was later expanded and strengthened in Copenhagen in 1992. [41] The amount of ozone-depleting substances close to Earth's surface consequently declined, whereas the amount in the upper atmosphere remained high. The persistence of such chemicals means it may take decades for the ozone layer to return to the density it had before 1980. The good news was that the rate of new destruction approached zero by 2006. [42] It is interesting to note that businesses opposed restrictions on CFC use until patent-protected alternative materials were available to substitute for CFCs in the market.

The increasingly global scale of environmental threats and the growing awareness among nations of the interrelated nature of economic development and stable functioning of natural systems led the United Nations to establish the World Commission on Environment and Development (WCED) in 1983. The commission was convened the following year, led by chairwoman Gro Harlem Brundtland, former prime minister of Norway. In 1987, the so-called Brundtland Commission produced a landmark report, **Our Common Future**, which tied together concerns for human development, economic development, and environmental protection with the concept of sustainable development. Although this was certainly not the first appearance of the term sustainable development, to many the commission's definition became a benchmark for moving forward: "Sustainable development is development that meets the needs of the present without compromising the ability of future generations to meet their own needs." Around that same time, the phrase environmental justice was coined to describe the patterns of locating hazardous industries or dumping hazardous wastes and toxins in regions predominantly home to poor people or racial and ethnic minorities.

Pollution Prevention

By the mid-1970s, companies had begun to act to prevent pollution rather than just mitigate the wastes already produced. **Pollution prevention** refers to actions inside a company and is called an in-the-pipe as opposed to an end-of-the-pipe method for environmental protection. Unlike pollution control, which only imposes costs, pollution prevention offers an opportunity for a company to save money and implement environmental protection simultaneously. Still used today, companies often enter this process tentatively, looking for quick payback. Over time it has been shown they can achieve significant positive financial and environmental results. When this happens it helps open minds within companies to the potential of environmentally sound process redesign or reengineering that contributes both ecological and health benefits as well as the bottom line of profitability.

There are four main categories of pollution prevention: good housekeeping, materials substitution, manufacturing modifications, and resource recovery. The objective of good housekeeping is for companies to operate their machinery and production systems as efficiently as possible. This requires an understanding and monitoring of material flows, impacts, and the sources and volume of wastes. Good housekeeping is a management issue that ensures preventable material losses are not occurring and all resources are used efficiently. Materials substitution seeks to identify and eliminate the sources of hazardous and toxic wastes such as heavy metals, volatile organic compounds, chlorofluorocarbons, and carcinogens. By substituting more environmentally friendly alternatives or reducing the amount of undesirable substances used and emitted, a company can bypass the need for expensive end-of-the-pipe treatments.

Manufacturing modifications involve process changes to simplify production technologies, introduce closed-loop processing, and reduce water and energy use. These steps can significantly lower emissions and reduce costs. Finally, resource recovery captures waste materials and seeks to reuse them in the same process, as inputs for another process within the production system, or as inputs for processes in other production systems. [43]

One of the earliest instances of pollution prevention in practice was 3M's Pollution Prevention Pays (3P) program, established in 1975. The program achieved savings of over half a billion dollars in capital and operating costs while eliminating 600,000 pounds of effluents, air emissions, and solid waste. This program continued to evolve within 3M and became integrated into incentive systems, rewarding employees for identifying and eliminating unnecessary waste. [44] Other companies, while not pursuing environmental objectives per se, have found that total quality management (TQM) programs can help achieve cost savings and resource efficiencies consistent with pollution prevention objectives through conscious efforts to reduce inputs and waste generation.

Though pollution prevention is a significant first step in corporate environmental protection, Joseph Fiksel identifies several limitations to pollution prevention as typically practiced. First, it only incrementally refines and improves existing processes. Second, it tends to focus on singular measures of improvement, such as waste volume reduction, rather than on adopting a systems view of environmental performance. Renowned systems analyst Donella Meadows offered a simple definition of a system as "any set of interconnected elements." A systems view emphasizes connections and relationships. [45] Third, as most of the gains are often in processes that were not previously optimized for efficiency, the improvements are not repeatable. Fourth, pollution prevention is detached from a company's business strategy and is performed on a piecemeal basis. [46]

KEY TAKEAWAYS

- In the 1970s, the federal government mandated certain standards and banned some chemicals outright in a command-and-control approach.
- Pollution prevention provided the first significant opportunity to reconcile business and environmental goals.
- Environmental problems grew in geographic scale and intensity through the 1980s, creating a growing awareness that more serious measures and new thinking about limits to growth were required.

EXERCISES

1. Compare and contrast pollution control and pollution prevention based on (a) their effectiveness and ease of administration as regulations, and (b) their effects on business processes and opportunities.

2. How did trends in environmental issues and regulations change and stay the same in the 1970s and 1980s as compared to earlier decades?

3. Do you see any overlap in circumstances today and the events and perspectives in the 1980s?

---

[1] Richard Nixon Foundation, "RN In '70—Launching the Decade of the Environment," *The New Nixon Blog*, January 1, 2010, accessed March 23, 2011, http://blog.nixonfoundation.org/2010/01/rn-in-70-the-decade-of-the-environment.

[2] See National Environmental Policy Act of 1969, 42 U.S.C. § 4321–47. GPO Access US Code Online, "42 USC 4331," January 3, 2007, accessed April 19, 2011, http://frwebgate.access.gpo.gov/cgi-bin/getdoc.cgi?dbname=browse_usc&docid=Cite:+42USC4331, Jan 3, 2007.

[3] Walter A. Rosenbaum, *Environmental Politics and Policy*, 2nd ed. (Washington, DC: Congressional Quarterly Press, 1991), 180–81.

[4] Gaylord Nelson, interview with Philip Shabecoff, quoted in Philip Shabecoff, *A Fierce Green Fire: The American Environmental Movement* (New York: Hill & Wang, 1993), 114–15.

[5] Hayes organized Earth Day while working for US Senator Gaylord Nelson. Hayes, a Stanford- and Harvard-educated activist with a law degree, helped found Green Seal, one of the most prominent ecolabeling systems in the United States, and directed the National Renewable Energy Laboratory under the Carter administration.

[6] Tyler Miller Jr., *Living in the Environment: Principles, Connections, and Solutions*, 9th ed. (Belmont, CA: Wadsworth, 1996), 42.

[7] Joseph Lelyveld, "Mood Is Joyful Here," *New York Times*, April 23, 1970, quoted in Philip Shabecoff, *A Fierce Green Fire: The American Environmental Movement* (New York: Hill & Wang, 1993), 113.

[8] Walter A. Rosenbaum, *Environmental Politics and Policy*, 2nd ed. (Washington, DC: Congressional Quarterly Press, 1991), 195–96.

[9] Walter A. Rosenbaum, *Environmental Politics and Policy*, 2nd ed. (Washington, DC: Congressional Quarterly Press, 1991), 206–7.

[10] Philip Shabecoff, *A Fierce Green Fire: The American Environmental Movement* (New York: Hill & Wang, 1993), 175.

[11] Philip Shabecoff, *A Fierce Green Fire: The American Environmental Movement* (New York: Hill & Wang, 1993), 46–47.

[12] Andrew J. Hoffman, *From Heresy to Dogma: An Institutional History of Corporate Environmentalism* (San Francisco: New Lexington Press, 1997), 81.

[13] Michael Porter and Claas van der Linde, "Green and Competitive: Ending the Stalemate," *Harvard Business Review* 73, no. 5 (September/October 1995): 120–34.

[14] US Congress, Office of Technology Assessment, *Serious Reduction of Hazardous Waste* (Washington, DC: US Government Printing Office, 1986), quoted in Stephan Schmidheiny, with the Business Council for Sustainable Development, *Changing Course* (Cambridge, MA: MIT Press, 1992), 106.

[15] Stephan Schmidheiny, with the Business Council for Sustainable Development, *Changing Course* (Cambridge, MA: MIT Press, 1992), 100.

[16] Michael Porter and Claas van der Linde, "Green and Competitive: Ending the Stalemate," *Harvard Business Review* 73, no. 5 (September/October 1995): 120–34.

[17] Philip Shabecoff, *A Fierce Green Fire: The American Environmental Movement* (New York: Hill & Wang, 1993), 96. Also see Donella H. Meadows, Dennis L. Meadows, Jørgen Randers, and William W. Behrens III, *The Limits to Growth* (New York: Universe Books, 1972), 23–24.

[18] Tyler Miller Jr., *Living in the Environment: Principles, Connections, and Solutions*, 9th ed. (Belmont, CA: Wadsworth, 1996), 42.

[19] Energy Information Administration, Department of Energy, "Petroleum," accessed November 29, 2010, http://www.eia.doe.gov/oil_gas/petroleum/info_glance/petroleum.html.

[20] Clive Ponting, *A Green History of the World* (New York: Penguin Books, 1991), 372–73.

[21] Andrew J. Hoffman, *From Heresy to Dogma: An Institutional History of Corporate Environmentalism* (San Francisco: New Lexington Press, 1997), 73.

[22] John F. Mahon and Richard A. McGowan, *Industry as a Player in the Political and Social Arena* (Westport, CT: Quorum Books, 1996), 144.

[23] Philip Shabecoff, *A Fierce Green Fire: The American Environmental Movement* (New York: Hill & Wang, 1993), 269.

[24] According to the US Environmental Protection Agency, "The Clean Water Act (CWA) establishes the basic structure for regulating discharges of pollutants into the waters of the United States and regulating quality standards for surface waters. The basis of the CWA was enacted in 1948 and was called the Federal Water Pollution Control Act, but the act was significantly reorganized and expanded in 1972. 'Clean Water Act' became the Act's common name with amendments in 1977." Under the CWA, industry wastewater and water quality standards were set for industry and all surface-water contaminants. In addition, permits were required to discharge pollutants under the EPA's National Pollutant Discharge Elimination System (NPDES) program. See US Environmental Protection Agency, "Laws and Regulations: Summary of the Clean Water Act," accessed March 7, 2011, http://www.epa.gov/lawsregs/laws/cwa.html.

[25] Tyler Miller Jr., *Living in the Environment: Principles, Connections, and Solutions*, 9th ed. (Belmont, CA: Wadsworth, 1996), 387.

[26] Tyler Miller Jr., *Living in the Environment: Principles, Connections, and Solutions*, 9th ed. (Belmont, CA: Wadsworth, 1996), 385.

[27] Energy Information Administration, Department of Energy, "U.S. Nuclear Reactors," accessed November 29, 2010, http://www.eia.doe.gov/cneaf/nuclear/page/nuc_reactors/reactsum.html.

[28] Andrew J. Hoffman, *From Heresy to Dogma: An Institutional History of Corporate Environmentalism* (San Francisco: New Lexington Press, 1997), 79.

[29] Aubrey Wallace, *Eco-Heroes* (San Francisco: Mercury House, 1993), 169–70.

[30] Andrew J. Hoffman, *From Heresy to Dogma: An Institutional History of Corporate Environmentalism* (San Francisco: New Lexington Press, 1997), 79.

[31] Andrew J. Hoffman, *From Heresy to Dogma: An Institutional History of Corporate Environmentalism* (San Francisco: New Lexington Press, 1997), 79.

[32] Denise Scheberle, *Federalism and Environmental Policy: Trust and the Politics of Implementation*, 2nd ed. (Washington, DC: Georgetown University Press, 2004), 5.

[33] United States Council on Environmental Quality and the Department of State, *The Global 2000 Report to the President* (Washington, DC: US Government Printing Office, 1980), 1.

[34] Andrew J. Hoffman, *From Heresy to Dogma: An Institutional History of Corporate Environmentalism* (San Francisco: New Lexington Press, 1997), 96.

[35] Walter A. Rosenbaum, *Environmental Politics and Policy*, 2nd ed. (Washington, DC: Congressional Quarterly Press, 1991), 80.

[36] Andrew J. Hoffman, *From Heresy to Dogma: An Institutional History of Corporate Environmentalism* (San Francisco: New Lexington Press, 1997), 179.

[37] Clive Ponting, *A Green History of the World* (New York: Penguin Books, 1991), 377; World Health Organization, "Health Effects of the Chernobyl Accident: An Overview," Fact sheet no. 303, April 2006, accessed April 19, 2011, http://www.who.int/mediacentre/factsheets/fs303/en/index.html.

[38] Tyler Miller Jr., *Living in the Environment: Principles, Connections, and Solutions*, 9th ed. (Belmont, CA: Wadsworth, 1996), 436.

[39] Clive Ponting, *A Green History of the World* (New York: Penguin Books, 1991), 367.

[40] Walter A. Rosenbaum, *Environmental Politics and Policy*, 2nd ed. (Washington, DC: Congressional Quarterly Press, 1991), 184.

[41] Tyler Miller Jr., *Living in the Environment: Principles, Connections, and Solutions*, 9th ed. (Belmont, CA: Wadsworth, 1996), 317–27.

[42] World Meteorological Organization, *Scientific Assessment of Ozone Depletion: 2006*, Global Ozone Research and Monitoring Project—Report No. 50 (Geneva, Switzerland: World Meteorological Organization, 2007), accessed November 29, 2010, http://www.wmo.ch/pages/prog/arep/gaw/ozone_2006/ozone_asst_report.html.

[43] Stephan Schmidheiny, with the Business Council for Sustainable Development, *Changing Course* (Cambridge, MA: MIT Press, 1992), 101–4.

[44] Joseph Fiksel, "Conceptual Principles of DFE," in *Design for Environment: Creating Eco-Efficient Products and Processes*, ed. Joseph Fiksel (New York: McGraw-Hill, 1996), 53.

[45] Donella H. Meadows, "Whole Earth Models and Systems," *Coevolution Quarterly* 34 (Summer 1982): 98–108, quoted in Joseph J. Romm, *Lean and Clean Management* (New York: Kodansha, 1994), 33.
[46] Joseph Fiksel, "Conceptual Principles of DFE," in *Design for Environment: Creating Eco-Efficient Products and Processes*, ed. Joseph Fiksel (New York: McGraw-Hill, 1996), 54.
[47] Robert U. Ayres, "Industrial Metabolism," in *Technology and Environment*, ed. Jesse H. Ausubel and Hedy E. Sladovich (Washington, DC: National Academy Press, 1989), 26; Robert Solow, "Sustainability: An Economist's Perspective," in *Economics of the Environment*, 3rd ed., ed. Robert Dorfman and Nancy S. Dorfman (New York: W. W. Norton, 1993), 181.

1.3 Pressures on Companies Continue

LEARNING OBJECTIVES

1. Understand how business opportunities arise from changes in environmental regulation as well as from the growing public demand to protect the environment and health.
2. Analyze how globalization and environmental hazards contributed to the development of sustainability as a framework for business and government.

In the United States, the slow pace of government action on environmental protection during the 1980s began to change with the Superfund reauthorization in 1986. The following year, Congress overrode President Reagan's veto to amend the Clean Water Act to control nonpoint sources of pollution such as fertilizer runoff. [1] As America's economy continued to expand during the 1980s, so did its solid waste problem. The issues of America's bulging landfills and throwaway economy were captured by the image of the Mobro 4000, a barge carrying 3,168 tons of trash that set sail from Islip, Long Island, New York, on March 22, 1987. [2] The barge spent the next fifty-five days in search of a suitable location to deposit its cargo while drawing significant media attention. [3] Meanwhile, New York City's Fresh Kills Landfill became the largest landfill in the world. The following summer, the issue of waste returned to the headlines when garbage and medical waste, including hypodermic needles, began washing onto beaches in New York and New Jersey, costing coastal counties in New Jersey an estimated $100 million in tourist revenue. Public outcry spurred the federal government to ban ocean dumping of municipal waste. The states of New York and New Jersey subsequently closed several coastal sewage treatment plants, upgraded others, and enacted laws for medical waste disposal. [4]

America's reliance on fossil fuels was brought to the forefront once again when the Exxon Valdez supertanker ran aground in Prince William Sound, Alaska, on March 24, 1989. Over 10 million gallons of crude oil spilled from the ship, polluting 1,200 miles of coastline. Approximately 350,000 sea birds, several thousand rare otters, and countless other animals were killed. In 2010, lasting damage from the spill was still documented. The accident coincided with and helped to further a generational peak in environmental awareness.

Improved regulatory design focused on goals and results rather than means and proscribed technical fixes, representing what many viewed as a positive policy strategy evolution. This adaptation by government occurred in part as a response to industry resistance to government imposition of "command and control" requirements. Often neglected in polarized discussions that simplistically frame business against government is the fact that governments are steadily adjusting, updating, and refining regulatory approaches to better reflect new knowledge, technology, and business realities. It should be kept in mind that the history of environmental and sustainability issues in business is an evolutionary process of constantly interacting and interdependent cross-sector participants that may collide but ultimately adapt and change. Just as the regulatory bodies have had to adapt to changing and emerging resource, waste stream, Earth system, and health problems, so too have environmental groups and companies had to acknowledge a novel cascade of problems associated with industrial production. Shifting, give-and-take, back-and-forth dynamics characterized the terrain even as new participants emerged. Examples of this evolution were the rising numbers of health, equity, energy, and environmental nongovernmental activist organizations, many of which had lost faith in governments' capacities to solve problems. However, pressures on government by such groups might cause a regulatory response that creates an unintended new pollution problem. For example, does a focus on reducing large particulate matter in the air from vehicle emissions drive higher emissions of microsized particles that create a new set of medical challenges and respiratory afflictions? In addition, the environmental community is not monolithic.

These organizations range from law-defying extreme activists attacking corporations to pragmatic, collaborative science-based nongovernmental organizations (NGOs) working closely with companies to generate solutions. Despite this rich evolutionary adaptive phenomenon across sectors, for the most part companies remained relatively resistant to environmental groups through the 1990s.

Compliance was still the primary goal, and companies combining forces to set industry standards became a method of forestalling regulation. Unless they were singled out due to their industry's visibility or poor reputation, most companies continued to see health and environmental issues as a burden and additional cost. Environmentalism was associated with tree-huggers, altruists, overhead cost burdens, and public sector fines and regulation.

As if on a parallel yet nonintersecting path, in 1989, a special issue of the Scientific American journal articulated the state of scientific understanding of the growing global collision and the urgency of addressing the clashes among human economic growth patterns, ecological limits, and population growth. For the first time, the need to address dominant policies and economic growth models was being raised in a leading US scientific journal.

In fact, debate on scientific evidence and necessary global action was expanding to challenge the one-dimensional view held by most corporate leaders. With the rise in environmental problems at the global scale, the United Nations (UN) convened a conference on the environment in Rio de Janeiro in June of 1992, which became known as the **Rio Earth Summit**. Attending this unprecedented forum were more than 100 heads of state, representatives from 178 nations, and 18,000 people from 7,000 NGOs. Major results included a nonbinding charter for guiding environmental policies toward sustainable development, a nonbinding agreement on forestry management and protection, the establishment of the UN Commission on Sustainable Development, and conventions on climate change and biodiversity that have not yet been ratified by enough nations to go into effect. Despite the lack of binding treaties, the Rio Earth Summit succeeded in articulating general global environmental principles and guidelines in a consensus-driven setting involving participation by most of the world's nations. [6]

While there may have been less activity in the United States at the time, a new era was under way internationally. Creation of the World Business Council for Sustainable Development (WBCSD) marked a turning point in global business engagement. In preparation for the Rio Earth Summit, Swiss industrialist Stephan Schmidheiny organized the WBCSD in 1990. The council featured over fifty business leaders from around the world. Their task was without precedent, as Schmidheiny explained: "This is the first time that an important group of business leaders has looked at these environmental issues from a global perspective and reached major agreements on the need for an integrated approach in confronting the challenges of economic development and the environment." [7]

The WBCSD published a book in 1992 titled Changing Course, in which the objectives of business and the environment were argued to be compatible. Schmidheiny wrote that business must "devise strategies to maximize added value while minimizing resource and energy use," and that "given the large technological and productive capacity of business, any progress toward sustainable development requires its active leadership." [8] This language represented a mainstreaming of what is called **eco-efficiency** in business. The WBCSD opened new doors. Its work signaled acceptance of the new term sustainable business and hinted at sustainability as a term that referred to an alternative economic growth pattern. Sustainable business, defined as improving the efficiency of resource use, was beginning to be recognized by global business leaders as an activity in which corporations could legitimately engage. The important shift under way was that the notion of sustainability was moving from small pockets of visionary business leaders and development specialists to the broader international business community.

It made sense. World population growth trajectories predicted emerging economies growing at an accelerating rate. Their societies' legitimate aspirations to live according to Western developed economies' standards would require a tremendous acceleration in the throughput of raw materials, massive growth in industrial activity, and unprecedented demand for energy. People were beginning to wonder how that growth would be achieved in a way that preserved ecological systems, protected human health, and supported stable, viable communities. Figure 1.8 "Actual and Predicted Global Population Growth, 1750-2050 (billions)" shows the significant increases in emerging economy populations compared to developed countries after 1950.

Of no small significance, certain publications emerged and within a few years were read widely by those interested in the debates over economic growth and population trajectories. In 1993, Paul Hawken authored The Ecology of Commerce, which brought to the public's attention an alternative model of commerce without waste that relies on renewable energy sources, eliminates toxins, and thrives on biodiversity.

Hawken moved beyond the WBCSD goals of minimization (eco-efficiency) by suggesting a restorative economy "that is so intelligently designed and constructed that it mimics nature at every step, a symbiosis of company and customer and ecology." [9] Written for a broad audience, Hawken's book became a must-read for those trying to grasp the tensions among economic growth, the viability of natural systems, and the possibilities for change. An entrepreneur himself, Hawken looked to markets, firms, and an entrepreneurial mind-set to solve many of the problems.

Figure 1.8 Actual and Predicted Global Population Growth, 1750–2050 (billions)

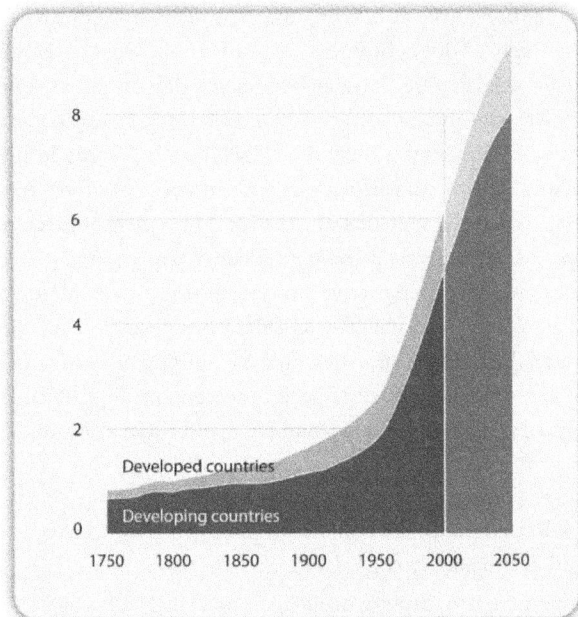

Source: UNEP/GRID-Arendal, "Trends in Population, Developed and Developing Countries, 1750–2050 (Estimates and Projections)." UNEP/GRID-Arendal Maps and Graphics Library, accessed March 14, 2011,http://maps.grida.no/go/graphic/trends-in-population-developed-and-developing-countries-1750-2050-estimates-and-projections.

In 1991, strategy thinker and Harvard Business School professor Michael Porter published articles about green strategy in Scientific American, and in 1995 his article with Claas van der Linde called "Green and Competitive: Ending the Stalemate" appeared in the Harvard Business Review. [10] Publication in a top business journal read by executives was important because it sent a strong signal to business that new ideas were emerging, in other words, that integrating environmental and health concerns into strategy could enhance a company's competitive position. Business-executive-turned-educator Robert Frosch had already published his ideas about recovering waste materials in closed-loop systems in "Closing the Loop on Waste Materials." [11] For a former executive of a major

corporation to talk about recovering and using waste streams as assets and inputs for other production processes represented a breakthrough. Earlier classics such as Garrett Hardin's "The Tragedy of the Commons" and Kenneth Boulding's "The Economics of the Coming Spaceship Earth" continued to serve as foundations for new thinking about the contours of future business growth.[12] A body of research and new reasoning was accumulating and diffusing, driving change in how people thought.

Even as the relationship among conventional business perspectives and environmental, health, and social issues shifted, albeit slowly, global problems continued to mount. Climate change debate moved from exclusively scientific conversations to mainstream media outlets. In the summer of 1988, an unprecedented heat wave attacked the United States, killing livestock by the thousands and wiping out a third of the country's grain crop. The issue of global warming or, more appropriately, global climate change entered the headlines with new force. [13] During the heat wave, Dr. James E. Hansen of the National Aeronautics and Space Administration (NASA) warned a Senate committee that the greenhouse effect—the process by which excessive levels of various gases in the atmosphere cause changes in the world's climate—had probably already arrived. [14] The United Nations and the World Meteorological Organization established the Intergovernmental Panel on Climate Change (IPCC) in 1988 to study climate change. With input from over nine hundred scientists, the IPCC published its first report in 1995, which concluded that by the year 2100, temperatures could increase from 2°F to 6°F, causing seas to rise from 6 to 38 inches with changes in drought and flooding frequency. Citing a 30 percent rise in atmospheric carbon dioxide since the dawn of the Industrial Age, the IPCC reported that "the balance of evidence suggests a discernable human influence on global climate." Twenty-four hundred scientists endorsed these findings. [15]

As with the issue of ozone depletion, an international conference was convened in December 1997 in Kyoto, Japan, to address the problem of global climate change. Representatives from over 160 nations hammered out an agreement known as the **Kyoto Protocol** to the United Nations Framework Convention on Climate Change (UNFCCC). The protocol, seen as a first step in addressing climate change issues, required developed nations to reduce their emissions of greenhouse gases by an average of 5.2 percent below 1990 levels by the years 2008 to 2012. Regulated greenhouse gases included carbon dioxide, nitrogen oxides, methane, hydrofluorocarbons, perfluorocarbons, and sulfur hexafluoride. To date, the US

Senate has not ratified the agreement, and President Bush rejected the Kyoto Protocol.

The first IPCC report was followed by subsequent IPCC reports to refine the predictions for particular regions of the world; the last one was published in 2007. Other materials followed, such as the National Academy Press publication The Industrial Green Game in 1997, as leading scientists and business experts spoke out together about a need for new thinking. The book highlighted issues of national if not international concern, such as product redesigns and management reforms whose intent was to avoid environmental and health problems before they arose. A full life-cycle approach and systems thinking, deemed essential to the new industrial green game, were fundamental to the evolving alternative paradigm.

Unfortunately, most leaders in the business community and business schools were not ready to discuss the scientific evidence and its implications. In the US business community, where the prior politics of environmentalism and business resistance to the threat of regulation had polarized debate, the conversations were not productive. Top business schools followed mainstream business thinking well into the first decade of the twenty-first century, marginalizing the topics as side issues to be dealt with exclusively by ethics professors or shunting them to courses or even other schools that focused on regulation, public policy, or nonprofit management.

Slowly, however, the groundwork was laid for significant and prevalent changes in how businesses relate to the environment. The commission wrote, "Many essential human needs can be met only through goods and services provided by industry....Industry extracts materials from the natural resource base and inserts both products and pollution into the human environment. It has the power to enhance or degrade the environment; it invariably does both." [20]

Embedded within the statement was a particular linkage among previously conflicting interests. This would usher in a new way of doing business. As Mohan Munasinghe of the IPCC explained, "sustainable development necessarily involves the pursuit of economic efficiency, social equity, and environmental protection." [21] Thus, beginning in the 1990s, thanks to the efforts of a small number of pioneering firms and spokespersons able to span the science-business gap, sustainability as a business strategy was emerging as a powerful new perspective to create value for multiple stakeholders. A sustainable business perspective—and the sustainability innovations created by entrepreneurs—is the current evolutionary stage in an increasingly sophisticated corporate response to environmental and social concerns.

KEY TAKEAWAYS

- In the 1980s and 1990s, population growth and the scale of industrialization and concomitant environmental concerns led to the pursuit of "sustainable" business models that acknowledged health and ecological system constraints.
- Pressure on companies grew due to scientific discoveries about pollutants, waste disposal challenges, oil spills, and other accidents.
- Proliferation and diffusion of reports educated the public and government officials, resulting in increased pressure for regulatory action and corporate response.

EXERCISES

1. What opportunities for business innovation and entrepreneurship can you identify given the trends and historical information?
2. What implications can you deduce from the population growth trends projected for the next fifty years?
3. If entrepreneurial opportunity is a response to inefficiencies in the market, what inefficiencies can you identify?
4. Summarize the mind-set of someone born in the 1960s with respect to knowledge and attitudes about sustainability compared to someone born in the late 1980s or 1990s.

Table 1.1 An Overview of the Historical Context for Sustainable Business in the United States, 1960–2000

Year	Event	Legislation	Environmental Framework for Business [22]
1962	*Silent Spring*		
1963	New York City smog-related fatalities		
1964	Mississippi River fish kills		
1969	Cuyahoga River fire; Santa Barbara oil spill; Moon landing		
1970	First Earth Day	National Environmental Policy Act (NEPA); Clean Air Act (CAA)	Pollution control
1972	The limits of growth	Federal Water Pollution Control Act (FWPCA; became Clean Water Act); Federal Insecticide, Fungicide, and Rodenticide Act (FIFRA)	
1973	"Oil shock"	Endangered Species Act (ESA)	
1974		Safe Drinking Water Act (SDWA)	
1975			Pollution prevention
1976	Seveso explosion	Toxic Substance Control Act (TSCA); Resource Conservation and Recovery Act (RCRA)	
1977		Clean Air Act Amendments of 1990; Clean Water Act amendments	
1978	Love Canal; Second "oil shock"		
1979	Three Mile Island		
1980	*Global 2000 Report*	Comprehensive Environmental Response, Compensation, and Liability Act (CERCLA, a.k.a. Superfund)	
1983	Federal acid rain studies		
1984	Bhopal		
1985	Ozone hole over Antarctica discovered		
1986	Chernobyl	Superfund Amendments and Reauthorization Act (SARA)	
1987	Mobro 4000 trash barge; Montreal Protocol; *Our Common Future*	Clean Water Act amendments	Sustainable development
1988	Medical waste on NY and NJ beaches; Global warming		
1989	*Exxon Valdez*		Industrial ecology; The Natural Step
1990	World Business Council for Sustainable Development (WBCSD)	Clean Air Act Amendments of 1990	

	formed		
1992	Rio Earth Summit; *Changing Course*		Design for Environment (DfE); Eco-efficiency
1993	*The Ecology of Commerce*		Sustainable design
1996	*Our Stolen Future*		
1997	Kyoto Protocol		
2001	Toxic dust from World Trade Center and Pentagon attacks		
2002	Cradle to Grave: Remaking the Way We Make Things		Eco-e
2005	*Capitalism at the Crossroads;* EU begins greenhouse gas emission trading scheme		Beyond greening
2006	*An Inconvenient Truth*		
2007	Melamine-tainted pet food and leaded toys from China	Supreme Court rules in *Massachusetts v. Environmental Protection Agency* (EPA) that EPA should regulate carbon dioxide and greenhouse gases under CAA	
2008	Summer gas prices exceed $4 per gallon	Consumer Product Safety Act	
2009	Regional Greenhouse Gas Initiative begins trading		

[1] Philip Shabecoff, *A Fierce Green Fire: The American Environmental Movement* (New York: Hill & Wang, 1993), 230.

[2] William Rathje and Cullen Murphy, *Rubbish!* (New York: Harper Perennial, 1992), 28.

[3] Philip Shabecoff, *A Fierce Green Fire: The American Environmental Movement* (New York: Hill & Wang, 1993), 271.

[4] Andrew J. Hoffman, *From Heresy to Dogma: An Institutional History of Corporate Environmentalism* (San Francisco: New Lexington Press, 1997), 120–21.

[5] Andrew J. Hoffman, *From Heresy to Dogma: An Institutional History of Corporate Environmentalism* (San Francisco: New Lexington Press, 1997), 121–22.

[6] Tyler Miller Jr., *Living in the Environment: Principles, Connections, and Solutions*, 9th ed. (Belmont, CA: Wadsworth, 1996), 706.

[7] Stephan Schmidheiny, with the Business Council for Sustainable Development, *Changing Course* (Cambridge, MA: MIT Press, 1992), xxi.

[8] Stephan Schmidheiny, with the Business Council for Sustainable Development, *Changing Course* (Cambridge, MA: MIT Press, 1992), 9.

[9] Paul Hawken, *The Ecology of Commerce* (New York: Harper Business, 1993), 12, 15.

[10] Michael E. Porter and Claas van der Linde, "Green and Competitive: Ending the Stalemate," *Harvard Business Review* 73, no. 5 (September/October 1995): 120–34.

[11] Robert A. Frosch, "Closing the Loop on Waste Materials," in *The Industrial Green Game* (Washington, DC: National Academy Press, 1997), 37–47.

[12] Garrett Hardin, "The Tragedy of the Commons," *Science* 16 (1968): 1243–48; Kenneth Boulding, "The Economics of the Coming Spaceship Earth" (paper presented at the Sixth Resources for the Future Forum on Environmental Quality in a Growing Economy, Washington, DC, March 8, 1966).

[13] Kirkpatrick Sale, *The Green Revolution: The American Environmental Movement, 1962–1992* (New York: Hill & Wang, 1993), 71.

[14] Philip Shabecoff, *A Fierce Green Fire: The American Environmental Movement* (New York: Hill & Wang, 1993), 196.

[15] Paul Raeburn, "Global Warming: Is There Still Room for Doubt?" *BusinessWeek*, November 3, 1997, 158.

[16] Theo Colborn, Dianne Dumanoski, and John Peterson Myers, *Our Stolen Future* (New York: Dutton, 1996), vi.

[17] From the US Centers for Disease Control and Prevention, "National Report on Human Exposure to Environmental Chemicals," accessed December 29, 2010, http://www.cdc.gov/exposurereport; "The *Fourth National Report on Human Exposure to Environmental Chemicals* is the most comprehensive assessment to date of the exposure of the U.S. population to chemicals in our environment. CDC has measured 212 chemicals in people's blood or urine—75 of which have never before been measured in the U.S. population. *What's new in the Fourth Report*: The blood and urine samples were collected from participants in CDC's National Health and Nutrition Examination Survey, which is an ongoing survey that samples the U.S. population every two years. Each two year sample consists of about 2,400 persons. The *Fourth Report* includes findings from national samples for 1999–2000, 2001–2002, and 2003–2004. The data are analyzed separately by age, sex and race/ethnicity groups. The *Updated Tables, July 2010* provides additional data from the 2005-2006 survey period for 51 of the chemicals previously reported through 2004 in the *Fourth Report* and the new addition of four parabens and two phthalate metabolites in 2005–2006."

[18] Sara Goodman, "Tests Find More Than 200 Chemicals in Newborn Umbilical Cord Blood," *Scientific American*, December 2, 2009, accessed March 7, 2011, http://www.scientificamerican.com/article.cfm?id=newborn-babies-chemicals-exposure-bpa.

[19] *Our Stolen Future*, "Semen Quality Decreases in Men with Higher Levels of Phthalate," http://www.ourstolenfuture.org/newscience/oncompounds/phthalates/2006/2006-1101hauseretal.html.

[20] World Commission on Environment and Development, *Our Common Future* (New York: Oxford University Press, 1987), 206.

[21] Mohan Munasinghe, Wilfrido Cruz, and Jeremy Warford, "Are Economy-wide Policies Good for the Environment?" *Finance and Development* 30, no. 3 (September 1993): 40.

[22] See Richard R. Johnson, {Author's Name Retracted as requested by the work's original creator or licensee}, and Elizabeth Teisberg, *The Path to Sustainable Business: Environmental Frameworks, Practices and Related Tools*, UVA-ENT-0033 (Charlottesville, VA: Darden Business Publishing, University of Virginia, 1997); updated by author {Author's Name Retracted as requested by the work's original creator or licensee} to 2009. See comprehensive update: {Author's Name Retracted as requested by the work's original creator or licensee}, *Sustainability and Innovation: Frameworks, Concepts, and Tools for Product and Strategy Redesign*, UVA-ENT-0138 (Charlottesville, VA: Darden Business Publishing, University of Virginia, January 2010).

NOTES:

NOTES:

Chapter 2:

Sustainability Innovation in Business

2.1 Energy and Materials: New Challenges in the First Decade of the Twenty-first Century and Limits to the Conventional Growth Model

LEARNING OBJECTIVES

1. Appreciate the scope and complexity of the challenges that have recently spurred sustainability innovation with respect to energy and materials.

2. Gain insight into the fundamental drivers creating opportunities for entrepreneurs and new ventures in the sustainability innovation arena.

Sustainability innovators create new products and services designed to solve the problems created by the collision of economic growth, population growth, and natural systems. They seek integrated solutions that offer financial renumeration, ecological system protection, and improved human health performance, all of which contribute to community prosperity. Sustainability innovation, growing from early ripples of change in the 1980s and 1990s, now constitutes a wave of creativity led by a growing population of entrepreneurial individuals and ventures. This form of creativity applies to raw materials selection, energy use, and product design as well as company strategies across supply chains. It encompasses renewable energy technologies to reduce pollution and climate impacts as well as the safer design of molecular materials used in common household products. Today's tough economic times and need for job creation, while seemingly detracting from environmental concerns, in fact underscore the importance of monitoring energy and material input and waste cost-reduction measures; these are made visible through a sustainability lens. In addition, because the environmental health and ecological system degradation issues will only increase with economic growth, and public concern is unlikely to fade, those firms that explore sustainability efficiencies and differentiation opportunities now will be better positioned to weather the economic downturn.

Research indicates that individuals and ventures that pursue these objectives often work through networks of diverse supply-chain collaborations to realize new and better ways of providing goods and services. As a result, a plethora of substitute products, technologies, and innovative ways of organizing that address pollution, health, resource use, and equity concerns are being introduced and tested in the marketplace. This is the challenge and the excitement of sustainability innovation. In this chapter we look more

closely at sustainability innovation. What forces have driven it, and how is it being defined?

Two areas, energy and materials, provide useful entry points for exploring why businesses are increasingly using sustainability frameworks for thinking about the redesign of their products and operations. However, in the first decade of the twenty-first century, the media and public increasingly focused on climate change as the top environmental issue. Severe storms and other extreme weather patterns predicted by climate change scientists had become more evident. Hurricane Katrina in New Orleans, accelerated Arctic and Antarctic warming, rising ocean levels, and increasing carbon dioxide (CO_2) concentrations were discussed widely in the scientific reports and the mainstream media as examples of how human actions shaped natural systems' dynamics. At the biological level, accumulating industrial chemicals in adults' and children's bodies were reported as one of the wide-ranging examples of system equilibrium disruptions. There was growing discussion of tipping points and ways to contain change within an acceptable range of variation for continued human prosperity.

Partly in response to this growing concern, globally and within nation-states, markets for carbon; clean and more efficient energy; and safer, cleaner products have grown rapidly. These markets will continue to expand given economic growth trajectories, the rapid movement of more people into a global middle class, and the constrained capacities of natural systems, including our bodies, to absorb the impacts.

While some hear only negative news in these words, entrepreneurs and innovators typically do not spend much time on the negative messages. They use innovation to create alternatives. They envision new and better possibilities. They take action to address perceived inefficiencies and to solve problems. Health and environmental problems, the inefficiencies related to pollution, and the newly understood health threats are viewed as opportunities for entrepreneurially minded individuals and ventures to offer substitutes.

The shift in perception about industrial and commercial pollution and adverse impacts has been augmented by a new appreciation of the scale and scope of human activity. For example, a short time ago pollution was considered a manageable local problem (and even a visible indicator of economic progress). Today our scientific knowledge has advanced to see not just visible acute pollution challenges as health problems but also molecular depositions far from their source; in other words, problems stretching across local, regional, and even global scales are major unintended effects of industrialization.

Table 2.1 Changes in the Character of the Ecological and Health Challenges, Pre-1980s vs. Post-1980s

Pre-1980s	Post-1980s
Minor	Systemic
Localized	Global
Dispersed and separate	Tightly coupled
Simple	Complex
Isolated	Ubiquitous
Stable and visible	Turbulent and hard to discern
Slow-moving	Accelerated

By 2010 there was a scientific and policy acknowledgement about the physical impossibility of maintaining ecosystems' stability in the face of the existing and the anticipated scale and scope of pollution levels. A biosphere that seemed a short time ago to be infinite in its capacity to absorb waste and provide ecosystem services showed growing evidence of limits. Thus today, satisfying the legitimate material and energy demands of billions of upwardly mobile people in the global community, without severely disrupting ecosystem functions and exacting harsh human costs, is a first-order challenge for economic and business design. This problem is soluble, but it requires creativity that reaches beyond conventional thinking to imagine new models for economic growth and for business. In fact, in increasing numbers companies are now adopting sustainability principles in their product designs and strategies. Recognizing the problem-complexity shift represented by the second column in Table 2.1 "Changes in the Character of the Ecological and Health Challenges, Pre-1980s versus Post-1980s", companies are taking on what can be called a sustainability view of their world. The changes under way are captured in Table 2.2 "Traditional View versus Sustainability View", which compares the old business approach, defined by more narrowly framed environmental issues, and leading entrepreneurial innovators' perspectives on sustainability challenges.

Table 2.2 Traditional View versus Sustainability View

Traditional view	Sustainability view
Rhetoric and greenwash	Operational excellence
Cost burden	Efficiencies
Compliance	Cost competitiveness/strategic advantage
Doing good/altruism	Strong financial performance
Peripheral to the business	Core to the business
Technology fix	Frameworks, tools, and programs
Reactive	Innovative and entrepreneurial

Let's start at a more macro level of analysis that allows us to track the reframing of what historically have been called environmental concerns. To better understand the functioning and interdependencies of the natural and human-created systems of which we are a part, we can look at basic energy and material flows. Even a cursory look reveals some of the major challenges. Fossil fuel energy consumption is closely linked to local and global climate modification, ocean acidification (and consequently coral reef degradation that undermines ocean food supplies), and ground-level air pollution, among other problems. Materials extraction and use are tightly coupled with unprecedented waste disposal challenges and dispersed toxins. Furthermore, in our search for energy and materials to fuel economic growth and feed more people, we have been systematically eliminating the habitat and ecosystems on which our future prosperity depends.

Americans have long voiced support for environmental issues in public opinion polls. That concern has grown, especially as human-influenced climate change became increasingly apparent and a harbinger of broader ecological and health challenges. Even as the US economy faltered dramatically in late 2008, 41 percent of respondents to a survey for the Pew Research Center stated in January 2009 that the environment should remain the president's top priority, while 63 percent thought the same when President Bush was in office in 2001. [1] In a different series of polls conducted by Pew between June 2006 and April 2008, over 70 percent of Americans consistently said there is "solid evidence" that global warming is occurring, and between 41 and 50 percent said human activity is the main cause. Independents and Democrats were one and one-half times to twice as likely as Republicans to agree to the statements, indicating ongoing political divisions over the credibility or impartiality of science and how it should inform our response to climate change. [2] Regardless of climate change public opinion polls, however, by 2010 energy issues had gained national attention for an ever-broadening set of reasons.

In fact, by 2010 climate change often was linked to energy independence and energy efficiency as the preferred strategy to get both liberals and conservatives to address global warming. This approach emphasized saving money by saving energy and deploying innovative technology rather than relying on federal mandates and changes to social behavior to curb emissions. The federal government was asked to do more under President Obama. Energy independence included reduced reliance on imported oil as well as nurturing renewable energy and technologies and local solutions to electricity, heating and cooling, and transportation needs. The Energy Security and Independence Act of 2007, among other things, increased fuel economy standards for cars, funded green job training programs, phased out incandescent light bulbs, and committed new and renovated federal buildings to being carbon-neutral by 2030.

Meanwhile, renewable energy sources continue to inch upward. By 2007, just over 71 quadrillion British thermal units of energy were produced in total in the United States. About 9.5 percent of that energy came from renewable sources: hydroelectric (dams), geothermal, solar, wind, and wood or other biomass. Indeed, wood and biomass accounted for about 52 percent of all renewable energy production, while hydroelectric power represented another 36 percent. Wind power represented about 5 percent of renewable energy and solar 1 percent. [3] The numbers were relatively small, but each of these markets was experiencing double-digit growth rates, offering significant opportunities to investors, entrepreneurs, and firms that wanted to contribute to cleaner energy and reduced fossil fuel dependence.

In fact, climate change took center stage among environmental issues in the first decade of this century, with public awareness of climate change heightened by unusual weather patterns. Hurricane Katrina, which devastated New Orleans in 2005, was interpreted as a sign of worse storms to come. The Intergovernmental Panel on Climate Change (IPCC) released its Fourth Assessment Report in 2007. This report affirmed global climate change was largely anthropogenic (caused by human activity) and indicated that change was occurring more rapidly than anticipated. Almost a doubling of the rate of sea level rise was recorded from 1993 to 2003 compared to earlier rates, and a steady increase in the ocean's acidity was verified. [4] The 2006 Stern Review on the Economics of Climate Change, commissioned by the Treasury of the United Kingdom, attempted to put a cost on the price of business as usual in the face of climate change. It estimated climate change could incur expenses equivalent to 5 to 20 percent of the global gross domestic product (GDP) in the coming decades if nothing changed in our practices, whereas acting now to mitigate the impact of climate change would cost only about 1 percent of global GDP. As the report concluded, "Climate change is the greatest market failure the world has ever seen." [5]

Also in 2007, former vice president Al Gore's documentary on climate change, An Inconvenient Truth, won an Oscar for best feature documentary, while Gore and the IPCC were jointly awarded the Nobel Peace Prize. Although debates over the science continued, the consensus of thousands of scientists worldwide that the atmospheric concentrations of CO_2 were at least in part man-made firmly placed global climate and fossil fuel use on the agenda. National policies and the US military engagements related to securing and stabilizing oil imports and prices focused attention further on avoiding oil dependency. Indicating resource issues' close link to social conflicts, in 2008 the National Intelligence Estimate report from the CIA and other agencies warned climate change could trigger massive upheaval, whether from natural disasters and droughts that destabilized governments or increased flows of climate refugees, both the result of and cause of competition over resources and civil unrest.

The 2008 Olympic Games in Beijing, meanwhile, highlighted the increasing pollution from high-growth industrializing countries. That year China eclipsed the United States as the leading emitter of CO2, while Chinese officials had to take steps to prevent athletes and tourists from choking in Beijing's notorious smog. To reduce the worst vehicle emissions in the days leading up to the games, cars with even license plate numbers could drive one day, odd the next, and factories were shut down. [6] India also has struggled to curb pollution as its industrialization accelerates. The World Bank estimated India's natural resources will be more strained than any other country's by 2020. [7]

To those living in a developed country, particularly in the United States where climate change continues to be debated, warming temperatures can seem somewhat abstract. The following links provide narratives and visual appreciation for how climate change actually influences many people around the world.

Broad scientific consensus on climate change and its origin, the increased concentration of greenhouse gases (GHGs) in the atmosphere, has motivated hundreds of US cities, from Chicago to Charlottesville, to pledge to follow the Kyoto Protocol to reduce emissions within their municipalities through a variety of mechanisms including setting green building standards. The Kyoto Protocol is an international agreement among countries formally initiated in 1997 whose goal is to reduce (GHGs).

For CO_2 from these mobile sources, in 2009 President Obama asked the EPA to reconsider California's request to regulate GHG emissions from vehicles, a request initially denied under the Bush administration despite a 2007 Supreme Court ruling that required the EPA to regulate GHGs under the Clean Air Act. Assuming California adopts stricter vehicle emissions standards, almost twenty other states will adopt those standards. Moreover, the American Recovery and Reinvestment Act of 2009 appropriated billions of dollars for green infrastructure, including high-speed rail.

The Kyoto Protocol itself, nonetheless, faced an uncertain fate under the Obama administration. Discussions for the successor to Kyoto were held in December 2009 in Copenhagen. In the interim between those two frameworks, over 180 nations plus nongovernmental organizations (NGOs)—many criticized for the carbon footprint of traveling in private jets—attended the UN Bali Climate Change Conference in December 2007.

As climate change and its consequences have become increasingly accepted as real, more people and institutions are considering their "carbon footprints," the levels of CO_2 associated with a given activity. A number of voluntary programs, such as the Climate Registry, ISO 14000 for Environmental Management, and the Global Reporting Initiative, emerged to allow organizations and businesses to record and publicize their footprint and other environmental performance tracking. To assess and abet such efforts, in 2000 the US Green Building Council introduced a rating system called **Leadership in Energy and Environmental Design (LEED)**. Buildings earn points for energy efficiency, preserving green space, and so on; points then convert to a certification from basic to platinum. The 7 World Trade Center building, for instance, was gold certified upon its reconstruction in 2006. [11] Other green building programs have appeared, while groups such as TerraPass and CarbonFund began selling carbon offsets for people to reduce the impact of their local pollution. Investors also have jumped in. Sustainable-investment funds allow people to buy stocks in companies screened for environmental practices and to press shareholder resolutions. For example, institutional investors representing state retirement funds have asked for evidence that management is fulfilling its fiduciary responsibility to protect the stock price against climate change impacts and other unexpected ecological and related political surprises. The Social Investment Forum's *2007 Report on Socially Responsible Investing Trends in the United States* noted that about 11 percent of investments under professional management in the United States—$2.7 trillion—adhered to one or more strategies of "socially responsible investment," a category encompassing governance, ecological, health, and safety concerns. [12]

Materials and Chemicals

In conjunction with threats to the globe's ecosystems (a somewhat removed and therefore abstract notion for many), people became increasingly aware of threats to their personal health. This concern shifts attention from climate and energy issues at a more macro level to the material aspects of pollution and resource management.

The national Centers for Disease Control and Prevention began periodic national health and exposure reports soon after the publication of *Our Stolen Future*, authored by Theo Colborn, Dianne Dumanoski, and John Peterson Myers. [14] Considered by many as the 1990s sequel to Rachel Carson's groundbreaking 1962 book *Silent Spring*, which informed and mobilized the public about pesticide impacts, *Our Stolen Future* linked toxins from industrial activity to widespread and growing human health problems including compromises in immune and reproductive system functions. In 2005, the federal government's *Third National Report on Human Exposure to Environmental Chemicals* found American adults' bodies contained noticeable levels of over one hundred toxins (our so-called **body burden**), including the neurotoxin mercury taken up in our bodies through eating fish and absorbing air particulates (from fossil fuel combustion) and phthalates (synthetic materials used in production of personal care products, pharmaceuticals, plastics, and coatings such as varnishes and lacquers). Phthalates are associated with cancer outcomes and fetal development modifications.

BPA, an endocrine-disrupting chemical that can influence human development even at very low levels of exposure, has been associated with abnormal genital development in males, neurobehavioral problems such as attention deficit/hyperactivity disorder (ADHD), type 2 diabetes, and hormonally mediated cancers such as prostate and breast cancers. [15]

A recent update found three-fourths of Americans had triclosan in their urine, with wealthier Americans having higher levels. [16] This antibiotic is added to soaps, deodorants, toothpastes, and other products. In the first decade of the twenty-first century, pharmaceutical companies were coming under greater scrutiny as antibiotics and birth control hormones were found in city water supplies; the companies had to begin to assess their role in what has come to be called the PIE (pharmaceuticals in the environment) problem. Children, because of their higher consumption of food and water per body weight and their still-vulnerable and developing neurological, immune, and reproductive systems, are especially at risk.

Europe has led the world in its public policy response to reduce the health risks of chemicals. After many years of debate and discussion with labor, business, and government, the EU adopted the **"precautionary principle"** in 2007, requiring manufacturers to show chemicals were safe before they could be introduced on a wide scale. [18] The REACH directive—Registration, Evaluation, Authorization, and Restriction of Chemicals—will be phased into full force by 2018. REACH requires manufacturers and importers to collect and submit information on chemicals' hazards and practices for safe handling. It also requires the most dangerous chemicals to be replaced as safer alternatives are found.

The opposite system, which gathers toxicological information after chemicals have spread, prevails in the United States. Hence only after a spate of contaminated products imported from China sickened children and pets did Congress pass the US Consumer Product Safety Act amendments in 2008 to ban lead and six phthalates from children's toys. However, another phthalate additive, BPA, was not banned. Often found in #7 plastics, including popular water bottles seen on college campuses around the country, BPA was linked to neurological and prostate problems by the National Toxicology Program. [19] Although the US Food and Drug Administration (FDA), unlike its EU and Canadian counterparts, chose not to ban the chemical, many companies stopped selling products with BPA.

Indeed, consumers have been increasingly wary of materials that inadvertently enter their bodies through the products they use, the air they breathe, and what they put into their bodies by diet. Sales of organic and local foods have been rising rapidly in numbers and prominence since the 1990s due to a greater focus on health. According to the Organic Trade Association, organic food sales climbed from $1 billion in 1990 to $20 billion in 2007. [20] Once found only in natural food stores, organic foods have been sold predominantly in conventional supermarkets since 2000. [21] Meanwhile, community-supported agriculture by 2007 encompassed nearly 13,000 farms as people grew more interested in sourcing from their local food shed. [22] In addition to protection against food supply disruption due to fuel price volatility, terrorist attack, or severe weather (most foods are transported over 1,000 miles to their ultimate point of consumption, creating what many view as undesirable distribution system vulnerabilities), local food production ensures traceability (important for health protection), higher nutritional content, fewer or no chemical preservatives to extend shelf life, and better taste while providing local economic development and job creation.

Whether from energy production or materials processing, a major challenge across the board is where to put the waste. As visible and molecular waste accumulates, there are fewer places to dispose of it. Global carbon sinks, the natural systems (oceans and forests) that can absorb GHGs, show signs of stress. Oceans may have reached their peak absorption as they acidify and municipal waste washes onshore. Forests continue to shrink, unable to absorb additional CO_2 emissions still being pumped into the atmosphere. The United Nations' Food and Agriculture Organization reported that from 1900 to 2005, Africa lost about 3.1 percent of its forests; South America lost around

2.5 percent; and Central America, which had the highest regional rate of deforestation, lost nearly 6.2 percent of its forests. Individual countries have been hit particularly hard: Honduras lost 37 percent of its forests in those 15 years, and Togo lost a full 44 percent. However, the largest absolute loss of forests continues in Brazil, home of the Amazon rain forest. Brazil's forests have been shrinking annually since 1990 by about three million hectares—an area about the size of Connecticut and Massachusetts combined. [23]

Bottled water may now face a similar fate because of the tremendous increase in trash from plastic bottles and the resources consumed to create, fill, and ship those bottles. [28] New York City, following San Francisco; Seattle; Fayetteville, Arkansas; and other cities, has curbed buying bottled water with city money. [29] The inability of natural systems to absorb the flow of synthetic waste was dramatically communicated with reports and pictures of the Great Pacific Garbage Patch, also known as the North Pacific Gyre. Pacific Ocean currents create huge eddies where plastic waste is deposited and remains in floating islands of garbage.

Although manufacturers of other products from CDs to laundry detergent have already decreased the amount of packaging they use, and although many American municipalities have increased their recycling capacity, the results are far less than what is required to achieve sustainability, and they still lag behind Europe's progress. The European Parliament and Council Directive 94/62/EC of December 1994 set targets for recycling and incinerating packaging to create energy. By 2002, recycling rates in the EU exceeded 55 percent for glass, paper, and metals, although only about 24 percent of plastic was being recycled. [30] An EU directive from 2003 addressed electronic waste specifically, requiring manufacturers of electronic equipment to set up a system to recycle their products. Target recycling rates were initially set at 70 percent by weight for small, household electronics and 80 percent for large appliances, with separate rates for recycling or reusing individual components. [31] The United States as of March 2009 had no federal mandate for reclaiming electronic waste (e-waste), although some states had implemented their own rules. [32] Companies such as Dell, criticized for their lack of attention to e-waste, responded to NGO and public concern with creative solutions. Working with citizen groups, Dell was able to shift from viewing e-waste as someone else's problem to developing a profit-making internal venture that reused many electronic devices, put disassembled component materials back into secondary markets, and reduced the dumping of e-waste into poor countries.

KEY TAKEAWAYS

- The world is composed of energy and materials, and how we design business activity defines the ways we use energy and materials.
- There is growing concern that our current patterns of use for energy and materials are not sustainable. Waste streams are the focus of much of this concern.

EXERCISES

1. Propose an idea for a product that has sustainability concepts designed in from the outset. How does this change your thinking about resources you might use? How might it change processes of decision making within the firm and across supply chains?
2. What key elements characterize the standard model of business? What barriers can you list that would need to be overcome to move a mainstream business to a sustainability view?

[1] Pew Research Center for the People and the Press, "Economy, Jobs Trump All Other Policy Priorities in 2009," news release, January 22, 2009, accessed March 27, 2009, http://people-press.org/report/485/economy-top-policy-priority.
[2] Pew Research Center for the People and the Press, "A Deeper Partisan Divide over Global Warming," news release, May 8, 2008, accessed March 27, 2009, http://people-press.org/reports/pdf/417.pdf.
[3] Energy Information Administration, Department of Energy, "Table 1.2: Primary Energy Production by Source, 1949–2009," *Annual Energy Review*, accessed March 27, 2009, http://www.eia.doe.gov/emeu/aer/txt/ptb0102.html.
[4] Rajendra K. Pachauri, and Andy Reisinger, eds. (core writing team), *Climate Change 2007: Synthesis Report* (Geneva, Switzerland: Intergovernmental Panel on Climate Change, 2008), accessed November 30, 2010, http://www.ipcc.ch/publications_and_data/publications_ipcc_fourth_assessment_report_synthesis_report.htm. The ocean's pH decreased about 0.04 pH units from 1984 to 2005. Acidity is measured on a logarithmic scale from 0 to 14, with a one pH unit increase meaning a tenfold increase in acidity.
[5] Sir Nicholas Stern, *Stern Review on the Economics of Climate Change* (London: HM Treasury, 2006), viii, accessed March 26, 2009, http://www.hm-treasury.gov.uk/sternreview_index.htm.
[6] Paul Kelso, "Olympics: Pollution over Beijing? Don't Worry, It's Only Mist, Say Officials," *Guardian* (London), August 6, 2008, accessed November 30, 2010, http://www.guardian.co.uk/sport/2008/aug/06/olympics2008.china; Talea Miller, "Beijing Pollution Poses Challenge to Olympic Athletes," *PBS NewsHour*, May 16, 2008, accessed November 30, 2010, http://www.pbs.org/newshour/indepth_coverage/asia/china/2008/athletes.html.

[7] "India and Pollution: Up to Their Necks in It," *Economist*, July 17, 2008, accessed November 30, 2010, http://www.economist.com/world/asia/displaystory.cfm?story_id=11751397.

[8] Pew Center on Global Climate Change, "Renewable & Alternative Energy Portfolio Standards," October 27, 2010, accessed November 30, 2010, http://www.pewclimate.org/what_s_being_done/in_the_states/rps.cfm.

[9] US Environmental Protection Agency, Office of Transportation and Air Quality, "Transportation and Climate: Basic Information," last modified September 14, 2010, accessed November 30, 2010, http://www.epa.gov/OMS/climate/basicinfo.htm.

[10] United Nations Environment Programme, Partnership for Clean Fuels and Vehicles, "Background," accessed November 30, 2010, http://www.unep.org/pcfv/about/bkground.asp.

[11] Taryn Holowka, "7 World Trade Center Earns LEED Gold," *US Green Building Council*, March 27, 2006, accessed March 27, 2009, http://www.usgbc.org/News/USGBCNewsDetails.aspx?ID=2225.

[12] Social Investment Forum, *2007 Report on Socially Responsible Investing Trends in the United States* (Washington, DC: Social Investment Forum Foundation, 2007), accessed March 27, 2009, http://www.socialinvest.org/resources/research.

[13] The US Department of Health and Human Services offers suggestions to parents to avoid exposure to children. See US Department of Health and Human Services, "Bisphenol A (BPA) Information for Parents," accessed November 30, 2010, http://www.hhs.gov/safety/bpa.

[14] See the home page for the book: "Our Stolen Future," accessed March 7, 2011, http://www.ourstolenfuture.org

[15] Frederick S. vom Saal, Benson T. Akingbemi, Scott M. Belcher, Linda S. Birnbaum, D. Andrew Crain, Marcus Eriksen, Francesca Farabollini, et al., "Chapel Hill Bisphenol A Expert Panel Consensus Statement: Integration of Mechanisms, Effects in Animals and Potential to Impact Human Health at Current Levels of Exposure," *Reproductive Toxicology* 24, no. 2 (August/September 2007): 131–38, accessed November 30, 2010, http://www.ewg.org/files/BPAConsensus.pdf.

[16] The report and updates are available from Centers for Disease Control and Prevention (CDC). See Centers for Disease Control and Prevention, "National Report on Human Exposure to Environmental Chemicals," last modified October 12, 2010, accessed November 30, 2010, http://www.cdc.gov/exposurereport.

[17] C. Lock, "Portrait of Pollution: Nation's Freshwater Gets Checkup," *Science News*, May 22, 2004, accessed March 7, 2011, http://findarticles.com/p/articles/mi_m1200/is_21_165/ai_n6110353.

[18] European Commission, "What Is REACH?," last modified May 20, 2010, accessed November 30, 2010, http://ec.europa.eu/environment/chemicals/reach/reach_intro.htm.

[19] National Institute of Environmental Health Sciences, National Toxicology Program, *Bisphenol A (BPA)* (Research Triangle Park, NC: National Institutes of Health, US Department of Health and Human Services, 2010), accessed November 30, 2010, http://www.niehs.nih.gov/health/docs/bpa-factsheet.pdf.

[20] Organic Trade Association, "Industry Statistics and Projected Growth," June 2010, accessed November 30, 2010, http://www.ota.com/organic/mt/business.html.

[21] Carolyn Dimitri and Catherine Greene, *Recent Growth Patterns in the U.S. Organic Foods Market*, Agriculture Information Bulletin No. AIB-777 (Washington, DC: US Department of Agriculture, Economic Research Service, 2002), accessed December 1, 2010, http://www.ers.usda.gov/publications/aib777/aib777.pdf.

[22] US Department of Agriculture, "Community Supported Agriculture," last modified April 28, 2010, accessed November 30, 2010, http://www.nal.usda.gov/afsic/pubs/csa/csa.shtml.

[23] Food and Agriculture Organization of the United Nations, "Global Forest Resources Assessment 2005," last modified November 10, 2005, accessed March 26, 2009, http://www.fao.org/forestry/32033/en.

[24] John Roach, "Are Plastic Grocery Bags Sacking the Environment?," *National Geographic News*, September 2, 2003, accessed November 30, 2010, http://news.nationalgeographic.com/news/2003/09/0902_030902_plasticbags.html; "The List: Products in Peril," *Foreign Policy*, April 2, 2007, accessed March 25, 2008, http://www.foreignpolicy.com/story/cms.php?story_id=3762.

[25] "The List: Products in Peril," *Foreign Policy*, April 2, 2007, accessed March 25, 2008, http://www.foreignpolicy.com/story/cms.php?story_id=3762; "China Bans Free Plastic Shopping Bags," *International Herald Tribune*, January 9, 2008, accessed November 30, 2010, http://www.iht.com/articles/2008/01/09/asia/plastic.php.

[26] Charlie Goodyear, "S.F. First City to Ban Plastic Shopping Bags," *San Francisco Chronicle*, March 28, 2007, accessed March 25, 2009, http://www.sfgate.com/cgi-bin/article.cgi?file=/c/a/2007/03/28/MNGDROT5QN1.DTL.

[27] David Zahniser, "City Council Will Ban Plastic Bags If the State Doesn't Act," *Los Angeles Times*, July 23, 2008, accessed March 25, 2009, http://articles.latimes.com/2008/jul/23/local/me-plastic23.

[28] Charles Fishman, "Message in a Bottle," *Fast Company*, July 1, 2007, accessed March 26, 2009, http://www.fastcompany.com/magazine/117/features-message-in-a-bottle.html.

[29] Jennifer Lee, "City Council Shuns Bottles in Favor of Water from Tap," *New York Times*, June 17, 2008, accessed March 26, 2009, http://www.nytimes.com/2008/06/17/nyregion/17water.html.

[30] Europa, "Packaging and Packaging Waste," accessed March 27, 2009, http://europa.eu/scadplus/leg/en/lvb/l21207.htm#AMENDINGACT.

[31] Europa, "Waste Electrical and Electronic Equipment," last modified January 6, 2010, accessed November 30, 2010, http://europa.eu/scadplus/leg/en/lvb/l21210.htm.

[32] US Environmental Protection Agency, "eCycling: Regulations/Standards," last modified February 23, 2010, accessed November 30, 2010, http://www.epa.gov/epawaste/conserve/materials/ecycling/rules.htm.

2.2 Defining Sustainability Innovation

LEARNING OBJECTIVES

1. Understand how sustainability innovation has been defined.

2. Begin to apply the basic ideas and concepts of sustainability design.

Recognition that the global economy is processing the world's natural resources and generating waste streams at an unprecedented scale and scope calls for the redesign of commercial activity. Reconfiguring how we conduct business and implementing business practices that preserve the world's natural resources for today's communities and the economic, environmental, and social health and vitality of future generations only recently has become a priority. This notion lies at the heart of sustainability. Sustainability in the business sense is not about altruism and doing what is right for its own sake. Businesses with successful sustainability strategies are profitable because they integrate consideration of clean design and resource conservation throughout product life cycles and supply chains in ways that make economic sense. Sustainability innovation is about defining economic development as the creation of private and social wealth to ultimately eliminate harmful impacts on ecological systems, human health, and communities.

Awareness of the problem of pollution and resource limits has existed for decades but until now only in fragmented ways across informed academic and scientific subcommunities. Today it is becoming self-evident that our past patterns of energy and material use must be transformed. While some still question the seriousness of the challenges, governments and companies are responding. Government is imposing more environmental, health, and safety regulatory constraints on business. However, while regulation may be an important part of problem solving, it is not the answer. Fortunately, businesses are stepping up to the challenge. In fact, the inherent inefficiencies and blind spots that are built into the accepted business and growth models that have been debated and discussed for many years are beginning to be addressed by business. Entrepreneurial innovators are creating solutions that move us away from needing regulation. In addition, recently the critiques have moved from periphery to mainstream as it has become increasingly clear to the educated public that the economic practices that brought us to this point are not sufficient to carry us forward. Since governments alone cannot solve the problems, it will take the ingenuity of people across sectors to generate progress. Sustainability innovation offers a frame for thinking about how entrepreneurial individuals and firms can contribute.

The new models of business sustainability are emerging. They are based on current science, pressure from governments, and citizen demand and envision a world in which human economic development can continue to be sustained by natural systems while delivering improved living standards for more people. That is the goal; however, it takes concrete actions striving toward that ideal to make headway. Those entrepreneurs and ventures embodying the ideal of sustainability have found creative ways to achieve financial success by offering products that improve our natural environment and protect and preserve human health, equity, and community vitality. We will now explore this term, sustainability, and its significance in entrepreneurial thinking.

General Definition

Sustainability innovation reflects the next generation of economic development thinking. It couples environmentalism's protection of natural systems with the notion of business innovation while delivering essential goods and services that serve social goals of human health, equity, and environmental justice. It is the wave of innovation pushing society toward clean technology, the green economy, and clean commerce. It is the combined positive, pragmatic, and optimistic efforts of people around the world to refashion economic development into a process that addresses the fundamental challenges of poverty, environmental justice, and resource scarcity. At the organizational level, the term sustainability innovation applies to product/service and process design as well as company strategy.

Sustainability and sustainability innovation have been defined by different individuals representing diverse disciplines and institutions. Certain fundamentals lie at the concepts' core, however, and we illuminate these fundamentals in the discussion that follows. Keep in mind that any given definition's precision is less important than the vision and framework that guide actions in the direction of enduring healthy economic development. Later we will examine concepts and tools that are used to operationalize sustainability strategy and design. It is by combining existing definitions with an understanding of sustainability's drivers and then studying how entrepreneurial innovators implement the concept that you gain the full appreciation for the change sustainability represents. Note that you will find the terms sustainability, sustainable business, and even sustainability innovation used loosely in the media and sometimes applied to activities that are only continued ("sustained") as opposed to the meaning of sustainability we work with in this text. Our definition addresses the systemic endurance and smooth functioning of ecological systems and the preservation of carrying capacities, together with protection of human health, social justice, and vibrant communities. We are interested in entrepreneurial and innovative disruption that can accelerate progress along this path.

Sustainability: Variations on a Theme

Paul E. Gray, a former president of the Massachusetts Institute of Technology (MIT), stated in 1989 that "furthering technological and economic development in a socially and environmentally responsible manner is not only feasible, it is the great challenge we face as engineers, as engineering institutions, and as a society." [1] This was his expression of what it meant for MIT to pursue sustainability ideas.

The Natural Step, a framework to guide decision making and an educational foundation with global reach based in Stockholm, Sweden, offers a scientific, consensus-based articulation of what it would mean for sustainability to be achieved by society and for humans to prosper and coexist compatibly with natural systems. Natural and man-made materials would not be extracted, distributed, and built up in the world at a rate exceeding the capacity of nature to absorb and regenerate those materials; habitat and ecological systems would be preserved; and actions that create poverty by undermining people's capacity to meet fundamental human needs (for subsistence, protection, identity, or freedom) would not be pursued. These requisite system conditions acknowledge the physical realities of resource overuse and pollution as well as the inherent threat to social and political stability when human needs are systematically denied.

Examining innovative leaders provides a window into the future through which we can see new possibilities for how goods and services can be delivered if sufficient human ingenuity is applied. The approach extends the premises of entrepreneurial innovation, a long-standing driver of social and economic change, to consider natural system viability and community health. Drawing on systems thinking, ecological and environmental health sciences, and the equitable availability of clean commerce economic development opportunities, sustainability innovation offers a fast-growing market space within which entrepreneurial leaders are offering solutions and paths forward to address some of society's most critical challenges.

It is important to recognize sustainability's cross-disciplinary approach. Sustainability in business is about designing strategies for value creation through innovation using an interdisciplinary lens. Specialization and grounding in established disciplines provide requisite know-how, but sustainability innovation requires the ability to bridge disciplines and to rise above the narrow bounds and myopia of specialized training in conventional economic models to envision new possibilities. Sustainability innovation occurs when entrepreneurs and ventures stretch toward a better future to offer distinctly new products, technologies, and ways of conducting business. The empirical evidence suggests that while entrepreneurs who succeed typically bring their uniquely specialized know-how to the table, they also have a systems view that welcomes and mixes diverse perspectives to create change.

Business has traveled a long distance from the adversarial pollution control days of the 1970s in the United States, when systemic ecological problems were first acknowledged. Companies were asked to bear the costs of environmental degradation yet often lacked the ability or know-how to realize any rewards for those investments. Decades ago, the goals were narrow: compliance and cost avoidance. Today the intersecting environmental, health, and social challenges are understood as more complex. Community prosperity requires a far broader view of economic development. It requires a sustainability mind-set. While the challenges are undeniably serious, as our examples will show, the entrepreneurial mind sees wide open opportunities.

A growing number of companies now recognize that improving performance and innovation across the full sustainability agenda—financial, ecological, environmental, and social health and prosperity—can grow revenues, improve profitability, and enhance their brands. Sustainability strategies and innovations also position businesses favorably in markets, as their slower-learning competitors fail to develop internal and supply-chain competencies to compete. We predict that within a relatively short period of time what is now considered sustainability innovation will become mainstream business operation.

The entrepreneurial leaders forging ahead with sustainability innovation understand the value of partnerships with supply-chain vendors and customers, nongovernmental organizations (NGOs), public policy agencies, and academia in pursuing product designs and strategies. Many of their innovations are designed to avoid the need for regulation by steadily reducing adverse ecological and health impacts, with the goal of eliminating negative impacts altogether. Significantly, environmental and associated health, community, and equity issues are integrated into core business strategy and thus into the operations of the firm and its supply chains.

Start-up firms and small to midsized companies have always been major movers of entrepreneurial innovation and will continue to lead in sustainability innovation. However, even large firms can offer innovative examples. Indeed, Stuart Hart in his 2005 book Capitalism at the Crossroads: The Unlimited Business Opportunities in Solving the World's Most Difficult Problems argues that multinational corporations have the capacity and qualities to address the complicated problems of resource constraints, poverty, and growth. [5] According to analysts of what is termed "bottom of the pyramid" markets where over two billion people live on one to two dollars a day, developing countries represent both a market for goods and the potential to introduce sustainable practices and products on a massive scale.

By the first decade of the twenty-first century, a growing number of business executives believed that sustainability should play a role in their work. PricewaterhouseCoopers found that in 2003, 70 percent of CEOs surveyed believed that environmental sustainability was important to overall profit. By 2005, that number had climbed to 87 percent. [6] In a later PricewaterhouseCoopers survey of technology executives, 71 percent said they did not believe their company was particularly harmful to the environment, yet 61 percent said it was nonetheless important that they reduce their company's environmental impact. The majority of executives also believed strong demand existed for "green" and cleaner products and that demand would only increase. [7]

Such employers as well as employees have begun striving toward sustainability. Labor unions and environmentalists, once at odds, jointly created the Apollo Alliance to promote the transition to a clean energy environment under the slogan "Clean Energy, Good Jobs." Van Jones, formerly with the Obama administration, led Green For All, an organization that proposed the new green economy tackle poverty and pollution at the same time through business collaboration in cities to provide clean energy jobs.

Meanwhile, numerous large and well-known companies, including DuPont, 3M, General Electric, Walmart, and FedEx, have taken steps to save money by using less energy and material or to increase market share by producing more environmental products. Walmart, for instance, stated that as of 2009 its "environmental goals are simple and straightforward: to be supplied 100 percent by renewable energy; to create zero waste; and to sell products that sustain our natural resources and the environment." [8] But transitioning from a wasteful economic system to one that conserves energy and materials and dramatically reduces hazardous waste, ultimately reversing the ecological degradation and social inequity often associated with economic growth, takes a major shift in the collective state of mind.

Assumptions that Earth systems, regional and local ecological systems, and even the human body can be sustained and can regenerate in the face of negative impacts from energy and material consumption have proven wrong. Linear processes of extracting or synthetically producing raw materials, converting them into products, using those products, and throwing them away to landfills and

incinerators increasingly are viewed as antiquated, old-world designs that must be replaced by systems thinking and life-cycle analysis. These new models will explicitly consider poverty alleviation, equity, health, ecological restoration, and smart energy and materials management as integrated considerations. The precise outline of the new approach remains ambiguous, but the direction and trajectory are clear. While government policies may contribute guidelines and requirements for a more sustainable economic infrastructure, the business community is the most powerful driver of rapid innovation and change. The entrepreneurs are leading the way.

In conclusion, economic development trajectories both in the United States and worldwide are now recognized as incompatible with ecological systems' viability and long-term human health and social stability. Wetlands, coastal zones, are rain forests are deteriorating, while toxins and air and water pollution harm human health and drive political unrest and social instability; witness the growing numbers of environmental refugees. Even large Earth systems, such as the atmosphere and nitrogen and carbon cycles, are endangered. The business models we created in the nineteenth and twentieth centuries that succeeded in delivering prosperity to ever greater numbers of people did not anticipate the exponential population explosion, technological capability to extract and process ever-greater volumes of materials, natural resource demand, growing constraints on resources, political unrest, fuel cost volatility, and limits of ecological systems and human bodies to assimilate industrial waste.

Scholars and students of business will look back on the early decades of the twenty-first century as a transition as the human community responded to scientific feedback from natural systems and took to heart the desire to extend true prosperity to greater numbers by redesigning business. To the extent that this effort will be deemed successful, much of the credit will go to the entrepreneurial efforts to experiment with new ideas and to drive the desired change. No single venture or individual can address the wide range of sustainability concerns. It is the combination of large and small efforts across sectors and industries around the world that will create an alternative future. That is how change happens—and entrepreneurs are at the cutting edge.

KEY TAKEAWAYS

- Sustainability innovation provides new ways to deliver goods and services that are explicitly designed to create a healthier, more equitable, and prosperous global community.
- The sustainability design criteria differ from conventional business approaches by their concurrent and integrated incorporation of economic performance goals, ecological system protection, human health promotion, and community vitality. A new model is emerging through the efforts of entrepreneurial leaders.

EXERCISES

1. Identify an ecological, equity, health, or product safety problem you see that might be addressed through a sustainability innovation approach. What causes the problem? What kind of shift in mind-set may be required to generate possible solutions?

---

[1] Paul E. Gray, "The Paradox of Technological Development," in Technology and Environment (Washington, DC: National Academy Press, 1989), 192–204.
[2] Bhavik R. Bakshi and Joseph Fiksel, "The Quest for Sustainability: Challenges for Process Systems. Engineering," AIChE Journal 49, no. 6 (2003): 1350.
[3] Karl-Heinrik Robert, The Natural Step: A Framework for Achieving Sustainability in Our Organizations (Cambridge, MA: Pegasus, 1997).
[4] Andrea L. Larson, Elizabeth Olmsted Teisberg, and Richard R. Johnson, "Sustainable Business: Opportunity and Value Creation," Interfaces: International Journal of the Institute for Operations Research and the Management Sciences 30, no. 3 (May/June 2000), 2.
[5] Stuart L. Hart, Capitalism at the Crossroads (Upper Saddle River, NJ: Wharton School Publishing, 2005).
[6] Karen Krebsbach, "The Green Revolution: Are Banks Sacrificing Profits for Activists' Principles?" US Banker, December 1, 2005, accessed March 27, 2009, http://www.accessmylibrary.com/coms2/summary_0286-12108489_ITM.
[7] PricewaterhouseCoopers, "Going Green: Sustainable Growth Strategies," Technology Executive Connections 5 (February 2008), accessed March 27, 2009, http://www.pwc.com/images/techconnect/TEC5.pdf.
[8] Walmart, "Sustainability," accessed March 27, 2009, http://walmartstores.com/Sustainability.

NOTES:

NOTES:

Chapter 3:

Framing Sustainability Innovation and Entrepreneurship

3.1 Evolutionary Adaptation

LEARNING OBJECTIVES

1. Provide an overview of the basic stages of corporate engagement.

2. Explore the evolutionary character of private sector adaptation.

During the 1990s and the first decade of the twenty-first century, start-up ventures and large corporations adopted a variety of approaches to shape what we now call sustainability-based product and strategy designs. A sustainability approach acknowledges the interdependencies among healthy economic growth and healthy social and ecological systems. **Sustainability innovation and entrepreneurship** seeks to optimize performance across economic, social, and ecological business dimensions. Applied broadly across countries, this effort will evolve a design of commerce aligned and compatible with human and ecosystem health. A growing number of firms are applying creative practices demonstrating the compatibility of profit, community health, and viable natural systems. This discussion provides an introduction to some of the most important approaches used by firms to guide firms. [1]

The spectrum of approaches can be viewed along a continuum toward the ideal of sustainability. Imagine a timeline. The Industrial Revolution has unfolded on the left side with time moving toward the right on a continuum. We are quickly learning how and why our industrial system, as currently designed, can undermine biosphere systems such as the atmosphere, water tables, fisheries, or soil fertility. With entrepreneurial actors leading the way, our response is to adapt our institutions and our mind-sets. Ultimately the evolution of new knowledge will create new rules for commerce, driving a redesign of our commercial systems to coevolve more compatibly with the natural world and human health requirements. Currently we are in a transition from the left side of the continuum to the right. On the far right of the continuum is the ideal state in which we achieve a design of commerce compatible with human prosperity and ecosystem health. This ideal state includes provision of goods and services to support a peaceful global community, one that is not undermined by violence and civil unrest due to income and resource disparities. Is this ideal state unrealistic? Having a human being walk on the moon was

once thought impossible. Electricity was once unknown. Global treaties were considered impossible before they were achieved. Humans shape their future every day, and they can shape this future. In fact, the author's decades of research show people are already shaping it. It's a question of whether the reader wants to join in.

Looking at the timeline—or continuum—as a whole, the transition from the Industrial Revolution toward the ideal state can be characterized by imagining a "filter" of environmental and health protection imposed on manufacturing processes. This process is well under way around the world. The filter first appeared at the "end of the pipe" where waste pollution moved from a facility to the surrounding water, air, and soil. With the first round of US regulations in the 1970s (mirrored by public policies in many other countries in the intervening years), typical end-of-the-pipe solutions included scrubbers, filters, or on-site waste treatment and incineration. These are called **pollution control** techniques, and regulations often specified the solution through fiat or "command and control" legislation.

Over time, as laws became more stringent, the conceptual filter for pollution control moved from filters on smokestacks outside a firm to operating and production processes inside. These in-the-pipe techniques constitute **pollution prevention** measures in manufacturing and processing that minimize waste and tweak the production system to operate as efficiently as possible. Pollution prevention measures repeatedly have been shown in practice to reduce costs and risks, offering improvements in financial performance and even the quality and desirability of the final products.

In the third and final stage of social and ecological protection, the stage in which sustainability innovation thrives, the conceptual filter is incorporated into the minds of product designers, senior management, and employees. Thus the possibilities for ecological disruption and human health degradation can be removed at the early design stages by the application of human ingenuity. Fostered by a systems mind-set and informed by current science, this ingenuity enables an evolutionary adaptation of firms toward the ideal sustainability state. Seeing this design creativity at work—for example, producing clean renewable energy for electricity and benign, recyclable materials—provides a window to a future landscape in which the original Industrial Revolution is rapidly evolving to its next chapter.

Eco-efficiency describes many companies' first efforts to reduce waste and use fewer energy and material inputs. Eco-efficiency can reduce materials and energy consumed over the product life cycle, thus minimizing waste and costs while boosting profits. Considering eco-efficiency beyond the level of the individual company leads to rethinking the industrial sector. Instead of individual firms maximizing profits, we see a web of interconnected corporations—an industrial ecosystem—through which a metabolism of materials and energy unfolds, analogous to the material and energy flows of the natural world. The tools for design for environment (DfE) and **life-cycle analysis** (LCA) from the field of industrial ecology provide information on the complete environmental impact of a product or process from material extraction to disposal. Other approaches to product design, such as **concurrent engineering**, aid in placing the filter of environmental protection in a design process that invites full design participation from manufacturing, operations, and marketing representatives as well as research and development designers.

When powerful new business perspectives emerge, they often appear to be fads. Concentrating on quality, for example, seemed faddish as the movement emerged in the 1980s. Over time, however, total quality as a concept and total quality management (TQM) programs became standard practice. Now, over two decades after the quality "fad" was introduced to managers around the world, product quality assurance methods are part of the business fundamentals that good managers understand and pursue. Similarly, sustainability has been viewed as a fad. In fact, as its parameters are more carefully defined, it is increasingly understood as an emerging tenet of excellence. [2]

When we look at the emerging wave of sustainability innovation, we can view it as an adaptive process indicating that businesses are moving toward more intelligent interdependencies with natural systems. It is clear that companies are under growing pressure to offer cleaner and safer alternatives to existing products and services. This is in large part because the footprint, or cumulative impact, of business activity is becoming clearer. Pressures on companies to be transparent and factor in full costs, driven by a wide range of converging and increasingly urgent challenges from climate change and environmental health problems to regulation and resource competition, now accelerate change and drive innovation. Furthermore, growing demand for fresh water, food, and energy puts the need for innovative solutions front and center in business. In this chapter, we will look at the major shifts occurring and consider the role of paradigms and mind-sets. A presentation of core concepts, practical frameworks, and tools follows.

Table 3.1 Approximate Timing of Major Approaches/Frameworks

Framework	Approximate Date of Emergence	Perspective
Pollution control (reactive)	1970s	Comply with regulations (clean up the pollution) using technologies specified by government.
Pollution prevention (proactive)	1980s	Manage resources to minimize waste based on better operating practices (prevent pollution); consistent with existing total quality management efforts.
Eco-efficiency	1990s	Maximize the efficiency of inputs, processing steps, waste disposal, and so forth, because it reduces costs and boosts profits.

Industrial ecology, green chemistry and engineering, design for environment, life-cycle analysis, concurrent engineering	1990s	Incorporate ecological/health impact considerations into product design stage; extend this analysis to the full product life cycle.
Sustainability innovation	2000s	Combine all the above in a systems thinking approach that drives entrepreneurial innovation.

KEY TAKEAWAYS

- Business practices have moved along a continuum, with an increasing attention to environmental, social, and health concerns.

- Corporate practice has evolved from rudimentary pollution control to product design changes that take into consideration the full life cycle of products including their energy and material inputs.

- As a consequence of new knowledge and evolutionary learning, sustainability issues are now in the forefront as companies experiment with ways to optimize performance across economic, social, and environmental factors.

EXERCISES

1. Identify a business and describe what operational changes would be made if senior management applied life-cycle analysis sequentially to its operations and supply chain.

2. Select a product that you use. Identify as many inputs (energy, materials, and labor) as you can that enable that product to be available to you. Where and how might you apply these ideas to the production and delivery of the product?

---

[1] Some topics discussed here have well-developed research literature and are taught as courses in engineering, chemistry, and executive business programs. A word of caution: terms do not have precise or universal meanings. Different academics and practitioners offer alternative views, and thus definitions may vary; this overview employs a consensus definition of a tool or concept as it is expressed by the author or authors primarily responsible for creating that tool or concept.
[2] For a comprehensive discussion of sustainability as an emerging tenet of excellence, see {Author's Name Retracted as requested by the work's original creator or licensee} and Elizabeth Teisberg, eds., "Sustainable Business," special issue, Interfaces: International Journal of the Institute for Operations Research and the Management Sciences 30, no. 3 (May/June 2000).

3.2 Paradigms and Mind-Sets

LEARNING OBJECTIVES

1. Explain how paradigms and innovation affect our perception of the possibilities for sustainable business.

2. Understand why new ideas, often introduced through innovative thinking and action, can meet with initial resistance.

The early decades of the twenty-first century will mark a transition period in which conventional economic models that assume infinite capacities of natural systems to provide resources and absorb waste no longer adequately reflect the reality of growth and its related environmental and health challenges. Providing material goods and creating prosperous communities for expanding populations in ways that are compatible with healthy communities and ecosystems are the core challenges of this century.

Not surprisingly, entrepreneurial innovators are stepping up to provide alternatives better aligned with the constraints of population growth, material demand, and limited resources. This activity is consistent with the role of society's entrepreneurs. They are the societal subgroup that recognizes new needs and offers creative solutions in the marketplace. However, innovators and their new ways are often misunderstood and rejected, at least initially. Understanding the challenges facing the sustainability entrepreneurs who produce new products and technologies is enhanced by understanding how a paradigm is created and replaced.

Education, cultural messages (conveyed through family, media, and politics), and social context provide us with ideas about how the world works and shape our mind-sets. Formalized and sanctioned by academic fields and canonical textbooks, assumptions become set paradigms through which we understand the world, including our role in it and the possibilities for change. Despite new knowledge, the reality of daily living, and the results of scientific research generating empirical evidence that can challenge core assumptions, it is well known that individuals and societies resist change and hold fast to their known paradigms. Why? Because the unquestioned assumptions have functioned well for many in the population, inertia is powerful, and often we lack alternatives that will explain and bring order to what appears to be contradictory information about how new or unprecedented events are unfolding.

The fact that reality does not correspond to our assumptions can be ignored or denied for a long time if no alternative path is perceived. For years, pollution was acknowledged and accepted as the price of progress, the cost that must be paid to keep people employed and maintain economic growth. "Clean commerce" was an oxymoron. Furthermore, specialized disciplines in academia create narrow intellectual silos that become impediments to broader systems views. In business, functional silos emerge as companies grow. Communication between research and development and manufacturing breaks down, manufacturing experts and marketing staff are removed from each other's work and even geographically separate, and sales departments rarely have the opportunity to provide feedback to designers. These realities present barriers to understanding the complex nature–human relationship shift in which we are now engaged.

It is only when the incongruity between reality and our perceived understanding of that same world presents a preponderance of data and experience to challenge accepted thought patterns that new explanations are permitted to surface, seriously discussed, and legitimized by the mainstream institutions (universities, corporations, and governments). Recently, climate change, toxin-containing household products, the collapse of ocean fisheries, the global asthma epidemic, and other challenges for which no simple answers seem possible have provided incentives for people to imagine and begin to build a different business model.

In fact, business consultants, architects, engineers, chemists, economists, and nonprofit activists have been grappling for many decades with limits to economic growth. Interdisciplinary science has become increasingly popular, and higher funding levels signal recognition that research and solutions need to bridge conventionally segregated and bound areas of thought (e.g., economics, biology, psychology, engineering, chemistry, and ecology). The new approaches to resource use, pollution, and environmental and equity concerns have opened new avenues for thought and action.

A body of ideas and approaches reflects movement toward inter- and even metadisciplinary understanding. Similarities across these approaches will be readily apparent. In fact, in combination, each of these seemingly disparate efforts to close the gap between what we have been taught about economic growth and what we have observed in the last few decades reveals common themes to guide entrepreneurial innovation and business strategy.

KEY TAKEAWAYS

- Educational institutions, cultural values, and everyday practices create and sustain assumptions that become paradigms, which then influence what we consider possible.
- The 1990s and first decade of the twenty-first century witnessed a variety of difficult and growing environmental and social problems and, in response, the introduction of new concepts for business. These sustainability concepts may offer an approach more attuned to the problems businesses face now and will face in the future.

EXERCISES

1. How do paradigms and entrepreneurial innovation interact?
2. What are the advantages and disadvantages of specialization when thinking about social and environmental issues and business?

3.3 Core Ideas and Metaconcepts

LEARNING OBJECTIVES

1. Identify the roles of carrying capacity and equity in the four key metaconcepts of sustainability.

2. Compare and contrast the four key metaconcepts, including their assumptions, emphases, and implications.

3. Apply the metaconcepts to identify sustainable business practices.

An educated entrepreneur or business leader interested in sustainability innovation should understand two core ideas. The first is that sustainability innovation ultimately contributes to preservation and restoration of nature's carrying capacity. **Carrying capacity** refers to the ability of the natural system to sustain demands placed upon it while still retaining the self-regenerative processes that preserve the system's viability indefinitely. Note that human bodies have carrying capacities, and thus we are included in this notion of natural carrying capacities. For example, similarly to groundwater supplies or coastal estuaries, children's bodies can be burdened with pollutants only up to a point, beyond which the system collapses into dysfunction and disease.

The second core idea is **equity**, leading to our discussion of environmental justice as the second metaconcept category. Prosperity achieved by preserving and restoring natural system carrying capacities that structurally exclude many people from realizing the benefits of that prosperity is not sustainable, practically or morally. Sustainability scholars have suggested that a "fortress" future lies ahead if equity issues are not considered core to sustainability goals. The wealthy will need to defend their wealth from gated communities, while the poor live with illness, pollution, and resource scarcity.

Sustainability innovations guided by the following approaches aim to sustain biological carrying capacities *and* healthy human communities that strive toward equity. The ideal is that we tap into every person's creativity and bring it to bear on how we learn to live on what scientists now call our "full Earth."

Each of our four key metaconcepts—sustainable development, environmental justice, earth systems engineering and management, and sustainability science—addresses ideas of equity and carrying capacity in a slightly different way. Earth Systems Engineering and management and sustainability science focus on technology and carrying capacity, while sustainable development and environmental justice emphasize social structures and equity. Yet each metaconcept realizes equity and carrying capacity are linked;

humans have both social and material aspirations that must be met within the finite resources of the environment.

Sustainable Development

Sustainable development refers to a socioeconomic development paradigm that achieves more widespread human prosperity while sustaining nature's life-support systems. Under sustainable development, the next generation's choices are extended rather than attenuated; therefore, sustainable development addresses equity issues across generations to not impoverish those generations that follow. Introduced in the Brundtland Commission's 1983 report, which focused attention on the interrelated and deteriorating environmental and social conditions worldwide, sustainable development would balance the carrying capacities of natural systems (environmental sustainability) with sociopolitical well-being. While debate continues on the challenges' details and possible solutions, there is widespread scientific consensus that continued escalation in scale and scope of resource and energy consumption cannot be maintained without significant risk of ecological degradation accompanied by potentially severe economic and sociopolitical disruption. In 1992, the Economic Commission for Europe described societal transformation toward sustainable development moving through stages, from ignorance (problems are not widely known or understood) and lack of concern, to hope in technology-based fixes ("technology will solve our problems"), to eventual conversion of economic activities from their current separation from ecological and human health goals of society to new forms appropriately adapted to ecological laws and the promotion of community well-being. The goal of sustainable development, though perhaps impossible to reach, would be a smooth transition to a stable carrying capacity and leveling of population growth. Societies would evolve toward more compatible integration and coevolution of natural systems with industrial activity. Because corporations are among the most powerful institutions in the world today, they are viewed as instrumental in creating the transition from the current unsustainable growth trajectory to sustainable development.

Environmental Justice

Environmental justice emerged as a mainstream concept in the 1980s. Broad population segments in the United States and elsewhere increasingly acknowledged that racial and ethnic minorities and the poor (groups that often overlap) suffered greater exposure to environmental hazards and environmental degradation than the general population. Following pressure from the Congressional Black Caucus and other groups, the US Environmental Protection Agency (EPA) incorporated environmental justice into its program goals in the early 1990s. The EPA defined environmental justice as "the fair treatment and meaningful involvement of all people regardless of race, color, national origin, or income with respect to the development, implementation, and enforcement of environmental laws, regulations, and policies." The EPA also stated that environmental justice "will be achieved when everyone enjoys the same degree of protection from environmental and health hazards and equal access to the decision-making process to have a healthy environment in which to live, learn, and work." [1] Other definitions of environmental justice similarly include an emphasis on stakeholder participation in decisions and an equitable distribution of environmental risks and benefits.

Environmental justice in the United States grew out of a civil rights framework that guarantees equal protection under the law, which globally translated into the framework of universal human rights. It crystallized as a movement in the years 1982–83, when hundreds of people were jailed for protesting the location of a hazardous waste dump in a predominantly black community in North Carolina. [2] In 1991, the National People of Color Environmental Leadership Summit first convened and drafted the "Principles of Environmental Justice," which were later circulated at the 1992 Rio Earth Summit. [3] The 2002 UN World Conference against Racism, Racial Discrimination, Xenophobia, and Related Intolerance also embraced environmental justice in its final report. [4]

Although the placement of hazardous waste dumps and heavily polluting industries in areas predominantly inhabited by minorities, such as incinerators in the Bronx in New York City and petrochemical plants along Louisiana's Cancer Alley, remains the most glaring example of environmental injustice, the concept encompasses myriad problems. For instance, housing in which minorities and the poor are concentrated may have lead paint (now a known neurotoxin) and proximity to the diesel exhaust of freeways and shipping terminals. [5] Migrant agricultural laborers are regularly exposed to higher concentrations of pesticides. As heavy industries relocate to areas where labor is cheaper, those regions and countries must shoulder more of the environmental and health burdens, even though most of their products are exported. For instance, demand for bananas and biodiesel in the Northern Hemisphere may accelerate deforestation in the tropics.

Climate change has also broadened the scope of environmental justice. Poor and indigenous people will suffer more from global warming: rising waters in the Pacific Ocean could eliminate island societies and inundate countries such as Bangladesh, cause warming in the Arctic, or cause droughts in Africa. Hurricane Katrina, which some scientists saw as a signal of the growing force of storms, was a dramatic reminder of how poor people have more limited access to assistance during "natural" disasters. In addition, those groups least able to avoid the consequences of pollution often enjoy less of the lifestyle that caused that pollution in the first place.

Spotting environmental injustice can sometimes be simple. However, to quantify environmental justice or its opposite, often called environmental racism, demographic variables frequently are correlated to health outcomes and environmental risk factors with an accepted degree of statistical significance. Rates of asthma, cancer, and absence from work and school are common health indicators. Information from the EPA's Toxic Release Inventory or Air Quality Index can be combined with census data to suggest disproportionate exposure to pollution. For example, children attending schools close to major highways (often found in low-income neighborhoods) experience decreased lung health and capacity.

Earth Systems Engineering and Management

With discussion of earth systems engineering (ESE), we transition from social and community concerns to human impacts on large-scale natural systems. Sometimes referred to as *Earth Systems Engineering and management*, ESE is a broad concept that builds from these basic premises:

1. People have altered the earth for millennia, often in unintended ways with enduring effects, such as the early deforestation of ancient Greece.
2. The scale of that alteration has increased dramatically with industrialization and the population growth of the twentieth century.
3. Our institutions, ethics, and other behaviors have yet to catch up to the power of our technology.
4. Since the world has become increasingly less natural and more—or entirely—an artifact of human activity, we should use technology to help us understand the impact

of our alterations in the long and short terms. Instead of desisting from current practice, we should continue to use technology to intervene in the environment albeit in more conscious, sustainable ways. However, the interactions of human and natural systems are complex, so we must improve our ability to manage each by better understanding the science of how they operate and interact, building better tools to manage them, and creating better policies to guide us. [7]

In 2000, Nobel laureate Paul Crutzen coined the term "anthropocene" to describe the intense impact of humanity upon the world. Anthropocene designates a new geological era with the advent of the Industrial Revolution. In this era, as opposed to the previous Holocene era, humans increasingly dominate the chemical and geologic processes of Earth, and they may continue to do so for tens of thousands of years as increased concentrations of GHGs linger in the atmosphere.

Professor Braden Allenby, a former vice president of AT&T who holds degrees in law, economics, and environmental science, argues we must embrace this anthropogenic (human-designed) world and make the most of it. An early and consistent proponent of ESE, he wrote in 2000, "The issue is not whether the earth will be engineered by the human species, it is whether humans will do so rationally, intelligently, and ethically." [9] Thus ESE differs from other sustainability concepts and frameworks that seek to reduce humanity's impact on nature and to return nature to a more equal relationship with people. Allenby believes technology gives people options, and investing in new technologies to make human life sustainable will have a greater impact than trying to change people's behaviors through laws or other social pressures.

ESE could be deployed at various scales. One of the more extreme is reengineering, which emerged in the 1970s and resurfaced after 2000 as efforts to curb greenhouse gas emissions floundered and people reconsidered ways to arrest or reverse climate change. Geoengineering would manipulate the global climate directly and massively, either by injecting particles such as sulfur dioxide into the atmosphere to block sunlight or by sowing oceans with iron to encourage the growth of algae that consume carbon dioxide (CO_2). The potential for catastrophic consequences has often undermined geoengineering schemes, many of which are already technologically feasible and relatively cheap. On the scale of individual organisms, ESE could turn to genetic engineering, such as creating drought-resistant plants or trees that sequester more CO_2.

Sustainability Science

Sustainability science was codified as a multidisciplinary academic field between 2000 and 2009 with the creation of a journal called *Sustainability Science*, a study section within the US National Academy of Sciences and the Forum on Science and Innovation for Sustainable Development, which links various sustainability efforts and individuals around the world. Sustainability science aims to bring scientific and technical knowledge to bear on problems of sustainability, including assessing the resilience of ecosystems, informing policy on poverty alleviation, and inventing technologies to sequester CO_2 and purify drinking water. William C. Clark, associate editor of the *Proceedings of the National Academy of Sciences*, writes, "Like 'agricultural science' and 'health science,' sustainability science is a field defined by the problems it addresses rather than by the disciplines it employs. In particular, the field seeks to facilitate what the National Research Council has called a 'transition toward sustainability,' improving society's capacity to use the earth in ways that simultaneously 'meet the needs of a much larger but stabilizing human population…sustain the life support systems of the planet, and…substantially reduce hunger and poverty.'" [10]

Like ecological economics, sustainability science seeks to overcome the splintering of knowledge and perspectives by emphasizing a transdisciplinary, systems-level approach to sustainability. In contrast to ecological economics, sustainability science often brings together researchers from a broader base and focuses on devising practical solutions. Clark calls it the "use-inspired research" typified by Louis Pasteur.

Sustainability science arose largely in response to the increasing call for sustainable development in the late 1980s and early 1990s. The core question became *how?* The number of scholarly articles on sustainability science increased throughout the 1990s. In 1999, the National Research Council published *Our Common Journey: A Transition Toward Sustainability*. The report investigated how science could assist "the reconciliation of society's development goals with the planet's environmental limits over the long term." It set three main goals for sustainability science research: "Develop a research framework that integrates global and local perspectives to shape a 'place-based' understanding of the interactions between environment and society….Initiate focused research programs on a small set of understudied questions that are central to a deeper understanding of interactions between society and the environment….Promote better utilization of existing tools and processes for linking knowledge to action in pursuit of a transition to sustainability." [11]

Shortly thereafter, an article in *Science* attempted to define the core questions of sustainability science, again focusing on themes of integrating research, policy, and practical action across a variety of geographic and temporal scales. [12]

At about the same time, groups such as the Alliance for Global Sustainability (AGS) formed. AGS is an academic collaboration among the Massachusetts Institute of Technology, the University of Tokyo, the Swiss Federal Institute of Technology, and Chalmers University of

Technology in Sweden. The alliance seeks to inject scientific information into largely political debates on sustainability. Members of the alliance also created the journal *Sustainability Science*. Writing in the inaugural edition, Hiroshi Komiyama and Kazuhiko Takeuchi described sustainability science as broadly addressing three levels of analysis and their interactions: (1) global, primarily the natural environment and its life-support systems; (2) social, primarily comprising human institutions and collective activities; and (3) human, largely addressing questions of individual health, happiness, and prosperity. [13]

KEY TAKEAWAYS

- The broad metaconcepts in sustainability emphasize equity and maintenance of the earth's carrying capacity, despite an increased human population.
- Sustainability metaconcepts focus on balancing the needs of humans and their environment, present and future generations, and research and policy. These problems are complex, and the metaconcepts therefore tend to endorse an interdisciplinary, systems-level view.
- Equity considerations as design criteria offer opportunities for novel approaches to product and business competitiveness while preserving socially and politically stable communities.

EXERCISES

1. Make a diagram comparing and contrasting the four metaconcepts, including their implications, assumptions, and past successes. Then present to others the framework you find most compelling and explain why. If you prefer, synthesize a fifth metaconcept to present.
2. Select an industry and briefly research how the four metaconcepts have changed its practices and may guide future changes.

[1] US Environmental Protection Agency, "Compliance and Enforcement: Environmental Justice," last updated November 24, 2010, accessed December 3, 2010, http://www.epa.gov/oecaerth/environmentaljustice.
[2] April Mosley, "Why Blacks Should Be Concerned about the Environment: An Interview with Dr. Robert Bullard," November 1999, Environmental Justice Resource Center at Clark Atlanta University, accessed July 2, 2009, http://www.ejrc.cau.edu/nov99interv.htm.
[3] United Church of Christ, Toxic Wastes and Race at Twenty: 1987–2007 (Cleveland, OH: United Church of Christ, 2007), 2.
[4] United Nations, United Nations Report of the World Conference against Racism, Racial Discrimination, Xenophobia and Related Intolerance (Durban, South Africa: United Nations, 2001), accessed December 3, 2010, http://www.un.org/WCAR/aconf189_12.pdf.
[5] David Pace, "More Blacks Live with Pollution," Associated Press, December 13, 2005, accessed December 1, 2010, http://www.precaution.org/lib/05/more_blacks_live_with_pollution.051213.htm; American Lung Association, "Comments to the Environmental Protection Agency re: Ocean Going Vessels," September 28, 2009, accessed April 19, 2011, http://www.lungusa.org/get-involved/advocate/advocacy-documents/Comments-to-the-Environmental-Protection-Agency-re-Ocean-Going-Vessels.pdf.
[6] United Church of Christ, Toxic Wastes and Race at Twenty: 1987–2007 (Cleveland, OH: United Church of Christ, 2007), 143.
[7] National Academy of Engineering, Engineering and Environmental Challenges: Technical Symposium on Earth Systems Engineering (Washington, DC: National Academy Press, 2000), viii.
[8] National Academies of Science, Engineering and Environmental Challenges: Technical Symposium on Earth Systems Engineering (Washington, DC: National Academies Press, 2000), viii.
[9] Braden Allenby, "Earth Systems Engineering and Management," IEEE Technology and Society Magazine 19, no. 4 (Winter 2000–2001): 10–24.
[10] William C. Clark, "Sustainability Science: A Room of Its Own," Proceedings of the National Academy of Sciences 104, no. 6 (February 6, 2007): 1737–38.
[11] National Research Council, Our Common Journey: A Transition toward Sustainability (Washington, DC: National Academy Press, 1999), 2, 10–11.
[12] Robert W. Kates, William C. Clark, Robert Corell, J. Michael Hall, Carlo C. Jaeger, Ian Lowe, James J. McCarthy, et al., "Sustainability Science," Science 292, no. 5517 (April 27, 2000): 641–42.
[13] Hiroshi Komiyama and Kazuhiko Takeuchi, "Sustainability Science: Building a New Discipline," Sustainability Science 1, no. 1 (October 2006): 1–6.

3.4 Practical Frameworks and Tools

LEARNING OBJECTIVES

1. Understand the core premises of each framework or tool.

2. Compare and contrast the frameworks and tools to evaluate the contributions of each to sustainability thinking.

3. Apply the frameworks and tools to improve existing products and services or to create new ones.

This section lists and discusses a set of frameworks and tools available to business decision makers. Those who are starting companies or those inside established firms can draw from these ideas and conduct further research into any tool that is of particular interest. Our purpose is to educate the reader about the variety and content of tools being applied by firms that are active in the sustainability innovation space. Each tool is somewhat different in its substance and applicability. The following discussion moves from the most general to the most specific. For example, The Natural Step (TNS) is a broad framework used by firms, municipalities, and nonprofit organizations, whereas industrial ecology is an academic field that has provided overarching concepts as well as developed product design tools. Natural capitalism is a framework developed by well-known energy and systems expert Amory Lovins together with L. Hunter Lovins and author-consultant Paul Hawken. Ecological economics is a branch of economics that combines analysis of environmental systems with economic systems, while cradle-to-cradle is a design protocol with conceptual roots in the field of industrial ecology. Nature's services refers to the ability of natural systems to ameliorate human waste impacts, and the related concept of ecosystem service markets references the burgeoning arena of markets for the services natural systems provide to business and society. The biomimicry approach calls for greater appreciation of nature's design models as the inspiration for human-designed technology. Green chemistry is a fast-expanding challenge to the conventional field of chemistry. It invites use of a set of twelve principles for the design of chemical compounds. Green engineering offers guiding design parameters for sustainability applied to engineering education. Life-cycle analysis, design for environment, concurrent engineering, and carbon footprint analysis are tools for analysis and decision making at various levels of business activity including within the firm and extending to supply chains. There is no "right" framework or tool. It depends on the specific task at hand. Furthermore, some of these tools share common assumptions and may overlap. However, this is a useful sample of the types of frameworks and tools in use. Reviewing the list provides the reader with insights into the nature and direction of sustainability innovation and entrepreneurship.

The Natural Step

TNS is both a framework for understanding ecological principles and environmental problems and an international nonprofit education, consultation, and research institution based in Sweden. TNS was founded in 1989 by Swedish pediatric oncologist Dr. Karl-Henrik Robèrt. In his medical practice, Dr. Robèrt observed an increase of rare cancers in children who were too young to have their cells damaged through lifestyle choices. He began to explore human-caused pollution (environmental) causes—outcomes of industrial and commercial activity. Once engaged in the process and frustrated by the polarized public and scientific debates over pollution, Dr. Robèrt began enlisting leading Swedish scientists to identify irrefutable principles from which productive debate could follow. These principles became the basis for TNS framework now used by many businesses worldwide to guide strategy and product design. [1]

The principles the scientists distinguished during the consensus-building process are three well-known and very basic physical laws. The first law of thermodynamics, also known as the law of conservation of energy, states that energy cannot be created or destroyed, only changed in form. Whether electrical, chemical, kinetic, heat, or light, the total energy remains constant. Similarly, the law of conservation of matter tells us that the total amount of matter is constant and cannot be created or destroyed. [2] Finally, by the second law of thermodynamics, we know that matter and energy tend to disperse. Greater entropy, or disorder, is the inevitable outcome. Think about the decomposition of discarded items. Over time, they lose their structure, order, and concentration; in other words, they lose their quality.

In our biosphere, these laws imply things do not appear or disappear; they only take on different forms. All energy and matter remain, either captured temporarily in products or dispersed into the air, water, and soil. The matter humans introduce into the biosphere from the earth's crust (e.g., by mining and drilling) or from corporate research laboratories (synthetic compounds) eventually is released and dispersed into the larger natural systems, including the air we breathe, water we drink, and food we eat. Furthermore, humans do not literally "consume" products. We only consume or use up their quality, their purity, and their manufactured temporary structure. Thus there is no "away" when we throw things away.

However, if the law of entropy dictates that matter and energy tend toward disorder rather than toward complex materials and ecosystems, what keeps the earth's systems running? An outside energy input is needed to create order. That energy is the sun. While the earth is essentially a closed system with respect to matter, it is an open system with respect to energy. Hence net increases in material quality on Earth ultimately derive from solar energy, present or ancient. [3]

Green plant cells, as loci of photosynthesis, curb entropy by using sunlight to generate order. The cells produce more structure, quality, and order than they destroy through dissipation. Plants thereby regulate the biosphere by capturing carbon dioxide (CO_2), producing oxygen for animal life, and creating food. Fossil fuels, meanwhile, are simply that: the end products of photosynthesis in fossil form.

Cyclical systems lie at the heart of TNS framework. While the natural world operates in a continuously regenerative cyclical process—photosynthesis produces oxygen and absorbs CO_2; plants are consumed, die, and decay, becoming food for microbial life; and the cycle continues—humankind has typically used resources in a linear fashion, producing waste streams both visible and molecular (invisible) that cannot all be absorbed and reassimilated by nature, at least not within time frames relevant for preservation of human health and extension of prosperity to billions more who demand a better life. The result is increasing accumulations of pollution and waste coupled with a declining stock of natural resources. [5] In the case of oil, global society must address both declining resources and control of existing resources by either unstable governments or regimes whose aims can oppose their own populations' and other countries' well-being.

TNS System Conditions

With foundational scientific principles dictating a compelling logic that guides decision making, a framework of system conditions followed to form *TNS system conditions*:

1. The first system condition states that "substances from the earth's crust must not systematically increase in the ecosphere." This means that the rate of extraction of fossil fuels, metals, and other minerals must not exceed

the pace of their slow redeposit and reintegration into the earth's crust. The phrase "systematically increase" in the systems conditions deserves elaboration. The natural system complexity that has built and sustains the biosphere maintains systemic equilibrium within a certain range. We now recognize that humans contribute to CO_2 atmospheric buildup, potentially tipping climate to a new equilibrium to which we must adapt.

2. The second system condition requires that "substances produced by society must not systematically increase in the ecosphere." These substances, synthetic compounds created in laboratories, must be produced, used, and released at a rate that does not exceed the rate with which they can be broken down and integrated into natural cycles or safely incorporated in the earth's crust (soil, water).

3. The third condition states that "the physical basis for productivity and diversity of nature must not be systematically diminished." This requirement protects the productive capacity and diversity of the earth's ecosystems as well as the green plant cells, the photosynthesizers on which the larger ecological systems depend.

4. Finally, the fourth system condition, a consideration of justice, calls for the "fair and efficient use of resources with respect to meeting human needs."

Under TNS framework, these four system conditions act as a compass that can guide companies, governments, nonprofit organizations, and even individuals toward sustainability practices and innovation. [6] Here, "sustainability" explicitly refers to a carrying capacity or ability of natural systems to continue the age-old regenerative processes that have maintained the requisite chemistry and systems balance to support life as we know it.

TNS framework has been applied in many corporations and is seen by some as a logical extension of quality management and strategic systems thinking. [7] It incorporates environmental and health protection into decision making by using scientific principles. TNS allows a company to understand the physical laws that drive environmental problems and defines the broad system conditions that form a "sustainable" society. These conditions provide a vehicle to assess progress, and from them companies can develop a strategy applicable to their products and services. Design teams can ask whether particular product designs, materials selection, and manufacturing processes meet each of the system conditions and can adjust in "natural steps"—that is, steps that are consistent with financially sound decision making in the direction of meeting the system conditions. TNS does not provide a detailed how-to regarding specific product design; however, with the knowledge and framework provided by TNS, companies can develop a more informed approach and strategic position and begin to take concrete steps customized to their unique circumstance with respect to natural resource use and waste streams.

Industrial Ecology

Business activity currently generates waste and by-products. Unlike natural systems, modern human societies process resources in a linear fashion, creating waste faster than it can be reconstituted into reusable resources. According to the National Academy of Engineering, on average 94 percent of raw materials used in a product ends up as waste; only 6 percent ends up in the final product. Whereas pollution control and prevention focus on minimizing waste, industrial ecology allows for inevitable waste streams since they become useful inputs to other industrial and commercial processes. Continued provision of needed goods and services to growing populations in a finite biosphere becomes at least conceptually possible if all waste generated by business and consumer behavior is taken up by other industrial and commercial processes or safely returned to nature.

Consequently, the field of industrial ecology assumes the industrial system exists as a human-produced ecosystem with distinct material, energy, and information flows similar to any other ecosystem within the biosphere. It therefore must meet the same physical constraints as other ecosystems to survive. As a systems approach to understanding the interaction between industry and the natural world, industrial ecology looks beyond the linear cradle-to-grave viewpoint of design—you source materials, build the product, use the product, and throw it away—and imagines business as a series of **energy and material flows** in which ideally the wastes of one process serve as the feedstock of another. Accordingly, nature's processes and business activities are seen as interacting systems rather than separate components. They form an industrial web analogous to but separate from the natural web from which they may nonetheless draw inspiration. [8]

Clinton Andrews, a professor of environmental and urban planning, suggested a series of themes for industrial ecology based on natural metaphors: "Nutrients and wastes become raw materials for other processes, and the system runs almost entirely on solar energy. The analogy suggests that a sustainable industrial system would be one in which nearly complete recycling of materials is achieved." Andrews

described the present industrial systems as having "primitive metabolisms," which will be "forced by environmental and social constraints to evolve more sophisticated metabolisms….Inexhaustibility, recycling, and robustness are central themes in the industrial ecology agenda." [9] Theoretically, restructuring industry for compatibility with natural ecosystems' self-regulation and self-renewal would reduce the current human activity that undermines natural systems and creates the growing environmental health problems we face.

In 1977, American geochemist Preston Cloud observed that "materials and energy are the interdependent feedstocks of economic systems, and thermodynamics is their moderator." [10] Cloud's point about thermodynamics anticipates TNS, and he was perhaps the first person to use the term "industrial ecosystem." [11] Despite earlier analogies between the human economy and natural systems, this correspondence did not gain widespread currency until 1989 when business executive Robert Frosch and Nicholas Gallopoulos first coined the term "industrial ecology" [12] and described it in *Scientific American* as follows:

> In nature an ecological system operates through a web of connections in which organisms live and consume each other and each other's waste. The system has evolved so that the characteristic of communities of living organisms seems to be that nothing that contains available energy or useful material will be lost. There will evolve some organism that will manage to make its living by dealing with any waste product that provides available energy or usable material. Ecologists talk of a food web: an interconnection of uses of both organisms and their wastes. In the industrial context we may think of this as being use of products and waste products. The system structure of a natural ecology and the structure of an industrial system, or an economic system, are extremely similar. [13]

Professor Robert U. Ayres clarified process flows within the natural and industrial systems by naming them the "biological metabolism" and the "industrial metabolism." [14] The feedstocks of these systems are known as "biological nutrients" and "industrial nutrients," respectively, when they act in a closed cycle (which is always the case in nature, and rarely the case in industry). [15] In an ideal industrial ecosystem, there would be, as Hardin Tibbs wrote, "no such thing as 'waste' in the sense of something that cannot be absorbed constructively somewhere else in the system." This suggests that "the key to creating industrial ecosystems is to reconceptualize wastes as products." [16]

Others have pointed out that "materials and material products (unlike pure services) are not really consumed. The only thing consumed is their 'utility.'" [17] This concept has led to selling the utilization of products rather than the products themselves, thus creating a closed-loop product cycle in which manufacturers maintain ownership of the product. For example, a company could lease the service of floor coverings rather than sell carpeting. The responsibility for creating a system of product reuse, reconditioning, and other forms of product life extension, or waste disposal, then falls on the owner of the product—the manufacturer—not the user. [18] This product life cycle can be described as being "from cradle back to cradle," rather than from cradle to grave, which is of primary importance in establishing a well-functioning industrial ecosystem. [19] The cradle-to-cradle life cycle became so important to some practitioners that it emerged as an independent concern.

The challenges to establishing a sophisticated industrial ecosystem are many, including identifying appropriate input opportunities for waste products amid ownership, geographic, jurisdictional, informational, operational, regulatory, and economic hurdles. Although industrial ecology could theoretically link industries around the globe, it has also been used at a local scale to mitigate some of these challenges. Several eco-industrial parks are currently in development (Kallundborg, Denmark, is the well-known historical example) where industries are intentionally sited together based on their waste products and input material requirements. If the interdependent system components at the site are functioning properly, the emissions from the industrial park are zero or almost zero. Problems arise when companies change processes, move facilities, or go out of business. This disrupts the ordered and tightly coupled chain of interdependency, much as when a species disappears from a natural ecosystem. Industrial ecology thus provides a broad framework and suggests practical solutions.

Natural Capitalism

Natural capitalism is a broad social and economic framework that attempts to integrate insights from eco-efficiency, nature's services, biomimicry, and other realms to create a plan for a sustainable, more equitable, and productive world. Paul Hawken, author of *The Ecology of Commerce*, and Amory Lovins and L. Hunter Lovins, cofounders of the Rocky Mountain Institute for resource analysis and coauthors with Ernest von Weizsäcker of *Factor Four: Doubling Wealth, Halving Resource Use*, were independently looking for an overall framework to implement the environmental business gains they had studied and advocated. After learning of each other's projects, they decided in 1994 to collaborate on *Natural Capitalism*:

Some very simple changes to the way we run our businesses, built on advanced techniques for making resources more productive, can yield startling benefits both for today's shareholders and for future generations. This approach is called natural capitalism because it's what capitalism might become if its largest category of capital— the "natural capital" of ecosystem services—were properly valued. The journey to natural capitalism involves four major shifts in business practices, all vitally interlinked:

- *Dramatically increase the productivity of natural resources....*
- *Shift to biologically inspired production models....*
- *Move to a solution-based business model....*
- *Reinvest in natural capital....* [20]

Natural capitalism emphasizes a broad and integrated approach to sustainable human activity. Although economic, environmental, and social goals had been conventionally seen in conflict, natural capitalism argues, "The best solutions are based not on tradeoffs or 'balance' between these objectives but on design integration achieving all of them together." [22] Hence, by considering all facets of the problem in advance, business can yield dramatic, multiple improvements and will drive environmental progress. For perhaps the simplest example, using more sunlight and less artificial light in buildings lowers energy costs, reduces pollution, and improves workers' outlook and satisfaction, and hence their productivity and retention rates.

Like similar broad frameworks for sustainability, natural capitalism perceives a variety of current structures, rather than lack of knowledge or opportunity for profit, as obstacles to progress: perverse incentives from government tax policy hamper change, the division of labor and capital investments among different groups does not reward efficiency for the entire system but only the cheapest choice for each individual, companies do not know how to value natural capital properly, and so on.

Natural capitalism also criticizes eco-efficiency as too narrow: "Eco-efficiency, an increasingly popular concept used by business to describe incremental improvements in materials use and environmental impact, is only one small part of a richer and more complex web of ideas and solutions....More efficient production by itself could become not the servant but the enemy of a durable economy." [23]

Natural capitalism does, however, see eco-efficiency as one important component of curbing environmental degradation. Adapting the best-available technology and designing entire systems, rather than just pieces, to function efficiently from the outset saves money quickly. That money can be invested in other changes. Indeed, natural capitalism's case studies argue major gains in productivity by reconceiving entire systems are often cheaper than minor gains from incremental improvements.

Natural capitalism's three other principles emphasize eliminating waste entirely and uniting environmental and economic gains. For instance, mimicking natural production systems means waste from one process equals food for another in a **closed loop**. Shifting from providing goods to providing services holds manufacturers accountable for their products and allows them to benefit from their design innovations while eliminating the waste inherent in planned obsolescence. Finally, companies can reinvest in natural capital to replenish, sustain, and expand the services and goods ecosystems provide. Beyond mimicry, letting nature do the work in the first place means that benign, efficient processes, such as using wetlands to process sewage, can replace artificial and often more dangerous and energy-intensive practices.

For example, a study of forests around the Mediterranean suggested that preserving forests may provide greater economic value than consuming those forests for timber and grazing land. Forests contribute immensely to clean waterways by limiting erosion and filtering pollutants. They can also sequester CO_2, provide habitats for other valuable plants and animals, and encourage recreation and tourism. Investing in forests could therefore return dividends in various ways.

Ecological Economics

Ecological economics as a field of study was formalized in 1989 with the foundation of the International Society for Ecological Economics (ISEE) and the first publication of the journal *Ecological Economics*. The move toward ecological economics had roots in the classical economics, natural sciences, and sociology of the mid-nineteenth century but gained significant momentum in the 1970s [24] as the strain between human activity (economics) and natural systems (ecology) intensified but no discipline or even group of disciplines examined the interaction of those two systems specifically. Robert Costanza commented on the problem and the need for a new approach: "Environmental and resource economics, as it is currently practiced, covers only the application of neoclassical economics to environmental and resource problems. Ecology, as it is currently practiced, sometimes deals with human impacts on ecosystems, but the more common tendency is to stick to 'natural' systems....[Ecological economics] is intended to be a new

approach to *both* ecology and economics that recognizes the need to make economics more cognizant of ecological impacts and dependencies; the need to make ecology more sensitive to economic forces, incentives, and constraints." [25]

Ecological economics examines how economies influence ecologies and vice versa. It sees economic activity as occurring only within the confines of Earth's processes for maintaining life and equilibrium and ecology as overwhelmingly influenced by humans, even if they are but one species among many. In short, the global economy is a subset of Earth systems, not a distinct, unfettered entity. Earth's processes and resultant equilibrium are threatened by massive material extraction from and waste disposal into the environment, while material inequality among societies and people threatens long-term prosperity and social stability. Hence the constitution of the ISEE propounds the "advancement of our understanding of the relationships among ecological, social, and economic systems and the application of this understanding to the mutual well-being of nature and people, especially that of the most vulnerable including future generations." [26] The field continues to emphasize broadly and rigorously investigating interdependent systems and their material and energy flows.

Indeed, ecological economics began as a transdisciplinary venture. That variety in academic disciplines is reflected in the field's seminal figures: Robert Costanza earned a master's degree in urban and regional planning and a doctorate in systems ecology, Paul Ehrlich was a lepidopterist, Herman Daly was a World Bank economist, and Richard Norgaard an academic one. Diversity and breadth were enshrined in the ISEE constitution because "in an interconnected evolving world, reductionist science has pushed out the envelope of knowledge in many different directions, but it has left us bereft of ideas as to how to formulate and solve problems that stem from the interactions between humans and the natural world." [27] Hence ecological economics has studied an array of issues, frequently including equitable economic development in poorer countries and questions of sustainable scale within closed systems.

Nonetheless, there has been some discussion of whether ecological economics should remain an eclectic category or become a defined specialty with concomitant methodologies. [28] Ecological economics tends to use different models than mainstream economics and has a normative inclination toward sustainability and justice over individual preference or maximizing return on investments. [29] Moreover, while mainstream economics continues not to require an environmental education for a degree, some doctoral programs now grant a separate degree in ecological economics, while others offer it as a field for specialization. The location of ecological economics courses within university economics departments, however, suggests that contrary to the founding aspirations of the field, ecological economics has become the purview of economists more than ecologists in the United States.

Cradle-to-Cradle

Cradle-to-cradle is a design philosophy articulated in the book of the same name by William McDonough and Michael Braungart in 2002. [30] As of 2005, cradle-to-cradle is also a certification system for products tested by McDonough Braungart Design Chemistry (MBDC) to meet cradle-to-cradle principles. The basic premise of cradle-to-cradle is that for most of industrial history, we have failed to plan for the safe reuse of materials or their reintegration into the environment. This failure, born of ignorance rather than malevolence, wastes the value of processed goods, such as purified metals or synthesized plastics, and threatens human and environmental health. Hence McDonough and Braungart propose "a radically different approach for designing and producing the objects we use and enjoy…founded on nature's surprisingly effective design principles, on human creativity and prosperity, and on respect, fair play, and good will." [31]

In this approach, ecology, economy, and equity occupy equally important vertices of a triangle of human activity, and waste is eliminated as a concept in advance, as all products should be designed to become harmless feedstocks or "nutrients" for other biological or industrial processes. These closed loops acknowledge matter is finite on Earth, Earth is ultimately humanity's only home, and the only new energy comes from the sun. Cradle-to-cradle thus shares and elaborates some of the basic understandings of TNS and industrial ecology albeit with an emphasis on product design and life cycle.

McDonough is an architect who was inspired by elegant solutions to resource scarcity that he observed in Japan and Jordan. In the United States, he was frustrated by the dearth of options for improving indoor air quality in buildings in the 1980s. He also was frustrated with eco-efficiency's "failure of imagination," although eco-efficiency was a trendsetting business approach at the time. Eco-efficiency stressed doing "less bad" but still accepted the proposition that industry would harm the environment; hence, eco-efficiency would, at best, merely delay the worst consequences or, at worst, accelerate them. Furthermore, it implied economic activity was intrinsically negative. McDonough specified his personal frustration: "I was tired of working hard to be less bad. I wanted to be involved in making buildings, even products, with completely positive intentions." [33]

Braungart, meanwhile, was a German chemist active in the Green Party and with Greenpeace: "I soon realized that protest wasn't enough. We needed to develop a process for change." [34] He created the Environmental Protection Encouragement Agency (EPEA) in Hamburg, Germany, to promote change but found few chemists had any concern for environmental design, while industrialists and environmentalists mutually demonized each other.

After Braungart and McDonough met in 1991, they drafted cradle-to-cradle principles and founded MBDC in 1994 to help enact them. One of their early successes was redesigning the manufacture of carpets for Swiss Rohner Textil AG. The use of recycled plastics in manufacturing carpet was rejected, as the plastic itself is hazardous; humans inhale or ingest plastics as they are abraded and otherwise degraded. Hence McDonough and Braungart designed a product safe enough to eat. They used natural fibers and a process that made effluent from the factory cleaner than the incoming water. This redesign exemplified McDonough and Braungart's idea of "eco-effectiveness," in which "the key is not to make human industries and systems smaller, as efficiency advocates propound, but to design them to get bigger and better in a way that replenishes, restores, and nourishes the rest of the world" and that returns humans to a positive "dynamic interdependence" with rather than dominance over nature. [35]

McDonough and Braungart's efforts proved that cradle-to-cradle design was possible, concretely illustrating concepts important to cradle-to-cradle design while affirming the prior decades of conceptual work. The first concept of eco-effectiveness or ecological intelligence to be realized in cradle-to-cradle was the sense of nature and industry as metabolic systems, fed by "biological nutrients" in the "biosphere" and "technical nutrients" in the "technosphere," or industry. "With the right design, all of the products and materials of industry will feed these two metabolisms, providing nourishment for something new," thereby eliminating waste. [36]

McDonough and Braungart operationalized and popularized the concept of "waste equals food," and by that phrase they mean that the waste of one system or process must be the "food" or feedstock of another. They were drawing on the industrial ecology writing of Robert Ayres, Hardin Tibbs, and others, since in a closed loop the waste is a nutrient (and an asset) rather than a problem for disposal. Hence waste equals food. [37] A core goal of sustainable design is to eliminate the concept of waste so that all products nourish a metabolism. Although lowering resource consumption has its own returns to the system, the waste-equals-food notion allows the possibility for nontoxic "waste" to be produced without guilt as long as the waste feeds another product or process.

To explain further the implications of designing into the two metabolisms, McDonough and Braungart and Justus Englefried of the EPEA developed the Intelligent Product System, which is a typology of three fundamental products that guides design to meet the waste-equals-food test. The product types are consumables, products of service, and unsalables. [38]

A "consumable" is a product that is intended to be literally consumed, such as food, or designed to safely return to the biological (or organic) metabolism where it becomes a nutrient for other living things. [39] McDonough added that "the things we design to go into the organic metabolism should not contain mutagens, carcinogens, heavy metals, persistent toxins, bio-accumulative substances or endocrine disrupters." [40]

A "product of service," on the other hand, provides a service, as suggested by Walter Stahel and Max Börlin, among others. [41] Examples of service products include television sets (which provide the service of news and entertainment), washing machines (which provide clean clothes), computers, automobiles, and so on. These products would be leased, not sold, to a customer, and when the customer no longer required the service of the product or wanted to upgrade the service, the item would be returned to the producer to serve as a nutrient to the industrial metabolism. This system of design and policy provides an incentive for the producer to use design for environment (DfE) and concurrent engineering to design for refurbishing, disassembly, remanufacture, and so forth. Braungart suggests that "waste supermarkets" could provide centralized locations for customer "de-shopping," where used service products are returned and sorted for reclamation by the producer. [42]

An "unsalable," also known as an "unmarketable," is a product that does not feed metabolism in either the technosphere or the biosphere and thus should not be made. Unsalables include products that incorporate dangerous (radioactive, toxic, carcinogenic, etc.) materials or that combine both biological and technical nutrients in such a way that they cannot be separated. These latter combinations

are "monstrous hybrids" from the cradle-to-cradle perspective or "products plus"—something we want plus a toxin we do not. Recycling, as Ayres explained, has become more difficult due to increasingly complex materials forming increasingly complex products. His example was the once-profitable wool recycling industry, which has now virtually disappeared because most new clothes are blends of fibers from both the natural and industrial metabolisms that cannot be separated and reprocessed economically. [43]

In a sustainable economy, unsalables would not be manufactured. During the transition, unsalables, as a matter of business and public policy, would always belong to the original manufacturer. To guarantee that unsalables are not dumped or otherwise discharged into the environment in irretrievable locations, "waste parking lots" operated perhaps by a public utility would be established so that these products can be stored safely. The original manufacturers of the unsalables would be charged rent for the storage until such time when processes were developed to detoxify their products. All toxic chemicals would contain chemical markers that identify the chemical's owner, and the owner would be responsible for retrieving, mitigating, or cleaning up its toxins should they be discovered in lakes, wells, soil, birds, or people. [44]

The second principle of ecological intelligence, "use current solar income," is derived from the second law of thermodynamics. Though the earth is a closed system with respect to matter, it is an open system with respect to energy, thanks to the sun. This situation implies that a sustainable, steady-state economy is possible on Earth as long as the sun continues to shine. [45] Using current solar income requires that Earth capital not be depleted—generally mined and burned—as a way to release energy. Thus all energy must be either solar or from solar-derived sources such as wind power, photovoltaic cells, geothermal, tidal power, and biomass fuels. [46] Fossilized animals and plants, namely oil and coal, while technically solar sources, fail the *current* solar income test, and their use violates the imperative to preserve healthy natural system functioning since burning fossil fuels alters climate systems and produces acid rain among other adverse impacts.

The third principle of ecological intelligence is "respect diversity." Biodiversity, the characteristic that sustains the natural metabolism, must be encouraged through conscious design. Diversity in nature increases overall ecosystem resilience to exogenous shocks. Clinton Andrews, Frans Berkhout, and Valerie Thomas suggest applying this characteristic to the industrial metabolism to develop a similar robustness. [47] (See Andrews's guiding metaphors for industrial ecology earlier in this section.) Respecting diversity, however, has a broader interpretation than just biological diversity. In its broadest sense, "respect diversity" means "one size does not fit all." Every location has different material flows, energy flows, culture, and character. [48] Therefore, this principle attempts to take into account the uniqueness of place by celebrating differences rather than promoting uniformity and monocultures.

In addition to the requirement of ecological intelligence, an additional criterion similar to the fourth system condition of TNS asks of the design, "Is it just?" Justice from a design perspective can be tricky to define or quantify and instead lends itself to qualitative reflection. However, the sustainable design framework forces an intergenerational perspective of justice through its design principles and product typology. As William McDonough explains, products designed to fit neither the biological nor industrial metabolism inflict "remote tyranny" on future generations as they will be left with the challenges of depleted Earth capital and wastes that are completely useless and often dangerous. [49]

Finally, cradle-to-cradle eco-effectiveness "sees commerce as the engine of change" rather than the inherent enemy of the environment and "honors its ability to function quickly and productively." [50] Companies should make money, but they must also protect local cultural and environmental diversity, promote justice, and in McDonough's world, be fun.

Nature's Services

Nature's services emerged in the late 1990s as a practical framework to put a monetary value on the services that ecosystems provide to humans to better weigh the trade-offs involved with preserving an ecosystem or converting it to a different use. The nature's services outlook posits two things. First, "the goods and services flowing from natural ecosystems are greatly undervalued by society…[and] the benefits of those ecosystems are not traded in formal markets and do not send price signals." [51] Second, we are rapidly reaching a point of no return, where we will have despoiled or destroyed so many ecosystems that the earth can no longer sustain the burgeoning human population. Nature's systems are too complex for humans to understand entirely, let alone replace if the systems fail. Indeed, Stanford biology professor Gretchen Daily was inspired to edit the book *Nature's Services*, published in 1997, after "a small group of us [scientists] gathered to lament the near total lack of public appreciation of societal dependence upon natural ecosystems." [52] Daily expanded on these concepts in the 2002 book *The New Economy of Nature*.

Nature's services consist primarily of "ecosystem goods" and "ecosystem services." Natural systems have developed synergistic and tightly intertwined structures and processes within which species thrive, wastes are converted to useful inputs, and the entire system sustains itself, sustaining human life and activity as a subset. For instance, ecosystems services include the carbon and nitrogen cycles, pollination of crops, or the safe decomposition of wastes, all of which can involve species from bacteria to trees to bees. Healthy ecosystems also provide "ecosystem goods, such as seafood, forage, timber, biomass fuels, natural fibers, and many pharmaceuticals, industrial products, and their precursors." [54] In short, ecosystems provide raw materials for the human economy or provide the conditions that allow humans to have economy in the first place.

Although these natural goods and services can be valued "biocentrically" (i.e., for their intrinsic worth) or "anthropocentrically" (i.e., for their value to humans), the nature's services framework focuses on the latter because its audience needs a way to incorporate ecosystems into conventional, cost-benefit calculations for human projects. For instance, if a field is "just there," the conventional calculation of the cost of converting it to a parking lot will focus much more on the price of asphalt and contractors than on the value lost when the field can no longer filter water, support plants and wildlife, grow food, or provide aesthetic pleasure. A nature's services outlook instead captures the value of the functioning field so that it can be directly compared to the value of a parking lot.

Anthropocentric valuation schemes can take numerous forms. They can consider how ecosystems contribute to broad goals of sustainability, fairness, and efficiency or more direct economic activity. For instance, a farmer could calculate the avoided cost of applying pesticides whenever a sound ecosystem or biological method instead controls pests. A state forestry agency could calculate the direct value of consuming ecosystem products, such as the value of trees cut and ultimately sold as lumber, or it could calculate the indirect value of using the same forest for recreation and tourism, perhaps by calculating travel costs and other fees people are willing to bear to use that forest.

Estimating the value of nature can be difficult, especially because we are not used to thinking about buying and selling its services, such as clean air and clean water, or we see them as so basic that we want them to be free to all. Moreover, most people do not even know the services nature provides or how those services interact. Nonetheless, in addition to the aforementioned methods, economists and others trying to use nature's services often survey people's willingness to pay for nature, such as using their willingness to protect an endangered animal as a proxy for their attitude toward that animal's ecosystem as a whole.

In addition to the uncertainty of ascertaining values for everything an ecosystem can do, nature's services face the issues of whether some people's needs should be valued more than others' and of how present choices will constrain future options. Nature's services practitioners also must be able to calculate changes in value from incremental damage, not just the total value of an ecosystem. For example, clear-cutting one hundred acres of rain forest to plant palm trees is one problem; eradicating the entire Amazon rain forest is quite another. Destroying the first hundred acres might have a very different cost than destroying the last hundred. Hence the nature's services approach attempts to characterize with ever greater resolution ecosystems, their goods and services, and the **systems interdependence** to include the results in economic calculations. Finally, once those values are quantified, their corresponding ecosystems need to be protected as would any other asset. Systems for monitoring and safeguarding nature's services must emerge concurrently with estimates of their worth.

Robert Costanza and collaborating scientists and economists wrote one of the first papers on the financial value of ecosystems, "The Value of Ecosystem Services: Putting the Issues in Perspective," published in *Ecological Economics* in 1998. [55] It and the review article "The Nature and Value of Ecosystem Services" by Kate Brauman, Gretchen Daily, T. Ka'eo Duarte, and Harold Mooney are worth reading for an accessible discussion of ecosystem services. [56]

Biomimicry

Biomimicry, expounded by Janine Benyus in a book of the same name, is "the conscious emulation of life's genius" to solve human problems in design, industry, and elsewhere. [57] Biomimicry also spawned a consultancy and nonprofit organization, both based in Montana. The Biomimicry Guild helps companies apply biomimicry's principles, while the Biomimicry Institute aspires to educate a broad audience and spread those principles. Biomimicry's core assumption is that four billion years of natural selection and evolution have yielded sophisticated, sustainable, diverse, and efficient answers to problems such as energy use and sustainable population growth. Humans now have the technology to understand many of nature's solutions and to apply similar ideas in our societies from the level of materials, such as mimicking spider silk or deriving pharmaceuticals from plants, to the level of ecosystems and the biosphere, such as improving our agriculture by learning from prairies and

forests or reducing our greenhouse gas emissions by shifting toward solar energy.

Biomimicry does not, however, merely exploit nature's design secrets in conventional industry, whether to make Velcro or genetically engineered corn. Instead, biomimicry requires us to assume a sustainable place within nature by recognizing ourselves as inextricably part of it. Biomimicry focuses "not on what we can extract from the natural world, but on what we can learn from it." [58] This emphasis leads to three precepts: nature is a model for sustainable designs and processes, nature is the measure for successful solutions, and nature is our mentor. It also lends urgency to protecting ecosystems and cataloguing their species and interdependencies so that we may continue to be inspired, aided, and instructed by nature's ingenuity. In these respects, biomimicry most resembles industrial ecology and nature's services but clearly shares traits with other frameworks and concepts.

Nature's ingenuity, meanwhile, displays recurrent "laws, strategies, and principles":

Nature

- *runs on sunlight.*
- *uses only the energy it needs.*
- *fits form to function.*
- *recycles everything.*
- *rewards cooperation.*
- *banks on diversity.*
- *demands local expertise.*
- *curbs excesses from within.*
- *taps the power of limits.* [60]

Benyus was frustrated that her academic training in forestry, in contrast, focused on analyzing discrete pieces, which initially prevented her and others from seeing principles that emerge from analyzing entire systems. Similarly, solutions to problems of waste and energy need to operate with the big picture in mind. Benyus explicitly allied biomimicry with industrial ecology and elucidated ten principles of an economy that mimicked nature: [61]

1. **Use waste as a resource.** Whether at the scale of integrated business parks or the global economy, "all waste is food, and everybody winds up reincarnated inside somebody else. The only thing the community imports in any appreciable amount is energy in the form of sunlight, and the only thing it exports is the by-product of its energy use, heat." [62]

2. **Diversify and cooperate to fully use the habitat.** Symbiosis and specialization within niches assure nothing is wasted and provide benefits to other species or parts of the ecosystem just as it does to other companies or parts of industry when businesses collaborate to facilitate efficiency, remanufacturing, and other changes.

3. **Gather and use energy efficiently.** Use fossil fuels more efficiently and invest them in producing what truly matters in the long run while shifting to solar and other renewable resources.

4. **Optimize rather than maximize.** Focus on quality over quantity.

5. **Use materials sparingly.** Dematerialize products and reduce packaging; reconceptualize business as providing services instead of selling goods.

6. **Don't foul the nests.** Reduce toxins and decentralize production of goods and energy.

7. **Don't draw down resources.** Shift to renewable feedstocks but use them at a low enough rate that they can regenerate. Invest in ecological capital.

8. **Remain in balance with the biosphere.** Limit emissions of greenhouse gases, chlorofluorocarbons, and other pollutants that severely disrupt natural cycles.

9. **Run on information.** Create feedback loops to improve processes and reward environmental behavior.

10. **Shop locally.** Using local resources constrains regional populations to sizes that can be supported, reduces transportation needs, and lets people see the impact of their consumption on the environment and suppliers.

While biomimicry's concepts can be used at different scales, they have already been directly applied to improve many conventional products. Butterflies alone have provided much help. For example, Lotusan paint uses lessons from the surface structure of butterfly wings to shed dirt and stay cleaner, obviating the need for detergents, while Qualcomm examined how butterfly wings scatter light to develop its low-energy and highly reflective Mirasol display for mobile phones and other electronics. These and other products have been catalogued by the Biomimicry Institute at AskNature.org.

Green Chemistry

Green chemistry, now a recognized field of research and design activity, grew from the awareness that conventional ways to synthesize chemicals consumed large amounts of energy and materials and generated hazardous waste, while the final products themselves were often toxic to humans and other life and persisted in the environment. Hence green chemistry seeks to produce safer chemicals in more efficient and benign ways as well as to neutralize existing contaminants. Such green chemicals typically emulate the nontoxic components and reactions of nature.

Green chemistry emerged as a field after the US Environmental Protection Agency (EPA) began the program "Alternative Synthetic Pathways for Pollution Prevention" in response to the 1990 Pollution Prevention Act. In 1993 the program, renamed "Green Chemistry," established the Presidential Green Chemistry Challenge Award to encourage and recognize research that replaces dangerous chemicals and manufacturing processes with safer alternatives. Recent winners of the award have created ways to make cosmetics and personal products without solvents and an efficient way to convert plant sugars into biofuels. [63] In 1997, the nonprofit Green Chemistry Institute was established and would later become part of the American Chemistry Society. The following year, the Organization for European Economic Development (OECD) created the Sustainable Chemistry Initiative Steering Group, and Paul Anastas and John Warner's book *Green Chemistry: Theory and Practice* established twelve principles for green chemistry. [64] Recognized as leaders in the green chemistry field, Anastas and Warner have continued to advance the ideas through innovation, education, and policy, with Warner helping to create the Warner Babcock Institute to support this mission. Paul Anastas, meanwhile, was confirmed as head of the EPA's Office of Research and Development in 2010. Their green chemistry principles are reflected in a hierarchy of goals set by the Green Chemistry program:

1. *Green Chemistry: Source Reduction/Prevention of Chemical Hazards*

   - *Design chemical products to be less hazardous to human health and the environment**
   - *Use feedstocks and reagents that are less hazardous to human health and the environment**
   - *Design syntheses and other processes to be less energy and materials intensive (high atom economy, low feed factor)*
   - *Use feedstocks derived from annually renewable resources or from abundant waste*
   - *Design chemical products for increased, more facile reuse or recycling*

2. *Reuse or Recycle Chemicals*
3. *Treat Chemicals to Render Them Less Hazardous*
4. *Dispose of Chemicals Properly*

Chemicals that are less hazardous to human health and the environment are:

- *Less toxic to organisms and ecosystems*
- *Not persistent or bioaccumulative in organisms or the environment*
- *Inherently safer with respect to handling and use* [65]

Green chemistry also refers to a journal devoted to the topic (*Green Chemistry*), and one of its associate editors, Terry Collins, has identified steps to expand green chemistry. First, incorporate environmental considerations and sustainability ethics into the training of all chemists and their decisions in the laboratory. Second, be honest about the terms *green* or *sustainable* and the evidence for the harm chemicals cause. For instance, a cleaner, more efficient way to produce a certain product may be progress, but if the product itself remains highly toxic and persistent in the environment, it is not exactly green. Consequently, "since many chemical sustainability goals such as those associated with solar energy conversion call for ambitious, highly creative research approaches, short-term and myopic thinking must be avoided. Government, universities, and industry must learn to value and support research programs that do not rapidly produce publications, but instead present reasonable promise of promoting sustainability." [66]

Collins has devised ways to degrade toxic chemicals already in the environment. He formed a spin-off from Carnegie Mellon University, GreenOx Catalysts, to develop and market his products, which have safely broken down anthrax as well as hazardous waste from paper pulp mills. Green chemistry, however, does not exist merely in government or university enclaves. In 2006, the Dow Chemical Company, with annual sales over $50 billion, declared sustainable chemistry as part of its corporate strategy. [67] DuPont, meanwhile, created a Bio-Based Materials division that has focused on using corn instead of petroleum to produce polymers for a variety of applications, from carpets to medical equipment, while also reducing greenhouse gas emissions. [68] Since synthetic chemicals are the basic building blocks of most modern products, from shoes to iPhones to food preservatives, green chemistry can play a significant role in sustainability. Cradle-to-cradle design, earth systems engineering, and virtually every other framework and tool can benefit from more environmentally friendly materials at the molecular level. As John Warner, a key figure in educating companies about green chemistry providing innovation and new materials across sectors, states,

The field of chemistry has been around in a modern interpretation for about 150 years, [and] we have invented our pharmaceuticals, our cosmetics, our materials, in a mindset that has never really focused on sustainability, toxicity and environmental impact. When one shifts to thinking in that way, it actually puts you in a new innovative space. In that new innovative space, that is the hallmark of creativity. What companies find is instead of it slowing them down, it accelerates time to market because they run into less hurdles in the regulatory process and in the manufacturing process. And it puts them in spaces that they weren't normally in because they've approached it from another angle. Chemicals policy creates the demand. Green chemistry is not chemical policy. Green chemistry is the supply side, the science of identifying those alternatives. And so hand in hand, those two efforts accomplish the goals of more sustainable futures. But they're not the same. [69]

Green Engineering

Green engineering, as articulated by Paul Anastas and Julie Zimmerman, is a framework that can be applied at scales ranging from molecules to cities to improve the sustainability of products and processes. Green engineering works from a systems viewpoint and is organized around twelve principles that should be optimized as a system. For instance, one should not design a product for maximum separation and purification of its components (principle 3) if that choice would actually degrade the product's overall sustainability.

Green engineering considers two basic priorities above all others: "life-cycle considerations" and "inherency." Life-cycle considerations require engineers and designers to understand and assess the entire context and impact of their products from creation to end of use. Inherency means using and producing inherently safe and renewable or reusable materials and energies. Inherency sees external ways to control pollution or contain hazards as a problem because they can fail and tend to tolerate or generate waste. In this sense, inherency is a stringent form of pollution prevention.

Meanwhile, waste is a concept important in many of the principles of green engineering. As Anastas and Zimmerman explain, "An important point, often overlooked, is that the concept of waste is human. In other words, there is nothing inherent about energy or a substance that makes it a waste. Rather it results from a lack of use that has yet to be imagined or implemented." [71] Waste often has been designed into systems as a tolerable nuisance, but increasingly, we cannot deal with our waste, whether toxins, trash, or ineffective uses of energy and resources. To avoid material waste, for example, we can design products to safely decompose shortly after their useful lifetime has passed (e.g., there is no point in having disposable diapers that outlast infancy by millennia). To avoid wastes within larger systems, we can stop overdesigning them based on worst-case scenarios. Instead, we should design flexibility into the system and look to exploit local inputs and outputs, as the way a hybrid car recovers energy from braking to recharge its battery whereas a conventional car loses that energy as heat. We can also recognize that some highly complex objects such as computer chips may be better off being collected and reused, whereas simpler objects such as paper bags may be better off being destroyed and recycled. In essence, green engineering advocates avoiding waste and hazards to move toward sustainability through more thorough, creative planning and design.

Table 3.2 Summary of Perspective of Green Engineering

	Input	Output
Material	Renewable/recycled, nontoxic	Easily separable and recyclable/reusable, nontoxic, no waste (eliminated or feedstock for something else)
Energy	Renewable, not destructive to obtain	No waste (lost heat, etc.), nontoxic (no pollution, etc.)
Human intelligence	Creative, systems-level design to avoid waste, renew resources, and so forth in new products and processes	Sustainability

Life-Cycle Analysis

Life-cycle analysis (LCA) methods are analytical tools for determining the environmental and health impacts of products and processes from material extraction to disposal. Engaging in the LCA process helps reveal the complex resource web that fully describes the life of a product and aids designers (among others) in finding ways to reduce or eliminate sources of waste and pollution. A cup of coffee is commonly used to illustrate the resource web of a product life cycle.

The journey of the cup of coffee begins with the clearing of forests in Colombia to plant coffee trees. The coffee trees are sprayed with insecticides manufactured in the Rhine River Valley of Europe; effluents from the production process make the Rhine one of the most polluted rivers in the world, with much of its downstream wildlife destroyed. When sprayed, the insecticides are inadvertently inhaled by Colombian farmers, and the residues are washed into rivers, adversely affecting downstream ecosystems. Each coffee tree yields beans for about forty cups of coffee annually. The harvested beans are shipped to New Orleans in a Japanese-constructed freighter made from Korean steel, the ore of which is mined on tribal lands in Papua New Guinea. In New Orleans, the beans are roasted and then packaged in bags containing layers of polyethylene, nylon, aluminum foil, and polyester. The three plastic layers were fabricated in factories along Louisiana's infamous "Cancer Corridor," where polluting industries are located disproportionately in African American neighborhoods. The plastic was made from oil shipped in tankers from Saudi Arabia. The aluminum foil was made from Australian bauxite strip-mined on aboriginal ancestral land and then shipped in barges fueled by Indonesian oil to refining facilities in the Pacific Northwest. These facilities derive their energy from the hydroelectric dams of the Columbia River, which have destroyed salmon fishing runs considered sacred by Native American groups. The bags of coffee beans are then shipped across the United States in trucks powered by gasoline from Gulf of Mexico oil refined near Philadelphia, a process that has contributed to serious air and water pollution, fish contamination, and the decline of wildlife in the Delaware River basin. And all of this ignores the cup that holds the coffee. [72]

The coffee example illustrates the complexity in conducting an LCA. The LCA provides a systems perspective but is essentially an accounting system. It attempts to account for the entire resource web and all associated points of impact and thus is understandably difficult to measure with complete accuracy. The Society for Environmental Chemistry has developed a standard methodology for LCA. The following are the objectives of this process: [73]

- Develop an inventory of the environmental impacts of a product, process, or activity by identifying and measuring the materials and energy used as well as the wastes released into the environment.

- Assess the impact on the environment of the materials and energy used and released.
- Evaluate and implement strategies for environmental improvement.

The process of conducting an LCA often reveals sources of waste and opportunities for redesign that would otherwise remain unnoticed. As Massachusetts Institute of Technology professor and author John Ehrenfeld points out, "Simply invoking the idea of a life cycle sets the broad dimensions of the framework for whatever follows and, at this current stage in ecological thinking, tends to expand the boundaries of the actors' environmental world." [74] LCAs can be used not only as a tool during the design phase to identify environmental hotspots in need of attention but also as a tool to evaluate existing products and processes. LCA may also be used to compare products. However, one must be careful that the same LCA methodologies are used for each item compared to guarantee accurate relative results.

LCA has several limitations. The shortcomings most commonly cited include the following:

- Defining system boundaries for LCA is controversial.
- LCA is data-intensive and expensive to conduct.
- Inventory assessment alone is inadequate for meaningful comparison, yet impact assessment is fraught with scientific difficulties.
- LCA does not account for other, nonenvironmental aspects of product quality and cost.
- LCA cannot capture the dynamics of changing markets and technologies.
- LCA results may be inappropriate for use in eco-labeling. [75]

Concurrent Engineering

Concurrent engineering is a design philosophy that brings together the players in a product's life cycle during the design stage. It presents an opportunity to integrate environmental protection in the design process with input from representatives across the entire product life cycle. Participants in a concurrent engineering design team include representatives of management, sales and marketing, design, research and development, manufacturing, resource management, finance, field service, customer interests, and supplier interests. The team's goal is to improve the quality and usability of product designs, improve customer satisfaction, reduce cost, and ease the transition of the product from design to production. Definitions of concurrent engineering vary, but the key concepts include using a team to represent all aspects of the product life cycle, focusing on customer requirements and developing production and field support systems early in the design process. [76]

While seemingly a commonsense approach to design, concurrent engineering is far from typical in industry. The traditional procedure for product design is linear, where individuals are responsible only for their specific function, and designs are passed from one functional area (e.g., manufacturing, research and development, etc.) to the next. This approach can be characterized as throwing designs "over the wall." For example, an architect may design a building shell, such as a steel skyscraper around an elevator core, and then pass the plans to a construction engineer who has to figure out how to route the heating, ventilating, and air-conditioning ducts and other building components. This disjunction can create inefficiency. Concurrent engineering instead would consider the many services a building provides—for example, lighting, heating, cooling, and work space—and determine the most efficient ways to achieve them all from the very beginning. Concurrent engineering therefore shortens the product development cycle by increasing communication early, resulting in fewer design iterations. [77]

Companies that employ a concurrent engineering design philosophy feature empowered design teams that are open to interaction, new ideas, and differing viewpoints. [78] Concurrent engineering then is an effective vehicle to implement product design frameworks such as DfE, sustainable design, and even the process-oriented tool TNS, which is not a design framework *per se* but can be used effectively as a guide to change decision making during design.

Design for Environment

DfE is an eco-efficiency strategy that allows a company to move beyond end-of-the-pipe and in-the-pipe concepts like pollution control and pollution prevention to a systems-based, strategic, and competitively critical approach to environmental management and protection. [79] It is a proactive approach to environmental protection in which the entire life-cycle environmental impact of a product is considered during its design. [80] DfE is intended to be a subset of the Design for X system, where X may be assembly, compliance, environment, manufacturability, material logistics and component applicability, orderability, reliability, safety and liability prevention, serviceability, and testability.

[81] Design for an end goal allows properties necessary to achieve that goal to be integrated most efficiently into a product's life cycle. Hence DfE, like concurrent engineering, becomes a critical tool for realizing many aspirations of frameworks, such as cradle-to-cradle, or other tools, such as green supply chains.

Within the domain of DfE are such concepts as design for disassembly, refurbishment, component recyclability, and materials recyclability. These concepts apply to reverse logistics, which allow materials to be collected, sorted, and reintegrated into the manufacturing supply stream to reduce waste. Reverse logistics become especially important for green supply chains.

DfE originated in 1992, mostly through the efforts of a few electronics firms, and is described by Joseph Fiksel as "the design of safe and eco-efficient products." [82] These products should minimize environmental impact, be safe, and meet or exceed all applicable regulations; be designed to be reused or recycled; reduce material and energy consumption to optimal levels; and ultimately be environmentally safe when disposed. In accomplishing this, the products should also provide a competitive advantage for a company. [83]

Green Supply Chain

Green supply-chain management requires that sustainability criteria be considered by every participant in a supply chain at every step from design to material extraction, manufacture, processing, transportation, storage, use, and eventual disposal or recycling. A green supply-chain approach takes a broader systems view than conventional supply-chain management, which assumes basically that different entities take raw materials at the beginning of the supply chain and transform them into a product at the end of the supply chain, with environmental costs to be borne by other companies, countries, or consumers, since each link in the supply chain receives an input without asking about its origins and forgets about the output once it's out the door. In contrast, the green supply chain considers the entire pathway and internalizes some of these environmental costs to ultimately turn them into sources of value.

Green supply chains thus modify conventional supply chains in two significant ways: they increase sustainability and efficiency in the existing forward supply chain and add an entirely new reverse supply chain. A green supply chain encourages collaboration among members of the chain to understand and share sustainability performance standards, best practices, innovations, and technology while the product moves through the chain. It also seeks to reduce waste along the forward supply chain and to reduce and ideally eliminate hazardous or toxic materials, replacing them with safer ones whenever possible. Finally, through the reverse supply chain, green supply chains seek to recover materials after consumption rather than return them to the environment as waste.

Expanded reverse logistics would ultimately replace the linearity of most production methods—raw materials, processing, further conversions and modification, ultimate product, use, disposal—with a cradle-to-cradle, cyclical path or closed loop that begins with the return of used, outmoded, out of fashion, and otherwise "consumed" products. The products are either recycled and placed back into the manufacturing stream or broken down into compostable materials. The cycle is never ending as materials return in safe molecular structures to the land (taken up and used by organisms as biological nutrients) or are perpetually used within the economy as input for new products (technical nutrients). Consequently, green supply chains appear implicitly in many conceptual frameworks while drawing on various sustainability tools, such as LCA and DfE.

Companies typically funnel spent items from consumers into the reverse supply chain by either leasing their products or providing collection points or other means to recover the items once their service life has ended. [84] Once collected, whether by the original manufacturer or a third party, the products can be inspected and sorted. Some items may return quickly to the supply chain with only minimal repair or replacement of certain components, whereas other products may need to be disassembled, remanufactured, or cannibalized for salvageable parts while the remnant is recycled or sent to a landfill or incinerator.

Concern for green supply-chain topics emerged in the 1990s as globalization and outsourcing made supply networks increasingly complex and diverse while new laws and consumer expectations demanded companies take more responsibility for their product across the product's entire life. [85] The green supply chain responds to these complex interacting systems to reduce waste, mitigate legal and environmental risks, reduce adverse health impacts throughout the value added process, improve the reputations of companies and their products, and enable compliance with increasingly stringent regulations and societal expectations. Thus green supply chains can boost efficiency, value, and access to markets, which then boost a company's environmental, social, and economic performance.

Carbon Footprint Analysis

Carbon footprint analysis is a tool that organizations can use to measure direct and indirect emissions of greenhouse gases associated with their provision of goods and services. Carbon footprint analysis is also known as a greenhouse gas inventory, while greenhouse gas accounting describes the general practice of measuring corporate greenhouse gas emissions. The measurement of greenhouse gas emissions (1) allows voluntarily disclosure of data to organizations such as the Carbon Disclosure Project, (2) facilitates participation in mandatory emissions regulatory systems such as the Regional Greenhouse Gas Initiative, and (3) encourages the collection of key operational data that can be used to implement business improvement projects.

Similar to generally accepted accounting principles in the financial world, a set of standards and principles has emerged that guide data collection and reporting in this new area. In general, companies and individuals calculate their corporate emissions footprint for a twelve-month period. They are also increasingly calculating the footprint of individual products, services, events, and so forth. Established guidelines for greenhouse gas accounting, such as the Greenhouse Gas Protocol, define the scope and methodology of the footprint calculation.

The Greenhouse Gas Protocol, one commonly accepted methodology, is an ongoing initiative of the World Resources Institute and the World Business Council for Sustainable Development. [86] The Greenhouse Gas Protocol explains how to do the following:

1. **Determine organizational boundaries.** Corporate structures are complex and include wholly owned operations, joint ventures, and other entities. The protocol helps managers define which elements compose the "company" for emissions quantification.
2. **Determine operational boundaries.** Once managers identify which branches of the organization are to be included, they must identify and evaluate which specific emissions sources will be included.
3. **Identify indirect sources.** Sources that are not directly owned or controlled by the company but that are nonetheless influenced by its actions are called indirect sources, for instance, electricity purchased from utilities that produce indirect emissions at the power plant or emissions from employee commuting, suppliers' activities, and so forth.

4. **Track emissions over time.** Companies must select a "base year" against which future emissions will be measured, establish an accounting cycle, and determine other aspects of how they will track emissions over time.
5. **Collect data and calculate emissions.** The protocol provides specific guidance about how to collect source data and calculate emissions of greenhouse gases. As a rule of thumb, the amount of energy consumed is multiplied by a series of source-specific "emissions factors" to estimate the quantity of each greenhouse gas produced by the source. Because multiple greenhouse gases are measured in the inventory process, the emissions for each type of gas are then multiplied by a "global warming potential" (GWP) to generate a "CO_2 equivalent" to facilitate streamlined reporting of a single emissions number. CO_2 is the base because it is the most abundant greenhouse gas and also the least potent one. [87] For instance, over a century, methane would cause over twenty times more warming than an equal mass of CO_2:

Total emissions in CO_2eq = σ(fuel consumed × fuel emissions factor × GWP).

The method for calculating emissions from a single facility or vehicle is the same as that for calculating emissions for thousands of retail stores or long-haul trucks; hence, quantifying the emissions of a *Fortune* 500 firm or a small employee-owned business involves the same process.

Companies can reduce their carbon footprint by reducing emissions or acquiring "offsets," actions taken by an organization or individual to counterbalance the emissions, by either preventing emissions somewhere else or removing CO_2 from the air, such as by planting trees. Offsets are traded in both regulated (i.e., government-mandated) and unregulated (i.e., voluntary) markets, although standards for the verification of offsets continue to evolve due to questions about the quality and validity of some products. A company can theoretically be characterized as "carbon neutral" if it causes no net emissions over a designated time period, meaning that for every unit of emissions released an equivalent unit of emissions has been offset through other reduction measures or that the company uses energy only from nonpolluting sources.

KEY TAKEAWAYS

- Business systems and the economy are subsystems of the biosphere.
- Businesses, including companies and supply chains and their interdependent ties to natural systems, like those natural systems, are composed of material, energy, and information flows.
- Mutually reinforcing compatibility between business and natural systems supports prosperity while sustaining and expanding the goods and services ecosystem services provide.
- Biologically inspired business models and product designs can offer profitable paths forward.
- Constraints, rather than limiting possibilities, can open up new space for business innovation and design.

EXERCISES

1. Select a product you use frequently. Describe its current life cycle and component and material composition based on what you know and can determine from a short search for information. Then describe how this same product would be designed, used, and handled through the end of its life if the product's designers used the ideas introduced in this chapter. Be specific about what concepts and tools you are applying to your analysis.

2. Explain what is meant by this quotation from Chapter 3 "Framing Sustainability Innovation and Entrepreneurship", Section 3.4 "Practical Frameworks and Tools": "Eco-efficiency, an increasingly popular concept used by business to describe incremental improvements in material use and environmental impact, is only one small part of a richer and more complex web of ideas and solutions....more efficient production by itself could become not the servant but the enemy of a durable economy."

3. Describe the ramifications when a company's activities are not all at the same location along the continuum of sustainability.

4. Where have you seen the sustainability design ideas discussed in this chapter applied? Write a paragraph describing your observations. What new insights have you gained through exposure to these ideas?

Footnotes

[1] {Author's Name Retracted as requested by the work's original creator or licensee} and Wendy Warren, The Natural Step, UVA–G–0507 (Charlottesville: Darden Business Publishing, University of Virginia, 1997), 1–3.

[2] These two laws assume that matter and energy are not being converted into each other through nuclear processes, but when fission and fusion are taken into account, mass-energy becomes the new conserved quantity.

[3] Karl-Henrik Robèrt, Herman Daly, Paul Hawken, and John Holmberg, "A Compass for Sustainable Development," Natural Step News 1 (Winter 1996): 4.

[4] Brian Nattrass and Mary Altomare, The Natural Step for Business (Gabriola Island, BC: New Society Publishers, 1999), 35.

[5] {Author's Name Retracted as requested by the work's original creator or licensee} and Joel Reichert, IKEA and the Natural Step, UVA-G-0501 (Washington, DC: World Resources Institute and Darden Graduate School of Business Administration, 1998), 18.

[6] Karl-Henrik Robèrt, Herman Daly, Paul Hawken, and John Holmberg, "A Compass for Sustainable Development," Natural Step News 1 (Winter 1996): 4–5.

[7] {Author's Name Retracted as requested by the work's original creator or licensee} and Wendy Warren, The Natural Step, UVA–G–0507 (Charlottesville: Darden Business Publishing, University of Virginia, 1997), 2.

[8] Hardin B. C. Tibbs, "Industrial Ecology: An Environmental Agenda for Industry," Whole Earth Review 4, no. 16 (Winter 1992): 4–19; Deanna J. Richards, Braden Allenby, and Robert A. Frosch, "The Greening of Industrial Ecosystems: Overview and Perspective," in The Greening of Industrial Ecosystems, ed. Deanna J. Richards and Braden Allenby (Washington, DC: National Academy Press, 1994), 3.

[9] Clinton Andrews, Frans Berkhout, and Valerie Thomas, "The Industrial Ecology Agenda," in Industrial Ecology and Global Change, ed. Robert Socolow, Clinton Andrews, Frans Berkhout, and Valerie Thomas (Cambridge: Cambridge University Press, 1994), 471–72.

[10] Suren Erkman, "Industrial Ecology: An Historical View," Journal of Cleaner Production 5, no. 1–2 (1997): 1–10.

[11] Preston Cloud, "Entropy, Materials and Posterity," Geologische Rundschau 66, no. 3 (1977): 678–96, quoted and cited in John Ehrenfeld and Nicholas Gertler, "Industrial Ecology in Practice: The Evolution of Interdependence at Kalundborg," Journal of Industrial Ecology 1, no. 1 (Winter 1997): 67–79.

[12] Robert A. Frosch and Nicholas E. Gallopoulos, "Strategies for Manufacturing," Scientific American 261, no. 3 (September 1989): 144–52.

[13] Robert A. Frosch, "Industrial Ecology: A Philosophical Introduction," Proceedings of the National Academy of Sciences, USA, vol. 89 (February 1992): 800–803.

[14] Ayres coined the term "industrial metabolism" at a conference at the United Nations University in 1987. The proceedings of this conference were published in Robert U. Ayres and Udo Ernst Simonis, eds., Industrial Metabolism (Tokyo: United Nations University Press, 1994).

[15] See Robert U. Ayres, "Industrial Metabolism: Theory and Practice," in The Greening of Industrial Ecosystems, ed. Deanna J. Richards and Braden Allenby (Washington, DC: National Academy Press, 1994), 25; Robert U. Ayres and Udo Ernst Simonis, eds., Industrial Metabolism (Tokyo: United Nations University Press, 1994).

[16] Hardin B. C. Tibbs, "Industrial Ecology: An Environmental Agenda for Industry," Whole Earth Review 4, no. 16 (Winter 1992): 4–19.

[17] Robert U. Ayres and Allen V. Kneese, "Externalities: Economics and Thermodynamics," in Economy and Ecology: Towards Sustainable Development, ed. Franco Archibugi and Peter Nijkamp (Dordrecht, Netherlands: Kluwer Academic Publishers, 1989), 90.

[18] Walter R. Stahel, "The Utilization-Focused Service Economy: Resource Efficiency and Product-Life Extension," in The Greening of Industrial Ecosystems, ed. Deanna J. Richards and Braden Allenby (Washington, DC: National Academy Press, 1994), 183.

[19] Walter R. Stahel, "The Utilization-Focused Service Economy: Resource Efficiency and Product-Life Extension," in The Greening of Industrial Ecosystems, ed. Deanna J. Richards and Braden Allenby (Washington, DC: National Academy Press, 1994), 183.

[20] Amory Lovins, L. Hunter Lovins, and Paul Hawken, "A Road Map for Natural Capitalism," Harvard Business Review 77, no. 3 (May–June 1999): 146–48.

[21] Paul Hawken, Amory Lovins, and L. Hunter Lovins, Natural Capitalism: Creating the Next Industrial Revolution (Boston: Little, Brown, 1999), xii–xiii.

[22] Paul Hawken, Amory Lovins, and L. Hunter Lovins, Natural Capitalism: Creating the Next Industrial Revolution (Boston: Little, Brown, 1999), xi.

[23] Paul Hawken, Amory Lovins, and L. Hunter Lovins, Natural Capitalism: Creating the Next Industrial Revolution (Boston: Little, Brown, 1999), xi–xii.

[24] Juan Martinez-Alier with Klaus Schlüpmann, Ecological Economics: Energy, Environment and Society (Oxford: Basil Blackwell, 1987).

[25] Robert Costanza, "What Is Ecological Economics?," Ecological Economics 1 (1989): 1.

[26] International Society for Ecological Economics, "Constitution: Article II. Purpose," accessed December 1, 2010, http://www.ecoeco.org/content/about/constitution.

[27] International Society for Ecological Economics, "Constitution: Article II. Purpose," accessed December 1, 2010, http://www.ecoeco.org/content/about/constitution.

[28] Richard B. Norgaard, "Ecological Economics: A Short Description," Forum on Religion and Ecology, Yale University, 2000, accessed June 25, 2009, http://fore.research.yale.edu/disciplines/economics/index.html.

[29] Mick Common and Sigrid Stagl, Ecological Economics: An Introduction (Cambridge: Cambridge University Press, 2005), 10; Paul Ehrlich, "The Limits to Substitution: Meta-Resource Depletion and a New Economic-Ecological Paradigm," Ecological Economics 1 (1989): 11.

[30] William McDonough and Michael Braungart, Cradle to Cradle: Remaking the Way We Make Things (New York: North Point Press, 2002).

[31] William McDonough and Michael Braungart, Cradle to Cradle: Remaking the Way We Make Things (New York: North Point Press, 2002), 6.

[32] William McDonough and Michael Braungart, Cradle to Cradle: Remaking the Way We Make Things (New York: North Pont Press, 2002), 16.

[33] William McDonough and Michael Braungart, Cradle to Cradle: Remaking the Way We Make Things (New York: North Point Press, 2002), 10.

[34] William McDonough and Michael Braungart, Cradle to Cradle: Remaking the Way We Make Things (New York: North Point Press, 2002), 11.

[35] William McDonough and Michael Braungart, Cradle to Cradle: Remaking the Way We Make Things (New York: North Point Press, 2002), 78, 80.

[36] William McDonough and Michael Braungart, Cradle to Cradle: Remaking the Way We Make Things (New York: North Point Press, 2002), 104.

[37] Paul Hawken, Amory Lovins, and L. Hunter Lovins, Natural Capitalism: Creating the Next Industrial Revolution (Boston: Little, Brown, 1999), 12. Also see Paul Hawken and William McDonough, "Seven Steps to Doing Good Business," Inc., November 1993, 81; William McDonough Architects, The Hannover Principles: Design for Sustainability (Charlottesville, VA: William McDonough Architects, 1992), 7.

[38] Paul Hawken, Amory Lovins, and L. Hunter Lovins, Natural Capitalism: Creating the Next Industrial Revolution (Boston: Little, Brown, 1999), 67; William McDonough, "A Boat for Thoreau: A Discourse on Ecology, Ethics, and the Making of Things," in The Business of Consumption: Environmental Ethics and the Global Economy, ed. Laura Westra and Patricia H. Werhane (Lanham, MD: Rowman and Littlefield, 1998), 297–317.

[39] Paul Hawken and William McDonough, "Seven Steps to Doing Good Business," Inc., November 1993, 81.

[40] William McDonough, "A Boat for Thoreau: A Discourse on Ecology, Ethics, and the Making of Things," in The Business of Consumption: Environmental Ethics and the Global Economy, ed. Laura Westra and Patricia H. Werhane (Lanham, MD: Rowman and Littlefield, 1998), 297–317. For an explanation of endocrine disrupters, see Theo Colburn, Dianne Dumanoski, and John Peterson Myers, Our Stolen Future (New York: Dutton, 1996).

[41] Walter R. Stahel, "The Utilization-Focused Service Economy: Resource Efficiency and Product-Life Extension," in The Greening of Industrial Ecosystems, ed. Deanna J. Richards and Braden Allenby (Washington, DC: National Academy Press, 1994), 183; Robert U. Ayres and Allen V. Kneese, "Externalities: Economics and Thermodynamics," in Economy and Ecology: Towards Sustainable Development, ed. Franco Archibugi and Peter Nijkamp (Dordrecht, Netherlands: Kluwer Academic Publishers, 1989), 90.

[42] Paul Hawken and William McDonough, "Seven Steps to Doing Good Business," Inc., November 1993, 81; Michael Braungart, "Product Life-Cycle Management to Replace Waste Management," Industrial Ecology and Global Change, ed. Robert Socolow, Clinton Andrews, Frans Berkhout, and Valerie Thomas (Cambridge: Cambridge University Press, 1994), 335–37.

[43] Robert U. Ayres, "Industrial Metabolism: Theory and Practice," in The Greening of Industrial Ecosystems, ed. Deanna J. Richards and Braden Allenby (Washington, DC: National Academy Press, 1994), 34–35.

[44] Paul Hawken and William McDonough, "Seven Steps to Doing Good Business," Inc., November 1993, 81; Michael Braungart, "Product Life-Cycle Management to Replace Waste Management," Industrial Ecology and Global Change, ed. Robert Socolow, Clinton Andrews, Frans Berkhout, and Valerie Thomas (Cambridge: Cambridge University Press, 1994), 335–37.

[45] Robert U. Ayres and Allen V. Kneese, "Externalities: Economics and Thermodynamics," in Economy and Ecology: Towards Sustainable Development, ed. Franco Archibugi and Peter Nijkamp (Dordrecht, Netherlands: Kluwer Academic Publishers, 1989), 105.

[46] Geothermal power, although perhaps more plentiful than other sources, ultimately derives from heat within Earth's mantle and is thus not technically solar derived.

[47] Clinton Andrews, Frans Berkhout, and Valerie Thomas, "The Industrial Ecology Agenda," in Industrial Ecology and Global Change, ed. Robert Socolow, Clinton Andrews, Frans Berkhout, and Valerie Thomas (Cambridge: Cambridge University Press, 1994), 472–75.

[48] William McDonough, "A Boat for Thoreau: A Discourse on Ecology, Ethics, and the Making of Things," in The Business of Consumption: Environmental Ethics and the Global Economy, ed. Laura Westra and Patricia H. Werhane (Lanham, MD: Rowman and Littlefield, 1998), 297–317.

[49] William McDonough, "A Boat for Thoreau: A Discourse on Ecology, Ethics, and the Making of Things," in The Business of Consumption: Environmental Ethics and the Global Economy, ed. Laura Westra and Patricia H. Werhane (Lanham, MD: Rowman and Littlefield, 1998), 297–317.

[50] William McDonough and Michael Braungart, Cradle to Cradle: Remaking the Way We Make Things (New York: North Point Press, 2002), 150.

[51] Gretchen Daily, ed., Nature's Services: Societal Dependence on Natural Ecosystems (Washington, DC: Island Press, 1997), 2.

[52] Gretchen Daily, ed., Nature's Services: Societal Dependence on Natural Ecosystems (Washington, DC: Island Press, 1997), xv.

[53] Gretchen Daily, ed., Nature's Services: Societal Dependence on Natural Ecosystems (Washington, DC: Island Press, 1997), xx.

[54] Gretchen Daily, ed., Nature's Services: Societal Dependence on Natural Ecosystems (Washington, DC: Island Press, 1997), 3.

[55] Robert Costanza, Ralph d'Arge, Rudolf de Groot, Stephen Farber, Monica Grasso, Bruce Hannon, Karin Limburg, et al., "The Value of Ecosystem Services: Putting the Issues in Perspective," Ecological Economics 25, no. 1 (April 1998): 67–72, doi:10.1016/S0921-8009(98)00019-6.

[56] Kate A. Brauman, Gretchen C. Daily, T. Ka'eo Duarte, and Harold A. Mooney, "The Nature and Value of Ecosystem Services: An Overview Highlighting Hydrologic Services," Annual Review of Environment and Resources 32, no. 6 (2007): 1–32, doi:10.1146/annurev.energy.32.031306.102758.

[57] Janine M. Benyus, Biomimicry: Innovation Inspired by Nature (New York: William Morrow, 1997), 2.

[58] Janine M. Benyus, prologue to Biomimicry: Innovation Inspired by Nature (New York: William Morrow, 1997).

[59] Janine M. Benyus, Biomimicry: Innovation Inspired by Nature (New York: William Morrow, 1997), 2, 9.

[60] Janine M. Benyus, Biomimicry: Innovation Inspired by Nature (New York: William Morrow, 1997), 7.

[61] Janine M. Benyus, Biomimicry: Innovation Inspired by Nature (New York: William Morrow, 1997), 252–277. Italicized items in the list are Benyus's wording.

[62] Janine M. Benyus, Biomimicry: Innovation Inspired by Nature (New York: William Morrow, 1997), 255.

[63] US Environmental Protection Agency, "Presidential Green Chemistry Challenge: Award Winners," last updated July 28, 2010, accessed December 3, 2010, http://www.epa.gov/greenchemistry/pubs/pgcc/past.html.

[64] Paul T. Anastas and John C. Warner, Green Chemistry: Theory and Practice (Oxford: Oxford University Press, 1998). The principles are quoted on the EPA website, US Environmental Protection Agency, "Green Chemistry: Twelve Principles of Green Chemistry," last updated April 22, 2010, accessed December 1, 2010, http://www.epa.gov/greenchemistry/pubs/principles.html.

[65] US Environmental Protection Agency, "Introduction to the Concept of Green Chemistry: Sustainable Chemistry Hierarchy," last updated April 22, 2010, accessed December 1, 2010, http://www.epa.gov/greenchemistry/pubs/about_gc.html.

[66] Terry Collins, "Toward Sustainable Chemistry," Science 291, no. 5501 (2001): 48–49.

[67] Dow Chemical, "Innovative Insect Control Technology Earns Dow Another Green Chemistry Award," news release, June 26, 2008, accessed June 26, 2009, http://www.dow.com/news/corporate/2008/20080626a.htm; Dow Chemical, "Dow Sustainability—Sustainability at Dow," accessed June 26, 2009, http://www.dow.com/commitments/sustain.htm.

[68] DuPont, "DuPont Bio-Based Materials—Delivering Sustainable Innovations That Reduce Reliance on Fossil Fuels," fact sheet, accessed June 26, 2009, http://vocuspr.vocus.com/VocusPR30/Newsroom/MultiQuery.aspx?SiteName= DupontNew&Entity=PRAsset&SF_PRAsset_PRAssetID_EQ=101244&XSL=MediaRoomText_&PageTitle=_Fact%20Sheet&IncludeChildren=true&Cache=.

[69] Jonathan Bardelline interview of John Warner, "John Warner: Building Innovation Through Green Chemistry," October 18, 2010, accessed March 7, 2011, http://www.greenbiz.com/blog/2010/10/18/john-warner-building-innovation-_green-chemistry?page=0%2C1.

[70] Paul Anastas and Julie Zimmerman, "Design through the Twelve Principles of Green Engineering," Environmental Science and Technology 37, no. 5 (2003): 95A.

[71] Paul Anastas and Julie Zimmerman, "Design through the Twelve Principles of Green Engineering," Environmental Science and Technology 37, no. 5 (2003): 97A.

[72] Alan Thein Durning and Ed Ayres, "The History of a Cup of Coffee," World Watch 7, no. 5 (September/October 1994): 20–23.

[73] Joseph Fiksel, "Methods for Assessing and Improving Environmental Performance," in Design for Environment: Creating Eco-Efficient Products and Processes, ed. Joseph Fiksel (New York: McGraw Hill, 1996), 116–17.

[74] John Ehrenfeld, "The Importance of LCAs—Warts and All," Journal of Industrial Ecology 1, no. 2 (1997): 46.

[75] Joseph Fiksel, "Methods for Assessing and Improving Environmental Performance," in Design for Environment: Creating Eco-Efficient Products and Processes, ed. Joseph Fiksel (New York: McGraw Hill, 1996), 113.

[76] Susan E. Carlson and Natasha Ter-Minassian, "Planning for Concurrent Engineering," Medical Devices and Diagnostics Magazine, May 1996, 202–15.

[77] Susan E. Carlson and Natasha Ter-Minassian, "Planning for Concurrent Engineering," Medical Devices and Diagnostics Magazine, May 1996, 202–15.

[78] Susan Carlson-Skalak, lecture to Sustainable Business class (Darden Graduate School of Business Administration, University of Virginia, Charlottesville, VA, November 17, 1997).

[79] Braden R. Allenby, "Integrating Environment and Technology: Design for Environment," in The Greening of Industrial Ecosystems, ed. Deanna J. Richards and Braden Allenby (Washington, DC: National Academy Press, 1994), 140–41.

[80] Thomas E. Graedel, Paul Reaves Comrie, and Janine C. Sekutowski, "Green Product Design," AT&T Technical Journal 74, no. 6 (November/December 1995): 17.

[81] Thomas E. Graedel and Braden R. Allenby, Industrial Ecology (Englewood Cliffs, NJ: Prentice Hall, 1995), 186–87.

[82] Joseph Fiksel, "Introduction," in Design for Environment: Creating Eco-Efficient Products and Processes, ed. Joseph Fiksel (New York: McGraw Hill, 1996), 3; Joseph Fiksel, "Conceptual Principles of DFE," in Design for Environment: Creating Eco-Efficient Products and Processes, ed. Joseph Fiksel (New York: McGraw Hill, 1996), 51.

[83] Bruce Paton, "Design for Environment: A Management Perspective," in Industrial Ecology and Global Change, ed. Robert Socolow, Clinton Andrews, Frans Berkhout, and Valerie Thomas (Cambridge: Cambridge University Press, 1994), 350.

[84] Shad Dowlatshahi, "Developing a Theory of Reverse Logistics," Interfaces: International Journal of the Institute for Operations Research and the Management Sciences 30, no. 3 (May/June 2000): 143–55.

[85] Jonathan D. Linton, Robert Klassen, and Vaidyanathan Jayaraman, "Sustainable Supply Chains: An Introduction," Journal of Operations Management 25, no. 6 (November 2007): 1075–82; National Environmental Education and Training Foundation, Going Green Upstream: The Promise of Supplier Environmental Management (Washington, DC: National Environmental Education and Training Foundation, 2001).

[86] The Greenhouse Gas Protocol Initiative, "About the GHG Protocol," accessed July 2, 2009, http://www.ghgprotocol.org/about-ghgp.

[87] United Nations Framework Convention on Climate Change, "GHG Data: Global Warming Potentials," accessed July 2, 2009, http://unfccc.int/ghg_data/items/3825.php.

NOTES:

Chapter 4:

Entrepreneurship and Sustainability Innovation Analysis

4.1 Entrepreneurial Process

LEARNING OBJECTIVES

1. Understand the constituent elements of the entrepreneurial process.

2. Gain appreciation for how the elements fit together to form a whole.

In this chapter, we examine the ways in which entrepreneurial ventures combine the classic entrepreneurial process with sustainability concepts. This combination encompasses design approaches and corporate competencies that generate new offerings that achieve revenue growth and profitability while enhancing human health, supporting ecological system stability, and contributing to the vitality of local communities. This chapter shows the interconnections across sustainability, innovation, and entrepreneurship to give the reader greater understanding of a current global phenomenon: the search for new products, technologies, and ways of conducting business that will replace the old with designs intended to help solve some of society's most challenging issues.

When products are designed and business strategies are structured around systems thinking that is associated with sustainability, the outcome, as in any system composed of interacting and interdependent parts, emerges as larger than the sum of its constituent elements. So we should keep in mind, as we dissect the entrepreneurial process into its core elements, that we do so for analytic purposes—first to understand the individual parts and then to see how they come together. Once that picture is clear, the reader will have gained new insights into what entrepreneurs active in the sustainability innovation space actually do.

Bear in mind that sustainability, innovation, and entrepreneurship are terms used to represent a wide range of ideas, depending on the context. However, just because they have come into common use and have been interpreted broadly does not mean they cannot be defined in focused and practical ways to help guide entrepreneurial individuals in business. Individuals and companies are, in fact, implementing sustainability designs and strategies through the use of innovative initiatives. At the present time, these three terms—sustainability, innovation, and entrepreneurship—are our best and most accurate descriptors of what is happening in the marketplace. No one

term covers all the ground required. In the following sections, we examine entrepreneurial process and then discuss sustainability concepts to explain how the necessary parts merge to create a holistic picture.

Entrepreneurial activity can seem mysterious for those not familiar with the phenomenon. US culture has created heroic myths around its most famous entrepreneurs, reinforcing the idea that entrepreneurship is about individuals. As a consequence, many people believe those individuals are born entrepreneurs. In fact, it is more accurate to talk about entrepreneurship as a process. More frequently than not, a person becomes an entrepreneur because she or he is compelled to pursue a market opportunity. Through that activity—that process—entrepreneurship unfolds. A typical story of entrepreneurship is one in which the entrepreneur is influenced by his or her engagement with favorable conditions, circumstances in which an idea comes together successfully with a market opportunity. An individual has an idea or sees a problem needing a solution and generates a way to meet that need. A new venture is initiated and, if successful, an ongoing business created. Thus entrepreneurship—the creation of new ventures as either new companies or initiatives within larger organizations—is about the process of individuals coming together with opportunities, resulting in specific customers being provided with new goods and services.

For purposes of this discussion, entrepreneurship is not constrained to starting a company. While that definition is commonly assumed, entrepreneurship and entrepreneurial innovation can occur in a variety of settings including small or large companies, nonprofit organizations, and governmental agencies. Entrepreneurship emerges under widely diverse circumstances, typically in response to new conditions and in pursuit of newly perceived opportunities. We focus here not on the average new venture set up to compete under existing rules against existing companies and delivering products or services comparable to those already in the market. Rather, our focus is on entrepreneurial innovators who forge new paths and break with accepted ways of doing business, creating new combinations that result in novel technologies, products, services, and operating practices—that is, substantial innovation.

In that regard, our approach is aligned with entrepreneurship as defined by twentieth-century economist and entrepreneurship scholar Joseph Schumpeter, who pointed out that change in societies comes as a result of innovation created by entrepreneurs. His emphasis was on innovation and the entrepreneur's ability through innovation to generate new demand that results in significant wealth creation. Peter Drucker, a twentieth and twenty first century scholar of entrepreneurship, echoed similar ideas many decades later. Entrepreneurship is innovative change through new venture creation; it is the creation of *new* goods and services, processes, technologies, markets, and ways of organizing that offer alternatives with the intention of better meeting people's needs and improving their lives. Innovation encompasses the creative combination of old and novel ideas that enables individuals and organizations to offer desired alternatives and replacements for existing products and services. These innovative products and ways of doing business, typically led by independent-thinking entrepreneurial individuals, constitute the substitutions that eventually replace older products and ways of doing things. Sustainability entrepreneurship and innovation build on the basics of this accepted view of innovation and entrepreneurship and extend it to encompass life-cycle thinking, ecological rules, human health, and social equity considerations.

Understanding entrepreneurial processes and the larger industrial ecosystem at work requires that we break down the subject matter into separate pieces and then recombine them. The pieces need to be examined on their own merit and then understood in relation to one another. We start with understanding the entrepreneurial process and move to examining the elements of sustainability innovation. Each piece is a necessary, but not sufficient, part of the puzzle.

Bear in mind that the mental exercise required in the following discussion is useful not only as an analytic approach for entrepreneurs or investors but also to set out core business plan elements. Business plans require elaboration on the market opportunity, a thorough understanding of what the entrepreneur brings to the business and the qualifications of the management team, and a clear articulation of the product or service offered and why a customer would purchase it. The business plan also must discuss the resources needed to launch the business and the

market entry strategy proposed to establish early sales, lock in reliable suppliers, and provide a platform for growth. Thus learning and applying the analytical steps discussed in this section has direct synergies with writing a business plan.

Analysis of Entrepreneurial Process

Successful entrepreneurship occurs when creative individuals bring together a new way of meeting needs and a market opportunity. This is accomplished through a patterned process, one that mobilizes and directs resources to deliver a specific product or service to customers using a market entry strategy that shows investors financial promise of building enduring revenue and profitability streams. Sustainability adds to the design of a product and operations by applying the criteria of reaching toward benign (or at least considerably safer) energy and material use, a reduced resource footprint, and elimination of inequitable social impacts due to the venture's operations, including its supply-chain impacts.

Entrepreneurial innovation combined with sustainability principles can be broken down into the following five key pieces for analysis. Each one needs to be analyzed separately, and then the constellation of factors must fit together into a coherent whole. These five pieces are as follows:

- Opportunity
- Entrepreneur/team
- Product concept
- Resources
- Entry strategy

Successful ventures are characterized by coherence or "fit" across these pieces. The interests and skills of the entrepreneur must fit with the product design and offering; the team's qualifications should match the required knowledge needed to launch the venture. The market opportunity must fit with the product concept in that there must be demand in the market for the product or service, and of course, early customers (those willing to purchase) have to be identified. Finally, sufficient resources, including financial resources (e.g., operating capital), office space, equipment, production facilities, components, materials, and expertise, must be identified and brought to bear. Each piece is discussed in more detail in the sections that follow.

The Opportunity

The opportunity is a chance to engage in trades with customers that satisfy their desires while generating returns that enable you to continue to operate and to build your business over time. Many different conditions in society can create opportunities for new goods and services. As a prospective entrepreneur, the key questions are as follows:

- What are the conditions that have created a marketplace opportunity for my idea?
- Why do people want and need something new at this point in time?
- What are the factors that have opened up the opportunity?
- Will the opportunity be enduring, or is it a window that is open today but likely to close tomorrow?
- If you perceive an unmet need, can you deliver what the customer wants while generating durable margins and profits?

Sustainability considerations push this analysis further, asking how you can meet the market need with the smallest ecological footprint possible. Ideally, this need is met through material and energy choices that enhance natural systems; such systems include healthy human bodies and communities as well as environmental systems. Sustainability considerations include reducing negative impact as well as working to improve the larger system outcomes whenever and wherever financially possible. Let us examine the different pieces separately before we try to put them all together.

Opportunity conditions arise from a variety of sources. At a broad societal level, they are present as the result of forces such as shifting demographics, changes in knowledge and understanding due to scientific advances, a rebalancing or imbalance of political winds, or changing attitudes and norms that give rise to new needs. These macroforces constantly open up new opportunities for entrepreneurs. Demographic changes will dictate the expansion or contraction of market segments. For example, aging populations in industrialized countries need different products and services to meet their daily requirements, particularly if the trend to stay in their homes continues. Younger populations in emerging economies want products to meet a very different set of material needs and interests. Features for cell phones, advanced laptop computer designs, gaming software, and other entertainment delivery technologies are higher priorities to this demographic group.

Related to sustainability concerns, certain demographic shifts and pollution challenges create opportunities. With 50 percent of the world's population for the first time in history living in urban areas, city air quality improvement methods present opportunities. Furthermore, toxicological science tells us that industrial chemicals ingested by breathing polluted air, drinking unclean water, and eating microscopically contaminated food pass through the placenta into growing fetuses. We did not have this information ten years ago, but monitoring and detection technologies have improved significantly over a short time frame and such new information creates opportunities. When you combine enhanced public focus on health and wellness, advanced water treatment methods, clean combustion technologies, renewable "clean" energy sources, conversion of used packaging into new asset streams, benign chemical compounds for industrial processes, and local and sustainability grown organic food, you begin to see the wide range of opportunities that exist due to macrotrends.

When we speak of an opportunity, we mean the chance to satisfy a specific need for a customer. The customer has a problem that needs an answer or a solution. The opportunity first presents itself when the entrepreneur sees a way to innovatively solve that problem better than existing choices do and at a comparable price. Assuming there are many buyers who have the same problem and would purchase the solution offered, the opportunity becomes a true business and market opportunity. When opportunities are of a sufficient scale (in other words, enough customers can be attracted quickly), and revenues will cover your costs and promise in the near term to offer excess revenue after initial start-up investment expenditures are repaid, then you have a legitimate economic opportunity in the marketplace.

It is important to understand that ideas for businesses are not always actual opportunities; unless suppliers are available and customers can be identified and tapped, the ideas may not develop into opportunities. Furthermore, an opportunity has multiple dimensions that must be considered including its duration, the size of the targeted market segment, pricing options that enable you to cover expenses, and so forth. These dimensions must be explored and analyzed as rigorously as possible. While business plans can serve multiple purposes, the first and most important reason for writing a business plan is to test whether an idea is truly an economically promising market opportunity.

The Entrepreneur

The opportunity and the entrepreneur must be intertwined in a way that optimizes the probability for success. People often become entrepreneurs when they see an opportunity. They are compelled to start a venture to find out whether they can convert that opportunity into an ongoing business. That means that, ideally, the entrepreneur's life experience, education, skills, work exposure, and network of contacts align well with the opportunity.

However, before we talk about alignment, which is our ultimate destination, we look at the entrepreneur. Consider the individual entrepreneur as a distinct analytic category by considering the following questions:

- Who is this person?
- What does this person bring to the table?
- What education, skills, and expertise does this person possess?

Like the opportunity, the entrepreneur can be broken down into components. This analysis is essential to understanding the entrepreneur's commitment and motivations. Analysis of the entrepreneur also indicates the appropriateness of the individual's capacities to execute on a given business plan. The components are as follows:

- **Values.** What motivates the individual? What does he or she care enough about to devote the time required to create a new venture?
- **Education.** What training has the individual received, what level of formal education, and how relevant is it to the tasks the venture requires to successfully launch?
- **Work experience.** Formal education may be less relevant than work experience. What prior jobs has the individual held, and what responsibilities did he have? How did he perform in those positions? What has he learned?
- **Life experience.** What exposure to life's diversity has the individual had that might strengthen (or weaken) her competencies for building a viable business?
- **Networks.** What relationships does the individual bring to the venture? Have her prior experiences enabled her to be familiar and comfortable with a diverse mix of people and institutions so that she is able to call upon relevant outside resources that might assist with the venture's execution?

If any one category could claim dominance in shaping the outcome of an innovative venture, it is that of the entrepreneur. This is because investors invest in people first and foremost. A good business plan, an interesting product idea, and a promising opportunity are all positive, but in the end it is the ability of the entrepreneur to attract a team, get a product out, and sell it to customers that counts. While management teams must be recruited relatively quickly,

typically there is an individual who initially drives the process through his or her ability to mobilize resources and sometimes through sheer force of will, hard work, and determination to succeed. In challenging times it is the entrepreneur's vision and leadership abilities that can carry the day.

Ultimately, led by the entrepreneur, a team forms. As the business grows, the team becomes the key factor. The entrepreneur's skills, education, capabilities, and weaknesses must be augmented and complemented by the competencies of the team members he or she brings to the project. The following are important questions to ask:

- Does the team as a unit have the background, skills, and understanding of the opportunity to overcome obstacles?
- Can the team act as a collaborative unit with strong decision-making ability under fluid conditions?
- Can the team deal with conflict and disagreement as a normal and healthy aspect of working through complex decisions under ambiguity?

If a business has been established and the team has not yet been formed, these questions will be useful to help you understand what configuration of people might compose an effective team to carry the business through its early evolutionary stages.

Resources

Successful entrepreneurial processes require entrepreneurs and teams to mobilize a wide array of resources quickly and efficiently. All innovative and entrepreneurial ventures combine specific resources such as capital, talent and know-how (e.g., accountants, lawyers), equipment, and production facilities. Breaking down a venture's required resources into components can clarify what is needed and when it is needed. Although resource needs change during the early growth stages of a venture, at each stage the entrepreneur should be clear about the priority resources that enable or inhibit moving to the next stage of growth. What kinds of resources are needed? The following list provides guidance:

- **Capital.** What financial resources, in what form (e.g., equity, debt, family loans, angel capital, venture capital), are needed at the first stage? This requires an understanding of cash flow needs, break-even time frames, and other details. Back-of-the-envelope estimates must be converted to pro forma income statements to understand financial needs.

- **Know-how.** Record keeping and accounting and legal process and advice are essential resources that must be considered at the start of every venture. New ventures require legal incorporation, financial record keeping, and rudimentary systems. Resources to provide for these expenses must be built into the budget.

- **Facilities, equipment, and transport.** Does the venture need office space, production facilities, special equipment, or transportation? At the early stage of analysis, ownership of these resources does not need to be determined. The resource requirement, however, must be identified. Arrangements for leasing or owning, vendor negotiations, truck or rail transport, or temporary rental solutions are all decision options depending on the product or service provided. However, to start and launch the venture, the resources must be articulated and preliminary costs attached to them.

The Product/Service Concept

What are you selling? New ventures offer solutions to people's problems. This concept requires you to not only examine the item or service description but understand what your initial customers see themselves buying. A customer has a need to be met. He or she is hungry and needs food. Food solves the problem. Another customer faces the problem of transferring money electronically and needs an efficient solution, a service that satisfies the need. Automatic teller machines are developed and services are offered. Other buyers want electricity from a renewable energy source; their problem is that they want their monthly payments to encourage clean energy development, not fossil fuel–based electricity. In any of these situations, in any entrepreneurial innovation circumstance in fact, as the entrepreneur you must ask the following questions:

- What is the solution for which you want someone to pay?
- Is it a service or product, or some combination?
- To whom are you selling it? Is the buyer the actual user? Who makes the purchase decision?
- What is the customer's problem and how does your service or product address it?

Understanding what you are selling is not as obvious as it might sound. When you sell an electric vehicle you are not just selling transportation. The buyer is buying a package of attributes that might include cutting-edge technology, lower operating costs, and perhaps the satisfaction of being part of a solution to health, environmental, and energy security problems.

Entry Strategy

Another category to examine carefully at the outset of a venture is market entry strategy. Your goal is to create something where nothing previously existed. Mobilizing resources, analyzing your opportunity, producing your first products for sale—none of these proves the viability of your business. Only by selling to customers and collecting the payments, expanding from those earliest buyers to a broader customer base, and scaling up to sufficient revenue streams to break even and then profit do you prove the enduring viability of the enterprise. Even then, a one-product operation is not a successful business; it is too vulnerable. A successful entrepreneur should consider additional products or services. Living through the early stages of a venture educates you about the customer and market and can point you to new opportunities you were unable to see previously. Your product concept at the end of year two may be, and often is, different from your original vision and intent.

The process of entrepreneurship melds these pieces together in processes that unfold over weeks and months, and eventually years, if the business successful. Breaking down the process into categories and components helps you understand the pieces and how they fit together. What we find in retrospect with successful launches is a cohesive fit among the parts. The entrepreneur's skills and education match what the start-up needs. The opportunity can be optimally explored with the team and resources that are identified and mobilized. The resources must be brought to bear to launch the venture with an entry strategy that delivers the product or service that solves customers' problem. Disparities among these core elements are signs of trouble. If your product launch requires engineering and information technology expertise and your team has no one with that knowledge, your team does not "fit" with the product. If you launch the product and have insufficient funds to sustain operations, perhaps you did not adequately calculate the capital resources required to reach the break-even point. Each category must be analyzed and thoroughly understood and all puzzle pieces joined to create the integrated picture required for financial success.

- Entrepreneurship is the creation of new ways of meeting needs through novel products, processes, services, technologies, markets, and forms of organizing.
- Entrepreneurial ventures can be start-ups or occur within large companies.
- Entrepreneurship is an innovation *process* that mobilizes people and resources.
- Key to entrepreneurial success is the fit among the entrepreneur/team, the product concept, the opportunity, the resources, and the entry strategy.

EXERCISE

1. In small teams, identify a successful entrepreneurial venture in your community and interview the entrepreneur or members of the management team. Define and describe the key elements of the entrepreneurial process for this enterprise. Analyze the fit between the entrepreneurial founder and the product or service, the fit between the product and the opportunity, and the fit between the resources and the entry strategy.

4.2 Systems Thinking

LEARNING OBJECTIVES

1. Understand the elements of sustainability innovation.

2. Explain how they can apply to existing companies and new ventures.

In this section, we discuss the ways in which entrepreneurial organizations integrate sustainability ideas into their ventures. Five core elements are necessary—systems thinking, molecular thinking, leveraging weak ties, collaborative adaptation, and radical incrementalism. Each contributes to innovation by opening up new vistas for creativity. For example, systems thinking allows participants to see previously hidden linkages and opportunities within a broader context. Molecular thinking initiates possibilities for innovation through substitution of more benign materials. The use of outside ties contributes novel perspectives and information to the decision process. Collaboration across functional and organizational boundaries helps generate new solutions. Radical incrementalism leads to system-wide innovation. Each of the core elements will be discussed and illustrated with examples.

Systems Thinking

Perhaps the most fundamentally distinctive feature of those engaged with sustainability innovation is the notion of **systems thinking**. Systems thinking does not mean "systems analysis," which implies a more formal, mathematical tool. Nor is systems thinking one-dimensional, as we shall see. Systems thinking is best illustrated by contrasting it to *linear thinking*, the approach historically associated with business decision making. Linear thinking assumes businesses create and sell, each business focusing on its own operations. Supplier or customer activities are

relevant only to the extent that understanding them can generate greater sales and profitability. This linear approach frames business activity as making and selling products that customers use and throw away. Therefore, conventional linear thinking in business ignores consideration of the product's origins; the raw materials and labor input to make it; and the chemical, engineering, and energy-consuming processes required to convert raw materials into constituent components and the ultimate finished product. In addition, it does not consider the effects of the product's use and the impacts when it is discarded at the end of its useful life.

In contrast, systems thinking applied to new ventures reminds us that companies operate in complex sets of interlocking living and nonliving systems, including markets and supply chains as well as natural systems. These natural systems can range from the atmosphere, to a wetlands area, to a child's immune system. Bear in mind that systems thinking can be applied to new ventures whether the firm sells products or provides services. If the venture is a service business, conventional business thinking can obscure the fact that service delivery involves information technology including hardware, software, servers, and energy use (heating and cooling). Service businesses may use office buildings and have employees who travel daily to the office and deliver services using truck fleets. Thus service businesses and their related supply chains also can benefit from the application of sustainability thinking and systems thinking. In sum, every venture rests within and is increasingly buffeted by shifts in natural and commercial systems that may be influenced through the direct or indirect reach of its activities.

Taking a systems perspective reminds us that we are accustomed to thinking of businesses in terms of discrete units with clear boundaries between them. We forget that these boundaries exist primarily in our minds or as legal constructs. For example, we may view a venture or company as a discrete entity. By extension we perceive a boundary between the firm and its suppliers and customers. Yet research suggests that the most successful business innovations arise from activities that cross category boundaries. Thus if one's mental map imposes boundaries, options may be unnecessarily constrained. In fact, given the dominance of linear thinking in business, systems thinking can give you an advantage over your more narrowly focused competitor. Your linear-oriented competitor may target incremental improvements to existing processes and shortchange research and development investments in longer-term goals—and then be surprised by unanticipated innovations in the industry. However, because you perceive the larger systems in which the venture is embedded, you can anticipate opportunities and be poised to act. Not only does the broader systems view lead to more opportunities, enabling you to adapt your competencies, it also holds the potential of producing outcomes that better serve the needs of customers and employees, your community, and your shareholders.

In other words, systems thinking asks you to see the larger picture, which, in turn, opens up new opportunity space. Let's look more closely at the systems view through an analogy. When you imagine a river, what do you see? A winding line on a map? A favorite fishing spot? Or the tumbling, rushing water itself? Do you include the wetlands and its wildlife, visible and microscopic? Do you see the human communities along the water? Do you see the ultimate end points of the water flows—the estuaries, deltas, and the sea? Do you include the water cycle from the ocean, through evaporation raining in the mountains regenerating the headwaters of the river? In other words, do you see the river as its component parts or as an integrated living system?

Sustainability applied to new ventures incorporates systems thinking. If you think only about the fish or the single stream, you miss what makes the river alive; you miss what it feeds and what feeds it. Similarly, your venture is part of a set of interlocking and interdependent systems characterized by suppliers and buyers as well as by energy and material flows. The more you are aware of these systems and their relationships to your company, the more rigor you bring to product design and strategy development and the more sophisticated your analysis of how to move forward.

Another advantage of systems thinking is its invitation to jettison outdated ideas about the environment. The environment has, in the past, been considered "out there" somewhere, separate and apart from people and businesses. In reality, the environment is not external to business. Indeed, it is coming to comprise an integral new set of competitive factors that shape options and opportunities for entrepreneurs and firms. For ventures to successfully launch and grow in the twenty-first century, it is essential to understand this more expansive systems definition of the new competitive conditions.

When systems thinking guides strategy and action, the collision between business and natural systems becomes a frontier of opportunity. Systems thinking can encourage and institutionalize the natural ability of companies to evolve—not through small adaptations but through creative leaps. The companies discussed in this section demonstrate these tactics in action. For example, AT&T shows how a company can work from a systems view to optimize benefits across multiple systems. Shaw Industries underwent a profound strategic reorientation when it redesigned its products—carpets—not in the traditional linear make-use-waste model but in a new circular strategy. Shaw now takes back carpets at the end of their use life, disassembles them, and remanufactures them as new carpets. This is a radical rethinking of the value of a product. Coastwide Lab offers an example of a systems view that helped a smaller company generate systems solutions for customers, not just products. All three sustainability-inspired strategies indicate a stepped-up understanding of the broader systems in which the business operates. Systems thinking allowed each company to recognize new opportunities in its competitive terrain and to act on them in innovative ways that greatly improved its competitive position.

AT&T

In hindsight, it seems obvious that AT&T, a telecommunications company, should be an early advocate of its employees telecommuting to work. At the outset, however, there was more doubt than confidence in the telecommuting arrangement. Yet it was soon shown that AT&T's innovative policy—grounded in systems and sustainability thinking—resulted in productivity growth, lower overhead costs, greater employee retention, reduced air pollution, lower gasoline and thus oil consumption, and more satisfied employees.

Was telecommuting an environmental policy because it reduced pollution, a cost-cutting measure because overhead and real estate costs dropped, or a national security measure because it lowered oil consumption? Perhaps it was a human resources initiative since it resulted in more satisfied employees. All of these descriptions are accurate, yet no single measure fully captures the *systemic* nature and benefits of this sustainability approach to rethinking work. AT&T's telecommuting policy is an example of *systems thinking*. Between 1998 and 2004, then AT&T vice president Braden Allenby led the telecommuting initiative. [1] With his systems focus on linkages and interdependencies rather than emphasis on discrete units, Allenby looked to inputs and outputs, processes, and feedback, taking into consideration multiple viewpoints within and outside AT&T. Over time, analysis pinpointed a cross-cutting convergence of factors that, when targeted for optimization, produced positive benefits across the system of AT&T's financial performance, employees, communities, and air pollution emissions.

New questions were asked. What is the relationship among working at home, spending hours in a car, spending time at a remote AT&T site, and productivity? What gasoline volumes, carbon dioxide (CO_2) levels, greenhouse gas emissions, and dollar savings for AT&T are involved when telecommuting is an option for managers? If there are benefits for certain employees and the company, what about extending the policy to other employees? What is AT&T's contribution to urban vehicle congestion, and can a telecommuting program help reduce gasoline use in a way that reduces oil dependency while benefiting towns, employees, and the firm? We know intuitively that these factors are interrelated, but it is unusual for a senior corporate executive to examine them from a strategic perspective. In this case, the telecommuting policy saved the company millions of dollars while raising productivity and enhancing AT&T's reputation. Sustainability strategies will always be tailored to a venture's unique competencies and circumstances; it will grow organically from the business you are in, the products you make, and the employees you hire.

Braden Allenby is a trained systems thinker and has contributed extensive writings on industrial ecology. Allenby saw the opportunity for telecommuting to reduce costs for AT&T and reduce pollution while raising employee productivity and satisfaction. As the environment, health, and safety vice president at AT&T, Allenby took the strategic view as opposed to the compliance perspective proscribed for many environment, health, and safety office heads. By the late 1990s AT&T had moved out of manufacturing. The key to the company's success became

service, and the key to high-quality service was application of in-house technology know-how by productive, satisfied employees.

Allenby quietly and successfully promoted telecommuting within the firm for over ten years, despite opposition. It helped that the program was not seen as a conventional "environmental" one that some might have assumed imposed irretrievable overhead costs. Inevitable resistance included the usual institutional inertia against change but also managers' and employees' discomfort with unfamiliar telecommuting job structures and loss of easy metrics for productivity. "Time at desk" was still equated with individual productivity as though the assembly line mentality of "if I don't see you working, you probably aren't working" held firm in the twenty-first-century information-age economy. In addition, many questioned how telecommuting relates to environment, health, and safety. Furthermore, weak technology, such as limited home computer bandwidth and an insufficient number of individuals willing to lead, slowed the process.

Despite obstacles, over time significant benefits were returned to AT&T as well as to its employees, their families, and their communities. Real estate overhead costs decreased (offices could be closed down) while productivity and job satisfaction increased according to the company's Telework Center of Excellence studies. [2] Survey results showed that not having to commute and gaining uninterrupted time to concentrate increased each telecommuter's workday by one additional productive hour, translating to an approximate 12.5 percent productivity increase. Upgrades to communication technology enabled easier phone messaging through personal computers and saved about one hour per week, an approximate 2.5 percent increase in telecommuters' productivity.

The program expanded rapidly as financial and other advantages proved the efficacy of telecommuting. About 35,000 AT&T management employees were full-time telecommuters in 2002 representing 10 percent of the workforce. By 2004 that number had expanded to 30 percent. Another 41 percent worked from home one to two days a week. Detailed records were kept on the telecommuting program's benefits and costs. Records included the number of employees who telecommuted and how many days they telecommuted per month, whether on the road, at home, or in a telecenter or satellite office. An annual survey provided the quantitative data and subjective elements of participation, such as employee perceptions of the personal and professional benefits.

Important results relevant for other companies were described in the AT&T report: "Work/family balance and improved productivity remain the top-tier benefits. Typically, these two things are seen as mutually exclusive—spending more time with one's family while simultaneously getting more work done would seem to be impossible—but teleworkers are able to have their cake and eat it, too." [3] Feedback on disadvantages of telework was recorded and used to adjust the program optimally.

The positive externalities reported were reduced use of fossil fuel resources, reduced vehicular air pollution, reduced contribution to greenhouse gases and global climate change, reduced runoff of automobile fluids, and decreased air deposition of nitrogen oxides (NOx) that lead to water pollution. AT&T estimated that "since one gallon of gasoline produces 19 lbs. of carbon dioxide (CO_2), the 5.1 million gallons of gas our employee teleworkers didn't use in 2000 (by avoiding 110 million miles of driving by telecommuting) equate to almost 50,000 tons of CO_2. Similar benefits result from reductions in NOx and hydrocarbons." [4] Reduced emissions may provide AT&T with assets in the form of emission credits to be used as internal offsets or sold at market price.

Results of the telecommuting policy included the following:

- Reduced costs for real estate and overhead. [5]
- Employee productivity gains: AT&T estimated that increased productivity due to telework was worth $100 million a year. Eighty percent of employees surveyed said the change had improved their productivity.
- Improved employee quality of life and morale: Eliminating the stress and wasted time of commuting contributed to productivity.
- Employee retention and related cost savings: AT&T employees turned down other job offers in part because of the telecommuting options they enjoyed.
- Appropriate management metrics: AT&T accelerated a transition from time-at-desk management to management by results and, more broadly, learned how to effectively manage knowledge workers in a rapidly changing, increasingly knowledge-based economy (seen as a competitive advantage).
- Security: After the 9/11 attacks on the World Trade Center and the Pentagon, a more dispersed workforce was viewed as a way to increase institutional resiliency and limit the impact of an attack (or for that matter any disaster, natural or otherwise).

As the AT&T example shows, when systems thinking guides strategy and action, the collision between business and natural systems can become a frontier of opportunity. Systems thinking can encourage and institutionalize the natural ability of companies to evolve, not through small adaptations but through creative leaps.

Shaw Industries

Shaw Industries underwent a profound strategic reorientation and redesigned its products—carpets—not in the traditional linear make-use-waste model but in a sustainability-inspired circular strategy. Shaw now takes back products at the end of their useful life, disassembles them, and remanufactures them as new carpets. This is a radical rethinking of the value of a product using systems terms.

In 2003, Shaw's EcoWorx product won the US Green Chemistry Institute's Green Chemistry Award for Designing Safer Products. The company combined application of green chemistry principles with a cradle-to-cradle design approach to create new environmentally benign carpet tile. [6] The product met the rising demand for sustainable products, helping define a new market space that emerged in the late 1990s and 2000s as buyers became more cognizant of health hazards associated with building materials and furnishings. EcoWorx also educated the marketplace on the desirability of sustainable products as qualitatively, economically, and environmentally superior substitutes, in this case for a product that had been in place for thirty years. [7]

Carpeting is big business. In 2004, the global market for carpeting was about $26 billion, and it was expected to grow to $73 billion in 2007. Carpeting and rugs sectors expect a combined growth rate of 17 percent that year. Shaw Industries of Dalton, Georgia, was the world's largest carpet manufacturer in 2004. Its carpet brand names include Cabin Crafts, Queen, Designweave, Philadelphia, and ShawMark. The company sells residential products to distributors and retailers and offers commercial products directly to customers through Shaw Contract Flooring. The company also sells laminate, ceramic tile, and hardwood flooring. In 2003, Shaw recorded $4.7 billion in sales.

Now acknowledged as an innovator in sustainable product design and business strategy, by early 2005, Shaw had completed a successful transformation to an environmentally benign carpet tile system design. Customers self-selected EcoWorx over tiles containing polyvinyl chloride (PVC), driving the new technology to over 80 percent of Shaw's total carpet tile production. In retrospect, selecting carpet tiles as a key part of its sustainability strategy looks like a smart decision. In 2005, carpet tile was the fastest growing product category in the commercial carpet market.

In hindsight, Shaw's decision seems the only way forward in the highly competitive floor covering business. However, in 1999, Shaw Industries Vice President Steve Bradfield described the carpet industry as "a marketing landscape that looked increasingly like a quagmire of greenwash." Waste issues were putting pressure on the industry to clean up its act. Carpet took up considerable space in municipal landfills, took a long time to decompose, and was notoriously difficult to recycle. Moreover, carpet was coming under increasing scrutiny for its association with health problems.

In the late 1990s, companies vied to project the best image of environmental responsibility. However, Shaw Industries moved beyond marketing hype to a strategy that eliminated hazardous materials and recovered and reused carpet in a closed materials cycle. Shaw had to differentiate itself and create new capabilities and even new markets. EcoWorx, designed with cradle-to-cradle logic, required more innovation than simply the product. To implement its strategy, the company had to think in systems and design products not in the linear make-use-waste model but in cycles. For Shaw, this meant it must collect, disassemble, and reuse the old carpet tile material in new products. Moreover, the materials used in its products needed to be environmentally superior to anything used before.

Shaw was not the first company to think of this approach. In 1994, Ray Anderson of Interface Flooring Systems set the bar high for the industry by declaring sustainability as a corporate (and industry) goal. [8] While smaller in scale than Shaw Industries, Interface succeeded in changing the terms of the debate. For Shaw, the biggest player in the field, to not only rise to the challenge but to champion the way forward was not something one could necessarily predict.

Shaw's EcoWorx, the replacement system for the PVC-nylon incumbent system, drove double-digit growth for carpet tile after its introduction in 1999. The system made it possible to recycle both the nylon face and the backing components into next-generation face and backing materials for future EcoWorx carpet tile. Shaw used its own EcoSolution Q nylon 6 branded fiber that would be recycled as a technical nutrient through a recovery agreement with Honeywell's Arnprior depolymerization facility in Canada. The nylon experienced no loss of performance or quality reduction and cost the same or less.

Seeking every way possible to reduce materials use, remove hazardous inputs, and maintain or improve product performance, Shaw made the following changes:

- Replacement of PVC and phthalate plasticizer with an inert and nonhazardous mix of polymers ensuring material safety throughout the system. (PVC-contaminated nylon facing cannot be used for noncarpet applications of recycled materials.)
- Elimination of antimony trioxide flame retardant associated with harm to aquatic organisms.
- Dramatic reduction of waste during the processing phases by immediate recovery and use of the technical nutrients. (The production waste goal is zero.)
- A life-cycle inventory and mass flow analysis that captures systems impacts and material efficiencies compared with PVC backing.
- Efficiencies (energy and material reductions) in production, packaging, and distribution—40 percent lighter weight of EcoWorx tiles over PVC-backed tiles yields transport and handling (installation and removal/demolition) cost savings.
- Use of a minimum number of raw materials, none of which lose value, as all can be continuously disassembled and remanufactured.
- Use of a closed-loop, integrated plant-wide cooling water system providing chilled water for the extrusion process as well as the heating and cooling system.
- Provision of a toll-free phone number on every EcoWorx tile for the buyer to contact Shaw for removal of the material for recycling.

Models assessing comparative costs of the conventional versus the new system indicated the recycled components would be less costly to process than virgin materials. Essentially, EcoWorx tile remains a raw material indefinitely.

Moreover, as is typical of companies actively applying a systems-oriented innovation to product lines, Shaw has found other opportunities for cost reduction and new revenue. For example, Shaw projects $2.5 million in overall savings per year from a Dalton, Georgia, steam energy plant designed collaboratively with Siemens Building Technologies. Manufacturing waste by-products are converted into gas that fuels a boiler to produce fifty thousand pounds of steam per hour that will be used on-site for manufacturing. The facility lowers corporate plant emissions, eliminates postmanufacturing carpet waste, and provides the Dalton manufacturing site with a fixed-cost reliable energy source, which is no small benefit in a time of high and fluctuating energy prices.

Once the power of systems thinking becomes clear, returning to a compartmentalized or linear view becomes an irrational abandonment of essential knowledge. Systems thinking illuminates how the world actually works and how actions far beyond what we can see influence our decisions and choices. It frees us to imagine alternative future products and services and create positive outcomes for more stakeholders. For Shaw, the benefits of thinking in systems were clear. The takeaway is that breaking out of the traditional linear approach to products and designing from a systems perspective can lead to differentiation, new competitive advantage, and tangible results.

Coastwide Labs

Systems thinking encourages *systems solutions* for your customers. Once you see the broader systems context and tightly coupled interdependencies, you have the opportunity to simultaneously solve multiple customer problems and provide a comprehensive "answer" for which they could not even form the right question.

Coastwide Laboratories, when it was a stand-alone company before being acquired by Express and then Staples, sold systems solutions to its customers. Coastwide's approach was developed over several years and culminated in a complete strategic transformation in 2006. The change separated the firm from its competitors and enabled it to shape a regional market to its advantage. Rewards included customer retention, increased sales to existing customers, new customers, dominant market share in a seven-state region, and brand visibility. By selling systems solutions, Coastwide Labs reduced regulatory burdens for itself and its customers, reduced costs for both, and removed human health and environmental threats across the supply chain. The company tracked an array of trends and systems that influenced its market and customers. The resulting perspective put senior management in the driver's seat to benefit from and shape those trends in ways that also meet customers' latent needs.

Context is important. For decades, Coastwide's product formulations, typical for the industry, were consistent with expectations for old-style janitorial products. The company made or bought cleaners, disinfectants, floor finishes and sealers, and degreasers and provided a full line of sanitary maintenance equipment and supplies. Performing the cleaning function was the primary requirement; other health and ecosystem impact considerations did not emerge until years later.

Serving the US Pacific Northwest region, Coastwide competed in a growing market in the 1990s, driven by expanding high-tech firms that emerged or grew rapidly in the 1980s and 1990s (e.g., Microsoft, Intel, Amgen, and Boeing). By the 1990s, the growth of overall demand for cleaning products had tapered off and the products were essentially commodities. This meant that growth, improved sales, and profitability depended on either increasing market share or offering value-added services. The commercial and industrial cleaning products industry remained fragmented in 2000 with many small companies with less than $5 million in revenue competing as producers, distributors, or both.

However, this sleepy, traditional industry was about to wake up. In August 2002, Coastwide—by then a commercial and industrial cleaning product formulator and distributor—introduced the Sustainable Earth line of products. This experimental line was designed for performance efficacy, easy use, and low to zero toxicity. By 2006, the line had grown to dominate the company's strategy, positioning Coastwide as the largest provider of safe and "clean" cleaning products, janitorial supplies, and related services in the region. The market extended from southern Canada to central California and west to Idaho.

The Sustainable Earth line enabled Coastwide to lower its customers' costs for maintenance by offering system solutions. Higher dilution rates for chemicals, dispensing units that eliminate overuse, improved safety for the end user, and less employee lost-work time because of health problems associated with chemical exposure were reported. Higher dilutions also reduced the packaging waste stream, thereby reducing customer waste disposal fees. TriMet, the Portland, Oregon, metropolitan area's municipal bus and light rail system, reduced its number of cleaning products from twenty-two to four by switching to Sustainable Earth products. Initial cleaning chemical cost savings to the municipality amounted to 70 percent, not including training cost savings associated with the inventory simplification. In 2006, the Sustainable Earth line performed as well or better than the category leaders while realizing a gross margin over 40 percent higher than on its conventional cleaners.

Perhaps most telling, Coastwide's overall corporate strategy changed in 2006 to implement a corporate transformation to what the company terms "sustainability" products. All cleaning product lines were replaced with sustainably designed formulations and designs. It is important to keep in mind that health benefits and improved water quality in the region's cities were not the reasons to design this strategy; they characterized opportunities for innovation that drove lower costs for buyers and higher revenues for

Coastwide. Through carefully crafted positioning, this company has become a major player creating and shaping the market to its advantage.

Coastwide's strategic roots were in its early systems approach to meet customers' full-service needs, long before environmental and sustainability vocabulary entered the business mainstream. The corporate vision evolved from simply selling cleaning products to offering unique, nonhazardous cleaning formulations at the lowest "total cost" to the buyer. Eventually, Coastwide addressed its customers' *comprehensive* maintenance and cleaning needs—in other words, their system's needs—which only later included sustainability features.

The cleaning product markets are more complicated than one might suspect. Several factors shaped industry selling strategies. Customers needed multiple cleaning products and equipment for different applications. However, buyers had more than cleaning needs. Fast-growing and large electronics manufacturers with clean rooms had to protect their production processes from contaminants or suffer major financial losses from downtime, as much as a million dollars a day. In addition, a barrage of intensifying local, state, and federal regulatory requirements demanded safe handling, storage, and disposal of all toxic and hazardous materials. These legal mandates imposed additional costs such as protective clothing, training, and hazardous waste disposal fees. Adding complexity, historic buying patterns fragmented purchase decisions. One facility maintenance manager ordered a set of products from one supplier; a second ordered different products from another supplier. As a result, companies with geographically dispersed sites made nonoptimal choices from both a price and a systems sense. As in many compartmentalized companies, jobs were divided with people working against each other, sometimes under the same roof. Maintenance bought the products; the environment, health, and safety group was responsible for knowing what was in the products as well as for workers' safety and health; and manufacturing had to ensure pristine production.

Furthermore, all buyers contended with wastewater disposal regulations that forbade contaminated water from leaving the premises and entering the water supply system, but the requirements were different depending on the local or state regulations. Typically, minimal or no training was given maintenance staff members who actually used the hazardous cleaning chemicals. High janitorial employee turnover and low literacy rates made it expensive to hire and train employees. A 150 to 200 percent annual turnover rate was typical with this employee group, imposing its own unique

costs and health risks to the employer. The low status of the maintenance and janitorial function didn't help. The job was delegated in the organization to the staff that did the cleaning work, or one supervisory level above. In other words, despite many small areas needing the customer's attention as a complex set of interrelated factors (a system), responsibility was either nonexistent or fragmented across different departments that traditionally had no incentive to communicate.

More history magnifies the systems thinking in action. In the late 1990s, buyers wanted stockless systems with just-in-time delivery and single source purchasing to avoid dealing with seven or eight companies for ninety cleaning items. Coastwide had designed its first system-solution contract in the late 1980s when it contracted with Tektronix, a test, measurement, and monitoring computer equipment producer, then the largest Oregon employer and a high-tech company with a dozen operating locations. Coastwide offered to supply all Tektronix maintenance needs, including training personnel to use cleaning products safely. Getting Tektronix's business required knowing the company's different facilities, various manufacturing operations requirements, and maintenance standards. It also meant that Coastwide presented an analysis showing Tektronix the economics of why it made sense to outsource the company's system needs. Coastwide had to understand the buyer's internal use and purchasing systems, including its costs and chemical vulnerabilities.

Roger McFadden, Coastwide's chemist and senior product development person—the internal entrepreneur, or intrapreneur—took on the additional job of keeping a list of chemicals the buyer wanted kept out of its facilities due to clean room contamination risks. McFadden saw this change as an opportunity to look at a variety of suspect chemicals on various health, safety, and environmental lists. The lists were growing for the customer and regulatory agencies. Eventually Coastwide was asked to handle the complete health and safety functions for this customer and eventually for others because it could do so at a lower cost with customized analyses presented to each buyer, and with a systems perspective that optimized efficiencies across linked system parts with tagged areas for continuous improvement. Important interrelated issues for Roger McFadden included product contamination, regulations, customers' workers' compensation and injury liability, and chemical compound toxicity thresholds and cancer rates.

To compete with foresight Coastwide also had to stay current on and continuously adapt its solutions services to larger and increasingly more relevant trends. McFadden served on the Governor's Community Sustainability Taskforce for Oregon and in the process gained more information about the science of toxicity, state regulatory intentions, and changing governmental agency purchasing practices. This led to expanded sales to the state and city governments and to Nike, Hewlett-Packard, and Intel. Coastwide's involvement with broader community issues translated into flows of information to senior management that helped the firm position itself and learn despite constantly moving terrain.

McFadden's first step was to rethink the cleaning product formulations. The products had to work as well as not pose a risk or threat. The second step was to expand the product line so that customers would source a range of products solely from Coastwide, a step that provided customers with insurance that all cleaning products met uniform "clean" and low- or zero-toxicity specifications. Coastwide extended its "cleaner cleaners" criteria to auxiliary products. For example, PVC-containing buckets were rejected in favor of those made from safely reusable polyethylene. Used buckets were picked up by Coastwide's distribution arm, with the containers color coded to ensure no other containers (for which the company would not know the materials inside) would inadvertently be brought back.

Understanding the interconnections across systems continued to bring Coastwide financial and competitive benefits. By 2005 the major trade organization for the industrial cleaning industry, the International Sanitary Supply Association (ISSA), began highlighting members' green cleaning products and programs. Grant Watkinson, president of Coastwide, was featured on the organization's website. The American Association of Architects' US Green Building Council developed its Leadership in Energy and Environmental Design (LEED) program that set voluntary national standards for high-performance sustainable buildings. LEED assigned points that could be earned by organizations requesting certification if they integrated system-designed cleaning practices. Since many major corporations and organizations gain productivity and reputation advantages for having their buildings certified by LEED, Coastwide was positioned with more knowledge and media visibility as this market driver accelerated a transition to lower toxicity and more benign materials.

In addition, Coastwide was in a far better position than its competition when Executive Order 13148, Greening the Government Through Leadership in Environmental Management, appeared. This order set strict requirements for all federal agencies to "reduce [their] use of selected toxic chemicals, hazardous substances, and pollutants...at [their] facilities by 50 percent by December 31, 2006." [9]

By 2006 most of the major institutional cleaning-products companies across the country had "green" product offerings of some sort, but Coastwide already was well ahead of them. Building service contractor and property manager customers told Coastwide they were awarded new business because of the "green" package Coastwide offers. Some buyers use the Sustainable Earth line as part of their marketing program to differentiate and enhance the value of their services. The city of San Francisco specified Coastwide's line even though the company did not have sales representatives in that market (sales are through distributors). Inquiries from the US Midwest, South, and East Coast increased in 2006, and Roger McFadden and the firm's corporate director of sustainability were frequently invited to speak in various US and Canadian cities outside Coastwide's market area. In sum, by making sure it understood the dynamics of the relevant systems for its success and its customers' benefit, Coastwide created a successful strategy because, in the current competitive environment, it was just good business.

Results for Coastwide included the following:

- The industry average net operating income was 2 percent; Coastwide averaged double or triple that level.
- Sales in 2005 increased by 8 percent, driven by market share increases in segments where the most Sustainable Earth products were sold; operating profits rose by an even larger percentage.
- The number of new customers rose over 35 percent in 2005, largely attributable to Sustainable Earth product lines.

Coastwide's solution for buyers went further than any other firm's to blend problem solving around a company's unique needs with changing regulatory system requirements and emerging human health and ecosystem trends. Coastwide, through McFadden's entrepreneurial innovation, saw an opportunity in the complex corporate, regulatory, and ecological systems and in its customers' need for a sustainable response. By understanding the systems in which you operate, higher level solutions can emerge that will give you competitive advantage. By 2010 McFadden had become Stapless' senior scientist, advising the $27 billion office products company on its sustainability strategy.

In each instance of these instances, entrepreneurial (or intrapreneurial) leaders made decisions from a systems perspective. The individuals came to this understanding in different ways, but this way of seeing their companies' interdependencies with both living and nonliving systems allowed them to introduce innovative ways of doing business, create new product designs and operating structures, and generate new revenues. Systems analysis is an effective problem-solving tool in dynamic, complex circumstances where economic opportunities are not easily apparent. A systems perspective accommodates the constant changes that characterize the competitive terrain.

To recap, we provide the following tactics to help you think in systems terms:

- Design products in "circles," not lines.
- Optimize across multiple systems.

- Sell systems solutions.

This kind of broader systems-oriented strategy will be increasingly important for claiming market share in the new sustainability market space. Increasingly, senior management, and eventually everyone within firms and their supply chains, will understand that the future lies on a path toward benign products (no harm to existing natural systems) or products that—at the end of use—are returned so that their component parts can be used to make equal or better quality new products. [10] Systems thinking applied to entrepreneurial innovation is not merely a tool or theory—it is increasingly a mind-set, a survival skill, and key to strategic advantage.

KEY TAKEAWAYS

- A systems approach to business is a reminder that companies operate in complex sets of interlocking living and nonliving systems, including markets and supply chains as well as natural system.
- Systems thinking can open up new opportunities for product and process redesign and lead to innovative business models.
- Individuals with a creative bent can lead sustainability innovation changes inside small or large firms.

EXERCISE

1. In teams, identify a commonly used product. Try to name all the component parts and material inputs involved in bringing the product to market. list the ways in which producing that item likely depended on, drew from, and impacted natural systems over the product's life.

---

[1] Braden R. Allenby is currently professor of civil and environmental engineering and professor of law at Arizona State University and moved from his position as the environment, health, and safety vice president for AT&T in 2004. His systems thinking comes naturally as author of multiple publications on industrial ecology, design for the environment, and earth systems engineering and management. His coediting of *The Greening of Industrial Ecosystems*, published by the National Academy Press in 1994, and his authorship of *Environmental Threats and National Security: An International Challenge to Science and Technology*, published by Lawrence Livermore National Laboratory in 1994, and *Information Systems and the Environment*, published by the National Academy Press in 2001, also enhanced his ability to see natural systems as integral to corporate strategy.
[2] Joseph Roitz, Binny Nanavati, and George Levy, *Lessons Learned from the Network-Centric Organization: 2004 AT&T Employee Telework Results* (Bedminster, NJ: AT&T Telework Center of Excellence, 2005). Brad Allenby provided me with this source.
[3] Joseph Roitz, Binny Nanavati, and George Levy, *Lessons Learned from the Network-Centric Organization: 2004 AT&T Employee Telework Results* (Bedminster, NJ: AT&T Telework Center of Excellence, 2005). Brad Allenby provided me with this source.
[4] Braden Allenby, "Telework: The AT&T Experience" (testimony before the House Subcommittee on Technology and Procurement Policy, Washington, DC, March 22, 2001), accessed December 2, 2010, http://www.fluxx.net/toronto/soc4.html.
[5] AT&T estimated savings of $75 million a year when it first changed its policies to make salespeople and consultants mobile. Jennifer Bresnahan, "Why Telework?," *CIO Enterprise* 11, no. 7 (January 15, 1998): 28–34.
[6] Shaw Industries worked with William McDonough and Michael Braungart, an architect and chemist who conceived the cradle-to-cradle design approach that considers the ultimate end of products from the very beginning of their design in order to reduce waste and toxicity.
[7] See Jeffrey W. Segard, Steven Bradfield, Jeffrey J. White, and Mathew J. Realff, "EcoWorx, Green Engineering Principles in Practice," *Environmental Science and Technology* 37, no. 23 (2003): 5269–77.
[8] Ray Anderson, *Mid Course Correction: Toward a Sustainable Enterprise: The Interface Model* (Atlanta, GA: Peregrinzilla, 1998).
[9] National Environmental Policy Act, "Executive Order 13148," accessed March 7, 2011, http://ceq.hss.doe.gov/nepa/regs/eos/eo13148.html.
[10] The point is not the goal but the continuous effort.

4.3 Molecular Thinking

1. Explore systems thinking at the molecular level.

2. Focus on materials innovation.

3. Provide examples of green chemistry applications.

In this discussion, we encourage you to think on the micro level, as though you were a molecule. We tend to focus on what is visible to the human eye, forgetting that important human product design work takes place at scales invisible to human beings. Molecular thinking, as a metaphorical subset of systems thinking, provides a useful perspective by focusing attention on invisible material components and contaminants. In the first decade of the twenty-first century there has been heavy emphasis on clean energy in the media. Yet our world is composed of energy *and* materials. When we *do* examine materials we tend to focus on visible waste streams, such as the problems of municipal waste, forgetting that some of the most urgent environmental health problems are caused by microscopic, and perhaps nanoscale, compounds. These compounds contain persistent contaminants that remain invisible in the air, soil, and water and subsequently accumulate inside our bodies through ingestion of food and water. Thinking like a molecule can reveal efficiency and innovation opportunities that address hazardous materials exposure problems; the principles of **green chemistry** give you the tools to act on such opportunities. The companies discussed in this section provide examples of successful sustainability innovation efforts at the molecular level.

Green chemistry, an emerging area in science, is based on a set of twelve design principles. [1] Application of the principles can significantly reduce or even eliminate generation of hazardous substances in the design, manufacture, and application of chemical products. Green chemistry offers many business benefits. Its guiding principles drive design of new products and processes around health and environmental criteria and can help firms capture top (revenue) and bottom line (profitability) gains within the company and throughout value chains. As public demand and regulatory drivers for "clean" products and processes grow, molecular thinking enables entrepreneurs inside large and small companies to differentiate their businesses and gain competitive advantage over others who are less attuned to the changing market demands.

In the ideal environment, green chemistry products are derived from renewable feedstocks, and toxicity is deliberately prevented at the molecular level. Green chemistry also provides the means of shifting from a petrochemical-based economy based on oil feedstocks (from which virtually all plastics are derived) to a bio-based economy. This has profound consequences for a wide range of issues, including environmental health, worker safety, national security, and the agriculture sector. While no one scientific approach can supply all the answers, green chemistry plays a foundational role in enabling companies to realize concrete benefits from greener design.

What does it mean to pursue sustainability innovation at the molecular level? When chemicals and chemical processes are selected and designed to eliminate waste, minimize energy use, and degrade safely upon disposal, the result is a set of processes streamlined for maximum efficiency. In addition, hazards to those who handle the chemicals, along with the chemicals' inherent costs, are designed out of both products and processes. With the growing pressure on firms to take responsibility for the adverse impacts of business operations throughout their supply chain and the demand for greater transparency by corporations, forward-thinking organizations—whether start-ups or established firms—increasingly must assess products and process steps for inherent hazard and toxicity.

Molecular thinking, applied through the use of the green chemistry principles, guides you to examine the nature of material inputs to your products. Once again, a life-cycle approach is required to consider, from the outset, the ultimate fate of your waste outputs and products. This analysis can occur concurrently with delivering a high-quality product to the buyer. Thus thinking like a molecule asks business managers and executives to examine not only a product's immediate functionality but its entire molecular cycle from raw material, through manufacture and processing, to end of life and disposal. Smart decision makers will ask, Where do we get our feedstocks? Are they renewable or limited? Are they vulnerable to price and supply fluctuations? Are they vulnerable to emerging environmental health regulations? Are they inherently benign or does the management of risk incur costs in handling, processing, and disposal? Managers and sustainability entrepreneurs also must ask whether chemicals in their products accumulate in human tissue or biodegrade harmlessly. Where do the molecular materials go when thrown away? Do they remain stable in landfills, or do they break down to pollute local water supplies? Does their combination create new and more potent toxins when incinerated? If so, can air emissions be carried by wind currents and influence the healthy functioning of people and natural systems far from the source?

Until very recently these questions were not business concerns. Increasingly, however, circumstances demand that we think small (at the molecular and even nano levels) to think big (providing safe products for two to four billion aspiring middle-class citizens around the world). As we devise more effective monitoring devices that are better able to detect and analyze the negative health impacts of certain persistent chemical compounds, corporate tracking of product ingredients at the molecular level becomes imperative. Monitoring chemical materials to date has been driven primarily by increased regulation, product boycotts, and market campaigns by health-oriented nonprofit organizations. But instead of a reactive defense against these growing forces, forward-thinking entrepreneurial companies and individuals see new areas of business opportunity and growth represented by the updated science and shifting market conditions.

Green chemistry design principles are being applied by a range of leading companies across sectors including chemical giants Dow, DuPont, and Rohm and Haas and consumer product producers such as SC Johnson, Shaw Industries, and Merck & Co. Small and midsized businesses such as Ecover, Seventh Generation, Method, AgraQuest, and Metabolix also play a leading innovative role. (See the Presidential Green Chemistry Challenge Award winners for a detailed list of these businesses.) [3] Currently green chemistry–inspired design and innovation has made inroads into a range of applications, including the following:

Adhesives	Pesticides
Cleaning products	Pharmaceuticals
Fine chemicals	Plastics
Fuels and renewable energy technologies	Pulp and paper
Nanotechnologies	Textile manufacturing
Paints and coatings	Water purification

Included in green chemistry is the idea of the **atom economy**, which would have manufacturers use as fully as possible every input molecule in the final output product. The pharmaceutical industry, an early adopter of green chemistry efficiency principles in manufacturing processes, uses a metric called **E-factor** to measure the ratio of inputs to outputs in any given product. [4] In essence, an E-factor measurement tells you how many units of weight of output one gets per unit of weight of input. This figure gives managers a sense of process efficiency and the inherent costs associated with waste, energy, and other resources' rates of use. By applying green chemistry principles to pharmaceutical production processes, companies have been able to dramatically lower their E-factor—and significantly raise profits.

Merck & Co., for example, uncovered a highly innovative and efficient catalytic synthesis for sitagliptin, the active ingredient in Januvia, the company's new treatment for type 2 diabetes. This revolutionary synthesis generated 220 pounds less waste for each pound of sitagliptin manufactured and increased the overall yield by nearly 50 percent. Over the lifetime of Januvia, Merck expects to eliminate the formation of at least 330 million pounds of waste, including nearly 110 million pounds of aqueous waste. [5]

Pfizer

In 2002, pharmaceutical firm Pfizer won the US Presidential Green Chemistry Challenge Award for Alternative Synthetic Pathways for its innovation of the manufacturing process for sertraline hydrochloride (HCl). Sertraline HCl is the active ingredient in Zoloft, which is the most prescribed agent of its kind used to treat depression. In 2004, global sales of Zoloft were $3.4 billion. Pharmaceutical wisdom holds that companies compete on the nature of the drug primarily and on process secondarily, with "maximum yield" as the main objective. Green chemistry adds a new dimension to this calculus: Pfizer and other pharmaceutical companies are discovering that by thinking like a molecule and applying green chemistry process innovations, they see their atom economy exponentially improve.

In the case of Pfizer, the company saw that it could significantly cut input costs. The new commercial process offered dramatic pollution prevention benefits, reduced energy and water use, and improved safety and materials handling. As a consequence, Pfizer significantly improved worker and environmental safety while doubling product yield. This was achieved by analyzing each chemical step. The key improvement in the sertraline synthesis was reducing a three-step sequence in the original process to a single step. [6] Overall, the process changes reduced the solvent requirement from 60,000 gallons to 6,000 gallons per ton of sertraline. On an annual basis, the changes eliminated 440 metric tons of titanium dioxide-methylamine hydrochloride salt waste, 150 metric tons of 35 percent hydrochloric acid waste, and 100 metric tons of 50 percent sodium hydroxide waste. With hazardous waste disposal growing more costly, this represented real savings now and avoided possible future costs.

By redesigning the chemical process to be more efficient and produce fewer harmful and expensive waste products, the process of producing sertraline generated both economic and environmental/health benefits for Pfizer. Typically, 20 percent of the wholesale price is manufacturing costs, of which approximately 20 percent is the cost of the tablet or capsule with the remaining percentage representing all other materials, energy, water, and processing costs. Using green chemistry can reduce both of these input costs significantly. As patents expire and pharmaceutical products are challenged by cheaper generics, maintaining the most efficient, cost-effective manufacturing process will be the key to maintaining competitiveness.

As mentioned earlier, E-factor analysis offers the means for streamlining materials processing and capturing cost savings. An efficiency assessment tool for the pharmaceutical industry, E-factor is defined as the ratio of total kilograms of all input materials (raw materials, solvents, and processing chemicals) used per kilogram of active product ingredient (API) produced. A pivotal 1994 study indicated that as standard practice in the pharmaceutical industry, for every kilogram of API produced, between twenty-five and one hundred kilograms or more of waste was generated—a ratio still found in the industry. By the end of the decade, E-factors were being used more frequently to evaluate products. Firms were identifying drivers of high E-factor values and taking action to improve efficiency. Multiplying the E-factor by the estimated kilograms of API produced by the industry overall suggested that, for the year 2003, as much as 500 million to 2.5 billion kilograms of waste could be the by-product of pharmaceutical industry API manufacture. This waste represented a double penalty: the costs associated with purchasing chemicals that are ultimately diverted from API yield and the costs associated with disposing of this waste (ranging from one to five dollars per kilogram depending on the hazard). Very little information is released by competitors in this industry, but a published 2004 GlaxoSmithKline life-cycle assessment of its API manufacturing processes revealed approximately 75 to

80 percent of the waste produced was solvent (liquid) and 20 to 25 percent solids, of which a considerable proportion of both was likely hazardous under state and federal laws.

For years, the pharmaceutical industry stated it did not produce the significant product volumes needed to be concerned about toxicity and waste, particularly relative to commodity chemical producers. However, government and citizen concern about product safety and high levels of medications in wastewater combined with the growing cost of hazardous waste disposal is changing that picture relatively quickly. With favorable competitive conditions eroding, companies have been eager to find ways to cut costs, eliminate risk, innovate, and improve their image.

After implementing the green chemistry award-winning process as standard in sertraline HCl manufacture, Pfizer's experience indicated that green chemistry–guided process changes reduced E-factor ratios to ten to twenty kilograms. The potential to dramatically reduce E-factors through green chemistry could be significant. Other pharmaceutical companies that won Presidential Green Chemistry Challenge Awards between 1999 and 2010—Lilly, Roche, Bristol-Meyers Squibb, and Merck—reported improvements of this magnitude after the application of green chemistry principles. Additionally, Pfizer was awarded the prestigious UK environmental Crystal Faraday Award for innovation in the redesign of the manufacturing process of sildenafil citrate (the active ingredient in the product Viagra).

Not surprisingly, thinking like a molecule applied through use of green chemistry's twelve principles fits easily with existing corporate Six Sigma quality programs whose principles consider waste a process defect. "Right the first time" was an industry quality initiative backed strongly by the US Food and Drug Administration. Pfizer's Dr. Berkeley ("Buzz") Cue (retired but still actively advancing green chemistry in the industry), credited with introducing green chemistry ideas to the pharmaceutical industry, views these initiatives as a lens that allows the companies to look at processes and yield objectives in a more comprehensive way (a systems view), with quality programs dovetailing easily with the approach and even enhancing it.

Dr. Cue, looking back on his history with green chemistry and Pfizer, said, "The question is what has Pfizer learned through understanding Green Chemistry principles that not only advantages them in the short term, but positions them for future innovation and trends?" [7] This is an important question for entrepreneurs in small firms and large firms alike. If you think like a molecule, overlooked opportunities and differentiation possibilities present themselves. Are you calculating the ratio of inputs to outputs? Has your company captured obvious efficiency cost savings, increased product yield, and redesigned more customer and life-cycle effective molecules? Are you missing opportunities to reduce or eliminate regulatory oversight by replacing inherently hazardous and toxic inputs with benign materials? Regulatory compliance for hazardous chemical waste represents a significant budget item and cost burden. Those dollars would be more usefully spent elsewhere.

Green chemistry has generated breakthrough innovations in the agriculture sector as well. Growers face a suite of rising challenges connected with using traditional chemical pesticides. A primary concern is that pests are becoming increasingly resistant to conventional chemical pesticides. In some cases, pesticides must be applied two to five times to accomplish what a single application did in the 1970s. Moreover, pests can reproduce and mutate quickly enough to develop resistance to a pesticide within one growing season. Increased rates of pesticide usage deplete soil and contaminate water supplies, and these negative side effects and costs (so-called externalities) are shifted onto individuals while society bears the cost.

AgraQuest

AgraQuest is an innovative small company based in Davis, California. The company was founded by entrepreneur Pam Marrone, a PhD biochemist with a vision of commercially harnessing the power of naturally occurring plant defense systems. Marrone had left Monsanto, where she had originally been engaged to do this work, when that company shifted its strategic focus to genetically modified plants. Marrone looked for venture capital and ultimately launched AgraQuest, a privately held company, which in 2005 employed seventy-two people and expected sales of approximately $10 million.

AgraQuest strategically differentiated itself by offering products that provided the service of effective pest management while solving user problems of pest resistance, environmental impact, and worker health and safety. AgraQuest provides an exemplary case study of green chemistry technology developed and brought to market at a competitive cost. The company is also is a prime example of how a business markets a disruptive technology and grapples with the issues that face a challenge to the status quo.

Winner of the Presidential Green Chemistry Challenge Small Business Award in 2003 for its innovative enzymatic biotechnology process used to generate its products,

AgraQuest employed a proprietary technology to screen naturally occurring microorganisms to identify those that may have novel and effective pest management characteristics. [9] AgraQuest scientists traveled around the world searching out promising-looking microbes for analysis. AgraQuest scientists gathered microbe samples from around the world, identifying those that fight the diseases and pests that destroy crops. Once located, these microorganisms were screened, cultivated, and optimized in AgraQuest's facilities and then sent in powder or liquid form to growers. In field trials and in commercial use, AgraQuest's microbial pesticides have been shown to attack crop diseases and pests and then completely biodegrade, leaving no residue behind. Ironically, AgraQuest's first product was developed from a microbe found in the company's backyard—a nearby peach orchard. Once the microbe was identified, company biochemists analyzed and characterized the compound structures produced by selected microorganisms to ensure there were no toxins, confirm that the product biodegraded innocuously, and identify product candidates for development and commercialization.

The company, led by entrepreneur Marrone, has screened over twenty-three thousand microorganisms and identified more than twenty product candidates that display high levels of activity against insects, nematodes, and plant pathogens. These products include Serenade, Sonata, and Rhapsody biological fungicides; Virtuoso biological insecticide; and Arabesque biofumigant. The market opportunities for microbial-based pesticides are extensive. Furthermore, the booming $4 billion organic food industry generates rising demand for organic-certified pest management tools. As growers strive to increase yields to meet this expanding market, they require more effective, organic means of fighting crop threats. AgraQuest's fungicide Serenade is organic certified to serve this expanding market, and other products are in the pipeline.

The US Environmental Protection Agency (EPA) has streamlined the registration process for "reduced-risk" bio-based pesticides such as AgraQuest's to help move them to market faster. The Biopesticides and Pollution Prevention Division oversees regulation of all biopesticides and has accelerated its testing and registration processes. The average time from submission to registration is now twelve to fourteen months rather than five to seven years.

Moreover, since the products biodegrade and are inherently nontoxic to humans, they are exempt from testing for "tolerances"—that is, the threshold exposure to a toxic substance to which workers can legally be exposed. This means that workers are required to wait a minimum of four hours after use before entering the fields, whereas other conventional pesticides require a seventy-two-hour wait. The reduction of restricted entry intervals registers as time and money saved to growers. Therefore, AgraQuest products can act as "crop savers"—used immediately prior to harvest in the event of bad weather. To growers of certain products, such as wine grapes, this can mean the difference between success and failure for a season.

AgraQuest deployed exemplary green chemistry and sustainability innovation strategies. The opportunity presented by the problems associated with conventional chemical pesticides was relatively easy to perceive, but designing a viable alternative took real ingenuity and a dramatic diversion from well-worn industry norms. Thinking like a molecule in this context enabled the firm to challenge the existing industry pattern of applying toxins and instead examine how natural systems create safe pesticides. Marrone and her team have been able to invent entirely new biodegradable and benign products—and capitalize on rising market demand for the unique array of applications inherent in this type of product.

As the science linking cause and effect grows more sophisticated, public concern about the human health and environmental effects of pesticides is increasing. [10] Related to this is an international movement to phase out specific widely used pesticides such as DDT and methyl bromide. Moreover, a growing number of countries impose trade barriers on food imports due to residual pesticides on the products.

In this suite of challenges facing the food production industry, AgraQuest found opportunity. The logic behind AgraQuest's product line is simple: rather than rely solely on petrochemical-derived approaches to eradicating pests, AgraQuest products use microbes to fight microbes. Over millennia, microbes have evolved complex defense systems that we are only now beginning to understand. AgraQuest designs products that replicate and focus these natural defense systems on target pests. When used in combination with conventional pesticides, AgraQuest products are part of a highly effective pest management system that has the added benefit of lowering the overall chemical load released into natural systems. Because they are inherently benign, AgraQuest products biodegrade innocuously, avoiding the threats to human health and ecosystems—not to mention associated costs—that growers using traditional pesticides incur.

NatureWorks

In a final example, NatureWorks, Cargill's entrepreneurial biotechnology venture, designed plastics made from biomass, a renewable input. The genius of NatureWorks' biotechnology is that it uses a wide range of plant-based feedstocks and is not limited to corn, thus avoiding competition with food production. NatureWorks' innovative breakthroughs addressed the central environmental problem of conventional plastic. Derived from oil, conventional plastic, a nonrenewable resource associated with a long list of environmental, price, and national security concerns, has become a major health and waste disposal problem. By building a product around bio-based inputs, NatureWorks designed an alternative product that is competitive in both performance and price—one that circumvents the pollution and other concerns of oil-based plastics. As a result of its successful strategy, NatureWorks has shifted the market in its favor.

NatureWorks LLC received the 2002 Presidential Green Chemistry Challenge Award for its development of the first synthetic polymer class to be produced from renewable resources, specifically from corn grown in the American Midwest. At the Green Chemistry and Engineering conference and awards ceremony in Washington, DC, attended by the president of the US National Academy of Sciences, the White House science advisor, and other dignitaries from the National Academies and the American Chemical Society, the award recognized the company's major biochemistry innovation, achieved in large part under the guidance and inspiration of former NatureWorks technology vice president Patrick Gruber.

Gruber was an early champion of sustainability innovation. As an entrepreneur inside a large firm, he led the effort that resulted in NatureWorks' bio-based plastic. Together with a team of chemical engineers, biotechnology experts, and marketing strategists, Gruber spearheaded the effort to marry agricultural products giant Cargill with chemical company Dow to create the spin-off company originally known as Cargill Dow and renamed NatureWorks in January 2005. Gruber was the visionary who saw the potential for a bio-based plastic and the possibilities for a new enzymatic green chemistry process to manufacture it. He helped drive that process until it was cost-effective enough to produce products competitive with conventional products on the market.

NatureWorks' plastic, whose scientific name is polylactic acid (PLA), has the potential to revolutionize the plastics and agricultural industries by offering biomass-based biopolymers as a substitute for conventional petroleum-based plastics. NatureWorks resins were named and trademarked NatureWorks PLA for the polylactic acid that comprises the base plant sugars. In addition to replacing petroleum as the material feedstock, PLA resins have the added benefit of being compostable (safely biodegraded) or even infinitely recyclable, which means they can be reprocessed again and again. This provides a distinct environmental advantage, since recycling—or "down-cycling"—postconsumer or postindustrial conventional plastics into lower quality products only slows material flow to landfills; it does not prevent waste. Moreover, manufacturing plastic from corn field residues results in 30 to 50 percent fewer greenhouse gases when measured from "field to pellet." Additional life-cycle environmental and health benefits have been identified by a thorough life-cycle analysis. In addition, PLA resins, virgin and postconsumer, can be processed into a variety of end uses.

In 2005, NatureWorks CEO Kathleen Bader and Patrick Gruber were wrestling with a number of questions. NatureWorks' challenges were operational and strategic: how to take the successful product to high-volume production and how to market the unique resin in a mature plastics market. NatureWorks employed 230 people distributed almost equally among headquarters (labs and management offices), the plant, and international locations. As a joint venture, the enterprise had consumed close to $750 million dollars in capital and was not yet profitable, but it held the promise of tremendous growth that could transform a wide range of markets worldwide. In 2005, NatureWorks was still the only company in the world capable of producing large-scale corn-based resins that exhibited standard performance traits, such as durability, flexibility, resistance to chemicals, and strength—all at a competitive market price.

The plastics industry is the fourth largest manufacturing segment in the United States behind motor vehicles, electronics, and petroleum refining. Both the oil and chemical industries are mature and rely on commodities sold on thin margins. The combined efforts of a large-scale chemical company in Dow and an agricultural processor giant in Cargill suggested Cargill Dow—now NatureWorks—might be well suited for the mammoth task of challenging oil feedstocks. However, a question inside the business in 2005 was whether the company could grow beyond the market share that usually limited "environmental" products, considered somewhere between 2 and 5 percent of the market. Was PLA an "environmental product," or was it the result of strategy that anticipated profound market shifts?

NatureWorks brought its new product to market in the late 1990s and early 2000s at a time of shifting market dynamics and converging health, environmental, national security, and energy independence concerns. These market drivers gave NatureWorks a profound edge. Oil supplies and instability concerns loomed large in 2005 and have not subsided. Volatile oil prices and political instability in oil-producing countries argued for decreasing dependence on foreign oil to the extent possible. The volatility of petroleum prices between 1995 and 2005 wreaked havoc on the plastics industry. From 1998 to 2001, natural gas prices (which typically tracked oil prices) doubled, then quintupled, then returned to 1998 levels. The year 2003 was again a roller coaster of unpredictable fluctuations, causing a Huntsman Chemical Corp. official to lament, "The problem facing the polymers and petrochemicals industry in the U.S. is unprecedented. Rome is burning." [11] In contrast PLA, made from a renewable resource, offered performance, price, environmental compatibility, high visibility, and therefore significant value to certain buyers for whom this configuration of product characteristics is important.

Consumers are growing increasingly concerned about chemicals in products. This provides market space for companies who supply "clean materials." NatureWorks' strategists knew, for example, that certain plastics were under increasing public scrutiny. Health concerns, especially those of women and children, have put plastics under suspicion in the United States and abroad. The European Union and Japan have instituted bans and regulatory frameworks on some commonly used plastics and related chemicals. Plastic softeners such as phthalates, among the most commonly used additives, have been labeled in studies as potential carcinogens and endocrine disruptors. Several common flame retardants in plastic can cause developmental disorders in laboratory mice. Studies have found plastics and related chemicals in mothers' breast milk and babies' umbilical cord blood samples. [12]

Consumer concern about chemicals and health opens new markets for "clean" materials designed from a sustainability innovation perspective. In addition, international regulations are accelerating growth in the market. In 1999, the European Union banned the use of phthalates in children's toys and teething rings and in 2003 banned some phthalates for use in cosmetics. States such as California have taken steps to warn consumers of the suspected risk of some phthalates. The European Union, California, and Maine banned the production or sale of products using certain polybrominated diphenyl ethers (PDBEs) as flame retardants. In 2006, the European Union was in the final phases of legislative directives to require registration and testing of nearly ten thousand chemicals of concern. The act, called Registration, Evaluation, Authorization, and Restriction of Chemicals (REACH), became law in 2007 and regulates the manufacture, import, marketing, and use of chemicals. All imports into Europe need to meet REACH information requirements for toxicity and health impacts. Companies are required to demonstrate that a substance does not adversely affect human health, and chemical property and safe use information must be communicated up and down supply chains to protect workers, consumers, and the environment.

All of these drivers contributed to the molecular thinking that generated NatureWorks' corn-based plastics. The volatility of oil prices, growing consumer concerns about plastics and health, waste disposal issues, and changing international regulations are among the systemic issues creating a new competitive arena in which bio-based products based on green chemistry design principles can be successfully introduced.

Given higher levels of consumer awareness in Europe and Japan, NatureWorks' plastic initially received more attention in the international market than in the United States. In 2004, IPER, an Italian food market, sold "natural food in natural packaging" (made with PLA) and attributed a 4 percent increase in deli sales to the green packaging. [13] NatureWorks established a strategic partnership with Amprica SpA in Castelbelforte, Italy, a major European manufacturer of thermoformed packaging for the bakery and convenience food markets. Amprica was moving ahead with plans to replace the plastics it used, including polyethelene terephthalate (PET), polyvinyl chloride (PVC), and polystyrene with the PLA polymer.

In response to the national phaseout and ultimate ban of petroleum-based shopping bags and disposable tableware in Taiwan, Wei-Mon Industry (WMI) signed an exclusive agreement with NatureWorks to promote and distribute packaging articles made with PLA. [14] In other markets, Giorgio Armani released men's dress suits made completely of PLA fiber and Sony sold PLA Discman and Walkman products in Japan. Due to growing concerns about the health impacts of some flame-retardant additives, NEC Corp. of Tokyo combined PLA with a natural fiber called kenaf to make an ecologically and biologically neutral flame-resistant bioplastic. [15]

The US market has been slower to embrace PLA, but Walmart's purchasing decisions may change that. In fact, NatureWorks' product solves several of Walmart's problems. Walmart has battled corporate image problems on several fronts—in its treatment of employees, as a contributor to "big box" sprawl, and in its practice of outsourcing, among others. Sourcing NatureWorks' bio-based, American-grown, corn-based plastic not only fits into Walmart's larger corporate "sustainability" effort but addresses US dependence on foreign oil and supports the American farmer.

The spectrum of entrepreneurial activities in the sustainable materials arena is wide. While some entrepreneurs are early entrants who are fundamentally reconfiguring product systems, others take more incremental steps toward adopting cleaner, innovative materials and processes. However, incremental changes can be radical when taken cumulatively, as long as one constantly looks ahead toward the larger goal.

Many companies, within the chemical industry and outside, now understand that cost reductions and product/process improvements are available through green chemistry and other environmental efficiency policies. Documented cost savings in materials input, waste streams, and energy use are readily available. In recognition of the efficiency gains to be realized, as well as risk reduction and regulatory advantages, most firms acknowledge the benefits that result from developing a strategy with these goals in mind. In addition, companies know they can help avoid the adverse effects of ignoring theses issues, such as boycotts and stockholders' resolutions that generate negative publicity.

However, the efficiency improvement and risk reduction sides of environmental concerns and sustainability are only the leading edge of the opportunities possible. Sustainability strategies and innovative practices go beyond incremental improvement to existing products. This future-oriented business strategy—geared toward new processes, products, technologies, and markets—offers profound prospects for competitive advantage over rival firms.

As the molecular links among the things we make and macrolevel issues such as health, energy independence, and climate change become more widely understood, companies that think strategically about the chemical nature of their products and processes will emerge as leaders. A "think like a molecule" approach to designing materials, products, and processes gives entrepreneurs and product designers an advantage.

- Invisible design considerations—for example, the design of molecular materials—must be factored into consideration of sustainability design.
- Green chemistry offers principles to guide chemical design and production.
- Thinking like a molecule opens new avenues for progress toward safer product innovation.

EXERCISE

1. Contact your local government and ask about chemical compounds from industrial and commercial activity that end up in the water and air. What are the government's major concerns? What are the sources of problematic chemicals? What is being done to reduce their release? Go to http://blog.epa.gov/blog/2010/12/17/tri or http://www.epa.gov/tri to read about the Toxic Release Inventory. Search the inventory for evidence of hazardous chemicals used in your area.

[1] Paul T. Anastas and John C. Warner, *Green Chemistry: Theory and Practice* (Oxford: Oxford University Press, 1998).

[2] Paul T. Anastas and John C. Warner, *Green Chemistry: Theory and Practice* (Oxford: Oxford University Press, 1998), 30.

[3] US Environmental Protection Agency, "Presidential Green Chemistry Challenge: Award Winners," last updated July 28, 2010, accessed December 3, 2010, http://www.epa.gov/greenchemistry/pubs/pgcc/past.html.

[4] The definition of E-factor is evolving at this writing. Currently pharmaceutical companies engaged in green chemistry are debating whether to include input factors such as energy, water, and other nontraditional inputs.

[5] US Environmental Protection Agency, "Presidential GC Challenge: Past Awards: 2006 Greener Synthetic Pathways Award," last updated June 21, 2010, accessed December 2, 2010, http://www.epa.gov/greenchemistry/pubs/pgcc/winners/gspa06.html.

[6] Stephen K. Ritter, "Green Challenge," *Chemical & Engineering News*, 80, no. 26 (2009): 30.

[7] Phone interview with Berkeley Cue, retired Pfizer executive, July 16, 2003.

[8] {Author's Name Retracted as requested by the work's original creator or licensee} and Karen O'Brien, from field interviews; untitled/unpublished manuscript, 2006.

[9] US Environmental Protection Agency, "Green Chemistry: Award Winners," accessed July 28, 2010, http://www.epa.gov/gcc/pubs/pgcc/past.html.

[10] Rick A. Relyeaa, "The Impact of Insecticides and Herbicides on the Biodiversity and Productivity of Aquatic Communities," *Ecological Applications* 15, no. 2 (2005): 618–27; Xiaomei Ma, Patricia A. Buffler, Robert B. Gunier, Gary Dahl, Martyn T. Smith, Kyndaron Reinier, and Peggy Reynolds, "Critical Windows of Exposure to Household Pesticides and Risk of Childhood Leukemia," *Environmental Health Perspectives* 110, no. 9 (2002): 955–60; Anne R. Greenlee, Tammy M. Ellis, and Richard L. Berg, "Low-Dose Agrochemicals and Lawn-Care Pesticides Induce Developmental Toxicity in Murine Preimplantation Embryos," *Environmental Health Perspectives* 112, no. 6 (2004): 703–9.

[11] Reference for Business, "SIC 2821: Plastic Materials and Resins," accessed January 10, 2011, http://www.referenceforbusiness.com/industries/Chemicals-Allied/Plastic-Materials-Resins.html.

[12] Sara Goodman, "Tests Find More Than 200 Chemicals in Newborn Umbilical Cord Blood," *Scientific American*, December 2, 2009, accessed January 10, 2011, http://www.scientificamerican.com/article.cfm?id=newborn-babies-chemicals-exposure-bpa; Éric Dewailly Dallaire, Gina Muckle, and Pierre Ayotte, "Time Trends of Persistent Organic Pollutants and Heavy Metals in Umbilical Cord Blood of Inuit Infants Born in Nunavik (Québec, Canada) between 1994 and 2001," *Environmental Health Perspectives* 36, no. 13 (2003):1660–64.

[13] Carol Radice, "Packaging Prowess," *Grocery Headquarters*, August 2, 2010, accessed January 10, 2011, http://www.groceryheadquarters.com/articles/2010-08-02/Packaging-prowess.

[14] NatureWorks LLC, "First Launch by Local Companies of Environmentally Friendly Paper & Pulp Products with NatureWorks PLA," June 9, 2006, accessed January 7, 2011, http://www.natureworksllc.com/news-and-events/press-releases/2006/6-9-06-wei-mon-extrusion-coated-paper-launch.aspx.

[15] "NEC Develops Flame-Resistant Bio-Plastic," *GreenBiz*, January 26, 2004, accessed December 2, 2010, http://www.greenbiz.com/news/news_third.cfm?NewsID= 26360.

4.4 Weak Ties

LEARNING OBJECTIVES

1. Understand the notion of weak ties.

2. Know how and why weak ties contribute to innovation.

Firms that carve out positions on the cutting edge of sustainable business share a common feature. They reach out to attract new information from nontraditional sources. Developing the capacity to seek, absorb, and shape changing competitive conditions with respect to human activity and natural systems through weak tie [1] cultivation holds a key to successful innovation. This is not surprising. Business success depends on continuous revitalization of strategic capabilities. Good strategy creates the future in which a company will succeed.

Not all individuals or companies can embrace change, however. In the past, revitalization of existing firms meant analysis of standard factors: competitors, market size and growth, product attributes, past consumer behavior, pricing strategies, and marketing programs. We suggest that limiting yourself to conventional analysis constrains strategic options.

To compete in the sustainability arena, companies must go beyond what has worked in the past and seek perspectives outside the historically assumed subset. We argue that incorporating rigorous sustainability analysis into your market positioning is likely to yield opportunities that can be keys to future success. What does this mean when it comes to environmental topics, opportunities in green chemistry applications, implementing sustainability principles in operations, and the myriad other environmental and health imperatives that fall under the term *sustainability*? It means developing what are called, in the academic literature on networks, **weak ties** with unconventional partners who provide you with increasingly essential strategic information. This does not mean that "the answer" will be easily found. It does mean that the net must be thrown wider to access information relevant to strategic success.

Sustainability innovation and entrepreneurship involves traveling across new ground. Imagine you will be accompanying the early nineteenth-century explorers Lewis and Clarke to explore the unfamiliar territory of the American West. You will be the first European Americans to chart a course from the eastern seaboard to the Pacific Ocean. The year is 1803, and there are very few maps of the American interior. The ones that exist are sketchy at best. How would you prepare for such a journey? You might talk to your friends and acquaintances to learn what they know about the terrain you'll be covering. To get the information necessary to survive this foray into the unknown, however, you would probably go outside your immediate circle to talk with trappers, Native Americans, French traders, natural scientists, and other voyagers—people from diverse walks of life. You would need to build new relationships, or *weak ties*, to access a wide range of people who will provide you with the necessary information to move forward.

These ties are called "weak" not because they lack substance or will disappoint you but because they lie outside the traditional network of relationships on which you or the company depends. Contrasting weak ties with "strong ties" highlights their unique characteristics. Strong ties, as a category of network relations, have immediate currency and often long-standing rich histories with extensive mutual exchange. An example in an established company would be an existing relationship with a funder or supplier; for a start-up, it may be someone with whom the company has a history of successful collaboration. Typically, strong ties are to people and organizations you see often and to which you frequently turn for input. In the case of large firms, important strong ties may be those formed between heads of independent business units within the same organization. Alternatively, they might be ties to reliable suppliers or even to the board of directors and the people with whom that group associates.

Research indicates, however, that the longer the duration of strong ties between two entities, the more similar the entities' perspectives are. People from the same circles tend to share the same pools of information. Under normal circumstances this is fine; we augment and reinforce each other's understanding of how the known world works. However, it is likely that information from strong ties will add only minimal value to the information you already possess. When we want to take action in an arena outside the familiar terrain, information from strong ties often proves insufficient. We would argue, moreover, that relying solely on strong ties can actually deprive you of information, thereby insulating you from potentially important emergent data and trends.

In contrast, weak ties bring new or previously marginal information to the forefront. They enable you to reach outside the normal boundaries of "relevant" strategic information. Weak ties trigger innovative thinking because they bring in fresh ideas—viewpoints likely to diverge from yours or from senior management's—and data otherwise overlooked or dismissed because they have not been a priority historically. Sometimes the most fruitful weak ties are to individuals or organizations previously considered to be your adversaries. Not surprisingly, the most innovative ideas for success may well come from those quarters most critical of how business has traditionally been done.

To successfully traverse the relatively unfamiliar territory of entrepreneurship and sustainability, you need to seek information from weak ties to access emergent perspectives and new scientific data that make what used to be peripheral issues—as many ecological and environmental health issues have been—now salient to strategic success. Perspectives gained from weak ties enable discerning companies to differentiate themselves and gain relative to their competitors. They can be formed with a range of individuals and organizations—including academics, consultants, nonprofit research institutes, government research organizations, and nongovernmental organizations (NGOs). The latter community is often business's harshest critic on environmental issues. It is for this reason that business is increasingly forming weak ties to NGOs to engage them in thinking strategically about solutions.

Toward this end, it is important to understand that the NGO community is not homogeneous. There is a spectrum of groups active on environmental and sustainability issues. They range from those that view business as antithetical to social and ecological concerns to those that seek partnership and joint solutions. Certainly any weak tie relationship requires due diligence and partnerships must be considered carefully, but there is a wealth of untapped expertise and stakeholder value that is potentially available to you.

The accounts that follow illustrate effective use of weak ties to help craft sustainability strategies. Home Depot's president Arthur Blank found new perspectives through weak ties by seeking input from NGOs critical of the company's old-growth forest purchasing practices prior to 1999. That year Home Depot, the largest home improvement retailer in the United States, was also the largest lumber retailer in the world, selling between 5 and 10 percent of the global market. The company recorded $38 billion in sales and over 200,000 employees in 930 stores. It also had been repeatedly voted "Most Admired Specialty Retailer."

Faced with negative publicity and store boycotts by activist groups, however, the company's openness to learning about alternative sourcing opportunities led to invitations to NGO representatives to meet with Home Depot's senior management. Those new contacts—and the information flows they facilitated—helped put Home Depot on a track and timetable for dramatically reducing and ultimately ending old-growth forest wood purchasing and store sales. Stated Arthur Blank at the time, "Our pledge to our customers, associates and stockholders is that Home Depot will stop selling wood products from environmentally sensitive areas. Home Depot embraces its responsibility as a global leader to help protect endangered forests. By the end of 2002, we will eliminate from our stores wood from endangered areas—including certain lauan, redwood and cedar products—and give preference to 'certified' wood." [2]

Certified wood is defined as lumber tracked from the forest, through manufacturing and distribution, to the customer to assure that harvesting the wood takes into account a balance of social, economic, and environmental factors. Home Depot's ultimate goal was to sell only products made from certified lumber, but initially only about 1 percent of timber available was certified. How was Home Depot's demand—let alone the industry's—going to be met? The answer was

that Home Depot's decision moved markets. Vendors were asked to dramatically increase their supplies of certified lumber, driving demand back through the supply chain to lumber companies that expanded their activity in sustainably managed forestry.

Evidence that companies are seeking new perspectives grows each year as firms expand their range of conversations about improved practices to citizens groups, environmental scientists, and even international experts from other countries and industries. These groups are outsiders—examples of weak ties—because historically they have not been sought for strategically relevant information. However, this pattern has increasingly been shared by companies for which market scanning processes were previously limited to competitor and narrowly conceived industry trend data.

As the larger picture of economic activity's impact on nature's life support systems and the quality of life becomes more important to business, these ties now serve as conduits for knowledge on how and where the company might improve its overall strategy and performance. The known link of deforestation to climate change and species extinction combine with the implication of raw material processing methods in ecological and human health threats and known mutations to require—for fiduciary reasons—that companies buying and selling lumber pay attention to these issues. Firms that actively seek new perspectives that may have a bearing on their business success going forward will have a distinct advantage over those whose efforts are minimal, poorly designed, or viewed as marketing "greenwash." Gaining true strategic leverage requires leadership. Home Depot was fortunate to have a leader with the broad intellect capable of seeing and implementing a wise path for the firm.

General Electric, Dell, and IKEA each pursued different types of weak ties. General Electric (GE) publicly announced the integration of environmental issues into product research and development (R&D) strategy and pursued weak ties to help develop strategy both by systematically contacting outside experts and by convening a series of gatherings of national experts and senior GE executives. In the process, GE unearthed previously unappreciated areas of technical innovation of great current and potential value to the company and launched a new corporate R&D strategy called "Ecomagination." Dell worked with some of its harshest NGO critics to understand the emerging perspectives on managing electronic waste. The NGO links were Dell's weak ties. This process of engagement not only helped Dell manage a public relations problem but—much to the company's surprise—created a profitable new secondary service business that differentiated Dell as an industry leader in managing electronic waste. In another example, IKEA searched for assistance in its effort to reorient strategy after being embarrassed by a product that failed to meet European environmental regulatory requirements. IKEA's weak tie to NGO consultant The Natural Step not only helped IKEA solve immediate product issues but helped fundamentally reorient company strategy on materials. IKEA's openness to new information played a role in differentiating the company and augmented its existing reputation for design and low cost. The following sections include accounts of these company's activities with lessons to be learned about profitably pursuing weak ties.

GE

In June 2005, GE CEO Jeff Immelt announced GE's new sustainability strategy, "Ecomagination," at a press event with Jonathan Lash, executive director of the environmental nonprofit organization World Resources Institute. Ecomagination, said Immelt, aims to "focus our unique energy, technology, manufacturing, and infrastructure capabilities to develop tomorrow's solutions such as solar energy, hybrid locomotives, fuel cells, lower-emission aircraft engines, lighter and stronger materials, efficient lighting, and water purification technology." [4]

Specifically, GE announced it would more than double its research investment in cleaner technologies, from $700 million in 2004 to $1.5 billion by 2010. GE also pledged to improve its own environmental performance by "reducing its greenhouse gas emissions 1% by 2012 and the intensity of its greenhouse gas emissions 30% by 2008, both compared to 2004 (based on the company's projected growth, GE says its emissions would have otherwise risen 40% by 2012 without further action)." [5]

GE's 2005 strategy was driven to a large degree by the cultivation of weak ties. Characteristic of many large firms active in eco-efficiency, GE had long viewed itself as a leader in environmental productivity improvements because it built energy-efficient airplane engines and other smaller systems and appliances that dramatically reduced resource and electricity use. However, these were design improvements that lacked the broader sweep of a systems view. To bring in new thinking and develop a new competitive stance, GE's senior management aggressively sought perspectives from atypical sources. [6]

The Ecomagination story begins in 2003 and 2004 when three-year strategic plans drawn up by GE's business unit CEOs were presented to corporate CEO Jeff Immelt. These

indicated market opportunities in green-friendly products across all the units. Core customers were asking for products designed to address escalating resource scarcity and pollution pressures. Clean water and clean energy featured prominently. At the same time, Immelt had received periodic inquiries publicly (in the form of shareholder petitions) and privately as to how GE would respond in an increasingly resource-constrained world. What was GE's position on environmental issues? Did it have a position?

A project to research the questions and trends was assigned and scoped out. GE assembled a team to interview thought leaders and experts outside the company in a variety of sectors. Academic experts in many fields, futurists, other business leaders, and leading NGOs were systematically interviewed as part of the information gathering that ultimately informed top management.

Through this process, topics were identified as relevant to GE's markets and offerings. In 2004, GE hosted by-invitation-only meetings of top GE decision makers and a subset of outside experts to look at trends in water and energy concerns five to ten years out. Major customers, the dozen top executives at GE including the CEO, and a select group of outside expert advisors were present at the meetings from beginning to end, an attendance record unusual in the corporate world. In total, over one hundred experts inside and outside GE were consulted, forty leading companies studied, and multiple internal GE seminars and brainstorming sessions convened to discuss megatrends influencing GE's future businesses.

As a result of this process, GE found that it was already seeing $10 billion annual revenues from existing green technologies and services. The relative value of this activity was unexpected. Rather than being something foreign or new, GE was already seeing high returns from existing green technology innovations. This perspective, when combined with the outside expert feedback on likely trends, confirmed for GE management that their efforts should be redoubled to generate revenues of at least $20 billion by 2010, with application of more aggressive targets thereafter.

Clean Edge, a research and advisory firm, estimated in 2006 that global markets for three of GE's identified technologies—wind power, solar photovoltaics, and fuel cells—would grow to more than $100 billion within 10 years, from some $16 billion in 2006. This figure did not include clean-water technologies, in which GE has also invested heavily. A previous study predicted that the market for world water treatment technologies will reach $35 billion by 2007. [7]

Weak ties influenced GE's strategy formation in a number of ways. First, the ties helped GE design metrics to measure the current and potential values of some of its "green" technologies. One of GE's weak ties was to GreenOrder, a New York–based consultancy specializing in sustainable business. According to GreenOrder, GE identified 17 products representing about $10 billion in annual sales as part of the Ecomagination platform on which it planned to build. In doing so, the company undertook intensive processes to identify and qualify current Ecomagination products, analyzing the environmental attributes of GE products relative to benchmarks such as competitors' best products, the installed base of products, regulatory standards, and historical performance. For each Ecomagination product, GE created an extensive "scorecard" quantifying the product's environmental attributes, impacts, and benefits relative to comparable products. [8] Doing this analysis was one of the key roles played by GreenOrder.

As a result of these metrics, GE's corporate Global Research Center doubled its R&D spending on Ecomagination products and associated services. Business units are required to focus on enhanced internal environmental performance *and* new product offerings. By October 2005, a senior vice president and officer of the corporation was appointed who reported directly to the CEO and took responsibility for the quantitative tracking of business units' progress to both "walk the talk" internally and drive new product ideas.

The firm's strategy change was driven by a historically unprecedented search for new information that used many weak ties to gain emerging perspectives and new science data. This process gave senior management a broader view of global resource trends and allowed the company to gauge how it could best leverage its assets and capabilities to both profit from and contribute to solutions.

In contrast to many firms that are low-key about their environmental activities (to avoid criticism of falling short of the ideal), Jeff Immelt put GE out on a limb. The company, already criticized for environmental transgressions such as that in the Hudson River, [9] will be held to a higher, self-defined standard. There is reasoned debate, moreover, on the "greenness" of some of the technologies that GE is putting forward (nuclear power, "clean" coal, etc.). No company with a brand as well known as GE's can afford to not deliver. Time will tell how successful GE's strategy will be, but suffice it to say that a company such as GE does not make such a significant and public move without a thoroughly reasoned strategy. The GE example shows the formative role that weak ties can play in a company's strategic transformation.

Dell

Next, we look at Dell. The article read, "Las Vegas, Nevada, January 9, 2002, environmentalists dressed in prison uniforms circled a collection of dusty computers outside the Consumer Electronics Show…to protest Dell Computer's use of inmates to recycle computers. 'I lost my job. I robbed a store. Went to jail. I got my job back,' chanted five mock prisoners wearing 'Dell Recycling Team' signs and linked by chains. While Dell's executives gathered at the huge electronics convention, the 'high-tech chain gang,' members of the Silicon Valley Toxics Coalition, attracted a small crowd outside." [10] Dell executives were understandably embarrassed by this incident. The assumption inside the company was that the company was doing what it reasonably could do about product recycling—a thorn in the paw of the industry lion. However, this public relations fiasco drew attention to an issue that no one in the industry was adequately addressing: electronic waste is a burgeoning problem that, if not dealt with, would come back to all players in the industry.

Disposal of electronic products represents one of the fastest growing industrial waste streams. Roughly one thousand hazardous materials used in manufacturing personal computers alone pose problems of human exposure to heavy metals, drinking water contamination, and air quality problems. With the rapid retirement of old models, a staggering volume of computers and other electronic equipment now migrates around the world. Only a small fraction goes to reuse programs. The majority are shipped to landfills and incinerators, or sent as waste to foreign countries. In response to the public health threats from hazardous materials in electronics waste streams, the European Union, Japan, China, and states within the United States are regulating electronic waste. One such regulation in the European Union is the Restrictions on Hazardous Substances in Electrical and Electronic Equipment. [11] "Product take-back" laws—and the threat of more such regulations in the future—are stimulating companies to experiment with a variety of means to take back and reuse products. (See the sidebar in this section.) Whether you agree or disagree with these actions, they are one of many drivers of sustainability strategies today:

Dell is one of the largest personal computer manufacturers in the world. It is an information technology supplier and partner and sells a comprehensive portfolio of products and services directly to customers worldwide. Dell dealt with a US government contractor, UNICOR, which employed prison inmates to recycle outdated computers. The justification was cost; since recycling products was assumed to be a net cost to the company, efforts were made to cut associated expenses.

In February 2002, the Basel Action Network released an alarming report about end-of-life electronics exported and dumped in Asia. The report, "Exporting Harm: The High-Tech Trashing of Asia," focused a significant amount of media and NGO attention on what computer manufacturers were doing to offer customers options for responsible electronics disposal. Later that year, the Computer Take-Back Coalition launched its "Toxic Dude" website, targeting Dell for not doing enough on computer recycling and reuse. Socially responsible investors (SRIs) and a variety of NGOs, including the aforementioned Silicon Valley Toxics Coalition and the Texas Campaign for the Environment, increased pressure on Dell to do more about electronic waste issues.

Following the prison-garbed protest, Dell began engaging in frequent conversations with these and other NGOs. These were Dell's weak ties—new sources of information outside the company. Dell found that having conversations with these groups helped the company create a more strategically astute direction for its product end-of-life programs. Dell, a relatively young company that had grown rapidly, had not previously formed relationships with health and environmental NGOs. Through these conversations, Dell fundamentally reconfigured its recycling and reuse services for customers. As a leader in supply-chain management, productivity, and efficiency, the company designed an "asset recovery" program for end-of-life products—a program that would maximize quality and minimize costs for its recycling programs. Much to Dell's surprise, the program not only minimized cost but generated value while also enhancing Dell's brand and reputation as a responsible corporate citizen.

Early in 2003, Dell restructured its recycling program to make it easier for users and more proactive for the company. The "Dell Recycling" program was simplified and made more visible to customers. The company launched a national recycling tour consisting of one-day no-cost computer recycling events in cities across the country, with the objective of raising consumer awareness of computer recycling issues and solutions. When Dell first offered printers among its array of products, the company included free recycling of old printers. Ongoing discussions with NGOs informed the approaches chosen.

In late 2003 Dell broadened its national network of approved recyclers by partnering with two private companies to support its environmental programs for retiring, disassembling, reusing, and recycling obsolete computer equipment. Dell discontinued its partnership with UNICOR. These changes helped Dell grow its environmental programs more quickly and efficiently, improve the economics and convenience for customers, and properly dispose of customers' old systems with minimal environmental or health impact. Moreover, the company began to see value in reclaiming assets rather than just costs in disposing of waste, a fundamental reorientation that would not have been possible without the weak ties that helped the company rethink its relationship with waste.

Tod Arbogast, who led Dell's sustainable business efforts, stated,

> The early discussions we had with NGOs and SRIs led to brainstorming sessions both within the company and with these stakeholders. Stakeholder input helped shape what we are doing now and it continues to be a valuable dialogue to this day. We came to realize that we could meet both our business objectives as well as the environmental goals we were being asked to adopt with new product recovery services offered to our customers. For example, our product recovery programs for our business customers have both helped grow the amount of used computers we are recovering and have become profitable. We've taken this same focus of meeting both sustainability and business goals into many areas since then including workplace conditions in our supply chain, chemical use policies and regular transparent reporting on all of these efforts to a broad set of external stakeholders. Connecting our sustainability objectives to our business objectives helps us get a broader set of internal colleagues supporting our efforts and helps us continue to expand our sustainability programs. [13]

By engaging with vocal critics and environmental advocates and having open and honest dialogue with NGOs, the company effectively improved its end-of-life disposal offers by making them easier, more affordable, and more visible to customers. Dell was able to reach outside the company to get the additional information it needed to make this possible. By learning from the feedback it received and adjusting several of its tactics for raising awareness among consumers about responsible computer recycling, Dell created what is today one of the industry's most aggressive and comprehensive recycling offers. In addition to the positive brand enhancement that came with having an environmentally responsible business offer, Dell also gained from showing customers that it could manage the entire life cycle of its technology equipment.

The story of electronics waste is not over. Dell and other leading companies are under intense scrutiny by NGOs to fulfill their commitments on waste management and toxics issues. Moreover, as a society, we still have a long way to go. To inspire more corporate action, in 2005, Calvert Investments and other SRIs filed shareholder resolutions with six computer companies, asking them to begin planning for recycling and take-back. As a result, Dell was the first US computer company to commit to setting recycling and take-back goals for personal computers.

IKEA

Global home furnishings retailer IKEA was stunned by claims in the 1990s that one of its most popular products—the Billy bookcase—was off-gassing formaldehyde at levels above German government safety standards. The resulting crisis for this company led to IKEA's search for ways to prevent such an issue from happening in the future. After talking with different environmental groups and receiving much criticism but little concrete direction, IKEA turned to The Natural Step (TNS), an environmental educational organization headquartered in Stockholm, Sweden. Karl Henrik Robèrt, founder of TNS and an oncologist who became an environmental health activist due to children's inexplicably rising cancer rates, was repeatedly invited to talk with IKEA's senior management team and train them in TNS process. By teaching the group about overlooked market conditions that would increasingly impinge on IKEA's worldwide practices, Robèrt catalyzed the group to commit to the first step of designing a green furniture line offering—and this weak tie ultimately helped IKEA develop its overarching sustainability strategy.

The task of "fixing" the company after its regulatory embarrassment seemed enormous to senior executives at the time. But the basic environmental education and criteria for designing both products and strategy offered by TNS educational framework allowed the senior executives to see a path forward. The major learning point is that without seeking outside perspectives from the very groups that had been most critical of the corporation, IKEA would not have found Dr. Robèrt and TNS ideas that were eventually integrated into the company's strategy.

Working with Robèrt helped IKEA leaders see their industry from the outside; thereafter, they viewed steps transitioning toward "sustainable business" as noncontroversial. IKEA leaders were simply adapting to new scientific and health research data and integrating that data with their strategic choices. In their earliest experience with TNS, that meant certain chemicals known to be toxic to cells (causing cell mutation) would not be used in any production steps required to make residential household furniture. The

solution of removing unsafe materials fit with IKEA's corporate purpose of improving the lives of its customers.

The first concrete product that resulted from this solution was IKEA's "eco-furniture" line, but the perspectives on materials and IKEA's strategic positioning went far beyond one product line. IKEA continued to set some of the highest environmental strategy standards in the industry. As one of the first adopters of sustainability standards, IKEA has set the bar that others seek to match. The company's initial corporate environmental action plan was called Green Steps, which was based on four intended actions/conditions posed in the form of questions:

1. Is the company systematically reducing its dependency on mining and nonrenewable sources?
2. Is the company reducing the use of long-lasting, unnatural substances?
3. Is the company reducing its encroachment on nature and its functions?
4. Is the company reducing unnecessary use of resources?

To ensure this policy is followed, IKEA trains all employees and regularly provides them with clear and up-to-date environmental information. The company also established an internal Environment Council, and all business plans and reports describe environmental measures and costs pertaining to the Green Steps.

IKEA does not manufacture its own products but instead commands a large international supply chain. The IKEA Group has nearly 220 stores in 33 countries. Nearly 1,600 suppliers manufacture products for IKEA. IKEA's purchasing is carried out through 43 trading service offices around the world. IKEA mainly sources from European countries, but purchases from developing countries and countries in transition are rapidly increasing. A limited part of the supply comes from the industrial group of IKEA, Swedwood, which has 35 factories in 9 countries.

IKEA has taken steps to work with and educate current and potential suppliers on its environmental specifications and expectations. In this way, the company is shifting the industry standards, as captured in "The IKEA Way on Purchasing Home Furnishing Products" (IWAY). This guiding document supports the IKEA vision and business idea, outlining in great detail its expectations and procedures for suppliers. IWAY is administered and monitored by IKEA of Sweden Trading Services Office and by a global compliance group. [14]

IKEA has won many environmental business awards and is a leader in setting high standards for its products, particularly environmental standards. As one of the early adopters of a green strategic approach to how it conducts business, IKEA now enjoys brand recognition as the company that not only sells low cost, well-designed home furnishings but clean and safe products as well.

These examples illustrate senior managers responding to a changing business environment by establishing weak ties to outsiders who provide content on a new strategic direction for the company. These managers took advice from sources considered unconventional—even threatening—and used it for their companies' financial and strategic gain. In these cases, we see three types of weak ties: to professional experts, to NGOs, and to an environmental educational organization.

There is no way to predict what outside source will offer weak tie benefits to your venture. However, a good way to find such sources is to identify the pool of weak ties from among your insider strong-tie group to relevant outsider voices. As noted, environmental groups and other NGOs are not homogeneous; some are more willing and able to work with entrepreneurs and companies than others. Certain leaders and their organizations are well established and widely respected. You need to research the topics that represent opportunities for your venture and then identify individuals and organizations with whom conversation may be fruitful. Ideally, you want to initiate weak tie

conversations with individuals and groups aligned with sustainability solutions who do not take issue with your proposed or existing practices. You need a set of weak ties willing to join with you over time to help inform strategy.

In summary, if entrepreneurs do not seek outsider perspectives on the shifting state of the competitive game, they will be blinded to forces that hold, in some cases, the overnight potential to undermine the venture's efforts. On the positive side, access to emergent perspectives and new scientific data on sustainability issues holds promise of strategic advantage. Access to this information enables discerning entrepreneurs to gain relative to competitors

because information flows from weak ties bring tighter cohesion between a firm's strategic thinking and the shifting conditions that shape market opportunities. Weak ties are a bridge to innovation, competitive differentiation, and new market opportunities. [15] Using weak ties for sustainability innovation can be understood as a parallel to adaptation in biology. As the complexity of business decisions and market dynamics grows, the effective use of weak ties can mean the difference between learning and not learning, at the individual, corporate, and supply-chain levels. We would argue that in the twenty-first century, it is essential to seek better information drawn from wider sources logically linked to a firm's social and environmental footprint to adapt intelligently.

KEY TAKEAWAYS

- Incorporating sustainability considerations into business requires reaching out beyond conventional sources of business information.
- Entrepreneurs and businesses that tap into weak tie relationships around sustainability concerns can use them to find new ideas for products and services.
- Adaptation to the new business conditions in which environmental, health, and community concerns have become more important requires cultivation of weak ties.

EXERCISE

1. Identify a business you would like to create. What health, community, and environmental concerns might emerge as you imagine building your firm? Where would you turn for advice and information to anticipate how you should respond? Why?

---

[1] Mark Granovetter, "The Strength of Weak Ties," *American Journal of Sociology* 78, no. 6 (1973): 1360–80.
[2] CBC News, "Home Depot Going Green," November 10, 2000, accessed January 7, 2011, http://www.cbc.ca/money/story/1999/08/27/homedepot990827.html.
[3] Home Depot, "Wood Purchasing," accessed March 16, 2011, http://corporate.homedepot.com/wps/portal/Wood_Purchasing.
[4] Joel Makower, "'Ecomagination': Inside GE's Power Play," *GreenBiz*, May 10, 2005, accessed December 3, 2010, http://www.greenbiz.com/news/columns_third.cfm?NewsID=28061.
[5] Joel Makower, "'Ecomagination': Inside GE's Power Play," *GreenBiz*, May 10, 2005, accessed December 3, 2010, http://www.greenbiz.com/news/columns_third.cfm?NewsID=28061.
[6] Thanks to Jon Freedman at GE Water, formerly with GE corporate marketing and a leader in the Ecomagination policy development process, for information about GE's activity.

[7] Joel Makower, "'Ecomagination': Inside GE's Power Play," *GreenBiz*, May 10, 2005, accessed December 3, 2010, http://www.greenbiz.com/news/columns_third.cfm?NewsID=28061.

[8] Joel Makower, "'Ecomagination': Inside GE's Power Play," *GreenBiz*, May 10, 2005, accessed December 3, 2010, http://www.greenbiz.com/news/columns_third.cfm?NewsID=28061.

[9] In 2002 the EPA decided to dredge 2.65 million cubic yards of sediment—enough dirt to fill an area the size of ten football fields to a height of 145 feet—which is expected to cost GE about $460 million. The dredging is aimed at removing polychlorinated biphenyls (PCBs) dumped into the river from GE plants in Hudson Falls, New York, and Fort Edward, New York, from 1947 to 1977, before PCB use was banned. Deborah Brunswick, "EPA: Hudson River Dredging Delayed," *CNNMoney*, July 26, 2008, accessed December 3, 2010, http://money.cnn.com/2006/07/28/news/companies/hudson_river.

[10] Janelle Carter, "Senate Rejects Felon Vote Bid," *Associated Press*, February 15, 2002, accessed December 10, 2011, http://www.sjcite.info/prison.html.

[11] NetRegs, "Restriction Of Hazardous Substances in Electrical and Electronic Equipment (RoHS)," last updated October 15, 2010, accessed December 3, 2010, http://www.netregs.gov.uk/netregs/63025.aspx.

[12] Proposal for a Directive of the European Parliament and of the Council on Waste Electrical and Electronic Equipment and on the restriction of the use of certain hazardous substances in electrical and electronic equipment. European Commission, "Recast of the WEEE and RoHS Directives proposed," COM (2000), accessed March 16, 2011, http://ec.europa.eu/environment/waste/weee_index.htm.

[13] Tod Arbobast, interview by author in preparation of book manuscript, summer 2006.

[14] "IKEA & the Environment—An Interview with Anders Berglund," *EarthShare Washington*, accessed December 3, 2010, http://www.esw.org/giving/ikea.html.

[15] This discussion draws on the work of Mark Granovetter, "The Strength of Weak Ties: A Network Theory Revisited," *Sociological Theory* 1 (1983): 201–33, accessed March 7, 2011, http://www.si.umich.edu/~rfrost/courses/SI110/readings/In_Out_and_Beyond/Granovetter.pdf.

4.5 Adaptive Collaboration through Value-Added Networks

LEARNING OBJECTIVES

1. Understand how implementation is carried out.

2. Learn about collaborative processes for adaptation and innovation.

Value-added networks (VANs) are necessary to implement sustainability innovation strategies; VANs provide the horsepower to implement projects and are the means to translate your strategic vision into competitive products or services. VANs are action oriented and results driven.

VANs are distinct from weak ties. The primary contribution of weak ties is new and diverse information that links strategy more coherently with broader systemic forces. Weak ties bridge the corporation to the "outside" world's events and stakeholders. In contrast, VANs are composed of closer and stronger ties within your firm and its inner circle of collaborators. They are ties that can be intentionally and strategically joined to add value throughout the implementation process. Weak ties also differ from VANs in that they might be critics or even opponents of your company. The purpose of weak ties is information access beyond the known and the predictable, while the purpose of VANs is to take action. Weak ties serve an essential role for bringing creative alternative perspectives to the business at the options generation stage. VANs enable adaptive collaboration.

VANs can offer a wealth of creativity in the implementation process. VANs can be familiar faces in your backyard, or they might include suppliers or customers. They are an untapped, underappreciated resource for implementation ideas, feedback, and adaption as a plan is implemented. Rarely do company executives directly create and monitor

VANs. More often they create the circumstances and culture that allow VANs to form and the protection and incentives for them to be effective. Our research indicates that where sustainability innovation strategies are successfully implemented, a group had come together with sufficient senior backing and the skills, resources, and authority to drive the project forward. It should perhaps go without saying that VANs tend to be more successful in implementing sustainability innovations in companies already open to change and known to be culturally innovative.

Membership in VANs can be formal or informal. If sustainability goals have been embraced by a company, the process might be more formal. If sustainability is being explored by only a subset of the firm, but resources and legitimacy are present, the process may be more organic. Sometimes all that is lacking to catalyze a VAN is the context for the right question, for example, asking a long-standing supplier, "Can we do this better if we integrate environmental/sustainability attributes?" When asked to provide greener, more benign materials, a supplier replied to one of the managers interviewed for this book, "Yes, sure, we can do that. You just never asked before." In this situation, the collaborative VAN simply emerged, its leaders and other participants identifying themselves by stepping forward once the space is created for them to act and flourish.

VANs are often informal structures; they are interwoven in and under the firm's formal administrative and functional hierarchies. However VANs are structured for a firm's circumstances, there are certain things entrepreneurs and managers can do to provide conditions conducive to innovation. First, incentives for innovation and experimentation must be part of the picture. Making it safe to experiment is another essential element, as is fostering a culture where "there are no dumb questions" or "issues off the table." Creating special, finite committees or advisory panels may be an effective approach for your context; if it is, be sure you reward members for their participation.

The VANs discussed here are the sets of relationships mobilized around sustainability innovation that contribute specific resources to converting ideas into action. In short, VANs are your nearest and best resource for inspiration, input, and feedback on how you can improve what you do and for practical ideas on how to implement and modify sustainability practices.

The examples that follow illustrate companies and individuals able to implement sustainability strategies by drawing knowledge and resources from VANs. Walden Paddlers' VAN, under the direction of the entrepreneur-founder, illustrates that organizational boundaries—and as we will discuss, even the existence of an organization in some instances—are irrelevant to successful implementation. This example may seem odd to those unfamiliar with the rise of virtual organizations and virtual companies since the 1990s. The Walden Paddlers example is a powerful way of showing the effectiveness of determined efforts to employ VANs to implement sustainability strategy visions regardless of organizational structure.

Moreover, VANs can serve to implement strategy in diverse settings: Walden Paddlers was a fledgling enterprise and United Technologies Corporation (UTC) an established, multibillion-dollar global company. Walden had no existing procedures; UTC has decades of established operations procedures. Walden makes recreational kayaks; UTC makes massive industrial products. The companies have very different circumstances yet use similar strategies and tactics.

Walden illustrates how a sustainability innovation vision can create and mobilize a network and resources around cutting-edge product innovations. Perhaps because sustainability goals can resonate strongly with the values of contributors, VANs can build a distinct energy and momentum. The vision defined by sustainability objectives acts like an extra lift under a VAN's wings. The UTC example shows how VANs form between innovators across functionalities. To

borrow from UTC's experience: *work with innovators in other fields*. Differentiation is a moving target; your VAN can help you stay on top of it and continually redefine it.

There will always be pessimists, the lazy, the comfortable, and people whose income depends on continuing the existing way of doing business. These are not the people you want in your VANs. Their attitude is "no," and they bring imaginations to match. Entrepreneur Paul Farrow's launch, successful growth, and ultimate sale of Walden Paddlers provide an unusual illustration of building a VAN to successfully implement strategy. All new initiatives and fledgling enterprises are start-ups and need to recruit resource- and information-rich participants by building lateral networks. In most companies, implementing sustainability strategy will, to a certain extent, constitute a deviation from the norm because it represents a new activity with all the characteristics of entrepreneurial initiatives. This means creating networks of like-minded others who understand and rally behind a powerful vision.

This account provides the core steps that enabled this VAN to succeed. Grit and determination to proceed despite hearing repeated discouraging feedback is part of the process. VANs share this with any innovation process, but remember that strategy that incorporates sustainability values into the core represents a larger and more far-reaching innovation of knowledge and meaning than a new product alone.

Walden Paddlers

Walden Paddlers represented a sustainability-oriented company from its inception. Paul Farrow built his company and core VAN from scratch. One day, on vacation in Maine, he made a back-of-the-envelope calculation that the economics of recycled plastics made into recreational kayaks was a market opportunity—thirty-five pounds of forty cents per pound of plastic sold for more than four hundred dollars at retail. Farrow saw the possibility for a higher quality product at a lower price to the user, and a profitable company. The question he pondered was whether he could create a new market space for kayaks made from used milk bottles. All he knew at that point was that he had a business idea worth exploring. He knew nothing about kayaks (except enjoying them for recreation) or recycled plastic, but he did know a little about plastics manufacturing.

The project began as many sustainability initiatives do. He talked with people he expected to understand his vision, experts in plastics and material science. He was summarily informed by materials specialists from preeminent Boston-area academic establishments that no one could make high-performance plastic for recreational kayaks from recycled materials. It was common knowledge; the composition of recycled plastics made it impossible. The recycled resins, appropriate for downscaling into speed bumps or perhaps waste cans, would not yield high-performance, aesthetically attractive kayak hulls. Furthermore, the industry lacked equipment to handle the new material and specifications. In conclusion, it could not be done.

Challenging the received wisdom of experts requires reaching beyond them to more open-minded fellow travelers, those with less invested in existing knowledge, objectives, and methods. With only his aspiration of earning a living doing something he believed in and that would help protect the natural environment, and a vague picture of using recycled resins to create a kayak of some sort (for a market that might or might not exist), Paul Farrow kept talking to people about his idea and gathering data. He sought the advice of materials science experts who *would* take his ideas seriously. He conducted research on the prospective customer segment and communicated through his extended family and network of friends that he had this crazy idea. In the process, he found a few receptive individuals who were willing to talk with him and consider the possibilities.

Your VAN can take form from unexpected locations. Reminded by his wife that he had a brother-in-law attending Rensselaer Polytechnic Institute in New York state, Farrow made some phone calls. His brother-in-law had taken a course on materials with a nationally known professor. Through persistence, several phone calls later Farrow connected with the professor, who had recently started a company with one of his former engineering students, Jeff Allott. Allott, now a product designer for the company General Composites, was coincidentally a paddle sports enthusiast and was intrigued by Farrow's plan. Allott was also anticipating that the company's government contracts would taper off in the near future, and General Composites needed to diversify. Moreover, Allott liked the notion of designing an unprecedented material that the experts had deemed impossible to create. Why not create a high-performance, aesthetically attractive, inexpensive recreational kayak from recycled milk bottles? Why can't positive expectations for health, ecology, community, and financial gains be optimized simultaneously?

This was a typical entrepreneurial endeavor during which Farrow repeatedly heard "no" in response to his questions Eventually he received a "maybe" from a more imaginative individual who could see the new market space. The pattern of "no" and a few "maybes" repeated itself with manufacturers, national retailers, distributors, and

component suppliers. From his innumerable rejections, Farrow had collected valuable information about how to implement his vision that he used to refine and recalibrate his plan. In this learning process Farrow's VAN identified itself in a self-selection, self-organizing fashion typical of new enterprises.

Each node in the network was a person with close knowledge about how to implement the proposal. Each suggested ways forward and was willing to collaborate with untested strategy, design protocols, product ideas, and market segment definitions that had unknown but possibly significant returns. Farrow also tapped into each individual's sense of competitive challenge, fun, and creativity posed by accomplishing something the so-called experts said was impossible. The results of the process were a set of innovations, an award-winning kayak, and a profitable company.

This story teaches the necessity of carefully selecting VAN participants whose goals are aligned with yours. The first manufacturer to sign on was Hardigg Industries. Its manufacturing manager was curious about working with the new recycled plastic resins and driven by the economic pressure of unused plant capacity. This seasoned manager was also interested in the prospect of a growing a new customer base in recycled plastic molding. In fact, Hardigg's management was so motivated to try new approaches in recycled plastics that it contributed capital to the start-up by agreeing to generous terms that acknowledged the start-up's cash-strapped condition. Hardigg invested $200,000 in new equipment and drew up a flexible, informal contract based on shared returns and aligned future interests should the venture take off.

The start-up's next phase illustrates how sustainability innovations are created. Extensive experimentation with different plastic compounds and resin colors followed. There were adjustments to the equipment to modulate temperatures and vary cooling times and methods. Farrow, along with the manufacturer and the designer, spent many hours testing, analyzing, discussing, and retesting. It was a microcosm of any implementation situation characterized by innovation and entrepreneurial process: learn as you go, draw from the creativity and imagination of your partners, collaborate, adapt and incorporate new knowledge along the way, and allow the feedback and events to shape the path and even the destination.

Entrepreneurs need to keep searching for allies to fill in the VAN gaps. The right mix of recycled plastic had to be developed to match the materials specifications of the product and the high heat demands of the molding equipment. Turned down by multiple plastic recyclers, Farrow finally found a Connecticut recycler who was trying to build his business and had a reputation for being open to new ideas. That recycler joined the emerging VAN and experimented with different collected plastics, testing a variety of pellets for melt consistency, texture, and color. More weeks of prototype experimentation unfolded, involving Paul Farrow, Jeff Allott, the recycler, and the head of manufacturing at Hardigg designing and redesigning incrementally but ultimately successfully to produce the first kayak.

Now Farrow had to address how to sell the kayak. What was the least expensive and most leveraged way to test the market? Attracted to the idea of selling more environmentally responsible kayaks, leading national sports equipment retailers were open to Farrow's product ideas. Through extensive discussions with retailers like REI, Eastern Mountain Sports, L. L. Bean, and others emerged optimal pricing strategies at wholesale and retail, creative in-store marketing, and colorful packaging for the customer to protect the kayak when it is placed on a vehicle roof rack. In other words, the collaborative retailers literally told Farrow what decisions to make on pricing, marketing, and packaging to optimize sales.

A successful VAN process will elicit energy and initiative from those self-selected to be involved because they know that business, the environment, and communities are not separate. Explicit sustainability strategies attract committed people and release their creativity. Dale Vetter, an operations expert and Farrow's friend and former business colleague, was drawn into the business bringing operating skills that complemented Farrow's finance know-how and general management experience. Vetter's creative redesign of the transport system that moved the kayaks from the manufacturer to Walden's tiny warehouse and office headquarters outside Boston resulted in dramatically improved logistics efficiencies and reduced labor costs. The kayak seat supplier was persuaded by Farrow and Vetter to take back its packaging, ultimately saving itself money when it discovered a method to recycle its packaging materials. This allowed Walden to avoid expensive Boston-area waste disposal fees.

Farrow has downplayed the challenges of creating his company, yet in its time Walden Paddlers implemented an early model of sustainability innovation that functioned under an innovative corporate structure. The company was one of the earliest documented virtual corporations [1] and continued to innovate in materials, product design,

transportation system, vendor relations, and wholesale buyer collaborations. Farrow was a sincere, informed, and modest yet passionate catalyst. Each VAN participant got hooked on his vision, and Farrow worked to ensure their economic interests were aligned. Both vision and potential returns were critical.

VAN participants, along with Farrow, heard discouraging comments throughout the start-up's early stages. Farrow laughed as he said, "You have to get used to hearing 'no.' Your attitude has to be, 'so what'? So you hear 'no' repeatedly." [2] Farrow's casual way of talking about the implementation process masked his determination, persistence, and willingness to learn and adapt and to compromise when economic necessity required. The perfect would not shut out the good. His attitude was contagious and created the required commitment to make this idea fly. He commented on the people who said "no" to him: "Those people just have less imagination. But those aren't the ones you want to work with. Do people think I'm a little odd in my passion for the vision? Sure, but you keep talking to people until you find the right partners who believe and will work hard to make the impossible happen."

The Walden Paddlers case shows how you may need to create and inspire your VAN while you are on the journey. If there are no precedents, the VAN literally creates what it is doing as it goes forward. Farrow had only one of the requirements needed to build a company: a vague idea backed by some rough financial calculations. He needed a materials specialist to design the first kayak from recycled plastic because he knew nothing about designing kayaks and even less about materials science. He needed manufacturers with knowledge of molding equipment. He needed operations capability, administrative processes for health benefits and hiring, transportation services, and retail and wholesale outlets. Yet within eight years he had built a virtual corporation before "virtual" or "network" organizations were recognized as legitimate forms for business. He defied conventional wisdom on materials design and sold high-performance, aesthetically attractive, 100 percent recycled and recyclable recreational kayaks through nationally known retailer chains. In addition, he sold his company at an undisclosed price, gave himself time off to build a vacation home with his wife and three sons, then took on a new corporate sustainability challenge with a small, growing company. How did he do it? It was important that he didn't accept the notion that his vision could not be realized. He formed his VAN of like-minded others and together they made it real.

What else can we learn from this case? Farrow questioned the conventional business wisdom—a common practice among entrepreneurial individuals. Their commitment to the unproven premise can be intense, and they may seem as though they *will* vision into action and results. However, implementation needs and invites collaborators.

Another lesson from the Walden Paddlers' example is that it took patience to allow solutions to emerge and evolve from the network participants' contributions. All participants had to be open to learning and finding the right "partners" willing to go outside their comfort and expertise zones to invest time and resources in a new idea. Don't be surprised if it takes time to find willing partners. There are too many strong influences at work that cause people and firms to be insular.

Finally, you don't need extensive resources, just enough to get to the next step. At every stage, the VAN became more closely aligned, tapping into its growing collective wisdom, imagination, and resources. The most underrated resource for breakthrough ideas might be the network of people you already know inside your firm or the network you can build outside through your company's supplier and customer relationships.

Creativity and imagination drawn from people who initially may be considered outsiders can be pivotal to a company's success. These individuals and their institutions can come to have a strong stake in the outcome, and they have the knowledge to generate paths forward that otherwise would remain latent. In Paul Farrow's case, there were no vertically integrated functions; he was building from the ground up. Within an established firm, some functional activities in the VAN are typically incorporated into the formal boundaries of the organization (e.g., design, product development, manufacturing, marketing, sales). Others lie outside with suppliers and buyers or other key allies. Implementation requires you to ignore conventional corporate boundaries and view the VAN as a lateral web of information and material flows through which ideas and resources can be mobilized. There is no reason not to tap into this potential power.

United Technologies Corporation

United Technologies Corporation (UTC), despite its large size and dominance in mature markets with mature products, remains remarkably innovative, including its leadership in sustainability strategy. In the 1990s, UTC CEO George David announced the company's goal of reducing its environmental footprint by a factor of ten. Explicitly committed to sustainability from the top, UTC was ahead of its time for an aerospace and building products and services firm. Management has since driven resource use efficiency programs through the business units and transitioned into new product designs that provide the power and performance people want for vehicles and operations while delivering on sustainability's positive health, ecological, and overall natural system robustness agenda.

Its disciplined process of bringing innovative ideas to market explains UTC's success over the years. The keys to UTC's success were highly motivated VANs formed across business units and with outside customers and supply-chain participants that drove the new ideas to successful commercialization. These VANs are at the leading edge of solving problems with technology and market receptivity and are characterized by creative and innovative participants who bring extra dedication to sustainability ideas.

The company's alternative power products business unit, UTC Power, faced a challenge, however. UTC's goal for that unit was to shift the market paradigm for power generation in stationary applications and transportation. The issues for large power consumers are straightforward. Customers want energy efficiency and reliability, lower bills, and protection from grid outages. They need system *resiliency* to assure ongoing operations and customer satisfaction in case of weather or other disruptions. For example, supermarket chains, hotels, and hospitals experienced the impact of Hurricane Katrina and the human and financial losses when their doors had to be closed.

UTC Power has a portfolio of solutions that offers power generation solutions in a variety of new technology combinations. However, when you are working with new products and new markets, a paradigm shift requires extraordinary effort. In UTC Power's case, you see examples that build on the company's competencies in technology innovation and management of massive supply chains to form VANs with more creativity than the norm. Jan van Dokkum, president of the UTC Power business, described the unique VAN situation as follows: "We carefully analyze the market for opportunities to improve emissions and efficiency. We then work closely with UTRC [UTC Research Center], buy standard, volume-produced equipment, optimize the system, and, finally, work with the customer to deliver high levels of service." [3]

UTC's PureComfort heating and cooling energy system is a good example. The PureComfort system offers the customer three features in one: electrical power, heating, and cooling. The system operates either off the electrical grid or connected to it and thus can serve as a cheaper and more reliable ongoing operating power source, even when the grid goes out. Highly motivated existing VANs at UTC drive conventional products and markets effectively, but for a new product and new markets plus a sustainability focused change, there are extra drivers, particularly once the product goes to market. The PureComfort system project began under the leadership of the corporate UTRC, working with autonomous business units Carrier and UTC Power. The group brainstormed combining their expertise to produce new products for new markets. They looked for ways to improve building system efficiencies by using the "waste" from power generating equipment (e.g., microturbines or reciprocating engines) as a "fuel" for heating and cooling equipment. They collected the hot exhaust from the supplier-produced microturbines and ran it to a Carrier double-effect absorption chiller, which produces hot and cool water. They found the flow rate temperature ideal to generate cold or hot water, thus creating three-in-one equipment producing on-site electricity, hot water, and cold water for refrigeration.

The A&P supermarket chain installed a PureComfort system in its store in Mount Kisco, New York. A&P chose the highly efficient heating, cooling, and power system because it leads to energy savings and ultimately reduces the store's dependence on the grid. The new rooftop unit uses underground-supplied natural gas to generate electricity for the store. Then it generates cold water, runs it to refrigerator "chillers," and provides heat when needed. The UTC PureComfort unit produces combined power, heating, and cooling at greater than 80 percent efficiency rates compared to approximately 33 percent from the electric grid. Distance monitoring by UTC Power means the company's service people will be at the A&P store to fix a problem before the people at A&P even realize one exists.

Meeting customers' multiple cooling, heating, and power needs with an innovative integrated, reliable on-site system solution at a cost reduction from existing options addressed UTC Power's strategic goals to deliver new products and new revenues. At the same time these offerings provided very low emissions, reduced customers' energy costs, lowered grid dependence, and assured standby power supply. While it would not have necessarily called its strategy "green," and its sales force is not necessarily hearing the term "sustainability" from its customers, UTC Power nonetheless has incorporated the core ideas into its strategy. These products provide safer, cleaner, and more reliable power sources than the alternatives available, at commensurate prices that are less expensive when full costs are considered.

However, the issue was not whether the PureComfort system met buyer needs or satisfied sustainability requirements; it did. The challenge was whether customers' standard way of meeting power needs—paying for electricity from the grid—could change to a solution that required new purchase practices and economic calculations as well as different impacts on the company's profit and loss statement and balance sheets.

Breakthroughs happen when VAN teams can tap into an intangible creativity source in sustainability agendas: the energy, the extra little bit of horsepower, or a passion for the technology and market changes. UTC Power experienced this type of breakthrough in its work with the city of London and the Ritz Carlton hotel chain in San Francisco. In each situation the VAN participants were well known for being creative, innovative, and willing to spend extra time to find solutions. New competitive space and successful positioning in that space were realized by firms working with other firms also positioned in the same market frontier.

The catalyst for this creativity is the process dynamics of UTC Power's technology design to achieve clean, safe, reasonably priced products combined with supply-chain partners that want to save money and assure performance but also have an absolute commitment to creating sustainability solutions through redesign of products and procedures. This means there is more continuity and commitment in teams because participants are passionate about seeing their ideas come to fruition. VAN participants will go the extra distance. When innovators talk with other innovators about how to implement sustainability innovations, results are achieved.

UTC Power uses its internal, highly disciplined product development process and committed working relationships with buyers and original equipment manufacturers to accelerate learning and feedback and to improve its power products. UTRC also employs an innovation effort, working with the business units that have identified UTC technologies for new, market-ready products and markets. The PureComfort system process started with a small, multidivisional group looking at opportunities at the intersection of power, heating, and cooling.

Brainstorming engineers, who did not usually work together, found the intersection of power, heating, and cooling rife with possibilities and developed a second product, known as the PureCycle 200 system. Together they altered standard Carrier industrial cooling equipment by converting it to run "backward"; instead of using electricity to produce cooling, the system uses waste heat to produce electricity. The system uses field-tested Carrier technology to provide turnkey, zero-emission, reliable, low-cost electricity from various industrial heat sources. The electricity can be used on-site where it is produced or sold to the electric utility grid. Customers can potentially make money by offsetting traditional fossil fuel electricity generation. The payback and savings depend on the geographic location in the United States and the price of the displaced energy.

It is not necessarily easy building new types of supply-chain relationships to implement sustainability innovations. In UTC Power's case, cross-business unit sales and service provisions had to be tightly coordinated, and getting electric utilities to buy excess power from buyers has been an uphill battle. Even with these challenges, a major obstacle is in developing trust with the end users, specifically the facility leader who makes the purchase decision and who is paid to be conservative. It is a tough sell because the system (though not the components) is new. It is mechanical and therefore may need servicing. Facility managers fear the unit will fail, and they have to be educated about the system, which takes time. Finally, having the system installed may seem "inconvenient," as it can disrupt current operations during the switch.

Thus the value proposition has to be communicated effectively. UTC Power has developed economic models that show payback time frames for equipment installed in different geographic locations according to size of facility, electricity rates based on different fuel sources, and seasonal demand. In addition, a turnkey service contract is offered that monitors units from UTC centers in Charlotte or Hartford where operators have the technological ability to locate errors. As UTC Power continued to refine its extensive supply-chain coordination, more new opportunities for innovation emerged.

Fuel price volatility, changing and more violent weather patterns, deregulation, supply interruptions, and rolling blackouts and brownouts in the Northeast and California have generated considerable interest in distributed (nongrid, noncentralized), on-site, clean and reliable electricity, heat, and cooling power sources. To capture this interest while overcoming the natural resistance of cautious buyers is still a challenge. UTC Power and UTC are addressing this challenge by creating an "all in service" solution. Through a long-term contract, a customer avoids the up-front cash cost and spreads it over time, thereby better matching the cost with the energy savings.

Another value proposition involves public health. An important sign of change that should be noted by all managers is occurring in UTC Power's urban bus transportation markets. Buyers such as the city of London and AC Transit in Oakland, California, are building previously externalized health costs into their purchase decisions. A regional public transit authority, AC Transit considers the cost of respiratory and other air-pollution-related illness resulting from diesel gasoline combustion, particularly from buses. Incorporating more of the full system costs into the equation shifts the price-performance calculation for conventional bus drivetrains compared with fuel cell systems. The price of the latter looks more attractive when adjusted downward by health cost savings due to reduced particulate matter and other air pollutants from transportation.

Through product take-back, UTC Power is getting a handle on design for disassembly. The company's team must determine what parts are recoverable and recyclable and the economics of remanufacturing the leased units brought back for repair or at the end of their useful life. Extending this concept to field-installed stationary fuel cell power units, UTC Power found that the reverse logistics and reuse/recycling of materials and parts could actually make money. The notion of leasing transportation or stationary power plant fuel cell stacks has engaged UTC Power even more closely with its suppliers and buyers along the value chain to source recyclable materials and components. Successful supply-chain coordination within the company and outside is important to the success of any leasing solution and to the systems redesign for disassembly and recyclability.

Because new ideas that challenge existing ways of operating require early adopters, innovators initially tend to work with and sell to other innovators. UTC Power is building new markets through cooperation with forward-thinking internal UTC executives and staff in other business units, and combining that synergy with eager corporate buyers trying to solve urgent problems (e.g., harsh storms in tropical geographies, zero-downtime requirements for electrical power) or open-minded municipalities searching for creative cost-cutting measures.

Conclusion

As we noted at the outset of this section, VANs are necessary to implement sustainability strategies. VANs provide the horsepower to implement projects. They are the means to translate vision into competitive products or services. Whatever your business is, catalyzing VANs is essential to put your nascent strategy into action. The following are strategies for working with VANs:

- Start with a compelling vision.
- Don't take "no" for an answer; find people whose values align with yours.
- Work with innovators in other fields.

Since by definition you will be forging a new path, you will hear "no" a lot. Don't stop there: seek out those who understand the bigger vision and are inspired by the prospect of inventing the way forward with you. Source participants from your existing suppliers or find new ones inspired by your green strategic vision and the multiple gains, including financial, that would come to participating organizations that develop new capacities. Collaborate closely with other innovators in other functions or fields. Since differentiation is a moving target, call upon your VANs to help you continuously redesign and improve, moving individual participants in and out of the constellation of skill sets and leadership attributes you need. Implementing strategy requires new approaches to your existing relationships, tapping into the latent creativity that is there.

KEY TAKEAWAYS

- Innovation is carried out by teams working collaboratively.
- Create teams that foster creativity by including individuals who are open to change.

EXERCISE

1. Working with a partner, imagine a new product or process you want to create. Identify who would want it as well as what VANs and weak ties could help you implement it. How could they help? What would be the benefit for them?

---

[1] See also extensive literature on "network organizations." See Mark Granovetter, "Economic Action and Social Structure: A Theory of Embeddedness," *American Journal of Sociology* 91 (1985): 481–510; Walter W. Powell, "Neither Market Nor Hierarchy: Network Forms of Organization," in *Research in Organizational Behavior*, ed. Barry M. Staw and L. L. Cummings (Greenwich, CT: JAI, 1990), 12:295–336; {Author's Name Retracted as requested by the work's original creator or licensee}, "Social Control and Economic Exchange: Conceptualizing Network Organizational Forms" (paper presented at the Annual Meeting of the American Sociological Association, Washington, DC, August 1990); Walter W. Powell, "Hybrid Organizational Arrangements: New Form or Transitional Development?," *California Management Review* 30, no. 1 (1983): 67–87; H. B. Thorelli, "Networks: Between Markets and Hierarchies," *Strategic Management Journal* 7 (1986): 37–51; {Author's Name Retracted as requested by the work's original creator or licensee} with Jennifer Starr, "A Network Model of Organization Formation," *Entrepreneurship Theory and Practice* 17, no. 2 (Winter 1993): 5–15. {Author's Name Retracted as requested by the work's original creator or licensee}, "Network Dyads in Entrepreneurial Settings: A Study of the Governance of Exchange Relationships," *Administrative Science Quarterly* 37, no. 1 (March 1992): 76–104; {Author's Name Retracted as requested by the work's original creator or licensee}, "Partner Networks: Leveraging External Ties to Improve Entrepreneurial Performance," *Journal of Business Venturing* 6, no. 3 (May 1991): 173–88; {Author's Name Retracted as requested by the work's original creator or licensee}, "Strategic Alliances: A Study of Entrepreneurial Strategies for the 1990s" (paper presented at the Eleventh Annual Babson College Entrepreneurship Research Conference, Babson College, Babson Park, MA, 1991).
[2] Paul Farrow, interview with author, July 1996.
[3] Jan van Dokkum, phone interview with author, June 21, 2001.

4.6 Radical Incrementalism

LEARNING OBJECTIVES

1. Examine the role of incremental steps in innovation.

2. Understand how systems changes can result from combining small steps.

Some companies enter the market with a mission of challenging existing products with sustainable replacements. Their strategy is radical from the start. Others, typically larger established firms, gain momentum in sustainability innovation by building upon incremental improvements in products and systems. Business analysis often juxtaposes incremental change with radical or dramatic change; a common assumption is that the two are mutually exclusive. Moreover, literature in the sustainability field privileges the latter over the former, dismissing incremental change as timid at best and "greenwash" at worst—accusations that may indeed hold true at times. Separating the two concepts, incremental and radical, can be useful for heuristic purposes. Perhaps doing so is also psychologically satisfying; it's either this or it's that.

In real life, however, people in business make a series of small steps over time that add up to larger, more profound change. Sometimes early successes build momentum for bigger changes that previously were viewed as too radical or risky. Alternatively, incremental successes can build courage and internal support, stimulating requisite imagination and energy to design more radical and innovative changes. By consciously pursuing incremental changes with a radical ultimate goal and tracking progress, one can catalyze significant innovation and ultimately differentiate the firm.

Radical incrementalism involves small, carefully selected steps that result in learning that in turn reveals new opportunities. It means taking marginal, integrated progress toward more ambitious sustainability goals. Ideally, your whole company would participate in discussing and defining ideal characteristics of this goal, track milestones along the way, observe lessons, and feed this data back into the definition of the goal and the next steps forward.

Others have used the term *radical incrementalism* to describe a deliberate strategy for business operations (particularly in information technology) in which a series of small changes are enacted one after the other, resulting in radical cumulative changes in infrastructure. Our use of the concept differs in that while company strategists should have a vision of what sustainability means for their company, the incremental steps to get there necessarily shape the course. In other words, the feedback you get along the way will accelerate, alter, and inform your next actions. This is iterative and adaptive learning—one gains knowledge along the way that affects future decisions. The companies we examine here demonstrate this strategy.

Corporate adoption of green and sustainability strategies is gaining global momentum. Its implications are radical for firms, supply chains, and consumers because it represents a significant challenge to conventional ways of doing business. We present leaders here because they offer us a window to the future. In this section and the discussion of adaptive collaboration through value-added networks (VANs). The result, for those companies that successfully pursue it, is new market space shaped to the lead firm's advantage. However, just as the journey of one thousand miles begins with a single step, so does the radical shift toward sustainability involve incremental changes.

Kaiser Permanente

Kaiser Permanente (KP) deliberately adopted a radically incremental approach to implementing its strategy. The company has a sustainability perspective on its corporate purpose (health care) that widens the meaning of "health care" to include not only medical treatment but the broader community health impacts of its facilities and operations and

the materials it sources. We examine here one relatively small decision in KP's broader strategy: the company's decisions on the use of polyvinyl chloride (PVC), a material of increasing environmental concern. Specifically, we will look at KP's choices regarding flooring. KP measured everything it did to build the business case for greening each incremental step and discovered there were significant economic benefits to be gained by seemingly small changes. Moreover, these incremental decisions have had radical impacts on the company's success and have facilitated moving forward on other sustainability fronts. This discussion puts KP's incremental step on flooring in the wider context of green buildings as an important arena for companies to measure the collective impact of seemingly small decisions. We present the business case for greener buildings and the economic and environmental benefits that they generate for companies as an integral part of their strategy. Next, we will discuss SC Johnson's award-winning product sustainability assessment tool, Greenlist. As SC Johnson (SCJ) evolved its efforts to incorporate sustainability into its corporate strategy, it constructed a powerful tool to measure the range of environmental impacts of chemical inputs into its products. As a result, the company has significantly altered its environmental footprint, improved product performance, and achieved significant cost savings. Moreover, this tool has had broader catalytic effects on SCJ's supply chain and competitors. By patenting Greenlist, SCJ hopes to widen the circle even more.

Both of our company examples, KP and SCJ, illustrate the following three radically incremental tactics:

1. Set big goals but take moderate, integrated steps.
2. Measure everything—build your business case.
3. Incorporate knowledge gained back into new product and process design.

Both KP and SCJ illustrate the tactics we advocate: set big goals but take moderate, integrated steps to get there. Both companies have religiously monitored and measured their progress to build the business case for the next ambitious step. Now both are grappling with incorporating the knowledge gained from their earlier successes into future product designs, process designs, or both.

KP is the largest health management organization in the United States, with 8.2 million members and over 500 hospitals and medical buildings under management. KP's Green Building Committee first met in 2001 to determine priority projects it would take on. Seated at the table were representatives from interior design firms, construction companies, health nongovernmental organizations (NGOs), and architects, along with KP's national environment health and safety people (labor joined later). KP's interest focused on identifying an area where the firm could move relatively quickly to eliminate a problematic chemical and thereby make a demonstrable difference for human and community health and ecological well-being. The group made the decision to investigate PVC-free flooring. Given growing research on PVC's toxicity to humans throughout its life cycle, this choice met the groups' selection criteria. It was a radically incremental step.

KP does not move precipitously. Prudent spending and sound financial performance enable KP to deliver quality care, convenience, and access and affordability. KP is also dedicated to individual and community health and is science-driven and acutely sensitive to lowering the costs of health care. In this last respect, there is no choice in the health care industry; new drugs and procedures, health care worker shortages, provider consolidation, aging populations, and the rise of chronic health conditions across population segments continually drive costs up. Careful consideration of costs therefore must be part of the equation for procurement and strategic change. Strong core values, however, including resource stewardship and leadership in improving the quality of life of the communities in which it operates, were taken seriously by senior management.

John Kouletsis, director of strategic planning and design, called the organization "fearlessly incremental" in its strategic approach. Though it takes on big issues, the company is meticulous in accumulating quantitative and qualitative evidence to support decisions, especially major changes in purchasing. Company leadership is akin to the old political notion of statesmanship. The belief that what is good for the environment and the community is good for the health maintenance organization (HMO) members and therefore good for KP's financial success guides strategy. KP employs a systems view of health care, incorporating environmental and community aspects, and this wider perspective on health informs the company's green strategic decisions.

Jan Stensland was half of the duo in strategic sourcing and technology for KP. Her friendly, easy-going exterior belied intensity, intelligence, and absolute dedication to achieving the multidimensional objectives of her job. She conversed equally comfortably about material costs per square foot, parts per million contaminants, construction specifications, human health, and PVC exposure research. She also tracked internal rates of return for new decisions—for example, alternative flooring technology projects under consideration

to renovate dozens of medical buildings throughout California, ten states, and Washington, DC, where thousands of patients and staff would spend time over the next several decades. While health is in the forefront of her mind, her proposals must show how the company will save money or get better spaces for the same cost. The national health care crisis of escalating costs is the elephant in her office, and she stares it down with an optimizing strategy across financial, community, health, and environmental objectives.

Stensland's team sought ways to influence KP's suppliers' research and development (R&D) shops to redesign products so that health care facilities would be more effective measured in terms of patient treatment, disease prevention, and costs. Thus business effectiveness is viewed in a larger social context. Stensland thinks in terms of today and fifteen years out in talks with suppliers, working through negotiations to maximize health benefits and minimize costs for multiple stakeholders.

For example, 16 percent of KP's 8.2 million person membership suffers from asthma. The rate of children's asthma recently has risen to an epidemic level of 27 to 30 percent in some counties in California. Chronic respiratory and immune systems problems increasingly have been linked to low exposures to different chemical compounds. There are considerable health impacts and significant monies at stake; therefore, suppliers bid with particular attention to KP's interests. Moreover, the health care industry often follows KP's lead. When KP was first among HMOs to move away from PVC gloves due to escalating allergic reactions and their associated costs, the industry followed, opening up opportunities for firms able to provide substitutes. However, that was only KP's first effort involving PVC.

Stensland described the company's efforts on non-PVC flooring as an ongoing effort—one piece of a larger puzzle with short-term wins and long-term goals. Thinking this intently about materials takes time but yields good results. The subcommittee assigned to investigate whether substitutes were available for PVC flooring found the inexpensive per-square-foot price of vinyl did not reflect true life-cycle, health, and environmental costs. PVC flooring was discovered to carry high maintenance costs not previously considered because they were not included in the first-cost price of the flooring. True costs are often disguised when budgets are divided between purchasing for new construction or renovation, and ongoing operations once the flooring is installed.

KP conducted pilot projects in several of its medical office buildings and hospitals, administering tests and comparing maintenance budgets in vinyl and nonvinyl flooring buildings, and interviewed the people who cleaned the floors in those facilities. These investigations revealed that up to 80 percent of flooring maintenance costs could be eliminated with the use of a rubber flooring product (Nora, from Freudenberg Building Systems) and another non-PVC flooring product, Stratica, an ecopolymeric product. The rubber and non-PVC vinyl flooring products were more stain and slip resistant and had improved acoustic properties. But that was not the end of the story.

Qualitative issues related to flooring often translated into significant ongoing expenses. "Slips, trips, and falls" are major problems in buildings and an early indicator of problems with flooring. Accidents require expensive settlements awarded to employees and visitors to buildings. Stensland analyzed the square footage costs across buildings and examined data for two years running. The company's new attention to the nature of, and differences across, various flooring materials uncovered two KP locations where rubber flooring was installed and for which data showed *zero* slips, trips, and falls. Furthermore, data from nurses revealed the harder vinyl floors generated more complaints and work absences by nurses who are on their feet all day. Non-PVC rubber flooring improved conditions for nurses and accomplished the environmental and health strategic goals. Analyses were conducted at multiple facilities. The magnitude of the flooring issue was significant for the company and its contract suppliers; in 2005, the company managed sixty-four million square feet of flooring. By 2015, it expects to have eighty-four million square feet under management.

However, that doesn't solve the problem of flooring replacement in existing facilities. With regularly scheduled replacement of flooring in the more than five hundred medical buildings in the system, could PVC be eliminated there as well in a variety of areas? KP turned to the Collins and Aikman Corporation (C&A), its carpet supplier, and required that C&A develop a non-PVC carpet backing (the underlayer of carpeting contained most of the materials of concern), preferably at the same price. The manufacturer brought the new offering back to KP six months ahead of schedule. An equivalently priced new carpet backing whose performance exceeded the PVC-backed carpet was now available not just for KP but for all the manufacturer's customers. The new material used postconsumer recycled polyvinyl buterol, the film used on safety glass for windshields that protects car passengers from broken glass

in accidents. An enterprising engineer had discovered he could use the discarded sticky "waste" compound found at recyclers and brought it back into the materials stream for new applications.

By asking suppliers for alternative, safer products, KP—due to its size—has been driving the market toward products that reduce resource use and improve health conditions by eliminating chemical hazards and lowering maintenance expenses. Incremental steps are taken toward sustainability goals, pulling markets and supply chains along in what ultimately constitutes radical change: the substitution of a new, better product design for the old.

There are other examples. Refrigerants used in medical facility chiller systems have had the same problems as refrigerants in general use. When contracts for refrigerants came up for reconsideration, KP put bidders on notice that any problematic chemical in use or being phased out by 2008 could not be used in chillers. York Incorporated, an award-winning firm for its product efficiency and advanced technical designs, won the bid, producing new chillers with benign refrigerants in a unit that was 25 percent more energy efficient than the market standard. Thousands of chillers across hundreds of medical office buildings and hospitals now drive substitution of a radically more effective system for the existing products.

There are other examples of KP's radically incremental approach. One of the companies selected to provide KP's elevators produced a super energy-efficient design that addresses KP's goal for more energy-efficient equipment, helping drive and justify that supplier's improvements to its product design. Another elevator company had switched from petrochemical-based hydraulic fluids to soy-based fluids and was investigating more sustainable elevator car finish materials. In 2006 KP was talking with furniture and textile manufacturers to provide non-PVC upholstery. By 2005, KP was leading an effort to bring locally grown organic food into its hospitals, supporting local organic markets and working with food service suppliers like Sysco together with local growers to reduce fuel consumption in distribution. The goal is delivery of "clean" foods without chemical additives at reasonable cost to members and patients. The slow food movement, a grassroots and rapidly spreading effort to improve the quality of food through organic practices and limited radius distribution from the growing site, gains momentum when a company the size of KP focuses on locally grown organic produce. [1]

KP's incremental steps to upgrade facilities add up to radical change. KP has put sustainable building design and construction practices into all new construction and "rebuilds" (KP renovations) through facility templates. These practices incorporate the following:

- Implementing efficient water and energy systems
- Using the least toxic building materials
- Recycling demolition debris, diverting thousands of tons of materials from landfills
- Making use of daylight whenever possible
- Managing storm water to enhance surrounding habitats
- Reducing site development area (e.g., total gross square footage) to concentrate and limit total paving and other site disturbances
- Installing over fifty acres of reflective roofing
- Publishing an Eco Toolkit reference book and providing it to KP capital project team members and more than 50 architects and design alliance partners

KP also incorporates health and ecosystem considerations into national contracts. These considerations include the following:

- Reducing the toxicity and volume of waste
- Increasing postconsumer recycled content
- Selecting reusable and durable products
- Eliminating mercury content
- Selecting products free from PVC and di-2-ethylhexyl phthalate (DEHP)

Successful changes include replacing three DEHP-containing medical products in the neonatal intensive care units with alternatives, ensuring the continued elimination of mercury-containing medical equipment from standards, and negotiating a national recycling contract. KP's purchasing standards include 30 percent postconsumer content office paper and mercury-free and latex-free products.

In addition, KP facilities often partner with local community organizations to implement community initiatives. One example is a mercury thermometer exchange at Kaiser Permanente Riverside (CA) Medical Center. A total of 540 pounds of material were collected from 3,000 mercury thermometers. Over 1,200 digital thermometers were distributed. "Kaiser Permanente's accomplishments in environmental performance are impressive and unique," said Kathy Gerwig, director of environmental stewardship. "We hope that by changing our practices, we can drive change throughout the health care industry." [2]

KP's metrics demonstrating the benefits of its sustainability efforts include the following:

- In 2003, KP diverted 8,000 tons of solid waste from landfills.
- In 2003, KP reused or safely redeployed more than 40,000 pieces of electronic equipment, weighing 410 tons and containing 10,500 pounds of lead.
- KP eliminated 27,000 grams of mercury from KP health care operations by phasing out mercury-containing blood pressure devices, thermometers, and gastrointestinal equipment.
- KP phased out one hundred tons of single-use devices in 2003.

The impact of energy conservation measures at KP prevented the creation of more than seventy million pounds of air pollutants annually. The aggregate impact of pollution prevention activities eliminated the purchase and disposal of forty tons of hazardous chemicals. Other activities reported by the company in 2005 are as follows:

- Waste minimization resulting in the recycling of nine million pounds of solid waste
- Electronic equipment disposition resulting in the recycling of 36,000 electronic devices containing 10,500 pounds of lead
- Optimal reuse of products that led to reprocessing 53,851 pounds of medical devices and supplies
- Capital equipment redistribution
- Greening janitorial cleaning products, eliminating exposure risks for employees, lowering costs, gaining system efficiencies, and improving performance
- Recycling and reuse of 8,300 gallons of solvents
- Energy conservation resulting in the recycling of 30,000 spent fluorescent lamps

In conclusion, KP provides a compelling example of the immediate gains to be had through pursing sustainability practices in radically incremental steps. KP's senior management team works from the premise that human health and environmental health are the same thing. As an institution engaged with human health, it makes sense for KP to be active in resolving a paradox facing the health care industry: that hazardous chemicals used in medical products and buildings have harmful effects on patients and employees. It makes sense to coordinate purchasing across member medical centers and hospitals to ensure improved health conditions for members and the communities in which they live. The opportunities are vast for KP. That means the hundreds of suppliers that provide technical and routine needs for the company and the more than two thousand minor and major construction projects under way at any one time also can take advantage of new sustainability-inspired market space opportunities. The question is which ones will step up to the challenge and follow KP into the next generation of "good business"?

Radical incrementalism means taking small, carefully selected steps that result in learning that in turn reveals new opportunities. In this case a seemingly small decision on a seemingly innocuous issue—flooring—resulted in larger systemic changes across the company and its supply chains, even sending an urgent signal to the flooring industry. By greening its flooring, KP is improving health by eliminating a questionable material, improving working conditions and health for nurses, and reducing costs by bringing employee absences down and lowering accident liability costs. Putting the pieces together took time; KP staff members measured each step and outcome to evaluate the effects on cost and performance. Moreover, the results are driving bigger goals. Three years from the start-up of the project, KP made a new-construction standards change: no PVC vinyl flooring would be used in any future facilities. If we take into account all the other incremental changes KP is making, the systemic and company benefits are profound. KP's radically incremental steps are part of its strategy to better support community health while it grows its operations.

We turn next to sustainability ideas applied to facilities. Buildings are not just where your business activities happen. Your facilities—and the decisions you make about resources, energy, materials, and so forth—are a significant investment and can either add to or subtract from your bottom line. They can also add to or subtract from your overall strategy. Buildings and their operating systems are an excellent area in which you can realize the benefits of radically incremental steps.

Among the many industries developing innovative strategies to increase profits and address environmental and related community quality of life concerns, the building sector presents some of the most accessible incremental opportunities that can aggregate into radical returns. Compared to standard buildings, "green" buildings can provide greater economic and social benefits over the life of the structures, reduce or eliminate adverse human health effects, and even contribute to improved air and water quality. Opportunities for reducing both costs and natural system impacts include low-disturbance land use techniques, improved lighting design, high-performance water fixtures, careful materials selection, energy-efficient appliances and heating and cooling systems, and on-site water treatment and recycling. Less familiar innovations include natural ventilation and cooling without fans and air conditioners;

vegetative roofing systems that cool buildings, provide wildlife habitat, and reduce storm water runoff; and constructed wetlands that help preserve water quality while reducing water treatment costs.

The building industry and growing numbers of private companies are responding to these opportunities. Valuable economic benefits are being realized in improved employee health and productivity, lower costs, and enhanced community quality of life. Since 2000, adoption of green design and construction techniques has been greatly aided and accelerated by the Leadership in Energy and Environmental Design (LEED) rating system.

LEED is a voluntary green building rating system established by architects, interior designers, and the construction industry through a consensual process during the 1990s. The US Green Building Council (USGBC), a voluntary membership coalition, developed and continues to review the LEED standards. LEED guides building owners, architects, and construction firms to use industry standards and advances in those standards for environmental and health performance across a wide range of building criteria including site design, building materials selection, and energy systems. While each modification and upgrade to the building and site may seem small unto itself, the changes combine to create a dramatically more efficient building system with far lower operating costs and more satisfied owners over the life of the structure. While there is valid criticism about some of the specifications within LEED and its impact on innovation in the materials industry, overall the system has helped green the building industry. [3]

Green buildings perform the same functions and serve the same purposes as conventional buildings but with a smaller ecological footprint. They employ optimized and often innovative design features to reduce natural systems impacts throughout a building's life cycle and all across the supply chain of materials, components, and operations.

Green buildings provide a range of benefits to stakeholders, from developers and owners to occupants and communities. Structural, mechanical, and landscape design elements can maintain comfort and indoor air quality, conserve resources, and minimize use of toxic materials while reducing pollution and damage to local ecosystems. A broad range of green design techniques, technologies, and operational strategies are available to building architects, engineers, and owners. Every building is different, and there is no single green design formula. However, there are common design objectives and classes of benefits. The potential benefits of green building practices include the following:

- Less disruption of local ecosystems and habitats
- Resource conservation
- Decreased air, water, and noise pollution
- Superior indoor air quality
- Fewer transportation impacts

While they may entail higher up-front costs (but not necessarily [4]), in the long term, green buildings can make up the shortfall. Careful design choices for particular locations can reduce that difference to zero. Some of the economic benefits they generate include the following:

- **Lower capital costs.** With careful design, measures such as passive solar heating, natural ventilation, structural materials and design improvements, and energy and water efficiency can reduce the size and cost of heating and cooling systems and other infrastructure. A new bank in Boise, Idaho, was able to take advantage of such considerations to go from an initially planned LEED Silver to an actual LEED Platinum with no added cost. [5]

- **Lower operations and maintenance (O&M) costs.** On average, lower energy and water consumption reduces energy demand 25–45 percent per square foot for LEED buildings versus conventional buildings. [6] The US Environmental Protection Agency (EPA) reported that office buildings that meet the energy efficiency requirements of the Energy Star program use 40–50 percent less energy than other buildings. [7]

- **Increased market value.** Green buildings can increase market value through reduced operating costs, higher lease premiums, competitive features in tight markets, and increased residential resale value. For instance, a 2008 study of Energy Star and LEED-certified office buildings versus conventional ones found that the green office buildings had higher occupancy rates and could charge slightly higher rents, making the market value of a green building typically $5 million greater than its conventional equivalent. [8]

- **Less risk and liability.** Using best practices yields more predictable results, and healthier indoor environments reduce health hazards. Some insurers offer discounts for certified green buildings, and others offer to pay to rebuild to green standards after damage. [9]

- **Increased employee productivity.** Green buildings increase occupant productivity due to better lighting and more comfortable, quiet, and healthy work environments. This improvement can be at least equal to buildings' lifetime capital and O&M costs and is the largest potential economic benefit of green buildings. For example, a survey of employees at two companies that moved from conventional buildings into LEED-certified ones found the new buildings added on average about 40 hours per year per employee in increased productivity. [10] Nationwide, the value of improved office worker productivity from indoor environmental improvements is estimated to be in the range of $20–160 billion. [11]

- **Reduced absenteeism.** Lawrence Berkeley National Laboratory calculates that improvements to indoor environments could reduce health care cost and work losses by 9 percent to 20 percent from communicable respiratory diseases, 18 percent to 25 percent from reduced allergies and asthma, and 20 percent to 50 percent from other nonspecific health and discomfort effects, saving $17–48 billion annually. [12]

- **Market perception of quality.** Green buildings require careful design attention and the use of best practices and display superior performance.

- **Promotion of innovation.** Green buildings employ new ideas and methods that produce significant improvements.

- **Access to government incentives.** A growing number of federal, state, and local agencies require green features and offer tax credits and other incentives such as faster, less costly planning and permit approvals.

Green buildings provide a tangible means of measuring incremental steps that can aggregate into radical system-level benefits. Moreover, they are a visible area in which to demonstrate corporate sustainability strategy—the benefits derived from greening facilities and building systems add up to significant cost savings and represent a demonstrable area in which to see near-term return on investment in green technologies and operating systems.

SC Johnson

We turn next to the example of incremental changes creating system innovations at SC Johnson. By the mid-1990s, SC Johnson (SCJ) had a very respectable record on corporate environmental responsibility. In 1975, SCJ voluntarily removed ozone-threatening chlorofluorocarbon (CFC) propellants from its products worldwide. This was three years before the US government banned CFCs. In 1992, when eco-efficiency was introduced as a cost savings measure by the World Business Council for Sustainable Development (WBCSD), SCJ of the first companies to join the WBCSD. Millions of dollars of unnecessary costs were trimmed by using fewer resources far more efficiently. The company was able to eliminate over 420,000,000 pounds of waste from products and processes over the ten-year period prior to 2004, resulting in cost savings of more than $35 million.

In addition, the company built a landfill gas–powered turbine cogeneration energy plant that delivers 6.4 megawatts of electricity and some 40,000 pounds per hour of steam for SCJ's Waxdale manufacturing facility in Wisconsin. This energy project enabled SCJ to halve its use of coal-generated utility electricity and thereby cut its carbon emissions.

SCJ is a 120-year-old family-owned (sixth generation) firm with explicit commitments to innovation, high-quality products, environmental concerns, and the communities in which it operates. SCJ is a consumer packaged goods (CPG) company and a "chemical formulator"—a company that chooses from a menu of chemical inputs to make its consumer products. With such well-known brands as Pledge, Windex, and Ziploc, the company had over $6.5 billion in sales in 2006 and sold its products in more than 110 countries.

In holding up sustainability criteria as goals, SCJ had set off on a journey in which the end destination was not entirely clear, and by the new millennium company strategists knew it was time to evaluate the systems currently in place. SCJ's earlier positive results motivated the company to look for more opportunities, so it stepped back and looked at the progress it made over a decade. Company strategists discovered that while eco-efficiency had become second nature to product design at SCJ, strategy needed to shift beyond capturing relatively easy efficiencies and move deeper. They engaged outside expertise to help develop and introduce product design tools that could be used to build preferred ingredient choices into product and packaging design. The result of this assessment was the development of a new product evaluation tool, Greenlist.

Greenlist is a tool SCJ developed to improve the quality of its products through better understanding of the health and environmental impact of material inputs. In the Greenlist database are 2,300 chemicals including surfactants, insecticides, solvents, resins, propellants, and packaging. Criteria measured include the chemicals' biodegradability, aquatic toxicity, vapor pressure, and so forth. Through Greenlist, SCJ has reduced its environmental impact while simultaneously witnessing increases in production and sales growth.

Greenlist is a patented rating system (US Patent No. 6,973,362) that classifies raw materials used in SCJ's products according to their impact on the environment and human health. Greenlist has helped SCJ phase out certain raw materials and use materials considered to be environmentally "better" and "best." The result is a process that gives SCJ scientists access to ingredient ratings for any new product or reformulation and enables them to continuously improve the environmental profile of the company's products.

The Greenlist screening process covers over 90 percent of the company's raw materials volume and is continually updated as new findings emerge. Materials are assigned a score from a high of 3 to a low of 0. An ingredient with a 3 rating is considered "best," 2 is "better," and 1 is "acceptable." Any material receiving a 0 is called a restricted use material (RUM) and requires company vice presidential approval for use. If a material is unavoidable and has a low score, the goal is to reduce and eliminate its use as soon as substitutes are available. When existing products are reformulated, the scientist must include ingredients that have ratings equal to or higher than the original formula.

While some raw materials with a 0 score are not restricted by government regulatory requirements, over the years SCJ has elected to limit their use. SCJ replaces these 0-rated materials with materials that are more biodegradable and have a better environment and health profile.

An example of Greenlist in action involves one of SCJ's glass cleaner products. In 2002 and again in 2004, SCJ assessed the formulation of Windex blue glass cleaner to reduce volatile organic compounds. The reformulations reduced health and environmental impacts while increasing the product's cleaning performance by 40 percent and growing its market share by 4 percent.

When SCJ introduced Greenlist in 2001, the company set a goal to improve its baseline Greenlist score for all raw material purchases from 1.2 to 1.41 by 2007. This goal was accomplished in early 2005. In 2001, SCJ's use of "better" and "best" materials was at 9 percent of all raw materials scored, and by 2005, this number increased to 28 percent of all raw materials scored. The company uses an annual planning process to help drive these scores, and the Greenlist results are shared in the company's annual public report. [13]

Moreover, SCJ has eliminated all PVC packaging (a step taken to eliminate risk and liability) and, as performance results remain stable or improve, the company has moved to

10 percent of surfactants made from bio-based as opposed to oil-based materials. Each change required coordination with suppliers, which have made the more efficient or benign substitute available for other customers as demand for "clean" materials grows.

SCJ has patented Greenlist, but it has made the process licensable by other companies at no charge (although SCJ's formulations remain protected). The goal is to encourage application of Greenlist thinking and analysis across industry sectors. The company has already shared its Greenlist process with the US EPA, Environment Canada, the Chinese Environmental Protection Agency, industry associations, universities, and other corporations. Moreover, the company has been able to use insights from Greenlist to work with partner suppliers to help identify and develop ingredients that are more environmentally sustainable.

To date, "the company has been recognized with over 40 awards for corporate environmental leadership from governments and non-governmental organizations, including the World Environment Center Gold Medal, and Environment Canada's Corporate Achievement Award. SCJ received the first-ever Lifetime Atmospheric Achievement Award from the US Environmental Protection Agency." [14] In 2005, SCJ announced that it had entered into a voluntary partnership with the EPA under the agency's Design for the Environment (DfE) program. SCJ is the first major CPG company to partner with EPA on the program, which promotes innovative chemical products, technologies, and practices that benefit human health and the environment. In 2006, SCJ received the Presidential Green Chemistry Challenge Award for its Greenlist process.

SCJ has evolved its sustainability strategy from well-meant but relatively piecemeal efficiency efforts to developing an award-winning, innovative product assessment tool. The company has achieved real leadership in the world of consumer products manufacturing. Not only has the company strategically positioned itself ahead of the pack by anticipating regulatory restrictions before they happen, but it has developed enviable preferred purchaser relationships with its suppliers. SCJ has simplified its materials inputs list to fewer, greener inputs and is helping suppliers develop market leadership in supplying greener inputs. Moreover, SCJ is trying to teach the world how it does what it does—and it is doing this for free.

An area in which the company has recognized it needs to take further steps is in incorporating Greenlist further

upstream in the product design process. SCJ's goal is to use the tool not only to assess existing products but also to inspire breakthrough green innovations to capture new market space. Given the company's track record of conscious evolution of its strategy, this is not an unrealistic goal.

Radical incrementalism, as we have seen, offers a path that can both deliver real-time benefits and lead to market-shifting innovation. KP and SCJ demonstrate the tactics we advocate here: set big goals but take moderate, integrated steps to get there. Both companies have religiously monitored and measured their progress to build the business case for the next ambitious steps. Consequently, both now grapple with incorporating the knowledge gained from their earlier successes into future product designs, process designs, or both.

Being radically incremental requires having an ambitious goal of corporate sustainability, but it does not imply that you will be able to map out all the steps with clockwork accuracy. It does mean, however, that one's incremental steps must be integrated, that each success and failure must be evaluated, and that the road map under one's feet must be redrawn accordingly. Being radical takes courage but so does radical incrementalism. Courage and resolve builds, however, with each successful step.

KEY TAKEAWAY

Radically incremental tactics include the following:
1. Setting big goals but taking moderate, integrated steps toward those goals.
2. Measuring everything (metrics are critical)—to build your business case.
3. Incorporating knowledge gained back into the process for new product and process design.

EXERCISES

1. List the small incremental steps Kaiser Permanente and SC Johnson took and the larger changes they added up to over time.
2. Select a familiar product and list all the incremental and small steps that could be applied to its design, use and disposal that would reduce the product's ecological/health footprint. As you consider these changes, look for imaginative leaps you could make to redesign the entire product, provide for the buyer's need in new ways altogether,

or consolidate incremental changes into a systems redesign involving supply chain partners that could improve the product and lower costs at the same time.

---

[1] The head of Slow Food USA's office, and founder of Slow Food International, Carlo Petrini views the organic and local food movements that have reinvigorated farmers' markets and microbreweries across the United States as representative of a new dialogue emerging between traditional knowledge and advancing science knowledge that is creating a new business reality and a different model of business.

[2] GreenBiz Staff, "Kaiser Permanente Turns Green," *GreenBiz*, April 22, 2003, accessed January 7, 2011, http://www.greenbiz.com/news/2003/04/22/kaiser-permanente -turns-green.

[3] The Healthy Building Network criticizes the USGBC and LEED for continuing to include PVC in green building specifications. Others have criticized the LEED process for inhibiting innovation because it freezes the specific definition of "green" in a moment in time. This can mean that unforeseen, even greener, innovations will be left out of the criteria.

[4] Lisa Fay Matthiessen and Peter Morris, "Costing Green: A Comprehensive Cost Database and Budgeting Methodology," US Green Building Council, July 2004, accessed January 10, 2011, http://www.usgbc.org/Docs/Resources/Cost_of_Green_Full.pdf.

[5] US Green Building Council, "Banner Bank Building: Green Is Color of Money," 2006, available from the project profiles at http://www.usgbc.org/DisplayPage.aspx?CMSPageID=1721.

[6] Cathy Turner and Mark Frankel (New Buildings Institute), *Energy Performance of LEED for New Construction Buildings* (Washington DC: US Green Building Council, 2008), accessed January 31, 2011, http://www.usgbc.org/ShowFile.aspx?DocumentID=3930; Greg Kats, *Greening Our Built World: Costs, Benefits, and Strategies* (Washington, DC: Island Press, 2009).

[7] Energy Star is familiar to many people for rating the energy efficiency of appliances, but a separate Energy Star certification system also exists for entire buildings. For the comparison, see EPA, *Energy Star and Other Climate Protection Programs 2007 Annual*, October 2008, accessed January 11, 2011, http://www.energystar.gov/ia/news/downloads/annual_report_2007.pdf.

[8] Piet Eichholtz, Nils Kok, and John M. Quigley, "Doing Well by Doing Good? Green Office Buildings" (Program on Housing and Urban Policy Working Paper No. W08-001, Institute of Business and Economic Research, Fisher Center for Real Estate & Urban Economics, University of California, Berkeley, 2008), accessed January 28, 2011, http://www.jetsongreen.com/files/doing_well_by_doing_good_green__office_buildings.pdf.

[9] For instance, Fireman's Fund Insurance Company, "Insurers Offer Rewards for Going Green," 2010, accessed January 11, 2011, http://www.firemansfund.com/about-fireman-s-fund/our-commitments/about-our-green-insurance/Pages/insurers-offer-rewards-for-going-green.aspx; or Zurich in North America, "Green Buildings Insurance Article," 2010, accessed January 11, 2011, http://www.zurichna.com/zna/realestate/greenbuildingsinsurancearticle.htm.

[10] Amanjeet Singh, et al., "Effects of Green Buildings on Employee Health and Productivity," *American Journal of Public Health* 100, no. 9 (2010): 1665–68.

[11] William J. Fisk, "Health and Productivity Gains from Better Indoor Environments and Their Relationship with Building Energy Efficiency," *Annual Review of Energy and the Environment* 25 (2000): 537–66.

[12] William J. Fisk, "Health and Productivity Gains from Better Indoor Environments and Their Relationship with Building Energy Efficiency," *Annual Review of Energy and the Environment* 25 (2000): 537–66.

[13] SC Johnson, "RESPONSIBILITY = SCIENCE: SC Johnson Public Report 2009," accessed March 7, 2011, http://www.scjohnson.com/Libraries/Download_Documents/2009_SC_Johnson_Public_Report.sflb.ashx.

[14] Five Winds International, "Greening the Supply Chain at SC Johnson: A Case Study," accessed December 3, 2010, http://www.fivewinds.com/_uploads/documents/g60tzmxo.pdf.

NOTES:

Chapter 5:
Energy and Climate

5.1 Climate Change

1. Understand the basic causes and effects of climate change.

2. Know the regulatory frameworks governments have used to address climate change.

3. Identify business responses and opportunities related to climate change.

The thickness of the air, compared to the size of the Earth, is something like the thickness of a coat of shellac on a schoolroom globe. Many astronauts have reported seeing that delicate, thin, blue aura at the horizon of the daylit hemisphere and immediately, unbidden, began contemplating its fragility and vulnerability. They have reason to worry. [1]

- Carl Sagan

Since the beginning of their history, humans have altered their environment. Only recently, however, have we realized how human activities influence earth's terrestrial, hydrological, and atmospheric systems to the extent that these systems may no longer maintain the stable climate and services we have assumed as the basis of our economies. The science of climate change developed rapidly in the late twentieth century as researchers established a correlation between increasing atmospheric concentrations of certain gases, human activities emitting those gases, and a rapid increase in global temperatures. Many, but by no means all, international policy makers spurred research as it became apparent that impacts ranging from melting polar ice caps to acidified oceans and extreme weather patterns were attributed to anthropogenic (human) influences on climate. Global businesses, many of which initially balked at potential economic disruption from changes in the use of fossil fuel and other business practices, have largely acceded to the need for change. Nonetheless, the overall response to the challenge has been slow and not without resistance, thereby increasing the potential opportunities and urgency.

The Science of Global Climate Change

In the early 1820s, Joseph Fourier, the French pioneer in the mathematics of heat diffusion, became interested in why some heat from the sun was retained by the earth and its atmosphere rather than being reflected back into space. Fourier conceived of the atmosphere as a bell jar with the atmospheric gases retaining heat and thereby acting as the containing vessel. In 1896, Swedish Nobel laureate and physicist Svante August Arrhenius published a paper in which he calculated how carbon dioxide (CO_2) could affect the temperature of the earth. He and early atmospheric scientists recognized that normal carbon dioxide levels in the atmosphere contributed to making the earth habitable. Scientists also have known for some time that air pollution alters weather. For example, certain industrial air pollutants can significantly increase rainfall downwind of their source. As intensive agriculture and industrial activity have expanded very rapidly around the world since 1850 (Figure 5.1 "Increase in Global Carbon Emissions from Fossil Fuel Combustion, 1750–2006"), a growing body of scientific evidence has accumulated to suggest that humans influence global climate.

Figure 5.1 Increase in Global Carbon Emissions from Fossil Fuel Combustion, 1750-2006

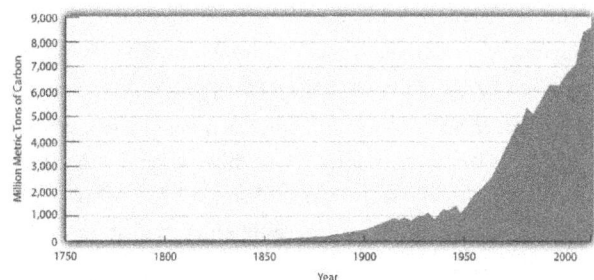

Units of carbon are often used instead of CO_2, which can be confusing. One ton of carbon equals 3.67 tons of CO_2. Hence emissions of CO_2 in 2006 were roughly eight billion tons of carbon, or twenty-nine billion tons of CO_2.
Source: Oak Ridge National Laboratory, Carbon Dioxide Information Analysis Center, accessed August 19, 2010,
http://cdiac.ornl.gov/trends/emis/graphics/global_ff_1751_2006.jpg.

The earth's climate has always varied, which initially raised doubts about the significance of human influences on climate or suggested our impact may have been positive.

Successive ice ages, after all, likely were triggered by subtle changes in the earth's orbit or atmosphere and would presumably recur. Indeed, changes in one earth system, such as solar energy reaching the earth's surface, can alter other systems, such as ocean circulation, through various feedback loops. The dinosaurs are thought to have gone extinct when a meteor struck the earth, causing tsunamis, earthquakes, fires, and palls of ash and dust that would have hindered photosynthesis and lowered oxygen levels and temperatures. Aside from acute catastrophes, however, climate has changed slowly, on the scale of tens of thousands to millions of years. The same paleoclimatological data also suggest a strong correlation between atmospheric CO_2 levels and surface temperatures over the past 400,000 years and indicate that the last 20 years have been the warmest of the previous 1,000. [2]

In the last decades of the twentieth century, scientists voiced concern over a rapid increase in "greenhouse gases." **Greenhouse gases (GHGs)** were named for their role in retaining heat in earth's atmosphere, causing a greenhouse effect similar to that in Fourier's bell jar. Increases in the atmospheric concentration of these gases, which could be measured directly in modern times and from ice core samples, were correlated with a significant warming of the earth's surface, monitored using meteorological stations, satellites, and other means.

The gases currently of most concern include CO_2, nitrous oxide (N_2O), methane (CH_4), and chlorofluorocarbons (CFCs). CO_2, largely a product of burning fossil fuels and deforestation, is by far the most prevalent GHG, albeit not the most potent. Methane, produced by livestock and decomposition in landfills and sewage treatment plants, contributes per unit twelve times as much to global warming than does CO_2. N_2O, created largely by fertilizers and coal or gasoline combustion, is 120 times as potent. CFCs, wholly synthetic in origin, have largely been phased out by the 1987 Montreal Protocol because they degraded the ozone layer that protected earth from ultraviolet radiation. The successor hydrochlorofluorocarbons (HCFCs), however, are GHGs with potencies one to two orders of magnitude greater than CO_2.

In response to such findings, the United Nations and other international organizations gathered in Geneva to convene the First World Climate Conference in 1979. In 1988, a year after the Brundtland Commission called for sustainable development, the World Meteorological Organization (WMO) and the United Nations Environment Programme (UNEP) created the **Intergovernmental Panel on Climate**

Change (IPCC). The IPCC gathered 2,500 scientific experts from 130 countries to assess the scientific, technical, and socioeconomic aspects of climate change, its risks, and possible mitigation. [3] The IPCC's First Assessment Report, published in 1990, concluded that the average global temperature was indeed rising and that human activity was to some degree responsible. This report laid the groundwork for negotiation of the Kyoto Protocol, an international treaty to reduce GHG emissions that met with limited success. Subsequent IPCC reports and myriad other studies indicated that climate change was occurring faster and with worse consequences than initially anticipated.

Effects and Predictions

The IPCC Fourth Assessment Report in 2007 summarized much of the current knowledge about global climate change, which included actual historical measurements as well as predictions based on increasingly detailed models. [5] These findings represent general scientific consensus and typically have 90 percent or greater statistical confidence.

The global average surface temperature increased 0.74°C ± 0.18°C (1.3°F ± 0.32°F) from 1906 to 2005, with temperatures in the upper latitudes (nearer the poles) and over land increasing even more. In the same period, natural solar and volcanic activity would have decreased global temperatures in the absence of human activity. Depending on future GHG emissions, the average global temperature is expected to rise an additional 0.5°C to 4°C by 2100, which could put over 30 percent of species at risk for extinction. Eleven of the twelve years from 1995 to 2006 were among the twelve warmest since 1850, when sufficient records were first kept. August 2009 had the hottest ocean temperatures and the second hottest land temperatures ever recorded for that month, and 2010 tied 2005 as the warmest year in the 131-year instrumental record for combined global land and ocean surface temperature. [6]

Seas have risen 20 to 40 centimeters over the past century as glaciers melted and water expanded from elevated temperatures. Sea levels rose at a rate of 1.8 (±0.5) millimeters per year from 1961 to 2003. From 1993 to 2003 alone, that rate was dramatically higher: 3.1 (±0.7) millimeters per year. An additional rise in sea level of 0.4 to 3.7 meters (1.3 to 12.1 feet) is expected by 2100. The former amount would threaten many coastal ecosystems and communities; [8] the latter would be enough to submerge completely the archipelago nation of the Maldives. If trends continue as predicted, inundation of global coastal areas and island communities may soon present major human migration and resettlement challenges. Many consider this the most critical climate change issue.

Trees are moving northward into the tundra. A thawing permafrost, meanwhile, would release enough methane to catastrophically accelerate global warming. [9] Other species, too, are migrating or threatened, such as the polar bear. The population of polar bears is expected to decline two-thirds by 2050 as their ice pack habitats disintegrate under current trends. [10] Warmer waters will also increase the range of cholera and other diseases and pests. [11]

At the same time that humans have increased production of GHGs, they have decreased the ability of the earth's ecosystems to reabsorb those gases. Deforestation and conversion of land from vegetation to built structures reduces the size of so-called carbon sinks. Moreover, conventional building materials such as pavement contribute to local areas of increased temperature, called heat islands, which in the evenings can be 12°C (22°F) hotter than surrounding areas. These elevated local temperatures further exacerbate the problems of climate change for communities through energy demand, higher air-conditioning costs, and heat-related health problems. [12]

By impairing natural systems, climate change impairs social systems. A shift in climate would alter distributions of population, natural resources, and political power. Droughts and rising seas that inundate populous coastal areas would force migration on a large scale. Unusually severe weather has already increased costs and death tolls from hurricanes, floods, heat waves, and other natural disasters. Melting Arctic ice packs have also led countries to scramble to discover and dominate possible new shipping routes. When the chairman of the Norwegian Nobel Committee awarded the 2007 Nobel Peace Prize to the IPCC and Al Gore, he said, "A goal in our modern world must be to maintain 'human security' in the broadest sense." Similarly, albeit with different interests in mind, the United States' 2008 National Intelligence Assessment, which analyzes emerging threats to national security, focused specifically on climate change. [13]

Scientists have tried to define acceptable atmospheric concentrations of CO_2 or temperature rises that would still avert the worst consequences of global warming while accepting we will likely not entirely undo our changes. NASA scientists and others have focused on the target of 350 parts per million (ppm) of CO_2 in the atmosphere. [14] Their paleoclimatological data suggest that a doubling of CO_2 in the atmosphere, which is well within some IPCC scenarios for 2100, would likely increase the global

temperature by 6°C (11°F). Atmospheric CO_2 levels, however, passed 350 ppm in 1990 and reached 388 ppm by early 2010. This concentration will continue to rise rapidly as emissions accumulate in the atmosphere. Worse, even if the CO_2 concentration stabilizes, temperatures will continue to rise for some centuries, much the way a pan on a stove keeps absorbing heat even if the flame is lowered. Hence scientists have begun to suggest that anything less than zero net emissions by 2050 will be too little, too late; policy makers have yet to embrace such aggressive action. [15]

International and US Policy Response

The primary international policy response to climate change was the **United Nations Framework Convention on Climate Change (UNFCCC)**. The convention was adopted in May 1992 and became the first binding international legal instrument dealing directly with climate change. It was presented for signature at the Earth Summit in Rio de Janeiro and went into force in March 1994 with signatures from 166 countries. By 2010 the convention had been accepted by 193 countries. [16] UNFCCC signatories met in 1997 in Kyoto and agreed to a schedule of reduction targets known as the Kyoto Protocol. Industrialized countries committed to reducing emissions of specific GHGs, averaged over 2008–12, to 5 percent below 1990 levels. The European Union (EU) committed to an 8 percent reduction and the United States to 7 percent. Other industrialized countries agreed to lesser reductions or to hold their emissions constant, while developing countries made no commitments but hoped to industrialize more cleanly than their predecessors. Partly to help developing countries, the Kyoto Protocol also created a market for trading GHG emission allowances. If one country developed a carbon sink, such as by planting a forest, another country could buy the amount of carbon sequestered and use it to negate the equivalent amount of its own emissions.

The Kyoto Protocol has ultimately suffered from a lack of political will in the United States and abroad. The United States signed it, but the Senate never ratified it. US President George W. Bush backed away from the emission reduction targets and eventually rejected them entirely. By the time he took office in 2001, a 7 percent reduction from 1990 levels for the United States would have translated into a 30 percent reduction from 2001 levels. US GHG emissions, instead of declining, rose 14 percent from 1990 to 2008. [17] Almost all other Kyoto signatories will also fail to meet their goals. The EU, in contrast, is on track to meet or exceed its Kyoto targets. [18] GHG pollution allowances for major stationary sources have been traded through the EU Emissions

Trading System since 2005. The consensus in Europe is that the Kyoto Protocol is necessary and action is required to reduce GHGs.

The Kyoto Protocol expires in 2012, so meetings have begun to negotiate new goals. In December 2007, UNFCCC countries met in Bali to discuss a successor treaty. The conference made little headway, and countries met again in December 2009 in Copenhagen. That conference again failed to generate legally binding reduction goals, but the countries confirmed the dangers of climate change and agreed to strive to limit temperature increases to no more than 2°C total. A subsequent meeting was held in Cancun, Mexico, in late 2010.

Individual countries and US states and agencies have acted, nonetheless, in the absence of broader leadership. In 2007, EU countries set their own future emissions reduction goals, the so-called 20-20-20 strategy of reducing emissions 20 percent from 1990 levels by 2020 while reducing energy demand 20 percent through efficiency and generating 20 percent of energy from renewable resources. In January 2008 the European Commission proposed binding legislation to implement the 20-20-20 targets. This "climate and energy package" was approved by the European Parliament and Council in December 2008. It became law in June 2009. [19] In the Northeast United States, ten states collaborated to form the Regional Greenhouse Gas Initiative (RGGI), which caps and gradually lowers GHG emissions from power plants by 10 percent from 2009 to 2018. A similar program, the Western Climate Initiative, is being prepared by several western US states and Canadian provinces, and California's Assembly Bill 32, the Global Warming Solutions Act, set a state GHG emissions limit for 2020. [20] Likewise, the federal government under President Barack Obama committed to reducing its emissions, while the US Environmental Protection Agency (EPA), in response to a 2007 lawsuit led by the state of Massachusetts, prepared to regulate GHGs under the Clean Air Act.

Members of Congress, however, have threatened to curtail the EPA's power to do so, either by altering the procedures for New Source Review that would require carbon controls or by legislatively decreeing that global warming does not endanger human health. [22] In contrast, one bill to combat climate change would have reduced US emissions by 80 percent from 2005 levels by 2050. It passed the House of Representatives in 2009 but failed to make it to a Senate vote.

Corporate Response and Opportunity

Certain industries are more vulnerable than others to the economic impacts of climate change. Industries that are highly dependent on fossil fuels and high CO_2 emitters, such as oil and gas companies, cement producers, automobile manufacturers, airlines, and power plant operators, are closely watching legislation related to GHGs. The reinsurance industry, which over the past several years has taken large financial losses due to extreme weather events, is deeply concerned about global climate change and liabilities for its impacts.

Given the potential costs of ignoring climate change, the costs of addressing it appear rather minimal. In 2006, the UK Treasury released the *Stern Review on the Economics of Climate Change*. The report estimated that the most immediate effects of global warming would cause damages of "at least 5% of global GDP each year, now and forever. If a wider range of risks and impacts is taken into account, the estimates of damage could rise to 20% of GDP or more." Actions to mitigate the change, in contrast, would cost only about 1 percent of global GDP between 2010 and 2030. [23]

Corporate reactions have ranged from taking action now to reduce or eliminate emissions of GHGs and active engagement with carbon trading markets to actively opposing new policies that might require changes in products or processes. Anticipatory firms are developing scenarios for potential threats and opportunities related to those policies, public opinion, and resource constraints. Among those companies actively pursuing a reduction in GHGs, some cite financial gains for their actions. Walmart and General Electric both committed to major sustainability efforts in the first decade of the twenty-first century as have many smaller corporations. Central to their strategies are GHG reduction tactics.

Excessive GHG emissions may reflect inefficient energy use or loss of valuable assets, such as when natural gas escapes during production or use. The Carbon Disclosure Project emerged in 2000 as a private organization to track GHG emissions for companies that volunteered to disclose their data. By 2010, over 1,500 companies belonged to the organization, and institutional investors used these and other data to screen companies for corporate social responsibility. Out of concern for good corporate citizenship and in anticipation of potential future regulation, GHG emissions trading has become a growing market involving many large corporations. The emissions trading process involves credits for renewable energy generation, carbon sequestration, and low-emission agricultural and industrial practices that are bought and sold or optioned in anticipation of variable abilities to reach emissions reduction targets. Some companies have enacted internal, competitive emissions reduction goals and trading schemes as a way to involve all corporate divisions in a search for efficiency, cleaner production methods, and identification of other opportunities for reducing their contribution to climate change.

In parallel to tracking GHG emissions, clean tech or clean commerce has become increasingly prevalent as a concept and a term to describe technologies, such as wind energy, and processes, such as more efficient electrical grids, that do not generate as much or any pollution. New investments in sustainable energy increased between 2002 and 2008, when total investments in sustainable energy projects and companies reached $155 billion, with wind power representing the largest share at $51.8 billion. [24] Also in 2008, sustainability-focused companies as identified by the Dow Jones Sustainability Index or Goldman Sachs SUSTAIN list outperformed their industries by 15 percent over a six-month period. [25]

Conclusion

Our climate may always be changing, but humans have changed it dramatically in a short time with potentially dire consequences. GHGs emitted from human activities have increased the global temperature and will continue to increase it, even if we ceased all emissions today. International policy makers have built consensus for the need to curb global climate change but have struggled to take specific, significant actions. In contrast, at a smaller scale,

local governments and corporations have attempted to mitigate and adapt to an altered future. Taking a proactive stance on climate change can make good business sense.

At a minimum, strategic planning should be informed by climate change concerns and the inherent liabilities and opportunities therein. Whether operationalized by large firms or smaller companies, one important form of entrepreneurial innovation inspired by climate change challenges today is to apply tools associated with reduced climate and resource footprints that result in systemic reduction of energy and material inputs. When applied within firms and across supply chains, such tools increase profitability by lowering costs. More important, these measures can lead to innovations made visible by the efforts. At minimum, opportunities for product design and process improvements that both reduce climate change impact and increase resource efficiency and consumer loyalty make sense. Companies that chart a course around the most likely set of future conditions with an eye to competitive advantage, good corporate citizenship, and stewardship of natural resources are likely to optimize their profitability and flexibility—and hence their strategic edge—in the future.

KEY TAKEAWAYS

- Scientific consensus concludes human activity now influences global climate.
- Greenhouse gases (GHGs), of which carbon dioxide (CO_2) is predominant, trap heat through their accumulation in the atmosphere.
- Governments at all levels and corporations are designing mechanisms and strategies for addressing climate change by monetizing impacts.
- Companies are well advised to stay current with the science and analyze their liabilities and opportunities as emissions restrictions are increasingly imposed through tax or market means.

EXERCISES

1. Gradual warming of the earth's temperature is one indication/prediction of climate scientists. What other impacts are being felt today, or are likely to be felt in the future?
2. Given the climate change trends, what social and environmental concerns appear most significant?
3. What are the implications of climate change, and of regulation of GHG emissions, for companies?
4. Under what conditions does a climate change strategy become an opportunity or otherwise make sense for a firm?

[1] Carl Sagan, *Billions and Billions* (New York, NY: Random House 1997), 86.

[2] National Oceanic and Atmospheric Administration Paleoclimatology, "A Paleo Perspective on Global Warming," July 13, 2009, accessed August 19, 2010, http://www.ncdc.noaa.gov/paleo/globalwarming/home.html.

[3] The IPCC comprises three working groups and a task force. Working Group I assesses the scientific aspects of the climate system and climate change. Working Group II addresses the vulnerability of socioeconomic and natural systems to climate change, negative and positive consequences of climate change,

and options for adapting to those consequences. Working Group III assesses options for limiting greenhouse gas emissions and otherwise mitigating climate change. The Task Force on National Greenhouse Gas Inventories implemented the National Greenhouse Gas Inventories Program. Each report has been written by several hundred scientists and other experts from academic, scientific, and other institutions, both private and public, and has been reviewed by hundreds of independent experts. These experts were neither employed nor compensated by the IPCC nor by the United Nations system for this work.

[4] Justin Gillis, "Temperature Rising: A Scientist, His Work and a Climate Reckoning," *New York Times*, December 21, 2010, http://www.nytimes.com/2010/12/22/science/earth/22carbon.html?_r=1&pagewanted=2.

[5] Rajendra K. Pachauri and Andy Reisinger, eds. (core writing team), *Climate Change 2007: Synthesis Report* (Geneva, Switzerland: Intergovernmental Panel on Climate Change, 2008). Available from the Intergovernmental Panel on Climate Change, "IPCC Fourth Assessment Report: Climate Change 2007," accessed August 19, 2010, http://www.ipcc.ch/publications_and_data/ar4/syr/en/contents.html. A fifth assessment report was begun in January 2010 but has yet to be completed. Unless otherwise footnoted, all numbers in this list are from the fourth IPCC assessment.

[6] Data more current than the fourth IPCC report are available from NASA and NOAA, among other sources, at NASA, "GISS Surface Temperature Analysis (GISTEMP)," accessed January 27, 2011, http://data.giss.nasa.gov/gistemp; and National Oceanic and Atmospheric Administration, "NOAA: Warmest Global Sea-Surface Temperatures for August and Summer," September 16, 2009, accessed January 27, 2011, http://www.noaanews.noaa.gov/stories2009/20090916_globalstats.html.

[7] Bryan Walsh, "Another Blizzard," *Time*, February 10, 2010, accessed January 7, 2011, http://www.time.com/time/health/article/0,8599,1962294,00.html.

[8] James G. Titus, K. Eric Anderson, Donald R. Cahoon, Dean B. Gesch, Stephen K. Gill, Benjamin T. Gutierrez, E. Robert Thieler, and S. Jeffress Williams (lead authors), *Coastal Elevations and Sensitivity to Sea-Level Rise: A Focus on the Mid-Atlantic Region* (Washington, DC: US Climate Change Science Program, 2009), accessed August 19, 2010, http://www.epa.gov/climatechange/effects/coastal/sap4-1.html.

[9] National Science Foundation, "Methane Releases from Arctic Shelf May Be Much Larger and Faster Than Anticipated," news release, March 4, 2010, accessed January 7, 2011, http://www.nsf.gov/news/news_images.jsp?cntn_id=116532&org=NSF and http://www.nsf.gov/news/news_summ.jsp?cntn_id=116532&org=NSF&from=news.

[10] US Geological Survey, "USGS Science to Inform U.S. Fish & Wildlife Service Decision Making on Polar Bears, Executive Summary," accessed January 27, 2011, http://www.usgs.gov/newsroom/special/polar_bears/docs/executive_summary.pdf.

[11] World Health Organization, "Cholera," June 2010, accessed August 19, 2010, http://www.who.int/mediacentre/factsheets/fs107/en/index.html.

[12] US Environmental Protection Agency, "Heat Island Effect," accessed January 27, 2011, http://www.epa.gov/heatisland.

[13] Ole Danbolt Mjøs, "Award Ceremony Speech" (presentation speech for the 2007 Nobel Peace Prize, Oslo, Norway, December 10, 2007), accessed January 7, 2011, http://nobelprize.org/nobel_prizes/peace/laureates/2007/presentation-speech.html.

[14] James Hansen, Makiko Sato, Pushker Kharecha, David Beerling, Valerie Masson-Delmotte, Mark Pagani, Maureen Raymo, Dana L. Royer, and James C. Zachos, "Target Atmospheric CO$_2$: Where Should Humanity Aim?" *The Open Atmospheric Science Journal* 2 (2008): 217–31.

[15] H. Damon Matthews and Ken Caldeira, "Stabilizing Climate Requires Near-Zero Emissions," *Geophysical Research Letters* 35, no. 4: L04705 (2008), 1–5.

[16] United Nations Framework Convention on Climate Change, "Status of Ratification of the Convention," accessed January 27, 2011, http://unfccc.int/kyoto_protocol/status_of_ratification/items/2613.php.

[17] US Environmental Protection Agency, *2010 Greenhouse Gas Inventory Report* (Washington, DC: US Environmental Protection Agency, 2010), accessed January 29, 2011, http://www.epa.gov/climatechange/emissions/downloads10/US-GHG-Inventory-2010_ExecutiveSummary.pdf.

[18] European Union, "Climate Change: Progress Report Shows EU on Track to Meet or Over-Achieve Kyoto Emissions Target," news release, November 12, 2009, accessed August 19, 2010, http://europa.eu/rapid/pressReleasesAction.do?reference=IP/09/1703&format=HTML&aged=0&language=EN&guiLanguage=en.

[19] European Commission, "The EU Climate and Energy Package," accessed January 29, 2011, http://ec.europa.eu/clima/policies/brief/eu/package_en.htm and http://ec.europa.eu/environment/climat/climate_action.htm.

[20] California Environmental Protection Agency Air Resources Board, "Assembly Bill 32: Global Warming Solutions Act," accessed August 19, 2010, http://www.arb.ca.gov/cc/ab32/ab32.htm.

[21] Matthew L. Wald, "E.P.A. Says It Will Press on With Greenhouse Gas Regulation," *New York Times*, December 23, 2010, http://www.nytimes.com/2010/12/24/science/earth/24epa.html?_r=1&ref=environmentalprotectionagency.

[22] "Coal State Senators Battle EPA to Control Greenhouse Gases," *Environmental News Service*, February 23, 2010, accessed January 7, 2011, http://www.ens-newswire.com/ens/feb2010/2010-02-23-093.html; Juliet Eilperin and David A. Fahrenthold, "Lawmakers Move to Restrain EPA on Climate Change," *Washington Post*, March 5, 2010, accessed January 7, 2011, http://www.washingtonpost.com/wp-dyn/content/article/2010/03/04/AR2010030404715.htm.

[23] Lord Stern, "Executive Summary," in *Stern Review on the Economics of Climate Change* (London: HM Treasury, 2006), 1, accessed January 7, 2011, http://www.hm-treasury.gov.uk/sternreview_index.htm.

[24] Rohan Boyle, Chris Greenwood, Alice Hohler, Michael Liebreich, Eric Usher, Alice Tyne, and Virginia Sonntag-O'Brien, *Global Trends in Sustainable Energy Investment 2009*, United Nations Environment Programme, 2008, accessed January 29, 2011, http://sefi.unep.org/fileadmin/media/sefi/docs/publications/Global_Trends_2008.pdf.

[25] Daniel Mahler, Jeremy Barker, Louis Belsand, and Otto Schulz, *Green Winners* (Chicago: A. T. Kearney, 2009), 2, http://www.atkearney.com/images/global/pdf/Green_winners.pdf.

5.2 East West Partners: Sustainability Strategy

LEARNING OBJECTIVES

1. Understand the conditions under which entrepreneurial leaders can work inside large companies.

2. Examine how and why sustainability implementation can require working with multiple stakeholders to increase social, environmental, and business benefits.

3. Identify how to translate sustainability thinking into viable corporate strategy.

4. Illustrate how to positively pair ecosystems, climate, sustainable development, and community contribution.

The first case looks at how a young entrepreneur, who recently completed his graduate training, successfully built an innovative pilot effort within a large real estate firm that manages real estate and ski resorts.

It might seem unlikely that a real estate developer, much less a project focused on expanding a ski resort, could provide a model of sustainable business practices, but real estate developer East West Partners (EWP) has done just that through its collaboration with a ski resort called Northstar Tahoe. Land conservation, waste reduction, and the adoption of wind energy are all part of EWP's incorporation of environmental and community considerations into every aspect of the project. At the same time the developer realizes significant cost savings and builds a reputation that enhances its competitive advantage. This was accomplished through top leadership's creating the opportunity for a young man with a newly minted MBA to innovatively integrate sustainability thinking into strategy.

East West Partners and the Northstar Development

East West Partners was founded in the 1970s by a group of real estate professionals working in the Richmond, Virginia, area. To "protect what we're here to enjoy" was a founding principle for EWP. In the mid-1980s, two senior EWP partners formed autonomous divisions in North Carolina and Colorado, maintaining a commitment to community and environmental quality and a loose affiliation with the Virginia group.

In 2000, Booth Creek Holdings, Northstar ski resort's parent company, approached EWP's Colorado office about a joint venture to develop land owned by the resort. Their subsequent agreement created East West Partners, Tahoe. EWP's initial decision to partner in the redevelopment of Northstar was based on the project's positive economic potential and sense of fit between EWP's and Northstar's business philosophy. The project was big. Northstar, a popular, family-oriented ski resort, owned hundreds of acres of land that could be developed into residential home sites, each with a market value of hundreds of thousands of dollars. The expansion and redevelopment of Northstar-at-Tahoe, which included a ski village with an ice rink and a massive increase in resort housing, including fractional-ownership condominiums, was expected to cost $2.7 billion over fifteen years. EWP would get zoning approvals, develop land, and build residences and commercial properties, profiting ultimately from property sales and management.

EWP Tahoe's chief executive, Roger Lessman, and project manager, David Tirman, reasoned that through careful design and the latest green building techniques they could develop new homes with limited environmental impact that would save money on owner operations, particularly energy and water costs. Furthermore, environmentally responsible development and a proactive approach with the local communities would enhance community relations, possibly ease government approvals, and add to the sales appeal of their properties.

By mid-2002, however, the importance of environmental performance and the level of effort necessary to incorporate it into branding and marketing had exceeded initial expectations. Within a year of helping area residents develop a new community plan, EWP discovered that a small but vocal group of citizens was unilaterally antigrowth and opposed to *any* development, regardless of efforts toward sustainability. It became clear to Lessman and Tirman that they would need help working with the community and establishing EWP as a resort development industry leader sensitive to local social and environmental concerns.

The Ski Resort Industry

In the early 1990s, no single ski company could claim more than 3 percent of the North American market. But industry shifts were under way and by 2002, about 20 percent of US ski resorts captured 80 percent of skier visits. The total for US ski visits in 2001–2 was 54,411,000, with the four largest companies accounting for about 15,000,000. The trends toward acquisitions and larger companies with multiple resorts were accelerating. So too were the industry's awareness and concern about global warming and its accompanying changing weather patterns influencing snowfalls and spring melts. Because of the industry's intimate links to well-functioning natural systems, its acute weather dependence, and the protection of aesthetic beauty associated with nature, which customers travel there to enjoy (and pay to surround themselves with), the term *sustainability* was an increasingly familiar one in ski resort strategy discussions.

During the 1990s the industry emphasized ski villages and on-mountain residences. The affluence of aging baby boom generation skiers and their growing affinity for amenities such as shopping, restaurant dining, and off-season recreation alternatives led to a development surge in ski area villages and mountain communities. Unfortunately, social and environmental issues developed alongside the economic windfall provided by ski area land development. The second homes and high-end shops that attracted wealthy skiers also displaced lower-income residents who lived and worked in or near resort areas. Wildlife that was dependent on the fragile mountain habitat was displaced as well.

Environmental groups issued scathing reports on the damage caused by ski area development and rated ski areas for their impacts on wildlife. In October 1998, environmental activists in Vail, Colorado, protested a ski area expansion into Canada lynx habitat by burning ski resort buildings in a $12 million fire. [1] Elsewhere, local citizen groups pursued less radical and perhaps more effective means of protecting mountain land and communities through actions that blocked, delayed, and limited development plan approvals by local zoning boards. In the California market, land developers faced very difficult government approval processes. Local government agencies and citizens were key players who could block or supply approvals for land development plans.

EWP's Approach

The proactive approach that EWP adopted—engaging all relevant actors in an open process—had both benefits and drawbacks. It seemed that a small group of citizens would inevitably oppose development of any kind, and keeping that group informed might not have been in a developer's best interest. On the other hand, a majority of nongovernmental organizations (NGOs) and local residents were likely to see the merit of socially and environmentally sustainable development, which argued for EWP's full disclosure of its plans with sustainability considerations factored in throughout. The trust of locals, won through an open and transparent planning process, seemed to speed approvals and inform and even attract customers. EWP's decision was to proceed with the sustainability-infused strategy and accept the risk that construction delays related to its proactive approach could cause added expenses, potentially overwhelming the benefits of goodwill, market acceptance, and premium pricing.

New Leadership Needed

EWP executives knew that environmental concerns were high on the list of factors they should consider in the Northstar development project given the area's high sensitivity to environmental health and preservation issues. Not only were prospective buyers more environmentally aware, but also, in the California market, land developers faced a very difficult government approval process relative to that in other states.

To address these concerns in the summer of 2002, Lessman hired Aaron Revere as director of environmental initiatives and made him responsible for ensuring that no opportunity for environmental sustainability was overlooked in building and operating the resort consortium. Revere, a recent University of Virginia environmental science and Darden School of Business MBA graduate, made it clear to subcontractors and materials suppliers that any attempt to

substitute techniques or materials that circumvented environmental design facets would not be overlooked or tolerated. With complete top management support, Revere's efforts met with little or no internal resistance. Coworkers wanted to help preserve the natural beauty of the areas they worked in and took a strong interest in new methods for reducing environmental impact.

In the new development model Revere proposed, sustainability would be a defining criterion from the outset. He presented top management with a business plan for making environmental amenities a central platform that differentiated EWP's project designs. He developed sustainability guidelines and outlined a strategy for making the Tahoe projects' environmental criteria a model for design and marketing. EWP would streamline government approvals by meeting with community stakeholders and outlining EWP's program for corporate responsibility before a project began. Contractors, subcontractors, suppliers, and maintenance services interested in working with an EWP project would know as much about a project's environmental and social criteria as they did about its economics. Marketing and sales personnel would be educated about the sustainability qualities of the project from the start and were expected to use those qualities to help generate sales. As the story unfolded, early tests of EWP's ability to translate ideals into concrete actions with measurable results came quickly.

A Cornerstone of Sustainable Development: LEED Certification

Revere was pleased to find that other top employees, particularly Northstar project manager David Tirman, had already written of EWP's intent to make environmental sustainability a key feature. The Leadership in Energy and Environmental Design (LEED) green building certification served as a cornerstone in these efforts. The LEED system was the result of a collaborative panel of respected green building specialists convened by the US Green Building Council (USGBC). The USGBC was formed in 1993 to address the growing US interest in sustainable building technology. The group was associated with the American Institute of Architects (AIA), the leading US architectural design organization. USGBC created the LEED system to provide unambiguous standards that would allow purchasers and end users to determine the validity of environmental claims made by builders and developers. Additionally, LEED provided conscientious industry players with a marketing tool that differentiated their products according to their efforts to minimize adverse health and environmental impacts while maintaining high standards for building quality and livability.

EWP expected to be among the largest builders of LEED-certified projects as that certification system branched into residential buildings. EWP encouraged customers who bought undeveloped lots to use LEED specifications and was offering guidelines and recommended suppliers and architects. By 2006, LEED certification was sought for all Northstar structures.

Successful projects implemented with LEED certification by 2007 included careful dismantling of the clock tower building at Northstar. EWP worked with the nonprofit group Institute for Local Self-Reliance (ILSR) to develop a deconstruction and sales strategy for the assets. Revere, who with three other EWP employees had become a LEED-certified practitioner, documented the percentage of waste diverted from the landfill, energy savings, and CO_2 offset credits that would result in tax benefits to EWP.

EWP's renovation of Sunset's restaurant on the shore of Lake Tahoe was already under way when Revere was hired. Revere nevertheless wanted to pursue LEED certification for every possible Tahoe Mountain Resorts structure. He soon became a familiar figure at the restaurant, finding design changes, products, and processes that captured environmentally effective building opportunities in the simplest and most efficient ways. His presence on the job enabled Revere to see new opportunities: A system for dispensing nonpolluting cleaning chemicals was installed; and "gray water" from sinks was drained separately, run through a special coagulation and filtration system, and reused for watering landscaping plants outside the restaurant. Sawdust from sanding the recycled redwood decking was captured and prevented from entering Lake Tahoe.

The end result of Revere's efforts and the enthusiastic participation of the architect, contractors, workers, and even the chefs was the first restaurant renovation to receive LEED certification and a marketing tool that appealed to the resort's environmentally aware clientele. By the time the renovation was completed, Revere estimated that the expense of seeking superior environmental performance was a negligible part of total renovation cost. Savings on operations—due to low energy-use lighting, maximum use of daylight and air circulation, natural cooling, and superior insulation—were expected to more than pay for the additional cost within the first two to three years.

Conservation and Development: Building Partnerships through an Oxymoron

While the pursuit of LEED certification for buildings was an excellent step toward reducing environmental impact, Revere and EWP management knew that they would have to do more to persuade the local community of their commitment. In 2002, the problem of habitat degradation from ski areas became the topic of considerable negative press. The environmental group Ski Area Citizens' Coalition (SACC) published claims that ski areas had transitioned from economically marginal winter recreation facilities to year-round resorts with premium real estate developments, mostly without sensitivity to environmental and social issues. The group went on to rate several prominent ski areas on environmental concerns, issuing grades from A to F, on its website. [2]

Since the SACC weighted its ratings heavily on habitat destruction, and new construction necessarily destroyed habitat, Northstar, which planned a 200-acre expansion of its ski area, a 21-acre village and a 345-acre subdivision, fared poorly. While other ski areas with more land and larger residential areas had disturbed more habitats, the SACC viewed past development as "water over the dam." In the eyes of the group, Northstar's planned expansion of both ski trails and housing overwhelmed any possible sustainable development efforts. Though the SACC rating would probably have little if any impact on the number of skiers visiting Northstar or the number of new homes sold, EWP executives were nevertheless annoyed. They were working hard to be good stewards of the land, determined to set an example for profitable, socially and environmentally responsible development and operations without giving up their planned projects.

Rather than ignore the SACC rating and environmentalists' concerns about development of any wilderness area, EWP management, under Aaron Revere's leadership, began an open and direct dialogue with conservation groups such as Sierra Watch and the Mountain Area Preservation Foundation. In March 2005, the groups reached what many termed as a precedent-setting agreement to limit Northstar's development of its eight thousand acres of land to fewer than eight hundred acres. In addition, the agreement required a transfer fee on all Northstar real estate sales to be used to purchase and protect sensitive wildlife habitat in the Martis Valley area of Tahoe. The fees were expected to total more than $30 million for the Martis Valley alone. In contrast, the previous two state conservation bonds raised $33 million for the entire Sierra mountain range.

In addition, the agreement called for a "habitat conservation plan" for the more than seven thousand acres of Northstar land not earmarked for residential and commercial development. EWP viewed that agreement as having dual benefits. Through the agreement, environmental and community groups dropped their opposition to the development projects proposed by Northstar, and a large tract of land was protected for the foreseeable future. The additional revenue generated for the purchase of more protected acreage allowed EWP to do more than simply responsibly develop land. Through the strategic intent to develop highly desirable and environmentally sustainable properties, the company had designed a new method of generating funds for the protection of the natural environment that is by definition key to its properties' success.

Measuring Success and Making a Difference

Aaron Revere's definition of his job with EWP included proving wherever possible the commercial viability of "doing the right thing." What preserved and enhanced the natural environmental systems on which the resort depended would serve the longer-term economic interests of the owner. But Revere was interested in the quantitative gains in the short and intermediate terms. He wanted to add to the growing pool of data in the ski industry on the cost differentials between typical construction and development practices and those that strived to incorporate sustainable design elements. Tahoe Mountain Resorts provided an ideal opportunity for tracking improvements and measuring the economic benefits that sustainable practices brought to the company. Metrics included biodiversity/natural capital (ecosystem, flora and fauna, and rare species assessments), air and water quality, and water and energy use. Revere's strategy included building an environmental initiation team within EWP/Northstar. He also sought early adopters in both Tahoe Mountain Resorts and nearby Booth Creek who would build sustainability into the corporate culture and brand. Sales and marketing people were encouraged to view sustainability features as what he termed "cooler and sexier" selling points that could command a premium price. Revere used weekly e-mail advisories to help keep implementation ideas fresh in the minds of his coworkers. He wanted to put local and organic food items on the menus of Tahoe Mountain Resort restaurants and eliminate the serving of threatened species such as Chilean sea bass and swordfish—the idea was to be consistent and authentic across operations. Advisories sent to colleagues included the following:

"Consider permeable paving stones or grass instead of asphalt, stockpiling snow from road-clearing above 'sinks' that would replenish aquifers, preformed walls, VOC [volatile organic compound]-free paints, stains, and sealants, water-conserving sensors on faucets and lights, and recyclable carpeting." [3]

The California Waste Management Board awarded EWP its Waste Reduction Awards Program's highest honor for eight consecutive years (1997–2004). Describing EWP, the board stated, "To date, East West Partners has achieved successful and unique waste reduction and recycling activities within its Coyote Moon golf course operations, Wild Goose restaurant operations, general office operations, and the planning of Old Greenwood and the Northstar Ski Village. From May 2002 to May 2003, East West Partners successfully diverted an estimated 12.5 tons of material from landfill. These efforts to 'remove the concept of waste' from their company vocabulary saved East West Partners thousands of dollars." [4]

Under Revere's direction, EWP achieved Audubon International's Gold Level certification for the Gray's Crossing Golf Course. Only three other golf courses in the nation had achieved this status for exceptional environmental sensitivity in the design and operations of both the facility and the community that surrounds it. Working with Revere and EWP's hand-picked contractors, the Audubon sustainable development experts were sufficiently impressed by the company's sincere efforts on sustainability as a strategic theme that they offered to work with EWP to make the redevelopment of a second course, the Old Greenwood Golf Course, a Gold Level project as well. Sustainable design principles applied to golf courses created significant cost and environmental savings, requiring only 50 percent as much water and fertilizer as conventional courses. Typical of the myriad implementation choices made across Revere's projects, cost savings, allocation of precious water to better purposes, and a halving of synthetic chemical use merged in what was ultimately seen as just good business.

KEY TAKEAWAYS

- Climate change is already influencing mountain ice packs and snowfall patterns, shortening ski seasons, and requiring ski resorts to adapt their strategies.
- Sincere efforts with stakeholders can create opportunities and help generate creative solutions.
- A committed, determined, educated entrepreneurial individual can create change within a large firm.

- Well-implemented sustainability concepts deliver concrete business benefits, both operational and strategic.

EXERCISES

1. What factors drove EWP to incorporate sustainability approaches into its strategy?

2. What are the roles of climate and climate change in shaping strategy for this company at the Tahoe location?

3. What are the changes Aaron Revere instituted? How did they contribute to operations and strategy for the firm? What learning could be transferred to other parts of the parent company's activities?

4. Given the tasks Aaron Revere had when he began his job, identify no less than five of the most significant challenges he faced in this job. Use the case information, your knowledge of business, and your own experience and imagination to anticipate what you believe Aaron would tell you were his major challenges.

5. Prepare an analysis of key factors that explain Revere's success. Come to class ready to present your analysis and defend your argument.

---

[1] Hal Clifford, "Downhill Slide," *Sierra*, January/February 2003, 35, accessed January 7, 2011, http://www.sierraclub.org/sierra/200301/ski.asp.

[2] Ski Area Citizens' Coalition, "Welcome to the 2011 Ski Area Report Card," accessed January 7, 2011, http://www.skiareacitizens.com.

[3] {Author's Name Retracted as requested by the work's original creator or licensee}, *East West Partners: Sustainable Business Strategy in Real Estate and Ski Resorts*, UVA-ENT-0093 (Charlottesville: Darden Business Publishing, University of Virginia, October 21, 2008).

[4] {Author's Name Retracted as requested by the work's original creator or licensee}, *East West Partners: Sustainable Business Strategy in Real Estate and Ski Resorts*, UVA-ENT-0093 (Charlottesville: Darden Business Publishing, University of Virginia, October 21, 2008).

5.3 Frito-Lay North America: The Making of a Net-Zero Snack Chip

LEARNING OBJECTIVES

1. Understand how measurable sustainability goals can drive business decisions.

2. Explain how projects within a company can contribute to larger changes in corporate culture and sustainability.

The second case, Frito-Lay (PepsiCo), examines innovative activity that has been ongoing for several years at a manufacturing facility in Arizona. Large firms typically struggle to implement significant change, yet this example shows how established companies can take steps that ultimately create innovative and systemic outcomes guided by sustainability principles that benefit multiple stakeholders.

It was late 2007, and Al Halvorsen had assembled his team of managers from across Frito-Lay North America (FLNA) to make a final decision on an ambitious proposal to take one of its nearly forty manufacturing plants "off the grid" [1] through the installation of cutting-edge energy- and water-saving technologies. After a decade of successful initiatives to improve the productivity of operations and to reduce the energy and other resources used in the production of the company's snack products, senior managers had decided that it was time to take their efforts to the next level.

Frito-Lay's resource conservation initiatives started in the late 1990s. Company managers recognized potential operating challenges as they faced rising utility rates for water, electricity, and natural gas; increasing resource constraints; and expected government-imposed limits on greenhouse gas (GHG) emissions. These challenges had implications for the company's ability to deliver sustained growth to its shareholders.

The programs the company put in place resulted in a decade of efficiency improvements, leading to incremental reductions in fuel consumption, water consumption, and GHG emissions. Each project's implementation helped the operations and engineering teams within the organization grow their institutional knowledge and expertise in a range of emerging technologies.

By 2007, managers were starting to wonder how far they could take efforts to improve the efficiency and environmental impact of operations. Al Halvorsen was several months into a new initiative to evaluate the feasibility of bundling several innovative technologies at one manufacturing facility to maximize the use of renewable energy and dramatically reduce the consumption of water. By leveraging the expertise of the in-house engineering team, and grouping a number of technologies that had been previously piloted in isolation at other facilities, Halvorsen believed that a superefficient facility prototype would emerge that could serve as a learning laboratory for the improvement of the company's overall manufacturing practices.

Halvorsen had asked the members of his cross-functional team of managers from across the organization to evaluate the broad scope of challenges involved with creating what was dubbed a "net-zero" facility. The project would likely push the boundaries of current financial hurdles for capital expenditure projects but would result in a number of tangible and intangible benefits. After months of evaluation, the time had come to decide whether to go forward with the project.

A Tasty History

Frito-Lay North America is one of the nation's best-known snack-food companies, with origins in the first half of the twentieth century. In 1932, Elmer Doolin started the Frito Company after purchasing manufacturing equipment, customer accounts, and a recipe from a small corn-chip manufacturer in San Antonio, Texas. That same year, Herman W. Lay of Nashville, Tennessee, started a business distributing potato chips for the Barrett Food Products Company.

The two companies experienced dramatic growth in the ensuing years. Herman Lay expanded his distribution business into new markets and in 1939 bought the manufacturing operations of Barrett Foods to establish the H. W. Lay Corporation. The Frito Company expanded production capacity and broadened its marketing presence by opening a western division in Los Angeles in 1941. Although the war years posed significant challenges, the two companies emerged intact and won the hearts of American GIs with products that provided a tasty reminder of home.

Both companies experienced rapid growth in the postwar boom years, fueled by an ever-expanding product selection and the development of innovative distribution networks. By the mid-1950s, the H. W. Lay Corporation was the largest manufacturer of snack foods in the United States, and the Frito Company had expanded its reach into all forty-eight states. As the two companies expanded nationally, they developed cooperative franchise arrangements. In 1961, after several years of collaboration, the companies merged to form Frito-Lay Inc., the nation's largest snack-food company.

In the years following the creation of Frito-Lay, the company continued to experience rapid growth and changes in its ownership structure. In 1965, a merger with Pepsi-Cola brought together two of the nation's leading snack and beverage companies under one roof. The resulting parent, PepsiCo Inc., was one of the world's leading food companies in 2007 and a consistent presence on *Fortune*'s "America's Most Admired Companies" list. The company includes a number of other iconic brands such as Tropicana juices, Gatorade sports drinks, and Quaker foods.

By 2007, the Frito-Lay business unit owned more than fifteen brands that each grossed more than $100 million in annual sales. The most well-known brands included Lay's potato chips, Fritos corn chips, Cheetos cheese-flavored snacks, Ruffles potato chips, Doritos and Tostitos tortilla chips, Baked Lay's potato crisps, SunChips multigrain snacks, and Rold Gold pretzels.

The Vision for a More Sustainable Snack Company

By the 1990s, PepsiCo's Frito-Lay business unit was experiencing healthy growth in earnings and was continuing to expand internationally. In the United States and Canada, Frito-Lay North America was operating more than forty manufacturing facilities, hundreds of distribution centers and sales offices, and a sizeable fleet of delivery vehicles. As the company grew, the costs associated with operating these assets increased as well.

Increasing resource costs, fuel price volatility, and emerging concerns about future resource availability started to worry managers during this time period. Members of the environmental compliance group took the initiative and expanded their traditional regulatory compliance role to also focus proactively on resource conservation as a cost-reduction strategy. Later, a resource conservation and energy team was formed at Frito-Lay's Plano, Texas, headquarters to coordinate efficiency initiatives across the portfolio of manufacturing and distribution facilities. At the facility level, "Green Teams" and "Energy Teams," consisting of plant operators and line workers, assembled to closely monitor daily energy and water usage and to identify and implement productivity-boosting resource conservation projects.

Initial results of the resource conservation program were positive, with projects paying back well within the corporate financial benchmark of two to three years and achieving incremental reductions in energy and water use. The company's senior management, including then CEO Al Bru, took notice of these results and set the stage for a more ambitious program at a time when competitors were only dabbling in the implementation of more efficient business processes.

In 1999, Senior Vice President of Operations Jim Rich challenged the team to expand its efforts into a company-wide effort to reduce resource use and costs. Managers at headquarters defined a set of stretch goals that, if achieved, would take the company's efforts to the cutting edge of what was feasible on the basis of available technologies while still meeting corporate financial hurdles for the approval of capital expense projects. This set of goals, affectionately known as the BHAGs ("Big Hairy Audacious Goals"), [2] called for the following efforts:

- A reduction in fuel consumption per pound of product (primarily natural gas) by 30 percent
- A reduction in water consumption per pound of product by 50 percent
- A reduction in electricity consumption per pound of product by 25 percent

Over the next eight years, the Resource Conservation Team and facility Green Teams set about designing, building, and implementing projects across the portfolio of FLNA facilities. Both new and established technologies were piloted, and responsibility was placed on line employees to implement improved operating practices and to monitor variances in resource usage from shift to shift. A growing group of in-house engineering experts—both at headquarters and at manufacturing facilities—oversaw these initiatives, bypassing the need to hire energy service companies (ESCOs), outside consultants often hired for these types of projects, and ensuring that FLNA developed and retained valuable institutional knowledge.

By 2007, the team estimated that it was saving the company $55 million annually in electricity, natural gas, and water expenses, compared with 1999 usage, as a result of the projects implemented to date. Piloted technologies included photovoltaic cells, solar concentrators, landfill gas capture, sky lighting, process steam recapture, and many other energy and water efficiency measures.

In 2006, Indra Nooyi was selected as the new chairman and CEO of the PepsiCo. As a thirteen-year veteran of the company, and the former CFO, she was supportive of the resource conservation initiatives at Frito-Lay and within other operating divisions. Nooyi set forth her vision for PepsiCo of "Performance with Purpose" in a speech on December 18, 2006, in New Delhi. "I am convinced that helping address societal problems is a responsibility of every business, big and small," she said. "Financial achievement can and must go hand-in-hand with social and environmental performance." [3] This statement established her triple-bottom-line vision for growth at the company. [4]

In line with this new vision, and with the support of the FLNA finance team, what started as a productivity initiative began to push the boundaries of traditional business thinking about the value of "sustainable" operating practices. By the end of the twenty-first century's first decade, all PepsiCo business units were adding environmental and resource conservation criteria to the capital expense approval process. With buy-in from the FLNA CFO, the benchmarks for capital expenditure projects were extended if a project could demonstrate additional benefits outside of traditional net present value calculations. This change was justified on the following grounds:

- New technological and manufacturing capabilities are of long-term value to the company and can result in future cost-cutting opportunities.
- Pilot projects that combine multiple technologies serve as a proof of concept for previously undiscovered operational synergies.
- Such projects are a part of overall corporate risk mitigation strategy to reduce dependence on water, energy, and raw materials in the face of resource cost pressures and an increasingly resource-constrained world.
- Sustainably manufactured products will have a place in the marketplace and will contribute to sales dollars, customer loyalty, and increased market share relative to competitors who do not innovate.
- Emerging government regulation, particularly with regard to carbon, could create additional value streams. For example, under a cap-and-trade system, projects that reduce net emissions would potentially generate carbon credits, which could be sold in a market.
- Water, electric, and natural gas inflation rates have been increasing even beyond expectations.

Measuring and Reporting GHG Emissions

A secondary benefit of FLNA's conservation initiatives was the collection of rich data about operations, productivity, and resource usage. The efforts of each facility Energy Team to implement the corporate resource conservation program resulted in an in-depth understanding of the impact each project had on fuel and electricity consumption in the manufacturing process. Managers at headquarters were able to piece together an aggregate picture of energy consumption across the organization.

Around the same time period, managers within the environmental compliance group started to voice their opinion that the company should be documenting its success in improving the energy efficiency of its operations. During the 1990s, the issue of climate change was receiving increased attention globally—and the Clinton administration was warning that reductions in US emissions of GHGs would be necessary in the future as a part of the solution to this emerging global problem. FLNA managers believed that future climate regulation was likely and were concerned that they might be penalized relative to their competitors in the event that the government limited GHG emissions from manufacturing operations. Future emissions caps were likely to freeze a company's emissions at their current levels or to mandate a reduction to a lower level. Managers were concerned that all the reductions in emissions made by the company prior to the establishment of a regulatory limit would be ignored. As a result, they sought out potential venues for documenting their successes.

Through dialogues with the US Environmental Protection Agency (EPA), the company learned about a new voluntary industry partnership program aimed at the disclosure and reduction of corporate emissions of GHGs. The Climate Leaders program was the flagship government initiative aimed at working with US companies to reduce GHG emissions, and it provided its partners with a number of benefits. The program, a government-sponsored forum for disclosure of emissions information, offered consulting assistance to companies in the creation of a GHG emissions inventory. In exchange for these benefits, Climate Leaders partners were required to annually disclose emissions and to set a meaningful goal and date by which they would achieve reductions.

In 2004, FLNA signed a partnership agreement with Climate Leaders—publicly disclosing its corporate emissions since 2002. [5] By joining the program, FLNA challenged itself to improve the efficiency of its operations even more. A corporate goal of reducing carbon dioxide (CO_2) equivalent emissions per ton of manufactured product by 14 percent from 2002 to 2010 was included as a part of the partnership agreement. Public inventory results through 2007 are provided in Table 5.1 "FLNA Public GHG Inventory Results, 2002–7" and include emissions from the following sources:

- **Scope 1.** [6] Natural gas, coal, fuel oil, gasoline, diesel, refrigerants (hydrofluorocarbons [HFCs], perfluorocarbons [PFCs]).
- **Scope 2.** Purchased electricity, purchased steam.

Table 5.1 FLNA Public GHG Inventory Results, 2002-7

	Scope 1 Emissions (Metric Tons CO2 Eq)	Scope 2 Emissions (Metric Tons CO2 Eq)	Total Emissions (Metric Tons CO2 Eq)	Metric Tons of Product Manufactured	Normalized Total
2002	1,072,667	459,088	1,530,755	1,287,069	1.19
2003	1,081,634	452,812	1,534,446	1,304,939	1.18
2004	1,066,906	455.122	1,522,028	1,324,137	1.15
2005	1,113,061	464,653	1,577,714	1,401,993	1.13
2006	1,076,939	456,466	1,533,405	1,394,632	1.10
2007 (Projected)	1,084,350	442,425	1,526,775	1,442,756	1.06

Source: PepsiCo Inc., Annual Reports, 2002–7, accessed March 14, 2011, http://pepsico.com/Investors/Annual-Reports.html; US EPA Climate Leaders inventory reporting, 2002–7; and Environmental Protection Agency, Climate Leaders, "Annual GHG Inventory Summary and Goal Tracking Form: Frito-Lay, Inc., 2002–2009," accessed March 17, 2011, http://www.epa.gov/climateleaders/documents/inventory/Public_GHG_Inventory_FritoLay.pdf.

Taking the Next Step

By 2007, FLNA was well on its way to achieving the goal of a 14 percent reduction in normalized emissions [7]—having reduced emissions by 11 percent in the prior five years. Resource conservation projects had been rolled out at plants and distribution centers across North America to improve the efficiency with which products were manufactured and distributed to retailers.

Over the same seven-year period, top-line sales grew by 35 percent. [8] As a result of the increase in sales and decrease in emissions intensity, absolute emissions, or the sum total of emissions from all sources, remained relatively flat during this period.

For most companies, this substantial reduction in emissions intensity per unit of production would be cause for celebration. Although FLNA managers were pleased with their progress, they were hopeful that future projects could reduce *absolute emissions*—enabling the company to meet or exceed future regulatory challenges by arresting the growth of GHG emissions while continuing to deliver sustained growth in earnings to shareholders. For the innovators at FLNA, and PepsiCo as a whole, this strategy was part of fulfilling the "Performance with a Purpose" vision set forth by their CEO.

It was time to set a new goal for the team. As they had done almost ten years before, members of the resource conservation team floated ideas about how they could push the limits of available technologies to achieve a new, more aggressive goal of cutting absolute resource usage without limiting future growth prospects. A variety of technologies was available to the team, many of which had been piloted separately at one or more facilities.

One manager asked the question, "What if we could package all these technologies together in one place? How far off the water, electricity, and natural gas grids could we take a facility?" [9] The team developed this kernel of an idea, which came to be the basis for what would be a new type of facility. The vision for this net-zero facility was simple: to maximize the use of renewable energy and to dramatically reduce the consumption of water in a manufacturing plant.

Going Net Zero at Casa Grande

Planning for its pilot net-zero facility began in earnest. Rather than build a new manufacturing facility, managers selected one of the company's existing plants for extensive upgrades. But selecting which plant to use for the pilot was in itself a challenge, due to the varying effectiveness of certain renewable technologies in different geographic regions, production line characteristics, plant size considerations, and other factors.

With the assistance of the National Renewable Energy Laboratory (NREL), members of the headquarters operations team began evaluating a preselected portfolio of seven plants on the basis of a number of key criteria. Available energy technologies were mapped over geographic facility locations to predict potential effectiveness (e.g., solar panels were more effective in sunnier locales). An existing software model was modified to determine the best combination of renewable technologies by location while minimizing life-cycle costs of the proposed projects.

The results of the NREL model, when combined with a number of other qualitative factors, pointed to the Casa Grande, Arizona, manufacturing plant as the best location to pilot the net-zero facility. Casa Grande's desert location in the distressed Colorado River watershed made it a great candidate for water-saving technologies, and the consistent sunlight of the Southwest made it a prime facility for solar energy technologies. Approximately one hundred acres of available land on the site provided plenty of space for deploying new projects. In addition, Casa Grande was a medium-size manufacturing operation, ensuring that the project would be tested at a significant scale to produce transferable results.

Casa Grande was a manufacturing location for Lay's potato chips, Doritos tortilla chips, Fritos corn chips, and Cheetos cheese-flavored snacks and was the planned location for a future SunChips multigrain snacks production line. Although the ingredients for each product were different, the production processes were somewhat similar. Water was used in the cleaning and processing of ingredients. Energy in the form of electricity and natural gas was used to power production equipment, heat ovens, and heat cooking oil.

Per the net-zero vision, a number of new technologies were being evaluated in concert as replacements for current technologies. These proposals included the following:

- A concentrated solar heating unit. Hundreds of mirrors positioned outside the facility would concentrate and redirect solar energy to heat water in a pipe to very high temperatures. The water would be pumped into the facility and used as process steam to heat fryer oil. Frito-Lay had successfully tested this technology at a Modesto, California, plant.
- Photovoltaic solar panels to generate electricity.
- A membrane bioreactor and nanofiltration system to recover and filter processing wastewater to drinking water quality for continuous reuse in the facility.
- A biomass-burning power plant to generate process steam or electricity. Sources of biomass for the plant could include crop waste from suppliers, waste from the production process, and sediments collected in the membrane bioreactor.

Although this combination of technologies had never before been piloted at a single facility, the results from individual projects at other facilities suggested that results at Casa Grande would be very promising. Based on these past experiences, the resource conservation team expected to achieve a 75 percent reduction in water use, an 80 percent reduction in natural gas consumption, and a 90 percent reduction in purchased electricity. Approximately 80 percent of the reduction in natural gas would come through the substitution of biomass fuels.

Making the Call: Evaluating the Project at Casa Grande

After months of preparation and discussions, the net-zero team gathered in Plano, Texas, and via teleconference to decide the fate of the Casa Grande project. In the room were representatives from Operations, Marketing, Finance, and Public Affairs. On the phone from Arizona was Jason Gray, chief engineer for the Casa Grande facility and head of its Green Team. Leading the discussion were Al Halvorsen, the Resource Conservation Team leader, and Dave Haft, group vice president for Sustainability and Productivity.

The meeting was called to order and Halvorsen welcomed the team members, who had spent several months evaluating Casa Grande's viability as the net-zero pilot facility. "Each of you was charged with investigating the relevant considerations on the basis of your functional areas of expertise," Halvorsen said. "I'd like to start by going around the table and hearing the one-minute version of your thoughts and concerns before digging into the details. Let's begin by hearing from the facility team." [10]

Each of the managers shared his or her synopsis.

Jason Gray, chief facility engineer at Casa Grande, said,

> There's a strong interest among the Green Team and our line workers about the possibility of being the proving ground for a new company-wide environmental initiative. But we need to recognize the potential challenges associated with layering in all these technologies together at once. In the past, our efficiency-related projects have involved proven technologies and were spread out incrementally over time. These projects will hit in rapid succession. That being said— we've always rallied around a challenge in the past. I imagine that we'll hit a few snags on the way, but we're up for it.

Larry Perry, group manager for environmental compliance and engineering, said,

> On the whole, we are very optimistic about the reductions in energy and water usage that can be achieved as a result of the proposed mix of technologies at the facility. These reductions will have a direct impact on our bottom line, taking operating costs out of the equation and further protecting the company against future spikes in resource prices. In addition, our improved energy management will yield significant reductions in greenhouse gas emissions—perhaps even opening the door

for our first absolute reductions of company-wide emissions. Although the carbon numbers are not yet finalized, we are working to understand the potential financial implications if future government regulations are imposed.

Anne Smith, brand manager, said,

> Casa Grande is the proposed site of a new manufacturing line for a new SunChips manufacturing line. Although this line won't account for all our production of SunChips snacks, it could strengthen our existing messaging tying the brand to our solar-energy-driven manufacturing initiatives. While we are optimistic that our sustainable manufacturing initiatives will drive increased sales and consumer brand loyalty, we have been unable to directly quantify the impact to our top line. As always, although we want to share our successes with the consumer, we want to continue to make marketing decisions that will not be construed as "green-washing."

Bill Franklin, financial analyst, said,

> I've put together a discounted cash-flow model for the proposed capital expense projects, and over the long term we just clear the hurdle. Although this is an NPV-positive project, we're a few years beyond our extended payback period for energy projects. I know there are additional value streams that are not included in my analysis. As a result, I've documented these qualitative benefits but have excluded any quantitative impacts from my DCF analysis.

Aurora Gonzalez, public affairs, said,

> As we look to the future, we all need to be aware that potential green-washing accusations are a primary concern. We must balance the desire to communicate our positive strides, while continuing to emphasize that our efforts in sustainability are a journey with an undetermined ending point.

Al Halvorson and David Haft listened attentively, aware that the decision had to accommodate the diverse perspectives and resonate strategically at the top level of the corporation. Discussion ensued, with strong opinions expressed. After the meeting ended, Halverson and Haft agreed to talk privately to reach a decision. An assessment of the facility's carbon footprint would be part of that decision.

The following discussion provides background and analytic guidance for understanding carbon footprint analysis. It can be used with the preceding case to provide students with the tools to calculate the facility's carbon footprint. The material is broadly applicable to any facility, thus the formulas provided in this section may be useful in applying carbon footprint analysis to any company's operations.

Corporate GHG Accounting: Carbon Footprint Analysis [11]

For much of the twentieth century, scientists speculated that human activities, such as the widespread burning of fossil fuels and large-scale clearing of land, were causing the earth's climate system to become unbalanced. In 1979, the United Nations took a preliminary step to address this issue when it convened the First World Climate Conference. In the years that followed, governments, scientists, and other organizations continued to debate the extent and significance of the so-called climate change phenomenon. During the 1990s, scientific consensus on climate change strengthened significantly. By the turn of the century, approximately 99 percent of peer-reviewed scientific articles on the subject agreed that human-induced climate change was a reality. [12] While modelers continued to refine their forecasts, a general consensus emerged among the governments of the world that immediate action must be taken to reduce human impacts on the climate system. [13]

Large numbers of businesses initially responded to the climate change issue with skepticism. The American environmental regulatory landscape of the 1970s and 1980s was tough on business, with sweeping legislative initiatives relating to air quality, water quality, and toxic waste remediation. Private industry was still reacting to this legislation when scientific consensus was building on climate change. Many companies were content to wait for scientists and government officials to reach an agreement on the best path forward before taking action or, in some instances, to directly challenge the mounting scientific evidence.

In recent years, however, a number of factors have contributed to a shift in corporate opinion. These factors include growing empirical data of human impacts on the global climate system, definitive reports by the UN Intergovernmental Panel on Climate Change, and increased media and government attention on the issue. Perhaps most significant, however, is the impact that rising energy costs and direct pressure from shareholders to disclose climate-related operating risks are having on business managers who can for the first time connect this scientific issue with financial considerations.

A number of leading companies and entrepreneurial start-ups are using the challenge of climate change as a motivating force to shift strategic direction. These companies are measuring their GHG emissions, aggressively pursuing actions that will reduce emissions, and shifting product and service offerings to meet new customer demands. In the process, they are cutting costs, reducing exposure to weather and raw material risks, and unlocking growth opportunities in the emerging markets for carbon trading.

This technical note introduces a number of concepts relating to how companies are responding to the issue of climate change, with the goal of helping business managers develop a practical understanding in several key areas. The purposes of this note are to (1) present a working language for discussing climate issues, (2) introduce the history and motivation behind corporate emissions disclosure, and (3) describe a basic calculation methodology used to estimate emissions.

Carbon, Footprints, and Offsets

As with any emerging policy issue, a vocabulary has evolved over time to support climate change discussions. Academics, policy makers, nongovernmental organizations (NGOs), and the media speak in a language that is at times confusing and foreign to the uninitiated. An exhaustive introduction of these terms is not possible in this section, but a handful of frequently used terms that are central to understanding the climate change issue in a business context are introduced in the following paragraphs.

The Greenhouse Effect

Earth's atmosphere allows sunlight to pass through it. Sunlight is absorbed and reflected off the planet's surfaces toward space. The atmosphere traps some of this reflecting energy, retaining it much like the glass walls of a greenhouse would and maintaining a range of temperatures on the planet that can support life. Climate scientists hypothesize that human activity has dramatically increased concentrations of certain gases in the atmosphere, blocking the return of solar energy to space and leading to higher average temperatures worldwide.

GHGs

The atmospheric gases that contribute to the greenhouse effect include (but are not limited to) CO_2, methane (CH_4), nitrous oxide (N_2O), and chlorofluorocarbons (CFCs). Note that not all the gases in earth's atmosphere are GHGs; for example, oxygen and nitrogen are widely present but do not contribute to the greenhouse effect.

Carbon

Carbon is a catchall term frequently used to describe all GHGs. "Carbon" is short for carbon dioxide, the most prevalent of all GHGs. Because carbon dioxide (CO_2) is the most prevalent GHG, it has become the standard by which emissions of other GHGs are reported. Emissions of gases such as methane are "converted" to a "CO_2 equivalent" in a process similar to converting foreign currencies into a base currency for financial reporting purposes. The conversion is made on the basis of the impact of each gas once it is released into the earth's atmosphere, as measured relative to the impact of CO_2.

Footprint

A footprint is the measurement of the GHG emissions resulting from a company's business activities over a given time period. In general, companies calculate their corporate emissions footprint for a twelve-month period. Established guidelines for GHG accounting are used to define the scope and methodology to be used in the creation of the footprint calculation. The term *carbon footprint* is sometimes used interchangeably with *greenhouse gas inventory*. In addition to enterprise-wide inventories, companies and individuals are increasingly calculating the footprint of individual products, services, events, and so forth.

Offset

In the most basic sense, an offset is an action taken by an organization or individual to counteract the emissions produced by a separate action. If, for example, a company wanted to offset the GHG emissions produced over a year at a manufacturing facility, it could either take direct actions to prevent the equivalent amount of emissions from entering the atmosphere from other activities *or* compensate another organization to take this action. This latter arrangement is a fundamental concept of some government-mandated emissions regulations. Within such a framework, a paper mill that switches from purchasing coal-generated electricity to generating on-site electricity from scrap-wood waste could generate offset credits and sell these credits to another company looking to offset its emissions. Offsets are known by a variety of names and are traded in both regulated (i.e., government-mandated) and unregulated (i.e., voluntary) markets. Standards for the verification of offsets continue to evolve due to questions that have been raised about the quality and validity of some products.

Carbon-Neutral

A company can theoretically be characterized as carbon-neutral if it causes no *net* emissions over a designated time period, meaning that for every unit of emissions released, an equivalent unit of emissions has been offset through other reduction measures. Companies that have made a carbon-neutrality commitment attempt to reduce their emissions by becoming as operationally efficient as possible and then purchasing offsets equivalent to the remaining balance of emissions each year. Although most companies today emit some level of GHGs via operations, carbon markets enable the neutralization of their environmental impact by paying another entity to reduce its emissions. In theory, such arrangements result in lower net global emissions of GHGs and thereby give companies some credibility to claim relative neutrality with regard to their impact on climate change.

Cap-and-Trade System

A number of policy solutions to the climate change challenge are currently under consideration by policy makers. A direct tax on carbon emissions is one solution. An alternative market-based policy that has received a great deal of attention in recent years is the cap-and-trade system. Under such a system, the government estimates the current level of a country's GHG emissions and sets a cap (an acceptable ceiling) on those emissions. The cap represents a target level of emissions at or below the current level. After setting this target, the government issues emissions permits (i.e., allowances) to companies in regulated industries. The permits provide the right to emit a certain quantity of GHGs in a single year. The permits in aggregate limit emissions to the level set by the cap.

Initial permit distribution approaches range from auctions to government allocation at no cost to individual firms. In either case, following the issuance of permits, a secondary market can be created in which companies can buy and sell permits. At the end of the year, companies without sufficient permits to cover annual corporate emissions of GHGs either purchase the necessary permits in the marketplace or are required to pay a penalty. Companies who have reduced their emissions at a marginal cost lower than the market price of permits typically choose to sell their allotted permits to create additional revenue streams. To steadily reduce economy-wide emissions over time, the government lowers the cap (and thus further restricts the supply of permits) each year, forcing regulated companies to become more efficient or pay penalties. The cap-and-trade approach is touted as an efficient, market-based solution to reducing the total emissions of an economy.

Corporate Climate Change

Corporate attitudes about climate change shifted dramatically between 2006 and 2009, with dozens of large companies announcing significant sustainability initiatives. During this time, major business periodicals such as *BusinessWeek* and *Fortune* for the first time devoted entire issues to "green" matters, and the *Wall Street Journal* launched an annual ECO:nomics conference to bring together corporate executives to answer questions on how their companies are solving environmental challenges. Today, a majority of large companies are measuring their carbon footprints and reporting the information to the public and shareholders through established channels. (See the discussion of the Carbon Disclosure Project later in this section.)

A number of companies that were silent or openly questioned the validity of climate science during the 1990s are now engaged in public dialogue and are finding ways to reduce emissions of GHGs. In 2007, a group including Alcoa, BP, Caterpillar, Duke Energy, DuPont, General Electric, and PG&E created the US Climate Action Partnership (USCAP) to lobby Congress to enact legislation that would significantly reduce US GHG emissions. By 2009, USCAP had added approximately twenty more prominent partners and taken steps to pressure legislators for a mandatory carbon cap-and-trade system. The organization included the Big Three US automakers, a number of major oil companies, and some leading NGOs.

In addition to financial considerations, the case for corporate action on climate change is strengthened by a number of other factors. First, the proliferation of emissions regulations around the world creates a great deal of uncertainty for US firms. A company operating in Europe, California, and New England could face three separate emissions regulatory regimes. Without a more coordinated effort on the part of the United States and other governments to create unified legislation, firms could face an even more kaleidoscopic combination of regulations. Business leaders are addressing these concerns by becoming more actively engaged in the policy debate.

A second motivator for corporate action is shareholder pressure for increased transparency on climate issues. As our understanding of climate change improves, it is clear that impacts in the natural world as well as government-imposed emissions regulations will have a tremendous effect on the way that companies operate. Climate change has emerged as a key source of risk—an uncertainty that shareholders feel entitled to more fully understand.

In 2002, a group of institutional investors united to fund the nonprofit Carbon Disclosure Project (CDP). The organization serves as a clearinghouse through which companies disclose emissions data and other qualitative information to investors. The CDP has become the industry standard for voluntary corporate emissions reporting, and each year the organization solicits survey questionnaire responses from more than three thousand firms. In 2008, three hundred institutional investors representing over $57 trillion in managed assets supported the CDP. [14]

In 2007, the CDP received survey responses from 55 percent of the companies in the *Fortune* 500 list. This high level of participation speaks to the seriousness with which many companies are addressing climate change.

The Greenhouse Gas Protocol

The measurement of GHG emissions is important for three reasons: (1) a complete accounting of emissions allows for voluntary disclosure of data to organizations such as the CDP, (2) it provides a data set that facilitates participation in mandatory emissions regulatory systems, and (3) it encourages the collection of key operational data that can be used to implement business improvement projects.

GHG accounting is the name given to the practice of measuring corporate emissions. Similar to *generally accepted accounting principles* in the financial world, it is a set of standards and principles that guide data collection and reporting in this new field. The Greenhouse Gas Protocol is one commonly accepted methodology for GHG accounting and is the basis for voluntary reporting initiatives such as the CDP. It is an ongoing initiative of the World Resources Institute and the World Business Council for Sustainable Development to provide a common standard by which companies and governments can measure and report emissions of GHGs.

The Greenhouse Gas Protocol provides critical guidance for companies attempting to create a credible inventory of emissions resulting from its operations. In particular, it explains how to do the following:

- **Determine** *organizational* **boundaries.** Corporate structures are complex and include wholly owned operations, joint ventures, subsidiaries, collaborations, and a number of other entities. The protocol helps managers define which elements compose the "company" for emissions quantification purposes. A large number of companies elect to include all activities over which they have "operational control" and can thus influence decision making about how business is conducted.

- **Determine** *operational* **boundaries.** Once managers identify which branches of the organization are to be included in the inventory, they must identify and evaluate which specific emissions sources will be included. The protocol identifies two major categories of sources:

Direct sources. These are sources owned or controlled by the company that produce emissions. Examples include boilers, furnaces, vehicles, and other production processes.

Indirect sources. These sources are not directly owned or controlled by the company but are nonetheless influenced by its actions. A good example is electricity purchased from utilities that produce indirect emissions at the power plant. Other indirect sources include employee commuting, emissions generated by suppliers, and activities that result from the customer use of products, services, or both.

- **Track emissions over time.** Companies must select a "base year" against which future emissions will be measured, establish an accounting cycle, and determine other aspects of how they will track emissions over time.
- **Collect data and calculate emissions.** The protocol provides specific guidance about how to collect source data and calculate emissions of GHGs. The next section provides an overview of these concepts.

A Basic Methodology for Calculating Emissions

The calculation of GHG emissions is a process that differs depending on the emissions source. [15] As a general rule of thumb, a consumption quantity (fuel, electricity, etc.) is multiplied by a series of source-specific "emissions factors" to estimate the quantity of each GHG produced by the source. Each **emissions factor** is a measure of the average amount of a given GHG, reported in weight, that is generated from the combustion of a unit of the energy source. For example, a gallon of gasoline produces on average 8.7 kg of CO_2 when combusted in a passenger vehicle engine. [16]

Because multiple GHGs are measured in the inventory process, the accounting process calculates emissions for each type of gas. As common practice, emissions of non-CO_2 gases are converted to a "CO_2 equivalent" to facilitate streamlined reporting of a single emissions number. In this conversion, emissions totals for a gas like methane are multiplied by a "global warming potential" to convert to a CO_2 equivalent.

Given the scale of many companies, it is easy to become overwhelmed by the prospect of accounting for all the GHG emissions produced in a given year. In reality, quantifying the emissions of a *Fortune* 50 firm or a small employee-owned business involves the same process. The methodology for calculating emissions from a single facility or vehicle is the same as that used to calculate emissions for thousands of retail stores or long-haul trucks.

For the purposes of this note, we will illustrate the inventory process for a sole proprietorship. The business owner is a skilled cabinetmaker who manufactures and installs custom kitchen cabinets, bookshelves, and other high-end products for homes. She leases several thousand square feet of shop space in High Point, North Carolina, and owns a single gasoline-powered pickup truck that is used for delivering products to customers.

The business owner consults the Greenhouse Gas Protocol and identifies three emissions sources. Direct emissions sources include the gasoline-powered truck and a number of natural-gas-powered tools on the shop floor. Indirect emissions sources include the electricity that the company purchases from the local utility on a monthly basis.

The owner starts by collecting utility usage data. She reviews accounts payable records for the past twelve months to determine the quantities of fuel and electricity purchased. The records reveal total purchases of 26,700 MMBtus of natural gas; 2,455 gallons of gasoline; and 115,400 kWh of electricity.

Source: {Author's Name Retracted as requested by the work's original creator or licensee} and William Teichman, "Corporate Greenhouse Gas Accounting: Carbon Footprint Analysis," UVA-ENT-0113 (Charlottesville: Darden Business Publishing, University of Virginia, May 4, 2009).

The total kilogram emissions from all three sources represent the total annual footprint for this business (subject to the boundary conditions defined in this exercise). This total is stated as "1,494,747 kg of CO_2 equivalent."

KEY TAKEAWAYS

- Efficiency improvements can lead to larger systems changes.
- Companies seek greater control over their energy and resource inputs and use to save costs, protect the environment, and improve their image.
- Firms can cooperate with and contribute to the communities in which they reside.
- Basic carbon footprint can be calculated for facilities or larger entities.

EXERCISES

1. If you are Al Halverson, what considerations are in the forefront of your mind as you consider the net-zero facility decision? If you oppose the idea, what arguments would you garner? If you favor the decision, what is your rationale?
2. Optional: For the Casa Grande facility, calculate the metric tons of GHG emissions from electricity and natural gas usage for each year from 2002 to 2007. (Pay close attention to units when applying emissions factors.)
3. Optional: Project the estimated reduction in GHG emissions and operating cost savings that will result from the proposed net zero project in years 2008-2010. Assume for the purposes of your analysis that all equipment upgrades are made immediately at the start of 2008.

---

[1] The expression "off the grid" means reducing or eliminating a facility's reliance on the electricity and natural gas grids and on water utilities for production inputs.

[2] The term "Big Hairy Audacious Goals" is borrowed from James Collins and Jerry Porras's book *Built to Last: Successful Habits of Visionary Companies* (New York: HarperCollins, 1997).

[3] Indra K. Nooyi, "Performance with a Purpose" (speech by PepsiCo President and CEO at the US Chamber of Commerce–India/Confederation of Indian Industry, New Delhi, India, December 18, 2006), accessed January 10, 2011, http://www.wbcsd.org/DocRoot/61wUYBaKS2N35f9b41ua/IKN-IndiaSpeechNum6FINAL.pdf.

[4] The term *triple-bottom-line* refers to a concept advanced by John Elkington in his book *Cannibals with Forks: The Triple Bottom Line of 21st Century Business* (Mankato, MN: Capstone Publishers, 1998). Companies that embrace triple-bottom-line thinking believe that to achieve sustained growth in the long term, they must demonstrate good financial, environmental, and social performance, also referred to as "sustainable business."

[5] The Climate Leaders program allowed individual business units or parent corporations to sign partnership agreements. In the years since FLNA signed its partnership with Climate Leaders, PepsiCo started reporting the aggregate emissions of all business units via the Carbon Disclosure Project (CDP). The emissions data presented in this case are included in the consolidated emissions reported by PepsiCo through the CDP.

[6] The terms *Scope 1* and *Scope 2* refer to categories of greenhouse gas emissions as defined by the World Business Council for Sustainable Development/World Resource Institute Greenhouse Gas Protocol, which is the accounting standard used by Climate Leaders, the Carbon Disclosure Project, and other organizations. Scope 1 emissions are direct. Scope 2 emissions are indirect.

[7] Emissions reduction goals are generally stated in either "absolute" or "normalized" terms. In the former, a company commits to reduce the total emissions generated over some period of time. In the latter, a commitment is made to reduce the emissions generated *per some unit of production* (e.g., pounds of product, units manufactured, etc.). A normalized emissions metric can illustrate increased efficiency in manufacturing a product or producing a service over time and is often preferred by businesses that are growth oriented.

[8] Sales data are extracted from publicly available PepsiCo Inc. annual reports, 2002–7. PepsiCo, "Annual Reports," accessed January 7, 2011, http://www.pepsico.com/Investors/Annual-Reports.html.

[9] {Author's Name Retracted as requested by the work's original creator or licensee}, *Frito-Lay North America: The Making of a Net Zero Snack Chip*, UVA-ENT-0112 (Charlottesville: Darden Business Publishing, University of Virginia, May 4, 2009).

[10] {Author's Name Retracted as requested by the work's original creator or licensee}, *Frito-Lay North America: The Making of a Net Zero Snack Chip*, UVA-ENT-0112 (Charlottesville: Darden Business Publishing, University of Virginia, May 4, 2009). Unless otherwise specified, quotations in this section are from this source.

[11] This section is a reprint of {Author's Name Retracted as requested by the work's original creator or licensee} and William Teichman, "Corporate Greenhouse Gas Accounting: Carbon Footprint Analysis," UVA-ENT-0113 (Charlottesville: Darden Business Publishing, University of Virginia, May 4, 2009).

[12] See Naomi Oreskes, "Beyond the Ivory Tower: The Scientific Consensus on Climate Change," *Science* 306, no. 5702 (December 3, 2004): 1686, accessed February 6, 2009, http://www.sciencemag.org/cgi/content/full/306/5702/1686; Cynthia Rosenzweig, David Karoly, Marta Vicarelli, Peter Neofotis, Qigang Wu, Gino Casassa, Annette Menzel, et al., "Attributing Physical and Biological Impacts to Anthropogenic Climate Change," *Nature* 453 (May 15, 2008): 353–57; National Academy of Sciences Committee on the Science of Climate Change, *Climate Change Science: An Analysis of Some Key Questions* (Washington, DC: National Academy Press, 2001); and Al Gore, *An Inconvenient Truth* (New York: Viking, 2006).

[13] A broader discussion of the history and science of climate change is beyond the scope of this note. For additional information synthesized for business students on this subject, see *Climate Change*, UVA-ENT-0157 (Charlottesville: Darden Business Publishing, University of Virginia, 2010).

[14] For details about the questionnaire, see the Carbon Disclosure Project, "Overview," https://www.cdproject.net/en-US/Respond/Pages/overview.aspx.

[15] Although fossil fuel combustion is one of the largest sources of anthropogenic GHG emissions, other sources include process emissions (released during chemical or manufacturing processes), landfills, wastewater, and fugitive refrigerants. For the purposes of this note, we only present energy-related emissions examples.

[16] Time for Change, "What Is a Carbon Footprint—Definition," accessed January 29, 2011, http://timeforchange.org/what-is-a-carbon-footprint-definition.

[17] For the purposes of this note, we assume that emissions of CH_4 and N_2O are so small from the combustion of gasoline that they amount to a negligible difference. For the purposes of estimating emissions from gasoline combustion, many technical experts take this approach. The omission of calculations for

CH_4 and N_2O is justified on the basis that the emissions factor used for CO_2 assumes that 100 percent of the fuel is converted into gas during the combustion process. In reality, combustion in a gasoline engine is imperfect, and close to 99 percent of the fuel is actually converted to gases (the rest remains as solid matter). The resulting overestimation of CO_2 emissions more than compensates for the omission of CH_4 and N_2O.

[18] Emissions factors for purchased electricity differ depending on the method of power production used by an electric utility (e.g., coal-fired boilers emit greenhouse gases, whereas hydroelectric generation does not). In the United States, region-specific emissions factors are published that reflect the mix of fuels used by electric utilities within a given region to generate electricity. An in-depth explanation of the process for deriving these emissions factors is beyond the scope of this note; however, a listing of recent regional emissions factors for purchased electricity is provided in Exhibit 3. For the purposes of this calculation, the emissions factors in Exhibit 3 were converted to provide an emission factor for kg CO_2/kWh.

5.4 Calera: Entrepreneurship, Innovation, and Sustainability

LEARNING OBJECTIVES

1. Give an example of how biomimicry can be used to help solve business problems.

2. Identify the unique challenges of a sustainability-oriented start-up in a mature and conservative industry.

3. Analyze how a highly innovative company, still in the research and demonstration stage, will identify early customers and generate revenues to prove the commercial viability of the technology.

In our last case, we have the opportunity to see the early stage challenges of a high-potential entrepreneurial venture in California. Based on the entrepreneur's patented scientific knowledge, this firm is scaling up technology to sequester carbon emissions.

Brent Constantz had three decades of entrepreneurial experience, starting with companies based on how cements formed in coral reefs and seashells. Yet those same reefs and shells were threatened by ocean acidification from anthropogenic carbon dioxide (CO_2) emissions. Constantz had a simple insight: if humans could make cement as marine life did (biomimicry), without burning fuel and converting minerals in high-temperature processes, then we could significantly reduce our greenhouse gas (GHG) emissions. With that idea, the Calera Corporation was born.

Calera's goal was to make synthetic limestone and a carbonate cement, both used as major feedstocks for concrete, by mimicking nature's low-energy process. Calera's process aimed to precipitate [1] carbonate cement from seawater (ideally retentate left by desalination) and combine it with a strong alkaline base. When Constantz accidentally discovered CO_2 could enhance his process, he sought a source of CO_2. When he brought his technology and his challenge to clean tech venture capitalist Vinod Khosla, Calera became a **carbon capture and sequestration (CCS)** technology company, one with massive storage potential if located proximate to point sources of pollution: power plants emitted 40 percent of US carbon dioxide in 2008 and industrial process facilities another 20 percent. Yet a high level of technical risk and a number of unknowns remained about the breadth of applicability due to the requirement for brines and alkaline materials. Khosla, as the principal

investor, shared Constantz's vision and saw the huge promise and the attendant risk of failure as a high-risk, high-impact home run to completely change assumptions about the power and cement industry or a strikeout swing.

In two and one-half years, Calera went from small batch processing in a lab as a proof of concept to constructing a continuously operating demonstration plant that suggested the feasibility of large-scale operations. In the process Constantz continued to uncover new possibilities. Since his process stripped magnesium and calcium ions from any water charged with minerals, such as seawater, some wastewaters, and brines, it could potentially yield potable water. Could the venture provide water purification technology as well? Could it be economic? Furthermore, wherever seawater and strong bases were not available, Calera needed to replace or produce them. Consequently, Calera developed a more energy-efficient process to use saltwater to produce sodium hydroxide, the base it needed. With that technology, Calera could potentially impact the mature chlor-alkali industry. There were also environmental remediation possibilities. Calera's initial process had used the base magnesium hydroxide that had been discarded by other companies at its Moss Landing demonstration site. In lieu of seawater, Calera could use subsurface brines, which were often left behind by oil and gas drilling as hazardous wastes. As Constantz and his growing team saw their opportunities expand, the company grew rapidly. If everything worked as hoped, Calera's method seemed a magic sponge capable of absorbing multiple pollutants and transforming them into desirable products. The reality, though full of possibilities, was complex with many practical hurdles.

Along the way, the Calera team had identified and added to the firm's multiple areas of expertise—often as the company ran into the complexity of a developing process. Calera also attracted a wide range of curious onlookers who could someday become prospective customers. Government agencies and other companies were eager to get in on the action. To position itself favorably, Calera needed to understand its core competencies and identify key collaborators to bring the new technology to full-scale operation at multiple sites. Simultaneously, it needed to protect its intellectual property and forge a defensible market position. As a high-risk, highly capital-intensive start-up with a huge number of uncertainties and potential ways to address many markets and positively affect the environment, what business model made sense?

The Cement Industry

CO_2-sequestering cement could make a significant impact. In 2008, 2.5 billion metric tons of Portland cement were produced with between 0.8 and 1 ton of CO_2 emitted for every ton of cement. [2] China produced nearly 1.4 billion tons of cement in 2008, followed by India (about 200 million tons) and the United States (100 million tons). [3] Consequently, production of Portland cement, the main binder for conventional concrete, accounted for between 5 and 8 percent of global GHG emissions, making it one of the more GHG-intense industries

Portland cement production generates CO_2 in two ways. The first source of emissions is calcination, which decomposes quarried limestone (calcium carbonate) into quicklime (calcium oxide) and releases CO_2 as a by-product. The second source is the heat needed to achieve calcination, which requires temperatures over 2700°F (1500°C), or almost one-third the surface temperature of the sun. These temperatures are generally achieved by burning fossil fuels or hazardous wastes containing carbon. Sustaining such temperatures consumes around 3 to 6 gigajoules (1,000 to 2,000 kWh) of energy per ton of cement, making energy costs around 14 percent of the value of total shipments. [4] (By comparison, the typical US home uses around 11,000 kWh per year. [5])

Since emissions from calcination are dictated by the chemistry of the reaction and cannot be changed, to save energy and lower emissions, kilns have striven to use heat more efficiently. In California, for instance, emissions from calcination remained steady at 0.52 tons of CO_2 per ton of cement from 1990 to 2005, while emissions from combustion declined from 0.40 tons of CO_2 per ton of

cement to 0.34 tons. [6] Lowering emissions further, however, had proven difficult.

Given the carbon intensity of cement production, governments increasingly have attended to emissions from cement kilns. Calcination alone emitted 0.7 percent of US CO_2 in 2007, a 34 percent increase since 1990 and the most of any other industrial process except energy generation and steel production. [7] California's Assembly Bill 32, the Global Warming Solutions Act of 2006, includes cement kilns under its GHG emissions reduction program, which would require kilns to further reduce their emissions starting in 2012. The EPA's Greenhouse Gas Reporting Rule from April 2009 also requires kilns to send data about their GHG emissions to the EPA, a prerequisite for any eventual mandatory emissions reductions.

In addition to being energy and CO_2 intense, cement production is also a capital-intense industry. A kiln and its concomitant quarrying operations may require an investment on the order of $1 billion. Consequently, about a dozen large multinational companies dominate the industry. In 2010 there were 113 cement plants in the United States in 36 states, but foreign-owned companies accounted for about 80 percent of US cement production.

Despite this ownership structure, actual cement production and consumption is largely regional. The cement industry moves almost 100 percent of its product by truck; the majority goes to ready-mix concrete operators, from plant to use. The entire US cement industry shipped $7.5 billion of products in 2009, a decline from $15 billion in 2006 since domestic construction had declined. [8] Worldwide, the cement industry represented a $140 billion market in 2009 with about 47 percent poured in China.

Although cement can be used to produce mortar, stucco, and grout, most cement is used to produce concrete. To make concrete, cement is mixed in various proportions with water and aggregates, including fine aggregates such as sand and coarse aggregates such as gravel and rocks. (Concrete cement is commonly called simply concrete, although asphalt is also technically a type of concrete where the binder is asphalt instead of Portland cement.) The cement itself comes in five basic classes, depending on the desired strength, time to set, resistance to corrosion, and heat emitted as the cement sets, or hydrates. Though cement plays a crucial role in the properties of concrete, the other ingredients also matter. Aggregates help give concrete its strength and appearance. Plasticizers can be added in smaller quantities, as can materials such as coal fly ash or slag from blast furnaces to vary the concrete's strength, weight, workability, and resistance to corrosion. Some states, such as California, require fly ash and slag be added to concrete to reduce its GHG intensity, improve the durability of the final material, and prevent these aggregates from entering landfills as waste materials.

A typical mix of concrete might contain by mass one part water, three parts cement, six parts fine aggregate, and nine parts coarse aggregate. Thus a cubic yard of concrete, which weighs roughly two and one-half tons (2,000 to 2,400 kg/m^3), would require approximately 300 pounds (36 gallons) of water, 900 pounds of cement (9.5 bags, or 9.5 cubic feet), and 4,500 pounds of total aggregates. Varying amounts of air can also be trapped, or entrained, in the product. Cement, at around $100/ton in 2010, is normally about 60 percent of the total cost of poured concrete. Aggregates, in contrast, cost closer to $10/ton.

Making concrete adds more GHG emissions from, for instance, quarrying and transporting stone and keeping the water at the right temperature (from 70 to 120°F) to mix effectively. As the cement in concrete cures, it carbonates, which is the process in which CO_2 interacts with the alkaline pore solutions in the concrete to form calcium carbonate. This process takes decades to occur and never accounts for more than a few percent of carbon sequestrations in cement.

By using less energy, Calera's process already promised lower emissions. More important, using a standard construction material, cement, to capture CO_2 would mean sequestration capacity scaled directly with economic activity as reflected in new construction. For instance, the Three Gorges Dam in China used approximately fifty-five million tons of concrete containing eight million tons of cement. The concrete in the dam is enough to pave a sixteen-lane highway from San Francisco to New York. [9] Hence if Calera cement had been used in that dam, it could have sequestered roughly four million tons of CO_2 rather than emitting approximately seven million additional tons of it, for a net difference of eleven million tons. If Calera had manufactured the stones used as aggregate in the dam's concrete, emissions potentially could have been reduced even more, so long as Calera's process produced fewer emissions than quarrying the equivalent aggregate. The promise remained but so did the question: in how many places was the Calera process viable, and where did the economics make sense?

Constantz Looks for an Opening

Brent Constantz had focused his career on how nature makes cements and how we can apply those techniques to other problems. He now faced the challenge of moving from niche markets for small-scale, specialty medical cements to the mainstream of international construction, commodity materials, and carbon sequestration. For these markets Calera's product promised negative net CO_2 emissions but first had to compete on cost, set time, strength, and durability. Calera would need to pass all appropriate standards as well as target applications for which people would be willing to pay a premium for carbon-negative concrete. In addition, the chain of liability often terminated at the cement producer in the highly litigious construction industry. Consequently, Calera cement had to be deemed beyond reproach to penetrate the market. But if it was, then its ability to reduce GHG emissions would appeal to many in the construction industry who sought to lower costs and improve their environmental image.

A rock climber and wind surfer, Constantz earned his BA in Geological Sciences and Aquatic Biology from the University of California–Santa Barbara in 1981 and went on to earn his master's (1984) and PhD (1986) in Earth Sciences from University of California–Santa Cruz. He received a US Geological Survey postdoctoral fellowship in Menlo Park, California, during which he studied isotope geochemistry. Next as a Fulbright Scholar in Israel, he studied the interaction of crystals and proteins during biomineralization. At that time, Constantz developed medical cements to help heal fractured or worn bones, and in 1988 he founded his first company, Norian Corporation, in Cupertino, California, to commercialize those medical cements. When Norian was sold in 1998 to Synthes, a company with $3.4 billion in sales in 2009, [10] Constantz became a consulting professor at Stanford University, where he continued to teach courses on biomineralization, carbonate sedimentology, and the "Role of Cement in Fracture Management" through 2010. [11]

During his time at Stanford, Constantz founded and provided leadership for three more medical cement companies: Corazon, bought by Johnson & Johnson; Skeletal Kinetics, bought by Colson Associates; and Biomineral Holdings, which Constantz still controlled. He served on the board of directors of the Stanford Environmental Molecular Science Institute and also won a variety of awards, including a University of California–Santa Cruz Alumni Achievement Award in 1998 and a Global Oceans Award in 2004 for advancing our understanding of and helping to conserve oceans.

Indeed, climate change's impact on oceans was increasingly on Constantz's mind. In an interview with the *San Francisco Chronicle*, Constantz stated, "Climate change is the largest challenge of our generation." [12] Constantz was concerned specifically with ocean acidification, which was destroying coral, the very topic that had inspired him for years. As CO_2 is emitted into the atmosphere, a portion is absorbed by the oceans, forming carbonic acid by roughly the same process that gives carbonated beverages their bubbles. Constantz recognized that the process threatened by CO_2 emissions—natural biomineralization—was also a solution. He founded Calera Corporation in 2007.

The name *Calera* is Spanish for lime kiln, but it also refers to a stratum of limestone underlying parts of California. That layer likely formed one hundred million years ago when seafloor vents triggered precipitation of calcium carbonate. Constantz found that a similar inorganic process to precipitate carbonates could make construction-grade cement. In fact, early lab work revealed the surprising finding that adding CO_2 could increase the reaction's yield eightfold. In one of his regular conversations with Khosla about the company, Constantz wondered out loud where to get more CO_2. Khosla, a prominent clean tech investor, immediately saw the answer: carbon sequestration. If Calera could make cement with CO_2, cement could now be produced that was, in fact, carbon negative. First-round funding for the enterprise came from Khosla in 2007. No business plan was written, and in 2010 there still was no formal board or enough clarity to develop a strategic plan.

Calera's method puts power plant flue gases that contain CO_2 in contact with concentrated brines or concentrated seawater, which contain dissolved magnesium and calcium ions. Hydroxides and other alkaline materials are added to the seawater to speed the reaction between the CO_2 and minerals. [13] That reaction precipitates carbonates of magnesium and calcium, the cementitious materials found in coral reefs and seashells, thus storing the CO_2 and leaving behind demineralized water. Unlike conventional cement kilns, Calera can produce its cement at temperatures below 200°F (90°C), dramatically lowering emissions of CO_2 from fuel combustion. In principle, Calera could produce and sell its aggregate, essentially manufactured stones; powdered stones, or cement, the binder in concretes; or supplementary cementitious material (SCM), an additive to improve the performance of concrete that can be added to the cement blend directly or later added to the concrete.

Yet in 2010, each of these materials was in the midst of optimization and testing. Some were early in their product development phase. Furthermore, even though Constantz held nearly two hundred patents or pending patents, including two for Calera's processes, one for producing the carbonate cement, and another for demineralizing water, the medical cements he was accustomed to in earlier ventures typically used grams or less at a time, not tons or kilotons, and did not require massive machinery, tracts of land, and large capital investments. Calera faced another challenge: the industrial ecosystem.

One practical application of industrial ecology concepts refers to the collocation of factories or processes that can use each others' wastes as feedstocks. When the waste stream of one plant becomes the material input of the next, the net effect is to save energy and material and reduce the necessary infrastructure. The most famous industrial ecology park, in Kalundborg, Denmark, included a power plant, a refinery, a pharmaceutical company, a drywall manufacturer, and a fish farm. [14] The power plant, for instance, treated its flue gas to trap sulfur dioxide emissions and thereby produced gypsum, the raw material for drywall. Hot water from the power station went to the fish farm, as did wastes from the pharmaceutical company that could be used as fertilizer. Constantz saw an existing symbiosis between cement plants, power stations, and water supplies, but he would have to plan carefully to insert Calera effectively into that ecology.

If he could enter the markets, Constantz felt the opportunity was there. He commented on the global market for Calera's technology:

> *Almost everywhere else in the world but the U.S. can projects get the value for carbon emission reductions. In cap and trade systems, the government sets a "cap" on emissions; if a business's emissions fall below the cap, it can sell the difference on the market to companies that want to exceed their cap. If Calera proves out, it can go anywhere, set up next to a power plant and get our revenue just by selling carbon credits. That means we could produce cement in a developing country where they basically can't afford concrete, so they otherwise couldn't build out their infrastructure or even build houses. And the more cement Calera produces, the more carbon dioxide we remove from the atmosphere.* [15]

At the federal level, Calera also lobbied to have the American Clean Energy and Security Act of 2009 (HR 2454, the Waxman-Markey Bill) include sequestration other than by solely geological means; otherwise, Calera would not be recognized as providing offsets worth allowances in a trading program. The bill exited committee in May 2009 with the expanded sequestration options but then stalled. Before that, carbon capture and sequestration (CCS) debates had focused on geological sequestration, but that solution was expensive, required massive federal subsidies to CO_2 emitters, and, according to a 2008 McKinsey & Company report, would not be commercially feasible for another twenty years. [18] Despite the enticing estimates that centuries' worth of CO_2 emissions could be stored underground, [19] skeptics wondered how long it would stay there, as a sudden release of stored CO_2 would be catastrophic. They further noted that gradual leaks would defeat the technology's purpose and potentially acidify groundwater, causing new problems. Everyone, meanwhile, agreed that much depended on the price of carbon, which was contingent on evolving carbon markets in the United States and Europe.

A new bill with a mix of carbon trading and taxes was in the works in March 2010, and in the absence of congressional action, the EPA was preparing to regulate CO_2 under the Clean Air Act per order of the Supreme Court in its 2007 decision *Massachusetts v. EPA*. [20] Despite the overall failure of the Copenhagen Climate Conference in December 2009—Constantz considered the attempt to negotiate a successor to the Kyoto Protocol "a joke" [21]—the United States did pledge, nonbindingly, to reduce its GHG emissions 17 percent from 2005 levels by 2020 and ultimately 83 percent by 2050, a significant departure from the previous Bush administration. In January 2010, President Obama announced via Executive Order 13514 that the federal government would reduce its GHG emissions 28 percent from 2008 levels by 2020. The federal government was the single largest consumer of energy in the United States. Nonetheless, Constantz claimed that even without climate change regulations, "We will be profitable, we don't care, we don't need a price on carbon."

Moss Landing

Aside from climate change legislation, Constantz witnessed regulatory agencies "bending over backward to help us. Fortunately, people are in favor of what we're doing because I think they see the higher purpose toward which we're dedicated." [22] Calera's process had proven effective, for instance, at trapping sulfur dioxide emissions, currently regulated in the United States under the Acid Rain Program and other standards. Water regulators and air boards alike, a total of nine agencies, eased the way for Calera's first plant at Moss Landing, California. The site, two hundred acres along Monterey Bay, had seven three-million-gallon tanks for storing seawater, a total volume equivalent to thirty Olympic swimming pools, and permits for pumping sixty million gallons of seawater per day, or nearly seven hundred

gallons per second, through the original World War II–era redwood pipe. The site also had five million tons of magnesium hydroxide left from earlier operations, which included making bombs.

In June 2008, Calera collaborated with the nearby Monterey Bay Aquarium Research Institute and Moss Landing Marine Lab to assess and minimize impacts on the bay's marine ecosystems. Water is a key element of the Calera process, and everything was done to minimize its use. Constantz told a local paper, "We wanted to make sure we weren't going to do any harm. We're right next to these world-class oceanographic institutions. These places can publish papers about [the process], whereas most parts of the world don't have scientists of that caliber to sign off on it." [23] Calera was interested in using the power plant's water, potentially reducing demand for and impacts on Monterey Bay water. Constantz knew Moss Landing would set the standard for future plants. In fact, turning a site with a negative environmental history into a location that demonstrated clean energy and potable water technologies was very appealing to the entire management team.

The magnesium hydroxide, meanwhile, formed a gray and white crust that stretched for hundreds of yards and was visible from the sky. It provided the alkalinity for Calera's early production. Massive metal sheds on the otherwise muddy soil housed a variety of production lines. Equally important, across the street stood the largest power plant on the West Coast, Dynegy's 2,500 MW natural gas-fired plant.

In August 2008, Calera opened its test cement production plant. In April 2009, it achieved continuous operation and was capturing with 70 percent efficiency CO_2 emissions from a simulated 0.5 MW coal-fired power plant. [24] In December 2009, Calera ran a pipe beneath the road to tap into Dynegy's flue stack, somewhat like sticking a straw in a drink, to capture emissions equivalent to a 10 MW plant as Calera moved up to a demonstration scale project. By spring 2010 the demonstration plant, twenty times the size of the pilot plant, had achieved continuous operation.

In addition to considering his suitors, material resources, and business opportunities, Constantz also had to consider his competition. Other companies were trying to make cement in innovative ways to reduce GHG emissions. In 1979, German-born architect Wolf Hilbertz had published a way to produce calcium carbonate from seawater via electrolysis. [29] That method had been commercialized as Biorock, also the name of the company, and used to help restore coral reefs by plating calcium carbonate onto rebar. The company Biorock, however, did not seem interested in pursuing terrestrial applications. In contrast, Novacem in England planned to use magnesium oxide and other additives to lower processing temperatures and obviate GHG emissions from cement kilns. Other companies were also attempting to sequester CO_2 in cement. Carbon Sciences of Santa Barbara planned to use mine slime (water plus magnesium and calcium residues left in mines) and flue gas to make cement, and Carbon Sense Solutions in Nova Scotia planned to use flue gases to cure cement, thereby absorbing CO_2. Nonetheless, Calera so far had kept ahead of these possible competitors and worked on ensuring that its products met familiar engineering performance standards to speed adoption.

Building performance aside, climate scientist Ken Caldeira at the Carnegie Institution's Department of Global Ecology had publicly doubted that the Calera process would reduce net carbon emissions, as it currently used magnesium or sodium hydroxides, which would have to be produced somehow and did not seem included in life-cycle analyses of carbon emissions. Caldeira had also said that Calera basically took dissolved limestone and converted it back into limestone, and there were active online discussions on this issue. [30] Calera simply waited for its patents to be published rather than directly refute the charge.

Portland cement was the industrial standard and had been since its invention in 1824. Any change was likely to encounter resistance from producers and consumers, and the standards-setting bodies were necessarily conservative and cautious. An array of organizations, from the American National Standards Institute's American Standards for Testing and Materials (ASTM) to the Portland Cement Association and American Concrete Institute, in addition to individual companies, conducted their own rigorous quality tests and set many standards.

Ironically, rather than seeing himself as an opponent of the Portland cement industry, Constantz considered himself an ally: "I think we're going to save their entire industry. As soon as there's carbon legislation, the asphalt industry is going to eat their lunch. The Portland cement industry is really in trouble without us and they know that. That's why they're calling us up." [31] After all, the industry had tried to reduce emissions by increasing efficiency but could only do so much. Calera's process appeared to be the breakthrough the industry needed. Moreover, the infrastructure already existed to link cement plants with power plants because the latter often have to dispose of fly ash. Likewise, power plants also consume lots of water, meaning the infrastructure

existed to supply the Calera process, presuming the water contained sufficient salts.

Constantz felt Calera could disrupt the carbon sequestration industry, primarily oil and gas exploration companies that had been advocating enhanced recovery through injecting CO_2 underground as a form of geological carbon sequestration: injecting compressed CO_2 underground forced more oil and gas to the surface. Khosla agreed but was uncertain about the breadth of applicability of the Calera process. An attractive business and a few plants were definitely possible, but Calera had yet to prove it was anything more than a solution for some special cases.

To do so, Calera hoped to outperform all other CCS options, especially retrofits of existing plants. Even if the technical and environmental problems could be solved for widespread CCS, it would be costly, especially in a world without a price on carbon. In April 2010, the US Interagency Task Force on Carbon Capture and Storage estimated the cost of building typical CCS into new coal-fired plants (greenfield development) to be $60 to $114 per metric ton of CO_2 avoided, and $103/ton for retrofitting existing plants. That translated into increased capital costs of 25–80 percent. Such plants were also expected to consume 35–90 percent more water than similar plants without CCS. [32]

Available CCS required much energy to operate, the so-called parasitic load it placed on power plants whose emissions it sequestered. This parasitic load represented a very high cost and penalty for the power plant as it was essentially lost electricity, translating directly into lost revenue. To cover the electricity needed to operate any system that trapped CO_2 emissions from the flue and still supply its other customers, the power plant would have to consume more coal and operate longer for the same income.

Constantz noted that geologic CCS typically had parasitic loads around 30 percent. To solve this issue, Calera's business model was to buy power at wholesale price, becoming the power plant's electricity customer. The plant could increase its capacity factor to cover this additional power demand or reduce its power sales to the grid without much of a revenue loss. From the plant's perspective, then, Calera did not alter revenue, unlike other options. Constantz believed Calera's energy consumption could be much lower than that of CCS assuming the right local mineral and brine inputs could be exploited. In addition, to optimize its power use and price, Calera was designing a process that could take advantage of off-peak power. However, it remained uncertain how many locations met mineral input requirements to make the Calera process economically attractive.

Calera could disrupt other conventional pollution control industries. Existing technologies to control sulfur oxides (SOx), mercury, and other emissions could be supplanted by Calera's technology. Such pollutants are currently subject to either cap-and-trade programs or Best Available Control Technology, which means companies have to install whatever available pollution control technology achieves the best results. The cost to power plants could be as high as $500 to $700 per kWh to remove these pollutants from their flue gas. [33] Early experiments suggested that Calera's process could trap these pollutants with over 90 percent efficiency in a single system, though nitrous oxides (NOx) would still need to be dealt with.

Conceivably, utilities could balk at the prospect of selling a large portion of their electricity to Calera, even if Calera set up shop where carbon was capped, such as the European Union, or approached companies wanting to reduce their emissions voluntarily. Utilities could switch to natural gas or find other ways to cut emissions. Calera, however, saw enough value in its own process and the coal-fired infrastructure that it had considered buying power plants outright and operating them itself.

Finally, Calera considered the possibility of providing a form of energy storage. Power plants could operate more at night, typically when demand was lower, to supply energy for Calera's electrochemistry process, effectively storing energy in the form of other chemicals. During the day, there would be no increased energy demand from Calera, thereby increasing a power plant's total energy output. In the same manner, Calera could also store energy from wind farms or other renewable sources.

Managing Growth

With many people eager to exploit Calera's technology, the company emphasized maintaining control. From the very beginning, Constantz limited outside investors to the well-known venture capital investor Vinod Khosla. Khosla cofounded Sun Microsystems in 1982 and left five years later for the venture capital firm Kleiner Perkins Caufield and Byers. Khosla founded his own firm, Khosla Ventures, in Menlo Park, California, in 2004, and invested his own money in sustainable and environmental business innovations. By May 2009, Khosla had made a significant investment in Calera. Despite two rounds of investments, adding seven seasoned vice presidents for functions ranging from intellectual property to government affairs, and successful

movement from batch process to continuous operation pilot plant to demonstration plant, Calera still had a board of only two members: Constantz and Samir Kaul of Khosla Ventures. Constantz believed "the largest risk of this company or any other company in this space is board problems. Because Calera had just one investor, it had been spared the problems of several board members, which can tank visionary start-ups." [34] Bad advice or conflicts posed a bigger threat than "the technology or the market," a lesson Constantz had taken to heart from his previous enterprises.

The company also protected itself from liability by creating special-purpose entities (SPEs) to operate individual projects. According to Constantz, "We're a corporation licensing its technology and intellectual property to other separate companies [SPEs] we've set up." [35] For example, the Moss Landing facility was owned and operated by the Moss Landing Cement Company, which, in turn, Calera owned. This division allowed Calera to reduce the threat of litigation and insurance costs at its office headquarters in nearby Los Gatos in Silicon Valley because cement production and associated construction were heavy industries in which equipment scale and complexity could involve expensive mistakes and working conditions posed many hazards. Everyone at the Moss Landing site was required to wear hard hats and safety glasses, and the sodium hydroxide produced by electrochemistry on-site was a toxic product.

The company also had grown to absorb more areas of technical expertise. Aurelia Setton came to Calera in mid-2008 as senior manager of corporate development after completing her MBA at Stanford Business School. She became director of strategic planning in the summer of 2009. Young and committed to sustainable business thinking, Setton had seen the company realize the implications of different technology applications and then move to recruit experts in those areas. First it was how to produce cement with less energy and then how to boost its ability to sequester CO_2. Then it was water purification. Then it was electrochemistry, the process of extracting chemicals through splitting them in solution. "If we see enough value in it, we bring it in-house," Setton said. [36]

Nonetheless, Calera had to recognize limits. For instance, Setton knew "we are not a manufacturing company. Those partnerships are very complicated. People are very interested in getting into our IP [intellectual property], and we need their help, but there's only one Calera and several of them." Hence Calera felt it could dictate its terms.

To facilitate deployment, Calera entered a worldwide strategic alliance with Bechtel in December 2009. Bechtel is a global engineering, procurement, and construction (EPC) firm with forty-nine thousand employees. Based in San Francisco, Bechtel operates in about fifty countries and generated $31.4 billion in revenues in 2008. Its past projects included the Channel Tunnel connecting England and France; the San Francisco–area metro system, Bay Area Rapid Transit (BART); and military bases, oil refineries, airports and seaports, nuclear and fossil-fuel-fired power plants, and railroad infrastructure. Calera worked closely with the Renewables and New Technology division in Bechtel's Power Business Unit. That division had experience with CCS and government grant applications and contracts, which could help Calera. Bechtel also offered a massive network of suppliers. "We didn't want to go out to a lot of EPC firms," Constantz explained. "We opted to just go to one firm and let them see what we're doing." [37] Bechtel advised Calera on the construction of its demonstration plant and played a pivotal role in worldwide deployment.

Calera pursued other possible collaborators. One was Schlumberger, the oil field and drilling firm with seventy-seven thousand employees and $27 billion in revenues in 2008. Calera sought Schlumberger's expertise in extracting subsurface brines, which were needed to replace seawater for Calera's process for inland locations. In early 2010, Calera was also in the midst of signing a deal with a big supplier for its electrochemistry operations. Finally, for power plants, Constantz considered Calera "just another industrial user. We can fight over who keeps carbon credits and all that, but the only time we have a relationship is if they invest in a plant, and we don't need them to invest." [38] Nonetheless, Setton believed Calera had leverage in negotiating the terms with a power plant for electricity and CO_2.

Quantifying Economic Opportunities

By mid-2010, Setton conceived of Calera's possible services as spanning four major categories: clean power, material efficiency, carbon management, and environmental sustainability. These opportunities were often interconnected, complex, and affected by changing regulations and markets, so to make money, the company had to manage this complexity and educate multiple audiences. It seemed a daunting, though exciting, balancing act for Setton. It was one she had a chance to hone when the Australian government and TRUEnergy wanted to see what Calera could do.

The Latrobe Valley, site of TRUEnergy's Yallourn Power Station in the state of Victoria, Australia, contains about 20 percent of the world's and over 90 percent of Australia's known reserves of lignite, or brown coal, an especially dirty

and consequently cheap coal. In 2006–2007, Australia produced 65.6 million metric tons of brown coal valued at A$820 million, or about US$10/ton. [39] Australia accounted for about 8 percent of the world's coal exports, and its lignite accounted for about 85 percent of electricity generation in Victoria. The Labor Government had proposed carbon trading in 2009, but that plan had been faltering through 2010. The coal industry nonetheless had invested in various demonstration projects to make brown coal a cleaner source of electricity. Bringing a Calera demonstration plant to the Yallourn Power Station was another such endeavor. The Calera project would eventually be increased to a scale of 200 MW.

The entire Yallourn Power Station had a capacity of 1,480 MW and voracious demand for resources. The plant needed thousands of tons of water per hour at full capacity. Some of that water would need to be sent to treatment afterward. The plant also had the low energy-conversion efficiency typical of coal-fired plants. Compounding that, the plant's brown coal had a low energy density, about 8.6 gigajoules per ton. In addition, combusting brown coal creates more SOx and NOx than other fuels, [40] and both pollutants were regulated in Australia.

Calera planned to look for local brines to provide alkalinity for its process. If they were unavailable, Calera would produce alkalinity with its proprietary electrochemistry process, which would increase the cost of cement production. The economics of the project would depend primarily on the price it could get for its cement. Calera had the potential to use wastewaters to provide calcium: about one hundred miles from the TRUEnergy plant, a large-scale desalination project was under construction, providing a potential feedstock for the Calera process. Utilizing such wastewater streams also offered potential revenue: as an example, in Europe, a desalination plant had to pay up to €200 per ton to dispose of its brine. Although prices would be different for Australia, Calera could be paid to take such waste brine for its process. Calera also considered using fly ash, a coal-combustion waste, for additional alkaline material.

With many variables and several unknowns, it was critical to determine the cost of each part of the process to determine the viability of the entire project. Nonetheless, the models depended on various assumptions, and those assumptions changed constantly as the project configuration and other factors changed. Nobody had ever built a Calera system in the field. That left much uncertainty in actual numbers. It also left uncertainty in broader strategies. Under many scenarios, Calera's energy demand would remain far less than the parasitic load of other CCS options. On the other hand, in some scenarios, Calera would need to have closer to 50 percent electrochemistry ions, which would represent a high energy requirement. How many sites could compete with CCS in terms of this energy requirement? How should that impact the business model and expansion plan of Calera?

TRUEnergy, for sure, could greatly benefit from Calera, beyond the CO_2 capture potential. TRUEnergy was a wholly owned subsidiary of the CLP Holdings Group, an electricity generation, distribution, and transmission investor based in Hong Kong with assets in India, China, Southeast Asia, and Australia. Lessons CLP learned now could pay dividends later, and the company had committed to lowering its carbon intensity. [41] The Yallourn Power Station, which could have an operating life of forty or more years, could attempt to gain a strategic advantage and improved public image by reducing its carbon emissions in anticipation of eventual regulation. The plant could also potentially use Calera's processes to lower SOx emissions. Calera's cement could directly trap these particulates. Indirectly, if Calera purchased power at night, the plant could decrease SOx emissions at times when they were most destructive—typically hot, sunny afternoons—and SOx controls typically most expensive. This load shifting could save money on pollution controls or new generation capacity.

Next Steps

Setton sat in her office, adjoining Constantz's in the building that Calera shared with the Los Gatos Public Library. Outside her door, a dozen employees worked at cubicles whose low, translucent partitions made them more side-by-side desks than cubicles. A light flashed in a bubble containing a toy-sized display in the foyer to represent CO_2 moving from a power plant to a Calera cement plant and then to a concrete mixer truck. Bits of chalky stones, like the ones in vials on Constantz's desk, represented Calera's product. The company had grown rapidly and showed enormous promise, but it had yet to build full-scale, commercial plants to fulfill that promise. Setton summarized the situation: "To innovate means you have to protect yourself, have to convince people, have to prove quickly, and have to deploy widely. Two strategic questions are important: one, what are the partnerships that will help us convince the world and bring it to reality, and second, how fast can we deploy. That means resources and allocation. How much do we keep in house, how much do we outsource without losing our protection. Those are key questions as we grow fast." [42]

The Calera case offers an example of an entrepreneur taking a process performed naturally, but at a small scale in coral reef formation, and applying the inherent principles to cement production on a large scale. This imitation of natural system chemistry and function represents a growing inspirational focus and concrete product design approach for innovation. The following discussion introduces students to the notion of biomimicry in business.

Biomimicry

What better models could there be?...This time, we come not to learn about nature so that we might circumvent or control her, but to learn from nature, so that we might fit in, at last and for good, on the Earth from which we sprang. [43]

- Janine Benyus

Humans have always imitated nature. Therefore, biomimicry is probably as old as humanity. Biomimicry as a formal concept is much newer, however. As a design philosophy, biomimicry draws upon nature to inspire and evaluate human-made products and strategies for growth. Biomimetic designers and engineers first examine how plants, animals, and ecosystems solve practical problems and then mimic those solutions or use them to spur innovation. Plants and animals have evolved in relation to each other and the physical world over billions of years. That evolution has yielded successful strategies for adaptation and survival that can, in turn, inform business products, practices, and strategic choices. Nature's sustainability strategies—a systems perspective, resource efficiency, and nontoxicity—form the core of biomimicry and offer a model on which to base sustainable innovations in commerce.

Key Concepts

Janine Benyus, a forester by training, is the central figure in articulating and advocating the principles of biomimicry. In her 1997 book *Biomimicry: Innovation Inspired by Nature*, she coined the term **biomimicry** and defined it as "the conscious emulation of life's genius" to solve human problems in design and industry. [44] Benyus has called it "innovation inspired by nature. It's a method, a way of asking nature for advice whenever you're designing something." [45] Benyus also founded the Biomimicry Guild, a consultancy that helps companies apply biomimetic principles, and the Biomimicry Institute, a nonprofit organization that aspires to educate a broad audience. [46]

Benyus was frustrated that her academic training focused on analyzing discrete pieces of life because it prevented her and others from seeing principles that emerge from analyzing entire systems. Nature is one such system, and Benyus calls for designers and businesses to consider nature as model, mentor, and measure. As she points out, four billion years of natural selection and evolution have yielded sophisticated, sustainable, diverse, and efficient answers to problems such as energy use and population growth. Humans now have the technology to understand many of nature's solutions and to apply similar ideas in our societies whether at the materials level, such as mimicking spider silk or deriving pharmaceuticals from plants, or at the level of ecosystems and the biosphere, such as improving agriculture by learning from prairies and forests or reducing our GHG emissions by shifting toward solar energy. As the final step, if we assess our own products and practices by comparing them with natural ones, we will have a good sense of how sustainable they ultimately are.

Indeed, Benyus identified a list of principles that make nature sustainable and could do the same for human economic activity:

- Runs on sunlight
- Uses only the energy it needs
- Fits form to function
- Recycles everything
- Rewards cooperation
- Banks on diversity
- Demands local expertise
- Curbs excesses from within
- Taps the power of limits [47]

Such biomimetic principles could be, and have been, exploited to make innovative products in conventional industries. For instance, an Italian ice-axe manufacturer modified its product design after studying woodpeckers. The new design proved more effective and generated higher sales. [48] Biomimicry notions can be extrapolated further and urge us to assume a sustainable place within nature by recognizing ourselves as inextricably part of nature. Biomimicry focuses "not on what we can extract from the natural world, but on what we can learn from it." [49] It also lends urgency to protecting ecosystems and cataloging their species and interdependencies so that we may continue to be inspired, aided, and instructed by nature's ingenuity.

In its broader, systems-conscious sense, biomimicry resembles industrial ecology and nature's services but clearly shares traits with William McDonough's concept of cradle-to-cradle design, Karl-Henrik Robèrt's Natural Step guidelines, and other sustainability strategies and theories. [50] Benyus has even explicitly aligned biomimicry with industrial ecology to enumerate ten principles of an economy that mimics nature. [51]

1. "Use waste as a resource," whether at the scale of integrated business parks or the global economy.
2. "Diversify and cooperate to fully use the habitat." Symbiosis and specialization within niches assures nothing is wasted and provides benefits to other companies or parts of industry.
3. "Gather and use energy efficiently." Use fossil fuels more efficiently while shifting to renewable resources.
4. "Optimize rather than maximize." Focus on quality over quantity.
5. "Use materials sparingly." Dematerialize products and reduce packaging; reconceptualize business as providing services instead of selling goods.
6. "Don't foul the nests." Reduce toxins and decentralize production of goods and energy.
7. "Don't draw down resources." Shift to renewable feedstocks, but use them at a low enough rate that they can regenerate. Invest in ecological capital.
8. "Remain in balance with the biosphere." Limit or eliminate pollution.
9. "Run on information." Create feedback loops to improve processes and reward environmentally restorative behavior.
10. "Shop locally." Use local resources for resiliency and to support regional populations, reduce transportation needs, build local economies, and let people see the impact of their consumption on the environment and local economic vitality.

Examples of Biomimetic Products

While biomimicry's concepts can be applied at various scales, they are most often considered at the level of individual products or technologies. Velcro is perhaps the best-known example. In the 1940s, Swiss engineer George de Mestral noticed burrs stuck to his clothes and his dog's fur after they went for a hike. He analyzed the burs and fabric under a microscope and saw how the hooks of the former tenaciously gripped the loops of the latter. He used this observation to invent Velcro, a name he derived from *velours* (French for velvet) and *crochet* (French for hook). Over the next several years, he switched from cotton to nylon to improve product durability and refined the process of making his microscopic arrays of hooks and loops. He then began to file patents worldwide. Velcro now is used in countless ways—including space suits, wallets, doll clothes, and athletic shoes.

Plants inspired another example of early design biomimicry. [52] Joseph Paxton, a gardener, was charged with caring for an English duke's giant Amazon water lily (*Victoria amazonica*), which British travelers had brought back from South America in the 1830s. The lily pads were so massive and buoyant that Paxton could put his young daughter on them and they would not sink. Intrigued, Paxton studied the underside of the water lily. He then used the rib-and-spine design that kept the water lilies afloat to build a greenhouse. A few years later, he applied the same principles to design the Crystal Palace for the 1851 Great Exhibition in London. The building relied on cast iron ribs to support glass plates and was a forerunner of modular design and modern greenhouses. [53]

Conclusion

Nature provides a rich source of ideas that can make human-designed products and corporate strategies more efficient and resilient, and less toxic—and therefore more sustainable. Nature's ecosystems avoid waste: what is discarded by one species is often used by another as input or nutrition. Nature solves problems with the materials at hand, the very building

blocks of life, rather than exotic and synthetic chemicals. Its systems are self-energizing; nature runs on sunlight, mediated by photosynthesis. When strategy executives or product designers operate from a biomimicry vantage point, considering its principles and the examples of plants and animals that apply, they can use nature's models to create sustainable business innovations.

KEY TAKEAWAYS

- Biomimicry can offer new ideas for solving some of our seemingly intractable ecological and environmental health problems.
- Entrepreneurs emerge from a wide variety of backgrounds; it is more a question of "fit" among the entrepreneur, the product/technology, and the market need that creates the opportunity.
- Success is not just about having a unique or superior technology; it is, perhaps most important, about finding early customers and generating revenue streams that satisfy investors.

EXERCISES

1. Describe each of the following for Calera:
   a. entrepreneur
   b. opportunity
   c. product
   d. concept
   e. resources
   f. market
   g. entry
2. What are Calera's major challenges now? What does the company have to et right in the short run to succeed? Prepare your analysis as a presentation with recommendations.
3. Name advantages or disadvantages in having the financial backing of Vinod Khosla.

---

[1] *Precipitate* means to separate from a solution or suspension, in this case to form solids from an aqueous solution.
[2] All tons indicate metric tons throughout this case. For production information, see Carrie Sturrock, "Green Cement May Set CO_2 Fate in Concrete," *San Francisco Chronicle*, September 2, 2008, accessed January 8, 2011, http://articles.sfgate.com/2008-09-02/news/17157439_1_cement-carbon-dioxide-power-plants. In 2001 in the United States, the world's third-largest producer of cement, the average CO_2 intensity of cement production was 0.97 tons CO_2/ton cement, ranging by kiln from 0.72 tons CO_2/ton cement to 1.41 tons CO_2/ton cement. Coal was the overwhelming energy source (71 percent) of cement kilns, followed by petroleum coke and other fuels. See Lisa Hanle, Kamala Jayaraman, and Joshua Smith, *CO_2 Emissions Profile of the U.S. Cement Industry* (Washington, DC: US Environmental Protection Agency, 2006), accessed January 8, 2011, http://www.epa.gov/ttnchie1/conference/ei13/ghg/hanle.pdf. Globally, the average CO_2 intensity for cement production in 2001 was around 0.82 tons CO_2/ton cement. See Ernst Worrell, Lynn Price, C. Hendricks, and L. Ozawa Meida, "Carbon Dioxide Emissions from the Global Cement Industry," *Annual Review of Energy and Environment* 26, no. LBNL-49097 (2001): 303–29, accessed January 8, 2011, http://industrial-energy.lbl.gov/node/193. Numbers from California alone in 2008 put CO_2 intensity there at 0.85 tons CO_2/ton cement. See California Environmental Protection Agency Air Resources Board, "Overview: AB 32 Implementation Status" (presentation at the California Cement Industry workgroup meeting, Sacramento, CA, April 10, 2008), accessed May 29, 2010, http://www.arb.ca.gov/cc/cement/meetings/041008/041008presentations.pdf.
[3] "Research Report on China's Cement Industry, 2009," Reuters, March 5, 2009, accessed January 8, 2011, http://www.reuters.com/article/pressRelease/idUS108100+05-Mar-2009+BW20090305; David Biello, "Cement from CO_2: A Concrete Cure for Global

Warming?" *Scientific American*, August 7, 2008, accessed January 8, 2011, http://www.scientificamerican.com/article.cfm?id=cement-from-carbon-dioxide; India Brand Equity Foundation, "Cement," accessed January 8, 2011, http://www.ibef.org/industry/cement.aspx.

[4] An alternative method, wet production, has largely been phased out due to its higher energy consumption. Ernst Worrell, "Energy Use and Efficiency of the U.S. Cement Industry" (presentation to the Policy Implementation Committee of the Energy Conservation and GHG Emissions Reduction in Chinese TVEs Project, Berkeley, CA, September 18, 2003).

[5] US Energy Information Administration, "Frequently Asked Questions," accessed January 29, 2011, http://www.eia.doe.gov/ask/electricity_faqs.asp#electricity_use_home.

[6] California Environmental Protection Agency Air Resources Board, "Overview: AB 32 Implementation Status" (presentation at the California Cement Industry workgroup meeting, Sacramento, CA, April 10, 2008), accessed May 29, 2009, http://www.arb.ca.gov/cc/cement/meetings/041008/041008presentations.pdf.

[7] US Environmental Protection Agency, *Fast Facts: Inventory of U.S. Greenhouse Gas Emissions and Sinks: 1990–2008* (Washington DC: US Environmental Protection Agency, 2010), accessed January 8, 2011, http://www.epa.gov/climatechange/emissions/downloads10/US-GHG-Inventory-Fast-Facts-2008.pdf.

[8] Portland Cement Association, "Overview of the Cement Industry: Economics of the U.S. Cement Industry," December 2009, accessed January 8, 2011, http://www.cement.org/basics/cementindustry.asp.

[9] Bruce Kennedy, "China's Three Gorges Dam," *CNN*, accessed January 8, 2011, http://www.cnn.com/SPECIALS/1999/china.50/asian.superpower/three.gorges. The comparison road value is derived from the Hoover Dam, which used approximately 6 million tons of concrete. US Department of the Interior, "Hoover Dam: Frequently Asked Questions and Answers," accessed January 8, 2011, http://www.usbr.gov/lc/hooverdam/faqs/damfaqs.html.

[10] Synthes, "Synthes Reports 2009 Results with 9% Sales Growth and 13% Net Earnings Growth in Local Currency (6% and 12% in US$)," news release, February 17, 2010, accessed January 8, 2011, http://www.synthes.com/html/News-Details.8013.0.html?&tx_synthesnewsbyxml_pi1[showUid]=39.

[11] Stanford biography at Stanford Biodesign, "People: Brent Constantz Ph.D.," accessed January 8, 2011, http://biodesign.stanford.edu/bdn/people/bconstantz.jsp.

[12] Carrie Sturrock, "Green Cement May Set CO_2 Fate in Concrete," *San Francisco Chronicle*, September 2, 2008, accessed January 8, 2011, http://articles.sfgate.com/2008-09-02/news/17157439_1_cement-carbon-dioxide-power-plants.

[13] See Brent R. Constantz, Cecily Ryan, and Laurence Clodic, Hydraulic cements comprising carbonate compound compositions, US Patent 7735274, filed May 23, 2008, and issued June 15, 2010.

[14] The park has a website: Industrial Symbiosis, "Welcome to the Industrial Symbiosis," accessed January 8, 2011, http://www.symbiosis.dk.

[15] {Author's Name Retracted as requested by the work's original creator or licensee} and Mark Meier, *Calera: Entrepreneurship, Innovation, and Sustainability*, UVA-ENT-0160 (Charlottesville: Darden Business Publishing, University of Virginia, September 21, 2010).

[16] {Author's Name Retracted as requested by the work's original creator or licensee} and Mark Meier, *Calera: Entrepreneurship, Innovation, and Sustainability*, UVA-ENT-0160 (Charlottesville: Darden Business Publishing, University of Virginia, September 21, 2010).

[17] European Energy Exchange, "Emission Rights," accessed January 10, 2011, http://www.eex.com/en; Regional Greenhouse Gas Initiative, "Auction Results: Auction 6," December 2, 2010, accessed January 10, 2011, http://www.rggi.org/market/co2_auctions/results/auction6.

[18] McKinsey Climate Change Initiative, *Carbon Capture and Storage: Assessing the Economics* (New York: McKinsey, 2008), accessed January 10, 2011, http://www.mckinsey.com/clientservice/sustainability/pdf/CCS_Assessing_the_Economics.pdf.

[19] Joseph B. Lassiter, Thomas J. Steenburgh, and Lauren Barley, *Calera Corporation*, case 9-810-030 (Boston: Harvard Business Publishing, 2009), 3, accessed January 10, 2011, http://www.ecch.com/casesearch/product_details.cfm?id=91925.

[20] Massachusetts v. Environmental Protection Agency, 549 US 497 (2007), accessed January 10, 2011, http://www.supremecourt.gov/opinions/06pdf/05-1120.pdf.

[21] {Author's Name Retracted as requested by the work's original creator or licensee} and Mark Meier, *Calera: Entrepreneurship, Innovation, and Sustainability*, UVA-ENT-0160 (Charlottesville: Darden Business Publishing, University of Virginia, September 21, 2010).

[22] {Author's Name Retracted as requested by the work's original creator or licensee} and Mark Meier, *Calera: Entrepreneurship, Innovation, and Sustainability*, UVA-ENT-0160 (Charlottesville: Darden Business Publishing, University of Virginia, September 21, 2010).

[23] Lizzie Buchen, "A Green Idea Set in Cement," *Monterey County Herald*, October 4, 2008, accessed January 10, 2011, http://www.montereyherald.com/news/ci_10637168.

[24] Joseph B. Lassiter, Thomas J. Steenburgh, and Lauren Barley, *Calera Corporation*, case 9-810-030 (Boston: Harvard Business Publishing, 2009), 1, accessed January 10, 2011, http://www.ecch.com/casesearch/product_details.cfm?id=91925.

[25] Jay Withgott and Scott Brennan, *Environment: The Science Behind the Stories*, 3rd ed. (San Francisco: Pearson Benjamin Cummings, 2008), 445.

[26] These values assume that Calera's cement is composed of calcium and magnesium carbonates. Calcium carbonate has a molecular weight of 100 grams per mole; magnesium carbonate has a molecular weight of 84 grams per mole. CO_2 thus represents almost exactly half of the weight of each ton of Calera cement produced from standard seawater. This CO_2 proportion, however, would not include emissions from energy needed to operate the plant.

[27] Ben Block, "Capturing Carbon Emissions…in Cement?" Worldwatch Institute, January 26, 2009, accessed May 25, 2009, http://www.worldwatch.org/node/5996.

[28] {Author's Name Retracted as requested by the work's original creator or licensee} and Mark Meier, *Calera: Entrepreneurship, Innovation, and Sustainability*, UVA-ENT-0160 (Charlottesville: Darden Business Publishing, University of Virginia, September 21, 2010).

[29] Wolf Hilbertz, "Electrodeposition of Minerals in Sea Water: Experiments and Applications," *IEEE Journal on Oceanic Engineering* 4, no. 3 (1979): 94–113, accessed January 10, 2011, http://www.globalcoral.org/IEEE_JOUR_1979small.pdf.

[30] The debate seems to occur mainly over e-mail and groups, for instance, Climate Intervention, "Calera—Fooling Schoolchildren?" accessed January 10, 2011, http://groups.google.com/group/climateintervention/browse_thread/thread/7b5ff4ee64ce759d?pli=1.

[31] {Author's Name Retracted as requested by the work's original creator or licensee} and Mark Meier, *Calera: Entrepreneurship, Innovation, and Sustainability*, UVA-ENT-0160 (Charlottesville: Darden Business Publishing, University of Virginia, September 21, 2010).

[32] Interagency Task Force on Carbon Capture and Storage, *Report of the Interagency Task Force on Carbon Capture and Storage* (Washington DC: US Environmental Protection Agency/US Department of Energy, 2010), 27, 33–35, accessed January 10, 2011, http://www.epa.gov/climatechange/downloads/CCS-Task-Force-Report-2010.pdf. The report did not consider a model like Calera's to be CCS; instead, it defined CCS only as geological sequestration.

[33] Joseph B. Lassiter, Thomas J. Steenburgh, and Lauren Barley, *Calera Corporation*, case 9-810-030 (Boston: Harvard Business Publishing, 2009), 7, accessed January 10, 2011, http://www.ecch.com/casesearch/product_details.cfm?id=91925.

[34] {Author's Name Retracted as requested by the work's original creator or licensee} and Mark Meier, *Calera: Entrepreneurship, Innovation, and Sustainability*, UVA-ENT-0160 (Charlottesville: Darden Business Publishing, University of Virginia, September 21, 2010).

[35] {Author's Name Retracted as requested by the work's original creator or licensee} and Mark Meier, *Calera: Entrepreneurship, Innovation, and Sustainability*, UVA-ENT-0160 (Charlottesville: Darden Business Publishing, University of Virginia, September 21, 2010).

[36] {Author's Name Retracted as requested by the work's original creator or licensee} and Mark Meier, *Calera: Entrepreneurship, Innovation, and Sustainability*, UVA-ENT-0160 (Charlottesville: Darden Business Publishing, University of Virginia, September 21, 2010).

[37] {Author's Name Retracted as requested by the work's original creator or licensee} and Mark Meier, *Calera: Entrepreneurship, Innovation, and Sustainability*, UVA-ENT-0160 (Charlottesville: Darden Business Publishing, University of Virginia, September 21, 2010).

[38] {Author's Name Retracted as requested by the work's original creator or licensee} and Mark Meier, *Calera: Entrepreneurship, Innovation, and Sustainability*, UVA-ENT-0160 (Charlottesville: Darden Business Publishing, University of Virginia, September 21, 2010).

[39] Ron Sait, "Brown Coal," Australian Atlas of Minerals Resources, Mines, and Processing Centers, accessed January 10, 2011, http://www.australianminesatlas.gov.au/aimr/commodity/brown_coal_10.jsp.

[40] The exact NOx and SOx emissions, before pollution control, depend on the design of the combustion unit, but for a variety of designs the US Environmental Protection Agency estimated SOx emissions to be 5 to 15 kg per ton of lignite burned and NOx emissions to be 1.8–7.5 kg per ton of lignite burned. See US Environmental Protection Agency, "Chapter 1: External Combustion Sources," in *AP 42, Compilation of Air Pollutant Emission Factors, Volume 1: Stationary Point and Area Sources*, 5th ed. (Research Triangle Park, NC: US Environmental Protection Agency, 1998), 7–8, accessed January 10, 2011, http://www.epa.gov/ttn/chief/ap42/ch01/index.html. Although it is difficult to put an exact price on the cost of controlling emissions in Australia, trading programs in the United States give some insight. The United States runs a cap-and-trade program for NOx and SOx for power plants on the east coast, and from January 2008 to July 2010, permits to emit one ton of SOx decreased from approximately $500 to $50 per ton, while NOx allowances started around $800 before peaking near $1,400 and decreasing to $50 per ton. See the Federal Energy Regulatory Commission, *Emissions Market: Emission Allowance Prices* (Washington, DC: Federal Energy Regulatory Commission, 2010), accessed January 10, 2011, http://www.ferc.gov/market-oversight/othr-mkts/emiss-allow/2010/07-2010-othr-emns-no-so-pr.pdf. Since the price of an allowance ideally represents the marginal cost to abate an additional ton of emissions, it reflects the cost of control technology. Calera claimed its process, as noted earlier, could achieve up to 90 percent CO_2 reduction and do so at a lower price if local resources could provide valuable feedstock.

[41] CLP Holdings, "Climate Vision," accessed January 10, 2011, https://www.clpgroup.com/ourvalues/environmental/climatevision/Pages/climatevision.aspx.

[42] {Author's Name Retracted as requested by the work's original creator or licensee} and Mark Meier, *Calera: Entrepreneurship, Innovation, and Sustainability*, UVA-ENT-0160 (Charlottesville: Darden Business Publishing, University of Virginia, September 21, 2010).

[43] Janine M. Benyus, *Biomimicry: Innovation Inspired by Nature* (New York: William Morrow, 1997), 2, 9.

[44] Janine M. Benyus, *Biomimicry: Innovation Inspired by Nature* (New York: William Morrow, 1997), 2.

[45] Michael Cervieri, "Float Like a Butterfly—With Janine Benyus," *ScribeMedia*, October 22, 2008, accessed April 12, 2010, http://www.scribemedia.org/2008/10/22/float-like-a-butterfly-with-janine-benyus.

[46] To view a twenty-three-minute video of Janine Benyus talking about biomimicry at the 2005 Technology, Entertainment, Design conference, see Janine Benyus, "Janine Benyus Shares Nature's Designs," filmed February 2005, TED video, 23:16, from a speech at the 2005 Technology, Entertainment, and Design conference, posted April 2007, accessed April 12, 2010, http://www.ted.com/talks/janine_benyus_shares_nature_s_designs.html.

[47] Janine M. Benyus, *Biomimicry: Innovation Inspired by Nature* (New York: William Morrow, 1997), 7.

[48] Kate Rockwood, "Biomimicry: Nature-Inspired Products," *Fast Company*, October 1, 2008.

[49] Janine M. Benyus, *Biomimicry: Innovation Inspired by Nature* (New York: William Morrow, 1997).

[50] Each of these concepts relates to sustainable business and each has its own heritage. Hence the concepts are summarized here with a suggestion for further reading. *Industrial ecology* refers to the industry practice of collocation, which uses wastes from one process as input for another, such as using gypsum recovered from scrubbing smokestack emissions to make drywall. See Thomas E. Graedel and Braden R. Allenby, *Industrial Ecology*, 2nd ed. (Upper Saddle River, NJ: Prentice Hall, 2003). *Nature's services* refer to the ways natural processes, such as photosynthesis and filtration in wetlands, provide goods and benefits to humans, such as clean air and clean water. See Gretchen Daily, ed., *Nature's Services: Societal Dependence on Natural Ecosystems* (Washington, DC: Island Press, 1997). *Cradle-to-cradle design* emphasizes that products should be made to be safely disassembled and reused, not discarded, at the end of their lives to become feedstocks for new products or nutrients for nature. See William McDonough and Michael Braungart, *Cradle to Cradle: Remaking the Way We Make Things* (New York: North Point Press, 2002). *The Natural Step* is a strategic framework that considers human economic activity within the broader material and energy balances of the earth; it holds that because we cannot exhaust resources or produce products that nature is unable to safely replenish or degrade, we must switch to renewable and nontoxic materials. See Karl-Henrik Robèrt, *The Natural Step Story: Seeding a Quiet Revolution* (Gabriola Island, Canada: New Society Publishers, 2008); Natural Step, "Home," accessed April 12, 2010, http://www.naturalstep.org; and Natural Step USA, "Home," accessed April 12, 2010, http://www.naturalstep.org/usa.

[51] Janine M. Benyus, *Biomimicry: Innovation Inspired by Nature* (New York: William Morrow, 1997), 252–77.

[52] Many examples of biomimicry can be found at the Biomimicry Institute's website, Ask Nature, "Home," accessed April 12, 2010, http://www.asknature.org. The 2009 Biomimicry Conference in San Diego included an overview of biomimetic products; footage from that conference is available: "Biomimicry Conference 2009—San Diego," YouTube video, 3:26, from the Zoological Society of San Diego's Biomimicry Educational Conference on October 1–2, 2009, posted by MEMSDisplayGuy, November 9, 2009, accessed April 8, 2010, http://www.youtube.com/v/r-WUPr5LUR8.

[53] Lucy Richmond, "The Giant Water Lily That Inspired the Crystal Palace," *Telegraph* (UK), May 7, 2009, accessed January 10, 2011, http://www.telegraph.co.uk/comment/letters/5285516/The-giant-water-lily-that-inspired-the-Crystal-Palace.html; "Leaves Given Structural Support: Giant Water-Lily," Ask Nature, accessed April 8, 2010, http://asknature.org/strategy/902666afb8d8548320ae0afcd54d02ae.

[54] "Eastgate Centre Building: Passive Heating and Cooling Saves Energy," Ask Nature, accessed November 16, 2009, http://www.asknature.org/product/373ec79cd6dba791bc00ed32203706a1; "Ventilated Nests Remove Heat and Gas: Mound-Building Termites," Ask Nature, accessed April 12, 2010, http://www.asknature.org/strategy/8a16bdffd27387cd2a3a995525ea08b3; Abigail Doan, "Green Building in Zimbabwe Modeled after Termite Mounds," *Inhabit*, December 10, 2007, accessed January 10, 2011, http://inhabitat.com/building-modelled-on-termites-eastgate-centre-in-zimbabwe.

[55] "i2™ Carpet and Flooring: As-Needed Tile Replacement Saves Resources," Ask Nature, accessed January 10, 2011, http://www.asknature.org/product/a84a9167f21f1cc690e0e673c4808833; InterfaceFLOR, "i2™ Modular Carpet—How Nature Would Design a Floor," accessed April 12, 2010, http://www.interfaceflor.com/Default.aspx?Section=3&Sub=11.

[56] Qualcomm, "Mobile Displays: Mirasol Display Technology," accessed January 10, 2011, http://www.qualcomm.com/products_services/consumer_electronics/displays/mirasol; "Mirasol Display Hands-On High-Res," YouTube video, 0:58, posted by engadget, January 8, 2010; accessed April 12, 2010, http://www.youtube.com/v/jmpBgaPGYKQ; Mirasol Displays, "How It Works," accessed January 10, 2011, http://www.mirasoldisplays.com/how-it-works; and Mirasol Displays, "Press Center: Awards," accessed January 10, 2011, http://www.mirasoldisplays.com/awards.

NOTES:

Chapter 6:

Clean Products and Health

6.1 Green Supply Chains

LEARNING OBJECTIVES

1. Learn the definition of a green supply chain.

2. Understand how integration of green and sustainability knowledge can improve the performance of supply chains.

3. Define reverse logistics, life cycle assessment, and design for environment in the context of supply chains.

4. Gain insight into the strategic value of greening your supply chain.

Regardless of how you might feel about Walmart, the effect of the company's sustainability policies are being felt worldwide through its supply chains. On February 1, 2007, Walmart President and CEO Lee Scott announced his company's "Sustainability 360" program would expand Walmart's sustainability efforts from its operations and into its supply chains by "tak[ing] in," as Scott said, "our entire company—our customer base, our supplier base, our associates, the products on our shelves, the communities we serve." [1] Walmart customers could now track the company's "Love, Earth" jewelry all the way back to the mine or buy fish certified by the Marine Stewardship Council. In 2010 the company announced the goal of a twenty-million-metric-ton greenhouse gas emission reduction from its global supply chain (encompassing over one hundred thousand suppliers). [2] Furthermore, Walmart enlisted the nonprofit Carbon Disclosure Project, institutional investors with $41 trillion in assets as of September 2007, to help Walmart's suppliers of DVDs, toothpaste, soap, milk, beer, vacuum cleaners, and soda to assess and reduce their carbon footprints. [3] Indeed, with roughly one hundred thousand suppliers, two million employees, and millions of customers per day, [4] Walmart's operations and those it encouraged, from product design and resource extraction through final consumption and disposal, could massively influence societies and the natural environment. As such impacts attracted attention, so did the benefits of and the need for greener supply networks.

Green supply chains (GSCs) became *Supply Chain Digest*'s number one supply-chain trend of 2006 as more companies such as Walmart embraced them. [5] Fully developed green supply chains consider sustainability for every participant at every step, from design to manufacture, transportation, storage, and use to eventual disposal or recycling. This attentiveness would reduce waste, mitigate legal and environmental risks, minimize and possibly eliminate adverse health impacts throughout the value-added process, improve the reputations of companies and their products (enhancing brands), and enable compliance with increasingly stringent regulations and societal expectations. Thus GSCs offer the opportunity to boost efficiency, value, and access to markets *through* improving a company's environmental, social, and economic performance.

Improving Conventional Supply Chains

In its simplest form, a conventional supply chain assumes that firms take raw materials at the beginning of the supply chain and transform them into a product at the end of the supply chain. Ultimately, the supply chain terminates at the point of the final buyer purchasing and using the product. Vertical integration absorbs steps in the supply chain within a single corporation that conducts exchange through internal transfer pricing agreements. Disaggregation maintains ownership in discrete businesses that determine prices through market-based transactions.

A company that sells a final product must meet certain requirements and interact with suppliers, third-party logistics providers, and other stakeholder groups that can influence the entire process. Each institution tries to shape the supply chain to its own advantage. As the product moves from design to consumption (black arrows), waste and other problems (gray arrows) accrue. Whether those problems are unfair wages, deforestation, or air pollution, these costs are not necessarily reflected in the price of the finished product but are instead externalized to the public in some fashion or expected to be borne by intermediate links in the conventional chain.

While the term *supply chain* implies a one-way, linear relationship among participants (e.g., from concept, to resource extraction, to processing, to component manufacturing, to system integration, to final assembly, etc.), the chain is more accurately described as a *network* of individuals and organizations. Managing such networks can become quite complex, especially as they sprawl over more of the globe. Conventional supply-chain management plans, implements, and controls the operations of the supply chain as efficiently as possible—typically, however, from a limited vantage point that ignores and externalizes many costs.

In contrast, a green supply chain takes a broader, systems view that internalizes some of these costs and ultimately turns them into sources of value. Green supply chains thus modify conventional supply chains in two significant ways: they increase sustainability and efficiency in the existing forward supply chain and add an entirely new reverse supply chain.

Improving Logistics

A company can select various ways to improve the sustainability of its logistics systems. The company may communicate sustainability standards backward to suppliers and require them to adopt environmental management systems or certifications, such as ISO 14001; survey and monitor suppliers' current practices or products for their sustainability and offer training, technology, and incentives to improve those practices or products; [6] require suppliers to avoid certain hazardous ingredients and label others; and/or ask suppliers and other supporting firms, such as transportation companies, to suggest ways to improve the efficiency and sustainability of the whole process. Hence companies "greening" their supply chains are likely to communicate and collaborate more with suppliers and subcontractors to innovate and find the best solutions. They might also reach out to nongovernmental organizations (NGOs) and government agencies for further assistance.

For example, US-based DesignTex, in the 1990s a leader in the contract textile industry and now a subsidiary of US commercial furniture manufacturer Steelcase, [7] chose to pursue an environmentally friendly commercial upholstery fabric. DesignTex collaborated with a small Swiss firm called Rohner Textil AG, chemical corporation Ciba Geigy, and the Environmental Protection Encouragement Agency (a German NGO) to determine product specifications, develop fabric requirements, and identify substitute benign chemicals for the toxic chemicals present along the fabric supply chain. [8] The new product's supply chain originated from the wool of free-range sheep and ramie grown without

pesticides to a yarn-twisting mill and dye manufacturers, with scraps of the textile generated along the way being sold to farmers and gardeners for mulch.

Surprisingly, the production changes did not just reduce DesignTex's environmental impact; they also added value: The factory's effluent became cleaner than the incoming water supply. Regulatory paperwork was eliminated. Workers no longer needed protective masks or gloves, which eliminated health risks and liability exposure. [9] Because of these decreased costs and the tax relief for the accompanying environmental investments, the innovation showed a payback period of only five years. [10] It also was an early, successful illustration of cradle-to-cradle design, the cyclical design protocol that allows biologically benign products to safely return to nature.

Reverse Logistics

In addition to dramatically improving conventional supply-chain logistics, green supply chains extend past the point of product use, where conventional chains end, and consider how to recover and reuse materials—questions of **reverse logistics**. Many companies already have rudimentary reverse logistics systems to deal with customers' returns of items they do not want or that were found defective or otherwise unsatisfactory. An expanded reverse logistics system would ultimately replace the linearity of most production methods—raw materials, to processing, to further conversions and modification, to ultimate product, to use, to disposal—with a cradle-to-cradle, cyclical path or closed loop that begins with the return of used, outmoded, out-of-fashion, and otherwise "consumed" products. The products are either recycled and placed back into the manufacturing stream or broken down into compostable materials. The cycle is never ending because materials return to the land in safe molecular structures (taken up and used by organisms as biological nutrients) or are perpetually used within the economy as input for new products (technical nutrients).

Companies typically funnel spent items from consumers into the reverse supply chain by leasing their products or providing collection points or by other means of recovering the items once their service life ends. [11] For example, Canon and Xerox provide free shipping to return used toner cartridges and have thus collectively recovered over one hundred thousand tons of ink and cartridges since 1990. [12]

Once collected, whether by the original manufacturer or a third party, the products could be inspected and sorted. Some items might return quickly to the supply chain with only minimal repair or replacement of certain components, whereas other products might need to be disassembled, remanufactured, or cannibalized for salvageable parts while the remnant is recycled or sent to a landfill or incinerator. "Companies that remanufacture are estimated to save 40–60 percent of the cost of manufacturing a completely new product…while requiring only 20 percent of the effort," leading to significant, structural savings, wrote Shad Dowlatshahi in *Interfaces*. [13] Moreover, the reverse supply chain might spawn new suppliers as well as other sources of revenue for companies that engage in collection, disassembly, and so on, making the entire network more efficient. [14] This concept of an eco-efficient closed loop thereby makes green supply chains a central piece of sustainable industrial ecosystems.

Life-Cycle Assessment and Design for Environment

The same techniques that improve the sustainability of conventional logistics also aid reverse logistics. In addition, green supply chains fundamentally require two tools: life-cycle assessment (LCA) and design for environment (DfE). According to the US Environmental Protection Agency's National Risk Management Research Laboratory, LCA takes the viewpoint of a product, process, or service by "(1) compiling an inventory of relevant energy and material inputs and environmental releases; (2) evaluating the potential environmental impacts associated with identified inputs and releases; [and] (3) interpreting the results to help you make an informed decision," typically to minimize negative impacts across the entire life of the product. [15] This analysis helps identify the points in the green supply chain that detract from ultimate sustainability and establishes a baseline for improvement. For example, Walmart's third-party logistics provider in Canada began using railways more than roads to supply ten stores, thereby cutting carbon emissions by 2,600 tons. The company estimated it would save another $4.5 million and prevent 1,400 tons of waste annually by switching from cardboard to plastic shipping crates. [16]

Application of DfE acknowledges that design determines a product's materials and the processes by which the product is made, shipped, used, and recovered. Hence DfE could be used to avoid toxic materials from the outset; minimize energy and material inputs; and facilitate disassembly, repair, and remanufacturing. For instance, Hewlett Packard (HP) used DfE "product stewards," whose role, HP explained, was as follows: "[Product stewards] are integrated into product design and research and development teams to identify, prioritize, and recommend environmental design innovations to make products easier to disassemble and recycle. Such features include modular designs, snap-in features that eliminate the need for glues and adhesives, fewer materials, and molded-in colors and finishes instead of paint, coatings, or plating." [17]

Conversely, process designs could influence product designs through new technology that implements an innovative idea. For example, in the Walden Paddlers case discussed in Section 4.5 "Adaptive Collaboration through Value-Added Networks", Hardigg Industries was a plastics-molding company that partnered with Clearvue Plastics to create plastic pellets with 50 percent recycled content, which Hardigg thought was impossible until it was encouraged by the entrepreneurial founder of Walden Paddlers. Later, Hardigg was able to change its rotomolding technology to allow for the use of 100 percent recycled resins. Through the use of recycled materials and Clearvue's innovation, Hardigg was able to lower costs, establish a competitive advantage within its industry, attract new customers, and increase customer satisfaction. [18]

Greener Supply Chains: Accelerating Response to Changed Context

Although green supply chains could present novel challenges, they had spread to address a convergence of legal requirements, consumer expectations, and competition for continued profitability. In 2001, a study of twenty-five suppliers showed 80 percent received significant requests to improve the environmental quality of their operations and products, and they in turn asked their suppliers to do the same. [19] A larger survey from 2008 indicated 82 percent of respondents were planning to implement or were already implementing green supply-chain management strategies. [20] The trend toward green supply chains was expected to continue.

Concern for green supply-chain topics emerged in the 1990s as, on one hand, globalization and outsourcing made supply networks increasingly complex and diverse and, on the other hand, new laws and consumer expectations increasingly demanded that companies take more responsibility for their products across the entire life of those products. [21] Companies had to more closely monitor their suppliers. Total quality management and conventional supply-chain management adapted to address some of these challenges in "a paradigm shift [that] occurred when the scope of analysis was broadened beyond what was customary [for operations analysts] at the time." [22] These broader management practices and ISO 9001 in turn laid the foundation for green supply-chain management and ISO 14001.

Between 2000 and 2009, the increased emphasis on sustainability expanded the scope further and deeper into environmental, public health, and community/social issues and embraced stakeholders beyond consumers and investors. [23] This new paradigm of "extended producer responsibility," which included a call for greater transparency and accountability, also compelled companies toward green supply-chain design. [24]

Laws to reduce human exposure to hazardous and toxic chemicals drive corporate attention to supply-chain materials use. Noncompliance with laws could hurt profits, market share, and brand image. For example, Dutch customs agents prevented approximately $160 million worth of Sony PlayStation consoles from entering Holland in December 2001 because cadmium levels in their wiring exceeded levels set by Dutch law. [25] Sony disputed the root cause with its Taiwanese cable supplier but nonetheless had to pay to store, refurbish, and repack the machines.

Most forward-thinking global firms moved toward adopting consistent standards across all their markets, as opposed to different standards for different countries. Hence the tightest rules from one place tended to become the de facto global standard. For example, the EU's directives 2002/95/EC on "the Restriction of the Use of certain Hazardous Substances in Electrical and Electronic Equipment" (RoHS) and 2002/96/EC on "Waste Electrical and Electronic Equipment" (WEEE) had many ramifications for suppliers and producers in the electronics industry. RoHS required all manufacturers of electronics and electrical equipment sold in Europe by July 2006 to substitute safer materials for six hazardous substances, such as lead and chromium. WEEE required producers to collect their electronic waste from consumers free of charge. [26] The EU's 2006 directive on "Registration, Evaluation, Authorization, and Restriction of Chemicals" (REACH) might further tighten global standards for producers and suppliers because it "gives greater responsibility to industry to manage the risks from chemicals and to provide safety information on the substances." [27] Similar efforts have begun in Asia with Japan's Green Procurement rules and China's Agenda 21 goals. [28]

Consumers and institutional investors, meanwhile, have exerted pressure on companies through a variety of tactics from socially responsible investment screening criteria to market campaigns for engaging in fair trade or ending sweatshop labor. Failure to publicly improve practices anywhere along the supply chain could hurt brand image and curtail access to markets. American universities and colleges founded the Worker Rights Consortium in 2000 "to assist universities with the enforcement of their labor rights codes of conduct, which were adopted to protect the rights of workers producing apparel and other goods bearing university names and logos." [29] Manufacturers such as Canada's Hudson Bay Company began to audit suppliers' factories for compliance with labor standards. [30] By 2005, the Investor Environmental Health Network, following the effective strategy of institutional investors negotiating with companies for more action and accountability on climate change, was encouraging investment managers and corporations to reduce high-risk toxic chemicals used in their products and used by companies in which they invest.

Successful Green Supply Chains Manage Added Complexity

Businesses might face novel challenges when implementing, operating, or auditing green supply chains. Given these challenges, businesses that already used an environmental management system were more equipped to build a green supply chain. [31] Nonetheless, all businesses could take steps to green their chains.

"Green" has become strategic. When sustainability is recognized as an operating and strategic opportunity, as in the cases of General Electric and Walmart, senior management supports green supply-chain initiatives and integrates them into the business's core capabilities. [32] In 2010, however, authority over green supply chains still tended to be held by a variety of groups, such as supply-chain managers, environmental health and safety offices, and sustainability divisions. [33] Personnel who might have once functioned separately within a company often had to collaborate and create new teams for green supply chains to work effectively, and those people needed time for the green supply chains to yield their maximum benefits.

Companies must actively include suppliers and service providers in greening supply chains so that they can build trust, lend their own expertise to increase sustainability, and receive adequate guidance and assistance in improving their operations. [34] Businesses must state clear and reasonable expectations and allow sufficient lead time for suppliers to respond. They must also be willing to listen to suppliers. [35] Furthermore, companies cannot simply issue guidelines from their headquarters; their representatives must instead be available on the ground and cooperating with local contacts to ensure results and prevent increased competition within the supply chain. [36] Indeed, suppliers need incentives and assurance that their share of the profit will be protected if they innovate to improve the process because maximizing the overall value of the supply chain may reduce value for individual links. [37] For example, a design for disassembly that relies on pieces that snap together may obviate the need for suppliers of adhesives, even if it may create demand for disassembly and remanufacturing services.

Reverse supply chains complicate the overall supply chain, and therefore they need to be carefully crafted and considered in overall product design, production, and distribution. Materials and components recovered from used products need to reenter the same forward supply chain as new materials or components. Hence companies must recover items efficiently, train employees or subcontractors to assess properly the condition of a recovered item and what is salvageable and what is not, and manage their inventory to even out variation in the rate and quality of returned items. [38] They must also balance the availability of salvaged components or recycled materials with the need for new components or materials, especially as certain proprietary parts become unavailable or production processes change. In cases when consumers may want the same item they had before with only minor changes, such as a vehicle, businesses will also have to track individual pieces through disassembly and refurbishment. [39]

After establishing a green supply chain, companies need to assess its performance. In their 2008 survey of seventy supply-chain executives, Lassar and Gonzalez noted, "Almost 40 percent of the 56 firms that are active with green activities do not have any metrics to measure green/sustainability results in their firms." [40] Companies with metrics tracked quantities such as fuel use, packaging, and so on. Another study corroborates this trend: what metrics companies do have tend to cluster around eco-efficiency indicators, such as packaging used or miles traveled, likely because those are the easiest to observe, quantify, and associate with specific actions. [41] Companies can, however, include broader measures such as customer satisfaction. However, even then a company may fall short. A systems, health-oriented, and green approach to design does not always work. Some view Frito-Lay's SunChips compostable bag (offered to the market consistent with biodegradable bags being the fastest growing segment in packaging) as having failed due to its loud noise when handled. Since the crinkling of the bags at up to eighty-five decibels is comparable to glass breaking or an engine revving, the company has gone back to the drawing board with this packaging design.

Fading Extrinsic Challenges

Finally, green supply chains had to overcome institutional inertia and confusion. First, large companies with financial and political resources tended to resist change, especially at the outset, because of the large capital and infrastructural investments in the status quo. Walmart's green initiative, however, appears to be the turning point that moves other large enterprises toward green supply chains.

Second, in 2009, no official criteria defined a green supply chain. Standards such as ISO 14000 usually focus on a single entity and not the supply chain, while legal requirements often focus on products and ingredients. ISO 14001, the core voluntary set of standards, is used by firms to design an environmental management system that provides internal monitoring and provides practices, procedures, and tools for systematic efforts to improve performance. However, nothing defines how much of the supply chain is required to have ISO 14000 or other certifications to qualify for the green supply chain label. When Home Depot solicited its suppliers for candidates to its Eco Options marketing campaign, one manufacturer praised the plastic handles of its paintbrushes as more environmentally sensitive than wooden handles, while another praised the wooden handles of its paintbrushes as environmentally better than plastic. [42]

The lack of standards could promote individual certification programs, such as the cradle-to-cradle certification provided by McDonough Braungart Design Chemistry, LLC, which implies a corresponding green supply chain. This program, however, is private, largely to protect the confidential business information of its clients to ensure their cooperation, and has therefore been criticized for its lack of transparency. [43] However, the cradle-to-cradle approach is now being explored in California as a statewide system to encourage safer, less polluting design protocols. In the worst cases, vague standards or opaque processes can lead to charges of "greenwashing," or exaggerating or fabricating environmental credentials. [44] Greenwashing distracts people who are serious about taking care of the environment with counterproductive activities, misinforms the public, and undermines the credibility of more substantial initiatives of others.

Nonetheless, resistance to change and lack of an official definition reflect extrinsic problems rather than problems intrinsic to the mechanics of green supply chains. Such problems are more about marketing than about function. As green supply chains prove themselves through superior performance, they will likely become more studied, better understood and defined, and more widely spread. Good starting points for firms that understand these issues as strategic are to look at the inherent risks of not examining their supply chains and to envision a future market position in which a green, differentiated product and brand will grow revenues.

Green Supply Chains Improve Performance

Green supply chains yield a wide range of benefits. They can reduce a company's negative environmental or social impact, decrease operating costs, increase customer service and sales, promote innovation, and mitigate regulatory risk. The most immediate benefits of green supply chains are reduced environmental harm and operations costs. For example, Fuji Xerox adopted a cradle-to-cradle philosophy that emphasized supporting document services over a life cycle rather than selling photocopiers and forgetting about them. Fuji Xerox leased equipment and recovered 99 percent of materials from used equipment in Asia in 2006, saving $13 million on new materials, generating an additional $5.4 million in revenue, and reducing raw material consumption by 2,000 tons at its factories in China. [45] Government institutions could also benefit. For example, Norway's health-care system saved money by refurbishing more medical equipment. [46] Decreased costs could even accrue to suppliers. [47]

Another benefit from green supply chains was increased innovation, largely because people worked together who had not done so before, or new challenges brought new answers. By collaborating with suppliers and designers to design its cradle-to-cradle system, Fuji Xerox saw the opportunity to make material and component improvements. The decision was made to redesign a spring and a roller, saving the US affiliate approximately $40 million annually. [48]

Moreover, green supply chains can lead to improved customer satisfaction and higher sales. Through product recovery programs, Dell increased sales and strengthened its brand reputation for customer satisfaction and corporate citizenship. Dell Asset Recovery Services (ARS) designed a customized solution that quickly recovered 2,300 servers from the Center for Computational Research at the University at Buffalo, SUNY. "That solves two problems for us," said SUNY's Tom Furlani. "It helps get rid of the old equipment in a cost-effective way, and it allows us to get new,

faster equipment that is under warranty." In addition to secure destruction of hard drive data, the Dell ARS maintains a zero landfill policy and a zero trash export policy. Unwanted equipment is disassembled into materials that reenter the manufacturing stream. [49] This step also placed Dell in a more favorable position with the Basel Action Network, an NGO that targeted the company as contributing to e-waste exports to emerging economies.

Finally, green supply chains mitigate regulatory burdens and litigation risk. With the increasing severity of environmental regulations in different regions of the world and the global scale of today's supply chains for even simple products (e.g., cloth from Latin America, cut and assembled into a shirt in China, and the product itself sold in Europe), green supply chains play a critical role in the operations strategy of multinational organizations. The consequences of not meeting regulations in a particular location can be major. For instance, Chinese suppliers have suffered from scandals over lead paint in toys and toxins in pet food and powdered milk, costing companies money in recalls and prompting calls for tighter regulation. In 2009, drywall produced in China was implicated in emissions of toxic sulfur compounds in homes built in America between 2004 and 2008, causing problems for homeowners, builders, and state regulatory agencies. [50]

Conclusion

Green supply chains have arisen in response to multiple, often interwoven problems: environmental degradation, rising prices for energy and raw materials, and global supply chains that link labor and environmental standards in one country with legal and consumer expectations in another. Green supply chains strive to ensure that value creation, rather than risk and waste, accumulates at each step from design to disposal and recovery. They have gained audience with large and small organizations across cultures, regions, and industries. Managing complex relationships and flows of materials across companies and cultures may pose a key challenge for green supply chains. Nonetheless, those challenges are not insurmountable, and the effort to green a supply chain can provide significant benefits.

KEY TAKEAWAY

- Green and sustainability thinking can improve supply-chain management to save money, improve products, and enhance brands.

EXERCISES

1. Select a common product and identify the many inputs and stages in its production that were required to deliver it to your hands.

2. Now analyze ways to "green" that supply chain; try to think of every possible way to apply sustainability concepts to optimize the supply-chain outcomes.
3. Discuss the barriers you might find in implementing that supply-chain strategy with real suppliers.
4. Go to the Green Design Institute at Carnegie Mellon University (http://www.eiolca.net) and explore the LCA method.

---

[1] Walmart, "Wal-Mart CEO Lee Scott Unveils 'Sustainability 360,'" news release, February 1, 2007, accessed January 10, 2011, http://walmartstores.com/pressroom/news/6237.aspx.
[2] Walmart, "Sustainability Fact Sheet: Wal-Mart Takes the Lead on Environmental Sustainability," news release, March 1, 2010, accessed January 30, 2011, http://walmartstores.com/download/2392.pdf.
[3] Ylan Q. Mui, "Wal-Mart Aims to Enlist Suppliers in Green Mission," *Washington Post*, September 25, 2007, accessed January 10, 2011, http://www.washingtonpost.com/wp-dyn/content/article/2007/09/24/AR2007092401435.html.
[4] Walmart, "Sustainability Fact Sheet: Wal-Mart Takes the Lead on Environmental Sustainability," news release, March 1, 2010, accessed January 30, 2011, http://walmartstores.com/download/2392.pdf.
[5] Dan Gilmore, "Top Ten Supply Chain Trends of 2006," *Supply Chain Digest*, January 4, 2006, accessed January 10, 2011, http://www.scdigest.com/assets/FirstThoughts/07-01-04.cfm?cid=871&ctype=content.
[6] According to the International Organization for Standardization, which established this qualification, ISO 14001 "gives the requirements for quality management systems [and] is now firmly established as the globally implemented standard for providing assurance about the ability to satisfy quality requirements and to enhance customer satisfaction in supplier–customer relationships." International Organization for Standardization, "ISO 14001:2004," accessed January 10, 2011, http://www.iso.org/iso/iso_catalogue/catalogue_tc/catalogue_detail.htm?csnumber=31807.
[7] DesignTex, "Designtex, A Steelcase Company: Our Company," accessed January 30, 2011, http://store.designtex.com/ourcompany.aspx?f=35398.
[8] Matthew M. Mehalik, "Sustainable Network Design: A Commercial Fabric Case Study," *Interfaces: International Journal of the Institute for Operations Research and the Management Sciences* 30, no. 3 (May/June 2000): 180–89.
[9] William McDonough and Michael Braungart, "Waste Equals Food," in *Cradle to Cradle: Remaking the Way We Make Things* (New York: North Point Press, 2002).
[10] Matthew M. Mehalik, "Sustainable Network Design: A Commercial Fabric Case Study," *Interfaces: International Journal of the Institute for Operations Research and the Management Sciences* 30, no. 3 (May/June 2000): 180–89.
[11] Shad Dowlatshahi, "Developing a Theory of Reverse Logistics," *Interfaces: International Journal of the Institute for Operations Research and the Management Sciences* 30, no. 3 (May/June 2000): 143–55.
[12] Canon, "Toner Cartridge Return Program," accessed October 2, 2009, http://www.usa.canon.com/templatedata/AboutCanon/ciwencrpr.html; Xerox, "Prevent and Manage Waste," accessed January 10, 2011, http://www.xerox.com/about-xerox/recycling/supplies/enus.html.
[13] Shad Dowlatshahi, "Developing a Theory of Reverse Logistics," *Interfaces: International Journal of the Institute for Operations Research and the Management Sciences* 30, no. 3 (May/June 2000): 144.
[14] Joy M. Field and Robert P. Sroufe, "The Use of Recycled Materials in Manufacturing: Implications for Supply Chain Management and Operations Strategy," *International Journal of Production Research* 45, no. 18–19 (October 2007): 4439–63.
[15] US Environmental Protection Agency, "Life-Cycle Assessment (LCA)," accessed January 10, 2011, http://www.epa.gov/ORD/NRMRL/lcaccess. For examples, see Maurizio Bevilacqua, Filippo Emanuele Ciarapica, and Giancarlo Giacchetta, "Development of a Sustainable Product Lifecycle in Manufacturing Firms: A Case Study," *International Journal of Production Research* 45, no. 18–19 (2007): 4073–98, as well as Stelvia Matos and Jeremy Hall, "Integrating Sustainable Development in the Supply Chain: The Case of Life Cycle Assessment in Oil and Gas and Agricultural Biotechnology," *Journal of Operations Management* 25, no. 6 (2007): 1083–82.
[16] "Wal-Mart's 'Green' Campaign Pays Off in Canada," *DC Velocity*, October 1, 2007, accessed October 2, 2009, http://www.dcvelocity.com/news/?article_id=1338.
[17] Hewlett-Packard, "HP to Eliminate Brominated Flame Retardants from External Case Parts of All New HP Brand Products," news release, November 1, 2005, accessed January 11, 2011, http://www.hp.com/hpinfo/newsroom/press/2005/051101a.html.
[18] Paul H. Farrow, Richard R. Johnson, and Andrea L. Larson, "Entrepreneurship, Innovation, and Sustainability Strategies at Walden Paddlers, Inc.," *Interfaces: International Journal of the Institute for Operations Research and the Management Sciences* 30, no. 3 (May/June 2000): 215–25.
[19] Business for Social Responsibility Education Fund, *Suppliers' Perspectives on Greening the Supply Chain* (San Francisco: Business for Social Responsibility Education Fund, 2001), accessed January 11, 2011, http://www.getf.org/file/toolmanager/O16F15429.pdf.
[20] Walfried M. Lassar and Adrian Gonzalez, *The State of Green Supply Chain Management: Survey Results* (Miami, FL: Ryder Center for Supply Chain Management, Florida International University, 2008), accessed January 11, 2011, http://grci.calpoly.edu/projects/sustaincommworld/pdfs/WP_Florida_Supply_Chain_Mgmt.pdf.
[21] Jonathan D. Linton, Robert Klassen, and Vaidyanathan Jayaraman, "Sustainable Supply Chains: An Introduction," *Journal of Operations Management* 25, no. 6 (November 2007): 1075–82; *Going Green Upstream: The Promise of Supplier Environmental Management* (Washington, DC: National Environmental Education and Training Foundation, 2001), accessed January 11, 2011, http://www.neefusa.org/pdf/SupplyChainStudy.pdf.
[22] Charles J. Corbett and Robert D. Klassen, "Expanding the Horizons: Environmental Excellence as Key to Improving Operations," *Manufacturing and Service Operations Management* 8, no. 1 (Winter 2006): 5–22.
[23] Charles J. Corbett and Robert D. Klassen, "Expanding the Horizons: Environmental Excellence as Key to Improving Operations," *Manufacturing and Service Operations Management* 8, no. 1 (Winter 2006): 5–22.
[24] Markus Klausner and Chris T. Hendrickson, "Reverse-Logistics Strategy for Product Take-Back," *Interfaces: International Journal of the Institute for Operations Research and the Management Sciences* 30, no. 3 (May/June 2000): 156–65.
[25] Adam Aston, Andy Reinhardt, and Rachel Tiplady, "Europe's Push for Less-Toxic Tech," *BusinessWeek*, August 9, 2005, accessed January 11, 2011, http://www.businessweek.com/technology/content/aug2005/tc2005089_9729_tc_215.htm.
[26] European Commission, "Environment: Waste Electrical and Electronic Equipment," accessed January 11, 2011, http://ec.europa.eu/environment/waste/weee/index_en.htm.
[27] European Commission, "Environment: REACH," accessed January 11, 2011, http://ec.europa.eu/environment/chemicals/reach/reach_intro.htm.
[28] Adam Aston, Andy Reinhardt, and Rachel Tiplady, "Europe's Push for Less-Toxic Tech," *BusinessWeek*, August 9, 2005, accessed January 11, 2011, http://www.businessweek.com/technology/content/aug2005/tc2005089_9729_tc_215.htm.
[29] Worker Rights Consortium, "Mission: History," accessed October 2, 2009, http://www.workersrights.org/about/history.asp.
[30] Tim Reeve and Jasper Steinhausen, "Sustainable Suppliers, Sustainable Markets," *CMA Management* 81, no. 2 (April 2007): 30–33.

[31] Nicole Darnall, G. Jason Jolley, and Robert Handfield, "Environmental Management Systems and Green Supply Chain Management: Compliments for Sustainability?" *Business Strategy and the Environment* 17, no. 1 (2008): 30–45; Toshi H. Arimura, Nicole Darnall, and Hajime Katayama, *Is ISO-14001 a Gateway to More Advanced Voluntary Action? A Case for Green Supply Chain Management*, RFF DP 09-05 (Washington, DC: Resources for the Future, 2009), accessed January 11, 2011, http://www.rff.org/documents/rff-dp-09-05.pdf.

[32] Terry F. Yosie, *Greening the Supply Chain in Emerging Markets: Some Lessons from the Field* (Oakland, CA: GreenBiz, 2008), accessed January 11, 2011, http://www.greenbiz.com/sites/default/files/document/GreenBiz_Report_Greening_the_Supply_Chain.pdf; Samir K. Srivastava, "Green Supply-Chain Management: A State-of-the-Art Literature Review," *International Journal of Management Reviews* 9, no. 1 (March 2007): 53–80.

[33] Walfried M. Lassar and Adrian Gonzalez, *The State of Green Supply Chain Management: Survey Results* (Miami, FL: Ryder Center for Supply Chain Management, Florida International University, 2008), accessed January 11, 2011, http://grci.calpoly.edu/projects/sustaincommworld/pdfs/WP_Florida_Supply_Chain_Mgmt.pdf.

[34] Mark P. Sharfman, Teresa M. Shaft, and Robert P. Anex Jr., "The Road to Cooperative Supply-Chain Environmental Management: Trust and Uncertainty among Pro-active Firms," *Business Strategy and the Environment* 18, no. 1 (January 2009): 1–13.

[35] Business for Social Responsibility Education Fund, *Suppliers' Perspectives on Greening the Supply Chain* (San Francisco: Business for Social Responsibility Education Fund, 2001), accessed January 11, 2011, http://www.getf.org/file/toolmanager/O16F15429.pdf.

[36] Terry F. Yosie, *Greening the Supply Chain in Emerging Markets: Some Lessons from the Field* (Oakland, CA: GreenBiz, 2008), accessed January 11, 2011, http://www.greenbiz.com/sites/default/files/document/GreenBiz_Report_Greening_the_Supply_Chain.pdf.

[37] Jonathan D. Linton, Robert Klassen, and Vaidyanathan Jayaraman, "Sustainable Supply Chains: An Introduction," *Journal of Operations Management* 25, no. 6 (November 2007): 1078.

[38] V. Daniel R. Guide Jr., Vaidyanathan Jayaraman, Rajesh Srivastava, and W. C. Benton, "Supply-Chain Management for Recoverable Manufacturing Systems," *Interfaces: International Journal of the Institute for Operations Research and the Management Sciences* 30, no. 3 (May/June 2000): 125–42; also Nils Rudi, David F. Pyke, and Per Olav Sporsheim, "Product Recovery at the Norwegian National Insurance Administration," *Interfaces: International Journal of the Institute for Operations Research and the Management Sciences* 30, no. 3 (May/June 2000): 166–79.

[39] V. Daniel R. Guide Jr., Vaidyanathan Jayaraman, Rajesh Srivastava, and W. C. Benton, "Supply-Chain Management for Recoverable Manufacturing Systems," *Interfaces: International Journal of the Institute for Operations Research and the Management Sciences* 30, no. 3 (May/June 2000): 125–42.

[40] Walfried M. Lassar and Adrian Gonzalez, *The State of Green Supply Chain Management: Survey Results* (Miami, FL: Ryder Center for Supply Chain Management, Florida International University, 2008), accessed January 11, 2011, http://grci.calpoly.edu/projects/sustaincommworld/pdfs/WP_Florida_Supply_Chain_Mgmt.pdf.

[41] Vesela Veleva, Maureen Hart, Tim Greiner, and Cathy Crumbley, "Indicators for Measuring Environmental Sustainability," *Benchmarking* 10, no. 2 (2003): 107–19.

[42] Clifford Krauss, "At Home Depot, How Green Is That Chainsaw?" *New York Times*, June 25, 2007, accessed January 11, 2011, http://www.nytimes.com/2007/06/25/business/25depot.html?_r=1.

[43] Danielle Sacks, "Green Guru William McDonough Must Change, Demand His Biggest Fans," *Fast Company*, February 26, 2009, accessed January 11, 2011, http://www.fastcompany.com/blog/danielle-sacks/ad-verse-effect/william-mcdonough-must-change; Diana den Held, "'Criticism on Cradle to Cradle? Right on Schedule,' Says Michael Braungart," *Duurzaam Gebouwd* (blog), March 20, 2009, accessed October 2, 2009, http://www.duurzaamgebouwd.nl/index.php?pageID=3946&messageID=1936.

[44] Melissa Whellams and Chris MacDonald, "What Is Greenwashing, and Why Is It a Problem?" *Business Ethics*, accessed October 2, 2009, http://www.businessethics.ca/greenwashing.

[45] Fuji Xerox Australia, "Fuji Xerox Innovation Makes Business and Environmental Sense," news release, September 25, 2007, accessed January 11, 2011, http://www.fujixerox.com.au/about/media/articles/546.

[46] Nils Rudi, David F. Pyke, and Per Olav Sporsheim, "Product Recovery at the Norwegian National Insurance Administration," *Interfaces: International Journal of the Institute for Operations Research and the Management Sciences* 30, no. 3 (May/June 2000): 166–79.

[47] Business for Social Responsibility Education Fund, *Suppliers' Perspectives on Greening the Supply Chain* (San Francisco: Business for Social Responsibility Education Fund, 2001), accessed January 11, 2011, http://www.getf.org/file/toolmanager/O16F15429.pdf.

[48] *Corporate Societal Responsibility: Knowledge Learning through Sustainable Global Supply Chain Management*, p 14, accessed April 2, 2011, http://www.reman.org/pdf/Fuji-Xerox.pdf.

[49] Dell, *That's Refreshing*, case study, November 2006, accessed January 11, 2011, http://www.dell.com/downloads/global/services/suny_ars_casestudy.pdf.

[50] Michael Corkery, "Chinese Drywall Cited in Building Woes," *Wall Street Journal*, January 12, 2009, accessed January 11, 2011, http://online.wsj.com/article/SB123171862994672097.html; Brian Skoloff and Cain Burdeau, Associated Press, "Chinese Drywall Poses Potential Risks," *US News and World Report*, April 11, 2009, accessed January 11, 2011, http://www.usnews.com/science/articles/2009/04/11/chinese-drywall-poses-potential-risks?PageNr=1.

6.2 Method: Entrepreneurial Innovation, Health, Environment, and Sustainable Business Design

LEARNING OBJECTIVES

1. Evaluate and explain the conditions under which sustainability strategies succeed.

2. Discuss health challenges that offer market opportunities.

3. Analyze factors that favor sustainability innovation processes.

In our first case we have the opportunity to track Method, an entrepreneurial consumer products company, through two stages in its early growth. The first case presents the company and its unique sustainability strategy, highlighting both the scope of its efforts and unanticipated challenges that arose. Technical notes are provided for background on health threats from exposure to toxic materials in everyday life. The second Method case provides a 2010 update on the company's activities and distinctive focus on innovation process. It is preceded by a discussion of toxicity issues intended to highlight Method's ongoing innovative efforts to differentiate itself as a company that is about supply-chain solutions to the chemical hazards increasingly on the minds of consumers and scientists.

It was spring 2007, and Method cofounder Adam Lowry was deep in thought over enchiladas at Mercedes, a restaurant a block from his company's office on Commercial Street in San Francisco. He began to sketch ideas on a piece of paper to sort the issues troubling him. As a company known for environmentally healthy household products with designer brand appeal, Method was eager to develop a biodegradable cleaning cloth. Sourcing polylactic acid (PLA) cloth from China had not been in his plans, but every US PLA manufacturer Lowry had talked to told him it was impossible for them to create the dry floor dusting cloth he wanted. There was also a genetic modification issue. US PLA producers did not screen their corn plant feedstock to determine whether it came from genetically modified organisms (GMOs). However, Lowry wondered, weren't *any* bio-based and biodegradable materials a better alternative than oil-based polyester, the material used by the competition? Yet certain major retailers were unwilling to stock products that weren't certifiably GMO-free. It was hard enough to manage a fast-growing new company, but why did some people seem willing to stop progress while they held out for perfection on the environmental front? The naysayers made Lowry think carefully about what it meant to be true to the environmental philosophy that formed the backbone of his business. He had often said that Method's business was to change the way business was conducted. But where should the company draw the line? [1]

As a hot new company that had received widespread publicity for its dedication to environmental values and healthy, clean production, use, and disposal of all its products, Method had set high standards. In a relatively short time, it had created a model for excellence in integrating health and environmental concerns into corporate strategy. From only a germ of an idea in 1999, Method had experienced explosive growth during the intervening years. The company proved that home cleaning products could evolve from toxic substances that had to be locked away from children and hidden in cupboards to nice-smelling, stylishly packaged, biodegradable, benign products that consumers proudly displayed on their countertops. In 2006, *Inc.* magazine listed Method at number seven of the five hundred fastest and most successfully growing firms in the United States. Method stood out in many ways from the typical entrepreneurial firm.

Leveraging only $300,000 in start-up capital, twentysomethings Adam Lowry and Eric Ryan caused small-scale "creative destruction" across a $17 billion industry in the United States by emphasizing the health, environmental, and emotional aspects of the most mundane of products: household cleaners. The company's differentiating characteristic? Lowry and Ryan assumed from the start that incorporating ecological and human health concerns into corporate strategy was simply good business. By 2007, Method was growing rapidly and was profitable with forty-five employees and annual revenues of more than $50 million. Its products were available in well-known distribution channels (drugstores, department stores, supermarkets, and other retail outlets) in the United States, Canada, Australia, and the United Kingdom. Customers embraced Method's products, giving the company live feedback on its website, praising the firm and providing tips for the future. They were a loyal crowd and a signal that the time was right for this kind of business model. They even requested T-shirts featuring the Method brand, and the company responded by offering two different shirts: one that said, "Cleans like a mother" and another that simply said, "Method," both with the company slogan—"People against dirty"—on the back. A baseball cap was also available.

Indeed, "People against dirty" was Method's stated mission. The company website explains it this way: "Dirty means the toxic chemicals that make up many household products, it means polluting our land with nonrecyclable materials, it means testing products on innocent animals….These things are dirty and we're against that." Under Lowry and Ryan's leadership, Method shook up the monolithic and staid cleaning-products markets by delivering high-performance products that appealed to consumers from a price, design, health, and ecological perspective—simultaneously. From the original offering of a clear cleaning spray, Method's product line had expanded by 2007 to a 125-product line of home solutions including dishwashing liquids and hand and body soaps. The "aircare" line, an array of air fresheners housed in innovatively designed dispensers, extended the product offerings in 2006, and the O-mop was added in 2007.

All products were made in alignment with Method's strategy. They had to be biodegradable; contain no propellants, aerosols, phosphates, or chlorine bleach; and be packaged in minimal and recyclable materials. Method used its product formulation, eye-catching design, and a lean outsourcing network of fifty suppliers to remain nimble and quick to market while building significant brand loyalty.

Method sold its products in the United States through several national and regional groceries, but one of the company's key relationships was with Target, the nation's number-two mass retailer in 2007. Through Target's 1,400 stores in 47 states, Method reached consumers across the

United States. International sales were expanding, and the firm was regularly in discussion with new distribution channels.

An Upstart Innovator in an Industry of Giants

The US market for soaps and cleaning products did not seem a likely industry for innovation and environmental consciousness. It was dominated by corporate giants, many of which were integral to its founding. Although the soap and cleaning product industry was fragmented around the edges, with a typical supermarket stocking up to forty brands, market share was dominated by companies such as SC Johnson, Procter & Gamble (P&G), Unilever, and Colgate-Palmolive.

To put Method's position in perspective, its total annual sales were approximately 10 percent of Procter & Gamble's sales *in dish detergent alone* ($317.6 million) (2006). P&G's total annual sales in the category were more than $1 billion. Furthermore, the market for cleaning products was under steady cost pressure from private-label brands, increasing raw materials prices and consumers' view of these products as commodities. Companies that reported positive numbers in the segment between 2000 and 2006 did so by cutting costs and consolidating operations. Startups such as Seventh Generation and others attempted to penetrate the mass market with "natural" products, but those products were largely relegated to health food stores and chains such as Whole Foods. For Method to have obtained any foothold in this heavily consolidated segment dominated by market giants seemed improbable at best. But for Method founders Lowry and Ryan, the massive scale and cost focus of their competitors offered an opportunity.

Method to Their Madness

"You have all your domestic experiences in that house or wherever you live," Ryan explained. And so, "from the furniture you buy to your kitchenware, you put a lot of thought and emotion into what you put in that space. Yet the commodity products that you use to maintain this very important space tend to be uninteresting, ugly, and toxic—and you hide them away." [2] Lowry and Ryan didn't understand why it had to be that way.

They decided to take the opposite approach; if they could create products that were harmless to humans and the natural environment and were attractively designed with interesting colors and aromas, they could disrupt an industry populated with dinosaurs. By differentiating themselves from the competition in a significant and meaningful way,

Lowry and Ryan hoped to offer an attractive alternative that also reduced the company's ecological footprint and had a positive environmental impact. "It's green clean for the mainstream," said Lowry, "which wouldn't happen if it wasn't *cool*." [3]

To make green cool, Method took a two-pronged approach. First, it formulated new product mixtures that performed as well as leading brands while minimizing environmental and health impacts. Cleaning product manufacturers had been the target of environmental complaints since the 1950s, when the federal government enacted the Federal Water Pollution Control Act in part to address the foaming of streams due to the use of surfactants, chemicals used in soaps and detergents to increase cleaning power. In addition to surfactants, household cleaners often contained phosphates, chemicals used as water softeners and that also acted as plant nutrients, providing an abundant food source for algae. Fast-growing algae resulted in algal blooms, which depleted oxygen levels and starved aquatic life. Water sources contaminated with phosphates were also toxic for animals to drink. Another environmentally problematic compound in cleaning products was chlorine bleach, which when released into the environment could react with other substances to create toxic compounds. According to the Method website, "A major problem with most household cleaners is that they biodegrade slowly, leading to an accumulation of toxins in the environment. The higher the concentration of toxins, the more dangerous they are to humans, animals, and plant life. The key is to create products that biodegrade into their natural components quickly and safely." [4]

With a degree in chemical engineering from Stanford University, experience researching "green" plastics, and a stint at a climate-change think tank, Lowry saw these issues as opportunities.

Method counted on the competition's seeing environmental and health issues as "problems." Doing so allowed Method to seize competitive advantage through designing out human health threats and ecological impacts from the start, while their larger competitors struggled to deal with increasing legislative and public image pressures. Method products sold at a slight premium to compensate for the extra effort. "I knew as a chemical engineer that there was no reason we couldn't design products that were nontoxic and used natural ingredients," Lowry said. "It would be more expensive to do it that way. But that was okay as long as we created a brand that had a 'premiumness' about it, where our margins would support our extra investments in product development and high-quality ingredients." [5]

The second prong of Method's attack on the entrenched cleaning products industry was to utilize design and brand to appeal to consumers tired of the same old products. In an industry rife with destructive price competition, Method realized it would have to be different. The founders believed that their competition was so focused on price that "they weren't able to invest in fragrance or interesting packaging or design." Lowry explained, "Our idea was to turn that reality on its head and come up with products that absolutely could connect with the emotion of the home. We wanted to make these products more like 'home accessories.' We believed there was an opportunity to really reinvent, and in the end, change the competitive landscape." [6]

By focusing their marketing and packaging as the solution "against dirty," they tapped into consumers' disquiet with the ingredients in their household cleaners. Through packaging that stood out from the rest, they created the opportunity to deliver the environmental and health message of the products' ingredients.

Design of packaging to deliver that message was integral to Method's success from its first sale. Method's home-brewed cleaning formulas for kitchen, shower, bath, and glass surfaces were originally packaged in clear bottles that stood out on a shelf. "The manager of the store just liked the way the packaging looked," said David Bennett, the co-owner of Mollie Stones, a San Francisco Bay–area grocer that was Method's first retail customer. "It looked like an upscale product that would meet our consumer demands, so we went with it." [7]

As design continued to be a key element of Method's appeal, the company recruited Karim Rashid, a renowned industrial designer who had worked with Prada and Armani. Rashid was responsible for bringing a heightened sense of style to Method's packaging while continuing to focus on environmental impact. This led to the use of easily recycled number one and number two plastics (the types of plastic most commonly accepted by municipal recycling centers). Method's approach seemed to represent a younger generation's more holistic mental model. This small firm seemed to provide a window into a future where health, environmental, and what were increasingly called "sustainability issues" would be assumed as part of business strategy and product design.

Wipes, the O-mop, and PLA Material

PLA was an innovative and relatively new plastic material derived from plants such as corn, rice, beets, and other starch-based agricultural crops. PLA biodegraded at the high temperatures and humidity levels found in most composting processes. NatureWorks was the first large-scale plant in the United States to produce PLA in resin (pellet) form, based on milled material made from farm-supplied corn and corn waste. The resin pellets went to a fiber manufacturer who made bales; those bales of PLA material went next to the nonwoven cloth manufacturer, which converted it into giant rolls of nonwoven cloth. Next, a converter took the bulk nonwoven cloth, cut it into shapes, and packaged it according to the specifications of a customer such as Method. When NatureWorks first began operations, demand was limited. That picture changed quickly between 2004 and 2006, and by 2007 the plant could not produce its PLA feedstock resins fast enough to meet worldwide demand. PLA came out of the facility in pellet form and was melted, extruded, spun, and otherwise manipulated by converters at different steps of the supply chain into a virtually endless spectrum of materials for different applications across a wide range of product categories.

As a replacement for ubiquitous oil-based plastic feedstock, PLA promised a departure from the petroleum-based plastic materials that had come to dominate since synthetic plastics were first developed in volume after World War II. PLA had proved itself a particularly high-performing and cost-effective raw material that was well suited as a substitute for polyethylene terephthalate (PET) in many applications. PET was the oil-based polymer known generically as polyester and used extensively in packaging, films, and fibers for textiles and clothing.

The competition's wipes and mop heads were made of petroleum-based nonbiodegradable plastic material, typically polyester or polypropylene. Although microfiber was quickly becoming commonplace, microfiber and the denier unit of measurement were first associated with material in women's hosiery. Technology advances permitted polyester microfiber production for very fine fiber applications, and just as microfiber had become common in clothing lines, it was also used as a more effective wiping and cleaning product. Microfiber was fiber with strands measured at less than one denier, a unit of weight used to describe extremely fine filaments and equal to a yarn weighing one gram per nine thousand meters. Whether made from corn or oil, microfiber material, used by most companies selling residential cleaning wipes by 2006, made an excellent cleaning cloth. Its structure enabled the fiber surface to more effectively pick up dirt and dust compared with conventional materials and methods. The microfiber wipes could be washed and reused, providing greater durability than alternative products that were typically thrown away immediately after use.

Consistent with Method's environmental and sustainability philosophy, Lowry wanted to use bio-based materials, specifically PLA nonwoven cloth, for the dry floor dusting product. Ultimately he wanted PLA to be the basis for all fibers used, both nonwoven disposable cloth and reusable woven microfiber. If customers weren't grabbed by the marketing message that the mop was sexy and hip (a message consistent with Method's playful tone), they might be pulled in by the ergonomic O-mop's more effective, biotech-based, and nontoxic floor cleaning.

Lowry knew most disposable wipes ended up in landfills, not compost piles, even with their extended life. So the company supported municipal recycling and composting infrastructure development in an effort to encourage cradle-to-cradle [8] resource use, or at least raise awareness and encourage behavior in that direction. Method estimated that eighty-three thousand tons of "wipe" material made of polyester or polypropylene plastic was ending up in landfills annually, enough to fill nine thousand tractor-trailers. If using PLA could reduce oil feedstock use even a little, he reasoned, it was an improvement. Even if the PLA fiber went to landfills, where temperature and humidity never reached the ideal composting levels that would quickly and thoroughly break it down, it would still decompose safely, perhaps after one to two months, unlike oil-based fibers, which could remain in landfill disposal sites in the same condition for thousands of years.

The market for bio-based plastic materials had taken off by 2007, but Lowry had had no luck finding a US manufacturer to create a PLA-based fabric suitable for the white, nonwoven, dry-floor duster cloth used with the O-mop. He had just talked with the last on his list of PLA manufacturers, and the answer was no. They had all told him it couldn't be done. The material was too brittle, they couldn't process it, it wouldn't run on their machines, and the strands were too weak. In short, PLA nonwoven cloth for this application was technologically impossible.

Lowry picked up the phone and placed a call to a company he knew in China—a departure from business as usual given that 90 percent of Method's inputs were sourced in the United States. Chinese suppliers often were excellent, but domestic sourcing was preferable to avoid the high transportation costs of moving product long distances. Typically the farther the transport requirement, the greater the fossil fuel use, so the choice seemed inconsistent with the firm's sustainability approach. But Lowry was sure the

dry-floor dusting cloth could be made with PLA resins, and the Chinese manufacturer confirmed it. Lowry placed the order. A Taiwanese fiber manufacturer would make the bales and send them to the Chinese nonwoven cloth manufacturer that would pass on the cloth to a nearby converter that would in turn cut and package it to meet Method's needs. Lowry knew the suppliers were good and reliable and that the product would arrive promptly. Perhaps all Method's PLA products would need to come from China. But was sourcing from the other side of the world "sustainable" in the sense that he and Ryan tried to apply sustainability principles to the company's operations?

The other issue on Lowry's mind was that Method's products could be deemed unacceptable in certain distribution channels that would not tolerate any GMOs in their products. PLA was produced from agricultural material (often corn or cornfield waste material) that was brought by farmers to a centrally located milling plant that converted it and separated out the components from which PLA was made. There was no monitoring of the corn coming into the milling facility; thus there was no guarantee that all inputs to the PLA resin-producing process were free of GMOs. If Lowry used PLA, it meant certain large and reputable buyers would refuse to put Method products on their shelves. Even so, to Lowry, it seemed preferable to substitute PLA for petroleum-derived products and compromise on the GMO issue for the time being. After a particularly discouraging conversation with a company that declined to do business with Method until it agreed to stop using GMO agricultural inputs, he decided to write out his thoughts in an essay, both to sort them out for himself and to draft a position paper that he could later post on the Method website.

As our knowledge base grows regarding exposure to toxins, we become more informed and better equipped to find solutions. We are capable of learning and absorbing feedback from the environment and our bodies. Lead was removed from gasoline in the United States and extensive efforts made to remove lead-based paint from older homes, thereby significantly reducing exposure to lead (a neurotoxin), particularly for children. Chlorofluorocarbons (CFCs), known to break down upper atmosphere ozone, were banned enabling recovery of the ozone layer and over time reducing the ozone hole that formed every year over parts of the Southern Hemisphere. As a species, we act, we receive feedback, we adjust and adapt. We are beginning to learn and adapt with respect to toxic chemicals exposure. However, materials toxicity and contamination is just starting to receive attention and still remains secondary in the media's attention due to the current focus on climate and energy issues (topics that also require attention to materials and toxic inputs/outputs). Nevertheless, materials issues will be acknowledged and addressed. The pattern will be similar to other arenas that challenge human ingenuity: most people will be overwhelmed by the problem scale, while others, the entrepreneurial individuals (and ventures they create), will drive innovation to create benign alternatives. [9]

The next two sections provide additional background information on toxic substances. They are followed by a second case on Method that demonstrates how forward-thinking companies work on an ongoing basis to eliminate questionable chemical compounds from their products through innovative processes that lead to breakthrough designs and safer products in the marketplace.

Toxic Chemicals: Responding to Challenges and Opportunities

In the early 1960s, US scientist and writer Rachel Carson spoke about the risks of toxic chemicals: "We are subjecting whole populations to exposure to chemicals which animal experiments have proved to be extremely poisonous and in many cases cumulative in their effect. These exposures now begin at or before birth and—unless we change our methods—continue through the lifetime of those now living. No one knows what the results will be, because we have no previous experience to guide us." [10]

We have made progress in the face of the abundant evidence that increases in cancer and other disease rates are the result of exposure to chemicals. The US Environmental Protection Agency (EPA) was established in 1970 partly in response to Carson and others who foresaw the dangers of society's ill-informed experimentation with toxic chemicals. Similar agencies now exist in most countries and the United Nations. Environmental and health nongovernmental organizations (NGOs) have become powerful change agents. Federal and state laws and international agreements have been passed banning or severely restricting the manufacture and use of certain exceptionally dangerous and persistent chemicals. However, progress is slow and public awareness insufficient. We remain vulnerable to both existing chemicals and hundreds of new ones that are invented and introduced into commerce daily. [11]

More than thirty years after Carson's book *Silent Spring* was published, scientists Theo Colborn and John Peterson Myers and a coauthor renewed the warning about widespread molecular toxins in the book *Our Stolen Future* (1996):

The 20th century marks a true watershed in the relationship between humans and the earth. The unprecedented and awesome power of science and technology, combined with the sheer number of people living on the planet, has transformed the scale of our impact from local and regional to global. With that transformation, we have been altering the fundamental systems that support life. These alterations amount to a great global experiment—with humanity and all life on earth as the unwitting subjects. Synthetic chemicals have been a major force in these alterations. Through the creation and release of billions of pounds of man-made chemicals over the past half-century, we have been making broad-scale changes to the earth's atmosphere and even in the chemistry of our own bodies....The global scale of the experiment makes it extremely difficult to assess the effects. Over the past fifty years, synthetic chemicals have become so pervasive in the environment and in our bodies that it is no longer possible to define a normal, unaltered human physiology. There is no clean, uncontaminated place, nor any human being who hasn't acquired a considerable load of persistent hormone-disrupting chemicals. In this experiment, we are all guinea pigs and, to make matters worse, we have no controls to help us understand what these chemicals are doing. [12]

Synthetic chemicals are everywhere—in the plastics used in packaging, cars, toys, clothing, and electronics and in glues, coatings, fertilizers, lubricants, fuels, and pesticides. We make or "synthesize" chemicals from elements present in nature. Many "organic" [13] or carbon-based chemicals are derived from petroleum. We use synthetics to serve many purposes that natural materials cannot serve as well, and industry and consumers often save money in the process. Without synthetics, we wouldn't have computers, television, and most drugs and medical equipment. Synthetic chemicals, however, have dangers as well as benefits. Those dangers are often unknown or even unsuspected when a chemical is first introduced. They may become evident only after thousands or even millions of pounds of that chemical have been released into the environment through industrial and agricultural processes and energy generation, or as products, emissions, or other wastes.

Synthetic chemicals' detrimental environmental and health consequences are unintentional. The pesticide dichloro-diphenyl-trichloroethane (DDT), for example, was never intended to kill bald eagles or robins. [14] The chlorine bleaching process used in paper mills wasn't meant to disrupt the endocrine systems of fish downstream. [15] Polychlorinated biphenols (PCBs) and pesticide residues weren't supposed to end up in human breast milk, nor were they supposed to affect the immune and endocrine systems or possibly cause sperm decline and even infertility in men. [16]

History

Synthetic chemicals were first produced in laboratories during the nineteenth century. DDT was invented in 1874 in Germany and began its infamous career as pesticide in the 1930s. Before World War II, pesticides consisted mainly of metals such as arsenic, copper, lead, manganese, and zinc and compounds found in plants such as rotenone, nicotine sulfate, and pyrethrum. Plastics from cellulose were first created in the 1890s. Beginning in about 1900, synthetic plastics produced from oil began to find their way into industry. Polyvinyl chloride (a.k.a. "vinyl" or PVC) was discovered in the 1920s. PCBs were introduced in the 1920s. Steady progress through the early twentieth century led to rapid breakthroughs during the World War II years and the creation of thousands of new chemicals every year since. Some toxic chemicals are not created intentionally. Dioxins, for example, are by-products from chlorine-product manufacturing, combustion (especially of plastics), and paper bleaching. [17]

For most people, it would be hard to deny the benefits of the chemical era. Pharmaceuticals, plastics, semiconductors, disinfectants, and food preservatives are just a few of the many synthetic chemical–based conveniences on which we have come to depend. However, rather like the famous story of the sorcerer's apprentice, the junior-level alchemist who knows enough to unleash the forces of magic but not enough to control them, we have the capacity to create a vast array of products with synthetic chemicals but are politically and technologically constrained in our ability to cope with the pollution and wastes we create along the way.

The chemists, physicists, engineers, and corporations who brought us the "green revolution" in agriculture, plastics, fuel for our vehicles, microchips, and myriad other useful products have also given us many unintended consequences. Even if you eat organic foods, prefer natural wood and leather furniture, and wear only organic cotton and wool clothing, the house you live in, the car you drive, and nearly everything else that you consume is dependent on synthetic chemicals at some point in its life cycle.

Impacts

Hazards associated with toxic ingredients in pesticides, solvents, lubricants, plastics, fuels, exhaust gases, cleaning fluids, and hundreds of other consumer and industrial substances are generally thought of in terms of impacts on human health, wildlife, and ecosystems. Human health impacts from toxic synthetic chemicals range from minor skin irritations and sinus conditions to chronic asthma, severe nervous system disorders, respiratory illnesses, cancers, and immune system dysfunction.

Ecological Impacts

Wildlife and ecosystems are often impaired by toxic chemical exposure long before we are aware that any damage has been done. In the mid-1980s, scientists found that the alligators in central Florida's Lake Apopka were born with faulty reproductive systems following an accidental spill from the Tower Chemical Company more than ten years earlier. In 1998, farmland near the lake was allowed to flood as part of a wetland restoration project. Years of pesticide-intensive farming had taken its toll. Vast numbers of fish-eating birds such as herons and egrets died in as toxic chemicals from flooded agricultural fields moved up the food chain from algae and small aquatic animals to the amphibians and fish species the birds ate. By the time the birds consumed the chemicals, they had bioaccumulated to concentrations that caused acute poisoning. [19]

Polar bears also are suffering from **bioaccumulation** of toxins, but their pollutants come from thousands of miles away, carried by ocean and air currents. The toxins are concentrated through the food chain until prey species such as seals have millions of times the amount of heavy metal or persistent organic chemical that is found in the water. [20]

Virtually no place on earth is free from contamination by synthetic chemicals. They have been found in water, air, and human beings all over the globe. Some of the highest concentrations have been found near the Arctic Circle in the breast milk of indigenous people. [21] Some lakes in Norway, Sweden, and northern Canada are essentially dead from acid rain caused by power plants hundreds of miles away. [22] Populations of amphibians, long considered an indicator species for pollution, are declining all over the world, even in remote Amazonian forests, in part because of pesticides and other pollutants. [23]

Tests for synthetic chemicals consistently find them in humans. For example, plastic additives providing flexibility, such as phthalates, are known for their endocrine-disrupting potential; they pass from tubing and bags used in intravenous medical preparations into the patients attached to them. [24] The same chemicals may end up in babies' mouths when they chew on a soft plastic toy. [25] Window blinds and other hard plastic products sometimes contain lead. Wells and municipal water supplies contain varying concentrations of chemical contaminants. It may be indicative of the complexity of testing for, and guarding against, hazardous pollutants in water supplies that the US EPA sets drinking water standards for only thirty-three of the hundreds of pesticides in current use. [26]

How Chemicals Cause Damage

Between fifty thousand and one hundred thousand synthetic chemicals are in commercial use, with more entering commerce every day. [27] The problem is that some of those chemicals cause illness or death to people, animals, and plants. Some, such as chemicals used in warfare and pesticides, were intended to kill or impair specific organisms, but the bulk of the harm from synthetic chemicals is unintended. Many of the consequences of our great experiment in chemical production and use have come as surprises to the scientists who created them.

Bioaccumulation

Traces of persistent synthetic chemicals are found in animals—in especially high concentration—at the top of the food chain. In a process known as bioaccumulation, persistent toxic wastes like PCBs, present in water and sediments, are eaten by phytoplankton and zooplankton that store them at about 250 and 500 times their ambient concentration. Those tiny creatures are in turn eaten by slightly larger animals such as microscopic shrimp, building PCB levels to tens of thousands of times that of the surrounding water. The shrimp are consumed by animals such as small fish, in whose tissues PCB concentrations may reach hundreds of thousands of times ambient levels. A larger fish eats the smaller fish and stores PCBs in concentrations millions of times higher. A top predator, such as a gull or a fish-eating eagle, eats the fish, accumulating up to twenty-five million times the original PCB concentration level. Finally, the chemical reaches a concentration where toxicity becomes manifest, and the gull can no longer produce viable offspring. [28] Human beings are not exempt from chemical bioaccumulation. Chemical pollutants are found in virtually all humans in our blood, fat tissues, and breast milk. The US Centers for Disease Control reports on pollutants present in human bodies, describing the "body burden" of accumulated chemicals.

Unfortunately, the old adage that "the dose makes the poison" doesn't always apply. That belief assumes that the lower the dose, the lower the adverse effect. We now find that very low and high exposure levels stimulate cellular change; however, little influence is discernable with midrange exposures. Some chemicals, including tetraethyl lead, many pesticides, and other persistent organic pollutants (POPs) are known to cause reproductive problems and developmental problems before birth and during the first few years of life. Those impacts may occur even with concentrations so small that they are measured in parts per trillion. For that reason, the EPA works under the assumption that there is no safe exposure level for chemicals classed as probable human carcinogens.

Impacts on Children and Pregnant Women

The study of chemical threats to children's health is still in an early stage. The EPA created the Office of Children's Health Protection in 1997 in recognition of the need to address risks to children that are potentially different from risks to adults.

EPA's traditional method of setting human health protection standards has relied almost exclusively on the assessment of risks to adults. That kind of broad focus is understandable, given how little was understood about environmental risk before 1970. It was assumed that people were comparable in terms of their response to exposures to pollution. As we learned more about the effects of environmental contaminants on human health, the differences among subsets of the population, particularly differences among children and adults, began to emerge.

A child's nervous system, reproductive organs, and immune system grow and develop rapidly during the first months and years of life. As organ structures develop, vital connections between cells are established. Those delicate developmental processes in children may easily and irreversibly be disrupted by toxic environmental substances such as lead.

Neurotoxins that may have only a temporary ill effect on an adult brain can cause enduring damage to a child's developing brain. The immaturity of children's internal systems, especially in the first few months of life, affects their ability to neutralize and rid their bodies of certain toxics. If cells in the developing brain are destroyed by lead, mercury, or other neurotoxic chemicals, or if vital connections between nerve cells fail to form, the damage is likely to be permanent and irreversible.

Increasing Regulations

Rapidly expanding scientific understanding of chemicals and their impacts has resulted in closer regulatory oversight.

The EPA has faced an embarrassing backlog of chemical risk assessments for many years. In 1998, the agency developed a system for high production volume (HPV) chemicals. The program was intended to move testing forward through voluntary cooperation from industry in assessing approximately three thousand chemicals produced in volumes of one million pounds per year or more. The EPA-sponsored national computerized database known as the Toxic Release Inventory (TRI) tracks toxic chemicals that are being used, manufactured, treated, transported, or released into the environment. Section 313 of the Emergency Planning and Community Right-to-Know Act (EPCRA) of 1986 specifically requires manufacturers to report releases of six hundred designated toxic chemicals into the environment. The reports are submitted to the EPA and state governments. EPA compiles this data in the online, publicly accessible TRI. [29]

There are five end points for the screening tests: acute toxicity, chronic toxicity, mutagenicity, ecotoxicity, and environmental fate. Of chemicals required for testing under the TRI requirements, only 55 percent or about 680 have been tested. [30] Seven percent of all other chemicals have complete test data. Only 25 percent of 491 chemicals examined by the EPA due to their use in consumer products brought into the home and used by children and families have data. Of the three thousand HPV chemicals imported or produced at over one million pounds annually by the United States, 43 percent have no basic toxicity testing data available. The government depends on companies to report; however, no testing data have been submitted by 148 of 830 companies producing chemicals in the high-volume range. A total of 459 companies sell products for which half or fewer chemicals used have been reported under the required testing protocols. Only twenty-one companies have submitted complete screening data for all chemicals they produce. The EPA observes that filling in the screening data gaps would cost about $427 million, or about 0.2 percent of annual sales for the top one hundred US chemical companies. [31]

A significant step toward international restrictions on some on the most hazardous chemicals is evident in the sequence of conventions on POPs. POPs are widely considered the least acceptable hazardous chemicals. They persist in the environment for decades without degrading into harmless substances, they are organic, and they are highly toxic pollutants. Some other chemicals that are themselves relatively harmless create persistent toxic by-products, such as dioxins, as they are combusted or degrade.

On May 22, 2001, delegates from 127 countries, including the United States, formally signed the international treaty on POPs in Stockholm, Sweden.

Acceptable Risk?

How much risk to our health and environment are we willing to accept and pass on to future generations in return for the benefits we expect from a new chemical? Many people would immediately answer, "None; it's unacceptable to pass on any risk!" Chemical industry advocates recommend applying cost-benefit analysis to hazardous chemicals. They point out that it may be reasonable to eliminate 80 percent of the risk of a substance, but it costs a great deal to eliminate the last 20 percent. They would prefer that we accept the remaining risk and spend the savings on other pressing concerns.

Chemical risks are associated with four main variables for human health: exposure to a chemical, toxicity of the chemical, dosage received, and response (acute or chronic illness). Multiple exposures to several different chemicals and possible synergistic effects are sometimes accounted for as well. Ecological impacts are an added concern reviewed in some risk assessments. The reality is that the US regulatory system for monitoring chemicals is insufficient for the scope of the task. Reform of the key legislation, the Toxic Substances Control Act, may not be possible under the current political polarization in the United States. Some people have concluded that while targeting more benign, or fully benign, chemical components for products in the private sector is to be commended, nothing will take the place of dramatic chemical regulatory reform at the federal level.

The challenges are significant. It is hard to know exactly the risk to which we are exposed. Whose responsibility is it to assess risks from chemicals and communicate them to end users and others who may share the impacts? Limits to environmental regulatory budgets, industry resistance to regulatory constraints, public debt and sentiment that larger government is not the right choice, and increasing complexity of toxicology science combine to make it difficult for government to provide reassuring answers.

Alternative Approaches

Should those who benefit from the sale and use of toxic chemicals be held accountable for damages they cause if they knew or suspected harmful impacts? What if they were unaware that they were doing harm?

What are the opportunities for firms in this arena? It is important to learn from our mistakes. Cleaning up a Superfund site [32] or settling lawsuits with survivors of chemical experiments such as those involving asbestos and diethylstylbestrol (DES) can bankrupt a company. Many women who took the fertility drug DES on the advice of their physicians gave birth to children with malformed reproductive organs and unusual reproductive system cancers. Worker exposure in asbestos insulation factories led to a signature form of deadly cancer known as mesothelioma, yet asbestos is still not banned.

The Precautionary Principle

In the future, given the right mix of politics, economics, public pressure, and tragic consequences, industry may find itself forced to change from a status quo of "make it now and find out what harm it does later" to something resembling the "precautionary principle" espoused by many governments and environmental groups and today the dominant paradigmatic approach in the European Union. The **precautionary principle** states that "even in the face of scientific uncertainty, the prudent stance is to restrict or even prohibit an activity that may cause long-term or irreversible harm." [33] That concept places the burden of proof on those who would create a potential risk rather than on those who would face its impacts. Currently, most environmental disputes follow an opposite pattern. Those who are concerned about a potentially hazardous activity must prove that unreasonably high risk exists before the advocates of the activity can be expected to change. Applied to synthetic chemicals, the precautionary principle might lead us to look for alternatives to certain classes of chemicals, such as organohalogens (organic compounds that contain chlorine, fluorine, bromine, iodine, or astatine), which have proven exceptionally dangerous.

You Make It, You Own It

An economy is posited where consumers lease products. Instead of owning the product, they buy only the services it provides. For example, many copier companies lease their machines, selling document reproduction services rather than copiers. A system has been proposed that tags chemicals (as "technical nutrients") with molecular markers. The materials remain the property of the manufacturer, which will own not only the product but also the waste, toxicity, and liability it may cause. Cradle-to-cradle product management would keep unavoidable toxins in closed-loop systems of cyclical use and reuse. Ideally companies would make either "biological nutrients" that return safely to the earth or "technical nutrients" that stay in technical cycles managed by the companies that use them. [34]

The Next Problem

If industry fails to reach such a level of self-regulation, mankind will undoubtedly face new surprises from our production and use of chemicals. The early pioneers of the internal combustion engine saw it as a cure for streets covered with horse manure, the pollutant of their day. They never dreamed that their innovation would produce the air pollution that now kills thousands of people every year. Without a more prudent approach, we may find that our new inventions create unforeseen dangers as well. A few of the many candidates for the next revolutions in chemical use include GMOs, nanoscale molecular machines, and exotic molecules such as buckyballs. Some of those will probably never do any harm and may prove valuable. Others may harm our bodies and the natural systems that we depend on in ways that we cannot foresee. Foresight requires considering an innovation's risk of doing harm at least as carefully as we explore its potential benefits.

Thoughts for Commercial Enterprises

Some of our past experiments with chemicals provide opportunities for future technology. For example, devices that "sniff out" explosives may be used to detect and destroy abandoned land mines. Nontoxic substitutes for innumerable cleaners, solvents, lubricants, adhesives, medicinal supplies, bleaches, disinfectants, and hundreds of other products are waiting to be discovered. Agriculture needs cleaner, cheaper, safer substitutes for its pesticides and chemical fertilizers.

Alternatives

There already are safer alternatives for many of the processes and products that involve toxic chemicals, and companies are working diligently to discover more. Clean energy generation, such as fuel cells, solar cells, and wind power, had become a hot topic on Wall Street by 2005. Yet all these energy technologies need assessment from a component toxicity perspective and life-cycle view as well. Integrated pest management and organic farming are gaining popularity as the local food movement accelerates. Scientists are looking to nature for solutions to industrial as well as agricultural problems. The budding field of biomimicry explores and seeks to mimic the processes in nature that create materials and energy at ambient temperatures without using toxic chemicals. For example, spiders make waterproof webs that are twice as strong as Kevlar without toxicity. Abalones create shatterproof ceramics using seawater as their raw material. Leaves create food and useful chemical energy from sunlight, water, and soil. [35] Some bacteria even digest toxic organic chemicals and excrete harmless substances in the process.

Challenges and Opportunities

Both challenges and opportunities lie in learning to assess risks and to develop a clear vision of the short- and long-term benefits and the legal, financial, and social risks associated with new chemicals and the technologies they enable. Many options exist to help businesses design environmental and social responsibility into their products and services. Proven techniques include pollution prevention (P2), design for environment (DfE), The Natural Step (TNS) framework, and cradle-to-cradle thinking. In some cases, those options include efficiency improvements that have short-term payback periods. Other techniques inspire valuable innovations with long-term financial benefits, improved public image, and employee morale—a stakeholder approach. P2 can save money by eliminating waste in industrial processes and avoiding costly regulatory requirements and toxic waste disposal costs. The DfE school of thought recommends adding design criteria that insist on processes and products that are free from toxic chemicals throughout the product life cycle. Dr. Karl-Henrick Robèrt, father of TNS, suggested asking six questions about a persistent toxin such as dioxin before continuing to use it: "Is the material natural? Is it stable? Does it degrade into harmless substances? Does it accumulate in bodily tissues? Is it possible to predict the acceptable tolerances? Can we continue to place this material safely in the environment" [36]

A Reason for Environmental Health Concerns: Chemicals in Breast Milk

Breast-feeding advocates often refer to breast milk as "liquid gold." Besides its direct benefit of feeding a growing baby, breast milk contains antibodies to protect infants from disease, nutrients to support organ development, and enzymes to aid digestion. Research has shown that the unique composition of human milk enhances brain development and lowers the risk and severity of a variety of serious childhood illnesses and chronic diseases, including diarrhea, lower respiratory infection, bacterial meningitis, urinary tract infections, lymphoma, and digestive diseases. [37] There are also significant benefits to women who breast-feed, such as reduced risk of breast and ovarian cancer and osteoporosis. [38]

Although breast milk is recognized by doctors, public health officials, and scientists as the best first food for an infant, it is not pure. Many synthetic chemicals released into the environment, intentionally or not, can be found in breast milk. Chemicals such as famous "bad actors" like DDT and PCBs, as well as less well-known substances such as flame retardants (polybrominated diphenyl ethers, or PBDEs), have been detected in human breast milk around the world. Many of those synthetic chemicals are known or suspected causes of cancer, and they have been linked to other health problems such as diabetes, reproductive disorders, and impaired brain development. The health benefits of breast-feeding far outweigh the possible negative effects of chemical contaminants in breast milk, but the presence of those chemicals remains a cause for concern.

Many of the synthetic chemicals that have been found in breast milk have some general properties in common. They can be described as bioaccumulative and persistent. A substance that bioaccumulates is one that, once introduced into the environment, collects in living organisms that are exposed by breathing air, eating plants that have taken up the chemical from the soil, or drinking water that is contaminated with the substance. Thus bioaccumulating chemicals find their way into and up the food chain. Many such chemicals are not soluble in water but rather are soluble in fat. That means that instead of being expelled, they bind to fatty tissue and remain in the body. A chemical that is termed "persistent" is just that: it stays around. Chemicals that are persistent take a long time to be broken down and expelled, if they ever are. Many such synthetic chemicals resemble natural hormones and chemicals in the human body, which is why they are not easily broken down and expelled by the body.

Breast milk has a high fat content, which means it draws certain synthetic chemicals to it. To produce milk, a mother's body utilizes stored fat, thus some of the synthetic chemicals that have accumulated in body fat over a woman's lifetime are released in the production of breast milk and passed on to nursing infants. In many cases, human milk contains chemical residues in excess of limits established for commercially marketed food. [39]

Few countries regularly track contaminants in breast milk, but recent studies from around the world show that synthetic chemicals can be found in breast milk in both industrialized and developing countries. From the Artic to Africa, in Europe, in the Americas, and in Asia, those chemicals have taken up residence in the environment and in human bodies.

The chemicals found in breast milk are of concern not simply because they demonstrate the global dispersal and persistence of some chemicals but also because exposure to them has been linked to negative health effects. It may be true that no study has ever shown that a child exposed to a specific chemical from breast milk will develop a specific disease, but a growing body of science tells us that there are links between human health and exposure to toxic chemicals in the environment.

The primary chemicals of concern that scientists have found in breast milk include dioxin, furans, and PCBs, as well as pesticide residues such as DDT, chlordane, aldrin, dieldrin, endrin, heptachlor, hexachlorobenzine, mirex, and toxaphene. Those chemicals, nine of which are pesticides, are recognized as highly toxic by the international health community and are scheduled for phaseout worldwide as part of the International Treaty on Persistent Organic Pollutants. Other chemicals found in breast milk include PBDEs, brominated flame retardants, solvents such as tetrachloroethylene, and metals such as lead, mercury, and cadmium. [40] Metals and solvents do not bind to fat, so they are not stored in the body for long; however, they do pass from the mother's blood into her breast milk and to her baby. Exposure to heavy metals and solvents, like exposure to POPs, has been linked to health effects.

To further explore the issue of synthetic chemicals in breast milk, let's look at three examples: dioxins, PBDEs, and dieldrin.

Dioxins

Dioxins are chemical by-products and comprise a number of chemicals with similar molecular structure, seventeen of which are considered to be highly toxic and cancer causing. They are not produced intentionally and are created in a range of manufacturing and combustion processes, including the following:

- Production of certain pesticides (the best-known dioxin is Agent Orange)
- Paper pulp bleaching
- Municipal waste incineration
- Hospital waste incineration
- Production and incineration of PVC
- Diesel engine exhaust

Humans are primarily exposed to dioxins and furans through the food they eat. Dioxins are released into the air, and then rain, snow, and other natural processes deposit them onto soil and water, where they combine with sediments and contaminate crops and animals. Dioxin binds tightly to fat and therefore quickly bioaccumulates and persists for a long time in the body. Because it is initially

airborne, dioxin has been detected in breast milk around the world, even in places with little or no industrial activity, such as the native Inuit villages in northern Canada.

Dioxin is one chemical that has been the subject of many studies. Exposure to low levels of dioxin, levels as low as those detected in breast milk, have been linked to impaired immune systems, leading to a higher prevalence of certain childhood conditions such as chest congestion. Scientists have found a correlation between high levels of dioxin in body fat and thyroid dysfunction. The thyroid hormone is important to proper brain development, especially early in life. Other studies have associated dioxin exposure to more feminized play behavior in boys and girls. Researchers have discovered that dioxin exposure may also increase the risk of diseases such as endometriosis and diabetes. Non-Hodgkin's lymphoma and cancers of the liver and stomach have also been connected to dioxin. [41]

Dioxin continues to be released into the environment from industrial processes, but efforts are being made to reduce levels released. The World Health Organization conducted two breast milk studies in Europe in 1986 and 1993. Comparing the two revealed a decrease in dioxin levels. [42] That result demonstrates that efforts to reduce the creation and release of dioxin do lessen the amount of the chemical accumulated in breast milk.

PBDEs

Unlike dioxin, little is known about the possible health effects of PBDEs. PBDEs are synthetic chemical fire retardants that are added to plastics, electronics, furniture, and many other home and office products. They are not actually bound to those products, so they are slowly released into the environment over time.

What *is* known about PBDEs is that they are "rapidly building up in the bodies of people and wildlife around the world." [43] In 2003, the European Union banned two PBDEs that were shown to be accumulating in human bodies; other countries outside Europe have yet to place any restrictions on PBDEs and their use continues to increase.

A study in Sweden demonstrated that there has been a steep increase in the levels of PBDEs measured in women's breast milk. [44] Sweden and other Scandinavian countries have been especially concerned with contaminants deposited by rain and snow by inevitable weather patterns that bring pollution from the countries to their south.

Very little is known about the specific ways PBDEs may contribute to human disease. PBDEs, however, demonstrate many properties that are very similar to dioxin and to PCBs. They persist a very long time in the environment and in the body. They are suspected of impairing thyroid function and brain development. Like dioxin, they are also suspected to cause cancer and have been linked to non-Hodgkin's lymphoma. [45]

As scientists uncover more information about how PBDEs are absorbed by the body and how such exposures might affect human health, the chemicals, like other POPs, may be subject to bans in many countries. Many European manufacturers are already scaling back use of some PBDEs based on what is already known about their health effects. [46]

Dieldrin

Dieldrin is an example of the many pesticides that have been banned or severely restricted worldwide. Dieldrin and its sister pesticides aldrin and endrin are banned from use in the United States. In some countries, they are permitted for specific uses under severe restriction. Dieldrin has been used in agriculture for soil and seed treatment as well as for control of mosquitoes and tsetse flies. Other uses for dieldrin include veterinary treatments for sheep, wood treatment against termites, and mothproofing of woolen products.

Dieldrin binds to soil and sediments. It is introduced to the human body primarily through eating contaminated fish, meat, and dairy products and through eating crops grown on soil treated with dieldrin. Dieldrin has been detected in 99 percent of breast milk samples tested for its presence. [47] Studies done over time show that levels of dieldrin have been decreasing since the chemical was banned. Dieldrin is in the same family of pesticides as DDT. Like DDT, dieldrin is a carcinogen and can interfere with the body's natural hormone system. Dieldrin is more toxic than DDT but does not persist as long in the environment. [48]

Conclusion

Even though it contains synthetic chemical contaminants, breast milk is still the best food for babies, according to research. Infant formulas are not a more healthful substitute; after all, most formulas have to be mixed with water or milk and therefore are not free of contaminants. Moreover, formulas lack many of the other nutrients, antibodies, and fats found in breast milk.

The presence of chemicals in breast milk shows that these chemicals are found in most people, particularly people in industrialized countries. Breast milk, then, is both a measure of what environmental exposures give cause for concern and a measure of the effectiveness of efforts to reduce the prevalence of these synthetic chemicals in the environment. As the body of science connecting childhood exposures to these toxic chemicals to human health effects grows, it appears that breast milk contamination will be a growing cause for concern.

KEY TAKEAWAYS

- By applying a sustainability approach, one can find opportunities even in mature industries dominated by global giants.
- Markets exist and are likely to grow for products that reduce exposure to toxic chemicals.
- Application of sustainability principles presents both opportunities and unique dilemmas.

EXERCISES

1. What is Method's strategy?
2. What role does sustainability innovation play in the company's strategy?
3. Why was Adam Lowry confronted with the PLA dilemma?
4. What should he do about PLA? Why?
5. How is the model of chemical development and deployment changing? How could that change be accelerated?

[1] {Author's Name Retracted as requested by the work's original creator or licensee}, *Method: Entrepreneurial Innovation, Health, Environment, and Sustainable Business Design*, UVA-ENT-0099 (Charlottesville: Darden Business Publishing, University of Virginia, March 26, 2007). All quotations and references in this section, unless otherwise noted, come from this case.

[2] {Author's Name Retracted as requested by the work's original creator or licensee}, *Method: Entrepreneurial Innovation, Health, Environment, and Sustainable Business Design*, UVA-ENT-0099 (Charlottesville: Darden Business Publishing, University of Virginia, March 26, 2007).

[3] {Author's Name Retracted as requested by the work's original creator or licensee}, *Method: Entrepreneurial Innovation, Health, Environment, and Sustainable Business Design*, UVA-ENT-0099 (Charlottesville: Darden Business Publishing, University of Virginia, March 26, 2007).

[4] {Author's Name Retracted as requested by the work's original creator or licensee}, *Method: Entrepreneurial Innovation, Health, Environment, and Sustainable Business Design*, UVA-ENT-0099 (Charlottesville: Darden Business Publishing, University of Virginia, March 26, 2007).

[5] {Author's Name Retracted as requested by the work's original creator or licensee}, *Method: Entrepreneurial Innovation, Health, Environment, and Sustainable Business Design*, UVA-ENT-0099 (Charlottesville: Darden Business Publishing, University of Virginia, March 26, 2007).

[6] {Author's Name Retracted as requested by the work's original creator or licensee}, *Method: Entrepreneurial Innovation, Health, Environment, and Sustainable Business Design*, UVA-ENT-0099 (Charlottesville: Darden Business Publishing, University of Virginia, March 26, 2007).

[7] {Author's Name Retracted as requested by the work's original creator or licensee}, *Method: Entrepreneurial Innovation, Health, Environment, and Sustainable Business Design*, UVA-ENT-0099 (Charlottesville: Darden Business Publishing, University of Virginia, March 26, 2007).

[8] *Cradle-to-cradle* was an increasingly popular term that referred to a product cycle in which materials could be manufactured, used, then broken down and used again with no loss of quality; for more information on this concept, see William McDonough and Michael Braungart, *Cradle to Cradle: Remaking the Way We Make Things* (New York: North Point Press, 2002).

[9] See http://www.warnerbabcock.com for an example of a company committed to change

[10] Rachel Carson, *Silent Spring* (New York: Houghton Mifflin, 1962).

[11] {Author's Name Retracted as requested by the work's original creator or licensee}, Darden Business School technical note, *Toxic Chemicals: Responding to Challenges and Opportunities*, UVA-ENT-0043 (Charlottesville: Darden Business Publishing, University of Virginia, 2004). Information presented in this section comes from this study.

[12] Theo Colborn, Dianne Dumanoski, and John Peterson Myers, *Our Stolen Future* (New York: Penguin Group, 1996), 239–40.

[13] "Organic" chemicals are chemicals that have a carbon backbone. Some occur naturally and some are synthetic. There is no connection between the term *organic* as it is used in chemistry and the use of the word in phrases such as *organic food* or *organic farming*.

[14] Rachel Carson, *Silent Spring* (New York: Houghton Mifflin, 1962), 118–22.

[15] Ann Platt McGinn, *Why Poison Ourselves? A Precautionary Approach to Synthetic Chemicals*, Worldwatch Paper #153 (Washington, DC: Worldwatch Institute, November 2000), 22.

[16] Theo Colborn, Dianne Dumanoski, and John Peterson Myers, *Our Stolen Future* (New York: Penguin Group, 1996), 178.

[17] Ann Platt McGinn, *Why Poison Ourselves? A Precautionary Approach to Synthetic Chemicals*, Worldwatch Paper #153 (Washington, DC: Worldwatch Institute, November 2000), 9.

[18] Peter H. Raven and George B. Johnson, *Biology*, 5th ed. (New York: McGraw Hill, 1999), 342, table 17.3.

[19] Ted Williams, "Lessons from Lake Apopka," *Audubon*, July–August 1999, 64–72.

[20] Theo Colborn, Dianne Dumanoski, and John Peterson Myers, *Our Stolen Future* (New York: Penguin Group, 1996), 88–91.

[21] Theo Colborn, Dianne Dumanoski, and John Peterson Myers, *Our Stolen Future* (New York: Penguin Group, 1996), 107.

[22] G. Tyler Miller, *Living in the Environment*, 10th ed. (Belmont, CA: Wadsworth, 1998), 481.

[23] Ashley Mattoon, "Deciphering Amphibian Declines," in *State of the World 2001* (Washington, DC: Worldwatch Institute, 2001), 63–82, accessed January 11, 2011, http://www.globalchange.umich.edu/gctext/Inquiries/Module%20Activities/State%20of%20the%20World/Amphibian%20Declines.pdf.

[24] Our Stolen Future, "About Phthalates," accessed January 30, 2011, http://www.ourstolenfuture.org/newscience/oncompounds/phthalates/phthalates.htm.

[25] Our Stolen Future, "About Phthalates," accessed January 30, 2011, http://www.ourstolenfuture.org/newscience/oncompounds/phthalates/phthalates.htm.

[26] Payal Sampat, *Deep Trouble: The Hidden Threat of Groundwater Pollution*, Worldwatch Paper #154 (Washington, DC: Worldwatch Institute, 2000), 27.

[27] Ann Platt McGinn, *Why Poison Ourselves? A Precautionary Approach to Synthetic Chemicals*, Worldwatch Paper #153 (Washington, DC: Worldwatch Institute, November 2000), 7.

[28] Theo Colborn, Dianne Dumanoski, and John Peterson Myers, *Our Stolen Future* (New York: Penguin Group, 1996), 27.

[29] US Environmental Protection Agency, "Toxics Release Inventory (TRI) Program," accessed January 31, 2011, http://www.epa.gov/tri.

[30] US Environmental Protection Agency, "Toxics Release Inventory (TRI) Program, TRI Chemical List," accessed January 30, 2011, http://www.epa.gov/tri/trichemicals.

[31] US Environmental Protection Agency, "HPV Chemical Hazard Data Availability Study: High Production Volume (HPV) Chemicals and SIDS Testing," accessed January 29, 2011, http://www.epa.gov/hpv/pubs/general/hazchem.htm.

[32] Superfund sites are highly polluted areas registered with the US Environmental Protection Agency. A multibillion-dollar fund for cleaning up those sites is financed by the companies that caused the pollution in accordance with the "polluter pays" principle.

[33] Ann Platt McGinn, *Why Poison Ourselves? A Precautionary Approach to Synthetic Chemicals*, Worldwatch Paper #153 (Washington, DC: Worldwatch Institute, November 2000), 17–18.

[34] Robert A. Frosch and Nicholas E. Gallopoulos, "Strategies for Manufacturing," *Scientific American* 261, no. 3 (September 1989): 144–52; Robert U. Ayres, "Industrial Metabolism," in *Technology and Environment*, ed. Jesse H. Ausubel and Hedy E. Sladovich (Washington, DC: National Academy Press, 1989).

[35] Janine Benyus, *Biomimicry: Innovation Inspired by Nature* (New York: William Morrow, 1997).

[36] Paul Hawken, *The Ecology of Commerce* (New York: Harper Business, 1993), 53.

[37] {Author's Name Retracted as requested by the work's original creator or licensee}, Darden Business School technical note, *Environmental Health: Chemicals in Breast Milk*, UVA-ENT-0078 (Charlottesville: Darden Business Publishing, University of Virginia, 2004). All information in this section by author.

[38] US Department of Health and Human Services, "The Surgeon General's Call to Action to Support Breastfeeding, 2011," accessed January 30, 2011, http://www.surgeongeneral.gov/topics/breastfeeding/calltoactiontosupport breastfeeding.pdf.

[39] Sandra Steingraber, *Living Downstream: An Ecologist Looks at Cancer and the Environment* (New York: Addison-Wesley, 1997), 168.

[40] Natural Resources Defense Council, "Healthy Milk, Healthy Baby: Chemical Pollution and Mother's Milk," accessed January 30, 2011, http://www.nrdc.org/breastmilk/chems.asp.

[41] Lois Marie Gibbs, *Dying from Dioxin* (Cambridge, MA: South End Press, 1995), 138.

[42] Gina M. Solomon and Pilar M. Weiss, "Chemical Contaminants in Breast Milk: Time Trends and Regional Variability," *Environmental Health Perspectives* 110, no. 6 (June 2002): 343.

[43] Marla Cone, "Cause for Alarm over Chemicals," *Los Angeles Times*, April 20, 2003, accessed January 11, 2011, http://articles.latimes.com/2003/apr/20/local/me-chemicals20.

[44] Natural Resources Defense Council, "Healthy Milk, Healthy Baby: Chemical Pollution and Mother's Milk," accessed January 11, 2011, http://www.nrdc.org/breastmilk/chems.asp.

[45] K. Hooper and T. A. McDonald, "The PBDEs: An Emerging Environmental Challenge and Another Reason for Breast-Milk Monitoring Programs," *Environmental Health Perspectives* 110, no. 6 (June 2002): A339–47, quoted in Gina M. Solomon, "Flame Retardant Chemical Detections Rising in Breast Milk," *Quarterly Review, Harvard Medical School Center for Health and the Global Environment* 2, no. 2 (2000), accessed January 30, 2011, http://www.ncbi.nlm.nih.gov/pmc/articles/PMC1240888.

[46] Marla Cone, "Cause for Alarm over Chemicals," *Los Angeles Times*, April 20, 2003, accessed January 11, 2011, http://articles.latimes.com/2003/apr/20/local/me-chemicals20.

[47] Natural Resources Defense Council, "Healthy Milk, Healthy Baby: Chemical Pollution and Mother's Milk," accessed January 11, 2011, http://www.nrdc.org/breastmilk/chems.asp.

[48] Natural Resources Defense Council, "Healthy Milk, Healthy Baby: Chemical Pollution and Mother's Milk," accessed January 11, 2011, http://www.nrdc.org/breastmilk/chems.asp.

6.3 The Method Company: Sustainability Innovation as Entrepreneurial Strategy

LEARNING OBJECTIVES

1. Analyze a company culture conducive to innovation.

2. Understand how collaborative innovation processes work.

3. Discuss emerging new models of business.

This second Method case examines the process by which the firm created a breakthrough product design in 2010. Method also became a B Corporation, joining a fast-growing number of other companies committed to making money *and* using business innovation to solve health, social, and environmental problems by paying attention to toxicity and broad stakeholder interests. (A detailed discussion of B Corporations follows the case.) Together the two Method cases offer insights into how entrepreneurially minded individuals can address chemical contamination and design concerns through innovative approaches.

Method Products Inc. had hit a sweet spot for its buyers by 2010. [1] Since its founding in 2000, the privately held Method had a clear mission: make good-smelling, high-performing household cleaners that were healthy throughout their material life spans and packaged in attractive, eye-catching, and eco-designed containers. Said Adam Lowry, cofounder and chief "greenskeeper": "We wanted to change the way people view home cleaning. There is a disconnect between the way people feel about and care for their homes and the design of the products they use to clean them. We set out to evolve the household cleaner from an object that lived under the sink to a countertop accessory and must-have item by providing cool-looking, effective, nontoxic products that are healthy for both the environment and the home." [2]

As scientific studies revealed growing health problems associated with chemical exposure and regulation of chemicals steadily rose around the world, more informed customers were seeking effective but healthier cleaning product options on retail shelves.

Despite the company's small size and entrepreneurially disruptive approach, Method's stylish cleaning products had quickly become state of the art in an industry moving toward sustainable business thinking. "We want to be thought leaders and we want to evoke change," said cofounder and design guru Eric Ryan. [3] Method had in fact altered the

once staid market for cleaning products in which large competitors traditionally fought over shelf facings, thin margins, and fractional market share points. Method introduced a three-times-more-concentrated laundry detergent in 2004 that met Walmart's requirement that all detergent suppliers concentrate their products to save resources on packaging and shipping. In 2006, Method began getting many of its products cradle-to-cradle certified by McDonough Braungart Design Chemistry. This certification meant the products were nontoxic and used fewer resources throughout their life cycles. The next year, Method became one of the founding **B Corporations**, a form of company that built environmental and social goals into its charter and passed third-party standards for sustainable practices. Method also worked through its public communications and website to express the goals and values that were an integral part of its company culture and products—that is, protecting health, children, and pets through eco-friendly and socially conscious products designed from a full life-cycle perspective.

Yet Lowry wanted to go further to catalyze the next wave of innovation within the company's product categories. He and the company aspired to launch two major products a year. In 2008, Method turned to laundry detergents, a several-billion-dollar market in the United States alone. It devised an eight-times-concentrated detergent in an encapsulated tablet, or monodose format, which would further save packaging and product materials and drastically reduce manufacturing and distribution of energy usage. The consumer could toss the tablet in the washing machine with a load of laundry. It was convenient, efficient, less messy, and prevented using excess soap in each laundry load.

At a critical point in the product development process, everything about the monodose was working except one thing: the gel that encapsulated the detergent didn't dissolve entirely in cold water, a result of the company's decision not to use animal-derived ingredients such as the gelatins most often used for capsules. A bit of the plant-based gel casing could remain in the washing machine during the rinse cycle. Could Method and its loyal customers accept the residue as the price for a much more concentrated and environmentally compatible detergent formulation? Method could turn to petroleum-derived or gelatin capsules rather than plant-based materials for the capsule to solve the problem. Alternatively, the company could abandon the monodose concept and its inherent benefits. Lowry and his team contemplated what to do.

The Emergence of Method

Adam Lowry and Eric Ryan knew each other growing up in Michigan, where their families had entrepreneurial companies that became significant suppliers to the automobile industry. Lowry earned his bachelor of science in chemical engineering from Stanford University and worked on climate change policy at the Carnegie Institution for Science, an organization that focused on innovation and discovery. There, he helped develop software tools for the study of global climate change. In his postcollege work experience, Lowry honed his unique approach to commercial environmentalism, which would form the basis of Method's success. Through his combined education and employment, Lowry became convinced that business was "the most powerful agent for positive change on the planet. But it's not business as we know it today. It is fundamentally and profoundly different. It is business redesigned." [4]

In 2006, Ryan was named one of *Time* magazine's eco-leaders and received similar accolades from *Vanity Fair*. Ryan attended the University of Rhode Island and went into marketing, eventually doing work for the Gap and Saturn. The old high school classmates ran into each other on an airplane in 1997 and realized they lived on the same block of Pine Street in San Francisco. They soon thereafter became roommates, helping to maintain a house full of college fraternity brothers. As the story went, no one liked to clean. The two spent time discussing what was cool and what was not in commercial markets—and hence ripe for innovation. The pair settled on cleaning products, a bastion of typically harsh, dangerous chemicals—definitely not cool.

Lowry and Ryan used their bathtub to mix their own cleaners from natural, fragrant, and gradually more benign and renewable ingredients. Initial funding of $300,000 was provided through convertible debt from friends and family. They filled one beer pitcher at a time with their cleaners and made their first sale in February 2001 to a local grocery store—an order they scrambled to fill from their bathtub. The next day, Lowry and Ryan hired their new boss, an entrepreneurial CEO with an MBA and years of experience in the consumer packaged goods industry.

The founders knew presentation would matter when it came to making an impression on customers. Lowry said, "[We want to] inspire a happy, healthy home revolution....We want it to be happy because, in our opinion, way too much of the green movement has been heavy handed in sort of an education-based instead of inspiration-based [way]. That's one of the reasons that you see us concentrating so much on making our products not only work great and be green but be beautiful as well." [5]

They cold-pitched New York–based industrial designer Karim Rashid, whose aesthetically appealing work had appeared in museums, and he accepted the offer to design for Method. Soon, his designs would appear on countertops across the country. Rashid's name and Ryan's contacts got the company a pilot deal with Target to sell Method products at two hundred stores around Chicago and San Francisco. Method found a contract manufacturer to scale up production. Method's commitment to excellence and attention to detail impressed Target, especially after a problem with leaky containers led Lowry and other Method employees to walk through Target and pull the leaky bottles off the shelves themselves; their container supplier quickly corrected the problem.

Method's growth accelerated even as the company stayed true to its core values of style and social and environmental soundness. Target decided to carry Method products in all its stores, and Method went from having $16 in cash, credit card debt, and arrears to vendors in 2001 to profitability in 2005. [6] In 2006, Method experienced rapid growth, ending the year with about forty-five employees, fifty vendors and suppliers, and a foothold in the United Kingdom. The next year pushed sales to $71 million. Method expanded rapidly from hand soaps and countertop cleaners to body washes, floor cleaners, dish soaps, and laundry detergents. These products were carried by large retail chains such as Costco, Target, Lowe's, and Whole Foods and generated over $100 million in revenue by 2010. Method's former CEO distilled the company's approach for success in 2006: "Method has to enter a category with a huge disruption. The story cannot be copied overnight or eroded by competitors. It has to have disruptive packaging, ingredients, and fragrance." [7]

The company also continued to use naturally occurring or naturally derived ingredients as much as possible. If synthetic ingredients were needed, they were screened for biodegradability and toxicity to humans and the environment but without the use of animal testing. People for the Ethical Treatment of Animals (PETA) gave Lowry and Ryan its 2006 award for Person of the Year. The founding duo wrote a guidebook in 2008 titled *Squeaky Green: The Method Guide to Detoxing Your Home*. Their company, meanwhile, strove to reduce its carbon footprint through efficiency, switching to biodiesel trucks, or buying offsets such as methane digesters for manure at three Pennsylvania dairy farms. It also became the first company to introduce a custom-made bottle manufactured from 100 percent post–consumer recycled (PCR) polyethylene terephthalate (PET), which has a recycling number, as part of the resin identification code, of one.

Despite its innovation, growth, and sterling public image, Method remained tiny relative to the competition. While Seventh Generation, an established producer of green cleaners and a fellow B Corporation, had sales comparable to Method's, generating $93 million in revenue in 2007 and over $120 million the following year, the makers of conventional cleaning products were orders of magnitude larger. One of the largest companies in the world, Procter & Gamble (P&G) had a market capitalization of $180 billion in April 2010, and its Household Care business unit alone had sales of $37.3 billion in 180 countries in 2009. P&G's laundry detergents in 2009 included Tide, the first synthetic heavy-duty detergent launched in 1946 and a now billion-dollar brand; Gain, another billion-dollar brand; Ace and Dash, each of which generated over $500 million in sales; and Cheer. [8] In short, P&G's laundry detergents dominated that market and by themselves generated more than thirty times Method's revenue.

Other giants with broad product portfolios operated in the laundry detergent market. In 2009, Unilever, also a food producer, had total sales of about $55 billion. Colgate-Palmolive, known for toothpastes and dish soaps, had sales of $15 billion. Clorox, best known for its chlorine bleach, had sales of $5.5 billion. Clorox also had proven particularly adroit at moving into the green cleaning market. It launched its Green Works line in the United States in 2008, rapidly expanded into fourteen countries, and, according to the company, captured 47 percent of the natural cleaner market from mid-2008 to mid-2009, more than doubling the closest competitor's share. Church & Dwight Co., makers of Arm & Hammer brand baking soda, pulled in another $2.5 billion in sales in 2009 and marketed a series of baking soda–based green cleaners and laundry detergents under its Arm & Hammer Essentials line. [9]

As Method mulled its own new laundry detergent, it remained very much aware of its smaller stature. As Eric Ryan told *Inc.* magazine in 2007, "When you run through the

legs of Goliath, you need to spend a lot of time thinking about how to act so you don't put yourself in a place you can be stepped on." [10] Josh Handy, the lead Method designer, made a similar point: "Where we've gone awry sometimes is when we've forgotten how small we are and therefore while we talked about ourselves as being the biggest green brand in the world, which typically we were, that's the wrong mindset for Method. What we are is the 35th-smallest cleaning products brand in the world." [11]

Handy understood that Method's work environment had to support the creativity required for David-esque innovation. After Handy came to Method, he actively encouraged people to break rules to innovate, at one point literally drawing on a piece of furniture. Other employees followed his lead, and soon a room of once-uniform and uncomfortable white furniture was thus decorated and dubbed "the Wiggle Room." Commitment to giving people and ideas room to "wiggle" was serious. The mission was stated as "Keep it weird, keep it real, keep it different," and, as Eric Ryan commented,

> We don't build rockets over here; we build soap. And it's hard to be different in soap. So ideas have to be flowing. We have to have an environment where people are comfortable sharing ideas. We do everything we can to make people as connected as possible. We have to have every brain in the game. The more different an idea, the more fragile it is and the more likely it is beaten down and doesn't go anywhere. We have to cultivate our ability to be different, to be open to ideas. It means putting as much work into the culture as the product you are creating. [12]

Concentrating the Formula and Pushing the Monodose to Failure

When Method decided to pursue an improved detergent in early 2008, it turned over the matter to its team of "green chefs," including Fred Holzhauer, whom Lowry characterized as being "as close to a true mad scientist as anyone I've ever met." Lowry gave the green chefs the mission of creating a better detergent and trusted them to figure out the details. "What we do is set up a system," Lowry explained, "a way of working, an environment that allows the innovation to occur within the boundaries that we want." [13] Drummond Lawson, Method's "Green Giant" (or director of sustainability) seconded that notion. Method's strategy was to hire creative people and then get out of their way. In the case of Holzhauer, Lawson said, "He has this opportunity to really play with everything in the lab, bring it through, and get some prototypes up to the point where we can take them and put them in other people's hands. Whereas if we mandate—go make this formulation with these characteristics—he'd be checked out and bored and gone. You'd end up with what you ask for instead of myriad opportunities." [14]

Method's green chefs decided to build upon the success of Method's three-times-concentrated detergent. Further concentration would decrease the water in the product, thereby decreasing volume, mass, packaging, storage space, and freight costs. Method also wanted to encapsulate the detergent in tablet form for the user's convenience and to reduce detergent wasted by inaccurate measurement. The green chefs listed their goals and all the tools at their disposal, including the conventional harsh, artificial tools. They focused initially on getting the detergent formula right. As Holzhauer explained,

The first thing you do is you build it the old way. You build it with all the nasty stuff that a competitor would and say, "What would be the highest performing biggest-payoff thing that we could build?" And you build it and then you say, "This stuff rocks. This is my benchmark. How close can I get using materials that are available with green?" Then there's the whole process of drawing lines through a whole bunch of stuff you wish you could use. And you're left with some holes. You're definitely left with some holes. [15]

Method, in collaboration with the Environmental Protection Encouragement Agency based in Hamburg, Germany, had amassed a list of safe, biodegradable chemicals to use as starting points for its products. Holzhauer had to ensure no unwanted interactions among those ingredients, but he also had to fill the holes in his toolkit to get the results he wanted. Method prized its products' effectiveness above all else. If the products didn't clean, it didn't matter that they were natural, nontoxic, and beautiful. Rather than limiting Method, other constraints aside from performance forced the company to be more innovative.

Lowry had once called trade-offs among these various qualities "just a symptom of poor design." In addition, Lowry considered it essential "to make sure that what you're doing is really compelling for reasons other than being green. It has to be great in its own right, and green has to be just another part of its quality. The whole idea of eco-entrepreneur should become the standard for entrepreneurship in general." [16] Therefore, the chefs pushed further. They began to consult their networks.

Holzhauer said, "This is where collaboration and innovation really pay off. You start asking people who make detergents, [who] know you're handy, and you leverage your relationships and you say, 'Hey, would you guys entertain this thought? You guys can make sodium laurel sulfate, but

nobody's making MIPA sulfate, and that's the kind of tool that would really make a difference in what I'm doing, and it's just not available commercially. How about you whip me up a lab sample, you know?' And [from that] you get a new tool and you try it."

The chefs continued to use their contacts, get new tools, and test and alter them. They eventually refined the formula, dubbed "smartclean," to be as effective as "the nasty stuff" yet naturally based and eight times as concentrated. They found their detergent showed nonlinear improvement; doubling the concentration more than doubled its effectiveness.

Unexpectedly, they had moved into a new realm of chemistry in which few people had any experience working with such concentrated liquids. They kept testing the formula until they understood at the molecular level exactly what was happening. They also realized that the increased effectiveness meant they needed far less of the detergent to do the job, which meant the product could now compete on cost. [17]

The gel capsule, however, continued to be a problem. Holzhauer talked to people in the paintball industry to get a sense of how big he could make a glycerin or gelatin capsule to hold the detergent. He wanted something that could fit in your hand, and the paintball people thought that could be done. Holzhauer concentrated the detergent enough so the capsule size would contain all the detergent needed. Yet the detergent was so effective that it dissolved the capsules as well unless they were made sufficiently thick, at which point they would not fully dissolve in cold-water wash conditions. Holzhauer tinkered with the formula. He knew petroleum-based and animal-derived ingredients could make it all work perfectly, but that violated Method's premise of sustainability and ethics. "We tried and tried and tried. We just never got where we wanted to go," Holzhauer said. [18]

Surviving Failure: Collaboration and the Container

Ever optimistic that a tablet/capsule solution would be found, the chefs still wanted to test the "smartclean" detergent itself. They thought of a diaper cream Method already sold and got a simple idea: put the detergent in the pump dispenser used for the diaper cream. Let people squirt the detergent straight into the washing machine instead of dissolving a tablet. Suddenly, the critical solution had taken hold in the chef group: a pump instead of a tablet for this detergent. Holzhauer talked with Josh Handy to refine the pump bottle. "If you get a bright idea," Holzhauer said, "you walk over to Josh's desk and you say, 'Hey, dude. I need one of these. Could you whip it up for me?' And he's like, 'Sure.' He'll ask a few questions about it and make sure it's worth the time, but he'll do it." [19] Handy began working on Holzhauer's pump and posted his drawings outside the bathroom so that employees from all over could see them and provide feedback.

The switch from gel tablet to pump sent Holzhauer back to the lab to refine the formula. The detergent was incredibly viscous and had to be tweaked to work in a pump. It also had to be uniformly mixed so that each squirt dispensed exactly the same proportion of ingredients; in the tablet the ingredients would mix eventually once the tablet dissolved and thus could start off unevenly dispersed. Holzhauer wanted to keep tweaking the formula, which he had already refined to 95 percent effectiveness using all benign and renewable ingredients, but Method was preparing to launch the product. Holzhauer patented his work to date and continued to work on a revised version for future release.

The new detergent formula appeared to work in the pump, so Method shifted emphasis to making sure it could get the container it needed. Handy's final design featured a pump mechanism that was easy to depress without Herculean strength. The pump would also encourage people to use the recommended amount, unlike conventional detergent container caps, which were designed to be much bigger than the amount of liquid actually needed and thus encouraged people to overuse detergent. A standard cap and bottle also made measurement a two-handed task, and a full bottle of typical two-times concentrate could easily weigh seven pounds or more. In contrast, Method's customer could hold a laundry basket or child in one hand and dispense the necessary smartclean detergent—four short squirts—with the other. Method's fifty-load smartclean container, when full, weighed less than two pounds.

Handy's design next had to be mass-produced. That task fell largely to the packaging engineering and project management teams. Collaboration was the key for these groups; said one packaging engineer, "I can literally turn my chair around and help contribute." [20] Method employees worked at common long tables rather than in cubicles, so they could overhear discussions and add to them. The project manager believed innovation was more important than strict adherence to procedures. The packaging engineers, known internally as plastic surgeons, found they could use a stock engine (the internal workings of the pump) for the detergent but needed a custom top to match Method's aesthetic and operating needs. They reached out to various suppliers and found only one willing to

collaborate on the custom design. Method agreed to pay for the tooling necessary to produce the top.

Method wanted the bottle itself to have transparent windows to show the contents and the newly designed angled dip tube that sucked in the detergent. That transparency would allow customers to ensure the tube always rested at the bottom of the container to extract all the detergent rather than leave some behind. Method selected an independent, California-based plastics manufacturer that produced almost two hundred million containers annually and had experience using post–consumer recycled number-two plastic, or high-density polyethylene (HDPE). Method pushed the recycled content as high as it could before it started sacrificing transparency. Hence the company ultimately settled on 50 percent virgin HDPE and 50 percent PCR HDPE.

Simultaneously, Method worked to produce the detergent in sufficient volume. Method's operations department began working with the contract manufacturer it selected to make the product, a supplier for almost all the biggest personal care and cleaner companies, including P&G, Unilever, and others. Method's operations team ushered the smartclean detergent from batches in Method's labs to identical but more massive batches in the factory. A pilot manufacturing run revealed new problems—and a new opportunity. The first factory batch was contaminated by dirt from the bottling equipment because the Method detergent was so powerful, it cleaned out the lines as it moved through the system. Although Method had to nix the batch, it stumbled into a potential market: industrial cleaners. Indeed, the manufacturer began using the smartclean laundry detergent as its default factory equipment cleaner.

Finally, Method needed new shrink-wrapping equipment to put a label around the bottle's unique shape and to keep the pump locked while allowing customers to unscrew the cap and sniff the detergent, a design requirement responding to the desire of many buyers to smell the contents. Method worked with the manufacturer to get the results it needed and invested in the new equipment.

Quantifying Sustainability

Moving through the development and production of the smartclean laundry detergent, Method wanted to assess the product's environmental impact. The first step was cradle-to-cradle certification, and smartclean was the first laundry detergent to obtain it. Smartclean also was recognized by the US Environmental Protection Agency's Design for Environment program because of its nontoxic, biodegradable formulation.

In addition, Method wanted to calculate the detergent's overall carbon footprint. It collaborated with Planet Metrics, a Silicon Valley start-up founded in 2008 with $2.3 million in venture capital Series A funding. The young company was eager to collaborate with a company such as Method to build its reputation and beta-test its Rapid Carbon Modeling software. The ultimate goal of the software was to give companies a quick way to calculate returns on investment for various sustainability options. It did so by measuring life-cycle carbon emissions from a product throughout Scopes 1, 2, and 3. Those scopes are defined by the Greenhouse Gas Protocol accounting method as follows:

- **Scope 1.** All direct GHG emissions.
- **Scope 2.** Indirect GHG emissions from consumption of purchased electricity, heat, or steam.
- **Scope 3.** Other indirect emissions, such as the extraction and production of purchased materials and fuels, transport-related activities in vehicles not owned or controlled by the reporting entity, electricity-related activities (e.g., transmission losses) not covered in Scope 2, outsourced activities, waste disposal, and so forth. [21]

Planet Metrics analyzed Method's detergent from cradle to gate: all the activities and material needed to produce the product and get it ready to ship to retailers. Of course, later carbon dioxide emissions would presumably be lower for shipment to retailers, recycling old bottles, and so on because the bottles used less material overall, which meant less energy and less mass to be moved around for an equivalent cleaning capacity. Looking just at cradle to gate, however, Method's smartclean detergent per load had a carbon footprint 35 percent smaller than the average two-times concentrated laundry detergent. It also used 36 percent less plastic and 33 percent less oil and energy. Finally, consumers would be more likely to use the appropriate amount of detergent, making the actual reductions even greater.

Conclusion

Reflecting on the path of the smartclean laundry detergent, Lowry considered it a success born of failure. People were given space to create and collaborate within Method and across its supply chain. They didn't shut down after encountering obstacles; they got more creative and talked to each other. Lowry noted that some workers in the factories where the detergent was made volunteered to work extra, unpaid shifts because they believed they were part of something bigger: a social change, not just another way to make money from people's dirty laundry. He said, "Cultures are the only sustainable competitive advantage. We don't see the innovation per se as the competitive advantage. We see the ability to innovate as the competitive advantage. If you're going to do that you've got to build a different type of company where you literally are built—the people and the culture of the place—around the ability to bring the best ideas forward and let them live and let them thrive. Each innovation gives us license to innovate again." [22]

By summer 2010, it appeared the new laundry detergent was a successful launch. What was the next focus for this young, fast-moving company? Typical growth challenges faced the firm and its entrepreneurial founders. As it grew from start-up to midsize, could its innovative output be maintained? How should management's attention be allocated across its innovation imperatives and its proliferation of product offerings and growth demands? And what was the end point? Was the goal to grow Method indefinitely?

Next we look more closely at the emerging category of B Corporations. Although the number of companies listed and requesting assessment as B Corporations remains relatively small, the high level of interest and rapid expansion of B Corporation designations for firms in the short time the classification has been available suggests growing interest in this alternative business model. B Corporation designation connects to entrepreneurial innovation favoring cleaner, more benign, and less destructive business footprints in its effort to legally protect a company's commitment to those strategic goals, even when the firm is acquired by a larger corporation that may not share the same values.

B Corporation: A New Sustainable Business Model

We envision a new sector of the economy which harnesses the power of private enterprise to create public benefit.

- B Lab, "Declaration of Interdependence," 2010

Jay Coen Gilbert and Bart Houlahan were friends as undergraduates at Stanford University. In 1993, a few years after graduation, they helped start the basketball shoe and apparel company AND1. As the company grew, cofounder Gilbert and president Houlahan emphasized financial success along with corporate social responsibility (also called triple-bottom-line strategy and sustainable business): AND1 paid employees respectable wages, donated 5 percent of profits to charity, and made sure factories in China met their standards. The company was generating close to $250 million in annual revenue when it was sold to American Sporting Goods Inc. in 2005. Gilbert and Houlahan were personally enriched but disempowered: they watched their effort to create an innovative business model vanish under the new owners. [23]

Gilbert and Houlahan were not alone. Ben & Jerry's, known for its ice cream and its social responsibility, was sold to Unilever in 2000. Although some board members had misgivings, they voted for the sale because Vermont, like most states, required the board to act in the interest of the shareholders, which meant accepting Unilever's exceptionally lucrative offer.

Gilbert and Houlahan wanted a way to protect the triple bottom line (combined financial, social, and environmental performance) of companies even as companies switched owners, evolved over time, or grappled with shareholders' desire for greater dividends. That desire motivated them to contact another Stanford classmate, Andrew Kassoy, a private equity investor with the MSD Capital real estate fund of the Michael & Susan Dell Foundation. Each man invested $1 million of his own money to start the nonprofit B Lab in 2006 to bring about their shared vision of capitalist corporations working simultaneously toward financial health and social and environmental benefits. [24]

With additional funding from the Rockefeller Foundation, B (as in benefit) Lab created various tools to help companies achieve these broader goals. B Lab developed the B Impact Rating System (BIRS), which companies could use to assess their social and environmental performance. B Lab also established standards for transparency and a basic legal framework that companies could incorporate into their articles of incorporation to safeguard their social and environmental goals, especially in times of transition. Finally, Gilbert, Houlahan, and Kassoy recruited eighty-one companies that scored high enough on the BIRS and were willing to commit formally to transparency and working for the greater public benefit. Thus, in late 2007, the first B Corporations appeared.

B Corporations were companies that were third-party-certified by B Lab, demonstrating they were serious about sustainability strategies and corporate social responsibility. They sought certification because they wanted to distinguish themselves from competitors, wanted to reassure consumers and investors, and fundamentally believed that "doing good" had to become part of business itself, not ancillary to it. Hence B Corporations shared "[a vision that] is simple yet ambitious: to create a new sector of the economy which uses the power of business to solve social and environmental problems....As a result, individuals and communities will have greater economic opportunity, society will have moved closer to achieving a positive environmental footprint, more people will be employed in great places to work, and we will have built more local living economies in the U.S. and across the world." [25]

Objectives and Advantages of B Corporation Status

B Corporations shifted the emphasis of business from shareholder value to stakeholder value. Employees, consumers, and communities, including the environment, should all benefit from economic activity. B Corporations hoped to create these benefits in three ways. First, in addition to financial goals, they established explicit social and environmental goals and strategies. Second, these companies were transparent about their operations and broader stakeholder goals, and they progressed toward those goals. To be certified as B Corporations, companies had to earn at least eighty of two hundred possible points on the BIRS survey and submit to random audits of their social and environmental performance. That way, investors and customers knew where their money really went, and the B Corporation could dissociate itself from "greenwashing" and other brand risks. Finally, B Corporations incorporated their sustainability principles explicitly into their governance documents. Formalizing these principles was believed to help these companies survive transitions and gave B Corporations some legal grounds for considering social and environmental consequences as well as shareholder returns in their decisions.

To be considered for certification, a company paid an application fee to B Lab and submitted its BIRS survey responses along with documentation for some of the answers. The BIRS survey covered an array of categories organized largely by stakeholders: Accountability, Employees, Consumers, Community, and Environment. For instance, under Employees, a series of questions covered employee benefits, including health insurance coverage and premiums, sick days and maternity leave, training opportunities, flexible schedules, and so on. Completing the BIRS took about sixty to ninety minutes, according to B Lab, and after submitting the survey to B Lab, companies received a report. Those companies that met or exceeded the eighty-point minimum could be certified. Through mid-2010, more than four-fifths of companies that applied for B Corporation status had been rejected. In addition to screening new companies, B Lab audited 10 percent of existing B Corporations in any given year, and any company that fell below acceptable performance standards had ninety days to correct the problem. [26]

The rating criteria were continually reviewed and revised by B Lab's Standards Advisory Council, which included one B Lab member and eight independent members from business, academic, and nonprofit organizations. In 2010, the BIRS was in version 2.0, with version 3.0 under development. The original version 1.0 was developed from various extant corporate social responsibility metrics plus input from more than six hundred reviewers. Since B Lab provided its rating system to anyone, not just applicants, more than one thousand companies used BIRS in 2009 to monitor their performances. In conjunction with private investment funds and government agencies, B Lab in 2010 was also developing a Global Impact Investing Rating System for investors. [27]

In exchange for working for the public benefit and submitting to greater transparency and scrutiny, B Corporations received a number of benefits. First, they reduced the effects of labor, environmental, and other problems to their companies' brands. Second, they shared ideas and services with each other. Indeed, in addition to routinely swapping best practices, B Corporations provided services to one another at a discount and helped each other find like-minded suppliers, consultants, and investors. Third, B Corporations had access to support from B Partners (non-B Corporations that nonetheless supported the concept) and the B Lab, which promoted B Corporations and helped devise metrics and attract investors and customers.

Among other things, B Lab advocated for state laws that favored B Corporations. As of 2010, no state recognized B Corporation as such, although the Maryland legislature passed a bill March 29, 2010, that would create separate legal recognition for B Corporations and give them some protection if shareholders sued to improve their returns at the expense of social and environmental goals. [28] Six other states were considering comparable laws, and the city of Philadelphia had already announced it would give $4,000 in tax breaks to twenty-five B Corporations in the years 2012 through 2017. Ultimately, B Lab hoped the IRS would recognize B Corporations with a different tax status and expected B Corporations to equal nonprofits' current share of GDP, about 5 percent, in twenty years. [29]

Other benefits may accrue to B Corporations. One may be attracting more talented and dedicated employees because potential employees are motivated to work for places that care about a triple (economic, social, environmental), not single, bottom line. Schools may help push their graduates in that direction. Already, the Yale School of Management has offered to forgive its graduates' loans if they work for B Corporations. [30]

The B Corporation Community

As of March 2010, 285 B Corporations existed in 54 industries in 27 states and the District of Columbia. Most were in California, which had 81 B Corporations, followed by Pennsylvania with 37, and New York with 20. One-third of all B Corporations were in financial or business-to-business services. Collectively, the B Corporation community generated $1.1 billion in revenues and saved more than $750,000 through discounts they offered each other. [31]

B Corporations encompassed a diverse group, including shoemaker Dansko, renewable energy contractors and lawyers, real estate management firms, banks, and tea distributor Numi Organic Tea. They ranged from older companies to relatively young entrepreneurial ventures and included both explicitly green service providers and more conventional service providers. B Corporations tended to be smaller, privately held, and incorporated in states that encouraged sustainable businesses. Several of them are profiled briefly here.

King Arthur Flour

Based in Norwich, Vermont, King Arthur Flour was 100 percent employee owned and the country's oldest flour maker, having operated continuously for more than two hundred years. It had gross sales of more than $3 million in 2009 at its flagship store and was "the number-one selling unbleached flour in every market where we have full distribution." [32] The company was committed to environmental stewardship and did not use chemical additives or genetically modified wheat in its flours. Employees could take forty paid hours each year to volunteer at nonprofit organizations, and the company donated 5 percent of profits to charities and offered free baking classes to children. The company won numerous awards for its efforts, including a 2008 *Wall Street Journal* Top Small Workplaces Award and a 2008 WorldBlu Most Democratic Workplaces Award. King Arthur Flour was a founding B Corporation, certified in June 2007. [33]

Seventh Generation

Seventh Generation had been making nontoxic, sustainability-oriented cleaning and household paper products since 1990. In 2008, the sale of its products saved more than fifty million gallons of water and one million gallons of petroleum compared with conventional products, and the company generated around $4 million in pretax profits, 10 percent of which was donated to charities.

Seventh Generation took its name from the Iroquois injunction to "consider the impact of our decisions on the next seven generations." [34]

Like King Arthur Flour, Seventh Generation was based in Vermont and became a founding B Corporation in June 2007. According to Jeffrey Hollender, "Executive Chairperson and Chief Inspired Protagonist," as well as the coauthor of *The Responsibility Revolution*, [35] "Seventh Generation decided to become a B Corporation because there needs to be standards around corporate responsibility. In a landscape in which every company now says they're a responsible business, there is no way for consumers, investors, and other stakeholders to tell real responsible businesses apart from those businesses that just say they are. The dual focus of B Corp, which involves a change to your bylaws and a comprehensive evaluation, is the best way to separate companies that really are responsible from ones that just pretend to be so." [36]

Trillium Asset Management

This Boston-based firm pioneered socially responsible investing in 1982 and in June 2008 became a B Corporation with a Composite B Score of 116.9 points. The company handled about $900 million in investments in 2009 from individuals and institutions and was "deeply committed to using the power of capital markets to move toward a sustainable economy that properly values people and planet." [37] Trillium's thirty employees included several people focused on ecological and social impact research, and all employees could benefit from generous profit sharing. In addition, Trillium purchased carbon offsets for its operations and took other steps to improve its own sustainability record.

Greenlight Apparel

Founded to combat child labor, Greenlight Apparel gave 5 percent of sales to charities that helped achieve its mission. The company garnered 76 percent of the possible BIRS points when it was certified in December 2009. Greenlight's interest was as follows: "[We] became a B Corporation because we wanted to add a third-party endorsement to our social and environmental efforts. Not only does it signify our

willingness to strive to be a better corporation by our internal measures, but also gives us an opportunity to measure our impact against our peers." [38]

The company, with headquarters in Fremont, California, began as a project for five business school students at the University of California–Davis after they observed labor conditions at apparel factories in Asia. The students assembled a business proposal that made it to the finals of the Global Social Venture Competition. Their first chance to prove their business model came when a Silicon Valley marathon race placed an order for shirts.

Deep Ecology

Deep Ecology was a scuba diving shop in Haleiwa, Hawaii, that was dedicated to protecting marine wildlife and habitats while providing divers of all levels with a great experience. Started in 1996 by Ken O'Keefe with $8,000, the shop regularly dispatched employees to pick up trash from the ocean and rescued animals trapped by debris or abandoned fishing lines and nets, so-called ghost nets. Eventually, O'Keefe realized an environmental focus could differentiate his company from other dive shops. He changed the company's name from North Shore Diving Headquarters to Deep Ecology because it would make it easier to franchise new shops "and more importantly, it reflects our unparalleled commitment to protection of the marine environment." [39] When Deep Ecology was certified as a B Corporation in December 2009, its rating was highest in the Environment category.

Conclusion

In 2010, B Corporation status was growing in importance as a reliable standard by which companies could demonstrate their commitment to social and environmental goals concurrently with their commitment to financial performance. That commitment to stakeholders, not just shareholders, was verified by the nonprofit B Lab and allowed B Corporations of all kinds to attract sustainability-conscious customers, investors, and vendors. That verification also allowed B Corporations to receive legal and technical support and various incentives to pursue their commitments over the long run.

KEY TAKEAWAYS

- When you are a small competitor challenging large incumbent firms, you must continue to innovate to differentiate your products. The innovation process requires input and creativity from a wide range of participants.
- "Failure" is another opportunity to learn and regroup; a culture that supports this view is more likely to foster institutional innovation and creativity.

EXERCISES

1. What cultural factors at Method help or hinder innovative initiatives?
2. Describe the innovation process for this new laundry detergent product introduction.
3. What is necessary to turn failure into success?
4. Imagine you are an executive who has to convince your board of directors to convert the company into a B Corporation. What would you argue? What would you expect the board to argue?

---

[1] {Author's Name Retracted as requested by the work's original creator or licensee} and Mark Meier, *Method Products: Sustainable Innovation as Entrepreneurial Strategy*, UVA-ENT-0159 (Charlottesville: Darden Business Publishing, University of Virginia, 2010).

[2] {Author's Name Retracted as requested by the work's original creator or licensee} and Mark Meier, *Method Products: Sustainable Innovation as Entrepreneurial Strategy*, UVA-ENT-0159 (Charlottesville: Darden Business Publishing, University of Virginia, 2010). All other quotations in this section not otherwise attributed come from this case study.

[3] {Author's Name Retracted as requested by the work's original creator or licensee} and Mark Meier, *Method Products: Sustainable Innovation as Entrepreneurial Strategy*, UVA-ENT-0159 (Charlottesville: Darden Business Publishing, University of Virginia, 2010).

[4] Method, "Methodology: Behind the Bottle," accessed August 24, 2010, http://www.methodhome.com/behind-the-bottle.

[5] "Adam Lowry, the Man Behind the Method (Cleaning Products)," interview by Jacob Gordon, *Treehugger Radio*, podcast audio and transcript, April 30, 2009, accessed August 24, 2010, http://www.treehugger.com/files/2009/04/th-radio-adam-lowry.php.

[6] "How Two Friends Built a $100 Million Company," *Inc.*, accessed January 11, 2011, http://www.inc.com/ss/how-two-friends-built-100-million-company.

[7] Stephanie Clifford, "Running Through the Legs of Goliath," *Inc.*, February 1, 2006, accessed January 12, 2011, http://www.inc.com/magazine/20060201/goliath.html.

[8] Jeffrey Hollender, "How I Did It: Giving Up the CEO Seat," *Harvard Business Review*, March 2010, accessed January 11, 2011, http://hbr.org/2010/03/how-i-did-it-giving-up-the-ceo-seat/ar/1; Procter & Gamble, *2009 Annual Report*, accessed January 11, 2011, http://www.pg.com/en_US/investors/financial_reporting/annual_reports.shtml.

[9] Unilever, *Annual Report and Accounts 2009*, accessed January 12, 2011, http://annualreport09.unilever.com; Colgate-Palmolive, *Colgate-Palmolive Company 2009 Annual Report*, accessed January 12, 2011, http://www.colgate.com/app/Colgate/US/Corp/Annual-Reports/2009/HomePage.cvsp; Clorox Company, "Financial Overview," accessed August 24, 2010, http://investors.thecloroxcompany.com/financials.cfm; Clorox Company, *2010 Annual Report to Shareholders and Employees*, accessed January 12, 2011, http://www.thecloroxcompany.com/investors/financialinfo/annreports/clxar10/ar10_complete.pdf; Church & Dwight, "Church & Dwight Reports 2009 Earnings per Share of $3.41," news release, February 9, 2010, accessed January 12, 2011, http://investor.churchdwight.com/phoenix.zhtml?c=110737&p=irol-newsArticle&t=Regular&id=1385342&.

[10] "How Two Friends Built a $100 Million Company," *Inc.*, accessed January 11, 2011, http://www.inc.com/ss/how-two-friends-built-100-million-company#4

[11] {Author's Name Retracted as requested by the work's original creator or licensee} and Mark Meier, *Method Products: Sustainable Innovation as Entrepreneurial Strategy*, UVA-ENT-0159 (Charlottesville: Darden Business Publishing, University of Virginia, 2010).

[12] {Author's Name Retracted as requested by the work's original creator or licensee} and Mark Meier, *Method Products: Sustainable Innovation as Entrepreneurial Strategy*, UVA-ENT-0159 (Charlottesville: Darden Business Publishing, University of Virginia, 2010).

[13] {Author's Name Retracted as requested by the work's original creator or licensee} and Mark Meier, *Method Products: Sustainable Innovation as Entrepreneurial Strategy*, UVA-ENT-0159 (Charlottesville: Darden Business Publishing, University of Virginia, 2010).

[14] Drummond Lawson, interview with author, San Francisco, January 19, 2010; unless otherwise indicated all subsequent attributions derive from this interview.

[15] Fred Holzhauer, interview with author, San Francisco, January 19, 2010; unless otherwise indicated all subsequent attributions derive from this interview.

[16] Susanna Schick, "Interview with OppGreen 2009 Speaker, Adam Lowry, Chief Greenskeeper of Method," *Opportunity Green*, November 3, 2009, accessed January 12, 2011, http://opportunitygreen.com/green-business-blog/2009/11/03/interview-with-oppgreen-2009-speaker-adam-lowry-chief-greenskeeper-of-method.

[17] On April 23, 2010, special sales excluded, Method's detergent sold on Amazon.com for about $0.31 per load, the same price as Tide with Febreze, while Seventh Generation sold for about $0.27 per load and Gain for $0.19 per load.

[18] {Author's Name Retracted as requested by the work's original creator or licensee} and Mark Meier, *Method Products: Sustainable Innovation as Entrepreneurial Strategy*, UVA-ENT-0159 (Charlottesville: Darden Business Publishing, University of Virginia, 2010).

[19] {Author's Name Retracted as requested by the work's original creator or licensee} and Mark Meier, *Method Products: Sustainable Innovation as Entrepreneurial Strategy*, UVA-ENT-0159 (Charlottesville: Darden Business Publishing, University of Virginia, 2010).

[20] {Author's Name Retracted as requested by the work's original creator or licensee} and Mark Meier, *Method Products: Sustainable Innovation as Entrepreneurial Strategy*, UVA-ENT-0159 (Charlottesville: Darden Business Publishing, University of Virginia, 2010).

[21] Greenhouse Gas Protocol Initiative, "Calculation Tools: FAQ," accessed August 24, 2010, http://www.ghgprotocol.org/calculation-tools/faq.

[22] {Author's Name Retracted as requested by the work's original creator or licensee} and Mark Meier, *Method Products: Sustainable Innovation as Entrepreneurial Strategy*, UVA-ENT-0159 (Charlottesville: Darden Business Publishing, University of Virginia, 2010).

[23] Susan Adams, "Capitalist Monkey Wrench," *Forbes*, March 25, 2010, accessed January 12, 2011, http://www.forbes.com/forbes/2010/0412/rebuilding-b-lab-corporate-citizenship-green-incorporation-mixed-motives.html; Peter Van Allen, "American Sporting Goods Buys AND1," *Philadelphia Business Journal*, May 18, 2005, accessed January 12, 2011, http://www.bizjournals.com/philadelphia/stories/2005/05/16/daily16.html.

[24] Susan Adams, "Capitalist Monkey Wrench," *Forbes*, March 25, 2010, accessed January 12, 2011, http://www.forbes.com/forbes/2010/0412/rebuilding-b-lab-corporate-citizenship-green-incorporation-mixed-motives.html; April Dembosky, "Protecting Companies that Mix Profitability, Values," *NPR Morning Edition*, March 9, 2010, accessed January 12, 2011 http://www.npr.org/templates/story/story.php?storyId=124468487; B Corporation, "About B Corp.: The Team," accessed April 18, 2010, http://www.bcorporation.net/index.cfm/nodeID/0360E845-9F78-4D71-8833-677CAC12CEF4/fuseaction/content.page.

[25] B Corporation, "Why B Corps Matter," accessed April 18, 2010, http://www.bcorporation.net/why.

[26] B Corporation, "The B Impact Rating System," accessed January 12, 2011, http://www.bcorporation.net/index.cfm/fuseaction/content.page/nodeID/f6780de0-cf1b-44a3-b8e4-195abbe68fb5; B Lab, *Large Manufacturer Impact Assessment: Version 2.0*, accessed January 12, 2011, http://www.bcorporation.net/resources/bcorp/documents/2010-B-Impact-Assessment%20%281%29.pdf; B Corporation, "Audits," accessed January 31, 2011, http://www.bcorporation.net/audits.

[27] B Corporation, *2009 B Corporation Annual Report*, 5, accessed January 12, 2011, http://www.bcorporation.net/index.cfm/fuseaction/content.page/nodeID/dec9e60f-392c-4207-8538-be73be69cf85/externalURL.

[28] Douglas Tallman, "Maryland in Line to Become B Corporations Pioneer," *Gazette.Net*, March 29, 2010, accessed January 12, 2011, http://www.gazette.net/stories/03292010/polinew175638_32561.php.

[29] "The B Corporation: A Business Model for the New Economy," *Impact Investor*, accessed January 12, 2011, http://www.theimpactinvestor.com/b-corp-model-rewrites-the-c.html; B Corporation, "Why B Corps Matter," accessed April 18, 2010, http://www.bcorporation.net/why.

[30] Carole Bass, "B School B Good," *Yale Alumni Magazine*, March 29, 2010.

[31] B Lab, "Home," accessed April 20, 2010, http://www.bcorporation.net.

[32] King Arthur Flour Company, "About the King Arthur Flour Company," accessed April 20, 2010, http://www.kingarthurflour.com/about.

[33] King Arthur Flour Company, "Good Works," accessed April 20, 2010, http://www.kingarthurflour.com/about/goodworks.html#a2; B Corporation, "King Arthur Flour," accessed January 12, 2011, http://www.bcorporation.net/kingarthurflour.

[34] Seventh Generation, *Corporate Responsibility 2.0: Our Corporate Consciousness Report, 2009*, accessed January 12, 2011, http://www.7genreport.com; Seventh Generation, "About Us: About Seventh Generation," accessed April 20, 2010, http://www.seventhgeneration.com/about?link-position=footer.

[35] Jeffrey Hollender, *The Responsibility Revolution: How the Next Generation of Businesses Will Win* (Hoboken, NJ: Jossey-Bass, 2010).

[36] B Corporation, *2009 B Corporation Annual Report*, 12, accessed January 12, 2011, http://www.bcorporation.net/index.cfm/fuseaction/content.page/nodeID/dec9e60f-392c-4207-8538-be73be69cf85/externalURL.

[37] B Corporation, "Trillium Asset Management," accessed April 18, 2010, http://www.bcorporation.net/trillium; Trillium Asset Management, "Trillium Asset Management Corporation Announces Hiring of Matthew Patsky as Its New CEO," news release, October 21, 2009, accessed January 12, 2011, http://trilliuminvest.com/news-articles-category/trillium-announces-hiring-of-matthew-patsky-as-its-new-ceo.

[38] B Corporation, "Greenlight Apparel," accessed April 18, 2010, http://www.bcorporation.net/greenlightapparel.

[39] Ken O'Keefe, "Our History," Deep Ecology, accessed April 18, 2010, http://www.oahuscubadive.com/our_history.html; B Corporation, "Deep Ecology," accessed April, 18, 2010, http://www.bcorporation.net/deepecology.

6.4 Pfizer Pharmaceuticals: Green Chemistry Innovation and Business Strategy

LEARNING OBJECTIVES

1. Examine the benefits of and barriers to a green chemistry innovation effort in the pharmaceutical industry.

2. Appreciate how health and environmental issues can be viewed as opportunities, not burdens.

3. Analyze the operating and financial benefits of green chemistry innovation.

At Pfizer, Yujie Wang reviewed the presentation she had prepared for the executive committee's strategy meeting later that afternoon. She wanted to build on the company's previous successes in green chemistry. Three of the committee members were familiar with the ideas, and she could count on their support. Four others had pushed for new ideas to be fed into their group over the last year. Depending on the strength of her argument this time, they might be persuaded to support the project. The remaining two members, who had significant responsibility for product development and operations, respectively, were somewhat less predictable. She had informed them of her progress during the project, but they seemed disinterested at best. Then again, they were busy people, and it had been hard to schedule the intermediate briefings she wanted to hold to update everyone. She knew the executives must be won over at least to a stance of "no opposition" to the proposal she would make.

Pharmaceuticals and Personal Care Products

The objective of an efficacious pharmaceutical is to make certain molecules biologically active in humans. Not surprisingly, however, the same molecules that can cause desired results can have adverse effects in the body as well

as postpatient—after the drug is expressed from the body and its active ingredients are released from disposal pipes into streams and other water bodies.

Regulations require extensive pretesting of toxins in drugs (typically conducted by subcontractors) on different aquatic and mammalian species. Some critics argue the tests are sufficient; others question how accurately those surrogate studies can predict real results. Sweden, a nation that has aggressively studied chemical impacts on health and ecological systems, actively restricts nonbenign drug manufacture and distribution, requiring labeling of environmental toxins and imposing sales caps and even bans. The European Union's 2005 Registration, Evaluation, Authorization, and Restriction of Chemicals (REACH) legislation would impose additional requirements on drug manufacturers (market size: 450 million).

According to the US Environmental Protection Agency (EPA), pharmaceuticals and personal care products (PPCPs) presented scientific concerns for the following reasons:

Large quantities of a wide spectrum of PPCPs (and their metabolites) can enter the environment following use by multitudes of individuals or domestic animals and subsequent discharge to (and incomplete removal by) sewage treatment systems. PPCP residues in treated sewage effluent (or in terrestrial runoff or directly discharged raw sewage) then enter the environment. All chemicals applied externally or ingested (and their bioactive transformation products) have the potential to be excreted or washed into sewage systems and from there discharged to the aquatic or terrestrial environments. Input to the environment is a function of the efficiency of human/animal absorption and metabolism and the efficiency of the waste treatment technologies employed—if any (sewage is sometimes discharged without treatment by storm overflow events, failure of systems, or "straight piping"). Removal efficiencies from treatment plants vary from chemical to chemical and between individual sewage treatment facilities (because of different technologies employed and because of operational fluctuations and "idiosyncrasies" of individual plants). Obviously, discharge of untreated sewage maximizes occurrence of PPCPs in the environment. No municipal sewage treatment plants are engineered for PPCP removal. The risks posed to aquatic organisms (by continual lifelong exposure) and to humans (by long-term consumption of minute quantities in drinking water) are essentially unknown. While the major concerns to date have been the promotion of pathogen resistance to antibiotics and disruption of endocrine systems by natural and synthetic sex steroids, many other PPCPs have unknown consequences. The latter are the focus of the ongoing U.S. EPA Office of Research and Development (ORD) work summarized here. [1]

Pfizer

In 2005 Pfizer employed fifteen thousand scientists and support staff in seven major labs around the world. Every weekday thirty-eight thousand sales representatives sold Pfizer products. The company's $3 billion annual advertising budget made it the fourth-largest US advertiser. In spring 2005 Pfizer was interviewing to fill the position of vice president of green chemistry. The new position reported to Dr. Kelvin Cooper, senior vice president, Worldwide Pharmaceutical Sciences, Pfizer Global R&D. The individual who would fill the position would need to examine the competitive challenges ahead, the internal progress to date, and ways to build on the Zoloft and Viagra innovation success stories in the context of a green chemistry embedded in corporate strategy. In the short run, how could the company take the lessons learned from those two cases and apply them beneficially elsewhere?

Exploring those questions had been Yujie Wang's task for the past two months. The innovations provided dramatic cost savings, and the removal of toxic materials reduced both costs and risk. Given growing global attention to corporate accountability, increased government scrutiny of pharma companies, and the fast-growing popularity of sustainable business strategy, could adoption of a green

chemistry strategy help Pfizer's reputation *and* offer growth as well as profit opportunities? In this industry, companies competed primarily on drug offerings and secondarily on process, with "maximum yield" as the main objective to maximize profitability.

Adding sustainability to the mix meant explicitly integrating human and community health as well as ecological system preservation into corporate performance. Sustainable development ideas introduced decades earlier had been transformed into business practices and were implemented through strategy by well-known global companies such as Toyota, General Electric, Walmart, Electrolux, and United Technologies. Walmart and General Electric announced sustainability as part of their core strategy in 2005. The goal was to achieve financial success concurrently with these broader objectives.

Debate on climate change and discussion of pollutants' effect on human health and the environment had raised awareness of the human influence on natural systems, and consequently financial institutions and insurance companies were paying more attention to firms' existing and future liabilities. In the face of increased scrutiny by governments and nongovernmental organizations (NGOs), firms were starting to assess their own vulnerabilities and opportunities with respect to such topics. *Sustainability* and *sustainable business* were two common terms in that discussion. Others in business used the phrase *triple bottom line*, which referred to performance across financial, social, and ecological standards, or strategy attuned to economy, equity, and environment.

According to Joanna Negri, a process chemist and manager, and a member of the company's green chemistry team, Pfizer "views sustainability and green chemistry as outcomes of good science—and this provides competitive business advantage through enhanced efficiency and safer processes." [2]

Green Chemistry at Pfizer

In 2002 Pfizer won the US Presidential Green Chemistry Award for Alternative Synthetic Pathways for its innovation of the manufacturing process for sertraline ("sir-tra-leen") hydrochloride (HCl). Sertraline HCl was the active ingredient in the pharmaceutical Zoloft. Zoloft, in 2005 the most prescribed agent of its kind, was used to treat clinical depression, a condition that struck more than twenty million US adults and cost society nearly $44 billion annually. As of February 2000, more than 115 million Zoloft prescriptions had been written in the United States; 2004 global sales grew to $3.11 billion. [3]

Applying the principles of green chemistry to the Zoloft line, Pfizer dramatically improved the commercial manufacturing process of sertraline HCl. After meticulously investigating each of the chemical steps, Pfizer implemented green chemistry technology for this complex commercial process, which required extremely pure product. As a result, Pfizer significantly improved both worker and environmental safety. The new commercial process (referred to as the "combined" process) offered dramatic pollution prevention benefits including improved safety and material handling, reduced energy and water use, and double overall product yield. [4] That success inspired green chemistry enthusiasts at Pfizer to look for other manufacturing processes to which the principles could be applied.

Complicating matters, however, was the state of the pharmaceutical industry in 2005: it was beleaguered by multiple issues affecting brand and profit margins, criticism of industry's policies on access to drugs in poorer communities, and lawsuits resulting from unexpected side effects. Could greener processes provide Pfizer an edge in this shifting landscape? Would they generate both the cost savings needed to justify the effort and the social capital that would support Pfizer's reputation, brand, and even its license to operate?

In 2001, informal conversations at a conference at the University of Massachusetts's Center for Sustainable Production had marked the beginning of Pfizer's involvement in green chemistry. While there, Dr. Berkeley Cue, then vice president of pharmaceutical sciences research at Groton Labs (reporting to Pfizer Global R&D's Cooper) was surprised to learn that some Pfizer environment and safety chemists in attendance shared his interest. Impressed by the green chemistry work of professor and chemist John Warner at University of Massachusetts, Cue believed the approach held potential for Pfizer.

During 2001 through 2004 Cue built a group at Groton, pulling in the discovery chemists from R&D to optimize products from the design stage. In talking with other R&D sites at Pfizer, the network quickly spread to the UK offices and to California's Pfizer R&D center in La Jolla. When Pfizer purchased Pharmacia in 2003, the company discovered that some of its new acquisition's R&D people were interested in green chemistry. Cue described his role as supporting a bottom-up initiative: "I brought people together in a tactical way and provided resources to give

them a strategy and a voice upwards in the organization, and out." [5]

In late 2003 a steering committee was formed to address the importance of the ideas for the corporation overall. Soon the active product ingredients (API) chemists joined in, and communication about the ideas expanded to legal and corporate affairs and R&D/manufacturing codevelopment teams. The committee communicated the message up and down the corporate hierarchy. Even the global marketing division was interested in the potential of this approach. By 2005, Pfizer had green chemistry activity in all seven of its R&D sites and had even begun to educate the federal oversight agency for the pharmaceutical industry, the Food and Drug Administration (FDA). (The FDA, with its legislative commitment to not compromise patient safety, was viewed by many as a demanding taskmaster that could dictate significant green chemistry changes to production that, although beneficial, would require long approval time frames.)

E-Factors and Atom Economy

Green chemistry is the design of chemical products or processes that eliminates or reduces the use and generation of hazardous substances. The application of green chemistry principles provided a road map that enabled designers to use more benign and efficient methods.

The industry used an assessment tool called E-factor to evaluate all major products. E-factor was defined in this industry as the ratio of total kilograms of all materials (raw materials, solvents, and processing chemicals) used per kilogram of API produced. Firms were identifying drivers of high E-factor values and taking actions to improve efficiency.

A pivotal 1994 study indicated that for every kilogram of API produced, between twenty-five and one hundred kilograms or more of waste was generated as standard practice in the pharmaceutical industry, a figure that was still common to the industry in 2005. Multiplying the E-factor by the estimate of kilograms of API produced by the industry overall suggested that for the year 2003 as much as 500 million to 2.5 billion kilograms of waste could be the by-product of pharma API manufacture. That waste represented a double penalty: costs associated with purchasing chemicals that are diverted from API yield and costs associated with disposing of that waste (ranging from $1 to $5 per kilogram). Very little information was released by industry competitors, but a published 2004 GlaxoSmithKline life-cycle assessment of its API manufacturing processes revealed that 75–80 percent of the waste produced was solvent (liquid) and 20–25 percent solid, of which a considerable proportion was likely hazardous under state and federal law.

For years pharma had said it did not produce significant enough product volumes to be concerned about toxicity and waste, particularly relative to commodity chemical producers. But with the competitive circumstances changing, companies were eager to find ways to cut costs, eliminate risk, and improve their image. After implementing its award-winning process as standard in sertraline manufacture, Pfizer's experience suggested the results of green chemistry–guided process changes brought E-factor ratios down to ten to twenty kilograms. The potential to dramatically reduce E-factors through "benign by design" principles could, indeed, be significant. Eli Lilly, Roche, and Bristol-Meyers Squibb—all winners of a Presidential Green Chemistry Award between 1999 and 2004—reported improvements of this magnitude after green chemistry principles had been applied.

Predictably, green chemistry also fit with Six Sigma, the principles of which considered waste a process defect. "Right the first time" was an industry initiative that the FDA backed strongly. Groton's Cue viewed green chemistry as a lens that allowed the company to look at processes and yield objectives in a more comprehensive way, with quality programs dovetailing easily with this approach.

Pfizer Company Background

Pfizer Inc., the world's largest drug company, was created in 1849 by Charles Pfizer and his cousin Charles Erhart in Brooklyn, New York. The company began its climb to the top of the industry in 1941, when it was asked to mass-produce penicillin for the war effort. In the 1950s, the company opened branches in Belgium, Canada, Cuba, Mexico, and the United Kingdom and began manufacturing in Asia, Europe, and South America. Pfizer expanded its research and development, introducing a range of drugs and acquiring consumer products such as Bengay and Desitin, and by the mid-1960s, Pfizer's annual worldwide sales had grown to $500 million. Pfizer engaged in the discovery, development, manufacturing, and marketing of prescription medicines, as well as over-the-counter products, for humans and animals. In 2003, 88 percent of Pfizer's revenue was generated from the human pharmaceuticals market, 6.5 percent from consumer health-care products, and 4 percent from animal health products. [6] Pfizer was traded on the New York Stock Exchange as ticker PFE. Its major competitors included Merck & Co. of Germany and Johnson & Johnson, GlaxoSmithKline Plc, and Novartis, all in the United States. [7]

Throughout the world, more than one billion prescriptions were written for Pfizer products in 2003. [8] In 2004, fourteen of Pfizer's drugs were top sellers in their therapeutic categories, including Zoloft, erectile dysfunction therapy Viagra, pain management medication Celebrex, and cholesterol-lowering drug Lipitor. [9] The company's many over-the-counter remedies included Benadryl and Sudafed. Subsidiaries in the Pfizer pharmaceutical group included Warner-Lambert, Parke-Davis, and Goedecke. In 2000, Pfizer merged with Warner-Lambert, making the company one of the top five drugmakers in the world. Pfizer then acquired pharmaceuticals company Pharmacia in 2003, making it the largest drug company in the world. This acquisition allowed Pfizer to diversify its product line because Pharmacia owned a range of therapeutic products in new areas, such as oncology, endocrinology, and ophthalmology. [10] The merger, which cost Pfizer $54 billion, also greatly expanded its pipeline through Pharmacia's research in atherosclerosis, diabetes, osteoporosis, breast cancer, neuropathic pain, epilepsy, anxiety disorders, and Parkinson's disease. By 2004, Pfizer had locations in 80 countries and sold products in 150 countries. In 2003, Pfizer also began selling some of its nonpharmaceutical businesses, such as the Adams confectionary unit (to Cadbury Schweppes) and Schick-Wilkenson Sword shaving products (to Energizer Holdings). [11] Pfizer was headquartered in New York and in 2005 had four subsidiaries involved in pharmaceuticals, consumer health care, and animal health care. Three subsidiaries conducted their business under the Pfizer company name, the fourth as Agouron Pharmaceuticals.

Pfizer posted total revenues for 2003 at $45.2 billion worldwide, an increase of 40 percent from 2002, and net income of $3.9 billion. While the company's largest market was in the United States, Pfizer's international market grew 56 percent in 2003, to revenues of $18 billion. According to Karen Katen, executive vice president of the company and president of Pfizer Global Pharmaceuticals, "[Pfizer's] portfolio of leading medicines, which spanned most major therapeutic categories, drove Pfizer's strong revenue growth in the fourth quarter and full-year 2003." [12] In fall 2004 Pfizer appeared well positioned for continued industry leadership and projected strong financial performance. The company had a target of $54 billion for its 2004 revenue and planned to spend about $7.9 billion in R&D during 2004. [13] "In the dynamic environment of today's worldwide pharmaceutical industry," said David Shedlarz, executive vice president and chief financial officer, "Pfizer is uniquely well-positioned to sustain our strong and balanced performance, leverage past and future opportunities, reinforce and extend our differentiation from others in the industry, and exploit both our operational flexibility and our proven abilities to execute." [14]

Industry Challenges

But despite Pfizer's optimism and past financial success, by early 2005 the entire pharmaceuticals industry was suffering from a devastating lack of customer trust. From 1990 to 2004, the industry experienced a series of well-publicized criticisms. Most contentious among these critiques was the accessibility of AIDS drugs to patients in southern Africa. Analysts such as Merrill Goozner, former chief economics correspondent for the *Chicago Tribune*, suggested in 1999 that private pharmaceutical companies contributed to the global AIDS crisis by claiming that lowering the price of drugs or easing patent protection for manufacturers in third-world countries would "stifle innovation." [15] In 2004 products from a flu vaccine production plant in the United Kingdom, critical to the US supply, were blocked due to health and safety concerns. The same year, New York Attorney General Elliot Spitzer filed suit against pharma giant GlaxoSmithKline, saying that the company concealed important information about the safety and efficacy of Paxil, an antidepressant drug. Adding to the controversy surrounding the pharmaceutical industry, popular filmmaker Michael Moore announced plans in 2005 to create a documentary called *Sicko*, which would use interviews with physicians, patients, and members of Congress to expose an industry that Moore claimed "benefits the few at the expense of the many." [16]

A poll conducted in December 2004 showed that Americans held pharmaceutical companies at the same low esteem as tobacco companies. [17] The pressure on Pfizer grew in late 2004 when prescriptions for its Celebrex pain relief and arthritis drug fell 56 percent in December following the company's announcement that the drug was linked to cardiovascular risk (heart attacks and strokes), a problem similar to Merck & Co.'s with its billion-dollar blockbuster drug Vioxx. (Merck, which was suspected of concealing Vioxx's potentially lethal side effects to maintain sales, had withdrawn the drug from the market in September 2004, undermining both public confidence in the pharma industry and the regulatory oversight of the US Food and Drug Administration.) [18] Pfizer ceased advertising Celebrex. In December 2004, the S&P 500 Pharmaceutical Subindustry Index was down 12.8 percent for the year, though the S&P 500 was up 6.8 percent.

The pharmaceutical industry was a high-risk, high-reward business. Consumers demanded lifesaving drug discoveries

that were safe and affordable. In the United States, drug patents only lasted for five to ten years, so pharmaceutical companies were constantly threatened by generic competition. In 2004, it cost an estimated $897 million to develop and test a new medicine; about 95 percent of chemical formulas failed during this process. In 2002, the FDA approved only seventeen new drugs, the lowest number since 1983. In an attempt to boost innovation, pharmaceutical R&D skyrocketed, with Pfizer investing $7 billion on R&D in 2003, leading the industry by a margin of several billion. [19]

In 2005, Pfizer managed the world's largest private pharmaceutical research effort, with more than thirteen thousand scientists worldwide. That tremendous investment, however, was not translating into drug output, which had been spiraling downward since 1996. In January 2005, Pfizer had 130 new molecules in its pipeline of new medicines, along with 95 projects to expand the use of therapies currently offered. [20] To meet its 2005 goal of double-digit growth of annual revenues, Pfizer planned to file applications for twenty new drugs before 2010. [21] Analysts viewed that unprecedented growth rate skeptically, saying that Pfizer had only seven drugs in the FDA testing phases.

From 1993 to 2003, Pfizer spent about $2 billion on drugs that failed in advanced human testing or were pulled off the market due to problems such as liver toxicity. Thus Pfizer decided in 2005 to shift its R&D focus to analyzing past failed drug experiments to find patterns that might help detect toxicity earlier in the expensive testing process.

From 1995 to 2005, pharma companies invested significant R&D funding into genomics experiments, which were very expensive and yielded less-than-revolutionary results. After a decade of investments in high-powered genomic tools, pharmaceutical companies were in their most prolonged and painful dry spell in years. "Genomics is not the savior of the industry. The renaissance is in chemistry," said Rod MacKenzie, Pfizer's vice president of discovery research in Ann Arbor, Michigan. [22]

Brand Protection

To counteract a growing reputation that Pfizer was unwilling to engage with certain NGOs, Pfizer was one of the earliest US signers of the voluntary UN Global Compact, which defined principles for corporate behavior including human rights, labor, and the environment. The UN Global Compact was designed to open dialogue among business, governments, NGOs, and society at large. The compact requires use of the precautionary principle, a guide to company decision making that assumed a "lack of full scientific certainty shall not be used as a reason for postponing cost-effective measures to prevent environmental degradation." [23] A study in 2003 by the International Institute for Management Development in Geneva found that stakeholders expect more social responsibility from the pharmaceutical sector than from any other industry. Pfizer transformed its quarterly financial report into a "performance report," which included updates on corporate citizenship. [24] The company was rated in the *Chronicle of Philanthropy* as "the world's most generous company." [25]

In the pharmaceuticals industry, innovation can be stifled by the complexity of global business, science, government, religion, and public response, all colliding over issues of life and death. AIDS was driving high demand for more breakthrough medicines but at an affordable price. "We have learned that no single entity—whether business, government, or NGO—can alone bridge the deep divides between poverty and affluence, health and disease, growth and stagnation. As the world's foremost pharmaceutical company, we have an important obligation to take a global leadership role," Pfizer chairman Hank McKinnell commented. [26]

In 2000, Pfizer conducted focus groups at several Pfizer locations around the world to create a new mission. First it was decided that Pfizer would measure itself on a combination of financial and nonfinancial measures, reflecting stakeholders' changing expectations of business. Second, Pfizer would no longer measure itself solely against others in the pharmaceuticals industry but against all other companies in all industries. The new mission statement was as follows: "We will become the world's most valued company to patients, customers, colleagues, investors, business partners and to the communities where we live. This is our shared promise to ourselves and to the people we serve. Pfizer's purpose is to dedicate ourselves to humanity's quest for longer, healthier, happier lives through innovation in pharmaceutical, consumer and animal health products." [27]

Pfizer stated that it measured progress as putting people and communities first, operating ethically, being sensitive to the needs of its colleagues, and preserving and protecting the environment.

In 2002, Pfizer donated $447 million to programs like its Diflucan Partnership Program, which provides health-care training and free medicine to treat HIV/AIDS-related infections to patients in Africa, Haiti, and Cambodia. That year Pfizer also held an internal symposium on green chemistry, a design approach that continued to drive manufacturing toward more benign material use.

In 2003, Pfizer became a member of the World Business Council for Sustainable Development, the International Business Leaders Forum, and Business for Social Responsibility, organizations that provide resources to firms to promote sustainable business practices internationally, sometimes referred to as triple-bottom-line performance (economy, environment, equity). Pfizer set a company goal for 2007 to reduce carbon dioxide emissions by 35 percent per million dollars of sales and, by 2010, to supply 35 percent of global energy needs through cleaner sources. Pfizer is a member of the EPA's Climate Leaders Program, a voluntary industry-government partnership. Pfizer was again included in the Dow Jones Sustainability Asset Management Index, a global index that tracks the performance of leading companies not only in economic terms but also against environmental and social standards.

Zoloft

Zoloft was released in 1992 and was approved for six mood and anxiety disorders, including depression, panic disorder, obsessive-compulsive disorder (OCD) in adults and children, post-traumatic stress disorder (PTSD), premenstrual dysphoric disorder (PMDD), and social anxiety disorder (SAD). [28] Zoloft was the most prescribed depression medication, with more than 115 million Zoloft prescriptions written in the United States in the drug's first seven years on the market. [29] According to Pfizer's 2003 filings, Zoloft brought in $3.1 million in worldwide revenue, with $2.5 million coming from the US market. Those revenues showed an increase of 16 percent worldwide, 14 percent in the United States, and 23 percent internationally during the fourth quarter of 2003 compared to the same period of the previous year. [30] Zoloft sales comprised approximately 9 percent of Pfizer's total US sales in 2003, second only in sales percentage to Lipitor.

In 2002, Pfizer was awarded the Green Chemistry Award for Alternative Synthetic Pathways. Pfizer received the award for its development of the sertraline process, an innovative process for deriving Zoloft, for which sertraline is the active ingredient. Since developing the new process in 1998, Pfizer successfully implemented it as the standard in sertraline manufacture. To make Zoloft, a pure output of sertraline must be isolated from a reaction that occurs in solvent (or in a combination of solvents). The "combined" process of isolating sertraline was the third redesign of the commercial chemical process since its invention in 1985. [31] Each of those redesigned reactions decreased the number of solvents used, thus simplifying both the process (through energy required and worker-safety precautions) and the resulting waste disposal. The traditional process used titanium tetrachloride, a liquid compound that was toxic, corrosive, and air sensitive (meaning it formed hydrochloric acid when it came in contact with air). [32] Titanium tetrachloride was used in one phase of the process to eliminate water, which reversed the desired reaction if it remained in the mix. In the process of "dehydrating" this step of the reaction, the titanium tetrachloride reacted to produce heat, hydrochloric acid, titanium oxychloride, and titanium dioxide. Those by-products were carefully recovered and disposed, which required an additional process (energy), inputs (washes and neutralizers), and costs (waste disposal). The new process blended the two starting materials in the benign solvent ethanol and relied on the regular solubility properties of the product to control the reaction. By completely eliminating the use of titanium tetrachloride, the "combined" process removed the hazards to workers and the environment associated with transport, handling, and disposal of titanium wastes. [33] Using ethanol as the solvent also significantly reduced the use of one of the starting materials, methyl methacrylate, and allowed this material to be recycled back into the process, increasing efficiency.

Another accomplishment of the new process was discovering a more selective catalyst. The original catalyst caused a reaction that created unwanted by-products. Removing these impurities required a large volume of solvent as well as substantial energy. Also, portions of the desired end product were lost during the purification process, decreasing overall yield. The new, more selective catalyst produced lower levels of impurities, which in turn had the effect of requiring less of the reactant (mandelic acid) for the next and final reaction in the process. Finally, the new catalyst was recovered and recycled, providing additional efficiency.

By redesigning the chemical process to be more efficient and produce less harmful or expensive waste products, the "combined" process of producing sertraline provided both economic and environmental/health benefits. Typically 20 percent of the wholesale price was manufacturing costs, of which approximately 20 percent was the cost of the tablet or capsule with the remaining percentage representing all other materials, energy, water, and processing costs. With generics on the horizon, achieving materials and processing cost reductions could prove a decisive capability differentiator.

Subsequent to receipt of the green chemistry award, Pfizer realized an even more efficient process driven off the earlier

successes. The starting material for sertraline, called tetralone, contained an equal mixture of two components. One produces sertraline and the other a by-product that must be removed, resulting in a process that is only half as productive. Using a cutting-edge separation technology called multiple-column chromatography (MCC), Pfizer scientists were able to fractionate the starting material into the pure component that results in sertraline. The other component can be recycled back to the original 1:1 mixture, which could be now mixed with virgin starting material and resubjected to MCC separation. This new process was reviewed and approved for use by the FDA. The net result was twice as much sertraline produced from a unit of starting material. Half the manufacturing plant capacity was required per unit of sertraline produced.

A Depressing Decree from the United Kingdom

In December 2003, the Medicines and Healthcare Products Regulatory Agency (MHRA) of the United Kingdom included Zoloft (sold in the United Kingdom as Lustral) on a list of antidepressants banned from use for the treatment of children and teenagers younger than age eighteen. [34] The safety and efficacy of the drugs was in question, a query brought to the attention of UK health officials after high rates of suicide were observed in patients taking certain antidepressants. Of the major antidepressants, only Eli Lilly's Prozac is currently permitted for use in treating UK children. [35] Pfizer immediately released a statement disagreeing with the findings of the MHRA, claiming that its "controlled clinical-trial data in pediatric and adolescent depression shows no statistically significant association between use of Zoloft and either suicidal ideation or suicidal behavior in depressed pediatric and adolescent populations." [36] After reviewing Pfizer's studies of Zoloft in pediatric populations, the FDA's office of pediatric therapeutics concluded in 2003 that there were no safety signals calling for FDA action beyond ongoing monitoring of adverse events. [37]

Conclusion

Market and industry turbulence was standard for pharma decision makers, but the confluence of regulation; distrust; technology improvement, medical, and ecological studies; costly company errors; economic decline; and prohibitive R&D investment requirements made the decision circumstances particularly constrained in 2005. What could green chemistry offer within that context, if anything? Yujie Wang made last-minute changes to her priority list of recommendations and saved the slide presentation to a Zip drive. It was time to head down the hall to the executive

committee meeting and try to convince the audience of the
value of green chemistry going forward.

KEY TAKEAWAY

- Green chemistry represents an opportunity for the pharmaceutical industry, which is relatively inefficient in its use of energy and materials, to find cost savings and stimulate innovation.

EXERCISES

1. How and why did this process innovation happen?
2. Estimate the potential savings (in dollars) of applying green chemistry innovations to Zoloft. Use information from the case (Zoloft sales, sales price per dose, average dose, waste disposal costs) and make reasonable assumptions if needed to determine your calculation. Be prepared to present your analysis to the class. What are the potential savings if this practice is implemented more broadly?
3. What drivers are in play with respect to green chemistry, inside and outside Pfizer?
4. Can you identify strategic opportunities for Pfizer? On what contingencies do they depend?
5. How would you define the responsibilities of Pfizer's new vice president? What priorities need attention first?

[1] US Environmental Protection Agency, "PPCPs: Frequent Questions," accessed January 12, 2011, http://www.epa.gov/ppcp/faq.html.

[2] Alia Anderson, {Author's Name Retracted as requested by the work's original creator or licensee}, and Karen O'Brien, *Pfizer Pharmaceuticals: Green Chemistry Innovation and Business Strategy*, UVA-ENT-0088 (Charlottesville: Darden Business Publishing, University of Virginia, January 22, 2007). Unless otherwise noted, other quotations in this section come from this case.

[3] Patrick Clinton and Mark Mozeson, "Pharm Exec 50," *PharmExec*, May 2010, accessed January 12, 2011, http://pharmexec.findpharma.com/pharmexec/data/articlestandard//pharmexec/222010/671415/article.pdf.

[4] US Environmental Protection Agency, "2002 Greener Synthetic Pathways Award," accessed January 31, 2011, http://www.epa.gov/gcc/pubs/pgcc/winners/gspa02.html.

[5] Alia Anderson, {Author's Name Retracted as requested by the work's original creator or licensee}, and Karen O'Brien, *Pfizer Pharmaceuticals: Green Chemistry Innovation and Business Strategy*, UVA-ENT-0088 (Charlottesville: Darden Business Publishing, University of Virginia, January 22, 2007).

[6] Pfizer, *8K Filing and 2003 Performance Report*, Exhibit 99, January 22, 2004.

[7] Business and Company Resource Center, Pharmaceuticals Industry Snapshot, 2002.

[8] Pfizer, *8K Filing and 2003 Performance Report*, Exhibit 99, January 22, 2004.

[9] Business and Company Resource Center, Pharmaceuticals Industry Snapshot, 2002.

[10] Business and Company Resource Center, Pharmaceuticals Industry Snapshot, 2002.

[11] Business and Company Resource Center, Pharmaceuticals Industry Snapshot, 2002.

[12] Alia Anderson, {Author's Name Retracted as requested by the work's original creator or licensee}, and Karen O'Brien, *Pfizer Pharmaceuticals: Green Chemistry Innovation and Business Strategy*, UVA-ENT-0088 (Charlottesville: Darden Business Publishing, University of Virginia, January 22, 2007).

[13] Pfizer, *8K Filing and 2003 Performance Report*, Exhibit 99, January 22, 2004.

[14] Pfizer, *8K Filing and 2003 Performance Report*, Exhibit 99, January 22, 2004.

[15] Merrill Goozner, "Third World Battles for AIDS Drugs," *Chicago Tribune*, April 28, 1999, accessed January 12, 2011, http://articles.chicagotribune.com/1999-04-28/news/9904280067_1_compulsory-licensing-south-africa-aids-drugs.

[16] Alissa Simon, quoted in BBC News, "Press Views: Michael Moore's *Sicko*," May 19, 2007, accessed January 31, 2011, http://news.bbc.co.uk/2/hi/6673039.stm.

[17] Marcia Angell, "Big Pharma Is a Two-Faced Friend," *Financial Times* (London), July 19, 2004, accessed January 12, 2011, http://www.globalaging.org/health/us/2004/pharma.htm.

[18] Theresa Agovino, "Pharmaceutical Industry Limps into 2005," *Boston Globe*, December 19, 2004, accessed January 31, 2011, http://www.boston.com/business/year_in_review/2004/articles/pharmaceutical_industry_limps_into_2005.

[19] David Rotman, "Can Pfizer Deliver?" *Technology Review*, February 2004, accessed January 12, 2011, http://www.techreview.com/biomedicine/13462/?mod=related.

[20] Nancy Nielson, "Pfizer, A New Mission in Action," in *Learning to Talk: Corporate Citizenship and the Development of the U.N. Global Compact* (Sheffield, UK: Greenleaf, 2004), 242–55.

[21] Nancy Nielson, "Pfizer, A New Mission in Action," in *Learning to Talk: Corporate Citizenship and the Development of the U.N. Global Compact* (Sheffield, UK: Greenleaf, 2004), 242–55.

[22] Alia Anderson, {Author's Name Retracted as requested by the work's original creator or licensee}, and Karen O'Brien, *Pfizer Pharmaceuticals: Green Chemistry Innovation and Business Strategy*, UVA-ENT-0088 (Charlottesville: Darden Business Publishing, University of Virginia, January 22, 2007).

[23] United Nations, *Report of the United Nations Conference on Environment and Development: Rio de Janeiro, 3–14 June 1992*, August 12, 1992, accessed January 12, 2011, http://www.un.org/documents/ga/conf151/aconf15126-1annex1.htm.

[24] Nancy Nielson, "Pfizer, A New Mission in Action," in *Learning to Talk: Corporate Citizenship and the Development of the U.N. Global Compact* (Sheffield, UK: Greenleaf, 2004), 242–55.

[25] Alia Anderson, {Author's Name Retracted as requested by the work's original creator or licensee}, and Karen O'Brien, *Pfizer Pharmaceuticals: Green Chemistry Innovation and Business Strategy*, UVA-ENT-0088 (Charlottesville: Darden Business Publishing, University of Virginia, January 22, 2007).

[26] Pfizer, *Medicines to Change the World: 2003 Annual Review*, accessed January 12, 2011, http://www.pfizer.nl/sites/nl/wiezijnwij/Documents/annualreportpfizer2003.pdf.

[27] Alia Anderson, {Author's Name Retracted as requested by the work's original creator or licensee}, and Karen O'Brien, *Pfizer Pharmaceuticals: Green Chemistry Innovation and Business Strategy*, UVA-ENT-0088 (Charlottesville: Darden Business Publishing, University of Virginia, January 22, 2007).

[28] Pfizer, *Medicines to Change the World: 2003 Annual Review*, accessed January 12, 2011,
http://www.pfizer.nl/sites/nl/wieziinwij/Documents/annualreportpfizer2003.pdf.
[29] US Environmental Protection Agency, "2002 Greener Synthetic Pathways Award: Pfizer, Inc.," accessed January 12, 2011,
http://www.epa.gov/greenchemistry/pubs/pgcc/winners/gspa02.html
[30] Pfizer, *8K Filing and 2003 Performance Report*, Exhibit 99, January 22, 2004.
[31] US Environmental Protection Agency, "2002 Greener Synthetic Pathways Award: Pfizer, Inc.," accessed January 31, 2011,
http://www.epa.gov/greenchemistry/pubs/pgcc/winners/gspa02.html.
[32] US Environmental Protection Agency, "2002 Greener Synthetic Pathways Award: Pfizer, Inc.," accessed January 31, 2011,
http://www.epa.gov/greenchemistry/pubs/pgcc/winners/gspa02.html.
[33] US Environmental Protection Agency, "2002 Greener Synthetic Pathways Award: Pfizer, Inc.," accessed January 31, 2011,
http://www.epa.gov/greenchemistry/pubs/pgcc/winners/gspa02.html.
[34] "UK Set to Ban Antidepressants for Children," *AFX International Focus*, December 10, 2003.
[35] "UK Set to Ban Antidepressants for Children," *AFX International Focus*, December 10, 2003.
[36] Pfizer, *8K Filing and 2003 Performance Report*, Exhibit 99, January 22, 2004.
[37] Pfizer, *8K Filing and 2003 Performance Report*, Exhibit 99, January 22, 2004.

NOTES:

Chapter 7:

Buildings

7.1 Project Frog: Sustainability and Innovation in Building Design

LEARNING OBJECTIVES

1. Evaluate opportunities and challenges for sustainability innovation within the modular building market.

2. Analyze the value of collaborations for innovation.

3. Examine the stages of growth for a start-up firm active in the sustainability space.

Introduction

Project Frog was an innovative designer of kits to rapidly build energy-efficient, greener, healthier, and affordable buildings. The company was transitioning from start-up to the next phase of growth just as the 2008–10 economic recession brought virtually all new building construction to a halt across the United States. Conditions forced the company to rethink strategy, conserve cash, and further refine its product and its processes. The company's Crissy Field project, completed in early 2010, provided a critically important demonstration of the company's designs, and as the economy began to turn around in 2010, geographic expansion and new markets segments—possibly government, retail, and health care—were planned. Architect, designer, and founder Mark Miller; president Adam Tibbs; and new CEO Ann Hand also hoped to meet more aggressive margin targets that would enable the company to triple revenue and be profitable early in 2011, only five years after start-up. **Venture capital** funding from RockPort Capital Partners and investor exit expectations required rapid ramping up of projects in the short run. Miller summarized the overlap of Project Frog's products and lead venture capital investor's interests: "Their vision for energy and resource efficiency and innovative products is perfectly aligned with the Project Frog approach: to be better, greener, faster and cheaper." [1]

In late spring 2010, having just moved from an operating role to a board position, Miller was focused on strategic concerns and how best to explain and sell his product to a broader range of buyers, including the military and potentially disaster-relief agencies. The Project Frog office, a short walk from San Francisco's Embarcadero district, was informal and open. Although Miller occupied the only office with a door, it was bounded by two glass walls and a clear acrylic panel he used as a whiteboard. He could often be found crisscrossing the office or standing at someone's workstation or at the table where Tibbs sat. Meanwhile, new CEO Ann Hand had set up her computer, sharing the long table with Tibbs. She sought to translate her experience at BP as senior vice president of global marketing and innovation into a strategy for Project Frog to build its brand and scale up. The senior team saw huge potential in Project Frog, but they had many decisions to make and priorities to set. Most important, they wanted to ensure Project Frog met key business goals as they focused on preparing to give the venture capital investors a successful exit in just a few years, either taking the company public or finding a buyer.

History

Mark Miller was no stranger to new design and enterprises in architecture. He graduated from Haverford College in 1984 and earned his master's in architecture and a prestigious Keasbey Fellowship at Cambridge University. He went to Kuala Lumpur as a Henry Luce Scholar, helping design refugee camps among other projects and deepening his strong interest in the relationship between culture and architecture. He also was certified by the American Institute of Architects. Miller later served as director of corporate and technology projects and director of the Asia Projects Group for the firm Kaplan McLaughlin Diaz in San Francisco, where his portfolio included Euro Disney. In 2000, he used $50,000 in personal savings to start MKThink, a design and architecture firm in San Francisco focused on innovative architectural design. Staff that included anthropologists conducted careful human behavior research to understand what people in work spaces truly need for high productivity and high performance. MKThink designed advanced offices and campuses for Sun Microsystems and General Electric's Warren Tech Center in Michigan and worked extensively with Stanford University on several projects, including a dozen at the law school, work for the education and engineering schools, and the business school's relocation analysis.

Around 2000, Miller began to think seriously about the education market and temporary or portable classrooms, the trailers that frequently begin as stopgaps and become permanent features of many schools despite their unhealthy interior environments and energy inefficiency. Miller said, "Design should speak to the issues of the day, and technology needs to enable the human condition, not dominate it. So what are the issues of today? Well, we've got a problem: 35% of the kids in the state of California go to school in out-of-date trailers. That's an issue of the day. It's how do you educate kids in public schools and what are their facilities like in solving that systematically? We have the technology, we have the knowledge. We can solve this." [2]

Solutions oriented, Miller saw an opportunity to meet the challenge. While relatively cheap, how well did existing buildings address how students learn and what teachers need to be high-performing instructors? How could technology and design come together to create healthier schools while addressing the desperate need for more classrooms as well as rising and more volatile energy costs? Why accept existing answers? Smart buildings were emerging as alternatives. Estimates were that school overcrowding and insufficient tax revenues to government to pay for new school facilities would continue to force public school students into trailer classrooms, and this was not just California's problem.

MKThink had always had a research component that enabled it to consider problems in its field, write half a dozen white papers a year, and present at conferences. By 2004, that research focused on the problem of unhealthy learning environments for children's education. After all, 60 percent of the firm's work was related to education. The group knew it had a solution, but not yet a new company, when it devised the basic idea for modular buildings that would be better places for kids to learn and more energy efficient. "I'm making a product that makes a system that becomes a kit. You could call it Lego and Tinker Toys on steroids," Miller said. Witnessing the devastation and aftermath of the 2004 Indonesian tsunami and Hurricane Katrina in 2005 in the United States confirmed for Miller that better buildings also needed to be constructed quickly. "That was the birth of Frog"—Flexible Response to Ongoing Growth—Miller told *GreenerBuildings* magazine. "Frogs are green. They only jump forward and—one of my favorites—each frog is a prince with the message, 'Do not be afraid of what's not familiar.' Because if you embrace it, it is a prince." [3]

By late 2005, Miller had decided to form a new company with two MKThink partners and two others, an industrial designer and a metal fabricator with a strong record of working well together. Together with angel investors, family and friends initially contributed $1.2 million to launch Project Frog in 2006. Their driving mantra was "better, greener, faster, cheaper." Their mission was to "provide global impact and market leadership in green building products and systems." Miller emphasized what Project Frog was not: "We are not a construction company. We are not about better trailers."

The metal fabricator, Bakir Begovic, became board vice chairman for Project Frog. He received his BS in mechanical, industrial, and manufacturing engineering from California Polytechnic State University in 1996. He had previous experience in various high-tech firms. Begovic was founding principal of B&H Engineering, a semiconductor manufacturing and technology firm with an emphasis on metal fabrication, manufacture, and assembly. He was also chair of the board of directors for Acteron, a coating company.

Indeed, Project Frog needed such architectural and high-tech manufacturing expertise because it hoped to combine and optimize the best of modular and traditional construction—cheap and mass-manufactured and also energy efficient and conducive to occupant comfort and productivity. To achieve all these results, Project Frog needed to innovate. Since 1947, productivity in manufacturing in the United States had increased sevenfold. In construction, in contrast, productivity had actually declined slightly. If Project Frog could harness the efficiency of manufacturing and bring it into the field of construction, the company could radically outperform the industry, which was used to margins of only a few percent. Instead of conceiving of a classroom as the culmination of a long, unique construction process involving myriad players, Miller conceived of it as a "technology-infused product," likening it to an iPhone, that could be produced from standardized parts and plans on a large scale in a variety of locations. Project Frog would thereby consolidate many tasks that were normally parceled among architects, engineers, and contractors, making the process more efficient and hence cheaper for the consumer and more profitable for Project Frog. In some sense, buying a Project Frog building was like purchasing a PC kit or an IKEA bookshelf: a lot of thought went into designing and configuring the components, but it was up to the end user to assemble them or hire someone who could.

The company's buildings, erected from standardized kits it designed and contractors assembled, would require less energy and materials to build and to operate. They offered spacious layouts designed to aid user productivity, health, and comfort. Units offered abundant natural light, state-of-the-art clean air systems, high-performance heating, ventilation, and air-conditioning (HVAC) systems, customized microclimate controls, and excellent acoustic performance. They also could be built faster because they did not require a new architectural design, engineering analysis, lengthy approval processes each time, nor did they require as much work and coordination of supplies from contractors. Project Frog modules also used recycled material, from steel beams to carpets and tiles, and were designed to support green "living" roofs and solar panels. Finally, more efficient design meant fewer machines and less labor were needed to assemble a building with fewer materials wasted. The net impact could be significant: even though construction was about 5 percent of the US economy, buildings accounted for about 40 percent of energy use and produced about two-thirds of landfill waste.

Sophisticated design and modeling software enabled this reconceptualization from construction process to manufactured product. Project Frog's engineering designers began with SolidWorks, software used to design products as diverse as airplanes and cell phones. The designers infused into their plans and predictive performance models data about the actual environmental performance of building materials—data that were regularly updated with measurements from new buildings. This design and analysis became the core of Project Frog's competence and intellectual property, which was the subject of several patent applications. The company also consulted Loisos+Ubbelohde, based in nearby Alameda, California, to help develop the energy modeling for its initial Project Frog kit system. That energy firm had previously worked on the Gap's headquarters in New York and Apple's Fifth Avenue store. [4] George Loisos and Susan Ubbelohde had directed significant government and university research programs on building energy use and efficiency, and their collaboration was a significant addition to the Frog design team.

Better control of manufacturing allowed Project Frog to use a set of basic parts with minor modifications to produce an array of products. Project Frog chose, however, to outsource the actual fabrication to others instead of having to build its own capacity. Project Frog sought partners to supply the steel structure, glass panels, curtain walls, ceilings, and finishing, such as external siding or carpets. A reporter for *Forbes* magazine described the result: "They snap together for a not bad look, as if a bunch of Swedish designers got hold of a really big Erector set." [5]

Miller chose to focus on the educational market in the early days of the company. Education is the largest segment of the $400 billion construction market, accounting for about one-fourth of both the traditional and modular market. Furthermore, few people are involved in making the decisions relative to the size of the project, schools generally desire to go green and efficient, and they don't have a lot of money but often need buildings quickly. Educational institutions have long needed to add or subtract space rapidly as schools and communities change. California had issued bonds at various times since 2002 to raise money to construct new schools to keep pace with its population. Compounding that growth, California was trying to reduce its average class size, requiring even more space. Hence when funding was available, construction could easily fall behind demand. Miller had seen Frog's previous portable, temporary choices.

Schools would also save time on design because they would choose from a limited number of prefabricated choices and configure and combine them as needed. Project Frog's designs were precertified in California by the Division of the State Architect, saving about six months on permitting individual projects. (The Division of the State Architect oversaw the design and construction of K−12 schools and community colleges and also developed and maintained building codes.) The State Allocation Board Office of Public School Construction noted that it took two to four years to design, build, and inhabit an average school for two thousand students, while portable classrooms took nine to fifteen months to plan and inhabit. Finally, students learned better when indoor air and light quality were better, thus schools had often been proponents of green construction.

Studies from 1999 through 2006 provided evidence of the link between green design and student performance. Window area correlated with improvement in math and reading, better air reduced asthma and other ailments that affected attendance, and improved temperature control increased the ability of students and teachers to concentrate. Meanwhile, money saved from operating more efficient buildings could be used to educate students. Project Frog thus used passive design, large windows and coatings, and other methods to improve learning and cut costs. California had strict energy-efficiency standards under Title 24, and the state specifically allotted $100 million in 2009 for High Performance Incentive grants to improve energy efficiency or maximize daylight in K−12 schools.

That grant, however, was still in the future when Project Frog began with two pilot projects in California, a preschool and racing school. The results pleased customers, but Project Frog was not making enough money from them. The company received $2.2 million from angel investors in 2007 and had revenue around $3.7 million with sixteen full-time employees. However, it was burning about $300,000 per month and had missed project completion deadlines. Nonetheless, in 2008 Miller projected to generate over $50 million in revenue by 2010. Then portents of a recession began to appear.

Completed Projects as of Spring 2010

Project Frog gained momentum with a number of projects. The following are the most notable ones:

- **Child Development Center at City College San Francisco, 2007.** Constructed 9,400 square feet of space for children, teachers, and administrators.
- **Jim Russell Racing Drivers School Learning and Technology Center, Sonoma, California, 2007.** Constructed 14,000 square feet of classroom and meeting space.
- **Greenbuild Conference Boston, 2008.** Constructed and unveiled the 1,280-square-foot Frog 2.0 in one week.
- **Jacoby Creek Charter School, Bayside, California, 2009.** Replaced a Northern California school's trailers with Frog classrooms, paid for by a state grant.
- **Vaughn Next Century Learning Center, Los Angeles, 2010.** Built a 3,000-square-foot structure for the charter school's Infrastructure Career Academy, designed to train students in green-collar jobs.
- **Crissy Field Center, San Francisco, 2010.** Built Golden Gate National Park a 7,400-square-foot education center to Leadership in Energy and Environmental Design (LEED) Gold standards, including classrooms, offices, and a café.
- **Watkinson School, classrooms for Global Studies Program, Connecticut, 2010.** Built 3,800 square feet of Frog Zero classroom and lab space.

Customers were pleased with the buildings' performance. Project Frog's purchase price was 25–40 percent lower than traditional construction. Operating costs could be as much as 50–70 percent lower than conventional or trailer construction. The new Frog Zero units could claim 75 percent energy demand reduction through use of occupancy and daylight sensors, smart wall panels that absorbed and reflected light, natural light optimization, glare control,

superior air quality, microclimate customization through advanced climate control technology, and enhanced acoustics. Carpeting and interiors were screened for toxicity. Conventional portables typically were equipped with pressed-wood furniture, vinyl walls, and new paint and carpet; these alternatives were superior to standard options, which could release invisible toxic gases known as volatile organic compounds (VOCs). The most advanced line, the Frog Zero buildings, produced more energy than they used and were energy neutral. Built from renewable or recyclable materials, the units could be disassembled easily and were designed with 100 percent recyclability potential.

However, the major appeal of any unconventional classroom construction was typically price. Project Frog's California prices were between prices for traditional construction and portable or trailer classrooms. In California, laws had actually mandated that 30 percent of new classroom construction be portables, to avoid overbuilding classrooms that would become vacant when birth rates declined. But some school districts facing unexpected and shifting population demographics found themselves housing 50 percent of their students in portables that ranged from relatively new to over forty years old. In Florida, 75 percent of portables that were intended as temporary structures were later classified as "permanent" classroom spaces. Estimates for 2009 placed six million students in portable classrooms. In 2003, it was estimated 220,000 portable classrooms served public school systems nationwide. Perception of lower quality was often justified; portables were poorly suited to music and language learning and they had heating and cooling inefficiencies, absence of natural light, and poor air quality, all of which undermined performance of students and teachers.

The Industry

As of June 2009, all but seven states had some kind of energy-efficiency requirements for government buildings. [6] About half those states required LEED Basic or equivalent certification specifically, and increasingly, states such as California and municipalities such as Boston and San Francisco required any large new construction or renovation to meet green building standards. LEED, created by the US Green Building Council (USGBC), was widely used to measure building efficiency and environmental impact and came in various levels, from Basic to Platinum. Other rating systems existed, especially as LEED Basic came to be considered too lax or inappropriate for homes or other structures, but LEED continued to be the industry norm. Buildings earned points toward certification based on site selection and design, environmental performance, and other attributes. The US General Services Administration (GSA), which oversaw many federal properties and purchases, began requiring LEED Silver certification in 2009. A study by McGraw-Hill Construction calculated the size of the green building market to be $10 billion in 2005 and $42 billion in 2009, and it estimated the market would be worth between $96 billion and $140 billion by 2013, with the education sector accounting for 15–30 percent of that market. [7]

Meeting those standards and the needs of the client, however, traditionally involved an array of people. Architects devised plans and construction engineers decided how to implement them safely. Government agencies had to approve those plans, and then an array of craftspeople—masons, carpenters, electricians, glaziers, and so on—were marshaled by a general contractor to execute the plans. Each new participant took a slice of the profit and decreased efficiency by not having an influence on the end-to-end life-cycle design but only on one small piece. Furthermore, involving more people increased the chance for delay and cost overruns, and the longer a project continued, the more likely weather or supply disruptions could slow it further. A single building could take years to plan and build. Hence construction typically had low margins and was unattractive to venture capitalists.

Indeed, when Project Frog sought investors, it found itself being compared to steel manufacturers. Investors had no idea how to value the company accurately: it wasn't traditional construction, nor was it traditional manufacturing. Project Frog combined many of the previously disparate aspects of construction in its predesigned, preapproved kit, which sped construction and limited the number of people involved, including distinct craft unions that would fight for their shares of the project. That increased the company's profit while decreasing cost to clients. Miller encountered one other problem he didn't anticipate: Project Frog was too fast. Schools typically forecast building new classrooms five to ten years out and had correspondingly sluggish procurement processes. Consequently, schools had a hard time determining how to buy something that could be standing and in use six months later.

Changes and Challenges

Project Frog president Adam Tibbs had shown a proclivity for entrepreneurial initiatives early, having started and sold a lawn-mowing company as a kid before earning his bachelor of arts in English from Columbia University in 1995. He worked as an editorial assistant for the Columbia University Press, where he gravitated toward digital publications, and

then joined Nicholson NY, an Internet and software consulting company, where he managed major projects from 1996 to 1998. In 1999 he founded Bluetip, a software development and incubator company. Bluetip spun off and sold several companies before Tibbs entered real estate development in New York and the Virgin Islands. He bought a house in the country and set out to write a novel. He also consulted for nonprofits and often borrowed Miller's office when he came to San Francisco, where his friend and eventual wife worked at MKThink. Eventually he went to work for Project Frog, where he arrived as president in June 2007.

In 2008 Project Frog began to redesign its base module and reorganize its business processes. Tibbs noticed that the original Project Frog designs were simply overbuilt; the same result could be achieved with less material and less design time. Tibbs was quick to note, "If you remove green from the table, the way we do things is still better. The innovation is business processes in an industry that doesn't have any business processes." Looking back, Tibbs recalled, "We stopped selling and redesigned from the ground up. We tried to bring intelligence in-house and keep it there." The international law firm Wilson Sonsini Goodrich & Rosati was brought in to "clean up" the company's procedures and documentation.

Meanwhile, Miller and his team examined their previous projects and relied on input from their own green material researchers as well as suppliers, especially steel manufacturer Tom Ahlborn, about how to improve environmental performance and efficiency. Ahlborn was based in California. He made the frame for the modules and also assembled them on-site. Hence his experience allowed engineers to make improvements along the entire life cycle of the project. After eighteen months of design, the 1,280-square-foot Frog 2.0 was unveiled at the Greenbuild Conference in Boston, where contractor Fisher Development Inc. assembled the demo module in only seven days to allay fears that Project Frog would miss deadlines again. The new design also earned California's Division of State Architect (DSA) precertification and an award from the Modular Building Institute. The new Frog 2.0 was anticipated to be 25–40 percent cheaper to build and 50–75 percent cheaper to operate, which meant it was baseline LEED Silver and could potentially be energy neutral when outfitted with photovoltaic panels (part of the Frog Zero option.) The components were recyclable or compostable and engineered for seismic design category E (which included San Francisco; the highest category was F.) Moreover, the building could withstand 110-mile-per-hour winds and be assembled in one-half to one-fifth the time of a traditional building. Since the basic plans had to be approved by engineering and architecture firms in fifty states, Frog 2.0 also streamlined documentation and certification.

On the financial side, the Wilson Sonsini law firm introduced Project Frog to a few venture capital companies. A deal for $8 million in Series B funding closed in November 2008. A partner from the venture capital fund joined Project Frog's board of directors. The partner said of the new partnership, "This is a truly pioneering company. Project FROG is developing dynamic concepts from a product design and manufacturing platform and applying those innovations to the building industry. Project FROG has a critical grasp on the technical and market advancements that will be game changers in the green building industry. These attributes solidify Project FROG's position as a leader in this fast growing marketplace." [8]

Though still $4 million short of its goal, Project Frog kept costs low and in 2010 raised an additional $5.2 million through debt financing and promissory notes. [9] In 2008, Project Frog won the Crunchies Award for Best Clean Tech company, given for compelling start-ups and Internet or technology innovation. Things continued to look up for the company when the Office of Naval Research asked the venture capital community about green buildings. The military was particularly interested in energy efficiency after paying exorbitant sums to keep fuel on the front lines in Iraq and Afghanistan. It had begun to see energy efficiency as a national security issue and sustainability (making sure the military had a positive footprint in terms of community, ecological, and health impacts of its operations) as key to continuing to operate bases in communities around the world. The investors recommended Project Frog, which eventually began work with the Navy on projects in Hawaii.

Even as Project Frog continually strove to distinguish itself from traditional trailer manufacturers, competition emerged from other modular groups. Miller believed that modular offerings sacrificed quality and green features. Nonetheless, they remained attractive to some clients such as cash-strapped schools.

New Hire, Next Steps, and Exit Strategy

Project Frog needed a way to stay ahead of the competition. Its improved Frog 2.0 certainly would help, and Frog Zero was the first energy-neutral building of its kind; streamlining business practices was now a priority. Project Frog turned to its supply chain to boost efficiency and profit.

Ash Notaney had worked with Booz Allen on strategy and supply-chain issues for twelve years. Through a mutual friend, he met Adam Tibbs and began to offer advice to the company about supply-chain management. In January 2010, he was hired. He noticed right away that people at Project Frog talked to one another; meetings were rare, which kept people available at their desks for interaction; the hierarchy was flat; and there were no corporate silos. "I don't think we even had an organizational chart until one of the investors asked to see one," Notaney recalled. [10] The spirit of collaboration was reflected in the office space: there were no cubicles, just tables where people worked side by side. Notaney literally sat with marketing to one side and the president to the other. Exposed HVAC conduits and hanging lights marked the building for what it was: a renovated roundhouse for streetcars that used to run along the Embarcadero. About two dozen employees were at work in the office on a given day, and probably two-thirds were under thirty years old. Clear plastic bins held sample materials from Project Frog buildings: exterior siding, interior wall, flooring, even bolts. Engineers continually manipulated plans on their SolidWorks screens.

Notaney began working with suppliers to collaborate more with Project Frog. The Crissy Field, Vaughan, and Jacoby projects used the same company to manufacture and assemble most of the kit. That company was Ahlborn Structural Steel. Tom Ahlborn, in particular, had been an excellent partner, continuing to suggest ways to improve the steel manufacture and assembly. Project Frog in return helped him cut costs and shared projected sales and volume of purchases over the coming year with increasingly detailed projections for closer time periods. Ahlborn became the preferred vendor for steel in any project unless contract stipulations or geography made it impossible. The company also used the same construction firm, Fisher Development Inc., for three of its installations. Fisher was based in San Francisco but worked nationally as a general contractor and construction manager. The company had worked with clients such as Williams-Sonoma and Hugo Boss and had assembled Project Frog's demonstration module at the Greenbuild Conference. Fisher had also worked on the Watkinson School in Connecticut. Although no single Project Frog building gave Fisher much money, he appreciated that construction was predictable and short, which allowed him to finish a project at a profit and move on. Moreover, he believed Project Frog was ripe to expand into markets beyond education and consequently all the small buildings would begin to add up.

Meanwhile, Project Frog worked with YKK and its partner Erie Architectural Products to procure exterior glass panels and curtain walls. The new glass panels could be installed legally and technically by steel unions, which meant Project Frog's contractors no longer needed to have glaziers on-site. The panels could also be modified for optimal performance in different environmental conditions. Roof panel suppliers were also involved, but to date the most effective relationships had been with Ahlborn and Fisher. Notaney was working to develop strategic partnerships with other suppliers.

The relationship with Fisher made sense for Tibbs as well. "We pick a guy we trust to fulfill our brand promise and make it a pleasurable experience," he said. After all, the company wanted to meet aggressive targets for margins and revenue. The company needed to sell the value of the learning experience its buildings created. Further, Tibbs wanted the company to grow not just by getting more deals in more markets but by keeping more of the money for Project Frog from each deal by integrating more features into its own manufactured kit. A switch to ceilings that integrated insulation and panels as well as the structural frame moved the company further along that path.

Tibbs continued to push for automating more of the design, improving algorithms, filing patents, and infringing on the company's earlier patents. He brought in GTC Law Group of Boston for patent advice. Tibbs wanted a way for clients to select features through online models and see the corresponding performance characteristics of the different designs. Once a plan was chosen, the computer could confirm the design, print a plan for the architect, and print any necessary parts designs and orders for suppliers.

In 2010, Project Frog raised an additional $5.2 million through convertible notes. That brought another venture capital director onto the company's board. He joined Ann Hand, who had a spot by virtue of being Project Frog's CEO; Miller, who had moved out of daily operations not long after Hand had arrived; and the lead venture capital partner from the B round. The fifth seat on the board, by charter designated for an independent member, remained vacant.

By summer of 2010, the market seemed to be improving, and Project Frog was on track to double its revenue that year. In fact, Project Frog was poised to flourish in a market that had changed radically from 2007. Miller said, "We mitigate risk. Clients are smarter and much more rigorous about goals and timeframes. Everyone wants to do green. That's changed. It has to be green, and it has to be cost-effective. They go together. That's just the way it is now."

The Crissy Field Center in Golden Gate National Park attracted 1,500 people to its grand opening and made a strong impression on visitors. Hundreds of people became Facebook fans of Project Frog. Guided tours of the center continued to draw many visitors through spring 2010 as did the building's café. Miller said with pride, "People walk into Crissy Field and say, 'I want one of these.' People don't usually buy buildings that way." But now with Project Frog, they could. In 2010 Project Frog had something very tangible and attractive to sell.

Miller continued to ponder how best to present his product. The company offered a unique synthesis of product and technology; sometimes he called it a product-oriented technology company. He liked the idea of portraying Project Frog as an integrated space and energy package in one leased product rather than a building with a mortgage that would also cut a client's energy costs. Furthermore, if prices reached the levels they had in 2007, breakeven could be cut in half. Miller wanted to underline that in a way people could understand and incorporate into their accounting. He worried, however, that the company might default downward into a conventional construction company if it did not maintain its industry expertise and vision for innovation at the edge of the industry.

The decision about an exit strategy also remained. Project Frog could go public. It also could court potential buyers. Yet many attitudes still reflected the confusion early investors felt about Project Frog's business. The venture capitalists struggled to find comps (comparable firms) to do the valuation. Various corporations with related business entities had expressed interest in investing in Project Frog. Each saw something it liked because the company integrated so many previously distinct businesses. Tibbs conjectured a global construction company or European modular building maker could make a bid. "We have about a three-year expectation to exit," Tibbs said. "I'm hoping to accelerate that." The whiteboard behind him was covered with red marker goals and graphs for the coming years. "If things go according to plan, we should be profitable by Q1 next year. For me, going public would be more fun because I've never done that before."

Project Frog and its venture capitalist investors appeared to share a business philosophy about green and what Mark Miller referred to as "edge of the grid energy areas"—the overlooked but attractive opportunities for innovation now that businesses and consumers were interested in saving energy and willing to invest in technology controls. The buyer had to get over the conventional "first cost" mentality, however. The new approach required monetizing the life cycle of the solution. It might mean taking facilities off the balance sheet.

Mark Miller was interested in these options, but his mind was focused on more immediate concerns:

> *We have to make sales and we have to execute. We have the product designed and defined. Now we need revenue. We're inventing a category though. The VCs understand that and they like us, but aren't sure how to think about us. We were one of the last VC deals done before the economy collapsed. And of course the market stopped for us too. I mean schools have no money and states are basically bailing out. And sales cycles are long because buyers have to be educated. We have our work cut out for us.*

Rating Environmental Performance in the Building Industry: Leadership in Energy and Environmental Design (LEED)

LEED provides building owners and operators a concise framework for identifying and implementing practical and measurable green building design, construction, operations and maintenance solutions. [15]

- US Green Building Council

Environmentally preferable, "sustainable," or "green" building uses optimal and innovative design and construction to provide economic, health, environmental, and social benefits. Green buildings cost little or nothing more to build than conventional facilities and typically cost significantly less to operate and maintain while having a smaller impact on the environment. [16] These savings plus a burnished environmental reputation and improved indoor comfort mean green buildings can command higher rents and improve occupant productivity. [17] In addition, green buildings' life-cycle costing provides a more accurate way to evaluate long-term benefits than the traditional focus on initial construction cost alone. [18]

Although many were interested in the idea of green building, in the early 1990s green building was difficult to define, which slowed the market adoption of its principles and practices. In response, the USGBC was formed in 1993 in association with the American Institute of Architects, the leading US architectural design organization. By 2000, USGBC had about 250 members that included property owners, designers, builders, brokers, product manufacturers, utilities, finance and insurance firms, professional societies, government agencies, environmental groups, and universities. Those council members helped create the LEED rating system, released to the public in 2000. The LEED standard intended to transform the building market by providing guidelines, certification, and education for green building. Thus architects, clients, and builders could identify and acquire points across a variety of environmental performance criteria and then apply for independent certification, which verified the green attributes of the building for others, such as buyers or occupants.

LEED quickly expanded as it filled the need for a reliable definition of green building. Within two years of its release, LEED captured 3 percent of the US market, including 6 percent of commercial and institutional buildings under design that year. By 2003, USGBC had more than three thousand members, more than fifty buildings had been LEED certified, and more than six hundred building projects totaling more than ninety-one million square feet were registered for future certification in fifty US states and fifteen countries. [19]

LEED found multiple proponents. In December 2005, USGBC made the *Scientific American* 50, the magazine's prestigious international list of "people and organizations worldwide whose research, policy, or business leadership has played a major role in bringing about the science and technology innovations that are improving the way we live and offer the greatest hopes for the future." [20] The federal government, through divisions such as the General Services Administration and US military, began providing incentives and requiring that its projects be LEED certified. The trademarked LEED certification became the de facto green building code for many locations, such as the cities of Santa Monica and San Francisco, or was rewarded with tax breaks, such as in New York, Indiana, and Massachusetts. Corporate and public sector organizations with certified or registered buildings soon included Genzyme, Honda, Toyota, Johnson & Johnson, IBM, Goldman Sachs, Ford, Visteon, MIT, and Herman Miller.

By July 2010, USGBC membership had jumped to over 30,000, more than 155,000 building professionals had been credentialed formally in the LEED system, and 6,000 buildings had been certified as meeting LEED criteria. The LEED system had been revised and expanded to include homes, renovation, and neighborhood development, not just individual, new commercial buildings. Almost half the states of the United States had begun to require LEED or equivalent certification for most state buildings. Hence, despite its shortcomings and competition, LEED remains the best-known green building program, and USGBC remains a committee-based, member-driven, and consensus-focused nonprofit coalition leading a national consensus to promote high-performance buildings that are environmentally responsible, profitable, and healthy places to live and work.

Why the Building Industry?

Buildings consume many resources and produce much waste. In the United States, buildings consume about 40 percent of all energy, including 72 percent of electricity, and 9 percent of all water, or forty trillion gallons daily. As a result, buildings produce about 40 percent of all greenhouse gas emissions. They also produce solid waste. A 2009 EPA study estimated that in one year, building construction, renovation, and demolition alone produced 170 million tons of debris, about half of which went straight to landfills. [21] Since Americans spend 90 percent of their time indoors, the building environment is also key to overall health.

The construction industry has major economic impacts. Construction and renovation is the largest sector of US manufacturing, and buildings and building products span more Standard Industrial Classification codes than any other industrial activity. The value of new construction put in place rose from $800 billion in 1993 to peak at nearly $1.2 trillion in 2006, equal to 5 to 8 percent of GDP over that span. About half of construction in the past two decades has been residential and about one-third commercial, manufacturing, office, or educational space. Including highways and other nonbuilding construction, total construction is roughly 70 percent private and 30 percent public. [22] Hence the building sector presents some of the most accessible opportunities to develop innovative strategies for increasing profits and addressing environmental and related community quality-of-life concerns.

Buildings, however, have some characteristics that can impede environmental design. They have a thirty- to forty-year life cycle from planning, design, and construction through operations and maintenance (O&M) and renovation to ultimate demolition or recycling. This long, varied life span requires advance planning to maximize environmental benefits and minimize harm and can lock older, less efficient, or hazardous technologies such as asbestos or lead paint in place. Indeed, advance planning is key. Structural and site design is the most important factor determining performance and cost throughout a building's life.

Buildings also involve multiple stakeholders, which can complicate optimization of the system. Costs are borne by one or more parties, such as owners, operators, and tenants.

This division can hamper maximizing the overall efficiency of the building, as various groups vie for their own advantage or simply fail to coordinate their efforts. Wages and benefits paid to occupant employees dwarf all other expenses but are typically not included in building life-cycle costs. Depending on the arrangement, a tenant may pay for most of O&M but have had no say in the original design or site selection. A system such as LEED can make all parties aware of environmental performance and thus help them collaborate to improve it while also assuring others that the building has been designed to a certain standard.

How LEED Works

USGBC created the LEED Green Building rating system to, in the council's words, transform the building market by doing the following:

- Defining *green building* by establishing a common standard of measurement
- Promoting integrated, whole-building design practices
- Recognizing environmental leadership in the building industry
- Stimulating competition
- Raising consumer awareness of green building benefits

To achieve these goals, LEED provides a comprehensive framework for assessing the environmental performance of a building over its lifetime as measured through the following categories:

- **Sustainable sites.** Minimizing disruption of the ecosystem and new development.
- **Water efficiency.** Using less water inside and in landscaping.
- **Energy and atmosphere.** Minimizing energy consumption and emissions of pollutants.
- **Materials and resources.** Using recycled or sustainable building materials and recycling construction debris.
- **Indoor environmental quality.** Maximizing indoor air quality, daylight, and comfort.
- **Innovation and design process.** Fostering breakthroughs and best practices.
- **Regional priorities.** Credits that vary by site to reward local priorities.

Projects within a given LEED rating system can earn points in each category and all points are equal, no matter the effort needed to achieve them. For instance, installing bike racks and a shower in an office building can earn one point for Sustainable Sites, as can redeveloping a brownfield. Merely including a LEED Accredited Professional (LEED AP) on the design team earns a point for Innovation and Design. The same action could also earn multiple points across categories. Installing a green roof could potentially manage storm water runoff, mitigate a local heat island, and restore wildlife habitat. The most points are concentrated in energy efficiency, which accounts for nearly one-third of all possible points. Under LEED 3, released in 2009, once a project gains 40 of the possible 110 points and meets certain prerequisites, such as collecting recyclable materials, it can apply for LEED Basic certification. (The criteria are slightly different for LEED for residences.) This point system makes LEED flexible about how goals are met, rewards innovative approaches, and recognizes regional differences. This systems perspective distinguishes LEED from conventional thinking.

Table 7.1 LEED for New Construction Rating System

Sustainable Sites		26
Prereq 1	Construction Activity Pollution Prevention	0
Credit 1	Site Selection	1
Credit 2	Development Density and Community Connectivity	5
Credit 3	Brownfield Redevelopment	1
Credit 4.1	Alternative Transportation—Public Transportation Access	6
Credit 4.2	Alternative Transportation—Bicycle Storage and Changing Rooms	1
Credit 4.3	Alternative Transportation—Low-Emitting and Fuel-Efficient Vehicles	3
Credit 4.4	Alternative Transportation—Parking Capacity	2
Credit 5.1	Site Development—Protect or Restore Habitat	1
Credit 5.2	Site Development—Maximize Open Space	1
Credit 6.1	Stormwater Design—Quantity Control	1
Credit 6.2	Stormwater Design—Quality Control	1
Credit 7.1	Heat Island Effect—Nonroof	1
Credit 7.2	Heat Island Effect—Roof	1
Credit 8	Light Pollution Reduction	1
Water Efficiency		**10**
Prereq 1	Water Use Reduction—20% Reduction	0
Credit 1	Water Efficient Landscaping	2 to 4
Credit 2	Innovative Wastewater Technologies	2
Credit 3	Water Use Reduction	2 to 4
Energy and Atmosphere		**35**
Prereq 1	Fundamental Commissioning of Building Energy Systems	0
Prereq 2	Minimum Energy Performance	0
Prereq 3	Fundamental Refrigerant Management	0
Credit 1	Optimize Energy Performance	1 to 19
Credit 2	On-Site Renewable Energy	1 to 7
Credit 3	Enhanced Commissioning	2
Credit 4	Enhanced Refrigerant Management	2
Credit 5	Measurement and Verification	3
Credit 6	Green Power	2
Materials and Resources		**14**

Prereq 1	Storage and Collection of Recyclables	0
Credit 1.1	Building Reuse—Maintain Existing Walls, Floors, and Roof	1 to 3
Credit 1.2	Building Reuse—Maintain 50% of Interior Nonstructural Elements	1
Credit 2	Construction Waste Management	1 to 2
Credit 3	Materials Reuse	1 to 2
Credit 4	Recycled Content	1 to 2
Credit 5	Regional Materials	1 to 2
Credit 6	Rapidly Renewable Materials	1
Credit 7	Certified Wood	1
Indoor Environmental Quality		**15**
Prereq 1	Minimum Indoor Air Quality Performance	0
Prereq 2	Environmental Tobacco Smoke (ETS) Control	0
Credit 1	Outdoor Air Delivery Monitoring	1
Credit 2	Increased Ventilation	1
Credit 3.1	Construction IAQ Management Plan—During Construction	1
Credit 3.2	Construction IAQ Management Plan—Before Occupancy	1
Credit 4.1	Low-Emitting Materials—Adhesives and Sealants	1
Credit 4.2	Low-Emitting Materials—Paints and Coatings	1
Credit 4.3	Low-Emitting Materials—Flooring Systems	1
Credit 4.4	Low-Emitting Materials—Composite Wood and Agrifiber Products	1
Credit 5	Indoor Chemical and Pollutant Source Control	1

Credit 6.1	Controllability of Systems—Lighting	1
Credit 6.2	Controllability of Systems—Thermal Comfort	1
Credit 7.1	Thermal Comfort—Design	1
Credit 7.2	Thermal Comfort—Verification	1
Credit 8.1	Daylight and Views—Daylight	1
Credit 8.2	Daylight and Views—Views	1
Innovation and Design Process		**6**
Credit 1.1	Innovation in Design: Specific Title	1
Credit 1.2	Innovation in Design: Specific Title	1
Credit 1.3	Innovation in Design: Specific Title	1
Credit 1.4	Innovation in Design: Specific Title	1
Credit 1.5	Innovation in Design: Specific Title	1
Credit 2	LEED Accredited Professional	1
Regional Priority Credits		**4**
Credit 1.1	Regional Priority: Specific Credit	1
Credit 1.2	Regional Priority: Specific Credit	1
Credit 1.3	Regional Priority: Specific Credit	1
Credit 1.4	Regional Priority: Specific Credit	1
Total		110

Source: US Green Building Council, "LEED for New Construction and Major Renovation," accessed March 7, 2011, http://www.usgbc.org/ShowFile.aspx?DocumentID=1095.

LEED has been amended regularly to respond to emerging needs. Partly in reaction to criticism that LEED focused too narrowly on new commercial construction, USGBC developed different LEED rating systems for different types of projects. In addition to the original LEED for New Construction and Major Renovation (LEED-NC), there are now LEED for Schools, LEED for Existing Building Operations and Maintenance (LEED-EB O&M), LEED for Commercial Interiors (LEED-CI), and LEED for Core and Shell (LEED-CS), all of which use the above categories and have similar, albeit slightly different, distributions of the 110 possible points among the categories. [23] The more recent LEED for Neighborhood Development (LEED-ND) and LEED for Homes have the same point approach but different categories. LEED-ND awards points for Innovation and Design and Regional Priorities plus Smart Location and Linkage, Neighborhood Pattern and Design, and Green Infrastructure and Buildings. LEED for Homes largely follows the categories of other building types but also has Locations and Linkages distinct from Sustainable Sites to encourage walking, infill, and so forth; Awareness and Education to encourage homeowners to educate others; and a Home Size Adjustment to acknowledge that bigger homes, efficiency notwithstanding, consume more resources than smaller ones. LEED for Homes also has 136, not 110, possible points with a lower threshold for Basic certification. LEED for Retail and LEED for Healthcare (versus more generic commercial buildings covered by LEED) were in development as of July 2010 and likely to be launched within a year.

To be LEED certified, a project is first registered for a few hundred dollars with the Green Building Certification Institute (GBCI), an independent spin-off of USGBC that assumed sole responsibility for LEED certifying buildings and training LEED APs in 2009. Documentation is gathered to demonstrate compliance with LEED criteria and then submitted to the GBCI along with another fee, over $2,000 for an average project, for certification. Bigger projects cost more to certify, and higher levels of certification are available with more points: 50 points earns Silver, 60 Gold, and 80 or more Platinum. Higher certification typically correlates with less energy use. A 2008 study by USGBC and the New Buildings Institute found that in the United States, newly built LEED Basic commercial buildings (including offices and laboratories) used 24 percent less energy per square foot than the average of all commercial building stock, while LEED Gold and Platinum buildings used 44 percent less energy than the average. Just over half of the LEED buildings, however, performed significantly better or worse than predicted at the outset of the project, with one quarter actually consuming more energy than the code baseline. [25]

LEED 3 was intended to address some of these prediction problems as well as criticisms that LEED could reward, for instance, a building for air-conditioning the desert as long as it did so more efficiently than comparable buildings. LEED

3 added online tools to facilitate planning and certification. It also harmonized criteria among its rating systems for different types of projects and added points to categories that made a larger overall difference in energy use, such as building near existing public transportation infrastructure instead of a more remote location. LEED already had been twice revised prior to LEED 3, and USGBC continues to support LEED as it evolves and expands.

To simplify use and speed adoption, LEED refers to existing industry standards of practice. LEED for Homes specifies ANSI (American National Standards Institute) Z765 for calculating square footage for the Home Size Adjustment. LEED for Operations and Maintenance adheres to ASHRAE (American Society of Heating, Refrigeration, and Air-Conditioning Engineers) standards for ventilation and various American Standards for Testing and Materials (ASTM) standards for lighting and reflectance.

Many credits require submission of a letter signed by the architect, engineer, owner, or responsible party and verification of the claims in language provided by a specific LEED template. To maintain the credibility of the third-party rating system, claims to credits are subject to auditing by GBCI.

Green Building Costs and Benefits

There are multiple aspects of green building cost and benefits. For LEED certification in particular, direct project costs include the administrative costs of the application process and fees, which can run into the thousands of dollars, as well as the financial impacts on building design, construction, and operation, due to implementation of LEED-related measures. These costs should be evaluated in terms of total cost of ownership, including both first costs and operating costs over the building's life cycle. Indirect costs are often harder to assess but are worthy of consideration.

Green building can add little to nothing to total design and construction cost, at least for the lower levels of LEED certification or equivalent green building codes. A study by global construction consultant Davis Langdon in 2006 found "no significant difference in average costs for green buildings as compared to nongreen buildings. Many project teams are building green buildings with little or no added cost to the amount a traditional building costs, and with budgets well within the cost range of nongreen buildings with similar programs." [26] Green design may require particular attention and effort in the initial phases, and design costs are generally higher, but more and more firms see green as part of the standard package, not an addition. Other studies of specific buildings by the GSA and various organizations found that green design might cost a few percentage points more but significantly reduced operating costs and improved occupant comfort. [27] The City of Portland, Oregon, for example, had eighteen LEED buildings in 2004 and saved more than $1 million per year in avoided wastewater treatment costs and another $1 million a year in lower energy bills. [28]

In some cases, highly innovative design features might retard both market and regulatory acceptance of green buildings (especially at the local level where green design knowledge may be low), slowing the project timetable and increasing costs. For example, regulators who are unfamiliar with constructed wetlands might doubt their effectiveness as a way to reduce the impacts of storm water runoff. Similarly, the real estate market in some areas, due to a lack of familiarity, might question the value of a geothermal heating system, or condo association rules might prohibit a supplemental solar electric system.

Nonetheless, green building, especially when certified to LEED or another standard, offers many benefits. Environmentally, it reduces the strain on the local ecosystem, conserves resources and habitat, and improves indoor air quality. Economically, green building lowers operating costs, can garner tax incentives, improves public image, can lower insurance costs, improves employee productivity and attendance, and increases market value. Indeed, in a 2008 study, Piet Eichholtz and collaborators compared 700 hundred Energy Star and LEED-certified office buildings to 7,500 conventional ones and found that the green office buildings had higher occupancy rates and could charge slightly higher rents, making the market value of a green building typically $5 million greater than its conventional equivalent. [29]

Given these benefits, green building will likely expand. With so much money on the line, the need for verified environmental performance and design standards will remain strong.

Alternatives to and Criticisms of LEED

Despite growth in the green building market, in 2009, $42 billion represented less than 10 percent of total building construction. One criticism of LEED is that as a voluntary standard, it does not force enough change fast enough. Public policy analyst David Hart concluded LEED "is inevitably bumping up against its limits" and does not "act assertively to pull along the trailing edge of 'brown building'

practice." [30] As more governments and organizations adopt LEED or similar standards because it gives them an established, reliable metric, the market could shift more quickly toward greener construction.

A second persistent criticism of LEED has been that basic certification doesn't represent much improvement over conventional building. As recently as 2010, renowned architect Frank Gehry criticized LEED for crediting "bogus stuff" that doesn't truly pay off. [31] LEED certification in this line of reasoning distracts people from more ambitious targets, and the money spent on registration and certification—ranging from about $2,000 for smaller buildings for USGBC members to $27,500 for larger buildings for nonmembers—could instead be spent on more environmental improvements. [32] Such fees also mean USGBC and GBCI have an economic stake in making LEED the dominant standard of certification. USGBC has even criticized California's State Building Code for the CalGreen label because USGBC feared the label would create confusion and detract from LEED's value. [33]

Finally, LEED unabashedly focuses on energy use as its main criterion for environmental performance. That has led to criticism from the nonprofit Environment and Human Health Inc. (EHHI) that LEED does too little to keep toxic materials out of buildings. An EHHI report from 2010 urged USGBC to discourage "chemicals of concern" such as phthalates and halogenated flame retardants and to include more medical professionals on its board. A USGBC vice president said he was willing to collaborate with critics to improve LEED, provided the expectations were reasonable: "LEED could say there should be no chemicals in any building and no energy used and no water and every building should give back water and energy. We could do all that, and no one would use the rating system. We can only take the market as far as it's willing to go." [34]

Yet LEED seems to have found just where the market is willing to go. Other certification systems exist but have not attained the status that LEED has. Green Globes, for instance, began in 2000, the same year as LEED, and had an online component from its inception. Green Globes offers a similar performance rating system, and certification is often cheaper than LEED. Green Globes is more prevalent in Canada, but in the United States it is being incorporated as ANSI's official green building standard. [35] The US EPA also awards Energy Star certification to buildings in the seventy-fifth or higher percentile for energy use in their category. Builders can apply by designing for Energy Star and completing an online application; actual operating data, however, are necessary to earn the final Energy Star label.

[36] There is no fee for certification. Finally, various regional certification programs exist, from EarthCraft in the southeast United States to Build It Green in California. These systems tend to be tailored more specifically to their locations.

Green building has become increasingly desirable. LEED and other certification systems have helped to make it even more desirable by creating trust. Builders, regulators, or the average person can know that LEED certification guarantees a modicum of environmental considerations without having to know a thing about what those are or how they work in the building. LEED in particular has proven powerful and flexible enough to spread internationally and to undergo frequent revision of its existing rating systems and expansion into brand new ones.

KEY TAKEAWAYS

- Challenging the building and construction industry and its submarkets with new products and unprecedented supply-chain requirements requires managing not only technology development but also market perception and accepted practices.
- Economic downturns add unique opportunities and challenges for new ventures.
- Meeting third-party standards offers market differentiation.

EXERCISES

1. Put together an analysis of the major elements of entrepreneurial venturing and sustainability innovation applied to Project Frog.
2. In teams, identify a differentiated and innovative company and interview senior management about their market and how they overcame challenges to convince early customers to accept their product or service.

[1] Project FROG, "Project FROG, Makers of Smart Building Systems, Closes Series B Funding with RockPort Capital Partners," news release, *Business Wire*, November 19, 2008, accessed January 28, 2011, http://www.thefreelibrary.com/Project+,+Makers+of+Smart+Building+Systems,+Closes+Series+B...-a0189242085.
[2] {Author's Name Retracted as requested by the work's original creator or licensee} and Mark Meier, *Project FROG: Sustainability and Innovation in Building Design*, UVA-ENT-0158 (Charlottesville: Darden Business Publishing, University of Virginia, 2010). Other quotations in this section, unless otherwise noted, also refer to this case study.
[3] Leslie Gueverra, "Project FROG Becomes a Cinderella Story for Modular Construction," *GreenerBuildings*, November 25, 2008, accessed January 28, 2011, http://www.greenbiz.com/news/2008/11/25/project-frog-becomes-cinderella-story-modular-construction.
[4] Sarah Rich, "Project Frog's 21st-Century Buildings," *Dwell*, April 1, 2009, accessed January 30, 2011, http://www.dwell.com/articles/project-frogs-21st-century-buildings.html.
[5] Quentin Hardy, "Ideas Worth Millions," *Forbes*, January 29, 2009, accessed January 30, 2011, http://www.forbes.com/2009/01/29/innovations-venture-capital-technology_0129_innovations.html.
[6] Pew Center on Global Climate Change, "Building Standards for State Buildings," June 16, 2009, accessed January 30, 2011, http://www.pewclimate.org/what_s_being_done/in_the_states/leed_state_buildings.cfm.
[7] McGraw-Hill Construction, *2009 Green Outlook: Trends Driving Change*, accessed January 26, 2011, http://construction.com/market_research/reports/GreenOutlook.asp.
[8] Rockport Capital, "Project FROG Closes $8MM Series B Financing Led by RockPort Capital Partners," press release, November 19, 2008, accessed January 30, 2011, http://www.rockportcap.com/press-releases/project-frog-closes-8mm-series-b-financing-led-by-rockport-capital-partners.
[9] Project FROG, "Project FROG, Makers of Smart Building Systems, Closes Series B Funding with RockPort Capital Partners," news release, *Business Wire*, November 19, 2008, accessed January 30, 2011, http://www.reuters.com/article/2008/11/19/idUS111863+19-Nov-2008+BW20081119.
[10] {Author's Name Retracted as requested by the work's original creator or licensee} and Mark Meier, *Project FROG: Sustainability and Innovation in Building Design*, UVA-ENT-0158 (Charlottesville: Darden Business Publishing, University of Virginia, 2010). Other quotations in this section, unless otherwise noted, also refer to this case study.
[11] Modular Business Institute, "City College of San Francisco—Child Development Center," accessed January 30, 2011, http://www.modular.org/Awards/AwardEntryDetail.aspx?awardentryid=370.
[12] Cleantech PR Wire, "Project FROG Wins 2008 Crunchies Award for 'Best Clean Tech,'" press release, January 13, 2009, accessed March 7, 2011, http://www.ct-si.org/news/press/item.html?id=5279.
[13] "Project Frog Building Systems for the Future," BlogsMonroe.com, March 23, 2010, accessed April 5, 2010, http://www.blogsmonroe.com/world/2010/03/project-frog-building-systems-for-the-future.
[14] Business Wire, "Ann Hand New CEO at Project FROG," news release, September 22, 2009, accessed September 1, 2010, http://www.businesswire.com/news/home/20090922005679/en/Ann-Hand-CEO-Project-FROG.
[15] US Green Building Council, "Intro—What LEED Is," accessed January 28, 2011, http://www.usgbc.org/DisplayPage.aspx?CMSPageID=1988.
[16] Davis Langdon, *Cost of Green Revisited: Reexamining the Feasibility and Cost Impact of Sustainable Design in the Light of Increased Market Adoption*, July 2007, accessed January 28, 2011, http://www.centerforgreenschools.org/docs/cost-of-green-revisited.pdf; Steven Winter Associates Inc., *GSA LEED Cost Study*, October 2004, accessed January 28, 2011, http://www.wbdg.org/ccb/GSAMAN/gsaleed.pdf; US Green Building Council–Chicago Chapter, *Regional Green Building Case Study Project: A Post-Occupancy Study of LEED Projects in Illinois*, Fall 2009, accessed January 28, 2011, http://www.usgbc-chicago.org/wp-content/uploads/2009/08/Regional-Green-Building-Case-Study-Project-Year-1-Report.pdf.
[17] Piet Eichholtz, Nils Kok, and John M. Quigley, "Doing Well by Doing Good? Green Office Buildings" (Program on Housing and Urban Policy Working Paper No. W08-001, Institute of Business and Economic Research, Fisher Center for Real Estate & Urban Economics, University of California, Berkeley, 2008), accessed January 28, 2011, http://www.jetsongreen.com/files/doing_well_by_doing_good_green_office_buildings.pdf

[18] {Author's Name Retracted as requested by the work's original creator or licensee}, Jeff York, and Mark Meier, "Rating Performance in the Building Industry: Leadership in Energy and Environmental Design" (UVA-ENT-0053), 2010 Darden Case Collection. All other references in this section, unless otherwise noted, come from this source.

[19] US Green Building Council, *Building Momentum: National Trends and Prospects for High-Performance Green Buildings*, February 2003, 1, 11, 13, accessed January 28, 2011, http://www.usgbc.org/Docs/Resources/043003_hpgb_whitepaper.pdf.

[20] US Green Building Council, "USGBC Named to '*Scientific American* 50,'" news release, January 1, 2006, accessed January 28, 2011, http://www.usgbc.org/News/PressReleaseDetails.aspx?ID=2045.

[21] D&R International Ltd., "1.1: Buildings Sector Energy Consumption," in *2009 Buildings Energy Data Book* (Silver Spring, MD: US Department of Energy, 2009), 1–10, accessed January 28, 2011, http://buildingsdatabook.eren.doe.gov/docs/DataBooks/2009_BEDB_Updated.pdf; D&R International Ltd., "8.1: Buildings Sector Water Consumption," in *2009 Buildings Energy Data Book* (Silver Spring, MD: US Department of Energy, 2009), 8-1, table 8.1.1, accessed January 28, 2011, http://buildingsdatabook.eren.doe.gov/docs/DataBooks/2009_BEDB_Updated.pdf; US Green Building Council, "Green Building Facts," accessed March 23, 2011, http://www.usgbc.org/ShowFile.aspx?DocumentID=5961; US Environmental Protection Agency, *Estimating 2003 Building-Related Construction and Demolition Materials Amounts*, accessed January 28, 2011, http://www.epa.gov/wastes/conserve/rrr/imr/cdm/pubs/cd-meas.pdf.

[22] US Census Bureau, "Construction Spending: Total Construction," accessed September 3, 2010, http://www.census.gov/const/www/totpage.html.

[23] Rating systems are available at US Green Building Council, "LEED Resources and Tools: LEED 2009 Addenda," accessed September 3, 2010, http://www.usgbc.org/DisplayPage.aspx?CMSPageID=2200#BD+C.

[24] Reprinted courtesy of the US Green Building Council, *LEED 2009 for New Construction and Major Renovations Rating System* (Washington DC: US Green Building Council, 2009), last updated October 2010, accessed January 31, 2011, http://www.usgbc.org/DisplayPage.aspx?CMSPageID=220&.

[25] Cathy Turner and Mark Frankel (New Buildings Institute), *Energy Performance of LEED for New Construction Buildings* (Washington DC: US Green Building Council, 2008), accessed January 31, 2011, http://www.usgbc.org/ShowFile.aspx?DocumentID=3930.

[26] Davis Langdon, *Cost of Green Revisited: Reexamining the Feasibility and Cost Impact of Sustainable Design in the Light of Increased Market Adoption*, July 2007, accessed January 28, 2011, http://www.centerforgreenschools.org/docs/cost-of-green-revisited.pdf.

[27] Steven Winter Associates Inc., *GSA LEED Cost Study*, October 2004, accessed January 28, 2011, http://www.wbdg.org/ccb/GSAMAN/gsaleed.pdf; US Green Building Council–Chicago Chapter, *Regional Green Building Case Study Project: A Post-Occupancy Study of LEED Projects in Illinois*, Fall 2009, accessed January 28, 2011, http://www.usgbc-chicago.org/wp-content/uploads/2009/08/Regional-Green-Building-Case-Study-Project-Year-1-Report.pdf.

[28] Mike Italiano (board member, US Green Building Council), personal communication, March 14, 2003.

[29] The report states, "The results show that large increases in the supply of green buildings during 2007–2009, and the recent downturns in property markets, have *not* significantly affected the rents of green buildings relative to those of comparable high quality property investments; the economic premium to green building has decreased slightly, but rents and occupancy rates are still higher than those of comparable properties." The report also concludes that green certification commands higher rental premiums and asset value at resale: "We find that green buildings have rents and asset prices that are significantly higher than those documented for conventional office space, while controlling specifically for differences in hedonic attributes and location using propensity score weights." Piet Eichholtz, Nils Kok, and John M. Quigley, *The Economics of Green Building*, 3, 20, accessed January 26, 2011, http://www.ctgbc.org/archive/EKQ_Economics.pdf.

[30] David M. Hart, "Don't Worry About the Government? The LEED-NC 'Green Building' Rating System and Energy Efficiency in US Commercial Buildings" (MIT-IPC-Energy Innovation Working Paper 09-001, Industrial Performance Center, Massachusetts Institute of Technology, 2009), accessed January 31, 2011, http://web.mit.edu/ipc/publications/pdf/09-001.pdf.

[31] Blair Kamin, "Frank Gehry Holds Forth on Millennium Park, the Modern Wing, and Why He's Not into Green Architecture," *Cityscapes* (blog), *Chicago Tribune*, April 7, 2010, accessed January 31, 2011, http://featuresblogs.chicagotribune.com/theskyline/2010/04/looking-down-on-the-stunning-view-of-the-frank-gehry-designed-pritzker-pavilion-from-the-art-institute-of-chicagos-renzo-pian.html.

[32] For costs, see Green Building Certification Institute, "Current Certification Fees," 2010, accessed January 31, 2011, http://www.gbci.org/main-nav/building-certification/resources/fees/current.aspx; and Green Building Certification Institute, "Registration Fees," accessed January 31, 2011, http://www.gbci.org/Certification/Resources/Registration-fees.aspx. For criticism, see Anya Kamenetz, "The Green Standard?," *Fast Company*, October 1, 2007, accessed January 31, 2011, http://www.fastcompany.com/magazine/119/the-green-standard.html?page=0%2C0.

[33] "California's Building Code Turns a Deeper Shade of Green," *Green Business*, January 14, 2010, accessed January 31, 2011, http://www.greenbiz.com/news/2010/01/14/californias-building-code-turns-deeper-shade-green.

[34] Suzanne Labarre, "LEED Buildings Rated Green…and Often Toxic," *Fast Company*, June 3, 2010, accessed January 31, 2011, http://www.fastcompany.com/1656162/are-leed-buildings-unhealthy. Also Tristan Roberts, "New Report Criticizes LEED on Public Health Issues," *Environmental Building News*, June 3, 2010, accessed January 31, 2011, http://www.buildinggreen.com/auth/article.cfm/2010/6/3/New-Report-Criticizes-LEED-on-Public-Health-Issues.

[35] Green Globes, "What Is Green Globes?," accessed September 3, 2010, http://www.greenglobes.com/about.asp.

[36] Energy Star, "The Energy Star for Buildings & Manufacturing Plants," accessed January 26, 2011, http://www.energystar.gov/index.cfm?c=business.bus_bldgs.

7.2 Greening Facilities: Hermes Microtech Inc.

LEARNING OBJECTIVES

1. Compare internal and external impediments to a company's shift toward a sustainability strategy for a new building design.

2. Understand how and why decision participants might end up at cross purposes in implementing green building designs.

3. Identify traits of successful sustainability innovation processes.

The next case is Hermes Microtech. [1] Created as an amalgam of various company experiences, this case shows the decision-making complexity of building design and construction. The viewpoints of various participants provide insights into why sustainability concerns change decision processes and therefore can be so difficult for conventional organizations.

Greening Facilities: Hermes Microtech Inc.

Heather Glen [2] pushed back in her chair in her office at Hermes Microtech Inc., which gave her a commanding view of the books, binders, notes, and messages piled around her computer. The sunset was fading out over the Pacific, and as the last of her colleagues left, she welcomed the quiet opportunity to contemplate the task before her. Hermes CEO Alden Torus had just approved the most important project in Glen's career to date, and she didn't want to waste any time getting started. Glen had one month to organize an initial meeting of all key participants involved in creating and building Hermes's new headquarters. For the first time, the company would bring together professionals from each phase of facilities design, construction, and operation to initiate project planning, and Glen would run the meeting. Although she was not the construction project manager, Glen was going to try to change the way her company built and ran its facilities to make them more environmentally friendly—and in the process transform the company itself.

Much had happened in the eighteen months since Glen had been appointed special projects coordinator by Sandy Strand, Hermes's executive vice president of environment and facilities (E&F). Strand had asked her to lead efforts to make environmental quality a higher priority in the company's buildings and facilities, a goal the CEO shared. Glen's work in implementing energy-efficiency improvements at one of their microchip factories had produced mixed results. She learned a great deal about the technical potential for improvement from that pilot project, but her most valuable lessons concerned the organizational dynamics of the design-build effort. She realized that the most important factors for success—as well as the greatest challenges—lay in renovating the decision-making process rather than in different design and technology choices.

As dusk fell and the cubicles outside her office sank into shadow, photo sensors increased the brightness of the fluorescent light fixtures above Glen's desk. She sipped another mouthful of coffee to stave off any drowsiness that might follow the meal she had just shared with Torus and Strand. Torus had called the dinner meeting to discuss how best to make the company's next planned facility an environmentally friendly or "green" building. He wanted that to happen because he believed it would benefit the company, and he had supported Strand and Glen's efforts. Yet Torus knew it would be a challenge to change the way the organization went about the design-build process.

"I am realistic about the constraints on my ability to effect change on this topic," Torus had told them. "My time and attention are consumed with more traditional core business issues. I can make it clear to others that I support the goal of environmental improvements, but I need to rely on you to make it happen." Torus asked Strand and Glen to suggest how best to proceed. He liked Glen's proposal that everyone involved in the full life cycle of the building join in an initial integrated design workshop to initiate the project. "I can't spare the time to attend the full meeting, but I can kick it off with introductory remarks," Torus said to her. "Send me a one-page memo with the three to five most important things you want me to say."

After dinner, Glen had returned to the office to draft an e-mail invitation to workshop participants. In her mind's eye, she saw their faces, and reviewed their roles in the project and in the greening efforts to date.

The Hermes Story

Hermes was a medium-sized microelectronics manufacturer based in California's Silicon Valley. The company started as a military contractor but grew to focus on consumer electronics through a series of mergers, acquisitions, and spin-offs. It made a mix of microchips spanning a range of capabilities and applications, from complex and costly chips for personal computers and cellular phones to simpler, cheaper devices for consumer appliances and automobiles. Hermes was essentially a component maker; almost all its customers were original equipment manufacturers (OEMs). Its ten manufacturing facilities, three R&D laboratories, and twenty sales offices in the United States, Europe, and Asia employed ten thousand people and generated annual revenues of $1 billion, with a net profit of $100 million.

Hermes CEO Alden Torus had been with the company since its founding twenty-five years earlier. The son of immigrants, he had started in the product development department and worked his way up through the ranks. Torus was an effective and charismatic engineer with a good head for business strategy and an encyclopedic memory for detail. He epitomized the corporate culture at Hermes: hardworking and production focused, he put in long hours to help develop and launch new products. Torus understood the importance of the first-mover advantage in the fast-paced microelectronics industry. Innovation was highly valued at Hermes, and product R&D was a spending priority.

Microchip Market Dynamics

Microchips were a commodity, competition was stiff, and profit margins were relatively narrow. The industry's business cycle was highly variable, typified by regular and significant swings in price and profits. The driving influence was the rapid pace of technological development, characterized by Moore's Law, which says computing processing power doubles every eighteen months. Racing each other as well as technical evolution, makers churned out increasingly sophisticated products, shrinking both transistor sizes and product development periods. Time to market was a critical competitive factor. The time available for new product launches did not often exceed eighteen months, including process and yield improvements. The sector was sensitive to macroeconomic conditions, particularly consumer spending. More than 85 percent of Hermes's revenues came from chips embedded in consumer products.

Another influence on supply and demand fluctuations was the uneven or "lumpy" process of step function increases in production capacity. Microchip manufacturing was capital intensive, and new fabrication facilities—"fabs"—took many months to bring online. When chip demand rose far enough, competing manufacturers responded quickly and invested in new capacity. Those fabs tended to come online at about the same time; the surge in supply depressed prices, inventories built up, and the market slumped. Eventually demand and prices rose again, followed by a new round of investment in manufacturing capacity for the latest products.

Chip fabs were costly and complex. Microchips were made on silicon wafers in a series of steps that were carried out within high-tech devices called tools, each of which cost millions of dollars. The tools operated inside carefully climate-controlled environments called clean rooms. Microelectronics production was very sensitive to disruption and contamination by microscopic particles. Line stoppages could ruin production batches and cost more than $1 million dollars per day or as much as tens of thousands of dollars per minute for some product lines. Clean rooms were isolated seismically from the rest of the fab on dedicated support pillars, so that vibrations from minor earthquakes or even nearby truck traffic did not disrupt the tools. Process water was deionized and highly filtered before being piped into the clean room and the tools.

Fabs had extensive HVAC systems with high-performance filters to maintain the clean room's temperature, humidity, and quantity of airborne particulates within stringent parameters. The air handlers, fans, pumps, furnaces, and chillers were located outside the clean room and delivered conditioned air and cooling water into the clean room via ducts and pipes. Those HVAC systems typically made up 40–50 percent of a fab's electricity consumption. Fab electricity use ranged from three million to fifteen million watts or megawatts (MW), depending on the size of the facility.

The Evolution of Hermes's Environmental Strategy

Microchip manufacturing involved numerous hazardous materials, toxic emissions, and energy-intensive processes. Maintaining worker safety and managing pollution was a critical function. Potentially dangerous emissions were highly regulated and strictly controlled. Traditionally, environmental health and safety (EHS) management and strategy had focused on end-of-the-pipe problems and solutions, such as treating acid-contaminated exhaust air before it was released into the atmosphere. More recently, increased attention and effort had focused on pollution prevention strategies that reduced dangerous emissions by changes in production processes. Such strategies could meet regulated emissions control requirements at less cost than end-of-the-pipe methods and often yielded economic benefits through waste reduction and other manufacturing improvements. Hermes's environmental activities were representative of the industry in that regard. In the mid-1990s, Hermes consolidated the EHS department and the maintenance department into one E&F department.

CEO Alden Torus did not pay much attention to environmental issues during most of his career. Like most of his colleagues, he regarded pollution control as a cost of doing business, driven by compliance with ever-increasing government regulations. He considered such matters to be the responsibility of the environment and facilities department but neither a high priority for senior management nor a central element of corporate strategy. He maintained that perspective during his tenure as VP of production and his early years as CEO.

Torus's perspective began to change when his young son developed a rare form of cancer. During the course of his son's treatment, he discovered that several other children in his neighborhood had the same type of cancer. His teenage daughter was passionate about environmental issues and had often complained about the extent of environmental contamination in Silicon Valley, asking her father to do something about it. Chemical feedstocks and by-products of electronics manufacturing had contaminated groundwater at more than one hundred locations. Santa Clara County had twenty-nine federally designated "Superfund" toxic waste sites, the highest concentration in the nation. Torus began to wonder if that had anything to do with his son's illness. His son recovered after long and difficult treatment, but other children with the same disease died. Although no link to any specific chemical or site was established, that family crisis prompted Torus to rethink his views on industrial pollution.

Prompted by his children, Torus began to explore new perspectives. His friend Sandy Strand, Hermes's VP of E&F, had long been interested in the potential business opportunities described by leading advocates of the integration of ecology and commerce. Strand introduced Torus to the writing of such thinkers as Paul Hawken, Amory Lovins, and William McDonough and the work of organizations such as The Natural Step, the Coalition for Environmentally Responsible Economies, and the World Business Council for Sustainable Development. Torus learned about new business tools and strategies, including environmental management systems, green design, and industrial ecology. He heard from other CEOs about businesses in a wide range of industries that were finding profit and competitive advantage through innovation and collaboration with leading practitioners. Soon Torus joined Strand in the belief that Hermes could realize many business benefits by incorporating more environmental and social factors with traditional economic considerations into what author John Elkington called a new "triple bottom line."

But where would they begin? Torus and Strand shared a long-term view of the transitional process of moving their industry (and the world economy) toward the vision of a more sustainable condition. Neither man advocated rapid change without regard to cost. They continued to believe that their priority was economic success and that building the business case for green business initiatives was essential. They recognized that they were well ahead of most of their colleagues on those issues and were pragmatic about the potential scope and pace of change, particularly within the managerial constraints of executive responsibility in a publicly traded company. They had limited time and attention to devote to a new strategic initiative, capital resources were perpetually constrained, and the company lacked experience with many of the promising approaches. Yet they wanted to start somewhere—and steadily, if slowly, develop momentum for organizational change.

Hermes's Green Initiatives

Torus began by sharing his vision of the future with the company and the public and declaring his support for prudent green business initiatives. His advocacy did not require much of his time, but it provided crucial top-level support for the employees who would carry most of the responsibility for project implementation. Initial efforts would pursue incremental improvements toward clear, measurable objectives. Those efforts would be supported by

education and training, recruitment of skilled staff, and outside expertise where necessary. Hermes had built its success on innovation and rigorous quality management.

Torus set two initial priorities: (1) development of a new, more environmentally friendly line of chips and (2) a 20 percent improvement in energy and water efficiency over five years. Those programs would have to pay for themselves within five years.

The green chip project would be implemented by the R&D and operations divisions of the production department, headed by Executive VP of Production Christopher "Chip" Smith. In addition to traditional areas of performance improvement, the new microprocessor had a design goal of using at least 15 percent less electricity than the previous model, which would appeal to OEM buyers and consumers because it would extend the battery life of portable devices such as laptops and cell phones. Manufacturing process improvements would reduce waste and toxic pollution. Hermes would advertise these attributes to differentiate their product, attract environmentally conscious consumers, and boost sales, thereby (hopefully) paying for the effort.

The energy and water efficiency effort would be implemented by the facilities maintenance division of the E&F department and the operations division of the production department. The program would pay for itself through avoided costs. The program would be headed up by Heather Glen, then a special assistant to Strand. At the time, Glen was a bright young electrical engineer and recent MBA graduate who had sought a position with Hermes because she had heard about the company's greening efforts and wanted to work in that field. She had been at Hermes for one year and had spent most of that time pulling together an overview of all its fabs' environmental performance and energy and water use. She had also initiated a pilot program to save energy through lighting retrofits at the company's headquarters and two other office spaces, which were successful though small in scope.

Initial Efforts: The F3 Fab Energy Survey

Strand hired a team of consultants led by Rocky Mountain Institute (RMI), a nonprofit research and consulting organization. He had seen a lecture by Amory Lovins, RMI's CEO and a resource efficiency pioneer, in which Lovins described RMI's energy-efficiency work in fabs that saved up to half of the HVAC energy cost-effectively. He invited Lovins to meet with Torus, who agreed to a pilot effort at Hermes's F3 fab near Dallas, Texas. Glen was designated project coordinator and liaison with RMI.

F3 was chosen because it was one of the most energy-intensive fabs in the company, water costs were relatively high, and a significant expansion was planned. The facility was built in the early 1970s by another firm and had been acquired by Hermes in the late 1980s. A renovation called Phase I was done in the late 1990s to accommodate a new production line, with only minor changes to the original HVAC system. A new addition was planned with another clean room and dedicated HVAC utilities, called Phase II. The initial drawings for Phase II had been completed by Expedia Design Company, Hermes's long-standing architectural and engineering design vendor. EDC was a fab design vendor to several firms in the industry and had a reputation for speed and competitive fees.

The RMI consulting team was led by Bill Greenman, an architect with an MBA and a background in green design. Technical services were provided by Peter Rumsey and John Blumberg from Rumsey Engineers, an engineering design firm and frequent RMI partner that specialized in energy-efficient HVAC systems for clean rooms and green buildings. Their objective was to briefly survey F3 to identify existing opportunities for improvement and conduct a streamlined design review of Expedia's plans for the rehab. The deliverable was a report with a list of recommendations that would be practical but general in nature, rather than a detailed engineering study based on performance measurements. The report would not include design plans or payback calculations. That introductory visit was intended to identify potential areas of improvement for further investigation and to provide an opportunity for the company and the consultants to learn more about each other. The limited scope of work also kept the consulting fees low.

Glen had been to the F3 site only once before, although she had worked with its facilities staff on her energy performance assessment. She flew from the company's headquarters in the Silicon Valley to Texas and met the RMI team there for the two-day survey. The team spent the first morning describing their approach and being briefed on the facility. They then toured the site for the rest of that day and much of the second, working with the chief engineer and facilities staff to understand HVAC and controls systems, water use, and operating procedures. At the end of the second day, the team presented its initial conclusions and recommendations in a meeting attended by facilities staff, the site's general manager Regina Shinelle, Expedia's Phase II project manager Art Schema, and Strand, who flew in for the occasion.

The RMI team estimated that low- and no-cost changes to F3's current operations could save up to 10 percent of the HVAC electricity almost immediately, such as utilizing evaporative "free" cooling in dry periods by operating all the cooling towers in parallel at low speed to reduce reliance on electric chillers. Another 15–25 percent savings were attainable with modest retrofit investments and estimated paybacks of two to three years, including pumping and fan system upgrades. Significant investments could reduce site HVAC energy use by more than 50 percent, requiring changes to Expedia's Phase II design to allow consolidation of the two clean rooms' independent process cooling systems into a centralized plant serving both buildings. The estimated payback period would be at least five years if it were to be conducted as a retrofit, once Phase II had been completed, or much sooner if combined with proposed Phase II energy-efficiency improvements.

The RMI team noted that significant opportunities for energy efficiency were not captured by the current Phase II design. These included larger low-friction air handlers with smaller fan motors and variable-speed drives, high-performance cooling towers, heat-reflective coatings on rooftop air intake ducts, and upgraded sensors and controls. Such measures would decrease HVAC energy use and cost by 30 to 60 percent, with paybacks ranging from immediate to several years depending on the measure. They would also increase construction costs, although some component capital costs would fall due to smaller equipment such as motors and chillers. The extent of this proposed redesign would be significant and would take weeks or even months.

With the exception of the centralized cooling plant, most recommended measures would not interrupt production and involved no intrusion into the clean room space. All the suggested methods had been demonstrated within the industry but not all in one place, and few had been tried within Hermes. RMI suggested that Hermes establish energy performance benchmarks to be used as guidelines for both existing fab operations and new design specifications.

Rumsey Engineers' Blumberg worked on water efficiency measures and proposed a method for reclaiming wastewater for evaporative cooling. But when he investigated techniques for reusing some of the acid rinse water that drained from a tool, the production manager rebuked him for interfering with manufacturing matters and the idea was dropped.

The Phase II review also noted that Expedia's design was an almost exact replica of another Hermes fab that was more than ten years old, which itself was based on blueprints from the 1970s. That became apparent when the team asked about a piping diagram showing an unusual zigzag in midair, and a facilities engineer named Steve Sparks replied that there was a structural pillar in that location in the fab these plans were drawn from—a pillar absent in Phase II. It did not appear to the RMI team that any performance improvements had been incorporated into the successive iterations of that design.

Such "copy exactly" practices were common in the microelectronics industry. Microchip manufacturing was extremely complicated. The sequence involved thousands of process variables and chemical interactions that were so complex as to defy full comprehension. Performance parameters and specifications were exacting, as minor deviations could be disastrous, and if problems occurred they needed to be isolated and identified. Time-to-market deadlines were unforgiving, and meeting them required an extraordinary level of control over process variables. Therefore, when something worked, it was copied exactly. A pilot production line for new product development was essentially "cloned" in numbers to create a high-volume manufacturing facility. That mind-set shaped all aspects facilities design, even areas outside the clean room that did not require such stringent inflexibility. "Copy exactly" reduced fab design effort, time, and cost but also hindered the adoption of technological and process improvements, including energy-conserving features.

Implementation Challenges

A few weeks after the survey in Texas, RMI and Rumsey Engineers submitted a brief report summarizing their observations and recommendations, which was circulated at the site and among senior management including Strand, Torus, and Smith. Meetings were held to discuss the recommendations and strategies for implementation. The reactions were mixed.

The RMI team had been greeted with initial skepticism by the site's facilities staff members, who were wary of outside interference, had never heard of RMI, and were confused about the unusual nonprofit-corporate consulting partnership. Chief Engineer Tom Dowit had been a particularly reluctant participant. It was rumored that Dowit had called the survey "just another far-fetched scheme of those environment division idealists" that was going to cost his facilities division money and distract him from his primary job of ensuring that the production division could maximize output. He was openly skeptical during RMI's initial presentations, although as the survey progressed, he grudgingly acknowledged the value of some of the team's observations, stating at one point that he would have made some of the same improvements if he'd been given permission and funding. But he grew defensive—and at one

point openly derisive—during the final presentation as the team described opportunities to save tens of thousands of dollars.

Glen realized that Dowit might have feared that the consultants were making him look bad by finding large cost savings he had not uncovered himself in recent years. But she also understood why he might have taken a highly cautious approach to new techniques. The facilities engineering staff had a difficult job, with a great deal of responsibility for maintaining highly complex and sensitive production equipment. They had limited input into tool selection and operation, yet when something went wrong, they often got the blame. The facilities department budget was constantly squeezed, pressuring engineers to cut corners. Many production managers viewed facilities as an overhead cost center that played a subordinate support role to manufacturing's revenue generation.

The rest of Dowit's staff agreed that many of the recommendations were technically feasible and had already successfully implemented some operational changes since the visit. Their initial skepticism about "a bunch of academics who were coming here to write on blackboards and waste our time" subsided over the course of the survey as the RMI team's skills became apparent, and most people quickly came to respect the consultants' abilities and ideas. The staff would need additional money for retrofits to capture further savings. A few of the consultants' ideas had been suggested in the past by site facilities staff, including measures used at other Hermes fabs, but most had been rejected because they did not meet the site's requirement that retrofit investments have a maximum payback period of eighteen months.

Facilities Engineer Steve Sparks enthusiastically supported the energy-efficiency efforts and confided in Glen. He lamented the inefficiency of F3's older equipment, pointing out that Dowit kept it running on a "shoestring budget." Dowit blamed the spending constraints on the comptroller, but Sparks suspected that Dowit was also currying favor with the production department by minimizing O&M spending. Sparks had worked at another fab just after Dowit had left there as chief engineer (the same facility Expedia had used as a template for Phase II). Sparks thought that Dowit's cost cutting might have helped him get promoted to this position at F3, but it had also run down the mechanical systems and left his successor with deferred upkeep costs. "To be fair," Sparks added, "Dowit is not unusual in this careful approach, he's good at it and he has been rewarded for it. This is typical of the facilities culture at Hermes."

F3 General Manager Shinelle had little interest in any project that diverted attention from production and no interest in slowing down the Phase II expansion. She did not meet the RMI team until their final presentation and did not say much then or in subsequent meetings; what she did say tended to agree with Dowit. "This facility works, and energy is 2 percent of the cost of our chips," she said. "I can't spend time worrying about it. We need to use our limited investment capital to get new, high-quality products quickly to market." Glen had the impression that Shinelle participated only reluctantly and would not have done so at all if it wasn't clear that Strand had requested she host the pilot energy survey. Ultimately, Shinelle agreed to direct Dowit's staff to select "a few" of the more cost-effective measures that met the site's eighteen-month payback criteria, and she would approve those facilities funding requests.

Nevertheless, Shinelle refused to make any changes to the Phase II design that would slow the project timeline. Nudged by Strand, she directed Dowit to check with Expedia and see if there was still time to order more efficient motors than the inexpensive but relatively low-efficiency types specified in the design—as long as the cost premium did not exceed 10 percent. "The production division can't afford to pay more for this expansion," she insisted. "We lose tens of thousands of dollars of sales revenue every week that we delay getting Phase II manufacturing up and running. We have to stay within budget and on schedule." Glen understood that Shinelle's annual performance bonus was probably tied to that very achievement and that in any event the facilities division would be paying the utility bills.

Expedia's Art Schema had been unsure how to respond to the design review comments during the on-site presentation. Although his primary clients Shinelle and Dowit seemed to think that the RMI team's input wouldn't change much if anything about Phase II, Schema could see that Strand supported the consultants' efforts. Schema limited his comments to polite expressions of interest in the findings and promised to give them detailed consideration.

Within a week of receiving the RMI report, Schema sent a critique of the design review to F3, and Shinelle e-mailed copies to Glen and Strand. Expedia's point-by-point response acknowledged the merit of a few of RMI's suggestions but dismissed most of the recommendations as too costly, impractical, or impossible. The tenor of the response was that half of RMI's recommendations were off-base and the other half were nothing new to Expedia. Schema's cover letter read in part: "Expedia provides superior reliability and security. Our architects and engineers have built our close relationship with Hermes by delivering

economical designs that work, as proven in previous projects. We leverage our skills and experience to consistently deliver low bids and rapid turnaround times, which benefit both Hermes and Expedia. We are open to discussions about changes to design criteria at any time with you, our valued clients."

Shinelle defended Expedia's approach and service in her attached e-mail. "Expedia has always been there for us and has never let us down. They have played a key role in Hermes's agility and speed in product development and launch. Let's not mess up a good partnership with untested ideas." It occurred to Glen that both Shinelle and Smith had risen through the ranks of the production department boosted by reputations as star managers of fab construction projects—success stories that Expedia had helped build. In addition, Shinelle's product quality and yield record at F3 was unmatched across Hermes's manufacturing sites for its consistency, and she had a reputation for bringing new products to market very rapidly.

Mixed Results

Six months later, Glen and Strand regarded the F3 survey as only a partial success. On the upside, technical results were positive. F3 facilities staff had successfully implemented most of the RMI team's low- and no-cost recommendations. Sparks and his colleagues were impressed by the new techniques, welcomed corporate-level support for investment in system improvements, and were openly supportive of the energy-efficiency efforts. They convinced Dowit to request that the RMI team return to conduct more detailed analysis of some of the more involved recommendations. The fact that Torus had mentioned the pilot effort at F3 in a companywide webcast address, praising the site manager and chief engineer's efforts, helped their cause. But unlike the first visit, which was underwritten by Strand's office, subsequent fees would have to come from the site's operating budget. Shinelle agreed to allocate them in principle but said no such expenditures could be undertaken until the following quarter at the earliest.

On the downside, F3's Phase II expansion project went ahead as designed. Some motor efficiency upgrades were incorporated at the last minute at minimal extra cost, but the scramble to change equipment orders at a late stage in a tight schedule resulted in some grumbling by Dowit and Schema.

Strand's environment department had engaged the RMI team to conduct similar general surveys at two more sites in Oregon and the Silicon Valley, accompanied by Glen in each case. The visits occurred three months after the F3 survey, and the team's recommendations had been submitted but not acted upon. Those visits had paralleled the experience at F3. The team worked with facilities division staff on energy improvements that did not risk interfering with production. (Manufacturing water efficiency was no longer investigated following Blumberg's rebuke at F3.) Technical efficiency opportunities were similar; so, too, were the political dynamics. Some facilities staff members were skeptical, but receptivity increased as awareness of the RMI team's capabilities spread by word of mouth and direct experience. Production staff members were more wary; the word going around the department was that the energy program was an expensive nuisance.

Expedia seemed to be torn about the energy program. Its design work was directly challenged by the consultants' critiques, its managers' personal networks and alliances were aligned with Hermes's production department (the one that hired it), and its designers were not keen to devote a great deal of effort to restructure its cost-effective copy-exactly approach. However, Expedia also wanted to please its client and recognized that Hermes's CEO was interested. Glen noted that Art Schema, the Hermes account manager at Expedia, had avoided directly criticizing the RMI team's work—that had been left to subordinates—and had signaled his openness to discussing new frameworks for doing business. In a brief aside as a meeting broke up, he told Glen, "We can design more energy-efficient systems; Hermes has never asked us to."

The Change Agent's Dilemma

Glen saw her task as essentially intrapreneurial. She was trying to harness resources to realize a new vision of the future. She marveled at how difficult it was to be innovative even in a company built around the creation of new ideas, techniques, and products. She faced a big challenge in trying to change business as usual, pushing against a persistent headwind of inertia and resistance to new methods. The semiconductor industry was typified by a very cautious and conservative corporate culture, stemming from exacting technical and process requirements, safety risks posed by hazardous materials, the high cost of downtime, and brutal competition in a fast-moving marketplace. (It wasn't for nothing that Intel CEO Andy Grove's book was titled *Only the Paranoid Survive*.)

Glen had to persuade many people to change the way they did things, both with different departments at Hermes and with outside vendors. She sometimes felt like an outsider herself during the site visits; even colleagues from the facilities division of her own department viewed her as an

environment division staffer from the corporate office. Glen was grateful that the RMI team could back up its claims with practical expertise. Her position afforded little formal authority to dictate change, although executive endorsement lent her informal authority, and her training provided only limited credibility with facilities engineers. The RMI team lacked authority but was building credibility with demonstrated skills, one site survey at a time, complementary to her strengths.

Her colleagues knew she had Strand and even Torus backing her, but executive time and attention was very limited, she was left to her own means to manage the process and implement change. Glen sensed that the production-focused skeptics in the opposing camp would respond positively to the energy program when she or Strand were present but would then return to the status quo as soon as the efficiency advocates weren't looking, hoping they could wait it out until the CEO retired and the issue dissipated. She recalled the Chinese saying about that attitude among middle management: "Heaven is high and the Emperor is far away."

A New Opportunity: The Green Headquarters Building

Despite his authority as CEO and personal credibility as a successful manager and leader, Alden Torus could not afford to dedicate much political and social capital to any efforts not directly focused on commercial success. Yet his interest in sustainable business opportunities remained strong, and he wanted to choose his interventions carefully to provide the greatest leverage for change. If he was going to risk his reputation and get out ahead of his colleagues on an unfamiliar issue, he wanted it to count. He was pleased with the early phases of the energy and water efficiency efforts, although it was becoming clear that the process of organizational learning and transformation would not be rapid. He wanted to expand awareness of—and attention to—environmental dimensions of commerce that went beyond using resources more efficiently.

One strategy under consideration was to establish companywide emissions reductions targets for gases that contributed to climate change. Specified targets could provide coherence to energy-efficiency efforts across the company's facilities and prevent individual sites from "cream skimming" only those opportunities with the most attractive paybacks—an approach that often rendered longer payoff measures uneconomic under current investment criteria. Torus suspected that bundling projects for investment would increase the average payback periods but yield larger overall emissions reductions. Internal emissions trading might further reduce the total cost of such efforts by directing funds to the highest-leverage opportunities.

Torus saw a good opportunity in the company's decision to consolidate the corporate headquarters and western US sales offices into one location. He asked the board of directors to support construction of a green building and invited RMI's Lovins and Greenman to the board meeting to describe the potential benefits. Green buildings used more environmentally friendly materials and design and construction practices and typically reduced utility bills by as much as 50 percent through energy and water efficiency. They did not have to cost more to build than conventional buildings, although they required careful design attention. The board was intrigued by research indicating that worker productivity typically increased in green buildings by an average of 5 percent, which would be even more valuable to the company than eliminating the utility bills entirely.

"But what constitutes 'green' building?" the board asked. Lovins and Greenman had said that each project was unique, and there were no simple standards to apply to a design, no Band-Aids that would make it green. However, third-party accreditation was available through the LEED rating system established in 2000 by the US Green Building Council (USGBC), a respected consensus coalition of stakeholders from all aspects of the building industry. LEED certification required that best practices be used in certain core aspects of building construction and operation. It provided a list of techniques and practices, most of which were rooted in existing industry standards. Designers and builders could incorporate features chosen from this menu of options to earn points toward certification. LEED provided a framework for action with defined objectives and established criteria for what was "green." USGBC data from scores of completed projects indicated that the basic level of certification added 0–5 percent to a building's initial cost (not factoring in typical operating cost savings), and the primary factor in that variability was the skill and experience of the design-build team. LEED was well received in the industry, grew rapidly, and within three years of its release was being applied to more than 5 percent of all planned commercial and institutional construction and major renovation projects in the United States.

The board approved the project. Torus believed the building would provide a potent educational symbol of the business benefits of green design and serve as a tool for organizational learning. He thought it likely that the new headquarters' innovative design approaches would appeal to Hermes's corporate culture, particularly that of the production department. He liked the idea that strategic planning and new product conceptual development would occur in a unique facility.

As with other Hermes facilities, the new office building development was being managed by the production department. (Most Hermes buildings projects were production related, so to simplify administration the production department oversaw all new construction.) Torus had decided to make the new headquarters a green building after the project had already begun. The plan had been to completely renovate a four-story, fifty-thousand-square-foot office building in the Silicon Valley. The project management team had been designated, and the design and construction contractors had already been chosen based on their conceptual design: Hermes's traditional partners, Expedia Design Company and Advanced Building Services (ABS). Art Schema was the Expedia project manager, and William Ditt was the ABS construction manager. Both had worked extensively with Hermes facilities in the past but had minimal experience with green building techniques. The next project milestone was to be a review of Expedia's initial plans for the building core and utilities, but Torus had put the process on hold when he decided to seek board approval to make the renovation a LEED building project. It was not too late to change the design to meet that new objective.

Torus decided to build on both the momentum of the energy-efficiency program and RMI's program. RMI and Rumsey Engineers would be retained as design consultants, based on their growing credibility in the company and reputation as leaders in the green design field. Glen was tasked with leading the greening effort toward the goal of attaining LEED certification and continuing her role as liaison to the RMI team.

Executive VP of Production Chip Smith had chosen Regina Shinelle as project manager and Tom Dowit as chief engineer. Glen could not help wondering whether that was a positive development and what Smith's true intentions were. Smith had not revealed much about his opinion of the greening efforts; although he acted supportive in Torus's presence, on most issues he embodied the production department's perspective. Now Glen would be working with the two people who had presented the most stubborn resistance to her efforts and who did not share her priorities. If the renovation failed to attain LEED certification or performed poorly, it would be a major setback to the sustainability program. But if the collaborative effort resulted in an economical, high-performance LEED building, it would bring positive recognition to all participants and perhaps create greater buy-in for sustainability efforts among the skeptics companywide.

Glen was pleased that Steve Sparks had been named facilities director for the new headquarters. He had been the most enthusiastic supporter of the efficiency efforts at F3, and his persistent efforts had played a key role in successful implementation of the recommended measures, despite more hesitant colleagues. Glen had suggested to Strand that Sparks would be an ideal internal candidate for the position. Sparks was excited about the promotion and the opportunity to be more involved in green design.

Greening Strategies

Glen's primary proposal as the project's sustainability coordinator was to arrange an integrated design process called a charrette. This multidisciplinary-facilitated meeting would bring together project participants, stakeholders, and outside experts in the same room (often around the same table) at the earliest practical point in a project. The goal was to clarify desired outcomes, identify obstacles, and devise strategies for attaining the best overall result. That integrative process helped participants to understand their differing perspectives and incentives, exchange ideas, build trust, work out problems, and create consensus. The approach took some time, but the investment of extra effort could significantly improve plans and specifications, streamline construction, reduce total costs, and increase building performance. "An axiom of design is that all the big mistakes are made on the first day," Greenman told Glen. "Most of a building's life-cycle cost is determined by the tiny fraction of the budget spent on initial design. Carpenters know it makes sense to measure twice and cut once. A charrette helps us to do that."

The charrette was to last for two days and would be held in Hermes's R&D center conference facilities. Hermes R&D staff had used similar techniques for product design, but it had never been tried in a facilities project. Participants commented that never before had all the parties spanning the service life of a Hermes building project met together simultaneously.

The meeting would begin with team introductions, followed by presentations on green design and LEED by the RMI team (which had obtained excellent results in past charrettes). Glen planned to describe the list of LEED requirements and the credit areas that she thought were best suited for exploration. There were several areas she identified as readily achievable and many more worthy of deeper exploration. The group would pick an initial set of LEED credit areas to pursue. That would take much of the first day.

The most detailed technical subject would be a collective consideration of HVAC design alternatives. Rumsey Engineers had reviewed the preliminary design drawn up by Expedia before the green objectives were set—now called the baseline case. Rumsey had submitted a proposal outlining recommendations for increasing the ventilation system efficiency. It involved spending more money on construction to save money on operation. The executive summary of recommendations and estimated costs and benefits was to be circulated to each participant. That discussion would begin on the first day and carry over to the second day if necessary.

The last and most difficult topic, but perhaps the most important, would concern potential policy and procedural changes that might foster more efficient facilities investments. Hermes's traditional approach to requiring, financing, designing, building, and operating its facilities was functional but not optimal. The energy-efficiency program of retrofit improvements had proven that there was widespread waste of energy and capital within the company's facilities. It had also highlighted aspects of the process that hindered improvement. It was in the interest of management and shareholders to create a more efficient process.

Most of those issues were not unique to Hermes but were characteristic of the industry. Buildings were made in a collective but not well-optimized production process. As Greenman put it, "If a camel is a horse designed by a committee, than most buildings are camels." Some decisions produced short-term savings for certain participants but degraded building performance or imposed long-term costs on the owners and occupants. Usually those choices made business sense to each decision maker and were not intended to cause problems elsewhere. Those challenges were a function of the rules of the game, and it was worth exploring whether changing any of those rules would produce better buildings. Glen's discussion would examine the participants' roles, incentives and disincentives, and the impact of financial and investment criteria. It had the potential to make some participants uncomfortable but also to yield significant process improvements.

Those thoughts were racing in Glen's mind on the night Torus had approved the charrette. She was excited and a little anxious as she set out to draft a meeting invitation and brief description. She hoped that the charrette would reduce rather than inflame any latent (or blatant) tensions and conflicts among participants. Greenman had assured her the process usually worked surprisingly well, but she could see how achieving consensus might also seem like herding cats. She considered the cast of characters she now had to work with, each representing a different organization or department, and made notes summarizing her interpretation of each participant's perspective going into the project.

She needed to identify the obstacles and opportunities in the group dynamic and select strategies that provided the highest leverage for change. The CEO had offered her the opportunity to try a few new approaches and policies that he could announce in his introductory remarks. She thought that a small number of well-targeted measures could "change the rules of the game" for key participants in the design-build process by providing different incentives or by removing important disincentives. That would help steer the group's decision toward a successful outcome for this project, and perhaps for future facilities as well.

Charrette Participants

Hermes Personnel

- **Regina Shinelle, project manager, production department, facilities division.** "I've got to get this facility built on time and under budget. The faster the construction and the lower the capital expenditure, the bigger my bonus. I've relied on Expedia Design contractors in the past for prompt and reliable service. There is no room in this process for trial and error."

- **Tom Dowit, project chief engineer, environment department, facilities division.** "It's my job to ensure facility operations support production, while minimizing risk and cost. I don't have the money or leeway to do anything expensive or risky. I've got to maintain the systems and pay the utility bills, and if my costs go down this year, my budget gets cut next year. Keep it simple, and if it ain't broke don't fix it—that's my philosophy. I've been doing this a long time, and my approach works. That's why I've been asked to oversee the design and construction process and contractors for this new building project. I use the value engineering process to review all aspects of design and construction, and either approve or reject proposed elements to control costs. Sure, there are some opportunities for improvement, but this green design stuff gets too much attention, costs too much, and slows me down. What a pain in the neck."

- **Steve Sparks, headquarters facilities director, environment department, facilities division.** "I will be responsible for the new building's operations and maintenance once it is completed. I am excited to work in a green building. I've seen some of those techniques work in practice and I believe there is great potential for facilities improvements. I'm surprised I was asked to

participate in this design meeting. Usually the production department calls us when a facility is built, hands us the keys at the ribbon-cutting, and says 'keep it clean and running.' Or they tell us 'new fab tools are going online in two weeks, make sure they have power and water.' I look forward to having a say in decisions that affect my job."

- **Susan Legume, comptroller, production department.** "My priority is cost control. I've got my eye on the bottom line and my mind on shareholder value. Capital spending is one area where costs can spiral, especially construction projects with multiple contractors. My job is to ride the project manager hard and squeeze the vendors harder. They can really nickel-and-dime the budget away if we don't watch out. The value engineering process gives us a chance to rein in runaway spending by cutting unnecessary purchases from the design or construction."

Design-Build Contractors

- **Art Schema, project manager for Expedia Design Company.** "We deliver reliability and security. Our architects and engineers have built this business by delivering economical designs that work, as proven in previous projects. We leverage our skills and experience to consistently deliver low bids and rapid turnaround times, which helps us win projects. Doing anything differently increases our costs; unfamiliar design techniques increase our risk exposure and project expense. As designer of record for this project, we would have to carefully consider whether we could sign off on any exotic features or plans. Of course, customer service is our number one priority and Hermes is a valued client, so we are open to whatever we are asked to do, as long as it is clearly defined and we are compensated for our efforts."

- **William Ditt, construction manager for Advanced Building Services.** "I cut this bid to the bone to get this contract. We'll make up for it by cutting a few corners, based on my experience where it will do the job. I've got to maintain cash flow by getting this done as fast as possible so I can move on to another project. I rely on my supplier network to get me the parts I need, quickly and at low cost. Any delays risk cutting into my thin profit margin and my tight schedule."

Green Design Consultants

- **Bill Greenman, consultant, Rocky Mountain Institute.** "Nonprofit organizations such as RMI can collaborate fruitfully with businesses to make money while protecting the environment. We are design consultants and process facilitators. Although we do not ourselves provide architectural plans or engineering designs, our partner Rumsey Engineers can do that. We can help with LEED certification and suggest ideas and best practices that we've seen used successfully elsewhere. Standard design-build practices do not produce green buildings. Green building is new to the industry as a whole, and we have experience with these innovative techniques. Green building can be profitable, but each case is unique and requires increased design effort and careful project management."

- **Peter Rumsey, consultant, Rumsey Engineers.** "We specialize in whole-systems energy-efficient design. We can deliver equivalent or superior HVAC performance at lower energy use and reduced cost of ownership (although our systems might cost more up front to build). It is always best to incorporate green techniques early in the project timeline, starting with the initial phases of design. All too often we're called in at the last minute when the plans have been completed and it is very difficult to make changes, at least at low cost and minimal hassle."

Environment, Entrepreneurship, and Innovation: Systems Efficiency Strategies for Industrial and Commercial Facilities

Many managers are unaware of the strategic advantages and cost savings possible through systems analysis applied to material, energy, and water use in building design and operation. This section provides whole-systems strategies for improving resource efficiency in industrial and commercial buildings. [3] Systems thinking and integrated, multidisciplinary methods are explained that can stimulate innovation in both the equipment (technical) systems that make up facilities as well as the human (organizational) systems involved in the design-build-operate process. Identifying and using key leverage points and systemic synergies can dramatically increase the performance of buildings and the groups of people who make and run them. In practice those approaches have saved money, reduced environmental impacts, improved worker health and productivity, attracted new employees, greatly decreased operating costs while adding little or nothing to initial costs, and in some cases even decreased capital costs.

Resource Efficiency: Doing More with Less

Resource efficiency (also called "resource productivity" and "eco-efficiency") provides cost-saving methods for reducing

a company's environmental and health impacts. Businesses consume resources to deliver goods and services and to create socioeconomic benefits. Primary resource inputs are materials, water, and energy. Their use directly links industrial activity to the earth through extraction, pollution, and waste generation. (Labor, money, and time are also economic inputs, although environmental and health impacts associated with their use are generally more indirect; we will focus on physical and energy resource use.) In any firm that manages for maximum efficiency, the life-cycle resource intensity and environmental "footprint" of a given product or company is evaluated across the supply chain, from the natural resource base through manufacturing and use to ultimate disposal or recycling.

Ideally resource efficiency enables the delivery of goods and services of equal or better quality while reducing both the costs and impacts of each unit of output. Systems efficiency strategies go beyond conservation by boosting productivity and differentiating the firm. When efficiency measurement stimulates innovation, doing more and better with less fosters revenue growth. Innovation and the entrepreneurial initiative that drives it result in the delivery to market of *new* goods and services with superior performance or other attributes that out-compete existing products and industries.

This Schumpeterian "creative destruction" (the creation of new products, processes, technologies, markets, and organizational forms) is fundamental to capitalism. A capitalist economizes on scarce capital resources by investing to improve productivity. The resource intensity of each unit of production tends to fall over time as knowledge and technology improve. Those dynamics have already increased resource productivity. For example, in the United States the amount of energy consumed per dollar of GDP has decreased in all but five of the years since 1976—for a total drop of more than 35 percent between 1973 and 2000. That improvement is good, but the reality is that standard practices have tended to prompt relatively incremental improvements. The potential for much greater productivity increases remains untapped, awaiting the systematic and synergistic application of best practices and better technologies. Unfortunately, market barriers and organizational behaviors maintain standard practices, thus hindering progress.

Overcoming those obstacles requires leadership, comprehensive strategies, and organizational change, but radical resource efficiency can be achieved. Radical resource efficiency results from effective management combined with innovative practices. Systems thinking and end-use, least-cost analysis (discussed later in this section) are essential conceptual frameworks for rapid improvement. Doing more with less is a basic and accepted business objective and a central concept of practices such as total quality management. Thus resource efficiency measures provide a familiar, practicable, and visibly beneficial first step.

"Greening" Facilities: A Good Place to Start

Buildings are one of an organization's primary interfaces with natural systems via the impacts of materials, energy, water, and land use. Consequently, they deserve attention from both systems dynamics and corporate strategy perspectives. Buildings and facilities are ideal sites for initial resource efficiency efforts in most companies. Every business uses buildings and pays literal overhead costs to keep the roof up. Yet often overlooked are the simultaneous financial, environmental, and health leverage that buildings offer.

Most buildings are relatively wasteful of money and resources, compared with state-of-the-art green building examples. Best practices can yield large improvements in building performance, occupant health and productivity, and environmental impacts. These benefits come with 30–50 percent lower operating costs and on average only 2–7 percent higher initial costs (and, in some cases, decreased capital costs). Those benefits have been widely demonstrated in environmentally preferable or "green" buildings certified by USGBC's **Leadership in Energy and Environmental Design (LEED)** rating system, and the US Department of Energy's Energy Star label.

There are many areas for performance improvement. The opportunities discussed here are primarily but not exclusively in energy use. Typically, those are the easiest opportunities to identify and offer the quickest benefits at the least risk to most businesses. The major categories of energy savings opportunities include lighting; motors; pumps and fans; heating, ventilation, and air-conditioning (HVAC) systems; building envelope; thermal integration of temperature differences and heat flows; load management; measurement and controls; and operational techniques. Keep in mind that the same systems thinking can be applied to other dimensions of a company's operations, including its supply chain.

Common resource efficiency opportunities in most building systems are quantifiable, proven, and relatively easy to understand and implement. Such opportunities are widespread due to technological improvements and because the design-build process consistently produces structural and mechanical systems that are relatively inefficient and overbuilt. Factories are particularly attractive subjects because manufacturing is a resource-intensive enterprise. Offices and other commercial buildings also offer potential. The economic and environmental gains are greatest in new design and construction, but retrofit opportunities abound.

Implementing a suite of proven best practices and technologies carries a high probability of yielding short-term cost-effective improvements. These measures increase profits directly, as each dollar of saved overhead goes straight to the bottom line. Although these savings convey more limited profit-growth potential than do sales, this oft-neglected frontier of cost reduction can add value at lower risk than launching new products and services, which only add to profits on the margin. In some cases, significant savings through more efficient resource use can make additional, relatively inexpensive capital available for higher priority investments.

Systems Thinking

Strategies discussed here are informed by systems thinking and the principles of system dynamics. These representative approaches to technology, design, and management have been successfully applied in a broad spectrum of facilities and contexts. As we have discussed, systems can be technical or organizational. Buildings are "technical" systems comprising subsystems such as climate control, water and plumbing, lighting, and others. Buildings are designed, built, and operated by "organizational" systems that include owners, architects, engineers, builders, tenants, and others. As with other manufacturing activities, this organizational system comprises different individuals, and teams execute an iterative process that results in a product (the building). Well-established systems analysis tells us that small changes at key nodes or input variables of complex systems can result in large changes in system outcomes. Thus identifying and using insights about key leverage points can significantly increase the performance of buildings as well as the groups that make and run them.

Implementation strategies typically are directed at creating change by making the business case for efficiency improvements and providing incentives for desired present and future behavior. As the reader knows, not all approaches will yield economic results in every context because conditions vary widely at different facilities and companies. There is no magic formula for success, nor can we provide an exhaustive list of opportunities. Rather, this discussion is intended as an introduction to representative opportunities and to methods for realizing their greatest value.

Leadership, Management, Innovation, and Entrepreneurship

Realizing those potential benefits requires that standard practices be changed. It is a leadership and management challenge that involves entrepreneurial innovation. Building design, construction, and operation is a complex process involving many participants, including developers, architects, contractors and subcontractors, clients, and end users. Greening that process encompasses design, engineering, and technology, and the management of information, money, and organizational behavior. The organizational learning value is high and spans a range of disciplines and enterprise functions. The successful integration of the varied participants involved in a building's life cycle is a primary challenge to green building champions and is perhaps the most influential factor in achieving radical improvements in building performance.

When it comes to adopting a green building design, differences between managers and leaders are also a consideration. Management strategies are arguably more conservative than leadership initiatives. Managers typically seek stability and risk reduction as they help steer an organization toward defined goals. Managers tend to favor slower, more incremental change. In contrast, the more entrepreneurial leaders are innovation oriented and take greater risks to move an organization farther and faster toward end states that radically differ from the existing patterns. These leaders often are not formal, official leaders. They may emerge as leaders of change. Acting as a change agent is essentially entrepreneurial because implementing significant organizational change requires vision and initiative, not a risk-reduction mind-set. Entrepreneurs have a vision of a new future reality and harness resources to realize that vision. Entrepreneurial leadership seeks to create innovative change in a company's products and services. Acting entrepreneurially within one's own organization is what consultant Gifford Pinchot III terms "intrapreneuring." [4] Sustaining innovation often requires organizational change, also potentially an innovative act.

A would-be change agent usually has limited resources with which to attain his or her objectives. He or she typically lacks formal authority over all the process participants whose cooperation is needed to reach a goal. Consequently, a systems perspective is valuable. An intrapreneur can identify and focus on leverage points in the system to effect the most change with limited resources. Identifying technical synergies can yield cost-effective performance improvements. (Examples are discussed later in this section.) Influencing the decision rules of participants can shift

organizational process outcomes. Persuasion can substitute for compulsion. Identifying benefits and incentives for the participant decision maker can help build buy-in to the change agent's approach.

Green buildings are innovative products with dramatically improved performance relative to standard buildings. Those improvements are heavily dependent on improvements in technical subsystems, such as energy and water use. They are determined by the actions and outcome of the organizational design-build-operate system, which is in effect the manufacturing process.

The economic benefits of greening facilities provide the strongest motivating factor and a common denominator for undertaking new practices involving disparate parties, unfamiliar methods, and the challenges of change. The dollar is the universal solvent, the value-neutral language of business. All participants can agree to the goal of cost cutting, regardless of their beliefs or perspectives on the environmental and social aspects.

Initial successes in green building can free up resources and build stakeholder knowledge, buy-in, and confidence. These traits are useful for further, more challenging steps toward sustainability, such as product and business model redesign.

This is not to say that efficiency measures are easy—they are not. The process requires unlearning old techniques and reforming the traditional process. Even modest changes can meet with significant resistance. But greening strategies use proven tools and techniques that can be discussed in quantifiable terms of engineering and financial analysis, simplifying the challenge of implementing new ways of doing things. Expert assistance is readily available, and successful systems and buildings provide literal examples. Skeptical participants might believe that certain measures "can't work here," but they can be shown buildings where such techniques have worked in a wide range of climates and structures. The merits can be presented with numbers rather than assertions.

Systematic Resistance

Green building is growing rapidly and moving into the mainstream of the construction industry. Nevertheless, many people continue to view it as a leading-edge activity and lacking standard practice, despite demonstrated benefits. The diffusion of this innovation is still in its early stages. As with many innovations, organizational behavior is the crux of the issue and has a larger impact than technology. It determines whether or not resource-efficient decisions are undertaken and implemented. That should not be surprising. After all, the usual ways of doing things seem to work. Buildings get built, their systems function, people occupy them and go about their business, and complaints are relatively few. Architects and engineers get paid and move on to the next project. Most of the parties involved are satisfied. If the system is not broken, why fix it?

Follow the Money to Find the Motives

Some might ask, if green building is so cost-effective, why isn't more of it happening in the free market? Surely if it were profitable, people would do it. But in the workaday world, green building experience is lacking and schedule and budget pressures limit the amount of effort that can be put into design and construction. If the owner doesn't ask for green features, it is up to another project participant to promote them. Champions of sustainable design face many obstacles to implementing their ideas, both in the marketplace and even within their own organizations. Selling environmentally friendly approaches and equipment to clients, managers, and colleagues often remains challenging, especially if taking those approaches or using that equipment asks them to do anything differently or spend more time and money. In addition, most design and construction professionals have little or no training or direct experience in sustainable building techniques. They don't see much incentive to try something new if they think it might increase the risk of a lost bid or an unhappy client. If common practices, habits, and perspectives don't prioritize green techniques then, as the saying goes, it can be hard to teach old dogs new tricks.

The picture is changing rapidly. Public agencies, architects, interior designers, construction companies, and other professionals are increasingly realizing the benefits of green buildings and are asking for—and getting—better results. Has it swept the country? No, but people are doing it and making money. There are many demonstrated economic benefits to more sustainable real estate development, but the problem is they don't all accrue to the same parties. Some benefits aren't counted directly in our economic system, such as reduced environmental impacts. But most important, we don't live in a free market; we live in the real world. Free markets exist only in theories and textbooks. Actual markets function under the influence of human and organizational behaviors and dynamics that prevent more optimal results.

In politics, it is said that if you want to know why something happens (or doesn't), follow the money. The same is true in building design and construction. We must look more closely at the economic incentives (and disincentives) facing the various parties to the design-build process to understand why more buildings aren't more sustainable.

Usually, several different companies and individuals are involved in a construction project. Sometimes one party profits at the expense of another party in the same project (even in the same firm). For example, a contractor or project manager might buy cheaper, less efficient mechanical equipment to save money or speed delivery. As a result, the tenant or facilities manager pays higher energy bills. For each decision or action, determine who benefits and you will often understand why a better outcome for society and the environment (if not for the owner) didn't occur.

Market dynamics and business models shape the decision rules of participants in the process and thus the outcomes. For example, the after-tax return on increasing the diameter of wire by just one size in a standard US office lighting circuit typically approaches 200 percent per year. The wire-size table in the National Electrical Code is meant only to help prevent fires, not save money, and hence specifies wire with half the diameter—and four times the electrical losses due to greater resistance—as would be economically desirable. However, an electrician altruistic enough to buy the larger (and more expensive) wire would no longer be the low bidder and wouldn't get the job. This example embodies two barriers to more efficient buildings: a life-safety minimum-requirement code misinterpreted as an economic optimum, and a split incentive between the party who chooses the wire size and the one who later pays the electric bills.

It is worthwhile to examine the incentives and disincentives faced by the various parties to the design-build process, and explore why standard practices and paradigms often block environmental improvements, to determine effective remedies.

The Current Design-Build Process Paradigm

Consider a representative list of the different parties involved in creating typical commercial buildings. The owner might be a building developer seeking to sell or lease the property, or it might be a business, public agency, educational institution, or other organization that owns its buildings. The project manager might be an employee of the owner or a general contractor. The design is created by contractors and consultants, or sometimes by staff of the business owner, including architects, structural engineers, and mechanical engineers. Construction is typically contracted out, or sometimes performed by a unit of the developer or business owner. Facility managers operate and maintain the buildings.

Now consider some of the common pressures and motivations that each of these parties faces. Any of them can champion sustainable design but also can undermine it—often unintentionally—by pursuing goals that their position or employer's policies dictate. Each project and decision maker is different, and generalizations are useful to a limited extent. Nevertheless, one can draw insights by considering typical incentives and disincentives that come with a given job description and role in the design-build process, regardless of the opinions and values of the person who is doing that particular job. Scholars of organizational behavior note that "where you stand depends on where you sit" applies.

Developers often build on speculation. They will find a buyer eventually. The lower their initial costs, the greater their potential profit from sale or lease. The structural shell is designed before tenants are found, and performance specifications are unlikely to exceed minimum building code requirements. Developers can buy low-quality equipment to save themselves money, and they don't ultimately pay the resulting higher energy bills. They might be experienced in green building techniques but probably are not. Many see little incentive to risk slowing their project turnover rate, increasing costs, or alienating potential customers with unfamiliar green features.

Tenants usually have little control over building design and tend to have a short-term perspective on costs. Even buyers of spec buildings often have no influence on the design or performance.

Organizations that own their buildings are more likely to take a more integrated, long-term perspective on life-cycle cost and performance (especially for new construction). They might be more interested in green building concepts than other players—or at least more likely to push for improvements. Even then, senior managers might share and communicate a greener vision but face competing pressures from project managers or department heads within their own firm or among their contractors.

Project managers are often rewarded for completing work ahead of schedule and under budget. This can provide incentives to cut corners, reject or redo design features and specifications (such "value engineering" often undermines integrated design), squeeze more out of contractors, and proceed with the most readily available options without pausing to make improvements or even to correct noncritical shortcomings and mistakes. If the manager's budget is funding construction but not building operation, there might be an incentive to use cheaper but lower-quality

materials and equipment and leave any increased maintenance or cost concerns to somebody else. These factors apply to both owners' employees and general contractors alike.

Architects are encouraged to innovate and are rewarded for interesting new designs with recognition and further work. However, environmental attributes do not often rank high in the review criteria of their clients and peers. Architects might have significant training or experience in whole-system, resource-efficient sustainable design but probably do not. If the client hasn't asked them to create a green building, they have little incentive to struggle to explain the potential benefits to the owner or contractor. When fees are based on a percentage of project cost, the compensation structure rewards architects for what they spend and not for what they save the client (or whoever ultimately pays the utility bills) in reduced energy or water use and costs.

Architects and engineers must work together on the same design, but that does not mean that they necessarily coordinate their efforts to produce an optimal building. In many cases, the architects and engineers are from different contractors. Even when they are from two departments within the same firm, all too often there is relatively little communication and harmonization of design approaches and equipment specifications. The architect completes the design with minimal input from the engineers and in effect rolls up the drawings and pushes them through a little hole in the wall into the engineering department to execute the next project phase. The design process is sequential rather than simultaneous.

There are two main types of engineers involved in building. Structural engineers are relatively conservative in their approach because if their design doesn't work, someone could die. Safety and consistency are prioritized over innovation. Mechanical engineers (MEs) face less pressure in that their worst-case design failure scenario is that building occupants might have to buy a fan or heater. But MEs are ultimately responsible for the majority of a building's energy use. For example, HVAC systems comprise almost half of the energy use of a typical San Francisco office building, the largest share of the load. (The next-largest energy consumer is lighting at more than one-fourth, and plug loads account for more than 10 percent of the building's total electricity use.) Yet better mechanical systems designs are typically invisible to users. Even if those paying the utility bills realize lower costs, unless they share the savings with the engineering team, the MEs are typically not rewarded for innovation or greater effort to green the design.

Both types of engineers face incentives to overdesign structural and mechanical systems, as excess capacity provides a margin of security (but often wastes resources). Both types labor under the same tight budgets and short timelines. They often specify average- rather than premium-quality equipment to cut initial costs and use design rules of thumb to save time. Indeed, if a problem arises, the engineer's best defense is that the design follows standard practice. Techniques that worked in the past (or at least did not fail) are copied and reused. Measurement and analysis of previous structures' actual performance is not commonly incorporated into improving the next similar design. Unlike architects, engineers are quite happy to make a building look and perform like the one next door. Those habitual approaches produce functional but overly energy-intensive designs.

Facility managers' experience and input are rarely solicited and incorporated into the design process. Typically, the managers are handed the keys after the building is complete and tasked with keeping the lights on and the floors clean on a limited budget. Increasingly, their function is outsourced. Their staff might not have the time or training to commission, maintain, and operate systems at peak environmental performance. They might not pay the utility bills or have much funding for investment in building improvements. Even if they do, they might not be inclined to increase energy and water efficiency and cut costs if their reward is a smaller budget next year.

Apart from the owner, no single participant in this group decision-making system has compelling authority over the others, and none can exert determining influence over the process. Even the owner must exert considerable effort to ensure that her objectives survive every step of the sequence. The typical result of this collective process is safe, sometimes interesting-looking structures with poor energy performance and average (frequently excessive) environmental impacts.

Most of the parties to design-build projects are used to these standard approaches and common dynamics, adhere to them habitually, and expect them intuitively. They see nothing abnormal and perceive little need for improvement, given that for the most part the end-user clients and occupants are satisfied or at least not complaining any more than usual. No market failures are required to explain this outcome, although it imposes unnecessary costs on society. All the participants in this process are acting in their economic rational self-interest, within the bounds of their knowledge. If a camel is "a horse designed by a committee," as the joke goes, then, in effect, all buildings are camels: their design intention has been subverted by the process.

Strategies for a Greener Facility Design-Build Process

The standard process produces suboptimal buildings because participants pursue their own objectives, even to a limited extent, rather than compromising more and cooperating in greater harmony to obtain optimal outcomes for building owners and users over the long term. Thus green building champions are necessarily change agents. Their challenge is to influence the organizational system by influencing the participants as well as technology and design. This experience can be as difficult as herding cats.

Only by providing participants with compelling reasons to change their approach, such as financial benefits and strategic advantage, can you foster lasting change.

The following paragraphs give a brief overview of some remedies to the common barriers to greener buildings.

Start early. It is very important to incorporate green elements from the very beginning of a project. An old design axiom says that all the really important mistakes are made on the first day. Even small decisions early in the process have significant influence on future building performance and costs. It is worthwhile to "measure twice and cut once" where building design and performance are concerned.

Increased awareness of green building techniques and demonstrated successes would benefit all the parties. Formal education plays a crucial role, but the pace of market transformation can be slow as graduates enter the workplace and make their mark. More and better in-service training and user-friendly resource materials for busy professionals can help shift existing practices faster. Positive, hands-on field experience with sustainable building is perhaps the most potent learning tool.

Encourage the use of outside energy-efficiency reviewers. Doing so can help establish a common baseline for design objectives and performance benchmarks. Authoritative third-party project assessments reinforce the importance of ensuring that specified and installed equipment and systems operate efficiently. For example, many energy companies provide energy-efficiency design assistance, useful resources and support, and sometimes economic incentives.

Building codes (such as California's stringent Title 24) and *voluntary guidelines* (such as LEED) can improve building design and performance as well as help educate practitioners. The LEED rating system provides a framework for setting shared goals, a template for project execution, and neutral evaluation criteria based on consensus best practices and measurable criteria.

Set targets and rewards for performance. Use specific metrics and performance criteria. Provide clear financial incentives for high-quality work. For example, provide a bonus payment if the building's performance exceeds California's Title 24 Energy Code by more than 40 percent or if LEED rating points are earned. Performance-based fees compensate architects and engineers in part based on measured savings in energy and water efficiency relative to preagreed building performance standards, an incentive for more efficient design.

The most effective approach is neither a technology nor a set of guidelines and benchmarks but rather to redesign the process itself. An *integrated design process* brings together project participants, stakeholders, and outside expertise at the earliest practical point in the project to collaborate, cocreate, and execute a shared vision. Often called a charrette, such an intensive, multidisciplinary-facilitated meeting can help identify and overcome many of the barriers to optimal green design.

This integrative process assists participants in articulating their differing perceptions and incentives and allows them to exchange ideas, work out problems, and establish common terminology and objectives. It creates a communication space in which to build mutual understanding and trust, clarifies owners' goals and options, and helps participants agree on any mutual trade-offs and concessions that might be required to achieve an optimal result. Those exercises can significantly improve plans and specifications, streamline construction, reduce total costs, and increase building performance—increasing the chances that systems will work as they are intended to, rather than just as they are *designed* to.

End-Use, Least-Cost Analysis

End-use, least-cost analysis is a core concept of whole-systems, resource-efficient design. Historically, energy resource discussions have focused on supply: where do we get more, and how much does it cost? But people don't want barrels of oil or kilowatt-hours of electricity per se; they want the services that energy ultimately provides, such as hot showers, cold beer, comfortable buildings, light, torque, and mobility. Considered from the demand as well as the supply side of the equation, least-cost analysis identifies the cheapest, cleanest way to deliver each of these services. Often the better, more cost-effective way is using less energy more productively, with smarter technologies. Efficient end use can thus compete with new supply as an energy resource and leverage bigger savings in resources, cost, and upstream pollution across the whole system.

Saving energy (especially electricity) is cheaper than consuming fuel to generate it. Surveys of utility-directed "demand-side management" efforts to save electricity show saved watts—or what Amory Lovins calls "negawatts"—typically cost from $0.025 to $0.02 per saved kilowatt-hour or less. That is less expensive than the marginal cost of electricity from all other sources of supply and unlike most types of generation does not emit any pollution. Although the potential savings are finite, they are significant.

Consider a pumping example. The end use is to move a unit of fluid through an industrial pipe. The pump runs on electricity. Thermal losses occur when coal is burned at a power plant to produce steam that a generator converts to electricity. Energy losses compound in transmission and distribution, in the motor and pump, the throttling balance valve, and pipe friction, until ultimately only 10 percent of the coal's embodied energy does the desired work.

Where is the biggest leverage point for resource efficiency? Conversion efficiency can be improved at the power plant (e.g., with heat recapture and cogeneration) and at other points along the delivery chain. Yet the biggest "bang for the buck" lies closest to the end-use application. For example, bigger pipes have less friction, reducing pumping requirements. That leverages upstream savings, turning losses into compounding savings. Each unit of conserved pumping energy in the pipe saves ten units of fuel, cost, and pollution at the power plant.

Generating Returns from Integrated Systems

Integrated design methodology optimizes the relationships among the components in technical systems as well as among a facility's component subsystems. The performance of many mechanical systems is undermined by design shortcuts, compromised layouts, and penny-wise, pound-foolish capital cost cutting. An integrated design approach can recognize and mitigate these effects at the same or reduced construction cost. It is much more cost-effective to integrate these elements into the initial design than to try to squeeze them into the project later—or retrofit them after completion. Maximum savings are achieved by first minimizing load at the end-use application, before selecting the energy supply or applying energy-conserving measures "upstream" toward the motor or other energy-conversion device.

Consider the following example. Bends in pipes or ducts increase friction and thus pumping power requirements. Optimal pipe and duct layouts eliminate bends. Larger-diameter pipe sizing is also very important because friction falls as nearly the fifth power of pipe diameter. Smaller pumping requirements enable smaller pumps, motors, and electrical systems, reducing capital costs. Larger pipes also maintain equivalent fluid flow at less velocity, enabling significant pumping energy savings. The "cube law" relationship between pump impeller power and fluid flow means that decreasing velocity by half drops pumping power use by almost seven-eighths. (Those same dynamics and potential savings also apply to ducts and fans.)

That approach was pioneered by Singaporean engineer Lee Eng Lock. Lee tutored Dutch engineer Jan Schilham at Interface Corporation, who applied those techniques to a pumping loop for a new carpet factory. A top European company designed the system to use pumps requiring a total of 95 horsepower. But before construction began, Schilham upsized the pipes and thus downsized the pumps. The original designer had chosen the smaller pipes because, according to the traditional cost-benefit analysis method, the extra cost of larger ones wasn't justified by the pumping energy savings.

Schilham further reduced friction with shorter, straighter pipes by laying out the pipes first, then positioning the equipment that they connected. Designers normally position production equipment without concern for efficient power configuration, and then have a pipe fitter connect the components with long runs and numerous bends. Those simple design changes cut the power requirement to only 7 horsepower—a 92 percent reduction. The redesigned system cost less to build and to operate, was easier to insulate, involved no new technology, and worked better in all respects. That small example has important implications: pumping is the largest application of motors, and motors use three-quarters of all industrial electricity in the United States, or three-fifths of all electricity.

Inventor Edwin Land said, "People who seem to have had a new idea have often simply stopped having an old idea." [5] The old idea is one of diminishing returns—that the greater the resource saving, the higher the cost. But that old idea is giving way to the new idea that innovative design can make big energy savings less expensive to attain than small savings. Such "tunneling through the cost barrier" has been proven in many kinds of technical systems. (A few other examples are highlighted later in this section.)

Noted green architect William McDonough said, "Our culture designs the same building for Reykjavik and Rangoon; we heat one and cool the other; why do we do it that way? I call this the 'Black Sun.'" [6] Facilities' energy intensity is chiefly in the HVAC systems that create interior comfort by compensating for climatic conditions and that provide (or remove) industrial process heat and cooling.

Cooling systems are typically designed to serve peak load, regardless of how frequently that occurs. The chilled water temperature is often determined by the most extreme thermal requirements of a small subset of the total load, such as one or two machines out of many. That results in excess cooling capacity and inefficient operation at partial loads. It is much more efficient to segregate the loads with parallel chilled water piping loops at two different temperatures. One higher-temperature loop with dedicated chillers optimized for that temperature can serve the majority of a facility's load. A second lower-temperature loop with a smaller high-efficiency chiller can serve the most demanding subset of the load. This can improve overall cooling plant efficiency by 25 percent or more. Higher temperature chillers cost less than lower temperature chillers of equal capacity.

"Thermal integration" leverages temperature differences. Many businesses consume energy to create heat and then spend even more energy removing waste heat from their processes and facilities, without matching up the two. Instead, they should strive to make full use of available energies before discarding them to the environment. Waste heat from an oven or boiler can be used to preheat wash water or intake air. Winter or night cool air, groundwater, or utility water can provide free cooling. Heat exchangers can allow energy transfer between media that should not mix. Such measures can reduce or eliminate HVAC capacity.

Lighting is generally one of the most cost-effective energy savings opportunities, due to the rapid pace of improvements in lighting technology and design. Retrofits usually offer attractive paybacks, averaging roughly 30 percent ROI. Yet the impact on building systems extends beyond illumination. Energy-efficient bulbs also emit less heat, thereby reducing facility cooling loads, enabling HVAC capacity cost savings.

Money

Making the business case for efficiency improvements is perhaps the most important yet most challenging task facing a sustainability champion. Most companies spend a small fraction of their costs on energy, and it does not command much executive attention. Facilities maintenance is a far lower priority to most senior managers than production, sales, and customer service. Yet saving 1–2 percent of total costs matters, even in financial terms alone.

Whole-Systems, Life-Cycle Costing

Green building experience shows that cost-effective energy savings of 30–50 percent are achievable in many facilities worldwide. Much of this wasted energy and excess mechanical and electrical systems capacity results from minimizing first cost instead of cost of ownership, especially in fast-track projects. High-efficiency design and equipment can cost more up front. Penny-wise, pound-foolish shortcuts and cost cutting degrade performance and increase energy bills for a facility's lifetime. Smart money looks at the big picture, not just the price tag.

Pervasive overemphasis on short-term first costs results in wasteful decisions. In facilities design and construction, the "value engineering" process is intended to save the owners money. Plans are reviewed and components are approved or rejected with a line-item-veto approach. Although that method can squeeze increments of capital cost out of a design, in actuality it undermines both long-term value and engineering integrity. A component-focused approach erodes design integration (and often function) and negates whole-systems benefits. Paying more for one component can often downsize or eliminate others, reducing total system capital cost as well as operating cost. Optimizing components for single benefits, not whole systems or multiple benefits, "pessimizes" the system. A first-cost approach might benefit one department's budget one time but imposes increased operating costs on the firm for decades to come. Look for the cheapest total cost of owning and operating the entire system of which the device is a component.

Whole-system, life-cycle costing incorporates both capital and operating costs (as well downtime costs, changes in output, the value of reliability, and other factors). It allows companies to assess the actual total cost of ownership, a better reflection of the financial impact of decisions on a company and its shareholders. Those techniques should credit savings from reduced infrastructure (recall the "big pipes, small pumps" example).

Some designers try to save money by using standard rules of thumb and even copying old designs without improving upon them. That helps them offer low bids to secure work. Facilities owners might find such practices appealing to reduce short-run costs or to help reduce construction project timelines. Although facilities construction timing is critical to some industries' profit model (e.g., electronics), fast-track design should not become standard procedure because speed comes at the price of lost efficiency and project value. Evaluate and improve upon past designs using operator feedback and careful measurement. Often the perceived need for fast design and construction is caused by lack of planning and preparation. Over time, fast design can inadvertently become a substitute for these vital steps.

Prioritization of Improvements

Whole-systems investment criteria are relevant to how proposed improvements are implemented. Green design consultants and champions often rank their suggestions according to their cost and **return on investment (ROI)**. Managers are tempted to go for the "low-hanging fruit" and select the most financially attractive measures first (or only), to reduce costs. This is also true of energy savings companies (ESCOs), which consult to firms on efficiency opportunities and often help implement the measures. Many ESCOs upgrade lighting, share the savings resulting from reduced bills with their clients—and stop there. But "cream-skimming" the most attractive savings only can render less financially attractive measures uneconomical when they are considered individually rather than as part of a systemic set of upgrades. This can make larger potential total savings of the whole set of opportunities difficult or impossible to attain. Maximize cost-effective improvements by considering all proposed green measures as a package, and reinvest the resources freed up via the larger cost reduction projects into other, less individually attractive projects. Only in that way will you be able to attain large systemic improvements cost effectively.

Investment Criteria: Payback and ROI

Retrofit improvements are often blocked by nonsensical financial hurdles. Upgrades are commonly held to higher ROI standards than are purchases of new equipment. Reexamine investment criteria to avoid distortions and inconsistencies. Most companies seem to apply an eighteen-month to two-year cap on payback periods for investments in efficiency, although the rationale for doing so remains unclear. This provides a much stricter standard than typical investment criteria for new capacity or supply investments, which is closer to the cost of capital (e.g., about 11–15 percent ROI). Harmonize payback and ROI requirements so that operating and financial people speak a common language; otherwise they can't compare investment opportunities on a level playing field. There are multiple approaches to calculating payback and ROI. Simplified methods are used here for the purposes of discussion.

The payback period for implementing an energy-efficiency measure can be calculated as the implementation costs divided by the energy savings in dollars. The resulting payback number represents the number of years of operation that is required to fully recover the capital investment costs. The ROI method used by the Department of Energy examines the projected annual cost after (CA) implementing a project, compared to a baseline annual cost before (CB) implementing the project. Expressed as a formula, ROI is the ratio of anticipated cost savings (CB − CA) to projected implementation cost (CI), expressed as a percentage.

Let us consider a hypothetical example of lighting and HVAC improvements. CA are energy costs after the energy-efficiency project is implemented, CB are the energy costs before implementing the project, and CI is the cost of the project.

The ROI is 33 percent and 37 percent for HVAC and lighting measures, respectively. That means that each year an average of 34 percent of the original investment is recovered through energy savings—several times higher than the typical ROI requirement for investments in new productive capacity. If a company's marginal cost of capital is, for example, 15 percent per year, that implies that the company is willing to accept a payback in the six- to seven-year range for additional capacity. Insisting that energy efficiency pay as much as $0.04 to $0.08 per kilowatt hour more for negawatts than for new electricity supply deprives shareholders of profits.

While building green may require collaboration among many different people at multiple points in the process, the effort can be well worth it. For little to no additional upfront costs, green buildings save operating costs and improve occupant productivity. The key, however, is to optimize the entire system rather than to view the design, construction, and operation of a building as unrelated parts.

KEY TAKEAWAYS

- A systems approach can significantly improve building designs and ongoing operating costs by optimizing performance across all aspects of the building system.
- Some barriers remain to green building, such as inadequate funding models and lack of knowledge, but those barriers are decreasing steadily.

EXERCISES

1. What are the major challenges facing Heather Glen?
2. What obstacles did she confront in the past, and how did those help prepare her for her current task?
3. What can she do to successfully implement this new project?

---

[1] This case was prepared by Batten fellow Chris Lotspeich in collaboration with author {Author's Name Retracted as requested by the work's original creator or licensee}. {Author's Name Retracted as requested by the work's original creator or licensee} and Chris Lotspeich, *"Greening" Facilities: Hermes Microtech, Inc.*, UVA-ENT-0054 (Charlottesville: Darden Business Publishing, University of Virginia, 2004). Case can be accessed through the Darden Case Collection at https://store.darden.virginia.edu.

[2] Name has been changed. This case is an amalgamation of different business scenarios that case researcher/writer Chris Lotspeich created. The case is not about one single company and none of the names are real; note tongue-in-cheek choice of names.

[3] This background note was prepared by Batten fellow Chris Lotspeich in collaboration with author {Author's Name Retracted as requested by the work's original creator or licensee}. {Author's Name Retracted as requested by the work's original creator or licensee} and Chris Lotspeich, *Environment, Entrepreneurship, and Innovation: Systems Efficiency Strategies for Industrial and Commercial Facilities*, UVA-ENT-0052 (Charlottesville: Darden Business Publishing, University of Virginia, 2008). Note can be accessed through the Darden Case Collection at https://store.darden.virginia.edu.

[4] Gifford Pinchot, *Intrapreneuring: Why You Don't Have to Leave the Corporation to Become an Entrepreneur* (New York: Harper & Row, 1985). See also Elizabeth Pinchot and Gifford Pinchot, *The Intelligent Organization* (San Francisco: Berrett-Koehler Publications, 1996); and Gifford Pinchot and Ron Pellman, *Intrapreneuring in Action: A Handbook for Business Innovation* (San Francisco: Berrett-Koehler Publications, 1999).

[5] {Author's Name Retracted as requested by the work's original creator or licensee} and Mark Meier, *Project FROG: Sustainability and Innovation in Building Design*, UVA-ENT-0158 (Charlottesville: Darden Business Publishing, University of Virginia, 2010).

[6] {Author's Name Retracted as requested by the work's original creator or licensee} and Mark Meier, *Project FROG: Sustainability and Innovation in Building Design*, UVA-ENT-0158 (Charlottesville: Darden Business Publishing, University of Virginia, 2010).

7.3 Shaw Industries: Sustainable Business, Entrepreneurial Innovation, and Green Chemistry

1. Analyze strategies to spur and sustain innovation within a mature industry.

2. Understand how a variety of innovations can accumulate to a significant breakthrough.

3. Examine how cradle-to-cradle design is implemented.

The carpet industry is the battlefield where the war for sustainability is being waged.

- Architect William McDonough

The Shaw Industries case examines the production of a cradle-to-cradle carpet product in which a waste stream becomes a material input stream. [1] In this situation we look at innovation challenges faced by a large global competitor.

In 2003 Shaw's EcoWorx carpet tiles won a US Green Chemistry Institute's Presidential Green Chemistry Challenge Award. The company had earned the award by combining the application of green chemistry and engineering principles (Table 7.5 "The Twelve Principles of Green Chemistry and Green Engineering") with a cradle-to-cradle design [2] (often called C2C) approach to create a closed-loop carpet tile system, a first in the industry. The product met the rising demand for "sustainable" innovations, helping to create a new market space in the late 1990s and 2000s as buyers became more cognizant of human health and ecosystem hazards associated with interior furnishings.

At the time, Steve Bradfield, Shaw's contract division vice president for environmental development, commented on the process of creating the EcoWorx innovation, a process that by no means was over: "The 12 Principles and C2C provide a framework for development of EcoWorx that incorporates anticipatory design, resource conservation, and material safety." [3] The framework was part of a larger sustainability strategic effort that the contract division was leading at Shaw. The company also needed to explain the benefits of the EcoWorx system and educate the marketplace on the desirability of sustainable products as qualitatively, economically, and environmentally superior replacements for a product system that had been in place for thirty years. Change was difficult, especially when the gains from a substitute product were not well understood by the end user or the independent distributor. It was also difficult internally for a Shaw culture that didn't fully comprehend the need to move beyond conservation.

Table 7.5 The Twelve Principles of Green Chemistry and Green Engineering

Green Chemistry	
1	**Prevention.** It is better to prevent waste than to treat it or clean it up after it has been created..
2	**Atom Economy.** Synthetic methods should be designed to maximize the incorporation of all materials used in the process into the final product.
3	**Less Hazardous Chemical Syntheses.** Wherever practicable, synthetic methods should be designed to use and generate substances that possess little or no toxicity to human health and the environment.
4	**Designing Safer Chemicals.** Chemical products should be designed to effect their desired function while minimizing their toxicity.
5	**Safer Solvents and Auxiliaries.** The use of auxiliary substances (e.g., solvents, separation agents, etc.) should be made unnecessary wherever possible and innocuous when used.
6	**Design for Energy Efficiency.** Energy requirements of chemical processes should be recognized for their environmental and economic impacts and should be minimized. If possible, synthetic methods should be conducted at ambient temperature and pressure.
7	**Use of Renewable Feedstocks.** A raw material or feedstock should be renewable rather than depleting whenever technically and economically practicable.
8	**Reduce Derivatives.** Unnecessary derivatization (use of blocking groups, protection/deprotection, temporary modification of physical/chemical

processes) should be minimized or avoided, if possible, because such steps require additional reagents and can generate waste.

9	**Catalysis.** Catalytic reagents (as selective as possible) are superior to stoichiometric reagents.	
10	**Design for Degradation.** Chemical products should be designed so that at the end of their function they break down into innocuous degradation products and do not persist in the environment.	
11	**Real-Time Analysis for Pollution Prevention.** Analytical methodologies need to be further developed to allow for real-time, in-process monitoring and control prior to the formation of hazardous substances.	
12	**Inherently Safer Chemistry for Accident Prevention.** Substances and the form of a substance used in a chemical process should be chosen to minimize the potential for chemical accidents, including releases, explosions, and fires.	

Green Engineering

1	**Inherent Rather Than Circumstantial.** Designers need to strive to ensure that all materials and energy inputs and outputs are as inherently nonhazardous as possible.
2	**Prevention Instead of Treatment.** It is better to prevent waste than to treat or clean up waste after it is formed.
3	**Design for Separation.** Separation and purification operations should be designed to minimize energy consumption and materials use.
4	**Maximize Efficiency.** Products, processes, and systems should be designed to maximize mass, energy, space, and time efficiency.
5	**Output Pulled versus Input Pushed.** Products, processes, and systems should be "output pulled" rather than "input pushed" through the use of energy and materials.
6	**Conserve Complexity.** Embedded entropy and complexity must be viewed as an investment when

making design choices on recycling, reuse, or beneficial disposition.

7	**Durability Rather Than Immortality.** Targeted durability, not immortality, should be a design goal.
8	**Meet Need, Minimize Excess.** Design for unnecessary capacity or capability (e.g., "one size fits all") solutions should be considered a design flaw.
9	**Minimize Material Diversity.** Material diversity in multicomponent products should be minimized to promote disassembly and value retention.
10	**Integrate Material and Energy Flows.** Design of products, processes, and systems must include integration and interconnectivity with available energy and materials flows.
11	**Design for Commercial "Afterlife."** Products, processes, and systems should be designed for performance in a commercial "afterlife."
12	**Renewable Inputs.** Material and energy inputs should be renewable rather than depleting.

Source: P. T. Anastas and J. C. Warner, *Green Chemistry: Theory and Practice* (New York: Oxford University Press, 1998), 30; and P. T. Anastas and J. B. Zimmerman, "Design through the 12 Principles of Green Engineering," *Environmental Science and Technology* 37, no. 5 (2003): 95–101. Used by permission.

The US Carpet Industry

World War II demanded wool, then the dominant carpet material, for military uniforms and blankets, providing an incentive for companies to research and create alternative fibers. This move toward alternatives was part of the general wartime drive that culminated in the introduction of synthetic materials (man-made) for many uses. After the war, manufacturers continued to develop various new natural and synthetic materials. By the 1960s, DuPont and Chemstrand's man-made nylon and acrylic materials supplied most of the growing carpet industry's textile fiber needs. An average American household could now afford machine-tufted synthetic carpets that replaced the expensive woven wool carpets of the past. By 2004 nylon accounted for 68 percent of the fibers used in carpet manufacturing, followed by 22 percent polypropylene and 9 percent polyester, with wool constituting less than 0.7 percent of the total.

By the 1970s, carpet flooring was the dominant aesthetic standard in a high proportion of industrialized countries for residential and commercial flooring markets. Historically, woven wool carpets (in which the carpet surface and backing were essentially one layer) gave way to tufted (fibers pulled through a matrix web) and needle-punched carpets bonded by a latex backing layer using an array of synthetic face fibers and backing materials. Carpet tiles, the fastest growing segment of the commercial carpeting industry, were expected to steadily replace much of the rolled broadloom carpet used historically in offices and other commercial locations. Regardless of design, all carpeting had traditionally been a complex matrix of dissimilar materials constructed without any thought of disassembly for recycling. [4]

Shaw Industries, Mohawk Industries, and Beaulieu of America were the three largest carpet producers in 2004. Interface was the largest carpet tile manufacturer. Invista, a fiber spin-off of DuPont, and Solutia were the sole US producers of Nylon 6.6, a type suitable for carpet. Honeywell and vertically integrated carpet giant Shaw Industries were the major producers of Nylon 6 for carpet use. Price competition, economic downturn, and overcapacity had taken a heavy toll on American fiber and carpet companies. Unlike the broader textile industry, the nylon fiber and carpet producers did not see an influx of low-cost imports due to high transportation costs, relatively low labor costs associated with US fiber and carpet production, and the difficulties in finding viable US distribution channels for imports. The industry was consolidating and companies vertically integrated, formed alliances, or organized around market niches as lower carpet and floor covering sales tracked personal income insecurity and general economic turbulence. The first few years of the twenty-first century witnessed the loss of more than 90,000 US textile jobs and 150 plant closings. The carpets and rugs sector experienced sluggish growth. Growth rebounded by 2005, but competition was fierce and buyers would not tolerate higher prices or lower product performance.

Shaw Industries

In 2006, Shaw Industries of Dalton, Georgia, was the world's largest carpet manufacturer, selling in Canada, Mexico, and the United States and exporting worldwide. The company's historic carpet brand names, including Cabin Crafts, Queen Carpet, Salem, Philadelphia Carpets, and ShawMark, were de-emphasized relative to the consolidated Shaw brand. Shaw sold residential products to large and small retailers and to the much smaller distributor channel. Shaw offered commercial products primarily to commercial dealers and contractors, including its own Spectra commercial contracting locations, through Shaw Contract, Patcraft, and Designweave. The company also sold laminate, ceramic tile, and hardwood flooring through its Shaw Hard

Surfaces division, and rugs through the Shaw Living division. Shaw Industries was publicly traded on the New York Stock Exchange (NYSE) until 2000, when it was purchased by Warren Buffet's Berkshire Hathaway Inc. Shaw's stock had been one of the best-performing stocks on the NYSE in the 1980s, but Wall Street's dot-com focus of the 1990s depressed the stock price of Shaw and other manufacturers. The Berkshire buyout took the Wall Street factor out of Shaw's management strategy, and 2001 through 2006 were record earnings years for the company.

Between 1985 and 2006, Shaw Industries made a string of acquisitions, including other large carpet makers, fiber-dyeing facilities, and fiber extrusion and yarn mills, moving steadily toward broad vertical integration of inputs and processes. The firm's expensive forays into retail stores ended, and Shaw concentrated on shifting its outside purchases of fiber to internal fiber production. Shaw polymerized, extruded, spun, twisted, and heat-set its own yarn and tufted, dyed, and finished the carpet. Several key acquisitions included the following:

- **Amoco's polypropylene operations, 1992.** Polypropylene fiber, used mainly in berber-style residential products, reached a high-water mark of approximately 30 percent of the fiber usage in the carpet industry. By purchasing the Amoco plants in Andalusia, Alabama, and Bainbridge, Georgia, in 1992, Shaw became the world's largest polypropylene carpet fiber producer, extruding all the fiber for its polypropylene carpets.

- **Queen Carpet, 1998.** Shaw purchased the fourth-largest manufacturer of carpets, Queen Carpet, which had $800 million in sales the previous year.

- **The Dixie Group, 2003.** The Dixie Group, one of the nation's biggest manufacturers of carpets for the mobile home and manufactured housing industry, sold six yarn-tufting, dyeing, finishing, and needlebond mills and distribution factories to Shaw for $180 million in October 2003. Included in the sale was a carpet recycling facility.

- **Honeywell Nylon 6 operations, 2005.** Shortly after its acquisition of the BASF carpet nylon business, Honeywell decided to exit the Nylon 6 carpet fiber business by selling to Shaw its South Carolina fiber mills at Anderson, Columbia, and Clemson. This made Shaw the world's largest producer of Nylon 6 carpet fiber. Honeywell's 50 percent interest in the Evergreen postconsumer Nylon 6 depolymerization facility was included in the deal.

- **Evergreen Nylon Recycling Facility, 2006.** Within

two months of closing the Honeywell acquisition, Shaw purchased the remaining 50 percent interest in the Augusta, Georgia, Evergreen caprolactam monomer recovery facility from Dutch State Mines (DSM). (Caprolactam was the monomer building block of Nylon 6.) This gave Shaw 100 percent ownership of the postconsumer Nylon 6 depolymerization facility, which had been closed since late 2001 due to low monomer prices. Shaw moved quickly to refurbish and restart the facility for production of thirty million pounds of caprolactam monomer by early 2007. This gave Shaw the only source of postconsumer Nylon 6 monomer, which could be continuously returned to carpet production.

Carpet Tile

For Shaw, the obvious place to start thinking about product redesign was at the top of the carpet hierarchy: carpet tile. Its high price in comparison with broadloom carpets, its thermoplastic polyvinyl chloride (PVC) plastisol backing, and its relative ease of recovery from commercial buildings where large volumes of product could be found made it the best hope for early success. That may have been the first and last point of agreement among fiber and carpet manufacturers as sustainability began to take on widely differing meanings. Given that lack of definition and standard measures of sustainability, marketing literature could be confusing for specifiers and end users looking to compare the environmental impacts of competitive carpet tiles.

Carpet tile as a product category bridged most commercial market segments (e.g., offices, hospitals, and universities). On the market for more than thirty years, it was introduced originally as a carpet innovation that enabled low-cost replacement of stained or damaged tiles, rotation of tiles in zones of high wear, and easy access to utility wiring beneath floors. Carpet tile's higher cost, high mass and embodied energy, more stringent backing adhesion performance specifications compared with broadloom, and double-digit market growth rate made it a logical focus for exploring alternative tile system designs.

Carpet tile was composed of two main elements, the face fiber and the backing. The face was made from yarn made of either Nylon 6 or Nylon 6.6 fiber, the only viable nylons in carpet use. US carpet tile was traditionally made with PVC plastisol backing systems, which provided the tile's mechanical properties and its dimensional stability. PVC was under suspicion, however, due to the potential of the plasticizer to migrate from the material, potentially causing

health problems and product failures. The vinyl chloride monomer in PVC was also a source of health concern for many. Most carpet tiles were made with a thin layer of fiberglass in the PVC backing to provide dimensional stability. These tiles ranged from eighteen inches to thirty-six inches square and required high dimensional stability to lay flat on the floor.

Backing provided functions that were subject to engineering specifications, such as compatibility with floor adhesives, dimensional stability, securing the face fibers in place, and more. Selecting backing materials and getting the chemistry and physical attributes right for the system's performance took time and resources, and added cost. Since the mid-1980s, the backing problems associated with PVC had led several companies, including Milliken, to seek PVC-alternative backings. In 1997, Shaw asked the Dow Chemical Company to provide new metallocene polyolefin polymers to meet Shaw's performance specifications for a thermoplastic extruded carpet tile backing. Shaw added a proprietary compounding process to complete the sustainable material design. Seeking every way possible to reduce materials use and remove hazardous inputs, yet maintain or improve product performance, Shaw made the following changes:

- Replacement of PVC and phthalate plasticizer with an inert and nonhazardous mix of polymers, ensuring material safety throughout the system (third-party tested for health and safety through the McDonough Braungart Design Chemistry toxicity protocol, which PVC cannot meet).
- Elimination of antimony trioxide flame retardant associated in research with harm to aquatic organisms (and replacement with benign aluminum trihydrate).
- Dramatic reduction of waste during the processing phases by immediate recovery and use of the technical nutrients resulting from on-site postindustrial recycling of backing waste. (The production waste goal is zero.)
- A life-cycle inventory and mass flow analysis that captures systems impacts and material efficiencies compared with PVC backing. (Carpet tile manufacturing energy was slightly lower for polyolefin, but polyolefin supply chain–embodied energy was more than 60 percent lower than PVC.)
- Efficiencies (energy and material reductions) in production, packaging, and distribution—40 percent lighter weight of EcoWorx tiles over PVC-backed carpet tiles yielded cost savings in transport and handling (installation and removal/demolition cost savings).

- Use of a minimum number of raw materials, none of which lose value, because all can be continuously disassembled and remanufactured through a process of grinding and airflow separation of fiber and backing, facilitating recycling of both major components.

- Use of a closed-loop, integrated, plantwide cooling water system providing chilled water for the extrusion process as well as the heating and cooling system (HVAC).

- Provision of a toll-free number on every EcoWorx tile for the buyer to contact Shaw for removal of the material for recycling at no cost to the consumer (supported by a written Shaw Environmental Guarantee).

Although Shaw had yet not begun to get carpet tiles back for recycling because of the minimum ten years of useful life, models assessing comparative costs of the conventional feedstock versus the new system indicated the recycled components would be less costly to process than virgin materials.

EcoWorx Innovation

The EcoWorx system developed by Shaw Industries offered a way to analyze and refine the C2C design of a carpet tile system without regard to technology constraints of the past. The Twelve Principles of Green Chemistry and Green Engineering and C2C provided a detailed framework in which to evaluate a new technology for engineering a successful carpet tile production, use, and recovery system. The EcoWorx system also utilized Shaw's EcoSolution Q Nylon 6 premium-branded fiber system, which was designed to use recycled Nylon 6 and in 2006 embodied 25 percent postindustrial recycled content in its makeup from blending and processing Nylon 6 fiber waste.

The EcoSolution Q Nylon 6 branded fiber system could be recycled as a technical nutrient through a reciprocal recovery agreement with Honeywell's Arnprior depolymerization facility in Canada without sacrificing performance or quality or increasing cost. But Shaw's original intention to take the Nylon 6 waste stream through the Evergreen Nylon Recycling Facility at Augusta, Georgia, was made possible with Shaw's purchase of the Honeywell/DSM joint venture. The depolymerization process was restarted in February 2007. That allowed Shaw's carpet tile products to make a cradle-to-cradle return to manufacturing, with nylon fiber from tile made into more nylon fiber and backing returned to backing.

Shaw's objective was to create technology for an infinitely recyclable carpet tile, one that could be entirely recycled with no loss in quality from one life cycle to the next. The notion of closed-cycle carpet tiles forced the complex issue of compatibility between face fiber (the soft side on which people walk) and the backing. As for which face fiber to use, current technology allowed only Nylon 6 fiber to be reprocessed. The Nylon 6 material retained its flexibility and structure through multiple reprocessing cycles by disassembling the Nylon 6 molecules with heat and pressure to yield the monomer building block, caprolactam. This recycled monomer was identical in chemical makeup to virgin caprolactam. In contrast, Nylon 6.6 could not be economically depolymerized due to its molecular structure. Nylon 6.6 incorporated two monomer building blocks resulting in greater disassembly cost and complexity.

In 1997 Bradfield and Shaw chemist Von Moody discussed a particular method of processing polyolefin resins that produced flexible, recyclable polymers. Polyolefins were an intriguing material for Shaw to explore as carpet backing, given the company's purchase of Amoco polypropylene (a type of polyolefin) extrusion facilities. After nearly $1 million invested in research and development and a pilot backing line, the tests suggested that polyolefins could be melted and separated from Nylon 6 and therefore successfully recycled into like-new materials. Shaw created the pilot backing line with the intention of "fast-prototyping" the polyolefin backing by modeling the performance attributes of Shaw's PVC backings. This prototyping risk might easily have failed but was instead the start of EcoWorx.

Shaw first introduced EcoWorx commercially in 1999. As a polyolefin-backed carpet tile, EcoWorx offered an alternative to the industry standard PVC backing at comparable cost, 40 percent less weight, and equal or improved effectiveness across all performance categories. EcoWorx earned the 1999 Best of Neocon Gold Award at the prestigious and largest annual interior furnishings and systems show in the United States. In 2002 the company's EcoWorx tile called "Dressed to Kill" won the carpet tile Neocon Gold Award for design, effectively mainstreaming the new material. By 2002, Shaw had announced EcoWorx as the standard backing for all its new carpet tile introductions. Indeed, customers preferred the new product; consequently, by 2004 EcoWorx accounted for 80 percent of carpet tile sold by Shaw—faster growth than anticipated. At the end of 2004, Shaw left PVC in favor of the EcoWorx backing, accomplishing a complete change in backing technology in a brief four years.

EcoWorx as a system of materials and processes proved significantly more efficient. The backing was dramatically lighter than that of PVC-backed tiles. The EcoWorx process, which used electric thermoplastic extrusion rather than a traditional gas-fired or forced-air oven, was more energy-efficient. The process combined an ethylene polymer base resin (developed by Dow Chemical) with high-density polyethylene (HDPE), fly ash for bulk (instead of the virgin calcium carbonate traditionally used), oil that improved the product's compatibility with the floor glue, antimicrobial properties, and black pigment in a proven nontoxic construction. This compound was applied to the carpet backs using a low-odor adhesive to maintain high indoor air quality standards. The backing material was combined with a nonwoven fiberglass mat for stability. Shaw's agreement with customers at the point of sale was that Shaw would pay to have the carpet returned to it. Back in its plant Shaw would shred the carpet and separate the backing stream from the fiber stream. The "infinitely recyclable" duo of Shaw's Nylon 6 fibers (marketed as EcoSolution Q) and EcoWorx backing received acclaim throughout the industry. Shaw's competitive cost and exceptional performance compared with traditional products allowed it to step beyond the limits of the "green" niche market. Especially important, Shaw's research showed that the cost of collection, transportation, elutriation, [5] and return to the respective nylon and EcoWorx manufacturing processes was less than the cost of using virgin raw materials. [6] Shaw tripled the production capacity in 2000, and by the end of 2002, shipments of EcoWorx tiles exceeded those of PVC-backed styles. [7] Shaw continued to expand its collection and recycling capacity in preparation for 2009, when the first round of EcoWorx carpet that was released in 1999 would reach the end of its *first* life cycle. It appeared that Shaw would be the first to close the industrial loop in the carpet tile industry.

The Recycling Challenge: Fits and Starts

Recycling carpet was a complex endeavor because carpet was composed of a complex composite of face fibers, glues, fillers, stabilizers, and backings, each with varying capacity to be melted and reused. Approximately 70 percent of the face fiber used in carpets was made of either Nylon 6 or Nylon 6.6, with each of these two types comprising an equal share of the nylon carpet fiber market. Neither fiber had the production capacity to serve the entire carpet industry.

Both nylons made excellent carpet. Although recovered Nylon 6.6 could be recycled into other materials (not carpeting), such as car parts and highway guard rails, the economic incentives for companies were low, and many people argued that "downcycling" in this way only postponed discarding the product in a landfill by one life cycle.

The development of technology for recycling Nylon 6 fibers into new carpet face fiber represented a major shift. Honeywell International Inc., a major supplier of the Nylon 6 fiber used by carpet manufacturers, was so confident about the market potential for recycled Nylon 6 fiber that it developed the $80 million Evergreen Nylon Recycling Facility in Augusta, Georgia, in 1999. Unfortunately, the cost of recycled caprolactam was not competitive with virgin caprolactam (used in making Nylon 6) at that point in time, and the plant closed in 2001. [8]

The Honeywell Evergreen Nylon 6 depolymerization unit was restarted in early 2007, but it was Shaw's purchase of Honeywell's carpet fiber facilities in 2006 that ultimately made that happen. After purchasing the Honeywell interest in Evergreen, negotiations for the DSM portion of the joint venture gave Shaw 100 percent ownership. In February 2007, Shaw reopened the Evergreen facility to produce caprolactam for Shaw Nylon 6 polymerization operations. In 2007, Shaw owned and operated the only commercially scaled postconsumer Nylon 6 monomer recycling facility in the world. Invista and Solutia, the only producers of Nylon 6.6, had a long history of technical development and response to competitive challenges. Promising work was under way in dissolution technologies that would allow postconsumer Nylon 6.6 to be recycled in an economical manner, restoring the uneasy balance between the two nylon types on the environmental front. Nylon 6.6 was here to stay, and industry observers said large-scale recycling of Nylon 6.6 was a matter of when, not if, the process was perfected. However, in 2007 no hint of plans for a Nylon 6.6 recycling facility had yet surfaced.

Environmental and Health Concerns Associated with Carpeting

After World War II, the design and manufacture of products from man-made and naturally occurring chemicals provided a wide range of inexpensive, convenient, and dependable consumer goods on which an increasing number of people relied worldwide. Behind the valuable medicines, plastics, fuels, fertilizers, and fabrics lay new chemicals and processes that were not time tested but appeared to have superior performance relative to prewar materials. Most of the polymer building blocks were developed by chemists between 1950 and 2000 as a result of and a driver of the post–World War II economic boom.

By the 1990s the growing rate of carpet usage had led to serious concern over waste disposal; 95 percent of carpet ended up in landfills. In 2001, this waste stream was reported at 4.6 billion pounds the United States. [9] Growing water quality, cost, and land-use issues related to carpet disposal generated significant pressure from government and commercial buyers for the development of carpet recycling technology. In January 2002, carpet and fiber manufacturers signed the National Carpet Recycling Agreement together with the Carpet and Rug Institute (the industry trade association), state governments, nongovernmental organizations (NGOs), and the EPA. This voluntary agreement established a ten-year schedule to increase the levels of recycling and reuse of postconsumer carpet and reduce the amount of waste carpet going to landfills. The agreement set a national goal of diverting 40 percent of end-of-life carpet from landfill disposal by 2012.

One result of the national agreement was the 2002 creation of the Carpet America Recovery Effort, a partnership of industry, government, and NGOs designed to enhance the collection infrastructure for postconsumer carpet and report on progress in the carpet industry toward meeting the national goals defined in the National Carpet Recycling Agreement. [10] In the late 1990s Presidential Executive Order 13101, a purchasing guide, was fueling demand for "environmentally preferable products" by government and by purchasers that received federal funds. This program introduced the idea of multiple-environmental-impact purchasing evaluations as a replacement for the outdated practice of relying solely on recycled content as the measure of product sustainability.

However, the problems with carpeting would not be addressed so easily. As monitoring equipment capabilities advanced between 1990 and 2005, new health and ecological impact hazards associated with certain widely used chemicals were identified. "Environment" was a topic that historically related to on-site toxins and compliance activity, with "health" referring to effects that surfaced *after* the product left the company; both concerns were relegated to the environment, health, and safety office inside a corporation. But scientists, design engineers, and increasingly middle and senior management needed to incorporate a broader understanding of such concerns into the ways products were designed and made. This was particularly true in the construction and home furnishing sectors, where greater use of chemicals combined with less than adequate ventilation and more architecturally tight building designs to create health problems.

As far back as 1987, the US Consumer Product Safety Commission, the federal agency that monitors commercial product safety, received more than 130 complaints about flu and allergy symptoms and eye and throat irritations that began directly following the installation of new carpet. Although that was a small number, this data often represented the tip of a health problem iceberg. Over the next few years, air quality research led to the well-publicized concept of "sick building syndrome"—a condition in which occupants experienced acute illness and discomfort linked to poor indoor air quality. Carpets were not the only culprits. Wall materials and wall coverings (paint and wallpaper) as well as various hardwood floor treatments also were implicated. To the industry's dismay, the EPA listed "chemical contaminants from indoor sources, including adhesives [and] carpeting…that may emit volatile organic compounds (VOCs)" as contributors to sick building syndrome. [11] It was not the building that was sick. At the time, the US Centers for Disease Control reported "body burdens" of chemicals in people's bloodstreams from unidentified sources. Under increasing study were babies' body burdens—the pollutants in infants' blood and organ tissues—later known to result from placental cycling of blood, oxygen, and nutrients between mother and child.

Simultaneously, concern was building throughout the 1990s concerning PVC plastic that contained phthalate plasticizers. Phthalates were added to PVC during processing to make the resulting plastic soft and flexible; however, researchers discovered that phthalate molecules did not structurally bind to PVC, which therefore leached out of products. Though there was debate about the level of harm that leaching caused humans, reputable studies linked phthalates to reproductive and endocrine disorders in animals. Environmental health science reports and concerns over PVC plasticizers grew steadily between 1995 and 2005. California planned to add di-2-ethylhexyl phthalate (DEHP) to a list of chemicals known to cause birth defects or reproductive harm. The list, contained in Proposition 65, followed on the heels of warnings from the Food and Drug Administration, National Toxicology Program, and Health Canada that DEHP may cause birth defects and other reproductive harm. Furthermore, incineration of PVC released highly toxic organochlorine by-products, including microscopic dioxins, into the atmosphere, where they moved with regional weather patterns, returning to the lower atmosphere and eventually to earth through the hydrologic cycle. Breathing in dioxins had been linked to cancer, growth disruptions, and developmental problems in humans for many years from laboratory and production worker data. By July 2005, links between commonly used chemicals, even in very low doses, and human health deficiencies were being discussed on the front page of the *Wall Street Journal*. Despite the evidence against PVC, the California Department of General Services (DGS) approved PVC carpet tile in its 2006 California Gold Carpet Standard and instituted a 10 percent postconsumer recycled content requirement for all state carpet purchases, which virtually guaranteed increased purchases of PVC carpets. The DGS also refused to allow exemptions for non-PVC materials that had not been on the market long enough to be recovering adequate quantities of postconsumer material.

Many carpet manufacturers focused their early environmental efforts on reducing trim waste from industrial and installation processes (eco-efficiency). Trim waste cost the industry an estimated $25 million per year in unused carpet production and disposal fees, but this represented only 2 percent of total carpet production and, though important, made a relatively small impact on the end-of-life waste volume issue. As efficiency strategies became more systems oriented, a competitive market grew for technology to recover and recycle postconsumer carpet.

Indeed, for many years real solutions to the problems of end-of-life recycling of carpet were lost in the clutter of the first and easiest step in environmental stewardship—reduction of materials, water, energy usage, and waste. Capabilities were developed—typically under a company's environment, health, and safety office—that essentially absorbed a quality and cost-cutting issue under the compliance function. With respect to carpeting materials, efforts were concentrated on the 2 percent of all carpet materials that remained as scrap in the manufacturing plants. More than 98 percent of all materials entering the carpet manufacturing stream were shipped to the customer as finished carpet. Once used and in need of replacement, this postconsumer carpet traditionally ended its life in landfills.

Other environmental efforts in the carpet industry focused on converting or recycling products such as polyethylene terephthalate (PET) plastic bottles (waste streams from other industries) into carpet fiber, incorporating the recovered materials into new products. This effort was encouraged by the Comprehensive Procurement Guideline (CPG) program (RCRA 6002, 1998), which required federal agencies to purchase items containing recovered and reused postconsumer materials. Of the forty-nine items listed in the program, PET carpet face fiber, carpet backing, and carpet cushioning were included. [12] EPA provided lists that gave priority to products containing a high percentage of postconsumer material. Shaw EcoWorx was not included on the vendor list because while it was an innovative

breakthrough that would achieve a 100 percent recovery rate, it had yet to complete its initial life cycle. The CPG proposed designation of nylon carpets (fiber and backing). However, due to the lack of postconsumer nylon availability in the market, the CPG designation would boost federal purchases of PVC carpets at a time when non-PVC carpets were increasing their market share but had not yet had time to see postconsumer material returned and to therefore achieve CPG compliance.

In 2006, recycled plastic remained more costly than virgin fibers, which limited the carpet industry's enthusiasm for this measure. But plastic came from oil, a feedstock source increasingly subject to price volatility and unstable supply. Crude oil prices rose from about $25 per barrel in the 1990s to more than $60 in 2006. In the face of this price uncertainty and consistent high oil prices, Shaw concentrated on and eventually achieved systems economics that resulted in the recovered EcoWorx materials coming back as feedstock under the price of virgin materials. Standards such as the CPG may have served as a disincentive to material innovation if first-generation products such as EcoWorx had to have significant postconsumer recycled content to qualify. The irony was that EcoWorx had won an EPA-sponsored Presidential Green Chemistry Challenge Award in 2003 in the safer chemicals category, yet an EPA nylon carpet CPG designation would effectively prevent federal agencies from purchasing it. Shaw and others devoted significant resources over a four-year period to persuade EPA to abandon the nylon carpet CPG designation in favor of a multiple impact assessment of carpet.

Green Building Council and LEED

Steve Bradfield was an early supporter of the US Green Building Council's (USGBC) Leadership in Energy and Environmental Design (LEED) program, which established standards for environmentally preferred building materials and construction. Bradfield had participated for several years in the architecture and building industries' movement to reduce and eliminate problematic materials that were increasingly linked with respiratory, allergy, and other human health problems. In 2003, Bradfield talked about Shaw's sustainability policy. (The following year, he would testify before Congress in support of green legislation.) Shaw's policy, Bradfield explained, articulated the firm's corporate strategy to move steadily toward a cradle-to-cradle and a solar-powered future.

In 2006 LEED requirements did not factor in EcoWorx's recovery and reuse benefits in awarding points to companies looking to achieve higher LEED rankings. But the USGBC had begun a dialogue on how to incorporate multiple metrics, including cradle-to-cradle design points, into the 2007 version of LEED. At the same time, many corporations that were committed to sustainability practices, or at least wanted to gain positive publicity for their efforts, were setting LEED certification levels among their goals for their headquarters buildings.

Environmental pressure had been mounting for several years in the carpet industry. Said William McDonough, architect, environmentalist, and promoter of the cradle-to-cradle design approach with Michael Braungart, "The carpet industry is the battlefield where the war for sustainability is being waged." [14] Indeed, so many carpet companies seemed to be actively marketing carpet sustainability in comparison with other industries that the question of "Why carpet?" is often asked. With Presidential Executive Order 13101, the purchasing mandate, and others fueling the demand for "environmentally preferable products" in government, a new breed of environmentalist had appeared by the late 1990s, ready to constructively engage with industry but still offering conflicting views of what constituted sustainable design in the absence of consensus on a national standard.

The first LEED Green Building Rating System was completed in 2000 and grew quickly into an internationally recognized certification program for environmentally sensitive design. Recognizing that buildings account for 30 percent of raw materials use and 30 percent of waste output (136 million tons annually) in the United States, [15] the USGBC, an organization affiliated with the American Association of Architects, gathered representatives from all sectors of the building industry to develop this voluntary and consensus-based rating system. By adhering to an extensive point system with categories such as Indoor Environmental Quality, Materials and Resources, and Water Efficiency, both new buildings and interior renovations could become LEED certified at different levels of excellence (Basic, Silver, Gold, and Platinum). Carpet selection became an integral element of LEED certification through materials requirements such as "Recycled Content," "Low-Emitting Materials–Flooring Systems," and Low-Emitting Materials–Adhesives and Sealants." [16] But LEED offered few incentives for other important environmental impact reductions.

Between 2000 and 2004, the LEED Green Building Rating System gathered more than 3,500 member organizations and certified projects in 49 states and 11 countries. [17] LEED's continued influence in the building industry was secured by policies in the US Department of the Interior, EPA, General Services Administration, Department of State, Air Force, Army, and Navy, mandating differing levels of LEED standards for future buildings. By 2005 California, Maine, Maryland, New Jersey, New York, Oregon, and many cities across the United States also had legislated LEED standards for construction and procurement at various levels, either through mandates on capital developments or tax credits to developers who met the requirements. [18]

Certifiers

Third-party organizations, both for profit and not for profit, were proliferating in 2005–6 in a bid to gather the critical mass necessary to be recognized as the certifier of choice for many different aspects of the environmental patchwork of metrics defining that elusive goal called sustainability. Even self-certification programs from various industry associations have attempted to build consensus. Recycled content seemed to be the path of least resistance, but life-cycle analysis, embodied energy studies, and variations on the complex theme of "closing the loop" proliferated and jockeyed for position in the new "industry" of environmental and health performance. Unfortunately, an inevitable "unintended consequence" of these efforts was confusion and controversy among stakeholders.

What Next?

As Steve Bradfield reflected on challenges in the near future, he said he hoped the innovations required to implement the EcoWorx strategy would continue to draw on the extensive capabilities of Shaw and its partner firms. Certainly whatever transpired had to be consistent with Shaw's Environmental Vision Statement. Questions went through his mind. Did the company fully anticipate the requirements of reverse logistics systems design? Had they identified the probable challenges and bottlenecks? Was the Shaw culture changing quickly enough to execute the strategy successfully? Would the company have sufficient capacity for the disassembly stage? The capacity of the elutriation system initially would allow Shaw to recycle 1.8 million square yards of carpet per year. This equipment enabled separation of the backing and fiber in a single pass and was expected to meet the anticipated future growth capacity requirement of the returned postconsumer material over the next five to ten years. But would the economics of the system meet the organization's expectations?

In 2007, Bradfield knew that EcoWorx had become a major driver in the phenomenal growth of Shaw's carpet tile business. In late 2006, the company had introduced EcoWorx broadloom, a twelve-foot roll version of the

EcoWorx technology that brought cradle-to-cradle design to the staid broadloom business. Bradfield's recent promotion to corporate director of environmental affairs for the $5.8 billion Shaw organization signaled the adoption of cradle-to-cradle goals across every division and functional area—a major achievement given the humble beginnings of what had started out as a commercial carpet initiative. A new Shaw environmental website, http://www.shawgreenedge.com, offered a single destination for anyone interested in the initiatives driving Shaw's sustainability efforts.

KEY TAKEAWAYS

- There are many drivers behind sustainability innovation changes in a large flooring firm.
- Cradle-to-cradle thinking can inform redesign and manufacturing of new flooring.
- Sustainability practices provide financial and strategic advantages.

EXERCISES

1. Create a graphic representation of the reverse supply chain. What challenges do you think Shaw will have going forward?
2. Describe what you see as innovative in the case and list the factors you believe were drivers of that innovation.
3. Analyze and assess Shaw's EcoWorx story as a strategy. What are the arguments in favor of it? Against it?
4. Explain the benefits to the firm of sustainable design using green chemistry principles and cradle-to-cradle thinking.
5. What, if any, accounting consideration must be given a product that is expected to return perpetually as a new raw material?
6. What use might the EcoWorx product, cradle-to-cradle, and green chemistry principles have to inform product and process design in other product markets? Bring an illustration to class to discuss.

---

[1] This case was written by Alia Anderson and Karen O'Brien under the supervision of author {Author's Name Retracted as requested by the work's original creator or licensee} and developed under a cooperative effort by the Batten Institute, the American Chemical Society, and the Environmental Protection Agency's Office of Pollution Prevention. Alia Anderson, {Author's Name Retracted as requested by the work's original creator or licensee}, and Karen O'Brien, *Shaw Industries: Sustainable Business, Entrepreneurial Innovation, and Green Chemistry*, UVA-ENT-0087 (Charlottesville: Darden Business Publishing, University of Virginia, 2006). Note can be accessed through the Darden Case Collection at https://store.darden.virginia.edu. Unless otherwise noted, quotations in this section refer to this case.

[2] See William McDonough and Michael Braungart, *Cradle to Cradle: Remaking the Way We Make Things* (New York: North Point Press, 2002) for extensive discussion of the C2C frame of reference. The field of industrial ecology provides a conceptual basis for this discussion; see Thomas E. Graedel and Braden R. Allenby, *Industrial Ecology* (Englewood Cliffs, NJ: Prentice Hall, 1995).

[3] Alia Anderson, {Author's Name Retracted as requested by the work's original creator or licensee}, and Karen O'Brien, *Shaw Industries: Sustainable Business, Entrepreneurial Innovation, and Green Chemistry*, UVA-ENT-0087 (Charlottesville: Darden Business Publishing, University of Virginia, 2006).

[4] It was not until 1994 that the industry began to take a more serious look at sustainability. One early adopter was the carpet tile innovator Interface Inc., which took steps to integrate sustainability throughout the company from top to bottom, reducing scrap waste, identifying operational inefficiencies, lowering energy use through solar and other innovations, and introducing a carpet leasing program through which it collected and recycled end-of-use carpet. Independently, however, other carpet producers began developing their own programs and initiatives, programs that some would contend exceeded the solutions Interface devised.

[5] Elutriation refers to the process of shredding returned tiles and their purification by washing, straining, or separating by weight.

[6] Steve Bradshaw (Shaw Industries), in discussion with author, March 2005.

[7] Steve Bradshaw (Shaw Industries), in discussion with author, March 2005.

[8] Katherine Salant, "Carpet Industry Makes Strides in Reducing Footprint, but Path Includes Several Obstacles," *Washington Post*, January 31, 2004.

[9] Carpet America Recovery Effort, "Memorandum of Understanding for Carpet Stewardship (MOU)," accessed January 31, 2011, http://www.carpetrecovery.org/mou.php#goals.

[10] Carpet America Recovery Effort, "Memorandum of Understanding for Carpet Stewardship (MOU)," accessed January 31, 2011, http://www.carpetrecovery.org/mou.php#goals.

[11] American Lung Association, American Medical Association, US Consumer Product Safety Commission, and US Environmental Protection Agency, *Indoor Air Pollution: An Introduction for Health Professionals*, accessed January 26, 2011, http://www.epa.gov/iaq/pdfs/indoor_air_pollution.pdf.

[12] US Environmental Protection Agency, "Indoor Air Quality: Indoor Air Facts No. 4 (Revised) Sick Building Syndrome," last updated September 30, 2010, accessed January 26, 2011, http://www.epa.gov/iaq/pubs/sbs.html.

[13] Testimony accessed March 7, 2011, http://www.gpo.gov/fdsys/pkg/CHRG-108hhrg92512/html/CHRG-108hhrg92512.htm.

[14] Alia Anderson, {Author's Name Retracted as requested by the work's original creator or licensee}, and Karen O'Brien, *Shaw Industries: Sustainable Business, Entrepreneurial Innovation, and Green Chemistry*, UVA-ENT-0087 (Charlottesville: Darden Business Publishing, University of Virginia, 2006).

[15] US Green Building Council, *An Introduction to the US Green Building Council*, accessed January 31, 2011, http://www.usgbc.org/Docs/About/usgbc_intro.ppt.

[16] See, for instance, US Green Building Council, "LEED 2009," accessed January 31, 2011, http://www.usgbc.org//ShowFile.aspx?DocumentID=5719.

[17] US Green Building Council, *An Introduction to the US Green Building Council*, accessed January 31, 2011, http://www.usgbc.org/Docs/About/usgbc_intro.ppt.

[18] US Green Building Council, *LEED Initiatives in Government by Type*, May 2007, accessed January 31, 2011, https://www.usgbc.org/ShowFile.aspx?DocumentID=1741.

[19] Shaw Industries, "Shaw Industries Announces New Environmental Policy to Drive Manufacturing Processes," press release, December 4, 2003, accessed March 7, 2011, http://www.shawcontractgroup.com/Contentpress_releases./pr_031204_Environmental.pdf.

NOTES:

Chapter 8:

Biomaterials

8.1 NatureWorks: Green Chemistry's Contribution to Biotechnology Innovation, Commercialization, and Strategic Planning

LEARNING OBJECTIVES

1. Become familiar with some key innovations and entrepreneurial opportunities in the biomaterials arena.

2. Analyze the possibilities of biomaterials as an alternative feedstock platform to fossil fuels.

3. Examine the barriers and opportunities in producing biomass feedstock through a venture inside a large corporation.

4. Compare the innovative venture inside a big firm with a subsequent stand-alone start-up.

In the NatureWorks [1] case, students examine challenges of commercializing polylactic acid (PLA), a disruptive technology innovation that substitutes corn-based biomass for oil-based feedstock. NatureWorks was the first US firm to create—and bring to commercial scale—biomass feedstock for a wide variety of applications including plastic components, thin film, and fabrics.

In 2002 a ten-year joint venture between US agricultural giant Cargill Inc. and Dow Chemical received the prestigious Presidential Green Chemistry Challenge Award from the American Chemical Society's (ACS) Green Chemistry Institute for its development of the first synthetic polymer class to be produced from renewable resources, specifically from corn grown in the American Midwest. The product was biomass material and held the potential to substitute a renewable feedstock (raw material) for petroleum-based polymers. Presented at the Green Chemistry and Engineering conference and awards ceremony in Washington, DC, attended by the president of the US National Academy of Sciences, the White House science advisor, and other dignitaries from the National Academies and the American Chemical Society, the award recognized the venture's innovative direction. In January 2005, Cargill chose to acquire Dow's share of the venture. Now the fledgling company had to learn to fly.

NatureWorks' bio-based plastic resins were named and trademarked NatureWorks PLA for the polylactic acid that composed the base plant sugars. In addition to replacing petroleum as the material feedstock, PLA resins had the added benefit of being compostable (safely biodegraded) or even infinitely recyclable, which meant they could be reprocessed into the same product again and again. That

feature provided a distinct environmental advantage over recycling, or "downcycling," postconsumer or postindustrial materials into lower-quality products, which merely slowed material flow to landfills by one or two product life cycles. Additional life-cycle environmental and health benefits had been identified by a thorough life-cycle analysis (LCA) from corn to pellets. PLA resins, virgin or postconsumer, could then be processed into a variety of end uses.

By early 2005, CEO Kathleen Bader and Chief Technical Officer Pat Gruber were wrestling with a number of questions. NatureWorks' challenges were both operational and strategic:

*   How to take the successful product to high-volume production
*   How to market the unique resin in a mature plastics market

With Cargill's January 2005 decision to acquire Dow's share of the venture, there were also questions about the structure of NatureWorks going forward.

Kathleen Bader had been at Dow for thirty years before joining NatureWorks in 2004. She had managed Dow's Styrenics and Engineered Products, a $4 billion business, between 1999 and 2003. She led Dow's Six Sigma program implementation. As a NatureWorks board member who had long championed the technology, Bader had confidence in its future and supported it from her budget at Dow. She was a logical fit at the helm. One of her first decisions involved selecting a retail alliance partner and narrowing a list of prospective customers. Limited resources constrained her choices.

There were other issues, including application challenges when converting PLA resins to different plastic forms, the controversy over **genetically modified organisms (GMOs)**, and appropriate market positioning for a "sustainable" product, still a vague concept to many. Many executives in the company knew all too well that positioning their new product would take far more than simply getting the technology right.

In spring 2005 NatureWorks employed 230 people, split almost equally among headquarters (labs and management offices), the plant, and the international division. International consisted primarily of the European Union; the Hong Kong representative who had worked with the Japanese market had been brought back to headquarters in early 2004. As a joint venture the enterprise had consumed close to $750 million dollars in capital, was not yet profitable, but held the promise of tremendous growth that could transform a wide range of markets worldwide. In 2005 NatureWorks was still the only company in the world capable of producing on a large-scale bio-based resins that exhibited standard performance traits such as durability, flexibility, and strength—all at a competitive market price.

The Plastics Industry

The plastics industry was the fourth-largest manufacturing segment in the United States behind motor vehicles, electronics, and petroleum refining. In 2001, the United States produced 101.1 million pounds of resins from oil and shipped $45.5 billion in plastic products. [2] Both the oil and chemical industries were mature and relied on commodities sold on thin margins. The combined efforts of a large-scale chemical company in Dow and an agricultural processor giant in Cargill suggested Cargill Dow—now NatureWorks—was in some ways well suited for the mammoth task of challenging oil feedstock. However, could the small company grow beyond the market share that usually limited environmental products, considered somewhere between 2 and 5 percent of the market? And for that matter, should PLA be considered an "environmental product"?

Wave of Change

The rising wave of interest and activity in biomaterials had pushed industrial biotechnology into the economic mainstream by 2005. Projects to convert renewable resources into industrial chemicals proliferated, funded by government, corporate, and private capital. Major agricultural companies and chemical giants had teamed up to produce carpeting, paint, inks, solvents, automobile panels, and roofing material made from plants. Production of plant-derived fuels, such as ethanol and biodiesel, was growing. Advocates described those as better *and* lower-cost products: less polluting, equally dependable, lower-cost feedstock; more environmentally friendly products and processes with fewer toxic by-products; a reduced reliance on imported oil; and a smaller environmental footprint.

McKinsey & Company (Zurich) estimated the 5 percent market share represented by biotechnology products in 2004 could jump to 10–20 percent by 2010, with the biggest shift occurring in biotech processes to make bulk chemicals, polymers, and specialty chemicals. Developments in enzymatic biocatalysis were already allowing for the production of new materials with improved properties compared to existing products. Bioprocesses enabled production of existing chemicals at lower cost. The textiles, energy, chemical, and pharmaceuticals industries were all transforming in the face of biotechnology advances. Within this larger dynamic, PLA was just one of many "platform" materials available to be converted into a range of derivative products.

NatureWorks was contributing to creating, and being carried forward by, this wave of biotechnology innovation. Factors were converging to create new markets worldwide. According to *Fortune* magazine (July 2003), "Sales that large [$280 billion by 2012] would displace a notable quantity of oil, freeing it up for other uses and helping keep prices down—though no one can yet estimate by how much. It would also shift the source of industrial chemicals from foreign countries to farm fields nearer the markets where the end products will be consumed. That would cut transportation costs and conceivably reduce dependence on foreign oil." [3]

Pat Gruber, chief technology officer for NatureWorks LLC, had known of biotechnology innovation's potential since his graduate school days in biochemistry. Gruber's interest in environmental issues had a long history, going back to high school, where he had enjoyed and shown an aptitude for biology and chemistry. He had always liked crossing between the systems perspective of biology and the molecular building-block orientation of chemistry.

In the same year that NatureWorks' achievements had been recognized by the Green Chemistry Challenge Award for innovation, the company brought online a plant with a capacity of 300 million pounds (140,000 metric tons) that promised to turn his team's breakthroughs into a viable and very large business. In 2003 the business went on to win the United Kingdom's Chemical Engineering prestigious

Kirkpatrick Award for Chemical Engineering Achievement for "bringing to market a technology that allows abundant, annually renewable resources to replace finite petroleum, to make consumer goods without sacrificing performance or price."

NatureWorks Pre-2005: The Cargill Dow Joint Venture (CD)

Cargill, the largest privately held company in the United States, was also the largest agricultural processor in the country, with 2004 revenues of $63 billion. The company served the food processing, food service, and retail food industries. The origins of NatureWorks went back to 1988, when Pat Gruber joined Cargill after graduate school. Sponsorship by Cargill's corn milling division launched what was then a small research project. During the 1990s Gruber and his team had acquired considerable biomaterials and bioprocessing expertise, but Cargill sought a polymer partner that would bring plastic processing and application knowledge as well as market know-how. Cargill processed and sold high-volume meats, corn, and other agricultural products to large customers such as Walmart and McDonald's but knew little about resin converters, thermomolding lines, or polymer science applications, traditional domains of the plastics industry. As a Cargill employee summed it up in the early 1990s, "We know food, we don't know chemicals." On the chemicals side, in the early 1990s, experts in the chemical industry generally did not believe it was possible to create carbohydrate feedstock (plant-based starches and sugars) that would perform the same as and be cost competitive with petroleum-originated plastics.

Ultimately Cargill found an interested partner in Dow Chemical, a $40 billion commodity chemical and plastics manufacturer. Dow was active in oil-based raw materials, plastics, additives, processing aids, and solvents applied across multiple industries. In 2004, Dow's commitment to its oil-based plastics businesses was expressed in plans to site large-scale plastics feedstock production facilities next to oil wells in the Arabian Peninsula. Dow also had major commitments to polypropylene (made from natural gas released in oil drilling) and polyethylene. Although Dow had considerable plastics science expertise, at the time Dow did not make polyethylene terephthalate (PET), the material PLA most likely would replace.

In 1995 the working partnership officially became a joint venture, a fifty-fifty undertaking between the two parent companies, Cargill and Dow. Though small, the enterprise was monitored closely because costs would show in red on the budgets of units within both companies. The initial $100 million investment carried with it the assumption that Cargill, primarily an agricultural commodity trading company, would contribute its corn and biological process expertise, while Dow brought polymer science, process control methods, and plastic supply-chain marketing knowledge from its commodity plastic polymer businesses. Dow also had a large biotech effort in its pharmaceutical intermediates business that could provide complementary knowledge for chemical production. The agreement between the two industry giants seemed ideal. Furthermore, the structure of the plastics industry, dominated by large companies generating high-volume, low-margin mature commodity plastics through established supply chains, virtually ensured that small players with limited capital would not last.

Board communications issues and the turnover of three CEOs, as well as four marketing VPs, between 1997 and 2004 had reduced the joint venture's effectiveness over its short life. Some thought the parent companies did not focus on the details of the business's unique challenges. Others believed the joint venture had served its useful life and a new ownership structure was necessary to move forward.

The assumption by many outside the company was that PLA would be adopted quickly. However, the complexity of differentiating the corn-based plastic pellets that left the Nebraska PLA plant, selling a sufficient volume to downstream buyers to increase plant capacity to greater than 70 percent, and selling the plastic as part of a buyer's sustainability strategy proved to be a tough challenge.

By 2005, when Cargill Dow became NatureWorks, it could claim more than fifteen years' experience in biopolymer technology and applications. However, some believed that Cargill still viewed Dow as the polymer company that provided the "technology." Managing under two different parent organizations created its own set of issues. Two accounting books had to be kept. Fiscal calendars and IT software systems were different. Dow required its process methods and proprietary software be purchased and incorporated by the joint venture. The plant was located on Cargill's property, thus Cargill was paid by NatureWorks for site management services in addition to the corn raw material, and the business tapped into Cargill's steam and electric infrastructure.

A member of the top management team commented in 2004 that until recently there had been no meaningful discussion between Cargill and Dow about what each of the investing parent companies wanted from its investment. Complicating matters was Cargill's historical unwillingness to discuss

GMOs and its general reluctance to engage in the public dialogue regarding environmental concerns, and sustainability in particular. Dow, on the other hand, understood the growing interest in the sustainability agenda and was experienced, although not necessarily successful with, environmental groups and the growing regulatory activity.

Making Plastic

The Cargill Dow undertaking was an industrial biotech project as opposed to *molecular* or gene-focused biotechnology that had evolved from Cargill's corn-milling business director's interest in finding new product opportunities for corn sugars. Among the key questions when the duo was considering the project in the 1990s were the following:

- Was it possible to create a cost- and performance-comparable plastic product using corn sugar instead of petroleum as the primary feedstock?
- And was there a business in bioplastics?

PLA innovation held the potential to revolutionize the plastics and agricultural industries by offering benign bio-based biopolymers to substitute for conventional petroleum-based plastics. In those days, however, plastics industry experts repeatedly told Pat Gruber and his small team that he would never find a low-cost biological supply for lactic acid production. They were informed that polymers from that source could never work in the variety of applications they had in mind. Yet the team of scientists Pat Gruber formed around the PLA project kept at their work, believing the technology could be developed and that markets would favor environmentally preferable and renewable resource–based materials. Using Cargill's corn-milling facility and a 34,000-ton-per-year prototype lactic acid pilot plant built in 1994, the small and expensive project moved determinedly forward.

PLA was not new. Wallace Corothers, the DuPont scientist who invented nylon, first discovered the lactic acid polymer in the 1920s and DuPont research continued through the 1930s. Plant sugars were processed into polymers in small volumes in the laboratory producing very similar characteristics to petroleum-based polymers, the traditional building blocks of commodity plastics. However, costs were orders-of-magnitude too high and the material's technical performance was not acceptable for large-scale plastics and fibers applications. While research continued on PLA and polylactides, the DuPont-ConAgra joint venture "Ecochem" in the early 1990s ultimately failed. Subsequently, only small

volumes of PLA plastic were produced for specialized applications in which the safe dissolution of the material was valued (implants and controlled drug release applications, for example). In the first decade of the twenty-first century, medical sutures made from PLA were sold by DuPont for $1,000 per kilo. Cost and technology constraints had prohibited PLA production in large volumes or for alternative uses.

Conventional plastic is made by cracking petroleum through heating and pressure. Long chains of hydrocarbons are extracted and combined with various additives to produce polymers that can be shaped and molded. The polymer material, called resin, comes in the form of pellets, powder, or granules and is sold by the chemical manufacturer to a processor. The processor, also called a converter, blends resins and additives to produce a buyer's desired product characteristics. For example, an automobile dashboard part needs to be flexible. The processor blends in plasticizer additives to make the resin more flexible and moldable. Plasticizers, often supplied by specialty chemical providers, are the most commonly used additives. Other additives include flame retardants, colorants, antioxidants, antifungal ingredients, impact modifiers (to increase materials' resistance to stress), heat or light stabilizers (to resist ultraviolet rays), and lubricants. In addition to those additives, some plastics also include fillers such as glass or particulate materials. First-tier processing companies typically sold resins with specific qualities in the form of rolled sheets or pellets. Additional converters along the supply chain melted the sheets or resin pellets and converted them by processes such as injection molding (for storage tubs such as yogurt containers or waste bins), blow molding (for plastic drink bottles), and extrusion (for films). [4]

In contrast, NatureWorks' process for creating a proprietary polylactide, trade named NatureWorks PLA (for plastics) and Ingeo (for fibers), was based on the fermentation, distillation, and polymerization of a simple plant sugar, corn dextrose. The process harvested the carbon stored in plant sugar and made a PLA polymer with characteristics similar to those of traditional thermoplastics. The production steps were as follows:

- Starch was separated from corn kernels.
- Enzymes converted starch to dextrose (a simple sugar).
- Bacterial culture fermented the dextrose into lactic acid in a biorefinery.
- A second plant used a solvent-free melt process to manufacture lactide polymers.
- Polymer emerged from the plant in the form of resin

pellets.

- Pellets had the design flexibility to be made into fibers, coatings, films, foams, and molded containers.

NatureWorks' manufacturing sequence reduced consumption of fossil fuel by 30–50 percent compared with oil-based conventional plastic resins. PLA plastic waste safely composted in about forty-five days if kept moist and warm (above 140 degrees Fahrenheit) or, once used, could be burned like paper, producing few by-products. PLA offered a renewable resource replacement material for PET and polyester, both used widely in common products such as packaging and clothing.

Field corn was the most abundant and cheapest source of fermentable sugar in the world, and the standard variety used by NatureWorks (yellow dent number 2) was commonly used to feed livestock. [5] The corn was sent to a mill, where it was ground and processed to isolate the sugar molecules (dextrose). Dextrose was purchased from Cargill and fermented using a process similar to that used in beer and wine production. That fermentation yielded lactic acid. The lactic acid was processed, purified, melted, cooled, and chopped into pellets. It was then ready for sale and to be made by processing companies along the supply chain into cups, plates, take-home containers, polyester-like fabrics, or laptop computer covers. Once the product was used, it could be either composted (meaning it would biodegrade) or melted down and recycled into equal quality products. [6] Though NatureWorks had the technical capacity to combine postconsumer PLA products with virgin corn feedstock to make new products, large-scale collection required a reverse logistics system. Bader and Gruber hoped that capability would someday exist, allowing them to close the loop of their industrial process and practice fully renewable, "cradle-to-cradle" [7] manufacturing, a new model then gaining credence as a substitute for the linear, cradle-to-grave industrial process that had traditionally characterized Western industrial economies.

A key breakthrough resulted in a dramatic cost reduction to manufacture the lactic acid for making PLA polymers. A new fermentation and distillation process enabled cheaper purification, better optical composition control, and significant yield increases over existing practice. In contrast, two-thirds of the material inputs in conventional PLA processing were lost to waste streams. The company's patented new process permitted the inexpensive production of different PLA grades for multiple markets in a flexible manufacturing system within the single plant, while adhering to environmentally sound practices throughout.

Buyers

Typically buyers such as food service companies (Cisco, Guest Services), restaurant chains, and supermarkets needing hundreds of thousands of drinking cups would contract with cup producers that had relationships with materials converters that had in turn purchased either plastic resins or previously fabricated plastic sheets, foams, or coatings. Some supply chains were simple, with only three steps from NatureWorks feedstock resins to the ultimate user. Other supply chains could be much longer and more complex. Long-established and preferential working relationships with plastic resins producers were standard, as were multiyear contracts and lines optimized for conventional materials. But converters could be persuaded to source differently and to change molds and even line equipment if customers demanded. Fortunately PLA could be dropped into PET molds and lines with only minor changes. It was harder to drop PLA into polystyrene lines, and optimizing for PLA might mean cutting new tools, new mold designs, or even new lines, depending on the application. For example, PLA thickness might be less than that of the conventional plastic sheets it replaced, requiring retooling to thinner sheets. Conversion to PLA could mean significant additional throughput or faster line times (cost savings), but it might also require expenditures of time and money. That could yield financial gains to converters, but few were interested in making changes when profit margins already were slim.

The Market

NatureWorks brought its new product to market in the late 1990s and early 2000s at a time of economic recession, uncertain market dynamics, and rapidly intersecting health, environmental, national security, and energy independence concerns. While the economy seemed to settle by 2005, oil supplies and dependency concerns loomed large, with oil prices exceeding $65 per barrel. Volatile oil prices and political instability in oil-producing countries argued for the US and other oil-dependent economies to decrease their oil dependence. European countries were moving more quickly than the United States, however.

Yet plastics were a visible reminder of societies' heavy reliance on petroleum-based materials. The US food industry and demographic trends were creating rapidly growing markets for convenient prepared foods, and clear plastic packaging helped get customers' attention at retail. Consumers had become increasingly well informed about chemicals in products and were becoming more aware that few had been tested for health impacts. Certain plastics known to leach contaminants even under normal use conditions were facing government and health nonprofits' scrutiny. Health concerns, in particular those related to infants, children, and pregnant women, had put plastics under the microscope in the United States, but nowhere near the microscopic focus plastics had received in the European Union and Japan, where materials bans and regulatory frameworks received significant citizen support. Strong interest in green building in China and Taiwan along with strong government motivations and incentives to reduce oil dependency (true also for Europe) drove international market buyers to find alternative feedstock for plastic.

The volatility of petroleum prices between 1995 and 2005 wreaked havoc on the plastics industry. From 1998 to 2001, natural gas prices (which typically tracked oil prices) doubled, then quintupled, then returned to 1998 levels. The year 2003 was again a roller-coaster of unpredictable fluctuations, causing a Huntsman Chemical Corp. official to lament, "The problem facing the polymers and petrochemicals industry in the United States is unprecedented. Rome is burning." [8] Others were assured that oil supplies, then central to plastics production, would be secured one way or another.

In contrast to petroleum-based plastics and fabrics, PLA, made from a renewable resource, offered performance, price, environmental compatibility, and high visibility, and therefore significant value to certain buyers and consumers for whom this configuration of product characteristics was important. But there was an information gap. Most late supply-chain buyers and individual consumers had to be reminded that plastics came from oil.

Competition

Several companies throughout the world had perfected and marketed corn-based plastic materials on a small scale. Japan was an early player in PLA technology. By the 1990s Shimadzu and MitsuiTuatsu in Japan were producing limited quantities of PLA and exploring commodity plastics applications. Their leadership reflected Japanese technological skills, greater public and government concern for environmental and related health issues, and greater waste disposal concerns given limited territory and a dense population. By 2004, Japanese companies were buying NatureWorks PLA and transporting the pellets to Chinese subsidiaries for research and production. Japan had already safely incinerated and composted PLA.

Larger companies were taking stabs at bio-based materials, but none was as far along or as targeted as NatureWorks. For example, Toyota had entered a joint venture with trading house Mitsui & Co. Ltd., which produced PLA from sweet potatoes. Toyota reportedly used PLA resins in its Prius hybrid car. Toyota announced plans in 2004 to construct a pilot plant to produce bioplastics made from vegetable matter. A new facility—to be built within an existing manufacturing plant in Japan—was expected to generate one thousand tons of the PLA plastics annually. Operations began in August 2004. Competitors and critics called these claims "greenwash": they were skeptical of Toyota's real intention to become a producer of its own plastic resins, a vertical integration step atypical of the auto company. But Toyota's Biogreen Division recently had purchased a biopolymer feedstock company.

DuPont had a seven-year research program with biotechnology company Genencor using its enzyme to create a predominantly corn-based fiber called Sorona [9] through a joint venture with Tate & Lyle. The Sorona polymer, expected to replace the company's more expensive petrochemical-based product, was to emerge from a new, 100-million-pound-capacity plant in 2005. Sorona was only half bio-based, however, still relying on petroleum for half its feedstock. DuPont's goal was to have 25 percent of its revenues derived from products made using renewable materials by 2015. Eastman Chemical Company's new product called "Eastar Bio GP & Ultra Copolyester" was designed to biodegrade to biomass, water, and carbon dioxide in a commercial composting environment in 180 days.

Metabolix (Cambridge, Massachusetts) was awarded $1.6 million from the Department of Commerce's Advanced Technology Program to help fund a project to improve the efficiency of a bioprocess to make polyhydroxyalkanoate (PHA) biodegradable plastics from corn-based sugars. Metabolix said it was engineering bacteria to make production of PHA cost competitive with petrochemical-based plastics. A report on Metabolix in 2002 stated,

> Genetically engineered microbes that produce thermoplastic polymers by fermenting cornstarch or sugar are going to start nibbling away at hydrocarbon-based resins more quickly than is generally expected. That is the view of James Barber, president of Metabolix Inc., whose company operates a pilot plant for polyhydroxyalkanoate (PHA) fermentation at its headquarters in Cambridge, Massachusetts. Metabolix was created in 1992 to develop PHA technology. In 2001, the company acquired Biopol technology from Monsanto. Biopol was originally developed by ICI in the 1980s. A recent $7.4 million grant to Metabolix by the U.S. Dept. of Energy will help develop a new route to bioproduction of PHA. Instead of fermentation, Metabolix will investigate making PHA through photosynthesis in the leaves or

roots of the switchgrass plant. This is a fast-growing, native American grass that grows relatively well even on marginal farmland. "Direct plant-grown PHA could allow us to challenge volume resins in lower-cost packaging and other markets," Barber says. [10]

Germany's BASF began R&D collaboration with Metabolix in 2003 to investigate PHA's materials and processing properties. However, much of that competitive activity was intended to forge "platform" technical capacities to use biomaterials and processing for wide varieties of pharmaceutical and industrial applications, was in its infancy stages, and was not necessarily seen as a threat to NatureWorks. In late 2004, agriculture giant Archer Daniels formed a fifty-fifty joint venture with Metabolix to make alternatives to petrochemical plastics.

In terms of its stage and scale of technology, NatureWorks was alone among companies in the emerging industry, a situation which caused it some additional challenges. Buyers preferred comparing the cost and performance of two products rather than having to choose the only product available. In addition, NatureWorks could hardly lobby for government subsidies or regulations for its industry, since it was the sole representative of that industry.

Yet factors continued to line up favorably. The chemically tough nature of oil-based plastic polymers was both their most desirable and most problematic trait. Plastic polymers can take hundreds and even thousands of years to break down. With steadily increasing consumption rates of plastics (predicted to be 2.58 billion tons between 2004 and 2015 [11]) and short product life spans (approximately 30 percent of plastic is used in packaging; this material is thrown away immediately), communities faced a significant solid waste problem. In 2004, plastic represented almost 40 percent of the municipal waste stream by tonnage. [12] The disposal issue had caused several countries to create a requirement for recyclability in plastic products. In 1994, the European Union passed the Packaging Recovery and Recycling Act, which required member nations to set targets for recovery and recycling of plastic wastes. By 2005, manufacturers had to take packaging back. The European Union also set a precedent with the Directive on End-of-Life Vehicles, which established a goal of 85 percent reuse and recycling (by weight of vehicle parts) by 2006. NatureWorks set up its EU office in 1996.

Similar laws followed in 1997 in Japan. One stated that the manufacturer was responsible for the cost of disposal of plastic packaging. Japan added to its waste regulations in 2001 by mandating that all electronics must contain 50–60 percent recyclable materials and that the manufacturers must take the electronic device back at the end of its useful life. This spurred the Japanese GreenPla designation (so named for green plastics, not PLA). This was a strict labeling program that identified products that met all government regulations for recyclability. The first product to receive the GreenPla designation was NatureWorks PLA resins.

In 2003, Taiwan initiated a phaseout of polystyrene foam and shopping bags. These regulations used the "polluter pays" approach, which made manufacturers responsible for the disposal and reuse of their products. The efforts were designed to inspire a movement toward the development of "readily recyclable" products, and two of three implementation phases were complete. The last phase would fine people for using nonbiodegradable materials. Whether termed sustainable business, triple bottom line (economic, social, and environmental performance), 3E's (economy, equity, ecology), or simply good business, drivers of change were growing.

Additives

No discussion of plastics can leave out the issue of additives and related health concerns. Chemical specialty companies provided packages of additives that converters incorporated into melted resins to achieve the customer's desired look and performance. One physical characteristic of plastic molecules is that the additives are not chemically bound in the polymers but rather physically bound (envision the additive molecule "sitting" inside a web of plastic molecules, rather than being molecularly "glued" in place). That means that as plastics undergo stress under normal use, such as heat or light, or pressure in a landfill, additive molecules are released into the environment. These "free-ranging" additives were causing scientists to raise questions about health impacts. Alarming data were accumulating from sources such as the American National Academy of Sciences and the US Centers for Disease Control. A 2005 Oakland Biomonitoring Project found evidence of the following chemicals in the blood of a twenty-month-old child in California: dichloro-diphenyl-trichloroethane (DDT), polychlorinated biphenyl (PCBs), mercury, cadmium, plasticizers, and flame retardants (polybrominated diphenyl ethers, or PBDEs); PBDEs, known to cause behavioral changes in rats at 300 parts per billion (ppb), registered at 838 ppb in the child.

Plasticizers, such as phthalates, were the most commonly used additives and had been labeled in studies as potential carcinogens and endocrine disruptors. Several common flame retardants regularly cause developmental disorders in laboratory mice. Possibly most startling were studies that found significant levels of phthalates, PDBEs, and other plastic additives in mothers' breast milk. Those findings were confirmed for women in several industrially developed economies including the United Kingdom, Germany, and the United States.

Science trends had led to a series of regulations that plastic producers and other companies active in the international market could not ignore. In 1999, the EU banned the use of phthalates in children's toys and teething rings and, in 2003, banned some phthalates for use in beauty products. California took steps to warn consumers of the suspected risk of some phthalates. The EU, California, and Maine banned the production or sale of products using certain PDBE flame retardants.

Attempting to address the fact that the majority of the thousands of chemical additives used in plastics have never been tested for health impacts, in 2005 the EU was in the final phases of legislative directives that required registration and testing of nearly ten thousand chemicals of concern. The act, called Registration, Evaluation, Authorization, and Restriction of Chemicals (REACH), was expected to become law in 2006. Imports into Europe would need to conform to REACH requirements for toxicity and health impacts. Europe used the precautionary principle in its decisions about chemicals use: unwilling to wait until conclusive scientific data proved causation, member countries decided that precautionary limits on, and monitoring of, chemicals would best protect human and ecological health.

Sales in Europe

NatureWorks' innovation had received more attention in the international market than in the United States. In 2004, IPER, an Italian food market, sold "natural food in natural packaging" (made with PLA) and attributed a 4 percent increase in deli sales to the green packaging. [13] NatureWorks established a strategic partnership with Amprica SpA in Castelbelforte, Italy, a major European manufacturer of thermoformed packaging for the bakery and convenience food markets. Amprica was moving ahead with plans to replace the plastics it used, including PET, polyvinyl chloride (PVC), and polystyrene with the PLA polymer. In response to the national phaseout and ultimate ban of petroleum-based shopping bags and disposable tableware, Taiwan-based Wei-Mon Industry signed an exclusive agreement with NatureWorks to promote and distribute packaging articles made with PLA. [14] In other markets, high-end clothing designer Giorgio Armani

released men's dress suits made completely of PLA fiber; Sony sold PLA Discman and Walkman stereos in Japan; and, due to growing concerns about the health impacts of some flame retardant additives, NEC Corp. of Tokyo had combined PLA with a natural fiber called kenaf to make an ecologically and biologically neutral flame-resistant bioplastic. [15]

Though the US market had not embraced PLA, there were signals that a market would evolve. In its eleven "green" grocery stores, Wild Oats Markets Inc.—a growing supermarket chain based in Portland, Oregon—switched to PLA packaging in its deli and salad bar. The stores advertised the corn-based material and had special recycling collection bins for the plastic tubs, which looked identical to petroleum-based containers. Wild Oats collected used PLA containers and sent them to a composting facility. The chain planned to expand that usage nationally to all seventy-seven Wild Oats stores, [16] scooping its larger rival, Whole Foods. Smaller businesses such as Mudhouse, a chain of homegrown coffee shops in Charlottesville, Virginia, had changed over to NatureWorks' PLA plastic clear containers for cold drinks, sourced from Plastics Place in Kalamazoo, Michigan, a company that stated its mission as "making things right."

NatureWorks marketing head Dennis McGrew noted that the more experimental companies and the firms trying to catch competitors were moving more quickly to explore PLA applications. It was significant that both smaller early adopter purchasers as well as large companies were interested. Soon, mainstream companies entered the mix. In 2004, Del Monte aced its rival Dole at the southern California food show with PLA fresh fruit packaging. Also that year, Marsh Supermarkets in Indianapolis agreed to use PLA packaging at its stores, representing an important new retail channel: the traditional supermarket. [17]

Clothing Fiber from PLA

Opportunities for fiber applications were growing. NatureWorks launched the Ingeo brand of PLA in January 2002, targeting fiber markets then dominated by PET, polyamide, and polypropylene fibers. Ingeo could be used for clothing, upholstery, carpets, and nonwoven furnishings as well as fiberfill for comforters and for industrial applications. By 2004 the company FIT had developed a range of man-made fibers derived from PLA polymers following the signing of a master license agreement between the Tennessee-based fiber maker and NatureWorks to produce and sell the fibers under the brand name Ingeo in North America and in select Asian markets. The agreement included technology licenses, brand rights, and raw material supply to manufacture and sell Ingeo. The US supply chain for apparel fiber had moved to Asia in the 1990s, making India and China the fabric markets to watch.

In 2004, Faribault Woolen Mill Company sold blankets and throws made with 100 percent PLA and a PLA/wool blend. Biocorp North America Inc., based in Louisiana, was one of a handful of companies producing compostable PLA cutlery and was able to offer the new product at a price competitive with conventional disposable knives, forks, and spoons. Biocorp had success selling its corn-based cutlery to sizable buyers such as Aramark and the US Environmental Protection Agency. In 2003, Ford introduced its Model U SUV, which boasted a range of "green" features such as a hydrogen engine; soy-based foam seating; and tires, roofing, and carpet mats all made with NatureWorks' PLA. [18] Though the new model was only a "concept vehicle," Ford claimed that it was using the same cradle-to-cradle approach to design a market-ready vehicle.

Genetically Modified Organisms (GMOs)

A significant obstacle to marketing NatureWorks PLA in the United States was that the corn feedstock included genetically modified (called GM or GMO) corn. That PLA was certified to be free of any detectible genetic material by GeneScan Inc. and that the base sugar source (GMO or not) had no impact on PLA performance did not persuade the naysayers. Furthermore, the business was not in a position to control the corn sources coming to the mill and GMO and non-GMO were typically intermixed.

When the revolutionary NatureWorks PLA product was initially released in 2002, outdoor clothing company Patagonia jumped at the chance to use it. After approving the suitability of PLA fibers for its products and moving toward a sizable partnership, Patagonia realized that the corn feedstock, like nearly all the corn produced in the United States, had been genetically modified to be more pest resistant. Patagonia shared the concerns of many environmental nongovernmental organizations throughout the world that GMO products had not received sufficient testing for full ecological and social impact. The uncertainty that still surrounded GMO products caused such groups to lobby for a total ban on GMOs until more sound investigations were conducted. Patagonia abandoned the NatureWorks partnership and launched a publicity campaign against PLA. Environmental groups also questioned the use of food material (the corn) as feedstock when hunger remained a seemingly intractable problem internationally. NatureWorks expected to spend about $2

billion on commercial development and production technology development to enable the conversion of other agriculturally based materials, such as corn stalks and other postharvest field waste, wheat straw, and grasses, into PLA.

Though NatureWorks would have preferred to produce GMO-free products, it was challenging to purchase separate quantities of non-GMO corn at a comparable price. In 2002 the company quantified the proportion of GMO/non-GMO corn in its final resin and designed a system of offsets to support customer choice regarding non-GMO sourcing. In this system, any PLA customer could pay $.10 more per pound of PLA. NatureWorks would use this money to buy an equivalent offset amount of non-GMO corn (per one pound of PLA) for the processing plant's primary feedstock. Though resin purchasers (under the direction of their buyers) could not guarantee that the product was 100 percent non-GMO, they could voice their preference for non-GMO corn. NatureWorks experts pointed out that since the genetically modified DNA was no longer present in the corn after it had been fermented, hydrolyzed, and distilled to make PLA, this system was the only way to work proactively on this customer issue. However, parent company Cargill had reservations about the program. Public Affairs and Communications Director Ann Tucker was working on reconfiguring the program on a more customer-directed and focused platform in early 2005. Sensitivity to the issues and the use of terms like *genetically modified* was not limited to Cargill. Dow had preferred that the company not say "from renewable resources."

In 2005 the plant was operating at a lower capacity than projected. Bader was hearing the refrain repeatedly: "You cost a lot of money, make the bleeding stop" and "Your product doesn't work because it does not offer a 'drop-in' (easily adopted) substitute for PET and polystyrene." It was hard to determine and stay focused on priorities. There was so much to be done simultaneously. The top management team had to constantly ask themselves what core issues should be tackled first and what strategy would generate essential sales volumes.

Marketing

After successfully overcoming the scientific and technological barriers of producing PLA on a large scale, the team now faced the challenge of creating and managing a new market, a challenge that had not been attempted for thirty years. Manufacturers did not understand how to reconfigure their machinery to handle this new polymer, and many customers needed convincing that sustainable products were worth the investment. The pilot plant in

Nebraska had the capacity to produce only 300,000 million pounds of plastic per year, hardly a contribution to the three billion oil-based pounds produced in the world annually.

Dennis McGrew, chief marketing officer, joined NatureWorks in April 2004 after twenty-one years at Dow in the plastics side of the business. McGrew was solutions oriented and brought with him considerable experience working on new business models for materials markets. The challenge as he described it was "taking PLA from niche to a broad market play." NatureWorks had a solution for companies that wanted to move in the direction of more sustainably designed corporate strategies. For McGrew the company was selling resin pellets, but really what it had to sell was environmental responsibility. McGrew had realigned commercialization to global markets where environmental concerns were more familiar concepts.

Formerly a marginal topic, by 2005 sustainable business practices had entered the mainstream. Although the definition of *sustainability* depended somewhat on one's perspective, it was clear insurers, investors, banks, end consumers, and governments worldwide were placing increasing emphasis on corporate accountability for the impact of their activities on communities, health, and the natural environment. Large companies were publishing social and environmental reports in response to investor demand, and there was a significant movement toward uniform international corporate reporting standards on what was called triple-bottom-line performance (economic, social, and environmental). The Dow Jones Sustainability Index tracked high performers in sustainable management practices. In April 2005, JPMorgan, the third-largest bank in the United States, announced a new policy of guidelines restricting lending and underwriting when projects harm the environment, following European financial institutions' strategies. As the first US financial institution to incorporate environmental risk management into the due diligence process of its private equity divisions, the signal sent a message far beyond financial markets. A negative reputation for a company going forward could result in more expensive capital, higher insurance premiums, costlier bank credit, lower stock price, and even consumer boycotts.

These larger trends might support initiatives by firms such as NatureWorks but seemed remote to Bader and her senior management team. To go from niche to mainstream with PLA, it was essential that NatureWorks create an ongoing profitable business. This meant going from tens of millions of pounds of PLA produced to hundreds of millions of pounds.

KEY TAKEAWAYS

- There are ways to decouple economic growth from fossil fuels through materials innovation based on sustainability principles.
- Entrepreneurs manage significant strategic and operating barriers that are further complicated when working with disruptive technology that must move from development to commercialization.
- Ventures within large companies face their own set of challenges due to the parent organization's scale, vested interests, and culture.
- Sustainability, a new branding and marketing category, faces challenges throughout the supply chain.

EXERCISES

1. What *is* this product in its markets? Is this a good opportunity? What is the potential for this product? Be specific about volume, markets, and applications.
2. What particular difficulties arise when working with innovative products such as PLA?
3. What does PLA displace; what does PLA complement? What are the implications of being a complement or a displacement?
4. What are the major marketing and sales (commercialization) challenges for NatureWorks?
5. What are the supply-chain issues? How might they be resolved?
6. How would you have managed the commercialization process differently?

---

[1] {Author's Name Retracted as requested by the work's original creator or licensee}, Alia Anderson, and Karen O'Brien, *Natureworks: Green Chemistry's Contribution to Biotechnology Innovation, Commercialization, and Strategic Positioning*, UVA-ENT-0089, 2006 (Charlottesville: Darden Business Publishing, University of Virginia, 2006). All quotations and references are from this source unless otherwise indicated.

[2] *Encyclopedia of Business*, 2nd ed., s.v. "SIC 2821: Plastic Materials and Resins," accessed January 31, 2011, http://www.referenceforbusiness.com/industries/Chemicals-Allied/Plastic-Materials-Resins.html.

[3] Stuart F. Brown, "Bioplastic Fantastic Bugs That Eat Sugar and Poop Polymers Could Transform Industry—and Cut Oil Use Too," *Fortune*, July 21, 2003, accessed March 8, 2011, http://money.cnn.com/magazines/fortune/fortune_archive/2003/07/21/346098/index.htm.

[4] *Encyclopedia of Business*, 2nd ed., s.v. "SIC 2821: Plastic Materials and Resins," accessed January 31, 2011, http://www.referenceforbusiness.com/industries/Chemicals-Allied/Plastic-Materials-Resins.html.

[5] Erwin T. H. Vink, Karl R. Rábago, David A. Glassner, and Patrick R. Gruber, "Applications of Life Cycle Assessment to NatureWorks[TM] Polylactide (PLA) Production," *Polymer Degradation and Stability*, 80 (2003): 403–19, accessed April 19, 2011, http://www.natureworksllc.com/the-ingeo-journey/eco-profile-and-lca/~/media/the_ingeo_journey/ecoprofile_lca/ecoprofile/ntr_completelca_ecoprofile_1102_pdf.

[6] Erwin T. H. Vink, Karl R. Rábago, David A. Glassner, and Patrick R. Gruber, "Applications of Life Cycle Assessment to NatureWorks[TM] Polylactide (PLA) Production," *Polymer Degradation and Stability*, 80 (2003): 403–19, accessed April 19, 2011, http://www.natureworksllc.com/the-ingeo-journey/eco-profile-and-lca/~/media/the_ingeo_journey/ecoprofile_lca/ecoprofile/ntr_completelca_ecoprofile_1102_pdf.

[7] Robert A. Frosch and Nicholas E. Gallopoulos, "Strategies for Manufacturing," *Scientific American* 261, no. 3 (September 1989): 144–52; see also William McDonough and Stanley Braungart, *Cradle to Cradle: Remaking the Way We Make Things* (New York: North Point Press, 2002).

[8] Robert A. Frosch and Nicholas E. Gallopoulos, "Strategies for Manufacturing," *Scientific American* 261, no. 3 (September 1989): 144–52.

[9] Peter Mapleston, "Automakers Work on Sustainable Platforms," *Modern Plastics* 80, no. 3 (March 2003): 45, accessed January 31, 2011, http://plasticstoday.com/articles/automakers-work-sustainable-platforms.

[10] "Low-Cost Biopolymers May Be Coming Soon," *Plastics Technology*, April 1, 2002, accessed January 31, 2011, http://www.thefreelibrary.com/Low-cost+biopolymers+may+be+coming+soon.+%28Your+Business+in+Brief%29.-a084944193.

[11] "Global Plastic Companies Plan to Make Biodegradable Products," *Financial Express* (Delhi), October 4, 2004, accessed January 31, 2011, http://www.financialexpress.com/news/global-plastic-companies-plan-to-make-biodegradable-products/57219/0.

[12] "Global Plastic Companies Plan to Make Biodegradable Products," *Financial Express* (Delhi), October 4, 2004, accessed January 31, 2011, http://www.financialexpress.com/news/global-plastic-companies-plan-to-make-biodegradable-products/57219/0.

[13] Carol Radice, "Packaging Prowess," *Grocery Headquarters*, August 2, 2010, accessed January 10, 2011, http://www.groceryheadquarters.com/articles/2010-08-02/Packaging-prowess.

[14] World Business Council for Sustainable Development, "NatureWorks[TM] by Cargill Dow LLC: Capturing Consumer Attention and Loyalty," accessed April 19, 2011, http://www.wbcsd.org/web/publications/case/marketing_natureworks_full_case_web.pdf.

[15] "NEC Develops Flame-Resistant Bio-Plastic," *GreenBiz*, January 26, 2004, accessed January 27, 2011, http://www.greenbiz.com/news/2004/01/26/nec-develops-flame-resistant-bio-plastic.

[16] World Business Council for Sustainable Development, "NatureWorks[TM] by Cargill Dow LLC: Capturing Consumer Attention and Loyalty," accessed April 19, 2011, http://www.wbcsd.org/web/publications/case/marketing_natureworks_full_case_web.pdf.

[17] Carol Radice, "Packaging Prowess," *Grocery Headquarters*, August 2, 2010, accessed January 10, 2011, http://www.groceryheadquarters.com/articles/2010-08-02/Packaging-prowess.

[18] Joann Muller, "Lean Green Machine," *Forbes*, February 3, 2003, accessed January 31, 2011, http://www.forbes.com/global/2003/0203/023.html.

NOTES: